Multidimensional Mathematical Demography

Academic Press Rapid Manuscript Reproduction

Proceedings of the Conference on Multidimensional Mathematical Demography held at the University of Maryland, College Park, Maryland, March 23–25, 1981, sponsored by the National Science Foundation.

This is a volume in
STUDIES IN POPULATION

A complete list of titles in this series appears at the end of this volume.

Multidimensional Mathematical Demography

Edited by

Kenneth C. Land

Department of Sociology and Population Research Center
University of Texas
Austin, Texas

Andrei Rogers

International Institute for Applied Systems Analysis
Schloss Laxenburg
Laxenburg, Austria

1982

ACADEMIC PRESS

A Subsidiary of Harcourt Brace Jovanovich, Publishers

New York London
Paris San Diego San Francisco São Paulo Sydney Tokyo Toronto

This volume resulted from a conference supported by the National Science Foundation under Grant No. SES-8016789. Any opinions, findings, and conclusions or recommendations expressed in this publication are those of the author(s) and do not reflect the views of the National Science Foundation.

ACADEMIC PRESS, INC.
111 Fifth Avenue, New York, New York 10003

United Kingdom Edition published by
ACADEMIC PRESS, INC. (LONDON) LTD.
24/28 Oval Road, London NW1 7DX

Library of Congress Cataloging in Publication Data
Main entry under title:

Multidimensional mathematical demography.

(Studies in population)
Papers presented at the Conference on Multidimensional Mathematical Demography, University of Maryland, College Park, Mar. 23-25, 1981, sponsored by the National Science Foundation.
Includes bibliographical references and index.
Contents: Multidimensional mathematical demography, an overview / Kenneth C. Land and Andrei Rogers -- Multidimensional population analysis with incomplete data / Frans Willekens -- Model schedules in multistate demographic analysis / Andrei Rogers and Luis J. Castro -- [etc.]
1. Demography--Mathematical models--Congresses. 2. Mortality-Tables--Congresses. I. Land, Kenneth C. II. Rogers, Andrei. III. Conference on Multidimensional Mathematical Demography (1981: University of Maryland, College Park) IV. National Science Foundation (U.S.) V. Series.
HB849.51.M84 304.6'072 82-6821
ISBN 0-12-435640-0 AACR2

PRINTED IN THE UNITED STATES OF AMERICA

82 83 84 85 9 8 7 6 5 4 3 2 1

Contents

Contributors

Numbers in parentheses indicate the pages on which the authors' contributions begin.

Luis J. Castro[1] (113), *International Institute for Applied Systems Analysis, Schloss Laxenburg, 2361 Laxenburg, Austria*

Joel E. Cohen (477), *Department of Populations, Rockefeller University, 1230 York Avenue, New York, New York 10021*

James J. Heckman (567), *Department of Economics, University of Chicago, 1126 East 59th Street, Chicago, Illinois 60637*

Jan M. Hoem[2] (155), *Laboratory of Actuarial Mathematics, University of Copenhagen, Universitetsparken 5, DK-2100 Copenhagen, Denmark*

Ulla Funck Jensen (155), *Institute of Mathematical Statistics, Universitetsparken 5, University of Copenhagen, DK-2100 Copenhagen, Denmark*

P. Kitsul[3] (505), *International Institute for Applied Systems Analysis, Schloss Laxenburg, 2361 Laxenburg, Austria*

Kenneth C. Land (1, 265), *Department of Sociology and Population Research Center, 1800 Main Building, University of Texas at Austin, Austin, Texas 78712*

Jacques Ledent[4] (347), *International Institute for Applied Systems Analysis, Schloss Laxenburg, 2361 Laxenburg Austria*

Charles J. Mode (535), *Department of Mathematics, Drexel University, Philadelphia, Pennsylvania 19104*

Dimiter Philipov (445, 505), *International Institute for Applied Systems Analysis, Schloss Laxenburg, 2361 Laxenburg Austria*

Andrei Rogers (1, 113, 445), *International Institute for Applied Systems Analysis, Schloss Laxenburg, 2361 Laxenburg Austria*

[1]Present address: *Population Division, United Nations, New York, New York 10017.*

[2]Present address: *Department of Statistics, University of Stockholm, S-113 85 Stockholm, Sweden.*

[3]Present address: *Institute for Control Sciences, USSR Academy of Sciences, Moscow, USSR 117342.*

[4]Present address: *INRS – Urbanisation, University of Quebec, 3465, rue Durocher, Montreal, Quebec H2X 2C6, Canada.*

Robert Schoen (265, 385), *Department of Sociology, University of Illinois, 702 S. Wright Street, Urbana, Illinois 61801*

Burton Singer[5] (567), *Department of Mathematical Statistics, Columbia University, New York, New York 10027*

Frans Willekens (43), *Netherlands Interuniversity Demographic Institute, 2270 AZ Voorburg, The Netherlands*

[5]Present address: *Department of Populations, Rockefeller University, 1230 York Avenue, New York, New York 10021.*

Preface

Contributions to the generalization of the stationary and stable population models of classical mathematical demography to include more than the single natality–mortality dimension have been appearing with increasing frequency in recent years. The result has been the creation of new methods, of considerable generality, for estimating life tables, generating population projections, and carrying out analyses of stable growth patterns. The emergence of new methods has been complemented by the appearance of innovative empirical applications to the study of interregional migration, marriage formation and dissolution, and labor-force participation. Yet, no systematic stock-taking, ordering, and assessment of these contributions has emerged; relationships to other bodies of research literature, such as the literature dealing with stochastic processes, have not been fully drawn out; and no charting of new important research questions to be addressed has been undertaken.

To respond to these needs, a conference on multidimensional mathematical demography was convened at the University of Maryland at College Park in March 1981. This conference brought together mathematicians, statisticians, mathematical demographers, and mathematical sociologists to evaluate recent research advances and successful substantive applications in the field. Papers prepared for the conference are contained herein to serve as a central reference for scholars in these disciplines who wish to pursue research on the subject. The volume also aims to serve as supplementary reading for graduate students in departments of sociology, geography, statistics, and demography. Finally, professionals in census bureaus and national statistical agencies will find material here that is pertinent in the search for improvements of their current traditional methods of organizing and analyzing demographic data.

The organizational plan of the volume follows the four major themes discussed at the conference. We begin with two essays on problems of demographic data, which consider available methods for dealing with data inaccuracy and unavailability. The transformation of data into probabilities, by means of life table methods, constitutes the second part of the book and is the subject of the next three chapters. This section is followed by three papers that focus on models of multidimensional population dynamics. The volume concludes with three essays on problems of heterogeneity.

The eleven chapters in this book are evidence that a new field of multidimensional mathematical demography has evolved during the past decade and a half. A body of theoretical models, empirical methods, and practical applications now exists. It is hoped that this volume will further promote the expansion and maturing of work in this area.

Acknowledgments

The conference on multidimensional mathematical demography described in this volume was financially supported by the National Science Foundation under Grant No. SES-8016789. We are grateful to the Foundation for this support and to Jim Zuiches for his assistance and encouragement. It should be emphasized, however, that the opinions, findings, and conclusions or recommendations expressed in this publication are those of the authors and do not necessarily reflect the views of the National Science Foundation. The International Institute for Applied Systems Analysis, in Laxenburg, Austria also provided support by extending travel grants and per diems to three of the participants.

1

Multidimensional Mathematical Demography: An Overview

Kenneth C. Land and Andrei Rogers

1. INTRODUCTION

A large and significant body of theory, methods, and applications in demography is concerned with the transitions that individuals experience during their lifetime, as they pass from one state of existence to another: for example, transitions from being single to being married, from being alive to being dead, from being in school to having graduated, from being out of the labor force to being in the

ISBN 0-12-435640-0

labor force, from living in one region to being a resident of another. A unifying analytic thread that runs throughout these substantively diverse problems is their description by a set of two or more "living" states (marital statuses, schooling statuses, labor force statuses, geographic regions), among which the members of a population make transitions, plus the absorbing state of death into which all individuals eventually enter. The analysis considers the evolution that arises as a consequence of the transitions that occur over successive periods of time and age.

Not only are these and similar problems of intrinsic substantive interest to demographers, but they often relate to

(a) other fundamental demographic phenomena (e.g., fertility);

(b) patterns of social and economic change (e.g., in family and household structures or in regional employment and economic growth);

(c) legal questions (e.g., estimating the expected number of remaining years of working life for a worker who is disabled on the job); and

(d) assorted social policy issues (e.g., ascertaining the impacts of employment and retirement trends on social security and pension systems).

The large numbers of uses and users of disaggregated multidimensional population projections have led national statistical agencies all over the world to expand their provision of such detailed totals. The U.S. Federal Government, for example, regularly issues a number of projections that are based on the Census Bureau's national population projections. These deal with fertility, mortality, immigration, school enrollment, educational attainment, family and household totals and composition, and the income distribution of households (Fig. 1). The only link between these different projection series is that in practice the exogenously projected rates are all applied to the same age-sex-race-specific population. No attempt has as yet been made to ensure that the rates used in projecting each series are consistent with those used in other series or with the level of the projected population. Thus, fertility rates may not be consistent with the proportion of ever-married women, and the size and composition of households may not be consistent with the level of educational attainment of household members. Yet the need for such consistencies is becoming ever more apparent as these projections are increasingly used to support planning and policy making.

Until relatively recently, demographers and agencies, such as the U.S. Bureau of the Census, have sought to introduce multidimensionality into their numerical projections by applying, more or less directly, the basic *single-decrement life table* and the associated *single-dimensional population projection model* of conventional demographic theory, as described, for example, in Keyfitz (1977) and in Shryock and Siegel (1973). But these *single-state* (living at age x) *models* exhibit one or both of the following deficiencies (Rogers, 1980, p. 497). First, single-state models

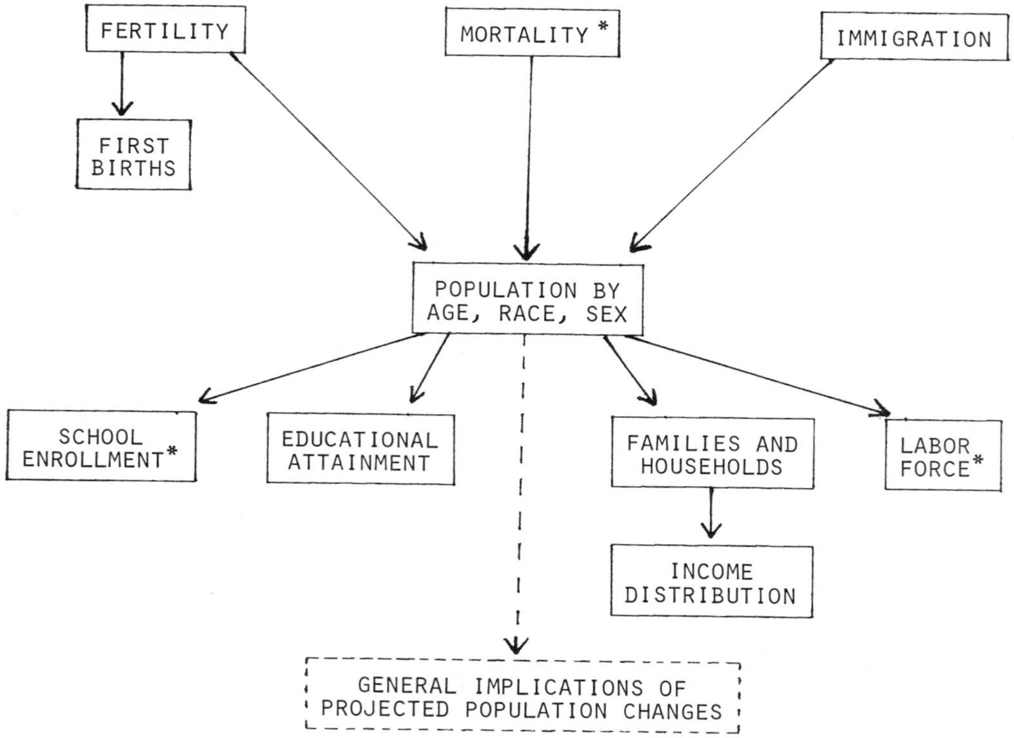

*Fig. 1. Demographic characteristic projections based on the Census Bureau's national population projections (Long, 1980). *Projections done by or in cooperation with other federal agencies.*

cannot incorporate interstate transfers differentiated by origins and destinations, and must therefore analyze changes in population stocks (i.e., the number of persons occupying various states at distinct points in time) by reference to *net* flows among the states, for example, net migration. Second, single-state models cannot follow individuals across several changes of state and therefore cannot disaggregate current or future stocks and flows by initially or previously occupied states.

Early efforts by actuarial scientists and demographers to generalize the single-state life table model led to the development of *multiple-decrement life tables*. They incorporate two or more forms of decrement from an initial status, such as mortality by cause of death, or attrition from the status of being single by mortality and nuptiality (Jordan, 1967, pp. 271-290; Preston *et al.*, 1972, pp. 13-20). More complex tables with secondary decrements (Jordan, 1967, pp. 291-304) or *hierarchical increment-decrement models* (Hoem, 1970a,b; Oechsli, 1975) were defined by chaining together a series of multiple-decrement tables in such a way as to allow successive transitions among living states, and hence increments into subsequently occupied states, but *no reentries* (with a given age interval) into a state previously occupied (e.g., from single to married to divorced back to married). Until about a decade ago, these hierchical increment-decrement models were the primary tools, other than single-decrement life tables, used by demographers for the construction of nuptiality tables, tables of working life, and tables of educational life (for a survey of this literature, see Shryock and Siegel, 1973, pp. 455-459). All such tables, however, suffer from the limited ability of these models to accommodate *reentrants* into states as well as decrements.[1]

The earliest extensions of the single-state population projection model focused on multiple states of residence and therefore were called *multiregional projection models* (Rogers, 1966, 1968; Feeney, 1970; Le Bras, 1971). Similar generalizations concerned with other classifications such as parity and occupational mobility appeared shortly thereafter (Goodman, 1969; Coleman, 1972). It then became clear that projections of populations classified by multiple states of existence could be carried out using a common methodology of multistate projection in which the core model of population dynamics was a multidimensional generalization either of the continuous age-time model of Lotka (Le Bras, 1971) or the discrete-age-time Leslie Model (Rogers, 1966; Goodman, 1969).

During the early 1970s, work on multistate life tables and on multistate projection models progressed rapidly, and the two streams of research were fused together to produce a consistent generalization of classical demographic techniques that unified many of the methods for dealing with transitions between multiple states of existence. This generalization of conventional analytical demography has produced

[1] *For thorough discussions of limitations in the "old" tables of working life constructed on the basis of hierarchical models and estimated from prevalence rates, see Hoem and Fong (1976), Schoen and Woodrow (1980), and Willekens (1980).*

(1) the specification of a general *nonhierarchical increment-decrement life table* (IDLT) *model* and an associated *multistate population projection model* capable of differentiating interstate transfers by both origin and destination states and that can accommodate reentrants into states;

(2) the development of *estimation and computational algorithms* to allow such models to be applied to the rather sketchy information demographers often confront; and

(3) the *empirical application* of these models to a growing range of substantive topics.

Because multistate models can be viewed as superimposing a set of two or more life (e.g., social, economic, health) statuses on the natality (birth)--alive at age x--mortality (death) continuum of the classic single-decrement life table model, thus combining the age dimension with one or more status dimensions, they also are called *multidimensional models*.[2] We (and the authors of chapters in the volume) use these terms interchangeably. In order to aid the reader in understanding the contributions of the chapters in the present volume to the state of the art in this field, we now turn to a brief account of the more recent historical development of multistate demographic models and their connections to other fields, such as mathematical statistics and biometrics.

[2] *Since they also combine the age dimension with one or more status dimensions, simple and hierarchical multiple-decrement life table models are multistate models, according to this definition. But the critical members of this class of models are the nonhierarchical models. The structure of the latter subclass is more complex, and it is in their specification, estimation, and use in projection that the critical advances of the past decade have been made.*

2. RECENT DEVELOPMENTS IN MULTISTATE DEMOGRAPHIC MODELS

2.1. *INCREMENT-DECREMENT LIFE TABLE MODELS*

The simplest possible mathematical framework suitable for specifying the stochastic process underlying a nonhierarchical multistate IDLT model is the *classic* discrete-state, continuous time *Markov chain* (Doob, 1953, pp. 235-255). A formal model of this type was studied in the context of disability insurance as long ago as Du Pasquier (1912, 1913). A similar Markov chain model was specified and applied to the study of recovery, relapse, death, and loss of patients by Fix and Neyman (1951). Sverdrup (1965) specified a three-state version of this model (two intercommunicating living states plus the absorbing state of death) and made a more systematic study of its statistical estimation and test procedures. While these are not the only analysts who developed statistical estimators applicable to this model, most other works (e.g., Meier, 1955; Zahl, 1955; Billingsley, 1961; Albert, 1962; Chiang, 1964) are based on an observation plan that assumes that all individuals can be observed over a fixed period [0,T]. Hoem (1971) noted that this assumption often is violated in demographic data (e.g., by censored or incomplete observations), extended Sverdrup's theory to a countably-infinite state-space, and suggested the application of the three-state model to the study of labor-force participation. But such an application was not published until Hoem and Fong (1976) constructed tables of working life for Denmark.

Given the existence of a model with long-standing foundations in actuarial science, mathematical statistics, and biomedical research, it might be assumed that mathematical demographers would regard the problem of specifying a model for multidimensional life tables as essentially resolved. For several reasons, however, this is not the case. First, because a nontrivial empirical application of the classic model did not appear until a few years ago, there was no common agreement that this model could be applied to the sketchy transition information typically available to demographers. Second, applications of multistate models especially in interregional migration studies often must deal with state spaces wherein the number of living states k is greater than two. However, the simple closed-form expressions for the transition probabilities and forces used by Hoem and Fong (1976) are based on a model with only two living states (e.g., in the labor force, not in the labor force) and nondifferential mortality into the absorbing state of death, and no explicit expressions are feasible when a model contains more than four intercommunicating living states.[3] Third, empirical applications of this classic model usually are based on the simplest possible time(age)-inhomogeneous Markov chain, namely, a chain that postulates *constant* instantaneous transition forces (intensities) within the age intervals over which the model is estimated. While this may be a tenable assumption for most demographic processes when the

[3]By "explicit," we mean expressions that involve only a finite number of algebraic operations. Thus, according to this convention, the matrix exponential (infinite series) solution of the classic homogeneous model for $k > 4$ intercommunicating states (applied, for example, to competing risks of illness and death by Chiang, 1964 and the marital status by Krishnamoorthy, 1979) does not produce explicit expressions for the transition probabilities and forces.

estimation-age-intervals are relatively short (e.g., single years), many mathematical demographers would not regard it as a sound basis for producing a sufficiently accurate IDLT when the age intervals are longer (e.g., 5 or 10 yr). In other words, while the piecewise-constant transition-forces multistate ife table model may be a reasonable specification for estimating an unabridged IDLT, it is less satisfactory for estimating an *abridged* IDLT.

These considerations help explain why demographers working on empirical multidimensional problems proceeded, in the early 1970s, to forge alternative multistate IDLT models and methods. For example, in the process of conducting research on inter-regional population growth and distribution, Andrei Rogers (1973a,b, 1975) developed and applied multiregional generalizations of the classic single-decrement life table. At about the same time, Robert Schoen performed a life table analysis of marriage, divorce, and mortality data (Schoen and Nelson, 1974) and investigated generalizations of the corresponding methods for constructing IDLTs (Schoen, 1975).

Both of these analysts replaced the piecewise-constant transition forces assumption of the classic model with a specification on the survivorship functions, namely, that they change (increase or decrease) linearly with distance into an age interval.[4] The resulting model has since become known as "the linear model" (for a brief review of this model, see Ledent, 1978 and Section 3.2 of the chapter by Land and Schoen in this

[4]*Schoen's (1975) algorithm actually is more general and potentially allows for other forms of the survivorship functions. But it is the linear model that he develops most fully.*

volume). But, because the form of data typically available to demographers for the study of migration in the United States (survivorship proportions from decennial censuses) differs from that typically available for the study of nuptiality (occurrence/exposure rates from vital event registers), the estimation methods of Rogers are somewhat different from those of Schoen.[5] Further, both Rogers, in his Option 1 method, and Schoen developed their estimation techniques initially in scalar form (Roger's Option 2 method, which focuses on the use of survivorship proportions, was expressed initially in matrix form).[6] However, after seeing Schoen's (1975) scalar expressions for the estimators of the "linear" version of this algorithm, Rogers and Ledent (1976) were able to derive a matrix estimator of interstate transition probabilities analogous to the scalar formula for survival probabilities in single-decrement theory when the survival function is assumed to be linear.[7] Nonetheless, be-

[5] *Even though Roger's Option 1 method deals with data in the form of occurrence/exposure rates, his assumption that individuals made only one state transition per estimation-age-interval (Rogers 1975, p. 59) makes his estimators differ from those of Schoen (1975).*

[6] *All life table functions originate from a set of transition probabilities, defined for all ages. In constructing such tables from the normal data on vital events and survivorship proportions, demographers frequently adopt one of two approaches: one that focuses on observed rates or one that considers observed proportions surviving. In Rogers (1975, p. 81) these two approaches are called the Option 1 and the Option 2 methods, respectively.*

[7] *Recall that this single-decrement formula for, say, 5-yr age intervals is*

$$_5p_x = \ell_{x+t}/\ell_x = (1 - (5/2)\,_5M_x)/(1 + (5/2)\,_5M_x)$$

(cf., Keyfitz, 1977, p. 20). The analogous formula for the linear IDLT is given, for example, as Eq. (3.13c) in the chapter by Land and Schoen in this volume.

cause neither Rogers nor Schoen had fully specified an underlying instantaneous process for their estimation algorithms, it was not clear exactly what was the underlying parametric counterpart of this matrix estimator. This question was addressed by Schoen and Land (1979), who specified a general continuous-time (age)-inhomogeneous Markov chain model for IDLTs and correspondingly modified the estimation algorithm of Schoen (1975).

Although a focus on transition probabilities and their underlying intensity functions has characterized the contributions of probabilists and statisticians to the construction of IDLTs, mathematical demographers have also directed their attention to other life table functions, such as expectations of life at various exact ages and age-group-specific survivorship proportions for use in population projection exercises. In Rogers (1973a,b, 1975), multistate generalizations for these functions were compactly expressed in matrix form, showing the resemblance to their corresponding conventional single-state counterparts. Further work on the use of survivorship proportions to calculate multistate life tables (the Option 2 method) was carried forward by Rees and Wilson (1977) and Ledent (1978, 1980). The latter author also contrasts the survivorship proportion approach with the more standard occurrence-exposure rate methods.

2.2. *MULTISTATE POPULATION PROJECTION MODELS*

An important and fundamental application of the survivorship probabilities and proportions provided by a multistate life table is to population projection. With the development of IDLTs, it became possible to generalize the demographer's conventional methods for estimating the elements of a population projection matrix to the multistate case in a consistent manner (Rogers, 1973a,b, 1975). The marriage of multistate life tables with multistate projection models and their expression in matrix form to show transparently their natural correspondence with widely accepted conventional single-state methods established multidimensional mathematical demography as a serious branch of analytical demography (Keyfitz, 1979; Rogers, 1980).

The distribution of a multistate population across its constituent states and the age compositions of its state-specific subpopulations are determined by the interactions of fertility, mortality, and propensities of interstate transfer. Individuals are born, age with the passage of time, reproduce, move between different states of existence, and ultimately die. Such a general perspective of the population projection process suggests a wide range of substantive applications. Regional population projections, generated simultaneously for a system of several interacting regional populations, instead of region-by-region, illustrated the first serious application of the new methodology (Rogers, 1975; Willekens and Rogers, 1978). More recently, multistate projection models of labor force totals have been proposed (Willekens, 1980), and multistate projections of the U.S. population by age and marital status are currently being developed (Espenshade, 1980). Thus, it appears that many of the categories of projections listed in Fig. 1, which generally have been calculated by applying extrapolated proportions and ratios to a projected population base, now can be produced using the models of multidimensional demography.

Such models seem to offer a fruitful direction of research for the internal consistency in projection exercises sought by government statistical agencies such as the U.S. Bureau of the Census:

> Perhaps the most striking results of this overview of projections methodologies are the lack of a mechanism for assuring consistency between projected variables and the apparent arbitrariness of many of the assumptions used to project (or more appropriately, to extrapolate) the proportions and ratios applied to the projected population base. Our interest at this point is to identify the most fruitful areas of research that may lead to specifying linkages between variables in the system, to estimating the parameters specified, and to devising a system or model for projecting these parameters (Long, 1980, pp. 14-15).

Studies of the asymptotic dynamics of the multistate projection model have shown that its ergodic properties can be analyzed by means of straightforward generalizations of the stable growth theory of conventional single-dimensional demography. It has been established, for example, that a multistate population system that is closed to external migration and subjected to an unchanging multistate schedule of mortality, fertility, and migration ultimately will converge to a stable constant age-by-state distribution that increases at a constant stable rate of growth (Rogers, 1966, 1975; Le Bras, 1971). Le Bras (1977) extended this proof to the case of weak ergodicity; and Liaw (1978) has demonstrated that, as in the case of the conventional single-state population projection model, the dominant root accounts for the part of an observed population distribution that is stable. The other positive roots transmit the redistributional effects of interstate transfers, and the negative and complex roots generate fluctuations in population totals and age profiles known as "waves."

3. THE CONFERENCE ON MULTIDIMENSIONAL MATHEMATICAL DEMOGRAPHY

There can be little doubt that the foregoing developments have greatly enriched the field of mathematical demography and expanded the range of application of its traditional analytic models. But these developments have left a number of questions unanswered. For instance, what is the precise relationship of the "linear" IDLT specification to the classic "constant-forces" model? More generally, how does each of these specifications relate to the underlying continuous-time Markov chain model that has come to be accepted as the mathematical basis for IDLTs? Are there other possible specifications that are better than these? What are the statistical properties of these and other models? For instance, does the linear model exhibit problems of embeddability, identification, and estimation-with-structural-zeros similar to those that have been discovered for the constant-forces model when applied to panel data? Can multistate models be extended to incorporate two sexes? Is there a multidimensional stochastic generalization of the ergodic theorems of classic stable population theory? How can recent developments on stochastic process models and methods on mathematical statistics and mathematical sociology be used to refine the models of multistate demography?

It was to address these and related theoretical and methodological questions and to stimulate further work on empirical applications that the editors of this volume organized and directed, on March 23 - 25, 1981, a conference on multidimensional mathematical demography.[8] The Conference brought together mathematical demographers, who had made prior contributions to multidimensional models, with other demographers, mathematical sociologists, and mathematical statisticians. This book is the product of that Conference.

To provide a focal point for Conference discussions, several participants were asked to prepare papers dealing with questions such as those raised above. Discussions on the first day were devoted primarily to essays on theoretical developments in, and empirical applications of, multidimensional demographic models, while those on the second day centered on multidimensional life table models and methods. Essays on the relationships of stochastic process models and methods (from mathematical statistics and mathematical sociology) to multidimensional demography were examamined on the morning of the third day. The Conference concluded with summaries of the principal sessions and a general discussion of needed research and next steps in multistate demography.

The diversity of disciplinary backgrounds and research interests of the Conference participants fostered a series of lively, intense, and fruitful discussions. It would be neither possible nor illuminating to give a detailed summary of these

[8] *The Conference was funded by Grant Number SES 80-16789 from the Sociology Program, Division of Social and Economic Science, National Science Foundation. It was held at the Center for Adult Education of the University of Maryland in College Park.*

discussions in this short chapter. Rather, in the remainder of this chapter, we shall focus on a description of the general issues and themes around which the Conference papers and discussions were organized and a statement of some possible next steps in research in multidimensional mathematical demography.

4. ORGANIZATION OF THE VOLUME

The papers collected in this volume are a selection of those presented at the "Conference on Multidimensional Mathematical Demography." They may be conveniently grouped into four major themes: data problems, life tables, population dynamics, and heterogeneity.[9]

4.1. DATA PROBLEMS

Empirical studies in multistate demography often begin with data, set out in tabular form, which describe changes in *stocks* that have occurred over two or more points in time. These changes arise as a consequence of increments and decrements associated with *events,* such as births and deaths, and with *flows* of individuals between different states of existence.

[9]*A list of participants and their current organization affiliations is included at the end of the volume. Four additional papers presented at the Conference were not revised for publication in this volume: "Estimating Individual-Level Transition Probabilities for Multistate Life Tables" by James S. Coleman; "Simplified Multiple Contingency Calculations" by Nathan Keyfitz and Andrei Rogers; "Constructing Multiregional Life Tables Using Place-of-Birth Specific Migration Data" by Jacques Ledent; and "Relations Between Individual Life Cycles and Population Characteristics" by Samuel H. Preston.*

The latter can be viewed either as events or as changes of state between two points in time (Ledent, 1978).

When all of the appropriate elements in such tables have been filled in with numbers, they generally are referred to as *accounts* (Stone, 1971, 1981; Rees and Wilson, 1977; Rees, 1980; Land and McMillen, 1981). And when, as is often the case, some data are unavailable, ingenuity and sophisticated fudging are used to supply the missing entries. Prominent among such techniques are various row and column balancing methods that have been successfully implemented in economics (input-output matrices), transportation planning (origin-destination traffic flows), and statistics (contingency tables). In the second chapter of this volume, Frans Willekens unifies much of this work showing that the underlying strategy in all of it is a search for missing elements in a flow matrix that preserves, in some sense, the structure of the whole data set. To accomplish this, Willekens adapts techniques used in demographic accounting and log-linear models of contingency table analysis.

To implement his procedure, Willekens focuses on two sets of accounts: an observed flow matrix, with its marginal totals, structural zeros, and subset of known elements, and an estimated flow matrix, with *all* of its flows specified. The elements in the latter are selected to reflect patterns of association that resemble those found in a similar but different problem setting, or they may reflect historical data or patterns suggested by cross tabulations of intermediate or explanatory variables.

Multidimensional demographic models require data on population flows for purposes of applying the methods of estimation that recently have been developed. But, for many phenomena, censuses and sample surveys provide only aggregate data. Consequently, techniques such as those presented by Willekens may become critical for converting existing data into a form that can be used in multistate demographic analyses.

Age-specific patterns of demographic events such as fertility or mortality exhibit remarkably persistent regularities (e.g., Coale and Demeny, 1966; Coale and Trussell, 1974). The age profiles of these schedules seem to be repeated, with only minor differences, almost everywhere. As a result, demographers have found it possible to summarize and capture such regularities by means of hypothetical schedules called *model* schedules.

Model schedules have two important applications in demography: (1) they may be used to infer the empirical schedules of populations for which the requisite data are unavailable or inaccurate; and (2) they can be applied in analytical studies of population dynamics arising out of growth regimes that may be defined in terms of a relatively limited set of model schedule parameters. Because the data requirements of multidimensional population analyses increase exponentially with the number of dimensions, the role of model schedules in such analyses is likely to be fundamental.

In Chapter 3, Andrei Rogers and Luis Castro focus on the development of hypothetical (synthetic) model schedules that reflect regularities in age profile found in empirical schedules of migration rates. They define two alternative perspectives for creating such synthetic schedules for use in situations where only inadequate or defective data on internal gross migration flows are available. The first associates variations in the parameters and variables of the model schedule to each other and then to age-specific migration rates; the second embodies different relationships between the model schedule parameters in several standard schedules and then associates the logits of the migration rates in the standard to those of the population in question. Preliminary tests of the proposed model schedules indicate that, although the quality of fits are satisfactory in describing internal migration flows in developed countries, further work will be needed if such approaches are to be of practical use in Third World population settings.

4.2. LIFE TABLES

The life table has been a central concept in classical demography. Its use to describe the facts of mortality in terms of probabilities and their combined impact on the lives of a hypothetical cohort of individuals born at the same moment has been so successful that, in the words of Keyfitz (1977, p. 3) "... we are incapable of thinking of population change and mortality from any other starting point." The natural starting point for thinking about multidimensional population change, therefore, is the multistate life table, its theoretical derivation, and its empirical calculation.

Chapters 4 - 6 deal with the methodology of constructing multidimensional life tables. Jan M. Hoem and Ulla Funck Jensen lead off this section with a critical overview of current multistate life table theory and estimation methods. Arguing from a probability theory/mathematical statistics perspective, they take the position that the proper place at which to begin the construction of an IDLT is with the specification of its state space and transition intensities. Furthermore, Hoem and Jensen maintain that the fundamental assumptions of a model specification should be made in those terms, and not in terms of transition probabilities or survival functions (as in the linear model), or other "derived" quantities. Given estimates of the transition intensities, the method they recommend for IDLT construction is to compute the transition probabilities and other quantities as a solution to the Kolmogorov equations. Hoem and Jensen also construct examples that show how the transition intensities in the linear model may violate fundamental theoretical requirements, such as nonnegativity constraints. Finally, they make a number of observations about general demographic methodology and present some results concerning observational plans and statistical inference in multistate life tables.

In Chapter 5, Kenneth C. Land and Robert Schoen identify their own set of shortcomings in existing methods of estimating IDLTs. One of the most serious of these is that existing methods *either* are capable of incorporating transition forces that increase, remain constant, or decrease within estimation-age-intervals *or* are capable of being put in explicit algebraic form, but they do not have both desirable features. To fill this gap in existing methods, Land and Schoen develop a new estimation method that is based on the specification of quadratic transition probabilities or gross flow functions. They also review the derivation of their general algorithm for estimating IDLTs (Schoen and Land, 1979) and show how the constant-forces, linear, and quadratic models can be estimated as special cases of this algorithm. In addition, Land and Schoen derive algebraic expressions for the classes of rational polynomial transition force functions corresponding to the linear and quadratic models. Referring to the pathologies concerning these induced transition forces discovered by Hoem and Jensen, Land and Schoen point out that these are nothing more than embeddability and estimation-with-structural-zero-constraints problems, and that the latter appear also in the approach of Hoem and Jensen when applied to similar data situations (e.g., in the application of the constant-forces model to panel data; see Singer and Spilerman, 1976b).

Both Hoem and Jensen and Schoen and Land deal with estimation problems created by mobility data in the form of events (*moves*) such as are typically obtained from population registers. In practice, however, there exists alternative sources, e.g., population censuses and surveys, which yield mobility data in the form of *movers*, i.e., interstate transfers defined by a comparison of the states in which individuals were present at two different points in time. Both Hoem and Jensen and Schoen and Land recognize the existence of these alternative forms of mobility data from which to estimate IDLTs and adapt their methods thereto. In addition, Jacques Ledent, in the final chapter of this section, focuses primarily on the problem of estimating transition probabilities from the latter type of data. Ledent first reviews two existing approaches and then attempts to develop them further.

As revised by Ledent, both estimation procedures require the following input data: (a) mortality rates as conventionally measured; and (b) mobility measures obtained by an appropriate transformation of the raw data on *movers*. The first of these procedures, originating from Roger's (1975) Option 1 method, calls for adequately estimated mobility propensities, whereas the second, following from Rogers's (1975) Option 2 method, requires transition probabilities conditional on survival. Of the two alternative approaches, Ledent appears to prefer the second one, because it relies on some additional information about stayers. Also, the latter method is more readily applicable to the calculation of increment-decrement life tables for open systems, e.g., to multiregional population systems that experience *international* (external) migration.

In general, these three chapters represent extensions of the existing theoretical and methodological streams in multistate demography summarized earlier herein. Based on the premise that estimation methods must be tailored to each type of available data, the paper by Ledent deals with the case of data coming in the form of counts of individuals who have moved. Methodological rather than theoretical in nature, it revises existing procedures of estimation from such data, with a special concern for ensuring agreement between some life table statistics and their observed counterparts.

The chapters by Hoem and Jensen and Land and Schoen are especially helpful in identifying the relationships of the constant-forces and linear survival function specifications to each other and to the corresponding Markov chain model. In brief, it now is clear that both specifications assume the same basic continuous-time(age)-inhomogeneous Markov chain. But, whereas the constant-forces approach deals with the age-inhomogeneity by dissecting an age range into age intervals that are sufficiently small that the transition forces can be approximated by constants, the linear specification approximates the solution of the Kolmogorov equations (over possibly longer age intervals) by linear functions. Thus, for example, the linear function defined by Eq. (3.45) of the chapter by Land and Schoen can be regarded as a Taylor polynomial approximation (to the linear term) of the (generally unknown and nonlinear) solution of the "true" Kolmogorov equations that generated the data. Similarly, the quadratic function defined by Land and Schoen's Eq. (3.38) can be regarded as a second-order Taylor polynomial approximation.

Clearly, these linear and quadratic approximations yield simple, algebraically explicit computation formulas. Furthermore, in the absence of embeddability and structural zeros problems, they appear to produce somewhat more accurate numerical estimates in *abridged* IDLTs than does the constant-forces model. Nonetheless, as the width of an estimation-age-interval decreases, the exponential, linear, and quadratic estimators will approach each other. For, in this case, the higher-order terms of the rational polynomial transition force functions of the former estimators will decrease toward zero so that the force functions will deviate less and less from a constant level over the age interval.

In our view, the ultimate conclusions to be drawn from these three chapters about "proper" methods of multistate life table estimation depend critically on the type of table to be constructed and the forms of data available for estimation. Clearly, the strong points of the classic constant-forces model are its well-developed foundation in mathematical statistics and its corresponding ability to deal with problems of statistical inference in sample data. In addition, the assumption of constant forces is least critical when the estimation-age-intervals of an IDLT can be made "small" relative to the local variability of the transition forces being modeled. Thus, we have no hesitation in recommending the use of this specification when the objective is the construction of an *unabridged* IDLT from data in which age intervals can be chosen optimally relative to the constant-forces assumption and for which statistical inferences are relevant.

On the other hand, when the objective is the construction of an *abridged* IDLT from population-level statistics or census data, particularly data in which the estimation-age-intervals are fixed in rather wide lengths, the polynomial gross flow specifications have two salient features. First, their more flexible specifications on the transition forces may yield more accurate estimates of transition probabilities than does the constant-forces specification. Second, they have the advantage of computational simplicity. Of course, the statistical theory for such specifications, embedded as it is in the theory of analytic graduation (Hoem, 1972b), may be less familiar to demographers than is that for the classical model. But statistical inferences traditionally have been more peripheral in the context described in this paragraph than that described in the preceding paragraph.

In the middle ground between these two extremes, the choice of estimation method is less clearcut. But, again, an optimal decision depends on whether the objective is an abridged or unabridged table, whether the age data are grouped or not, and on the relative importance of statistical inference versus computational simplicity. Note that these views on the estimation of *abridged* IDLTs are not greatly different from those of Hoem and Jensen (Section 4.4). The main difference is that the methods recommended here emphasize simple parametric forms of the solutions of the Kolmogorov equations, whereas those of Hoem and Jensen emphasize simple parametric forms for the transition forces. Since the emphasis in an abridged table is on producing accurate estimates of the transition probabilities, the former may seem more natural in this context.

4.3. POPULATION DYNAMICS

The chapters in the third group are concerned both with theoretical developments and with substantive applications of multidimensional demographic models. They deal with the evolution of multistate populations exposed to a given regime of growth and interstate mobility. Leading off is Robert Schoen's essay on the incorporation of the interaction between the sexes, in the form of nuptiality and fertility, in life table and stable population models. Using the harmonic mean as a mechanism for distributing the consequences of interactions between the sexes among the several states of the model, Schoen shows how the classic "problem of the sexes" is mathematical demography (Keyfitz, 1977, pp. 293-336) can be accommodated in multistate models. When the one-sex/two-sex dimension is combined with the stationary population/stable population and decrement/increment-decrement dimensions, ten distinct life table models arise. Schoen demonstrates how all ten models can be specified and constructed in terms of the same four sets of equations, and discusses some of the properties of each model.

As an illustration, a two-sex (fertility) increment-decrement stable population model is presented using birth, death, and migration rates for the United States and California, 1970.

Multistate population projection models disaggregate conventional population projections into a number of state-specific categories, such as state of current residence and state of birth, status at an earlier age, and duration of occupancy in the current state. If interstata transition probabilities vary significantly according to the chosen categories, then the disaggregated multistate projection models should produce more accurate results than aggregated models. In Chapter 8, Dimiter Philipov and Andrei Rogers explore the consequences of introducing several such state-specific categorizations of multiregional populations.

A number of studies have reported higher than average probabilities of migration to a given destination among those returning to their place of birth or region of previous residence (e.g., Ledent, 1981). Philipov and Rogers incorporate this characteristic into a multistate projection model that distinguishes between *native* and *alien* populations in each region of a multiregional system. Introducing higher transition probabilities for return migrants, they show that such native-dependent projections produce spatial distributions that differ significantly from those generated by a native-dependent multistate projection model. The latter consistently underestimate the fraction of natives in each regional population.

Concluding this group of essays, Joel Cohen's chapter considers the ergodic properties of multiregional population projection models with changing rates and stochastic patterns of behavior. In mathematical demography, ergodic theorems define long-run behavior that is independent of initial conditions. Weak ergodic theorems describe populations experiencing changing rates, and stochastic ergodic theorems assume that such rates are selected from a set of possible rates by some stochastic process. Building on extensions of his previous work in single-state ergodic theory, Cohen (1976, 1977a,b) develops four weak ergodic theorems and a stochastic ergodic theorem that assumes that a Markov chain selects the rates of transition from a set of alternatives.

4.4. *HETEROGENEITY*

Most of the models used in multidimensional demography assume that moves from one state to another are independent of each other, suppose that all of the individuals occupying a particular state at a given moment are homogeneous, and consider the evolution that would occur if the various probabilities of interstate transition were to remain constant over a time period. Yet it is widely accepted that the reverse is almost always a more accurate description of reality.

Blumen *et al.* (1955), in an early stochastic analysis of occupational mobility, posited a model of "movers" and "stayers" as a means for accommodating heterogeneity in simple Markov chain models. Their pioneering investigation stimulated a generation of studies, to which the chapter by Pavel Kitsul and Dimiter Philipov is the most recent addition. Kitsul and Philipov are motivated by the problem of analyzing mobility data collected over unit time intervals of different length. For example, in the case of interregional migration, registration systems in several countries (such as Sweden) can produce flow matrices every year. Censuses, on the other hand, usually provide such data over a fixed period (five years, say). How can the two alternative descriptions of the same mobility phenomenon be reconciled?

To address this problem analytically, the authors distinguish two homogeneous populations of movers: one with a high intensity of moving and the other with a low intensity. Representing the mobility process as a mixture of two Markovian processes, they introduce a few simplifying assumptions, which allow them to fit their model to British migration data for the five-year period from 1966 - 1971 and also for the single year 1970. They then demonstrate how their model can be used to transform data collected over one unit of time into comparable information covering a time period of different length.

Another stream of research that has grown out of the original Blumen *et al.*, investigations into the effects of population heterogeneity on mobility processes pertains to the use of semi-Markov, rather than Markov, specifications (see, for example, Ginsberg, 1971, 1972a,b; Hoem, 1972a). In Chapter 11, Charles J. Mode reviews a number of junctures at which semi-Markov process can be related to IDLTs from a sample path perspective. Underlying both IDLT methodology and semi-Markovian processes is the notion of a set of states among which an individual moves over a period of time. The set of states visited by an individual and the sojourn times in these states constitute the person's sample path. Mode discusses a class of stochastic processes based on probability distributions defined directly on the sample paths and relates these to problems of estimating IDLTs from microdata on sample paths.

Heterogeneity is also the focus of the chapter by James J. Heckman and Burton Singer, the final contribution to this volume. The two authors consider strategies for analyzing population heterogeneity in demographic studies using models that contain mixtures of Markov and semi-Markov processes. To illustrate the critical importance of this topic, Heckman and Singer show how different assumed choices of distributions of unobservable variables lead to substantively contradictory inferences in a structural model of waiting-time durations. They then derive a nonparametric estimator for mixing measures as a strategy to bypass the more traditional, but dangerous, *ad hoc* assumptions about mixing distributions used in most conventional modeling of duration data. Clearly, population heterogeneity is a data modeling problem of continuing relevance in multidimensional mathematical demography. Investigations such as Heckman's and Singer's, and those reported in their references, will therefore be of growing importance to the development and refinement of multistate demographic models.

5. CONCLUSIONS AND NEXT STEPS

The chapters of this volume, and the literature to which they refer, demonstrate that the field of multidimensional mathematical demography has come of age. A body of theoretical models, grounded in the mathematics of time-inhomogeneous Markov chains, now exists. Associated with this are several empirical methods, based on actuarial and statistical principles, for fitting these models to real data and for using their outputs to project the future evolution of multidimensional populations. Finally, a number of impressive empirical applications of nonhierarchical increment-decrement life tables and population projection models have been made. In some instances, these applications have appeared in substantive areas where no multistate analyses had existed before (e.g., interregional migration). In others, the new applications represent substantial improvements over the techniques that were previously available (e.g., nuptiality, labor-force participation).

It is remarkable that these accomplishments span little more than a decade. Clearly, this has been a very active period in the development and application of multidimensional generalizations of the models of classical mathematical demography. Furthermore, since many of the individuals who made contributions to this field during the past decade still are active researchers, and since others in related areas of demography, mathematical statistics, sociology, and geography, have been made aware of this area of applications and its problems, it is reasonable to expect that the near future will also exhibit a rapid rate of innovations. What are some promising lines of inquiry along which such developments may be expected to occur? Based in part on discussions of this topic by participants in the Conference, we see several important directions of theoretical-methodological research and of substantive applications.

A first, and most obvious, theme for future theoretical-methodological inquiry pertains to extensions and generalizations of ideas and methods summarized and developed in the chapters of this volume. For instance, given the computational simplifications and other desirable features of the polynomial gross flows methods for abridged IDLTs developed in the chapter by Land and Schoen, it might be useful to develop extensions of these specifications to IDLTs generated by semi-Markov processes (the approach that commences with a specification of the force functions has been extended to a semi-Markov framework by Hoem, 1972a). Such generalizations would help demographers to deal with the origin- and/or duration-dependence known to affect some mobility processes. Similarly, it is clear that studies of the effects of population heterogeneity in unobservables, such as those summarized by Heckman and Singer and Kitsul and Philipov, have a strategic importance for multidimensional demography. The extension of the life table model to capture the interactions between the sexes, as described by Schoen, opens up numerous theoretical and methodological issues. One of the most important questions is whether two-sex models exhibit weak or stochastic ergodicity. That is, can multistate ergodic theorems, such as those presented by Cohen chapter in this volume, be modified to apply to two-sex models? Since the rates defined in these models exhibit a complicated interactive interdependence, this question seems to require a nontrivial transformation of existing theory. Finally, several of the issues of statistical estimation and projection developed by Hoem and Jensen, Ledent, and Philipov and Rogers will provide a continuing source of problems for the attention of mathematical demographers and statisticians. As in any area of scientific inquiry, these issues are essentially open-ended and in need of continual development and refinement.

The second methodological innovation that we expect to unfold in the near future is an application to multistate models of methods of controlling for population heterogeneity in observable variables that have been developed in fields related to multidimensional demography. For example, in the context of single-decrement life tables, proportional hazards models have been created by statisticians and used by mathematical demographers to deal with heterogeneity in the presence of concomitant information on covariates (see, for example, Cox, 1972; Holford, 1976, 1980; Laird and Oliver, 1981; Manton and Stallard, 1981; Menken *et al.*, 1981). Other methods for coping with population heterogeneity have been developed by mathematical sociologists and statisticians in the context of applications of Markov chains to microdata from panel studies and event histories (see, for example, Coleman, 1964, 1981; Singer, 1981; Singer and Spilerman, 1976a,b; Cohen and Singer, 1979; Singer and Cohen, 1980; Tuma *et al.*, 1979). The latter methods seem especially applicable to IDLTs with little modification, at least in the case of piecewise-constant transition forces. For other specifications, new methodological developments may be required.

This development of methods for dealing with population heterogeneity in multistate models is related to one of the main substantive innovations that we see forthcoming, namely, the utilization of alternative data and the refinement of existing data sources. Up to now, multistate models have been constructed primarily from aggregate data with little or no cross classification other than by sex, age-interval, and one or two status dimensions (for example, region of residence by region of birth as in Ledent, 1981). But in order to apply the methods of "covariance analysis," additional information will be required on relevant "covariates." This may require the use of microdata sets in place of the aggregate tabulations that have been utilized heretofore.

At the same time, efforts should be made to upgrade the information gathered in vital statistics and other sources in order to take advantage of the power and flexibility of the new methods described in this volume. For instance, while it is now easy to incorporate differential mortality by labor-force participation status into tables of working life, available data typically do not allow this to be done because death certificates do not record the labor-force status of the deceased at the time of death. Similar comments on inadequacies of data on population flows from censuses and current population surveys could be compiled (see, for example, Land and McMillen, 1981). But the general point here is that the capacity of the models seems to have outstripped the data used in multidimensional demography. It is appropriate, therefore, to suggest that census and vital statisticians should consider what modifications of their data collection procedures would allow these models to be used to their full potential.

Because changes in established governmental data collection procedures take time to implement, methods of inferring data from inadequate or inaccurate sources, problems of missing data, and related topics in the design and use of model multistate schedules should become a central branch of multistate modeling in the future. The data requirements for such modeling activities are extensive and, even when available, multistate data are difficult to comprehend and manipulate. In the large majority of cases, however, multidimensional data are simply not available at the level of detail required and must be inferred from available sources by such means as multiproportional adjustment techniques and model schedules.

Another line of substantive research that we expect to grow pertains to an expansion of the range of applications of multistate models. One way in which this will occur is through the construction of multistate models for additional types of transitions (e.g., schooling), situations (e.g., the marriage squeeze), and populations (e.g., a criminal offender population). Other studies will apply multistate models to the study of economic-demographic interactions (e.g., in the tradition of Coale and Hoover, 1958), or, more generally, to the analysis of social change (e.g., as in Land, 1979).

In brief, research in multidimensional mathematical demography during the next decade can be expected to proceed apace along these and related lines. While some developments will be primarily methodological, they almost surely will be motivated by strong connections to the empirical transitions in multistate space that have characterized contributions to this field in the recent past.

REFERENCES

Albert, A. (1962). Estimating the infinitesimal generator of a continuous time, finite state Markov process. *Annals of Mathematical Statistics 33,* 727-753.

Billingsley, P. (1961). "Statistical inference for Markov processes." Chicago: University of Chicago Press.

Blumen, I., Kogan, M., and McCarthy, P. J. (1955). "The Industrial Mobility of Labor as a Probability Process," Vol. 6. Cornell Studies of Industrial and Labor Relations. Ithaca: Cornell University Press.

Chiang, C. L. (1964). A stochastic model of competing risks of illness and competing risks of death. *In* "Stochastic Models in Medicine and Biology" (J. Gurland, ed.), pp. 323-354. Madison: University of Wisconsin Press.

Coale, A. J., and Hoover, E. M. (1958). "Population Growth and Economic Development in Low-Income Countries." Princeton, New Jersey: Princeton University Press.

Coale, A. J., and Demeny, P. (1966). "Regional Model Life Tables and Stable Populations." Princeton, New Jersey: Princeton University Press.

Coale, A. J., and Trussell, T. J. (1974). Model fertility schedules: Variations in the age structure of childbearing in human populations. *Population Index 40,* 185-258.

Cohen, J. E. (1976). Ergodicity of age structure in populations with Markovian vital rates, I: Countable states. *Journal of the American Statistical Association 71,* 335-559.

Cohen, J. E. (1977a). Ergodicity of age structure in populations with Markovian vital rates, II: General states. *Advances in Applied Probability 9,* 18-37.

Cohen, J. E. (1977b). Ergodicity of age structures in populations with Markovian vital rates, III: Finite-state moments and growth rates; Illustration. *Advances in Applied Probability 3,* 462-475.

Cohen, J. E., and Singer, B. (1979). Malaria in Nigeria: Constrained continuous-time Markov models for discrete-time longitudinal data on human mixed-species infections. *Lectures on Mathematics in the Life Sciences 12,* 69-133.

Coleman, J. S. (1964). "Introduction to Mathematical Sociology." New York: Free Press.

Coleman, J. S. (1972). Flow models for occupational structure. *In* "Input-Output Techniques" (A. Brody and A. P. Carter, eds.), pp. 80-93. Amsterdam: North Holland.

Coleman, J. S. (1981). "Longitudinal Data Analysis." New York: Basic Books.

Cox, D. R. (1972). Regression models and life tables (with discussion). *Journal of the Royal Statistical Society (Series B) 34,* 187-220.

Doob, J. L. (1953). "Stochastic Processes." New York: Wiley.

Du Pasquier, L. G. (1912). Mathematische theorie der invalidätatsversicherung. *Mitt. Ver. Schweitzer, Versicherungsmath 7,* 1-7.

Du Pasquier, L. G. (1913). Mathematische theorie der invalidätatsversicherung. *Mitt. Ver. Schweitzer, Versicherungsmath 8,* 1-153.

Espenshade, T. (1980). Personal communication.

Feeney, G. M. (1970). Stable age by region distributions. *Demography 6,* 341-348.

Fix, E., and Neyman, J. (1951). A simple stochastic model of recovery, relapse, death and loss of patients. *Human Biology 23,* 205-41.

Ginsberg, R. B. (1971). Semi-Markov processes and mobility. *The Journal of Mathematical Sociology 1,* 233-262.

Ginsberg, R. B. (1972a). Critique of probabilistic model: Application of the semi-Markov model to migration. *The Journal of Mathematical Sociology 2,* 63-82.

Ginsberg, R. B. (1972b). Incorporating causal structure and exogenous information with probabilistic models: With special reference to choice, gravity, migration, and Markov chains. *The Journal of Mathematical Sociology 2,* 83-104.

Goodman, L. (1969). The analysis of population growth when the birth and death rates depend upon several factors. *Biometrics 25,* 659-681.

Hoem, J. M. (1970a). A probabilistic approach to nuptiality. *Biometrie-Praximetrie 11,* 3-9.

Hoem, J. M. (1970b). Probabilistic fertility models of the life table type. *Theoretical Population Biology 1,* 12-38.

Hoem, J. M. (1971). Point estimation of forces of transition in demographic models. *Journal of the Royal Statistical Society (Series B) 33,* 275-289.

Hoem, J. M. (1972a). Inhomogeneous semi-Markov processes, select actuarial tables, and duration-dependence in demography. *In* "Population Dynamics" (T. N. E. Greville, ed.), pp. 251-296. New York: Academic Press.

Hoem, J. M. (1972b). On the statistical theory of analytic graduation. *Proceedings of the Sixth Berkeley Symposium on Mathematical Statistics and Probability 1*, 569-600.

Hoem, J. M., and Fong, M. S. (1976). A Markov chain model of working life tables. Working Paper No. 2. Denmark: University of Copenhagen, Laboratory of Actuarial Mathematics.

Holford, T. R. (1976). Life tables with concomitant information. *Biometrics 32*, 587-597.

Holford, T. R. (1980). The analysis of rates and survivorship using log-linear models. *Biometrics 36*, 299-306.

Jordan, C. W. (1967). "Life Contingencies." Second Edition. Chicago: Society of Actuaries.

Keyfitz, N. (1977). "Introduction to the Mathematics of Population, with Revisions." Reading, Massachusetts: Addison-Wesley.

Keyfitz, N. (1979). Multidimensionality in population analysis. *Sociological Methodology 1980*, 191-218.

Krishnamoorthy, S. (1979). Classical approach to increment-decrement life tables: An application to the study of the marital status of United States females, 1970. *Mathematical Biosciences 44*, 139-154.

Laird, N., and Oliver, D. (1981). Covariance analysis of censored survival data using log-linear analysis techniques. *Journal of the American Statistical Association 76*, 231-240.

Land, K. C. (1979). Modeling macro social change. *Sociological Methodology 1980*, 219-279.

Land, K. C., and McMillen, M. M. (1981). Demographic accounts and the study of social change, with applications to the post-World War II United States. *In* "Social Accounting Systems" (F. T. Juster and K. C. Land, eds.). New York: Academic Press.

Le Bras, H. (1971). Equilibre et croissance de populations soumises à des migrations. *Theoretical Population Biology 2*, 100-121.

Le Bras, H. (1977). Une formulation générale de la dynamique des population. *Population* (special issue), 261-293.

Ledent, J. (1978). "Some Methodological and Empirical Considerations in the Construction of Increment-Decrement Life Tables." RM-78-25. Laxenburg, Austria: International Institute for Applied Systems Analysis.

Ledent, J. (1980). Multistate life tables: Movement versus transition perspectives. *Environment and Planning A 12*, 533-562.

Ledent, J. (1981). Constructing multiregional life tables using place-of-birth-specific migration data. *In* "Advances in Multiregional Demography" (A. Rogers, ed.), pp. 35-49. Laxenburg, Austria: International Institute for Applied Systems Analysis.

Liaw, K. L. (1978). Dynamic properties of the 1966-1971 Canadian population systems. *Environment and Planning A 10,* 389-398.

Long, J. (1980). Survey of federally-produced national level projections. Unpublished manuscript. Washington, D.C.: U.S. Bureau of the Census, Population Division.

Manton, K. G., and Stallard, E. (1981). Methods for the analysis of mortality risks across heterogeneous small populations: Examination of space-time gradients in cancer mortality in North Carolina counties. *Demography 18,* 217-230.

Meier, P. (1955). Note on estimation in a Markov process with constant transition rates. *Human Biology 27,* 121-124.

Menken, J., Trussell, J., Stempel, D., and Babakol, O. (1981). Proportional hazards life table models: An illustrative analysis of socio-demographic influences on marriage dissolution in the United States. *Demography 18,* 181-200.

Oechsli, F. W. (1975). A population model based on a life table that includes marriage and parity. *Theoretical Population Biology 7,* 229-245.

Preston, S., Keyfitz, N., and Schoen, R. (1972). "Causes of Death: Life Tables for National Populations." New York: Seminar Press.

Rees, P. (1980). Multistate demographic accounts. *Environment and Planning A12,* 499-531.

Rees, P., and Wilson, A. G. (1977). "Spatial Population Analysis." London: Edward Arnold.

Rogers, A. (1966). The multiregional matrix growth operator and the stable interregional age structure. *Demography 3,* 537-544.

Rogers, A. (1968). "Matrix Analysis of Interregional Population Growth and Distribution." Berkeley, California: University of California Press.

Rogers, A. (1973a). The mathematics of multiregional demographic growth. *Environment and Planning 5,* 3-29.

Rogers, A. (1973b). The multiregional life table. *The Journal of Mathematical Sociology 3,* 127-137.

Rogers, A. (1975). "Introduction to Multiregional Mathematical Demography." New York: Wiley.

Rogers, A. (1980). Introduction to multistate mathematical demography. *Environment and Planning A12*, 489-498.

Rogers, A., and Ledent, J. (1976). Increment-decrement life tables: A comment. *Demography 13*, 287-290.

Schoen, R. (1975). Constructing increment-decrement life tables. *Demography 12*, 313-324.

Schoen, R., and Land, K. C. (1979). A general algorithm for estimating a Markov-generated increment-decrement life table for applications to marital status patterns. *Journal of American Statistical Association 74*, 761-776.

Schoen, R., and Nelson, V. E. (1974). Marriage, divorce and mortality: a life table analysis. *Demography 11*, 267-290.

Schoen, R., and Woodrow, K. (1980). Labor force status life tables for the United States, 1972. *Demography 17*, 297-322.

Shryock, H. S., and Siegel, J. S. (1973). "The Methods and Materials of Demography." Two volumes. Washington, D.C.: U.S. Government Printing Office.

Singer, B. (1981). Estimation of nonstationary Markov chains from panel data. *Sociological Methodology 1981*, 319-337.

Singer, B., and Cohen, J. E. (1980). Estimating malaria incidence and recovery rates from panel surveys. *Mathematical Biosciences 49*, 273-305.

Singer, B., and Spilerman, S. (1976a). Some methodological issues in the analysis of longitudinal surveys. *Annals of Economic and Social Measurement 5*, 447-474.

Singer, B., and Spilerman, S. (1976b). The representation of social processes by Markov models. *American Journal of Sociology (July) 82*, 1-54.

Stone, R. (1971). "Demographic Accounting and Model-Building." Paris: Organization for Economic Cooperation and Development.

Stone, R. (1971). The relationship of demographic accounts to national income and product accounts. *In* "Social Accounting Systems" (F. T. Juster and K. C. Land, eds.). New York: Academic Press.

Sverdrup, E. (1965). Estimates and test procedures in connection with stochastic models for deaths, recoveries, and transfers between different states of health. *Skandinavisk Aktuarietidskrift 40*, 184-211.

Tuma, N. D., Hannan, M. T., and Groeneveld, L. P. (1979). Dynamic analysis of event histories. *American Journal of Sociology 84*, 820-854.

Willekens, F. (1980). Multistate analysis: Tables of working life. *Environment and Planning A12*, 563-589.

Willekens, F., and Rogers, A. (1978). "Spatial Population Analysis: Methods and Computer Programs." RR-78-18. Laxenburg, Austria: International Institute for Applied Systems Analysis.

Zahl, S. (1955). A Markov process model for follow-up studies. *Human Biology 27*, 90-120.

2

Multidimensional Population Analysis with Incomplete Data

Frans Willekens

1. INTRODUCTION

In multidimensional demography, various *dimensions* of a demographic system are studied simultaneously. In multiregional demography, the dimensions are age and region of residence. Demographic systems may also be defined along the dimensions age and marital status, age and labor force status, etc. For each dimension, several *states* or demographic categories may be distinguished, e.g., age groups of 5 years; marital states--never married, married, widowed, divorced. The states alive and death may also be considered to constitute a

This paper is part of a research project toward the development of a methodology for inferring detailed migration patterns from incomplete data; the project is carried out with financial assistance of the Netherlands Organization for the Advancement of Pure Research (Z.W.O.).

ISBN 0-12-435640-0

dimension. In this paper, it is not done however, because deaths are calculated as residuals, i.e., as persons who do not move on to any of the states in the system.

The application of multidimensional demography puts a heavy burden on data availability. Data requirement is a major drawback of multidimensional analysis. The opportunities of advanced techniques of demographic inquiry can only be fully explored if data are abundantly available or if adequate procedures for estimating missing data can be used. Recently, statistical offices throughout the developed world have started collection and tabulation, on a regular basis, of necessary data for multidimensional population analysis or are advised to do so. It is particularly interesting to follow discussions in statistical offices on whether it is sufficient to collect information on sizes and compositions of major subpopulations, or whether it is necessary to quantify the flows among relevant categories of the subpopulations. In Section 2, we review some positive developments on the data collection scene. Although the steps taken toward the solution of the data problem are encouraging, one has still a long way to go. Even the data collected may not be adequate for multidimensional analysis because of deficiencies in sample frame or in sample sizes. The available data must therefore be supplemented frequently by estimates.

This chapter addresses the problem of estimating flow data that are required for multidimensional population analysis. The estimation of flows or transitions is a relatively new problem in demography. It has however been investigated for many years in regional science (migration), transportation science (traffic between nodes on a transportation network), and economics (interindustry transactions in an input-output table). Statisticians have also devoted attention to this problem in information theory, in Bayesian statistics, and in contingency table analysis. We shall draw on this research to propose a strategy for estimating missing data in multidimensional population analysis. The main feature of this strategy is to derive the value of each missing element in the flow matrix from the structure of the whole data set. This means that individual elements are not considered on their own, but only in connection with the other elements, i.e., as components of a major structure. Accounting provides a framework for this structural representation.[1] The proposed strategy consists of five steps:

(a) Set up the accounting frame. Determine the dimensions (classifications) of the population system and the states (categories) in each dimension. The accounts studied in this paper are multidimensional cross classifications. As soon as the accounting frame is imposed, the location of the cells in the account tells something about the characteristics of the individuals falling into them. For instance, in a three-dimensional account individuals in a specific cell have a characteristic in common with individuals in all cells of the same row, another characteristic is common with all individuals in cells of the same column, and still another characteristic in common with all individuals in cells of the same layer.

[1]*A different, but not unrelated framework is provided by postulating an appropriate stochastic model. This approach is illustrated in Section 3.2 and is fully developed in de Jong (1981).*

(b) Develop a model of the data set in the account. In order to be able to consider individual elements in connection with other elements, the structural relationships in the data are represented by a parametric model. Various models of data structures may be imagined, but we shall limit ourselves to a log-linear model. It can be shown that models developed in the disciplines mentioned above are particular formulations of the log-linear model, as conceived in research on patterns of association in contingency tables.

(c) Enter the available data into the account, i.e., fill in the account as far as possible. In general, we do not know individual cell counts but only marginal totals. If some of the cell counts are observed, enter them into the account. Other prior information is listed separately.

(d) Determine the parameter values of the parametric model on the basis of the different types of prior information, supplemented by hypotheses about certain structural relationships in the data to be estimated. A hypothesis, frequently used when only aggregated data are available, is the assumption of independence between some of the variables. Model fitting and testing for independence are equivalent in the modeling perspective adopted in this chapter. This equivalence allows a remarkably simple and transparent approach to estimating missing elements in the account.

(e) Apply the model to infer the values of the missing elements.

In implementing this five-step procedure, methodological and practical problems may arise. Some of the potential problems are dealt with in this chapter. Section 2 focuses on data requirement and data availability. An illustrative overview is given of types of flow data that are available and of sources that may provide relevant data for multidimensional analysis. The overview is highly incomplete, but it demonstrates that it is worthwhile to search for additional and maybe uncommon data sources in order to fill the account as far as possible.

Section 3 discusses the log-linear model. Two model formulations are represented: the additive model is popular in interaction analyses; the multiplicative model may however be more appropriate in dealing with estimation problems. This section also reveals what information is sufficient to estimate the log-linear model parameters. These sufficiency conditions directly lead to the main theme of this paper, namely, the computation of expected cell counts from whatever data are available.

Different hypothetical situations of data availablity are considered in Section 4:

(i) marginal totals only;

(ii) marginal totals, supplemented by preliminary estimates of the cell counts

(iii) marginal totals and a few cell counts are given (i.e., exactly known).

These and related conditions of prior knowledge may be treated in a unified way, and a single multiproportional adjustment procedure for estimating the missing elements may be applied.

This general estimation technique is based on the log-linear analysis of the data sets and encompasses several approaches, found in the literature, to infer entries of an n-dimensional table from available data. Gravity modeling, entropy maximization, information gain minimization, and other popular estimation methods are equivalent to multiproportional adjustment. This equivalence indicates some interesting directions for further research aiming at the improvement of estimation techniques.

The techniques presented in this chapter, as well as some equivalent procedures, are applied to real data in Section 5. Two fields of application are selected: the estimation of social mobility tables and of migration tables.

2. DATA REQUIREMENTS AND DATA AVAILABILITY

Multidimensional demographic analysis requires gross flow data. Conventional demographic analysis of populations subdivided into subpopulations focuses on the size of each subpopulation and on changes in size. This stock perspective makes use of prevalence rates, which indicate the extent to which a particular characteristic is prevalent in the population (e.g., labor force participation rate, proportion of married population). In multidimensional analysis, population size is of secondary importance. The emphasis is on flows, i.e., passages among the various states; the magnitude of each subpopulation is merely an outcome of an initial condition and a flow mechanism. The rationale for adopting the flow perspective is that the dynamics underlying population change can more readily be represented. Entrances to and exits from each subpopulation are considered explicitly. The adoption of the flow perspective requires the existence of flow data. These data may be arranged in an accounting framework. The accounting framework is not only a convenient data-representation scheme, it is also a useful basis for the integration of data-estimation procedures. The accounting framework for multidimensional data representation and estimation is presented in Section 2.1. Section 2.2 gives an illustrative review of data sources for multidimensional population analysis and shows that the data problem is not all that bad. Several data sources with the right information have not yet been touched.

2.1. DATA REQUIREMENTS: AN ACCOUNTING FRAMEWORK

Multidimensional analysis requires age-specific flows among the various states considered in the analysis. The data may be arranged to constitute a multidimensional contingency table. This table represents the accounting framework in which the available information may be arranged and the estimation problem may be defined. In this chapter, we limit ourselves to a two-dimensional population system. One of the dimensions will be age. The findings may be generalized to any number of dimensions or, alternatively, a population system of a higher dimension can be reduced to two dimensions by increasing the number of states or categories in one or more dimensions (e.g., each of the four marital states may be sectioned by sex yielding eight states along the sex-marital status dimension).

For each age group, the number of passages from each state to any of the other states must be known. This information may be arranged in layers of two-way tables (Fig. 1). Let age (layer) be denoted by k, state of origin (row) by i, and state

Status of origin	Status of destination			
	1	2	3	Total
1	m_{11k}	m_{12k}	m_{13k}	$m_{1.k}$
2	m_{21k}	m_{22k}	m_{23k}	$m_{2.k}$
3	m_{31k}	m_{32k}	m_{33k}	$m_{3.k}$
Total	$m_{.1k}$	$m_{.2k}$	$m_{.3k}$	$m_{..k}$

Fig. 1. Account of passages for age group k.

of destination (column) by j. There are L age groups (layers), R origins (rows), and C destinations (columns) (R = C). The total number of cells in the account is therefore L × R × C. Let K, I, and J represent the index sets of, respectively, k, i, and j:

$$K = \{1,2,\ldots,k,\ldots L\},$$

$$I = \{1,2,\ldots,i,\ldots R\},$$

$$J = \{1,2,\ldots,j,\ldots C\}.$$

Some passages or aggregates of passages may be fixed, because they are actually known or observed, while others must be estimated. Let S be the set of cells in a multiway array or account that must be estimated. Formally, $S = \{(i,j,k) |$ passage from i to j by category k is possible, and not fixed$\}$. If the (i,j,k)-cell lies in S, we write $(i,j,k) \in S$. Reference will be made to four types of arrays: observed array $\{x_{ijk}\}$ containing the observed counts of the number of persons in category k passing from i to j; array of expected counts

$\{m_{ijk}\}$; prior array or array of preliminary estimates $\{m^0_{ijk}\}$ and array of maximum likelihood estimates (MLEs) of the expected counts, $\{\hat{m}_{ijk}\}$.

In practical applications, the array $\{x_{ijk}\}$ is not known, except for elements $(i,j,k) \notin S$, if any. The main use of an observed array lies in validity analyses of estimation methods.

Aggregations over the index sets I, J, or K are denoted by dots. For instance, the bivariate marginal $x_{.jk}$ is the marginal total of x_{ijk} over all $i \in I$. The unvariate marginal $x_{..k}$ is the sum of x_{ijk} over all $i \in I$ and $j \in J$. The overall total is $x_{...} = N$ and is equal to the total number of passages in the system. The marginal totals in the account are of particular relevance in multidimensional analysis with incomplete data since the information available of the passages generally is limited to aggregated flow values.

In this section, the term "passage" has not been defined. The definition very much depends on the way passages are measured and hence on the data collection system. In censuses and retrospective surveys, a passage is measured by comparing the status at the time of enumeration with the status at a prior date. In registration systems, however, each change in status is accounted for. Whatever passage definition is retained, the accounting framework is a useful strategy to integrate data availability and data estimation. Accounts also provide a logical connection between data and demographic models. Rees and Wilson (1977) and Rees (1980) elaborate on the advantages of accounting for demographic model building and propose some rules to designing accounts. The reader, interested in the problem of setting up an account, is referred to the literature, in particular to Rees (1980); in this chapter, we assume the accounting framework to be given and focus on the modeling of the data in the account and on the estimation of missing elements.

2.2. *ILLUSTRATIVE REVIEW OF SOURCES OF DATA FOR MULTIDIMENSIONAL POPULATION ANALYSIS*

In this section, we list some data sources that provide highly relevant data for multidimensional analysis. This review is not exhaustive, its only purpose is to illustrate the kind of data that are available and the types of estimation problems associated with it. Data availability is a fuzzy concept. Data may have been collected but not tabulated, or they may have been tabulated but not published. In the latter case, the data are generally available on microfiches; in the first case, they may be tabulated on request. This review considers data for multiregional analysis, labor force analysis, and marital status analysis. Some new areas of application of multidimensional demography are also discussed.

A. Multiregional analysis. Censuses and registration systems are the main sources of migration data. In several European countries, any change of residence must be registered. Central statistical offices collect the information from the local administration to prepare migration statistics. The "movement card" contains information on origin and destination, as well as on certain demographic characteristics such as age. The census is the main source of migration data in most countries. Relevant data may be derived from answers to such questions as age, place of enumeration, place of birth, place of previous residence, place of residence at a fixed prior date (1 or 5 yr ago), and duration of residence. An advantage of censuses is that they provide detailed information on migrant characteristics. A disadvantage, however, is that the information provided may not be up-to-date, because of the interval at which censuses are taken. Therefore, census data may be supplemented with migration information obtained through other sources such as household surveys and labor force surveys, which are also held at regular intervals. This poses the problem, however, of combining separate data sources; a problem that will be dealt with in this chapter.

B. Labor force analysis. Multidimensional tables of working life have been constructed for Denmark (Hoem and Fong, 1976; Willekens, 1980b) and for the United States (Schoen and Woodrow, 1980; Smith, 1980). Hoem and Fong use flow data generated by a special labor force survey in 1973-1974. The Schoen-Woodrow and Smith studies rely on Current Population Survey (CPS) data, provided by the Bureau of Census. Schoen and Woodrow give a detailed description of the data. Since January 1973, the CPS contains a retrospective question on the labor force status exactly one year ago. However, this question was only asked to persons aged 16 and over who are employed at the time of enumeration (about 60% of the total number of respondents). As a consequence, only part of the account can be filled with observed data. In the future, a more complete set of labor force flow data may become available in the U.S. The National Commission on Employment and Unemployment Statistics recently recommended that the CPS resume publication of gross flow data on occupational mobility and prepare monthly gross flow data time series tapes for public use. It also recommended that the next census questionnaire include a question on occupation, industry, and place of residence one year ago (Stein, 1980).

A potentially very useful data source for multidimensional labor force analysis is the biannual Labor Force Survey held since 1973 in each member country of the European Community. This survey distinguishes eight labor force statuses (of which one is employed) and contains for each status a retrospective question on the labor force status one year ago (since 1977, also the status two years ago is being asked). The survey, which is set up on a comparable basis in each country, provides rich demographic and socioeconomic information on the respondents. Care must however be given to extract only the information that is supported by the sample size. The Dutch National Program for Demographic Research initiated a project aiming at the development of multidimensional tables of working life for the Netherlands on the basis of the transition data provided by the Labor Force Survey. In a later stage, it will be investigated whether these data may also be used to project the labor force.

C. *Nuptiality analysis.* Flow data on marital formation and dissolution are more readily available than data for other applications of multidimensional analysis. The registration of changes in marital status is common in most countries. The Belgian and Dutch data situations are discussed in Willekens *et al.* (1979) and Koesoebjono (1981), respectively. Schoen and Nelson (1974) provide some insight into the kind of data on marital change available in the U.S.

D. Education analysis and other possible applications of multidimensional demography. Multiregional analysis, labor force, and nuptiality analysis, are only a few of the possibly many situations in which multidimensional demographic techniques may fruitfully be applied. In fact, any demographic investigation of renewable events may benefit from application of the increment-decrement life table model and hence from multidimensional demography. The growing number of retrospective surveys may furnish the required input data. Education analysis is one new possible field of application of multidimensional demography. In The Netherlands, data on flows to, from, and within the educational system were collected by the Central Bureau of Statistics in a retrospective survey of pupils in 1978. The survey inquired about type and level of education one year ago. The published flow matrix covers a large set of educational categories; the age dimension has however been neglected, but can easily be recovered. Other topics of analysis in which the application of multidimensional demographic techniques may lead to greater insight include the study of social mobility, family planning, and social security participation. For several of these studies, flow data may be available from retrospective surveys. If data availability is inadequate, however, multidimensional demography may still be considered. Appropriate estimation methods may infer the required data from the available knowledge. Such techniques are the subject of this chapter.

3. MODELING THE DATA IN THE ACCOUNT

The investigation of large data sets becomes relatively simple by fitting models to the data. During the past decade, the structural analysis of contingency tables attracted considerable interest, and the results of this research are well documented (Bishop *et al.*, 1975; Goodman, 1978; Gokhale and Kullback, 1978; Haberman, 1979). Analytical techniques, originally developed to identify patterns of associations among several categorical variables, may fruitfully be applied for estimation purposes.[2] The log-linear model is one of them. It is part of a class of generalized linear models, describing cell counts in terms of marginal totals and of interactions between cross-classified variables.

In Section 3.1, the log-linear model is presented; it is shown that it is an efficient tool for structural analysis of categorical data. Section 3.2 gives a simple rule for determining the necessary information to estimate the model parameters.

3.1. THE LOG-LINEAR MODEL

The log-linear model is not unknown in demography. Recently, an increasing number of authors is adopting this

[2] *In mathematical statistics, a distinction is made between "estimation" and "prediction." Estimation refers to model parameters, while prediction relates to the outcomes (of random variables) obtained by applying or postulating a particular model. In this chapter, no distinction is made because in the demographic literature "migration prediction" has a well-defined but different meaning. For the statistical theory of prediction as applied to migration, the reader is referred to de Jong (1981).*

modeling perspective to study dependencies among cross-tabulated demographic variables (Little, 1978, 1980; Little and Pullum, 1979; Hobcraft, 1978; Clogg, 1978, 1979; Fienberg and Mason, 1978).

The current formulation of the log-linear model is due to Birch (1963) and resembles the analysis-of-variance model. A neat review is by Payne (1977). Table 1 shows the model for the expected cell counts in two equivalent forms. The additive formulation is most popular since it closely resembles the analysis-of-variance paradigm. The multiplicative formulation is however convenient to solve estimation problems since it directly relates to conventional estimation models for flow data. This relationship to conventional models simplifies the interpretation of the model parameters in terms of available data. In addition, algorithms developed in regional science and transportation science may fruitfully be applied to solve estimation problems in multidimensional population analysis.

In both the additive and the multiplicative formulations, there are eight terms in the model. The number of terms depends on the dimension of the account and is unrelated to the number of cells or, equivalently, to the number of states or categories along the dimensions. The number of parameter-values, however, does depend on the number of cells in the account. In models (1) and (11), there are as many independent parameter-values as there are cells in the account. The model is therefore referred to as a *saturated log-linear model*. Each parameter in the model represents a particular structural effect on m_{ijk}. According to the log-linear model, the expected cell count is the sum of various effects. The overall

Figure 1. THE LOG-LINEAR MODEL

Multiplicative formulation

Model $m_{ijk} = w\, w_i^A w_j^B w_k^C w_{ij}^{AB} w_{ik}^{AC} w_{jk}^{BC} w_{ijk}^{ABC}$ (1)

Overall mean effect $w = \left[\prod_{i,j,k} m_{ijk} \right]^{\frac{1}{RCL}}$ (2)

Main effects $w_i^A = \frac{1}{w} \left[\prod_{j,k} m_{ijk} \right]^{\frac{1}{CL}}$ (3)

w_j^B and w_k^C: analogous

First-order interaction effects (two-way or pairwise interaction)

$$w_{ij}^{AB} = \frac{1}{z} \left[\prod_{k} m_{ijk} \right]^{\frac{1}{L}} \qquad (4)$$

with $z = w\, w_i^A w_j^B w_k^C$

w_{ik}^{AC} and w_{jk}^{BC}: analogous

Second-order interaction effects (three-way interaction)

$$w_{ijk}^{ABC} = \frac{1}{z'} m_{ijk}, \qquad (5)$$

with $z' = w\, w_i^A w_j^B w_k^C w_{ij}^{AB} w_{ik}^{AC} w_{jk}^{BC}$

Constraints $\prod_i w_i^A = \prod_j w_j^B = \prod_k w_k^C = 1$ (6)

$$\prod_i w_{ij}^{AB} = \prod_j w_{ij}^{AB} = \prod_i w_{ik}^{AC} = \prod_k w_{ik}^{AC} = \prod_j w_{jk}^{BC} = \prod_k w_{jk}^{BC} = 1 \qquad (7)$$

$$\prod_i w_{ijk}^{ABC} = \prod_j w_{ijk}^{ABC} = \prod_k w_{ijk}^{ABC} = 1 \qquad (8)$$

$$w = \exp u \qquad (9)$$

$$w_i^A = \exp u_i^A$$
$$w_{ij}^{AB} = \exp u_{ij}^{AB} \qquad (10)$$
$$w_{ijk}^{ABC} = \exp u_{ijk}^{ABC}$$

Additive formulation

$$\ln m_{ijk} = u + u_i^A + u_j^B + u_k^C + u_{ij}^{AB} + u_{ik}^{AC} + u_{jk}^{BC} + u_{ijk}^{ABC} \tag{11}$$

$$u = \frac{1}{RCL} \sum_{i,j,k} \ln m_{ijk} \tag{12}$$

$$u_i^A = \frac{1}{CL} \sum_{j,k} \ln m_{ijk} - u \tag{13}$$

u_j^B and u_k^C: analogous

$$u_{ij}^{AB} = \frac{1}{L} \sum_k \ln m_{ijk} - c \tag{14}$$

with $c = u + u_i^A + u_j^B + u_k^C$

u_{ik}^{AC} and u_{jk}^{BC}: analogous

$$u_{ijk}^{ABC} = \ln m_{ijk} - c', \tag{15}$$

with $c' = u + u_i^A + u_j^B + u_k^C + u_{ij}^{AB} + u_{ik}^{AC} + u_{jk}^{BC}$

$$\sum_i u_i^A = \sum_j u_j^B = \sum_k u_k^C = 0 \tag{16}$$

$$\sum_i u_{ij}^{AB} = \sum_j u_{ij}^{AB} = \sum_i {}_{ik}^{AC} = \sum_k u_{ik}^{AC} = \sum_j u_{jk}^{BC} = \sum_k u_{jk}^{BC} = 0 \tag{17}$$

$$\sum_i u_{ijk}^{ABC} = \sum_j u_{ijk}^{ABC} = \sum_k u_{ijk}^{ABC} = 0 \tag{18}$$

$$u = \ln w \tag{19}$$

$$u_i^A = \ln w_i^A$$
$$u_{ij}^{AB} = \ln w_{ij}^{AB} \tag{20}$$
$$u_{ijk}^{ABC} = \ln w_{ijk}^{ABC}$$

effect is a size-effect; it is the geometric mean of all cell counts. The main effects denote the effects on m_{ijk} of relative size differences between the various univariate marginals. For instance, w_k^C and u_k^C are the effects of the age classification on the number of passages m_{ijk}. Everything else equal, large age groups result in large values of m_{ijk}. The age effect is the ratio between the geometric mean of the k-th layer and the overall geometric mean. By comparing various geometric means, we can determine the range of effects exerted upon m_{ijk}. For example, to determine whether the age effect differs with the state of origin i, it suffices to calculate w_{ik}^{AC} or u_{ik}^{AC}. A nonzero value of u_{ik}^{AC} means the existence of an interaction between age and origin. Note that the pattern of interaction determined in this way represents the average interaction over all AC-tables (for all possible destination regions, i.e., j values of variable B). The pattern may differ for each level of B, resulting in a nonzero u_{ijk}^{ABC}. If $u_{ijk}^{ABC} \neq 0$, then the interaction between pairs of A, B, and C must also be nonzero. The principle that for any nonzero u-term its lower-order relatives must also be nonzero is referred to as the hierarchy principle (Bishop *et al.*, 1975, p. 34). Conversely, if any u-term is set equal to zero, its higher-order relatives must also be zero. In this chapter, only *hierarchical log-linear models* are considered.

By introducing the log-linear model, we have transformed the problem of estimating the cell counts into a problem of parameter-estimation, i.e., of quantifying the various effects. The effects are determined on the basis of available data augmented by assumption-making.

The following conclusion is the basis for the derivation of the estimation procedure. *To estimate the cell values in a multidimensional account, we must quantify the interaction effects. Hence data estimation is closely related to hypothesis testing.* If all data are available, i.e., if the array $\{x_{ijk}\}$ is known, then all parameter-values may be derived from the data. In Table 4 of Section 5, the parameters are shown of the log-linear model of a set of social mobility data. It can easily be seen that the saturated log-linear model replicates the observed data exactly, i.e.,

$$m_{ijk} = x_{ijk}.$$

In practical applications, $\{x_{ijk}\}$ is not known and the parameters must be calculated from whatever prior information exists. If certain parameters can not be estimated from available data, their value is set equal to zero, and the associated interaction effect is assumed to be absent. A log-linear model with certain terms absent is an *unsaturated model.* Section 3.2 describes an integrated approach to parameter estimation. It should be kept in mind that by estimating a log-linear model parameter, we are imposing a particular interaction pattern on the $\{m_{ijk}\}$-array. Conversely, if we want the estimates to express that certain variables depend on one another in a particular way, we must introduce this through appropriate values of the relevant model parameters.

3.2. *SUFFICIENT STATISTIC FOR OBTAINING CELL ESTIMATES*

First we determine what information is required for estimating the log-linear model parameters. To do this, we consider the account to be the outcome of a simple multinomial sampling scheme (sample in which the total sample size is fixed, say N, and each cell has an independent Poisson distribution). The account denotes then a multinomial distribution $M(N; m_{ijk}/m_{...})$ with probability density function (Fisher, 1922; Bishop *et al.*, 1975, p. 63):

$$P(X_{ijk} = x_{ijk} \text{ for all } i,j,k \mid X_{...} = N)$$

$$= \frac{N!}{\prod_{ijk} x_{ijk}!} \prod_{ijk} \left(\frac{m_{ijk}}{m_{...}}\right)^{x_{ijk}} . \tag{21}$$

The log-likelihood of the multinomial is

$$\ln\left\{\frac{N!}{\prod_{i,j,k} x_{ijk}!}\right\} + \sum_{i,j,k} x_{ijk} \ln m_{ijk} - N \ln m_{...} . \tag{22}$$

In maximizing the log-likelihood, under the assumption of $\sum_{ijk} (m_{ijk}/m_{...}) = 1$, we may disregard the first and third term and only consider the remaining term, the kernel of the log-likelihood function. The product-form of this kernel

$$W = \prod_{ijk} (m_{ijk})^{x_{ijk}} \tag{23}$$

represents the expected number of individuals falling into cell (i,j,k) if x_{ijk} members of the population of size N are randomly selected. The quantity W/N is, therefore, the probability that a randomly selected individual falls into the (i,j,k)-cell

Substituting $\ln m_{ijk}$ in the kernel for the log-linear model (11) gives:

$$\sum_{i,j,k} x_{ijk} \ln m_{ijk} = Nu + \sum_{i} x_{i..}\, u_i^A + \sum_{j} x_{.j.}\, u_j^B + \sum_{k} x_{..k}\, u_k^C + \sum_{i,j} x_{ij.}\, u_{ij}^{AB} + \sum_{i,k} x_{i.k}\, u_{ik}^{AB} + \sum_{j,k} x_{.jk}\, u_{jk}^{BC} + \sum_{i,j,k} x_{ijk}\, u_{ijk}^{ABC} . \qquad (24)$$

The sufficient statistic for estimating the parameters of the log-linear model consists of the x-terms adjacent to the unknown parameters. For instance, to determine the column effect u_j^B, we need to know the total $x_{.j.}$; and to determine the interaction between A and B, the marginal total $x_{ij.}$ must be known. Note that the interaction derived from $x_{ij.}$ is an average of the interaction patterns at various k-levels of the third variable C.

Knowledge of the bivariate marginal $x_{ij.}$ implies knowledge of the univariate marginals $x_{i..}$ and $x_{.j.}$ necessary to determine u_i^A and u_j^B, respectively. Hence we can define a minimal sufficient statistic (in this case $x_{ij.}$). In practice, the minimal sufficient statistic can be obtained by inspection of the log-linear model.

Expression (24) relates the log-linear model to the likelihood function. Birch (1963) has shown that there is a unique set of elementary cell-estimates that

(i) satisfies the conditions imposed by the form of the parametric model (log-linear);

(ii) satisfies the constraints that the marginal totals of the estimates m_{ijk} correspond to the given marginal totals ($x_{ij.}$, $x_{.j.}$, etc.); and

(iii) maximizes the likelihood function.

Hence, by applying the log-linear model, maximum likelihood estimates $\hat{m}_{ijk}$ of the expected counts m_{ijk} may be derived from the sufficient statistic alone. Formulated differently and more in line with the main theme of this chapter, application of the log-linear model to available data yields estimates that not only are consistent with what is known, but that also have a maximum likelihood of occurrence. The informed reader will notice the equivalence between these features and the characteristics of the estimates obtained by applying entropy maximization techniques, which have been developed by Wilson (1970) in the field of regional science. The equivalence between entropy maximization and maximum likelihood estimation is formally demonstrated by Batty and Mackie (1972) and Willekens (1980a).

4. PARAMETER ESTIMATION FROM AVAILABLE DATA

To estimate missing elements in the multidimensional account, a modeling approach was suggested and the log-linear model was selected as an adequate representation of the data. The functional form of the parametric model, underlying the estimation procedure, is therefore fixed. The sufficient statistic for estimating the model parameters consists of the x-terms adjacent to the unknown parameters. In this section, we review a procedure to derive parameter-values for this model from incomplete data. First, we assume that the prior information is limited to marginal totals only. Next, it will be shown how other types of prior information may be introduced. Whatever prior data are used, the estimation strategy is the same: prior knowledge yields estimates of log-linear model parameters and hence imposes a structure on the expected counts $\{m_{ijk}\}$. The better we can describe the structural relationship between the cross-classified variables, the better the estimates will be. If we are unable to obtain some parameter-values because of lack of information, observed or approximated, on the adjacent x-terms, the values are set equal to zero, implying the absence of the interaction pattern they represent.

4.1. *METHODS OF OBTAINING CELL ESTIMATES FROM MARGINAL TOTALS ONLY*

The MLEs we are looking for satisfy the log-linear model and the marginal constraints. The model and the constraints form a system of equations, the maximum likelihood equations, the solution of which yields the MLEs. In some cases, the MLE-equations have a closed-form solution.

A. *Closed-Form Expressions*

The estimates may be expressed in closed form if the known marginal totals satisfy particular conditions. For example, if the available information is limited to $x_{i..}$, $x_{.j.}$, and $x_{..k}$, then the MLEs $\hat{m}_{ijk}$ are the solution of the following system of equations:

Model equations:

$$m_{ijk} = w\ w_i^A w_j^B w_k^C$$

or

$$\ln m_{ijk} = u + u_i^A + u_j^B + u_k^C \tag{25}$$

with the w- and the u-parameters satisfying (6) and (16), respectively.

Minimal sufficient statistic equations:

$$\sum_{j,k} \hat{m}_{ijk} = x_{i..}\ , \tag{26}$$

$$\sum_{i,k} \hat{m}_{ijk} = x_{.j.}\ , \tag{27}$$

$$\sum_{i,j} \hat{m}_{ijk} = x_{..k}\ , \tag{28}$$

$$\sum_{i,j,k} \hat{m}_{ijk} = x_{...} = N\ . \tag{29}$$

The cell estimates for model (25) and the sufficient statistic consisting of (26) to (29) are

$$\hat{m}_{ijk} = \frac{x_{i..}\ x_{.j.}\ x_{..k}}{N^2}\ .$$

This formula provides a closed-form expression of MLEs in terms of sufficient statistics. It is the simplest illustration of the multidimensional estimation problem. Willekens *et al.* (1979) label this case the 3E (edge)-problem since the known information may be arranged on the edges of a box, the contents of which must be estimated. Several other closed-form estimates in three dimensions exist. They may be derived by solving the appropriate set of maximum likelihood equations. Table 2 summarizes the results. The available data are represented as a set of univariate and/or bivariate marginals. In a multiregional population system, for instance, a case could arise in which the migration pattern is known for the total population and only a single age structure of migrants is given. This prior information could be arranged on one face and one edge of a box and hence the label IFE (face-edge)-problem may be used. The MLE procedure reduces to applying the age composition $\frac{1}{N} x_{..k}$ to each of the elements of the migration matrix $x_{ij.}$. The application of a single age composition implies that in the m_{ijk} array, age is independent of region of origin and of region of destination. Although an unrealistic assumption, it is enforced on the model because of limited prior information. Since we do not have sufficient statistics to estimate all the parameters of the log-linear model, we postulate that some parameters are zero, with the consequence that the interaction effects they represent are absent. In the next section we shall see that even in the absence of "hard" data, we can impose some structure on the $\{m_{ijk}\}$ array by using "softer" information such as data collected at some prior date, expert opinion, relative measures obtained in sample surveys, etc.

The existence of closed-form expressions for the MLEs is very convenient in multidimensional analysis with incomplete data. Bishop *et al.* (1975, pp. 76-82) provide a few rules for detecting the existence of direct estimates. The interesting feature of these rules is that they apply to accounts of any dimension. The main idea is to delete the redundant configurations of available data or overlapping subconfigurations. If

TABLE 2. MLEs in Three-Dimensional Accounts

Case	Available data	Log-linear model	Closed-form cell estimates	Interpretation of log-linear
3E	{A, B, C}	$m_{ijk} = w\, w_i^A w_j^B w_k^C$	$\hat{m}_{ijk} = \frac{1}{N^2} x_{i..}\, x_{.j.}\, x_{..k}$	Mutual independence (variables A, B, and C are independent)
IFE	{AB, C}	$m_{ijk} = w\, w_i^A w_j^B w_k^C w_{ij}^{AB}$	$\hat{m}_{ijk} = \frac{1}{N} x_{ij.}\, x_{..k}$	Multiple independence (joint variable AB is independent of C)
2F	{AB, BC}	$m_{ijk} = w\, w_i^A w_j^B w_k^C w_{ij}^{AB} w_{jk}^{BC}$	$\hat{m}_{ijk} = x_{ij.}\, x_{.jk}/x_{.j.}$	Conditional independence (A independent of C, given B)
3F	{AB, AC, BC}	$m_{ijk} = w\, w_i^A w_j^B w_k^C w_{ij}^{AB} w_{jk}^{BC} w_{ik}^{AC}$	No closed-form solution	Pairwise association (each two-way interaction is independent of level of third variable)
CI	{ABC}	$m_{ijk} = w\, w_i^A w_j^B w_k^C w_{ij}^{AB} w_{jk}^{BC} w_{ik}^{AC} w_{ijk}^{ABC}$	$\hat{m}_{ijk} = x_{ijk}$	Three-way interaction (association between every pair of variables varies with level of third variable)

no more than two configurations remain, closed-form estimates exist. In general (for any dimension), it can be shown that this statement implies that at least one two-factor effect must be absent for direct estimates to exist. The general form of the direct estimates is predictable: the numerator has entries from each sufficient configuration; the denominator has entries from redundant configurations caused by overlapping; terms in powers of N ensure the right order of magnitude. The overlapping is illustrated in the 2F-case: the subscript j appears in both the AB and the BC configurations.

B. Iterative Fitting by Multiproportional Adjustment

To derive the MLEs, the 3F-problem requires a minimal sufficient statistic, consisting of three bivariate marginals. No closed-form solution exists, and iterative fitting of the sufficient configurations or prior data is the only way out. To start the procedure, we may choose any set of preliminary estimates that do not exhibit a three-factor effect ($u_{ijk}^{ABC} = 0$). For instance, the uniform distribution satisfies this condition, hence a convenient starting value is $m_{ijk}^{(0)} = 1$ for all i, j, and k.

The iterative algorithm goes as follows:

Step 0: $s = 0$

Step 1: Proportional adjustment along the C dimension

$$\hat{m}_{ijk}^{(3s+1)} = \hat{m}_{ijk}^{(3s)} \frac{x_{ij.}}{\sum_k \hat{m}_{ijk}^{(3s)}} .$$

Step 2: Proportional adjustment along the A dimension

$$\hat{m}_{ijk}^{(3s+2)} = \hat{m}_{ijk}^{(3s+1)} \frac{x_{.jk}}{\sum_i \hat{m}_{ijk}^{(3s+1)}} .$$

Step 3: Proportional adjustment along the B dimension

$$\hat{m}_{ijk}^{(3s+3)} = \hat{m}_{ijk}^{(3s+2)} \frac{x_{i.k}}{\sum_j \hat{m}_{ijk}^{(3s+2)}} .$$

If the stopping criterion

$$\left| \frac{\hat{m}_{ijk}^{(3s+3)}}{\hat{m}_{ijk}^{(3s+2)}} - 1 \right| \leq \varepsilon$$

for every i, j, and k is satisfied, then stop the iteration; otherwise s = s + 1 and go to step 1.

The algorithm is a special variant of a more general algorithm discussed in Section 4.2. This method of successive proportional adjustment is known under various names. It was originally developed by Bartlett in 1935, who called it the "no second-order interaction model." In contingency table analysis, it became known as the iterative proportional fitting (IPF) method (see, e.g., Bishop *et al.*, 1975, pp. 83-97). In this chapter, the algorithm is referred to as multiproportional adjustment (MAD) algorithm, for reasons that will become clear later. Applying the Rockafellar decomposition principle, Willekens *et al.* (1979) show that this algorithm may be derived from a maximization of the entropy function

$$\sum_{i,j,k} m_{ijk} \ln m_{ijk} , \qquad (30)$$

subject to the bivariate constraints {AB, AC, BC} and that the method converges to a unique solution (a number of other proofs of convergence of IPF exist; see references in Bishop *et al.*, 1975, p. 85). They demonstrate that the IPF algorithm is equivalent to the direct primal algorithm of the nonlinear mathematical programming problem. In addition, the authors derive an algorithm, based on the dual formulation of the programming problem. The advantage of this dual formulation is that it relates more directly to the parameters of the log-linear model. The dual will be discussed in the next section.

To show that MAD does not introduce a third-order effect, we may rewrite the estimates as a product of functions in two variables only:

$$\hat{m}_{ijk} = f_1(i,j) \cdot f_2(j,k) \cdot f_3(i,k), \tag{31}$$

with

$$f_1(i,j) = \prod_s \frac{\hat{m}_{ij.}}{\sum_k \hat{m}_{ijk}^{(3s)}},$$

$$f_2(j,k) = \prod_s \frac{\hat{m}_{.jk}}{\sum_i \hat{m}_{ijk}^{(3s+1)}},$$

$$f_3(i,k) = \prod_s \frac{\hat{m}_{i.k}}{\sum_j \hat{m}_{ijk}^{(3s+2)}},$$

where s denotes the iteration. Equivalent algorithms to calculate the bivariate functions of (31) are presented by Chilton and Poet (1973) and Caussinus and Thelot (1976).

4.2. METHODS OF OBTAINING CELL ESTIMATES FROM MARGINAL TOTALS SUPPLEMENTED BY OTHER PRIOR INFORMATION

The x-terms adjacent to the unknown parameters are sufficient for estimating the parameters of the log-linear model [see expression (24)]. In the previous section we assumed the parameters to be zero and the interaction pattern they represent to be absent, if the required x-term was not available. In particular, we were unable to assign any value to the u^{ABC}-term since the individual cell counts x_{ijk} were unknown. If some x-terms are not available, the parameter estimates may be derived from other sources of prior information. A combination of different data sources may permit the derivation of adequate estimates for log-linear model parameters and for cell counts. We shall call *main data source* to set of known x-terms; *auxiliary data sources* is (are) the prior information from which the model parameters are derived that cannot directly be obtained from the x-terms. Prior information may come in various ways. For instance, detailed mobility data may be lacking for one country, but may exist for another country. If the two countries are similar, then log-linear model parameters obtained for one country may be applied to derive mobility estimates for the other country. Analogously, similar data sources of different periods may be combined. Censuses may have the required detailed information for multidimensional population analysis, but the statistics may be outdated. A combination of census information and more recent data may yield an adequate data base for multidimensional analysis. Sometimes, expert opinion, intuition, and common sense may be introduced to increase the quality of the data base. We may know in advance that certain transitions are impossible or must take on certain values. For instance, reentrance into the state of never-married is impossible. In some cases, certain transitions are disregarded: in multiregional analysis, intraregional migrations are generally left out of consideration because they do not affect population redistribution. Fixed cell values arise when certain x_{ijk}-elements are observed. This is, for instance, illustrated by the data base used by Schoen and Woodrow (1980) to construct tables of working life. Labor force transitions were observed for a subgroup of the population only, namely, for those persons employed at the time of enumeration. The transitions made by persons in a different labor force category, had to be estimated.

The aim of this section is to show how an appropriate auxiliary data source may be generated if it does not exist, and how it may be combined with the main data source to yield accurate estimates for log-linear model parameters and cell counts. The main idea is that the parameters, which cannot be estimated from the main data source, are derived ("borrowed") from the auxiliary source.

4.2.1. Combining Separate Data Sources

The auxiliary data source is denoted by $\{x^0_{ijk}\}$ and it gives rise to the array or account of preliminary estimates $\{m^0_{ijk}\}$. The account is of the same dimension and magnitude as the $\{x_{ijk}\}$-account. If all x^0_{ijk} are observed, then $m^0_{ijk} = x^0_{ijk}$. In this chapter, we assume that all x^0_{ijk} are observed. Both the main and the auxiliary data sets may be modeled by the log-linear expressions:

$$\ln m_{ijk} = u + u_i^A + u_j^B + u_k^C + u_{ij}^{AB} + u_{ik}^{AC} + u_{jk}^{BC} + u_{ijk}^{ABC} , \quad (32)$$

$$\ln m_{ijk}^0 = {}^0u + {}^0u_i^A + {}^0u_j^B + {}^0u_k^C + {}^0u_{ij}^{AB} + {}^0u_{ik}^{AC} + {}^0u_{jk}^{BC} + {}^0u_{ijk}^{ABC} , \quad (33)$$

and

$$\ln \frac{m_{ijk}}{m_{ijk}^0} = {}^ru + {}^ru_i^A + {}^ru_j^B + {}^ru_k^C + {}^ru_{ij}^{AB} + {}^ru_{ik}^{AC} + {}^ru_{jk}^{BC} + {}^ru_{ijk}^{ABC} , \quad (34)$$

with

$$u = u - {}^0u ,$$

$${}^ru_i^A = u_i^A - {}^0u_i^A , \quad {}^ru_j^B = u_j^B - {}^0u_j^B , \quad {}^ru_k^C = u_k^C - {}^0u_k^C ,$$

$${}^ru_{ij}^{AB} = u_{ij}^{AB} - {}^0u_{ij}^{AB} , \quad {}^ru_{ik}^{AC} = u_{ik}^{AC} - {}^0u_{ik}^{AC} , \quad {}^ru_{jk}^{BC} = u_{jk}^{BC} - {}^0u_{jk}^{BC} ,$$

$${}^ru_{ijk}^{ABC} = u_{ijk}^{ABC} - {}^0u_{ijk}^{ABC} .$$

The multiplicative formulation of the log-linear model (34) is

$$m_{ijk} = m_{ijk}^0 \; {}^rw \; {}^rw_i^A \; {}^rw_j^B \; {}^rw_k^C \; {}^rw_{ij}^{AB} \; {}^rw_{ik}^{AC} \; {}^rw_{jk}^{BC} \; {}^rw_{ijk}^{ABC} , \quad (35)$$

where the superscript r denotes the ratio of the w-term in the log-linear model of the final estimates to the ${}^0w$-term in the log-linear model of the preliminary estimates. Assuming that the auxiliary account is completely observed ($m_{ijk}^0 = x_{ijk}^0$), the associated log-linear model is saturated and all the ${}^0u$-parameters, including the second-order interaction term, may be calculated from the preliminary estimates. Values of the u-parameters, on the other hand, are determined as follows:

(i) for available x-terms, the associated u-parameters are calculated from the main data source;

(ii) the u-parameters that cannot be determined from the main data source are set equal to the equivalent ^0u-terms.

According to this procedure, interaction patterns between variables in the $\{m_{ijk}\}$-account are derived from the main data source as far as possible; interaction patterns, which cannot be determined this way, are assumed to be equal to the interaction patterns observed in the auxiliary account. We may now answer an important question: How does the auxiliary data source contribute to the quality of the m_{ijk}-estimates? The auxiliary data set introduces interaction patterns into the final estimates that cannot be derived from the main data source. As a corollary, we may conclude that through a selection of an appropriate $\{m^0_{ijk}\}$-array, combined with the right set of x-terms, we can impose any desired higher-order interaction patterns onto the $\{m_{ijk}\}$-account. This approach may be of great use in multidimensional population analysis with incomplete data. The estimates obtained are MLEs or are approximations to MLEs depending on the data available (Haberman, 1979, pp. 519-540).

The $\{m_{ijk}\}$-account that satisfies the conditions spelled out above, may be obtained without calculation of the log-linear model parameters as an intermediate step. Proportional adjustments of the cells of the $\{m^0_{ijk}\}$-account to fit a set of predefined margins (x-terms) yield the appropriate estimates. If three bivariate marginal totals ($x_{ij.}$, $x_{i.k}$, $x_{.jk}$) are known, the algorithm closely resembles the Bartlett procedure, mentioned in the previous section and denoted as multiproportional adjustment. Instead of starting with the uniform distribution, yielding a "no second-order interaction" model, the $\{m^0_{ijk}\}$-array is used:

Step 0: $m^{(0)}_{ijk} = m^0_{ijk}$ for all $i,j,k \in S$

The algorithm converges to MLEs (Haberman, 1979, p. 540). In this 3F-case, the main effects and first-order interaction effects are derived from the given marginals; only the second-order interaction effects are "borrowed" from the $\{m^0_{ijk}\}$-array, i.e., $u^{ABC}_{ijk} = {}^0u^{ABC}_{ijk}$ and, hence, ${}^ru^{ABC}_{ijk} = 0$. The log-linear model of this 3F-case is easily derived from (34) by deleting the second-order interaction term. The log-linear model is equivalent to the expression obtained by Willekens *et al.* (1979, p. 23) through maximizing the dual of the entropy function

$$\sum_{i,j,k} m_{ijk} \ln(m_{ijk}/m^0_{ijk})$$

subject to the three sets of bivariate constraints that constitute the minimal sufficient statistic.

The solution of the dual entropy problem is

$$m_{ijk} = m^0_{ijk} \exp[-(1+\lambda_{ij}+\nu_{ik}+\xi_{jk})] \; , \tag{36}$$

with λ_{ij}, ν_{ik}, and ξ_{jk} the dual variables associated with the $x_{ij.}$, $x_{i.k}$, and $x_{.jk}$ constraints, respectively. Some analogies between log-linear modeling and entropy maximization were already shown in the previous section (see also Willekens, 1980a) The dual variables of the entropy maximization may be expressed in terms of the u-parameters of the log-linear model and vice versa. The multiproportional adjustment algorithm is slightly different if another combination of marginal totals is given. For instance, consider the 1FE-case, with $x_{ij.}$ and $x_{..k}$ given, the algorithm then goes as follows:

Step 0: $s = 0$

$$m_{ijk}^{(0)} = m_{ijk}^{0} \quad \text{for all } i,j,k \in S.$$

Step 1: For each k-value, adjust the (i,j)-matrix to the total $x_{..k}$

$$\hat{m}_{ijk}^{(2s+1)} = \hat{m}_{ijk}^{(2s)} \frac{x_{..k}}{\sum_{i,j} \hat{m}_{ijk}^{(2s)}} \quad \text{for all } k.$$

Step 2: Adjust along the age dimension k

$$\hat{m}_{ijk}^{(2s+2)} = \hat{m}_{ijk}^{(2s+1)} \frac{x_{ij.}}{\sum_{k} \hat{m}_{ijk}^{(2s+1)}} \quad \text{for all } i \text{ and } j.$$

Unless the stopping criterion is reached, $S = s + 1$ and go to step 1. The estimates are MLEs with main effects and the (AB)-interaction effect derived from the marginal totals and with the (AC), (BC), and (ABC) effects "borrowed" from the preliminary estimates, i.e., $u_{ik}^{AC} = {}^{0}u_{ik}^{AC}$; $u_{jk}^{BC} = {}^{0}u_{jk}^{BC}$ and $u_{ijk}^{ABC} = {}^{0}u_{ijk}^{ABC}$. The log-linear model (34) reduces to

$$\ln\left(m_{ijk}/m_{ijk}^{0}\right) = {}^{r}u + {}^{r}u_{i}^{A} + {}^{r}u_{j}^{B} + {}^{r}u_{k}^{C} + {}^{r}u_{ij}^{AB}$$

or

$$m_{ijk} = m_{ijk}^{0} \; {}^{r}w \; {}^{r}w_{i}^{A} \; {}^{r}w_{j}^{B} \; {}^{r}w_{k}^{C} \; {}^{r}w_{ij}^{AB} .$$

Analogously, an algorithm can be derived for the 3E-problem.

This problem was studied by Evans and Kirby (1974) in an attempt to generalize spatial interaction (gravity) models developed in transportation science in order to infer area-to-area traffic flows by types of goods. The Evans-Kirby model is as follows:

$$m_{ijk} = r_i s_j p_k m^0_{ijk} ,$$

with r_i, s_j, and p_k balancing factors. This model is nothing else but the log-linear model of the 3E-case, with only the main effects present in the x-terms.

Note that any set of preliminary estimates that exhibits the same interaction effects not found in the x-terms (marginals) leads to the same final estimates (for a formal proof, see Bishop *et al.*, 1975, p. 93). Hence, in the 3F-case, any array with given u^{ABC}_{ijk}-values yields the same estimates. This is not surprising since the only contribution of the initial array to the final estimates is the second-order interaction.

The multiproportional adjustment algorithm has a long history. In the statistical literature, it is often associated with Deming and Stephan (1940) and referred to as the "classical" iterative proportional fitting procedure (Bishop *et al.*, 1975, p. 84). For two-dimensional tables (matrices), however, the method was also independently developed in other areas of scientific inquiry to solve estimation problems. According to Murchland (1978), the earliest application of this technique of biproportional fitting was in forcasting telephone traffic to evaluate the needs for network expansion and dates back to 1937 (Kruithof, 1937). The algorithm is widely used in transportation science where it was introduced in 1954 by Fratar in an attempt to forecast area-to-area person transportation demand. Since then, transportation science, where the technique is also known as Furness procedure, elaborated the method in order to estimate spatial interaction flows. The direction of elaboration was a reformulation as a gravity model (see below). Transportation scientists also applied the gravity model to infer migration flows and the technique was later adopted by migration analysts. A further independent development of the biproportional adjustment procedure is due to Leontief (1940) and Stone (1962), both in the economic field. In input-output modeling, the technique is known as RAS method and associated with Stone, and as nonsurvey technique for estimating input-output tables. It has been investigated extensively (Bacharach, 1970; MacGill, 1977). The link with the log-linear model of categorical data has however not been made. As a consequence, the contribution of each source of prior information to the estimates could not be unraveled.

In the RAS technique, the model format is as follows (for a two-dimensional table):

$$m_{ij} = r_i s_j m_{ij}^0 \quad . \tag{37}$$

The balancing factors r_i and s_j must be determined from the data. Because the sum of row totals must be equal to the sum of column totals, the balancing factors are unique up to a scalar value. Various scaling procedures may be imagined. In the illustrations in Section 5, we postulate $s_1 = 1$. Stone (1962) suggested the following iterative procedure:

Step 0: s (step) = 0

$$r_i^{(0)} = 1 .$$

Step 1: $$s_j^{(2s+1)} = \frac{x_{.j}}{\sum_i r_i^{(2s)} m_{ij}^0} \quad \text{for } j = 2,3,\ldots C .$$

Step 2: $$r_i^{(2s+2)} = \frac{x_{i.}}{\sum_j s_j^{(2s+1)} m_{ij}^0} \quad \text{for } i = 1,2,\ldots R .$$

Unless the stopping criterion is reached, s = s + 1 and go to step 1. The Frater or Furness technique follows the same algorithm. As was already pointed out, the bi-(multi-)proportional adjustment problem may also be solved by maximizing an entropy function. In the two-dimensional case, the entropy solution is

$$m_{ij} = m_{ij}^0 \exp[-(1+\lambda_i+\mu_j)] , \tag{38}$$

where λ_i and μ_j are dual variables associated with the row constraints and column constraints, respectively.[3]

[3] *Sometimes, (38) is written as*

$$m_{ij} = m_{ij}^0 \exp[\hat{\lambda}_i+\hat{\mu}_j].$$

Both expressions are equivalent since one may define $\hat{\lambda}_i = 1 - \lambda_i$ *and* $\hat{\mu}_j = -\mu_j$. *Whereas (38) follows from maximizing the entropy*

$$W = \sum_{i,j} m_{ij} \ln(m_{ij}/m_{ij}^0) ,$$

the above expression follows from minimizing the negentropy (-W), also referred to as information gain or information divergence. The structural similarity between biproportional adjustment and information minimization is therefore also demonstrated.

The balancing factors of the RAS-technique and the dual variables or Lagrange multipliers of the entropy method are related to one another. We may write:

$$\lambda_i = -(1 + \ln r_i), \quad \mu_j = -\ln s_j.$$

By relating the multipliers and the balancing factors to the log-linear model parameters, they may be given a statistical interpretation. Since

$$-[1+\lambda_i+\mu_j] = {}^r u + {}^r u_i^A + {}^r u_j^B ,$$

and since $\sum_j {}^r u_j^B = 0$, we have

$$\sum_j - [1+\lambda_i+\mu_j] = C\,{}^r u + C\,{}^r u_i^A ,$$

and, consequently,

$$\lambda_i = -\left[1 + \frac{1}{C} \sum_j \mu_j + {}^r u + {}^r u_i^A\right],$$

$$\mu_j = -\left[1 + \frac{1}{R} \sum_i \lambda_i + {}^r u + {}^r u_j^B\right], \tag{39}$$

with C and R the number of, respectively, columns and rows in the matrix. Expressing the log-linear model parameters in terms of the Lagrange multipliers gives:

$${}^r u = -\left[1 + \frac{1}{R} \sum_i \lambda_i + \frac{1}{C} \sum_j \mu_j\right],$$

$${}^r u_i^A = -\left[1 + \lambda_i + \frac{1}{C} \sum_j \mu_j\right] - {}^r u$$

$${}^r u_j^B = -\left[1 + \frac{1}{R} \sum_i \lambda_i + \mu_j\right] - {}^r u . \tag{40}$$

The equalities hold for any scaling applied to the balancing factors and to the Lagrange multipliers.

4.2.2. *Obtaining Cell Estimates from Marginal Totals When Some Cell Values Are Fixed*

In the previous section it was assumed that none of the individual x_{ijk}-values was known exactly. In practice, it happens frequently that some cell counts are given. The data set used by Schoen and Woodrow (1980) is a case in point.

Recall that S is the set of (i,j,k)-cells that are not fixed. The treatment of $(i,j,k) \notin S$ is very simple. An $\{m^0_{ijk}\}$-array is constructed that contains a zero value in all (i,j,k)-cells not in S. To construct $\{m^0_{ijk}\}$, first all structural zeros ($x_{ijk} = 0$) are entered into the account of preliminary estimates. Next, non-zero x_{ijk}'s are subtracted from the associated marginal totals and then removed from the table; a zero is entered in the appropriate cells of the $\{m^0_{ijk}\}$-account. The remaining cells are given a value of one (or any value expressing a desired interaction effect). This procedure yields the following accounts:

(a) $m^0_{ijk} = 0$ for cells $(i,j,k) \notin S$,

$m^0_{ijk} = 1$ for cells $(i,j,k) \in S$,

(b) the $\{x_{ijk}\}$-account contains the revised marginal totals.

The expected m_{ijk}-values are computed by the multiproportional adjustment algorithm. However, only cells in S are taken into account and hence structural zeros are preserved in the estimation procedure. The interaction structure imposed on the estimates is one of *quasi-independence* (Bishop *et al.*, 1975,

p. 179). Quasi-independence implies independence between the cross-classified variables provided that we do not consider rows, columns, or layers that have structural zero entries in at least one of the cells. The log-linear model of a table containing structural zeros is defined for the subtable with cells $(i,j,k) \in S$; the parameters are computed on the basis of the nonzero cells only.

This simple procedure may pave the way for a new combination of observed and estimated data. Cell values for critical categories may be obtained from a special survey, whereas the remaining cell values can be estimated by other means. Hewings and Janson (1980) propose such a procedure for input-output analysis.

4.2.3. Constructing Accounts of Preliminary Estimates

Patterns of interaction between cross-classified variables, which are not contained in the x-terms, may be imposed on the final estimates through the account of preliminary estimates. Any $\{m^0_{ijk}\}$-account that exhibits the desired interaction patterns yields the same set of final estimates. In estimation problems, the true interaction patterns, i.e., those of the $\{x_{ijk}\}$-account, are not all known. In general, higher-order interaction patterns are unknown and can only be approximated by choosing an appropriate $\{m^0_{ijk}\}$-array. Several strategies may be adopted, only a few are mentioned here.

A. Outdated table. If structural change is minor, then the $\{m^0_{ijk}\}$-account may consist of a table collected at a prior data. The table as such may be outdated, but the interaction pattern may still be valid. By adjusting the old table to new marginals, the higher-order interaction pattern is kept. This procedure is generally followed in input-output analysis, where the preliminary estimates are generated by a survey held at a prior date, and the new marginals are taken from the national accounts. The same procedure is proposed by Shulman and Chaddha (1978) and Shulman (1979) to infer detailed population characteristics in an intercensal period from a combination of up-to-date aggregate data and outdated but detailed census-tabulations. In multidimensional population analysis, the data frequently come from censuses or special surveys held periodically but with intervals of considerable length. Adequate data sets may be generated by updating census information using recent aggregate data.

B. Table of intermediate/explanatory variables. Another approach is to derive a pattern of interaction from a cross classification of intermediate or explanatory variables. In this case, the account of preliminary estimates consists of intermediate or explanatory variables, and the higher-order interaction effects in this account are assumed to apply to the account of final estimates. This approach is widely used in spatial interaction analysis, although only implicitly. The spatial interaction models, developed in transportation science and regional science, have never been looked at as discrete multivariate analysis techniques. Only very recently were the analogies with models of categorical data realized (Willekens, 1980a). The disaggregated choice models for spatial interaction analysis, which are becoming increasingly popular, are also more closely tied to categorical data analysis, in particular to logit and probit analysis (McFadden, 1978).

In spatial interaction modeling, the challenge is to obtain accurate estimates of area-to-area flows of goods (transportation, traffic) or people (migration) on the basis of some aggregate data and some information on measures of spatial "friction," "impedance," or "deterrence." To derive these estimates, analysts have generally used the gravity model. The origin of the gravity model is not in statistics but in mechanics.

In the late nineteenth century, scientists such as Carey and Ravenstein pronounced the analogy between physical phenomena governed by Newton's law of gravity and social interactions. In 1948, Stewart formalized the idea by proposing that the interaction between place i and place j is directly related to the number of people in both places and is inversely related to the squared distance:

$$m_{ij} = gP_iP_j/d_{ij}^2 , \tag{41}$$

where g is a constant to be determined from the data. Several efforts have been devoted to modifying the social gravity model without endangering its fundamental structure. The gravity model is a log-linear-model and may be written in terms of the model discussed earlier:

$$m_{ij} = ww_i^A w_j^B m_{ij}^0 , \tag{42}$$

with $w = g$, $w_i^A = P_i$, $w_j^B = P_j$, and $m_{ij}^0 = d_{ij}^{-2}$. This transformation clarifies the role each term plays in the gravity model. The population figures generate the main effects; the distance term contributes the first-order interaction effect to the

$\{m_{ij}\}$-matrix. Distance is a spatial friction factor, inhibiting interaction. The modifications of the gravity model, made in an attempt to increase the accuracy of the estimates, affect the way the main effects are measured and the first-order interaction is described. A review of the approach may be found in Wilson (1970) and, more recently, in Hua and Porell (1979). Particularly interesting to follow are the designs of spatial distribution functions $\{m_{ij}^0\}$, normally represented as F_{ij}. March (1971) summarizes the main types of functions proposed in the literature. Some of the functions commonly used are

(i) Inverse power function

$$F_{ij} = d_{ij}^{-\gamma} \tag{43}$$

(ii) Negative exponential function

$$F_{ij} = \exp[-\delta d_{ij}] \tag{44}$$

(iii) Tanner function

$$F_{ij} = \exp[-\delta_1 d_{ij}] d_{ij}^{-\delta_2} , \tag{45}$$

where γ, δ, δ_1, and δ_2 are parameters to be estimated [Batty and Mackie (1972) provide an extensive overview of estimation procedures]. Instead of distance d_{ij}, transportation cost from i to j, c_{ij}, may be used. Whatever distribution function is used, its main purpose remains the same, namely, to get the best quantitative approximation of the higher-order interaction patterns, assumed to be present in the account to be estimated. The distribution function affects the estimates in a way which is completely analogous to the account of preliminary estimates.

As a result, research finding gathered in spatial interaction analysis may fruitfully be applied to categorical data analysis and vice versa.

5. NUMERICAL APPLICATIONS

To illustrate the techniques presented in this chapter, they are applied to two sets of mobility data. The first set consists of age-aggregated social mobility data of Britain and Denmark (Table 3). This simple application allows us to pay attention to the log-linear model parameters and their relationship to the balancing factors of the biproportional adjustment method and to the dual variables of the entropy maximization problem without getting lost in the cheer volume of numbers. The data set has already been thoroughly investigated by Bishop *et al.* (1975) from the perspective of testing for the presence of a particular pattern of interaction in the data.[4] In this chapter, the interest is in the estimation of missing elements. Comparison of the worked examples of both perspectives illustrates a major point made in this chapter, namely, that estimation of missing elements in cross-classified data is equivalent to testing hypotheses on statistical independence. An additional consideration for selecting this illustration is that the study of social mobility patterns is an area to which multidimensional demographic techniques may fruitfully be applied, if an age dimension can be added to

[4] *A similar analysis was carried out by Hauser (1979) for US-mobility data.*

TABLE 3. Observed Danish and British Social Mobility Data[a]

Father's status	Son's status					Total
	1	2	3	4	5	
A. Danish data						
1	18	17	16	4	2	57
2	24	105	109	59	21	318
3	23	84	289	217	95	708
4	8	49	175	348	198	778
5	6	8	69	201	246	530
Total	79	263	658	829	562	2391
B. British data						
1	50	45	8	18	8	129
2	28	174	84	154	55	495
3	11	78	110	223	96	518
4	14	150	185	714	447	1510
5	3	42	72	320	411	848
Total	106	489	459	1429	1017	3500

[a]*Source: Bishop et al., 1975, p. 100.*

social mobility tables (the mobility figures in Table 3 are life-time measures). The second data set consists of age-specific migration flows of Austria and Sweden. Both countries publish age-specific flows by region of origin and of destination. The $\{x_{ijk}\}$-account is therefore completely known. Willekens *et al.* (1979) used these data sets to test the validity of estimation methods they developed to infer the necessary migration data for multiregional population analysis. The main results are summarized here.

TABLE 4. Parameters of Saturated Log-Linear Model

Father's status	Son's status 1	2	3	4	5	Row effect
A. Danish social mobility table						
1	1.94	0.92	-0.07	-1.35	-1.46	-1.67
2	0.42	0.93	0.04	-0.47	-0.92	0.15
3	-0.33	0.00	0.31	0.13	-0.11	0.85
4	1.21	-0.36	-0.01	0.78	0.80	0.67
5	-0.82	-1.50	-0.27	0.90	1.69	0.00
Column effect	-1.17	-0.21	0.72	0.62	0.03	3.78
B. British social mobility table						
1	2.47	0.62	-0.83	-1.01	-1.24	-1.23
2	0.45	0.54	0.08	-0.31	-0.76	0.21
3	-0.38	-0.16	0.46	0.17	-0.09	0.10
4	-0.96	-0.33	0.15	0.51	0.62	0.92
5	-1.57	-0.67	0.14	0.64	1.47	0.00
Column effect	-1.51	0.23	-0.04	0.95	0.37	4.18

5.1. TWO-DIMENSIONAL SOCIAL MOBILITY TABLES

Table 4 shows the values of the parameters of the saturated log-linear model

$$\ln m_{ij} = u + u_i^A + u_j^B + u_{ij}^{AB} ,$$

where variable A is the father's status, variable B is the son's status. Note that the parameters of the multiplicative model can easily be derived from the u-parameters as shown in Table 1.

The parameter estimates are computed by the formula shown in Table 1, with the index set K = {1}, i.e., only a single layer is considered. A special computer program was developed, although the estimates could also be obtained by applying ECTA and GLIM packages. The program also computes indicators not given by the standard programs and allows a flexible entry of prior information. The overall effect u = 3.7831 is shown in the lower right corner. The last column contains the u_i^A-parameters; they represent the effect of size differences in social status categories of fathers (row effects). The last row shows the u_j^B-terms, which measure the effects of size differences in son's status categories. The interaction terms u_{ij}^{AB} constitute the matrix elements. A negative u_{ij}^{AB}-term indicates that less sons are in status j, given that the father's status was i, than one would expect if son's status and father's status would be independent. The parameter values demonstrate that most sons remain in their father's status and that, if they change status, the change is generally to an adjacent status. Note that

$$\sum_i u_i^A = \sum_j u_j^B = \sum_i u_{ij}^{AB} = \sum_j u_{ij}^{AB} = 0,$$

as requested by the constraint specifications in Table 1. Tables 5 and 6 present estimates of cell counts under varying conditions of information availability. To demonstrate the impact of incomplete data on the interaction patterns exhibited by the estimates ($\{m_{ij}\}$-account), the tables also give the log-linear model parameters associated with the various data availability conditions. In addition, the balancing factors of the adjustment model (RAS technique) adopted in the input-output analysis and the dual variables or Lagrange multipliers of the entropy method are shown.

TABLE 5. Danish Social Mobility Table Estimated from Marginal Totals Only ($m^0_{ij} = 1$ for i,j)

Father's status	Son's Status 1	2	3	4	5	Total
A. Estimates						
1	1.9	6.3	15.7	19.8	13.4	57
2	10.5	35.0	87.5	110.3	74.7	318
3	23.4	77.9	194.8	245.5	166.4	708
4	25.7	85.6	214.1	269.7	182.9	778
5	17.5	58.3	145.9	183.8	124.6	530
Total	79	263	658	829	562	2391

B. Log-linear model parameters						Row effect
1	0.00	0.00	0.00	0.00	0.00	1.82
2	0.00	0.00	0.00	0.00	0.00	-0.10
3	0.00	0.00	0.00	0.00	0.00	.70
4	0.00	0.00	0.00	0.00	0.00	.80
5	0.00	0.00	0.00	0.00	0.00	0.41
Column effect	-1.53	-0.32	0.59	0.82	0.44	3.98

C. Balancing factors (r_i, s_j) and Lagrange multipliers (λ_i, μ_j)

	r_i	λ_i	s_j	μ_j
1	1.88	-1.63	1.00	0.00
2	10.51	-3.35	3.33	-1.20
3	23.39	-4.15	8.33	-2.12
4	25.71	-4.25	10.49	-2.35
5	17.51	-3.86	7.11	-1.96

D. Goodness-of-fit

Pearson chi-square: 754 for ±6 degrees of freedom.

Table 5 shows that if prior information is limited to marginal totals only, the interaction effect will be absent in the estimates. The expected counts may be expressed as follows:

Table 6. Danish Social Mobility Table, Estimated from Marginal Totals Augmented by a British Social Mobility Table

Father's status	Son's status 1	2	3	4	5	Total
A. Estimates						
1	26.7	14.8	6.4	6.3	2.8	57
2	22.3	85.3	100.6	81.1	28.6	318
3	17.9	78.2	269.5	240.2	102.2	708
4	9.5	62.5	188.5	319.7	197.8	778
5	2.6	22.2	93.0	181.7	230.6	530
Total	79	263	658	829	562	2391
B. Log-linear model parameters						Row effect
1	2.47	0.62	-0.83	-1.01	-1.24	-1.68
2	0.45	0.54	0.08	-0.31	-0.76	0.16
3	-0.38	-0.16	0.46	0.17	-0.09	.77
4	-0.96	-0.33	0.15	0.51	0.62	.72
5	-1.57	-0.67	0.14	0.64	1.47	0.03
Column effect	-1.32	-0.07	0.55	0.72	0.13	3.82

C. Balancing factor (r_i, s_j) and Lagrange multipliers (λ_i, μ_j)

	r_i	λ_i	s_j	μ_j
1	0.53	-0.37	1.00	0.00
2	0.80	-0.77	0.62	0.49
3	1.63	-1.49	1.50	-0.41
4	0.68	-0.61	0.66	-0.41
5	0.86	-0.85	0.65	0.43

D. Goodness-of-fit

Pearson chi-square: 68

$$m_{ij} = \exp\left[u + u_i^A + u_j^B\right] .$$

For example,

$$m_{32} = \exp[3.9765+0.7030-0.3244] = 77.9 .$$

The estimates may also be expressed in terms of the balancing factors: $m_{ij} = r_i s_j$. For example, $m_{32} = 23.39 \times 3.33 = 77.9$, and in terms of the Lagrange multipliers, $m_{ij} = \exp[-(1+\lambda_i+\mu_j)]$, which gives $m_{32} = \exp[-(1-4.15-1.20)] = 77.9$. Table 5 illustrates how the quality of the estimates increases when a social mobility table of another country is added to the package of prior information. The chi-square value drops from 754 to 68. By comparing Tables 3 and 5, one observes that the British data contribute the first-order interaction parameters. The impact of the British data on overall, row and column effects are evaluated by comparing the parameter values of Tables 4 and 5. The expected counts may be expressed in the following terms:

Log-linear model parameters:

$$m_{ij} = m_{ij}^0 \exp\left[{}^r u + {}^r u_i^A + {}^r u_j^B\right] ,$$

$$\text{ex.:} \quad m_{32} = 78 \exp[(3.8189-4.1842) + (0.7712-0.1012) + (-0.0722-0.2300)]$$

$$= 78 \exp[-0.3653+0.6700-0.3022]$$

$$= 78 \exp(0.0025) = 78.2 .$$

Balancing factors:

$$m_{ij} = m^0_{ij} r_i s_j \ ,$$

$$\text{ex.:} \quad m_{32} = 78 \times 1.6302 \times 0.6150 = 78.2 \ .$$

Lagrange multipliers:

$$m_{ij} = m^0_{ij} \ \exp[-(1+\lambda_i+\mu_j)]$$

$$\text{ex.:} \quad m_{32} = 78 \ \exp[-(1-1.4887+0.4861)] = 78.2 \ .$$

5.2. *THREE-DIMENSIONAL MIGRATION TABLES*

The migration data required for multiregional population analysis consist of age-specific flow data by region of origin and region of destination. Few countries tabulate these data on a regular basis. In the context of the Comparative Migration and Settlement Study project at IIASA, which aimed at a comparative study of population distribution patterns in the 17 IIASA National Member Organization Countries applying multiregional demographic techniques, Willekens *et al.* (1979) developed a methodology to infer the necessary migration data from available information. The methodology was based on the principle of entropy maximization, but yields the same results as the perspective adopted in this paper. Assuming various combinations of marginal totals (x-terms), estimates of the detailed migration flows were obtained by the multiproportional adjustment algorithm and related procedures. Since no intraregional migration flows are considered in multiregional analysis, they were left out of the estimation problem. The array of preliminary estimates was as follows:

$$m^0_{ijk} = 1 \quad \text{for } i \neq j, \text{ for all } k.$$

$$m^0_{ijk} = 0 \quad \text{for } i = j, \text{ for all } k.$$

The log-linear model implicit in the analyses is therefore one of quasi-independence.

To test the validity of the techniques, an error (goodness-of-fit) analysis was carried out for Austrian and Swedish data.[5] The number of age groups was 18 in both data sets; the number of regions was 4 in Austria and 8 in Sweden. Table 7 summarizes the main results. The 3F-case yields estimates that are remarkably accurate. The Austrian estimates are given in Table 8. The estimates do not exhibit a second-order interaction effect (see the 3F-case in Table 2). The quality of the estimates may therefore be explained by the near absence of a second-order interaction effect in the observed data. This would mean that the pairwise interaction between origin (A) and destination (B) is the same in each age group (C); in other words, that the spatial mobility pattern is relatively independent of age. This is quite realistic. The error analysis of the Austrian 3F-case reveals that about half of the cells were estimated with less than 4% error and almost two-thirds of the migration volume has an estimation error of less than 4%. Table 9 gives the complete results of the error analysis. An important observation is that about 69% of the total absolute percentage error is due to the

[5] *The method (3F-case) was actually applied to estimate missing migration data for Bulgaria (Philipov, 1978), The Netherlands (Drewe and Willekens, 1980), and Belgium (Willekens, 1977; Tan, 1980).*

TABLE 7. Austrian and Swedish Migration Tables, Estimated from Various Combinations of Marginal Totals: Error Analysis

Case	Available data	Degrees of freedom[a]	Pearson chi-square		Average absolute % error	
			Austria	Sweden	Austria	Sweden
3E	$\{x_{i..}, x_{.j.}, x_{..k}\}$	$IJK - I - J - K + 2$	18590	-	31.09	34.58
1FE	$\{x_{ij.}, x_{..k}\}$	$(IJ-1)(K-1) - KI$	3662	-	16.24	15.26
2F	$\{x_{ij.}, x_{.jk}\}$	$(I-1)(J-1)K - KI$	2006	-	12.08	11.90
3F	$\{x_{ij.}, x_{i.k}, x_{.jk}\}$	$(I-1)(J-1)(K-1) - KI$	371	1262	4.27	6.32

[a] The number of d.f. associated with a fitted model is found by subtracting the number of independent parameters used in the model from the total number of cells to which the model is being fitted. For the quasi-independence model with no-zero entries in the marginal configurations, the number of d.f. is equal to the number of d.f. associated with the complete tabel, minus the number of structural zeros. For both Austria and Sweden, $K = 18$; for Austria $I = J = 4$; and for Sweden $I = J = 8$. Note: The 3E-case does not preserve the structural zeros.

TABLE 9. Error Analysis of (3F) Migration Estimates, Austria

A. Analysis by size class (flow volume) and migrant category

Size class	Number of flows[a] total	Number of flows[a] -%-	Volume of flows total	Volume of flows -%-	Cum. abs. % error value	Cum. abs. % error -%-	chi-square value	chi-square -%-
0- 200	112.	51.85	8452.	10.63	1043.	68.56	0.9121e 02	33.70
200- 400	45.	20.83	12742.	16.02	241.	15.81	0.5711e 02	21.10
400- 600	20.	9.26	9481.	11.92	74.	4.87	0.2255e 02	8.33
600- 800	11.	5.09	7687.	9.67	73.	4.81	0.4191e 02	15.49
800-1000	9.	4.17	7705.	9.69	36.	2.36	0.1924e 02	7.11
1000-1200	3.	1.39	3330.	4.19	8.	0.52	0.2466e 01	0.91
1200-1400	7.	3.24	9075.	11.41	25.	1.63	0.1295e 02	4.78
1400-1600	1.	0.46	1464.	1.84	1.	0.06	0.1074e 00	0.04
1600-1800	0.	0.00	0.	0.00	0.	0.00	0.0000e 00	0.00
1800-2000	2.	0.93	3811.	4.79	7.	0.43	0.4201e 01	1.55
2000+	6.	2.78	15769.	19.83	14.	0.95	0.1887e 02	6.97
Total	216.	100.00	79516.	100.00	1522.	100.00	0.2706e 03	100.00

B. Analysis by error category

Category	error %	Number of flows total	Number of flows -%-	Volume of flows total	Volume of flows -%-	Average flow
1	0- 2	46.	21.30	24037.	30.23	522.543
2	2- 4	57.	26.39	24756.	31.13	434.316
3	4- 6	31.	14.35	13604.	17.11	438.839
4	6- 8	18.	8.33	6463.	8.13	359.056
5	8- 10	12.	5.56	4026.	5.06	335.500
6	10- 15	28.	12.96	5021.	6.31	179.321
7	15- 20	10.	4.63	798.	1.00	79.800
8	20- 30	10.	4.63	650.	0.82	65.000
9	30- 40	3.	1.39	158.	0.20	52.667
10	40- 60	1.	0.46	3.	0.00	3.000
11	60-100	0.	0.00	0.	0.00	0.000
12	100+	0.	0.00	0.	0.00	0.000
Total		216.	100.00	79516.	100.00	368.130

Average absolute percentage error = 4.27%
(relative mean deviation)

C. Analysis by size class and error category

Size class	0-2	2-4	4-6	6-8	8-10	10-15	15-20	20-30	30-40	40-60	60-100	100+	Total
0- 200	21	23	13	8	4	20	10	9	3	1	0	0	112
200- 400	9	12	10	5	3	5	0	1	0	0	0	0	45
400- 600	6	9	0	2	2	1	0	0	0	0	0	0	20
600- 800	1	2	4	0	2	2	0	0	0	0	0	0	11
800-1000	2	4	0	2	1	0	0	0	0	0	0	0	9
1000-1200	1	2	0	0	0	0	0	0	0	0	0	0	3
1200-1400	1	3	3	0	0	0	0	0	0	0	0	0	7
1400-1600	1	0	0	0	0	0	0	0	0	0	0	0	1
1600-1800	0	0	0	0	0	0	0	0	0	0	0	0	0
1900-2000	0	2	0	0	0	0	0	0	0	0	0	0	2
2000-	4	0	1	1	0	0	0	0	0	0	0	0	6
Total	46	57	31	18	12	28	10	10	3	1	0	0	216

[a]The structurally zero flows are excluded.

TABLE 8. Observed and (3F) Estimated Migration Flows by Age, Austria, Four Regions, 1966-1971

		Migration from		East to				Migration from		South to	
	Total	East	South	North	West		Total	East	South	North	West
0	1783.	0.	674.	874.	234.	0	1909.	882.	0.	556.	471.
		0-	-670-	-877-	-236-			-853-	0-	-575-	-481-
5	930.	0.	328.	482.	120.	5	1115.	493.	0.	348.	274.
		0-	-328-	-468-	-134-			-530-	0-	-329-	-256-
10	1597.	0.	483.	821.	293.	10	3662	1371.	0.	1075.	1216.
		0-	-537-	-828-	-232-			-1342-	0-	-1044-	-1276-
15	4172.	0.	1351.	2029.	793.	15	8323.	3800.	0.	2022.	2501.
		0-	-1280-	-2192-	-700-			-3760-	0-	-1950-	-2613-
20	4227.	0.	1336.	2246.	645.	20	4625.	2097.	0.	1324.	1203
		0-	-1289-	-2231-	-707-			-2081-	0-	-1381-	-1163-
25	2807.	0.	939.	1477.	392.	25	2625	1187.	0.	781.	656.
		0-	-910-	-1464-	-433-			-1225-	0-	-800-	-600-
30	1123.	0.	378.	596.	149.	30	1062	465.	0.	333.	263.
		0-	-368-	-588-	-167-			-464-	0-	-346-	-252-
35	915.	0.	295.	493.	127.	35	903	392.	0.	281.	230.
		0-	-293-	-480-	-142-			-408-	0-	-276-	-219-
40	871	0.	280.	474.	117.	40	807.	409.	0.	223-	174.
		0-	-312-	-438-	-121-			-411-	0-	-240-	-156-
45	579	0.	204.	306.	69.	45	517.	277.	0.	140.	100.
		0-	-222-	-289-	-68-			-269-	0-	-149-	-99-
50	618.	0.	229.	314.	75.	50	514.	256.	0.	147.	111.
		0-	-241-	-312-	-65-			-263-	0-	-134-	-117-
55	689	0.	261.	346.	81.	55	521.	289.	0.	133.	99.
		0-	-280-	-331-	-78-			-296-	0-	-132-	-93-
60	700.	0.	259.	373.	67.	60	455.	246.	0.	133.	76.
		0-	-269-	-357-	-74-			-253-	0-	-137-	-65-
65	543.	0.	203.	290.	51.	65	340.	185.	0.	100.	55.
		0-	-210-	-280-	-53-			-190-	0-	-102-	-48-

70	353.	0.	131.	189.	33.	70	217.	118.	0.	64.	35.
		0-	-138-	-182-	-33-			-121-	0-	-65-	-31-
75	194.	0.	71.	105.	18.	75	118.	63.	0.	35.	19.
		0-	-74-	-101-	-19-			-65-	0-	-36-	-17-
80	68.	0.	24.	37.	6.	80	39.	22.	0.	11.	6.
		0-	-26-	-35-	-7-			-22-	0-	-12-	-5-
85	34.	0.	13.	18.	3.	85	21.	11.	0.	7.	3.
		0-	-13-	-18-	-3-			-11-	0-	-7-	-3-
Total	22203.	0.	7460.	11471.	3272.	Total	27773.	12564.	0.	7715.	7494.

		Migration from		North to				Migration from		South to	
	Total	East	South	North	West		Total	East	South	North	West
0	1445.	764.	402.	0.	280.	0	905	250.	352.	303.	0.
		-814-	-363-	0-	-268-			-229-	-395-	-281-	0-
5	917.	482.	252.	0.	184.	5	416.	111.	155.	150.	0.
		-448-	-282-	0-	-187-			-108-	-124-	-184-	0-
10	1568.	745.	371	0.	452.	10	568.	148.	197.	222.	0.
		-771-	-344-	0-	-453-			-151-	-171-	-246-	0-
15	5297.	2888.	1107.	0.	1302.	15	2240.	736.	754.	750.	0.
		-2892-	-1123-	0-	-1282-			-772-	-809-	-659-	0-
20	3250.	1806.	734.	0.	710.	20	2235.	678.	736.	821.	0.
		-1861-	-701-	0-	-688-			-640-	-816-	-779-	0-
25	1885.	1029.	466.	0.	390.	25	1373.	395.	479.	499.	0.
		-998-	-482-	0-	-405-			-389-	-491-	-493-	0-
30	924.	492.	241.	0.	191.	30	606.	165.	216.	226.	0.
		-485-	-255-	0-	-184-			-173-	-212-	-221-	0-
35	750.	402.	187.	0.	162.	35	408.	113.	140.	155.	0.
		-379-	-213-	0-	-158-			-119-	-116-	-173-	0-
40	688.	419.	146.	0.	122.	40.	361.	121.	113.	127.	0.
		-411-	-141-	0-	-136-			-128-	-87-	-146-	0-
45	447.	277.	101.	0.	68.	45	208.	71.	69.	69.	0.
		-275-	-102-	0-	-70-			-81-	-50-	-77-	0-
50	478.	273.	124.	0.	81.	50	241.	73.	88.	80.	0.
		-273-	-119-	0-	-86-			-65-	-81-	-95-	0-

	Total	Migration from East	South	North to North	West		Total	Migration from East	South	South to North	West
55	489.	304.	114.	0.	71.	55	237.	82.	82.	72.	0.
		-295-	-114-	0-	-80-			-84-	-64-	-89-	0-
60	439.	271.	110.	0.	58.	60	185.	59.	64.	61.	0.
		-263-	-114-	0-	-62-			-60-	-51-	-74-	0-
65	328	204.	83.	0.	41.	65	131.	42.	46.	43.	0.
		-198-	-84-	0-	-46-			-43-	-37-	-51-	0-
70	209.	130.	53.	0.	26.	70	82.	26.	29.	27.	0.
		-125-	-54-	0-	-30-			-28-	-21-	-33-	0-
75	109.	67.	27.	0.	14.	75	46.	15.	16.	16.	0.
		-66-	-27-	0-	-16-			-14-	-13-	-19-	0-
80	35.	22.	8.	0.	4.	80	14.	5.	5.	5.	0.
		-22-	-8-	0-	-5-			-5-	-3-	-6-	0-
85	19.	11.	6.	0.	2.	85	7.	2.	3.	2.	0.
		-11-	-6-	0-	-2-			-2-	-2-	-3-	0-
Total	19277.	10587.	4532.	0.	4158.	Total	10263.	3091.	3543.	3629.	0.

Source: Observed migration data: Sauberer (1981); Estimates: Willekens, Por, and Raquillet (1979, pp. 34-35).

minor migration flows (less than 200 migrants), representing only 11% of the flow volume (Table 9a). A similar pattern is obtained if the chi-square statistic is used. The error distribution is, however, more explicit: the minor flows account for 34% of the total chi-square value. The contribution of minor flows to the overall error is further illustrated by the cross classification of error categories and flow size classes (Table 9c). Minor flows are concentrated in the large error categories. A similar observation was made by Bacharach (1970), Hewings (1977), Hinojosa (1978), and others in an error analysis of input-output coefficients, estimated by the RAS-method. The error analysis of minor flows raises two additional problems: the validity of the error measures used, and the effect of rounding flow estimates to the nearest integer value. Both problems received attention in the statistical literature. Suggestions for substituting the chi-square measure in case of small cell counts are many, as are suggestions for adjusting small cell values (less than 5, say). A pragmatic solution to the problems encountered may be to force small flows to be equal to the preliminary estimates. Its effect on the overall outcome would be negligible, and it would simplify the comparative evaluation of estimation methods. Hewings and Janson (1980, p. 847) propose such a strategy for the prediction of input-output tables.

The error analyses of the social mobility data and of the migration data show that an increase of the prior information leads to better estimates. However, each piece of prior information does not contribute equally. In the migration analysis, we could, for instance, observe that the estimates did not improve substantially if we increased our knowledge of the age structure of inmigrants (compare 2F-case with 1FE-case), whereas information on the overall migration pattern was essential (1 FE versus 3E). In the Danish social mobility analysis, knowledge of the British social mobility table had a very significant impact on the quality of the estimates.

Other authors have experienced similar observations. Snickars and Weibull (1977) compared the descriptive capacity of four alternative models of trip distribution among 12 regions in the Stockholm county. Each model used different amounts of prior information. An interesting observation was that a biproportional adjustment of a historical trip matrix to new marginals (Fratar method) outperformed the classical gravity model, with distribution function $\exp[-\beta c_{ij}]$ and c_{ij} the transportation cost. The application of a historical matrix instead of a cost function reduced the mean absolute percentage deviation from 20% to 7%, while the chi-square dropped from 731 to 107. The result indicates that trip patterns are not primarily shaped by travel cost differentials. The interaction effects exhibited by the distribution function are therefore inappropriate to describe the travel pattern. The conclusion of the authors that the gravity model has a smaller descriptive capacity than the Fratar model is, strictly speaking, incorrect. The outcome is not determined by the difference in model structure but by the difference in preliminary estimates. The application of the Frater method with $m_{ij}^0 = \exp[-\beta c_{ij}]$ would give results identical to the gravity model. As these examples show, the value of each piece of prior information for estimation purposes is determined by the relevance of the interaction effect it exhibits and imposes onto the estimates. Prior knowledge has no value in itself; it only contributes through the interaction effects it carries. The closer the patterns of association in the prior estimates resemble those in the data to be estimated, the better the estimates will be.

6. CONCLUSION

Multidimensional demography provides new opportunities for gaining demographic insight. The opportunities, however, can only fully be explored if statistical data are abundantly available or if appropriate estimation methods can be applied. Although the steps taken by statistical offices throughout the world to solve the data problem are encouraging, the lack of adequate data remains a major drawback of multidimensional population analysis. Estimation methods are therefore needed that are adapted to any particular data situation. This paper suggests a unified perspective on estimation techniques for multidimensional analysis with incomplete data.

A key feature of the unified approach is its emphasis on data structures and not on the values of individual data elements. The data set is approached as an interdependent, hierarchical system that can be modeled. The model relates the values, individual data elements take on, to structural characteristics of the data system; it is an aid in exploring data structures. In this perspective, missing elements are nothing but expressions of our incomplete knowledge of the systems structure; and the problem of accurately estimating missing elements is a problem of hypothesizing the appropriate structure. To do this, optimal use should be made of all information available on the data system or on the phenomenon or process it represents. The techniques presented in this paper are intended to ease the formulation of structural hypotheses on the basis of the incomplete prior knowledge. An important advantage of the perspective and the techniques is that they are not only valid for conventional data sets (cross classifications of two or three variables), but that they can be applied equally well to multidimensional data sets.

To implement the unified perspective on estimating missing elements, an accounting framework is suggested. The advantages of accounts for multidimensional modeling and analysis were discussed by Rees (1980). Two types of accounts are distinguished. The first account contains what is known of the actual flow data. In general, prior knowledge is limited to marginal totals, structural zeros, and maybe a few elements. The second account contains preliminary estimates of the actual flows. The data in this account contribute to the quality of the estimates by imposing onto them patterns of association that are realistic but that cannot be derived from the limited information on the actual flows in consideration. How the mechanism works is easily seen from the log-linear models describing the two accounts (data sets). The introduction of an account of preliminary estimates m^0_{ijk} is a compromise between maximum likelihood estimation under the independence model and maximum likelihood estimation assuming a saturated model. Through the $\{m^0_{ijk}\}$-account, appropriate structural hypotheses with regard to the estimates can be formulated. It is shown that these hypotheses may be derived from analogous data of a different but similar country, from historical data or from cross tabulations of intermediate or explanatory variables. The classical gravity model for estimating migration is an illustration of the latter case.

The estimation algorithm presented in this chapter is very simple, and it is not required to calculate the log-linear model parameters in order to determine the expected cell counts.

Values of the most probable flows, given the limited prior knowledge, are obtained by multiproportional adjustment of the preliminary estimates until they exactly fit the given information on the actual flows (first account or main data source). Multiproportional adjustment is not the only way to infer the required estimates. Other algorithms are discussed in the literature, but they are less transparent and therefore less appropriate if one wants to explore the consequences for the data structure and through it, for the individual estimates, if the available statistical, factual, and other knowledge of the phenomenon or system changes. This type of exploratory data analysis is however crucial for determining the contribution of each piece of prior information to the final estimates and for evaluating how much information is actually needed to ensure that a data set, required for the application of multidimensional demographic techniques, can be estimated with an acceptable level of accuracy.

ACKNOWLEDGMENTS

I very much wish to thank Willem Schaafsma and Paul de Jong for extensive comments on an earlier draft. The contribution of Jaine Koendering, who transformed the manuscript into a skillfully typed version, is greatfully acknowledged.

REFERENCES

Bacharach, M. (1970). Biproportional Matrices and Input-Output Analysis. London: Cambridge University Press.

Batty, M. and Mackie, S. (1972). The calibration of gravity, entropy, and related models of spatial interaction. *Environment and Planning 4,* 205-233.

Birch, M. (1963). Maximum-likelihood in three-way contingency tables. *Journal of the Royal Statistical Society B 25,* 220-233.

Bishop, Y. M., Fienberg, S. E., and Holland, P. W. (1975). Discrete Multivariate Analysis: Theory and Practice. Cambridge, Massachusetts: MIT Press.

Caussinus, H. and Thelot, C. (1976). Note complémentaire sur l'analyse statistique des migrations. (Further note on the statistical analysis of migrations). *Annales de l'INSEE 22-23,* 135-146.

Chilton, R. and Poet, R. (1973). An entropy maximizing approach to the recovery of detailed migration patterns from aggregate census data. *Environment and Planning A 5,* 135-146.

Clogg, C. C. (1978). Adjustment of rates using multiplicative models. *Demography 15,* 523-539.

Clogg, C. C. (1979). Measuring Underemployment. Demographic Indicators for the United States. New York: Academic Press.

Deming, W. and Stephan, F. (1940). On a least square adjustment of a sampled frequency table when the expected marginal totals are known. *Annals of Mathematical Statistics 11,* 427-444.

Drewe, P. and Willekens, F. (1980). Maximum likelihood estimation of age-specific migration flows in the Netherlands. *Delft Progress Report 5,* 92-111.

Evans, S. P. and Kirby, H. R. (1974). A three-dimensional Furness procedure for calibrating gravity models. *Transportation Research 8,* 105-122.

Fienberg, S. E. and Mason, W. M. (1978). Identification and estimation of age-period-cohort models in the analysis of discrete archival data. *In* "Sociological Methodology 1979" (K. F. Schuessler, ed.), pp. 1-67. San Francisco: Jossey-Bass.

Fisher, R. A. (1922). On the interpretation of Chi-square from contingency tables, and the calculation of P. *Journal of the Royal Statistical Society 85,* 87-94.

Fratar, T. J. (1954). Forecasting distribution of interzonal vehicular trips by successive approximation. *Highway Research Board Proceedings 33,* 376-385.

Gokhale, D. and Kullback, S. (1978). The Information in Contingency Tables. New York: Dekker.

Goodman, L. (1978). Analyzing Qualitative/Cathegorical Data. Cambridge, Massachusetts, Abt Books, Abt Associates.

Haberman, S. J. (1979). Analysis of Qualitative Data (2 Vols). New York: Academic Press.

Hauser, R. M. (1979). Some exploratory methods for modeling mobility tables and other cross-classified data. *In* "Sociological Methodology 1980" (K. F. Schuessler, ed.), pp. 413-458. San Francisco: Jossey-Bass.

Hewings, G. J. D. (1977). Evaluating the possibilities for exchanging regional input-output coefficients. *Environment and Planning A 9,* 927-944.

Hewings, G. J. D. and Janson, B. N. (1980). Exchanging regional input-output coefficients: a reply and further comments. *Environment and Planning A 12,* 843-854.

Hinojosa, R. C. (1978). A performance test of the biproportional adjustment of input-output coefficients. *Environment and Planning A 10,* 1047-1052.

Hoem, J. and Fong, M. (1976). A Markov chain model of working life tables. Working Paper no. 2, Laboratory of Actuarial Mathematics. Copenhagen University.

Hua, C. and Porell, F. (1979). A critical review of the development of the gravity model. *International Regional Science Review 4,* 97-126.

Jong, P. M. de (1981). The reliability of methods for predicting missing figures in migration tables. Paper prepared for presentation at the Conference on the "Analysis of Multidimensional Contingency Tables," Rome, June 25-26, 1981.

Koesoebjono, S. (1981). Marital status life tables of female population in The Netherlands (1978); an application of the multidimensional demography. Working Paper no. 20, NIDI. Voorburg, The Netherlands.

Kruithof, J. (1937). Calculation of telephone traffic. *De Ingenieur 52,* E 15-E 25. English translation by UK Post Office Research Department Library (No. 2663). London, Dollis Hill.

Leontief, W. (1941). The Structure of the American Economy, 1919-1939. New York, Oxford University Press.

Little, R. J. A. (1978). Generalized linear models for cross-classified data from the WFS. Technical Bulletin no. 5/Tech. 834, World Fertility Survey, London.

Little, R. J. A. (1980). Linear models from WFS data. Technical Bulletin no. 9/Tech. 1282P. World Fertility Survey, London.

Little, R. J. A. and Pullum, T. W. (1979). The generalized linear model and direct standardization: a comparison. *Sociological Methods and Research 7*, 475-501.

MacGill, S. M. (1977). Theoretical properties of biproportional matrix adjustments. *Environment and Planning A 9*, 687-701.

MacFadden, D. (1978). Modelling the choice of residential location. *In* "Spatial Interaction Theory and Planning Models" (A. Karlqvist, L. Lundqvist, F. Snickars, and J. Weibull, eds.), pp. 75-96. Amsterdam: North-Holland.

March, L. (1971). Urban systems: A generalised distribution function. *In* "Urban and Regional Planning" (A. G. Wilson, ed.). (London Papers in Regional Science, Vol. 2). London: Pion Ltd.

Murchland, J. D. (1978). Application, History and Properties of Bi- and Multiproportional Models. London: University College, Traffic Studies Group, JDM-292.

Nijkamp, P. (1979). Gravity and entropy models: the state of the art. *In* "New Developments in Modelling Travel Demand and Urban Systems. Some Results of Recent Dutch Research" (G. R. M. Jansen, P. H. L. Bovy, J. P. J. M. Van Est, and F. le Clerq, eds.), pp. 281-319. Westmead, Farnborough, England: Saxon House.

Payne, C. (1977). The log-linear model of contingency tables. *In* "The Analysis of Survey Data. Vol. 2: Model Fitting" (C. O. Muircheartaigh and C. Payne, eds.), pp. 105-144. New York: Wiley.

Philipov, D. (1978). Migration and settlement in Bulgaria. *Environment and Planning 10*, 593-617.

Rees, P. H. (1980). Multistate demographic accounts: Measurement and estimation procedures. *Environment and Planning A 12*, 449-531.

Rees, P. H. and Wilson, A. G. (1977). Spatial Population Analysis. London: Edward Arnold.

Sauberer, M. (1981). Migration and settlement: Austria. Research Report, RR-81-16, IIASA, Laxenburg, Austria.

Schoen, R. and Nelson, V. (1974). Marriage, divorce and mortality: A life table analysis. *Demography 12*, 313-324.

Schoen, R. and Woodrow, K. (1980). Labor force status life tables for the United States, 1972. *Demography 17*, 297-322.

Shulman, S. A. (1979). Raking of state CPS labor force data. Proceedings of the 1979 Social Statistics Section, American Statistical Association, pp. 256-260.

Shulman, S. A. and Chaddha, R. L. (1978). Updating 1970 census data on the race-sex-occupation distribution of a state. Proceedings of the 1978 Social Statistics Section, American Statistical Association, pp. 607-611.

Smith, S. J. (1980). Tables of working life for the United States, 1977: Substantive and methodological implications. Paper presented at the annual meeting of the Population Association of America, Denver, Colorado, April 1980.

Snickars, F. and Weibull, J. W. (1977). A minimum information principle. Theory and practice. *Regional Science and Urban Economics 7*, 137-168.

Stein, R. L. (1980). National Commission recommends changes in labor force statistics. *Monthly Labor Review, April 1980*, 11-21.

Stewart, J. Q. (1948). Demographic gravitation: Evidence and application. *Sociometry 1*, 31-58.

Stone, R. (1962). Multiple classifications in social accounting. *Bulletin of the International Statistical Institute 39*, 215-233.

Tan, E. (1980). On the estimation of migration flows by migrant categories. MA Thesis, Interuniversity Programme in Demography, Brussels.

Willekens, F. (1977). The recovery of detailed migration patterns from aggregate data: An entropy-maximizing approach. Research Memorandum RM-77-58, IIASA, Laxenburg, Austria.

Willekens, F. (1980a). Entropy, multiproportional adjustment and analysis of contingency tables. *Systemi Urbani 2* (nr. 2-3), 171-201.

Willekens, F. (1980b). Multistate analysis: Tables of working life. *Environment and Planning 12*, 563-588.

Willekens, F., Por, A., and Raquillet, R. (1979). Entropy, multiproportional and quadratic techniques for inferring detailed migration patterns from aggregate data. Mathematical theories, algorithms, applications and computer programs. Working Paper WP-79-88, IIASA, Laxenburg, Austria (also published in *IIASA Reports 4* (1981), 83-124.

Willekens, F., Shah, I., Shah, J. M., and Ramachandran, P. (1980). Multistate analysis of marital status life tables. Theory and application. Working Paper no. 17, NIDI. Voorburg, The Netherlands. (Revised version published in *Population Studies 36* (1982), *129-144*.

Wilson, A. G. (1970). Entropy in Urban and Regional Modelling. London: Pion Ltd.

3

Model Schedules in Multistate Demographic Analysis: The Case of Migration

Andrei Rogers and Luis J. Castro

The age-specific fertility and mortality schedules of most human populations exhibit remarkably persistent regularities; consequently, demographers have found it possible to summarize and codify such regularities by means of hypothetical schedules called *model* schedules. Although the development of model fertility and mortality schedules has received considerable attention, the construction of model migration schedules has not, even though the techniques that have been successfully applied to treat the former can readily be extended to deal with the latter. The same may be said of model schedules of labor force entry and exit, and of marriage, divorce, and remarriage.[1]

[1] *There are a few notable exceptions, however, such as the paper on model divorce schedules by Krishnan and Kayani (1973).*

MULTIDIMENSIONAL MATHEMATICAL DEMOGRAPHY

ISBN 0-12-435640-0

In this chapter we consider the notion of model multistate schedules, focusing in particular on the development of a family of model migration schedules for use in situations where the available migration data are inadequate or inaccurate. To do this, we assume from the start that the regularities in age profile exhibited by empirical schedules of migration rates may be described by the following mathematical expression, called a *model migration schedule*:

$$M(x) = a_1\exp(-\alpha_1 x) + a_2\exp(-\alpha_2(x-\mu_2)-\exp[-\lambda_2(x-\mu_2)]) + a_3\exp(-\alpha_3(x-\mu_3)-\exp[-\lambda_3(x-\mu_3)]) + c \quad , x = 0,1,2,\ldots,z \tag{1}$$

The details of this formulation and its application are described elsewhere and are not considered further in this chapter (Rogers *et al.*, 1978; Castro and Rogers, 1979). The goal of this chapter, rather, is to set out two alternative approaches for generating families of hypothetical "synthetic" model migration schedules for migration patterns that follow the general age profile defined by the model migration schedule. Our conclusion is that although the idea has considerable promise, further work is needed if such approaches are to be of practical use in migration studies carried out in Third World population settings.

1. SYNTHETIC MODEL MIGRATION SCHEDULES: I. THE CORRELATIONAL PERSPECTIVE

A *synthetic* model schedule is a collection of age-specific rates that is based on patterns observed in various populations other than the one being studied and some incomplete data on the latter. The justification for such an approach is that age profiles of fertility, mortality, *and migration* vary within predetermined limits for most human populations. Birth, death, and migration rates for one age group are highly correlated with the corresponding rates for other age groups, and expressions of such interrelationships form the basis of model schedule construction. The use of these regularities to develop synthetic (hypothetical) schedules that are deemed to be close approximations of the unobserved schedules of populations lacking accurate vital and mobility registration statistics has been a rapidly growing area of contemporary demographic research.

1.1. INTRODUCTION: ALTERNATIVE PERSPECTIVES

The earliest efforts in the development of model schedules were based on only one parameter and, hence, had very little flexibility (United Nations, 1955). Demographers soon discovered that variations in the mortality and fertility regimes of different populations required more complex formulations. In mortality studies greater flexibility was introduced by providing families of schedules (Coale and Demeny, 1966) or by enlarging the number of parameters used to describe the age pattern (Brass, 1975). The latter strategy was also adopted in the creation of improved model fertility schedules and was augmented by the use of analytical descriptions of age profiles (Coale and Trussell, 1974).

Since the age patterns of migration normally exhibit a greater degree of variability across regions than do mortality and fertility schedules, it is to be expected that the development of an adequate set of model migration schedules will require a greater number both of families and of parameters. Although many alternative methods could be devised to summarize regularities in the form of families of model schedules defined by several parameters, three have received the widest popularity and dissemination:

(1) the regression approach of the Coale-Demeny model life tables (Coale and Demeny, 1966);

(2) the logit system of Brass (Brass, 1971); and

(3) the double-exponential graduation of Coale, McNeil, and Trussell (Coale, 1977; Coale and McNeil, 1972; and Coale and Trussell, 1974).

The regression approach embodies a *correlational* perspective that associates rates at different ages to an index of level, where the particular associations may differ from one "family" of schedules to another. For example, in the Coale-Demeny model life tables, the index of level is the expectation of remaining life at age 10, and a different set of regression equations is established for each of four "regions" of the world.[2]

[2] *Each of the four regions (North, South, East, and West) defines a collection of similar mortality schedules that are more uniform in pattern than the totality of observed life tables.*

Brass's logit system reflects a *relational* perspective in which rates at different ages are given by a standard schedule where shape and level may be suitably modified to be appropriate for a particular population.

The Coale-Trussell model fertility schedules are relational in perspective (they use a Swedish standard first-marriage schedule), but they also introduce an analytic description of the age profile by adopting a double exponential curve that defines the shape of the age-specific first-marriage function.

In this chapter we mix the above three approaches to define two alternative perspectives for creating synthetic model migration schedules to be used in situations where only inadequate or defective data on internal (origin-destination) migration flows are available. Both perspectives rely on the analytic (double plus single exponential) graduation defined by the basic model migration schedule set out in Rogers *et al.* (1978); they differ in the method by which a synthetic schedule is identified as being appropriate for a particular population. The first, the regression approach, associates variations in the parameters and derived variables of the model schedule to each other and then to age-specific migration rates. The second, the logit approach, embodies different relationships between the model schedule parameters in several standard schedules and then associates the logits of the migration rates in the standard to those of the population in question.

1.2. THE CORRELATIONAL PERSPECTIVE: THE REGRESSION MIGRATION SYSTEM

A straightforward way of obtaining a synthetic model migration schedule from limited observed data is to associate such data to the basic model schedule's parameters by means of regression equations. For example, given estimates of the migration rates of infants and young adults, M(0 - 4) and M(20 - 24), say, we may use equations of the form

$$Q_i = b_0[M(0\text{-}4)]^{b_1}[M(20\text{-}24)]^{b_2}$$

to estimate the set of parameters Q_i that define the model schedule. However, the parameters of the fitted model schedules are not independent of each other. For example, higher than average values of λ_2 were associated with lower than average values of a_1. The incorporation of such dependencies into the regression approach would surely improve the accuracy and consistency of the estimation procedure. An examination of empirical associations among model schedule parameters and variables, therefore, is a necessary first step.

Regularities in the covariations of the model schedule's parameters suggest a strategy of model schedule construction that builds on regression equations embodying these covariations. For example, if a_2 increases linearly with increasing values of α_2, then the linear regression equation

$$a_2 = b_0 + b_1\alpha_2$$

may adequately capture this pattern of covariation. For Swedish females this equation is estimated to be

$$a_2 = -0.006 + 0.645\ \alpha_2\ .$$

The correlation coefficient is 0.92, and the t-statistic of the regression coefficient associated with α_2 is 17.51

Table 1 presents regression equations, such as the one above, fitted to Swedish data on males and on females. The particular choice of variables and parameters included is, of course, only one of many possible alternatives, and it reflects a particular sequence of steps by which a complete model schedule with unit GMR can be inferred on the basis of estimates for δ_{12}, x_ℓ, and x_h.[3] Given values for these three variables, one can proceed to estimate μ_2, λ_2, σ_2, and β_{12}. Since $\sigma_2 = \lambda_2/\alpha_2$, we obtain, at the same time, an estimate for α_2, which we can then use to find a_2. With a_2 established, a_1 may be estimated by drawing on the definitional equation $\delta_{12} = a_1/a_2$, and α_1 may be found with the similar equation $\beta_{12} = \alpha_1/\alpha_2$. An initial estimate of c is obtained by setting $c = a_1/\delta_{1c}$, where δ_{1c} is estimated by regressing it on δ_{12}, and a_1, a_2, and c are scaled to give a GMR equal to unity.

Conceptually, this approach to model schedule construction begins with the labor force component and then appends to it the pre-labor force part of the curve. The value given for δ_{12} reflects the relative weights of these two components, with low values defining a labor-dominant curve and high values pointing to a family-dominant curve. (The behavior of the post-labor force curve is here assumed to be treated exogenously.)

[3] *The GMR is the gross migraproduction rate and describes the area under the age-specific migration schedule.*

TABLE 1. The Swedish Regression Equations: Males and Females

Dependent variables	Regression coefficients of independent variables[a]: Intercept	δ_{12}	α_2	x_ℓ	x_h	Multiple correlation coefficient r
Males						
μ_2	-5.037	-2.886		0.134	1.052	
		(-4.85)		(2.25)	(13.06)	0.90
σ_2	32.884	9.351		1.193	-2.164	
		(4.36)		(5.55)	(-7.45)	0.82
β_{12}	5.211	2.000		-0.186	-0.085	
		(8.00)		(-7.44)	(-2.52)	0.83
λ_2	2.239	0.172		0.104	-0.148	
		(1.40)		(8.43)	(-8.90)	0.87
a_2	0.007		0.576			
			(11.19)			0.86
δ_{1c}	9.725	-0.631				
		(-0.13)				0.02
Females						
μ_2	-1.080	-2.527		0.086	0.914	
		(-6.71)		(1.57)	(15.71)	0.92
σ_2	8.054	8.019		1.592	-1.423	
		(7.20)		(9.88)	(-8.28)	0.88
β_{12}	2.407	1.594		-0.147	0.005	
		(6.81)		(-4.33)	(0.14)	0.77
λ_2	1.759	0.192		0.155	-0.169	
		(2.38)		(13.27)	(-13.52)	0.93
a_2	-0.006		0.645			
			(17.51)			0.92
δ_{1c}	5.959	11.553				
		(1.93)				0.26

[a]Values in parentheses are t-statistics

We begin the calculations with μ_2 to establish the location of the curve on the age axis; is it an early- or late-peaking curve? Next, we turn to the determination of its two slope parameters λ_2 and α_2 by determining whether or not it is a labor-symmetric curve. Values of σ_2 between 1 and 2 generally characterize a labor-symmetric curve; higher values describe an asymmetric age profile. The regression of a_2 and α_2 produces the fourth parameter needed to define the labor force component. With values for μ_2, λ_2, α_2, and a_2 the construction procedure turns to the estimation of the pre-labor force curve, which is defined by the two parameters α_1 and a_1. Its relative share of the total unit area under the model migration schedule is set by the value given to δ_{12}.

Exhibit 1 demonstrates the sequence of calculations with the Stockholm model migration schedule for females. Figure 1 illustrates the resulting fit.[4]

1.2.1. *The Basic Regression Equations*

The collection of regression equations set out in Exhibit 1 may be defined to represent the "child-dependency" set, inasmuch as their central independent variable δ_{12} is the index of child dependency. It is, of course, also possible to replace this independent variable with others, such as σ_2 or β_{12}, for example, to create a "labor asymmetry" or a "parental regularity" set, respectively. Table 2 presents regression coefficients

[4] *The retirement peak is introduced exogenously by setting its parameters equal to those of the "observed" model migration schedule. An alternative specification for the post-labor force migrants is also introduced: the upward slope formulation that replaces the third component in Eq. (1) with* $a_3 exp(\alpha_3 x)$.

A. Inputs

$$\delta_{12} = 0.604 \quad x_\ell = 14.81 \quad x_h = 22.70$$

B. Outputs

B.1 Labor force component

$$\mu_2 = -1.080 - 2.527\,\delta_{12} + 0.086\,x_\ell + 0.914\,x_h$$
$$= 19.42$$

$$\delta_2 = 8.054 + 8.019\,\delta_{12} + 1.592\,x_\ell - 1.423\,x_h$$
$$= 4.17$$

$$\lambda_2 = 1.759 + 0.192\,\delta_{12} + 0.155\,x_\ell - 0.169\,x_h$$
$$= 0.334$$

$$\alpha_2 = \lambda_2/\sigma_2 = 0.080$$

$$a_2 = -0.006 + 0.645\,\alpha_2$$

$$= 0.046$$

B.2 Pre-labor force component

$$a_1 = a_2\delta_{12} = 0.028$$

$$\beta_{12} = 2.407 + 1.594\,\delta_{12} + 0.147\,x_\ell + 0.005\,x_h$$
$$= 1.31$$

$$\alpha_1 = \alpha_2\beta_{12} = 0.104$$

B.3 Constant component

$$\delta_{1c} = 5.959 + 11.553\,\delta_{12}$$
$$= 12.94$$

$$c = a_1/\delta_{1c} = 0.028/12.937 = 0.002$$

C. Goodness of Fit[a]

$$E = 8.50$$

Exhibit 1. The calculation sequence with the Swedish regressions: Stockholm females, GMR = 1.

[a] *The goodness-of-fit index E is the mean-absolute error expressed as a percentage of the observed mean.*

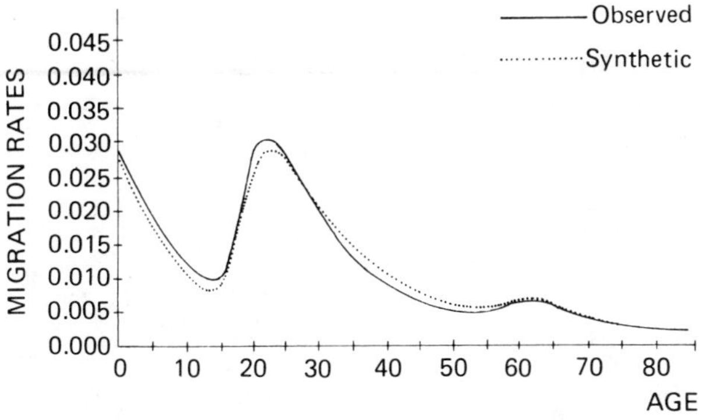

Fig. 1. The fit of the synthetic model migration schedule based on Swedish national regression equations; Stockholm females, 1974.

for all three variants, obtained using the age-specific interregional migration schedules (scaled to unit GMR) of Sweden, the United Kingdom, and Japan. Deleting schedules with a retirement peak leaves a total of 163 for males and 172 for females.

Tests of the three variants of the basic regressions using the data on Sweden, the United Kingdom, and Japan produced relatively satisfactory results, with the goodness-of-fit index E generally lying in the range of 5 and 35. Of the three variants, the child-dependency set gave the best fits in about a half of the female schedules tested, whereas the parental-regularity set was overwhelmingly the best-fitting variant for the male schedules.

1.2.2. Using the Basic Regression Equations

To use the basic regression equations presented in Table 2, one first needs to obtain estimates of δ_{12}, x_{ℓ}, and x_h.

TABLE 2. A Basic Set of Regression Equations

A. MALES

Dependent variables	Inter-cept	Regression coefficients of independent variables[a] δ_{12} σ_2 β_{12}	α_2	x_ℓ	x_h	Multiple correlation coefficient r
Child-dependency set (δ_{12})						
σ_2	16.42682	5.59390		0.89435	-1.17441	0.72
		(5.23)		(9.54)	(-11.14)	
β_{12}	1.90489	1.33191		-0.02651	-0.04019	
		(3.60)		(-0.82)	(-1.10)	0.28
λ_2	1.30848	0.15118		0.07617	-0.08963	
		(3.16)		(18.15)	(-19.00)	0.88
Labor-asymmetry set (σ_2)						
δ_{12}	-1.14777	0.02610		-0.01384	0.07039	
		(5.23)		(-1.74)	(9.01)	0.64
β_{12}	-1.42236	0.18826		-0.19178	0.19388	
		(8.70)		(-5.57)	(5.72)	0.57
λ_2	(Same equation as in the child-dependency set)					
Parental-regularity set (β_{12})						
δ_{12}	-0.88605	0.05634		0.01179	0.04530	
		(3.60)		(1.78)	(6.85)	0.60
σ_2	10.38013	1.70652		0.97656	-0.95133	
		(8.70)		(11.77)	-11.47)	0.78
λ_2	1.16111	0.02563		0.07816	-0.08316	
		(2.58)		(18.58)	(-19.77)	0.87
Equations common to all sets (δ_{12})						
μ_2	-3.26006	3.27947		-0.67070	1.39248	
		(2.77)		(-6.46)	(11.93)	0.77
a_2	0.03398		0.29713			
			(7.46)			0.51
δ_{1c}	9.41424	13.83372				0.05
		(0.63)				

B. FEMALES

Dependent variables	Inter-cept	Regression coefficients of independent variables[a]: δ_{12} / σ_2 / β_{12}	α_2	x_ℓ	x_h	Multiple correlation coefficient r
Child-dependency set (δ_{12})						
σ_2	10.96834	6.05257		0.63402	-0.84512	
		(9.85)		(11.47)	(-16.16)	0.82
β_{12}	1.82060	1.42203		-0.04282	-0.03911	
		(9.04)		(-3.02)	(-2.92)	0.58
λ_2	1.19343	0.12937		0.07635	-0.08650	
		(2.98)		(19.57)	(-23.45)	0.90
Labor-asymmetry set (σ_2)						
σ_{12}	-1.03192	0.06046		-0.02597	0.06933	
		(9.85)		(-3.66)	(10.81)	0.72
β_{12}	0.28708	0.09485		-0.08643	0.06544	
		(5.35)		(-4.22)	(3.53)	0.39
λ_2	(Same equation as in the child-dependency set)					
Parental-regularity set (β_{12})						
δ_{12}	-0.81011	0.22998		0.02297	0.02835	
		(9.04)		(4.12)	(5.60)	0.70
σ_2	5.92233	1.53566		0.77520	-0.67378	
		(5.35)		(12.34)	(-11.80)	0.75
λ_2	1.09905	0.01926		0.07916	-0.08282	
		(1.08)		(20.28)	(-23.33)	0.89
Equations common to all sets (δ_{12})						
μ_2	-7.69222	-2.14239		-0.52726	1.63218	
		(-2.37)		(-6.49)	(21.25)	0.86
a_2	0.03850		0.24908			
			(6.79)			0.46
δ_{1c}	0.18996	26.42951				
		(3.85)				0.28

Values for these three variables may be selected to reflect informed guesses, historical data, or empirical regularities between such model schedule variables and observed migration data.

For example, suppose that a fertility survey has produced a crude estimate of the ratio of infant-to-parent migration rates: $M = M(0-4)/M(20-24)$, say. A linear regression of δ_{12} on this M-ratio gives, for Swedish females,

$$ {}_F\hat{\delta}_{12} = -0.05562 + 0.79321\ M\ , $$

and a correlation coefficient of 0.92. Enlarging the data set to include also the United Kingdom and Japan reduces the correlation coefficient to 0.66, and gives

$$ {}_F\hat{\delta}_{12} = 0.10311 + 0.40811\ M\ . $$

Estimating the corresponding equation for males yields

$$ {}_M\hat{\delta}_{12} = -0.02066 + 0.68602\ M $$

and a correlation coefficient of 0.80. And repeating the above two regression calculations using data for single years of age (that is, $M = M(0-1)/M(20-21)$) gives

$$ {}_F\hat{\delta}_{12} = 0.18224 + 0.20346\ M\ , \qquad (r = 0.60) $$

and

$$ {}_M\hat{\delta}_{12} = 0.09318 + 0.35022\ M\ , \qquad (r = 0.74) $$

The correlation coefficients indicate that the fits for the five-year age groups are somewhat better for both males and females, and such data are generally more readily available. Moreover, tests of both pairs of regressions with data for

Sweden, the United Kingdom, and Japan consistently show that the two pairs produce virtually identical age profiles for fixed values of x_ℓ and x_h. Consequently we shall restrict our attention to the five-year age interval regression equations.

Figure 2 illustrates examples of the quality of fit provided by the synthetic schedules to the observed model migration data. Two sets of synthetic schedules are shown: those with the observed index of child dependency (δ_{12}) and those with the estimated index ($\hat{\delta}_{12}$), calculated using the five-year age group regressions.

1.2.3. Applications

A closer examination of the basic set of regression equations reveals several weaknesses. The equation for estimating β_{12} in the child-dependency set has a low coefficient of multiple correlation, $r = 0.28$. It would seem prudent to simply set β_{12} equal to a fixed value, say unity. A similar justification may be made for setting c equal to 0.003, say.

The male and female regression equations to calculate a_2 are similar enough to lead one to combine them to define the unisexual equation

$$a_2 = 0.04 + 0.27\,\alpha_2.$$

The regression equations for calculating μ_2, σ_2, and λ_2 remain as set out in Table 2.

Simplification of the M-ratio regression is also possible. Forcing the regression through the origin gives

$$_F\hat{\delta}_{12} = 0.549\ M$$

and

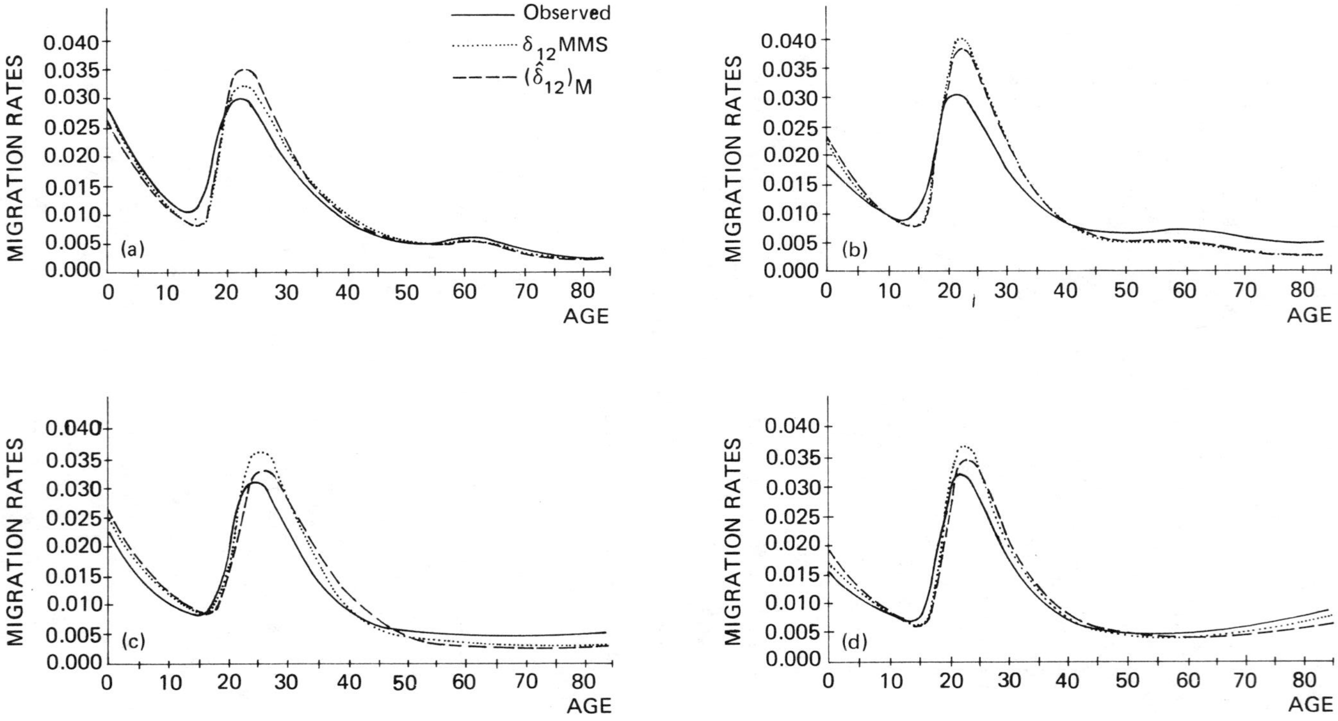

Fig. 2. The fits of correlational synthetic model migration schedules to data for the female populations of (a) Stockholm, (b) London, (c) Tokyo, and (d) Amsterdam.

$$M^{\hat{\delta}}_{12} = 0.654\ M\ .$$

Exhibit 2 presents the calculation sequence that uses the above equations to produce the synthetic model migration schedule for Philippine males illustrated in Fig. 3. The result is not very satisfactory and suggests that further research on the development of a basic set of regressions appropriate to Third World countries is needed.

2. SYNTHETIC MODEL MIGRATION SCHEDULES: II. THE RELATIONAL PERSPECTIVE

Two alternative perspectives for identifying an appropriate synthetic model migration schedule for a regional population with inadequate data were outlined at the beginning of the preceding section. Both ultimately depend on the availability of some limited data to obtain the appropriate model schedule, for example, at least two age-specific rates such as M(0-4) and M(20-24), and informed guesses regarding the values of a few key variables, such as the low and high points of the schedule.

Although the appropriate alternative will always depend on the particular situation at hand, it seems reasonable to expect that the relational logit system may turn out to be the more suitable approach in some particular instances. Therefore, we shall continue our discussion of synthetic schedules, in this section, by focusing on the development of a logit migration system.

A. Inputs

$$\frac{M(0\text{-}4)}{M(20\text{-}24)} = \frac{0.051}{0.132} = 0.386$$

$$\hat{\delta}_{12} = a_1 \frac{M(0\text{-}4)}{M(20\text{-}24)} = 0.654(0.386) = 0.252$$

$$x_\ell = 13.50$$

$$x_h = 23.00$$

B. Outputs

B.1 Labor force component

$$\mu_2 = -3.260 + 3.279\ \delta_{12} - 0.671\ x_\ell + 1.392\ x_h = 20.525$$

$$\sigma_2 = 16.427 + 5.594\ \delta_{12} + 0.894\ x_\ell - 1.174\ x_h = 2.906$$

$$\lambda_2 = 1.308 + 0.151\ \delta_{12} + 0.076\ x_\ell - 0.090\ x_h = 0.302$$

$$\alpha_2 = \frac{\lambda_2}{\sigma_2} = 0.104$$

$$a_2 = 0.04 + 0.27\ \alpha_2 = 0.068$$

B.2 Pre-labor force component

$$a_1 = a_2 \delta_{12} = 0.017$$

$$\beta_{12} = 1$$

$$\alpha_1 = \alpha_2 \beta_{12} = \alpha_2 = 0.104$$

B.3 Constant component

$$c = 0.003$$

C. Goodness of Fit

$$E = 35.10$$

Exhibit 2. The calculation sequence with the simplified version of the basic regressions: Philippine males.

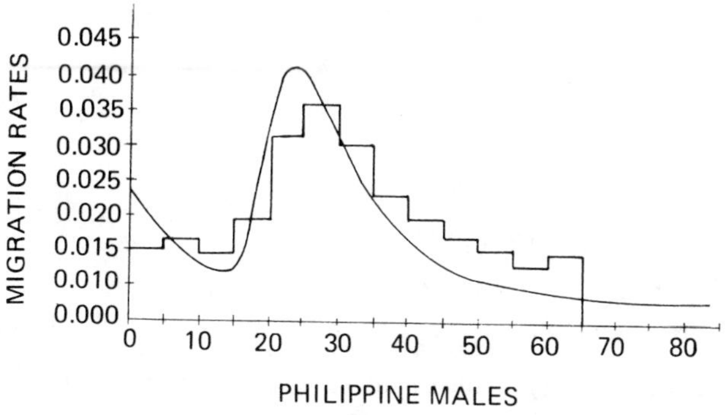

Fig. 3. A synthetic model migration schedule for Philippine males: the correlational approach (del Mar Pernia, 1977).

2.1. *INTRODUCTION: THE LOGIT APPROACH*

Among the most popular methods for estimating mortality from inadequate or defective data, is the so-called "logit system" developed by William Brass about 20 yr ago and now widely applied by demographers all over the world (Brass, 1971; Brass and Coale, 1968; Carrier and Hobcraft, 1971; Hill and Trussell, 1977; Zaba, 1979). The logit approach to model schedules is founded on the assumption that different mortality schedules can be related to each other by a linear transformation of the logits of their respective survivorship probabilities. That is, given an observed series of survivorship probabilities $\ell(x)$ for ages $x = 1,2,\ldots,\omega$, it is possible to associate these with a "standard" series $\ell_s(x)$ by means of the linear relationship

$$\text{logit}[1 - \ell(x)] = \gamma + \rho\ \text{logit}[1 - \ell_s(x)] ,$$

where

$$\text{logit}[y(x)] = \frac{1}{2}\,\ell n\left[\frac{y(x)}{1 - y(x)}\right] = Y(x) \quad \text{, say, } 0 < y(x) < 1 \text{ ,}$$

or

$$Y(x) = \gamma + \rho\, Y_s(x) \ .$$

The inverse of this function is

$$\ell(x) = 1/\{1 + \exp[2Y(x)]\}$$

The principal results of this mathematical transformation of the nonlinear $\ell(x)$ function is a more nearly linear function in x, with a range of $\pm\infty$ rather than unity and zero.

Given a standard schedule, such as the set of standard logits $Y_s(x)$, proposed by Brass, a life table can be created by selecting appropriate values for γ and ρ. In the Brass system, γ reflects the level of mortality and ρ defines the relationship between child and adult mortality. The closer γ is to zero and ρ to unity, the more like the standard is the synthetically created life table.

2.2. *THE RELATIONAL PERSPECTIVE: THE LOGIT MIGRATION SYSTEM*

As before, let ${}_uM(x)$ denote the age-specific migration rates of a schedule scaled to a unit gross migraproduction rate (GMR), and let ${}_uM_s(x)$ denote the corresponding standard schedule. Taking logits of both sets of rates gives the logit migration system,

$${}_uY(x) = \gamma + \rho\ {}_uY_s(x)$$

and

$${}_uM(x) = 1/\{1 + \exp(-2[\gamma + \rho\,{}_uY_s(x)])\} \ ,$$

where, for example,

$$\text{logit}[{}_uM_s(x)] = {}_uY_s(x) = \frac{1}{2} \ln \frac{{}_uM_s(x)}{1 - {}_uM_s(x)} , \quad 0 < {}_uM_s(x) < 1 .$$

The selection of a particular migration schedule as a standard reflects the belief that it is broadly representative of the age pattern of migration in the multiregional population system under consideration. To illustrate a number of calculations carried out with several sets of multiregional data, we shall adopt the national age profile as the standard in each case and strive to estimate regional outmigration age profiles by relating them to the national one. Specifically, given an m by m table of interregional migration flows for any age x, we divide each origin-destination-specific flow $O_{ij}(x)$ by the population in the origin region $K_i(x)$ to define the age-specific migration rate $M_{ij}(x)$. For the corresponding national rate, we define

$$M_{..}(x) = \sum_i \sum_j O_{ij}(x) / \sum_i K_i(x) , \qquad \text{for all } i \neq j .$$

Scaling all schedules to unit GMR gives

$${}_uM_{ij}(x) = M_{ij}(x) / \sum_x M_{ij}(x) = M_{ij}(x)/\text{GMR}_{ij} , \quad i \neq j ,$$

and

$${}_uM_{..}(x) = M_{..}(x) / \sum_x M_{..}(x) = M_{..}(x)/\text{GMR}_{..} .$$

Figure 4a illustrates the national migration rate schedule of Swedish males and females in 1974, scaled to unit GMR. The rates are for single years of age and describe

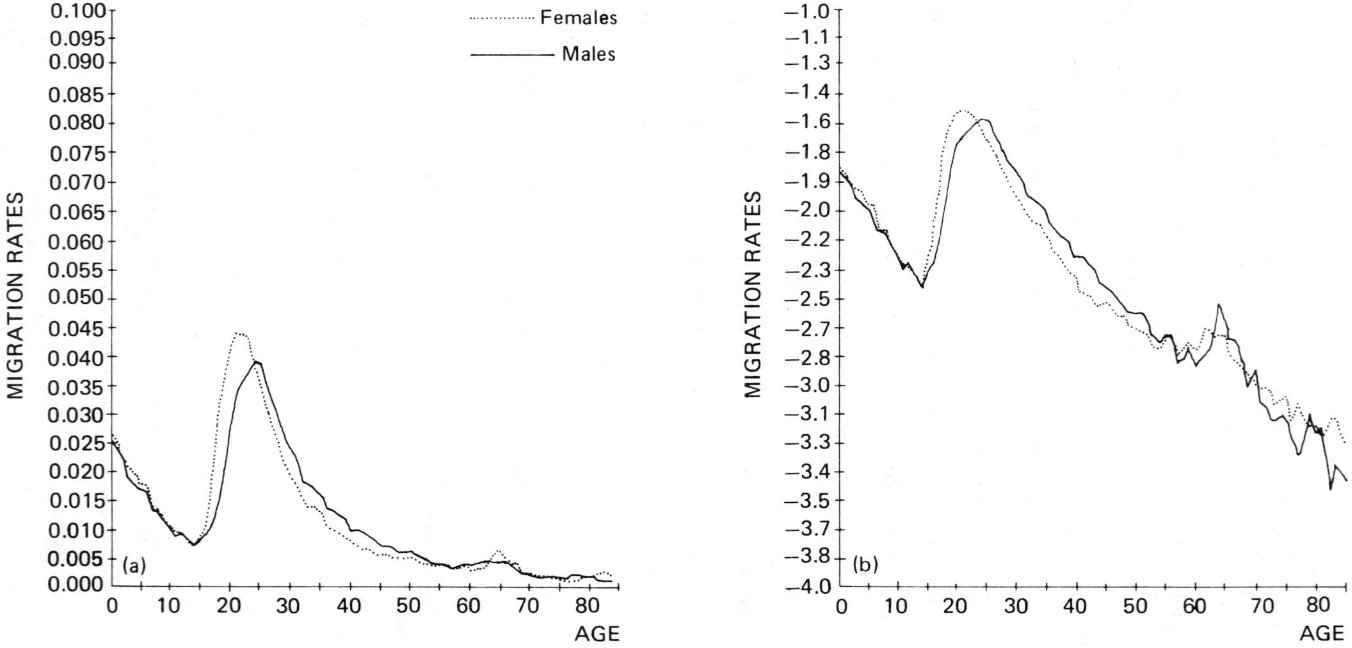

Fig. 4. National age-specific migration rates and standard logit values: Sweden 1974. (a) National age specific migration rates. (b) Standard logit values.

transfers across the regional boundaries of the eight-region system adopted in the comparative study.

Figure 4b graphs the age pattern of the logit values, $Y_s(x)$, of the national migration rates.[5] Regressing the set of 85 age-specific outmigration rates from Stockholm to the rest of the nation on these two standard schedules of logits, gives

$${}_uY(x) = -0.4871 + 0.7664\ Y_s(x)$$

for males, and

$${}_uY(x) = -0.3317 + 0.8362\ Y_s(x)$$

for females.

Alternatively, fitting the model migration schedule to the national standard with GMR set equal to unity, taking logits of these standard rates, and regressing Stockholm's model schedule outmigration rates (with GMR also equal to unity) on the standard logits, gives

$${}_uY(x) = -0.4978 + 0.7612\ Y_s(x)$$

for males, and

$${}_uY(x) = -0.3358 + 0.8345\ Y_s(x)$$

for females. The differences are minor for most of the Swedish data and so are their consequences for the fits of the synthetic Stockholm model schedules to the observed data and its graduated expression. Figure 5 illustrates both pairs of fits

[5] *Our standard schedules will always have a unit GMR, and, the left subscript on* ${}_uY_s(x)$ *will be dropped henceforth.*

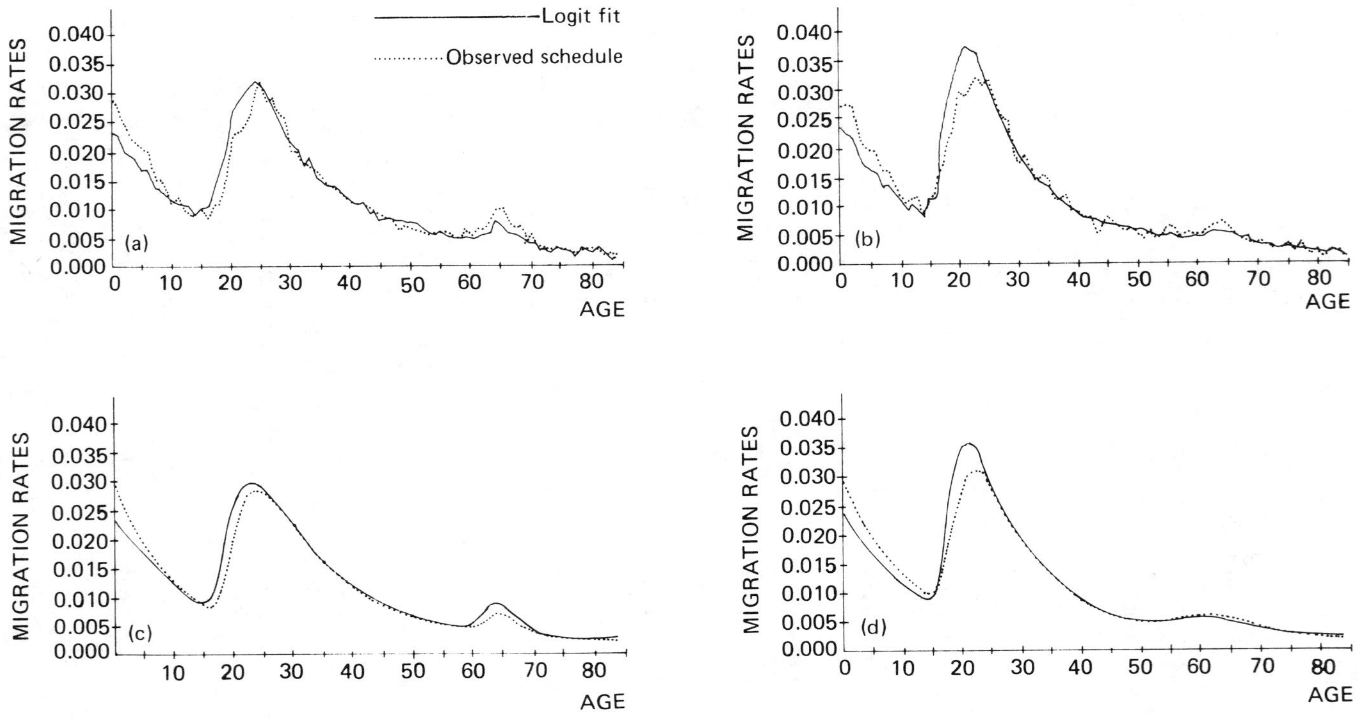

Fig. 5. Logit fits to observed and model migration schedules for males and females leaving Stockholm, 1974. (a) Males. (b) Females. (c) Males. (d) Females.

for Stockholm. Henceforth we shall deal only with graduated fits inasmuch as all of our non-Swedish data are for five-year age intervals and therefore need to be graduated first in order to provide single-year profiles by means of interpolation.

Figure 6 presents male national standards for Sweden, the United Kingdom, Japan, and The Netherlands. The differences in age profile are marked. Only the Swedish and the U.K. standards exhibit a retirement peak. Japan's profile is described without one because the age distribution of migrants given by the census data ends with the open interval of 65 yr and over. The data for The Netherlands, on the other hand, show a definite upward slope at the post-labor force ages and therefore have been graduated with the 9-parameter model schedule with an "upward slope."

Regressing the logits of the age-specific outmigration rates of each region on those of its national standard (the GMRs of both first being scaled to unity) gives the estimated values for γ and ρ that are set out in Table 3. Reversing the procedure and combining selected values of γ and ρ with a national standard of logit values, produces the GMRs set out in Table 4. The latter table identifies the following important regularity: *whenever $\gamma = 2(\rho-1)$, then the GMR of the synthetic model schedule is approximately unity.* Regressions of the form

$$\gamma = d_0 + d_1\rho$$

fitted to our data for Sweden, the U.K., Japan, and The Netherlands consistently produce estimates for d_0 and d_1 that are approximately equal to 2 in magnitude and that differ only in sign, i.e.,

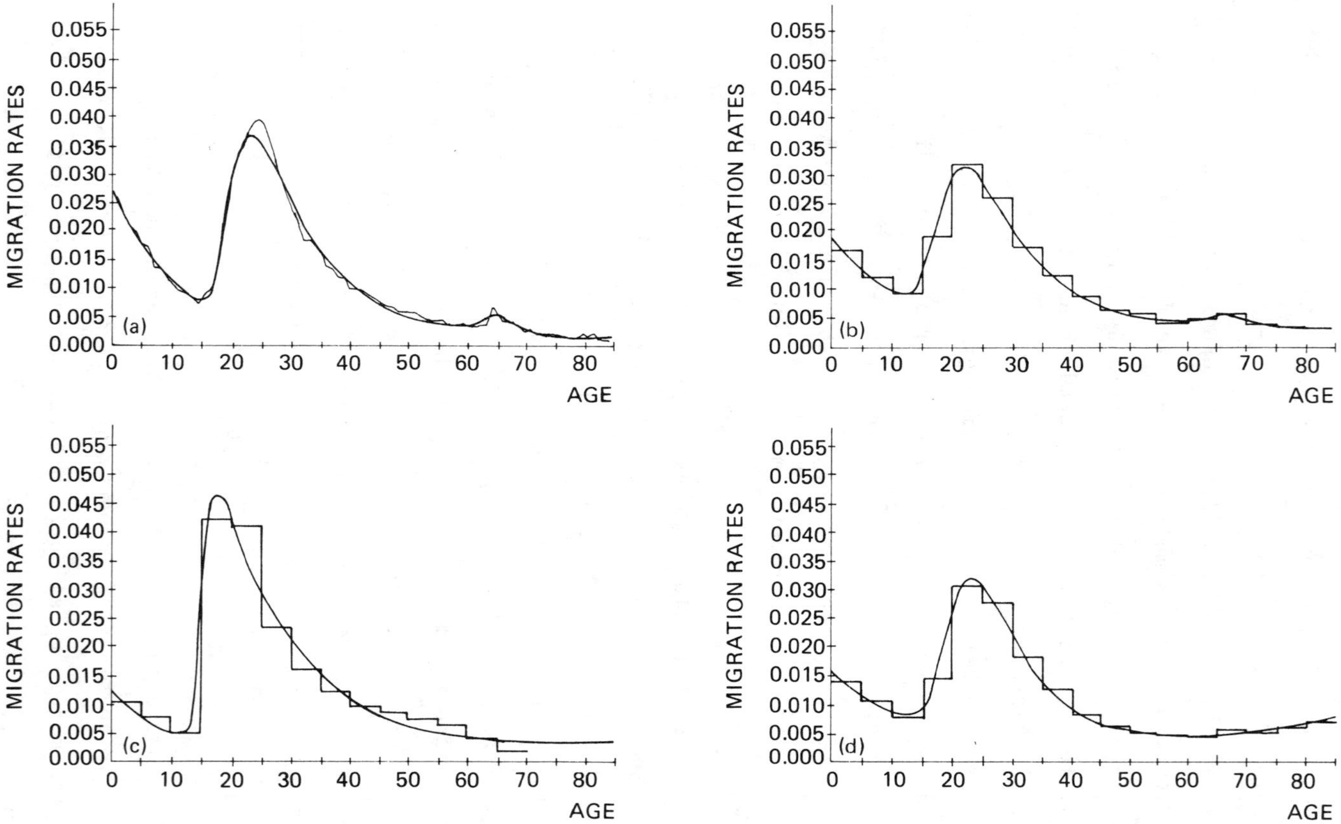

Fig. 6. National male standard schedules. (a) Sweden. (b) United Kingdom. (c) Japan. (c) The Netherlands.

TABLE 3. Estimated Logit Model Parameters

		γ		ρ	
		Males	Females	Males	Females
a.	Sweden				
1.	Stockholm	-0.4978	-0.3358	0.7612	0.8345
2.	East Middle	-0.1719	-0.0943	0.9214	0.9588
3.	South Middle	-0.0341	-0.0129	0.9939	1.0053
4.	South	-0.0669	-0.0005	0.9773	1.0090
5.	West	-0.0724	-0.0787	0.9697	0.9665
6.	North Middle	-0.0130	-0.0738	1.0051	0.9801
7.	Lower North	-0.0706	-0.0693	0.9852	0.9901
8.	Upper North	-0.2946	-0.2004	0.8767	0.9278
b.	United Kingdom				
1.	North	0.0604	0.0259	1.0326	1.0154
2.	Yorkshire	0.1464	0.2303	1.0699	1.1097
3.	North West	-0.2577	-0.0480	0.8826	0.9789
4.	East Middle	0.2730	0.1774	1.1276	1.0828
5.	West Middle	0.1768	0.1300	1.0816	1.0614
6.	East Anglia	0.0838	0.1966	1.0389	1.0918
7.	South East	-0.3324	-0.2959	0.8449	0.8626
8.	South West	0.3395	0.1247	1.1625	1.0588
9.	Wales	0.1416	-0.0144	1.0717	0.9976
10.	Scotland	0.5269	0.8599	1.2512	1.4074
c.	Japan				
1.	Hokkaido	-0.1075	-0.4254	0.9519	0.7931
2.	Tohoku	-0.6740	0.0975	0.7008	1.0747
3.	Kanto	-0.5251	-0.7071	0.7581	0.6753
4.	Chubu	0.2507	0.0984	1.1351	1.0509
5.	Kinki	0.1971	-0.3372	1.0916	0.8418
6.	Chugoku	0.3687	0.2055	1.1973	1.1066
7.	Shikoku	-0.0356	0.1680	1.0098	1.1009
8.	Kyushu	-0.2333	0.3389	0.9009	1.1738
d.	The Netherlands				
1.	Groningen	0.1434	0.1136	1.0705	1.0550
2.	Friesland	0.0222	-0.1122	1.0160	0.9507
3.	Drenthe	0.1835	-0.0103	1.0920	0.9982
4.	Overijssel	0.2430	0.2902	1.1445	1.1403
5.	Gelderland	0.1714	0.1103	1.0945	1.0541
6.	Utrecht	-0.0493	0.1539	1.0000	1.0762
7.	Noord-Holland	-0.1172	-0.2586	0.9549	0.8778
8.	Zuid-Holland	-0.1746	-0.2075	0.9292	0.9014
9.	Zeeland	0.3046	-0.0224	1.1537	0.9907
10.	Noord-Brabant	0.2353	0.0135	1.1427	1.0092
11.	Limburg	0.2923	0.1657	1.1679	1.0830

TABLE 4. Estimated GMRs for Different Logit Parameter Values and Male Standard Schedules

Sweden

		ρ		
		0.75	1.00	1.25
	-0.5	1.04	0.37	0.14
γ	0	2.74	1.00	0.37
	0.5	6.91	2.63	1.00

United Kingdom

		ρ		
		0.75	1.00	1.25
	-0.5	1.07	0.37	0.13
γ	0	2.82	1.00	0.36
	0.5	7.15	2.64	0.96

Japan

		ρ		
		0.75	1.00	1.25
	-0.5	1.04	0.37	0.14
γ	0	2.75	1.00	0.37
	0.5	6.94	2.62	1.00

The Netherlands

		ρ		
		0.75	1.00	1.25
	-0.5	1.08	0.37	0.13
γ	0	2.87	1.00	0.35
	0.5	7.32	2.65	0.94

$$\hat{d}_0 = -2 \quad \text{and} \quad \hat{d}_1 = +2 \ .$$

Thus,

$$\gamma = -2 + 2\rho = 2(\rho - 1) \ .$$

We have noted before that when $\gamma = 0$ and $\rho = 1$, the synthetic model schedule is identical to the standard. Moreover, since the GMR of the standard is always unity, values of γ and ρ that satisfy the equality $\gamma = 2(\rho-1)$ guarantee a GMR of unity for the synthetic schedule. What are the effects of other combinations of values for these two parameters?

Figure 7 illustrates how the Swedish male standard schedule is transformed when γ and ρ are assigned particular pairs of values. Figure 7a shows that fixing $\gamma = 0$ and increasing ρ from 0.75 to 1.25 lowers the schedule, giving migration rates that are smaller in value than those of the standard On the other hand, fixing $\rho = 0.75$, and increasing γ from -1 to

0 raises the schedule, according to Fig. 7b. Finally, fixing the GMR = 1 by selecting values of γ and ρ that satisfy the equality $\gamma = 2(\rho - 1)$ shows that as γ and ρ both increase, so does the degree of labor dominance exhibited by the synthetic schedule. For example, moving from a synthetic schedule with $\gamma = -0.5$ and $\rho = 0.75$ to one with $\gamma = 0.5$ and $\rho = 1.25$ does not alter the area under the curve (GMR = 1) but it does increase its labor dominance (Fig. 7c).

Figure 8 compares the behavior of the Swedish male standard with those of the U.K., Japan, and The Netherlands, as γ and ρ are assigned values of -0.5, 0, +0.5 and 0.75, 1.0, 1.25, respectively. In all cases, increases in γ and ρ values lead to more labor-dominant profiles. Note that, whereas the Swedish curve shows three points of intersection, the Japanese profile exhibits only two. This suggests that it might be useful to distinguish families of standard schedules according to the number and locations along the age axis of such intersection points.

2.3. THE BASIC STANDARD SCHEDULE

Available data on national and interregional migration patterns suggests at least three distinct families of age profiles. First, there is the 11-parameter *basic model migration schedule* with a retirement peak that describes adequately a large number of interregional flows, for example, the age profiles of outmigrants leaving capital regions such as Stockholm and London. The elimination of the retirement peak gives rise to the seven-parameter *reduced form* of this basic schedule, a form that can be used to describe a large number of labor-

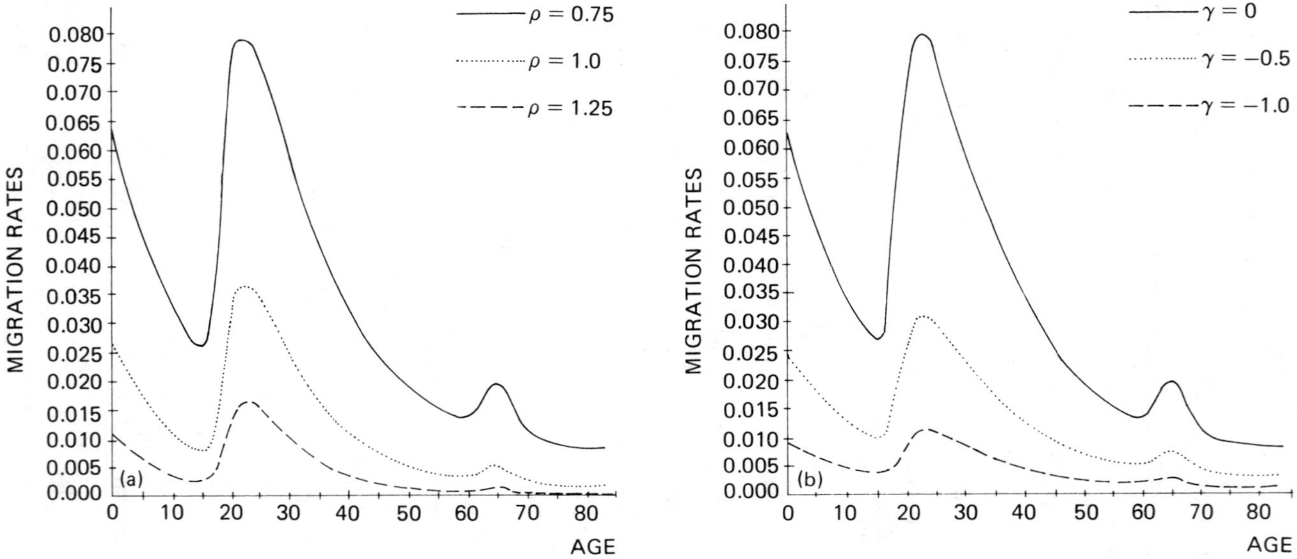

MIGRATION RATES
0.080
0.075
0.070
0.065
0.060
0.055
0.050
0.045
0.040
0.035
0.030
0.025
0.020
0.015
0.010
0.005
0.000
0
10
20
30
40
50
60
70
80
AGE
(a)
$\rho = 0.75$
$\rho = 1.0$
$\rho = 1.25$
(b)
$\gamma = 0$
$\gamma = -0.5$
$\gamma = -1.0$

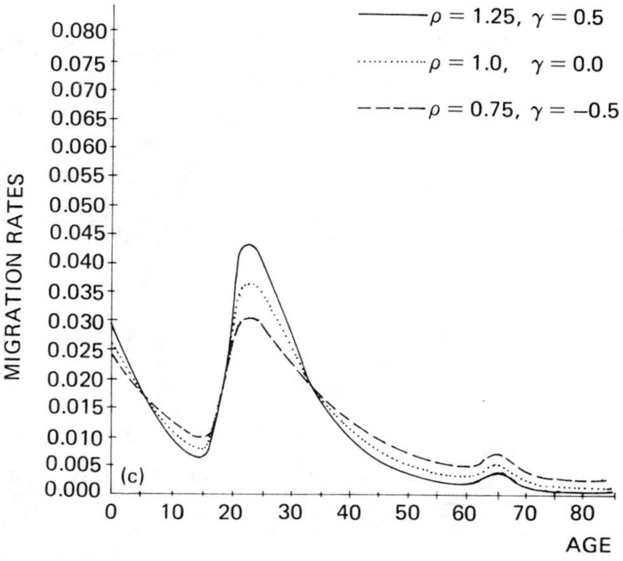

Fig. 7. Sensitivity of logit model schedule to variations in γ and ρ: Swedish male standard schedules. (a) Fixed γ and varying ρ; (b) fixed ρ and varying γ; (c) varying γ and ρ.

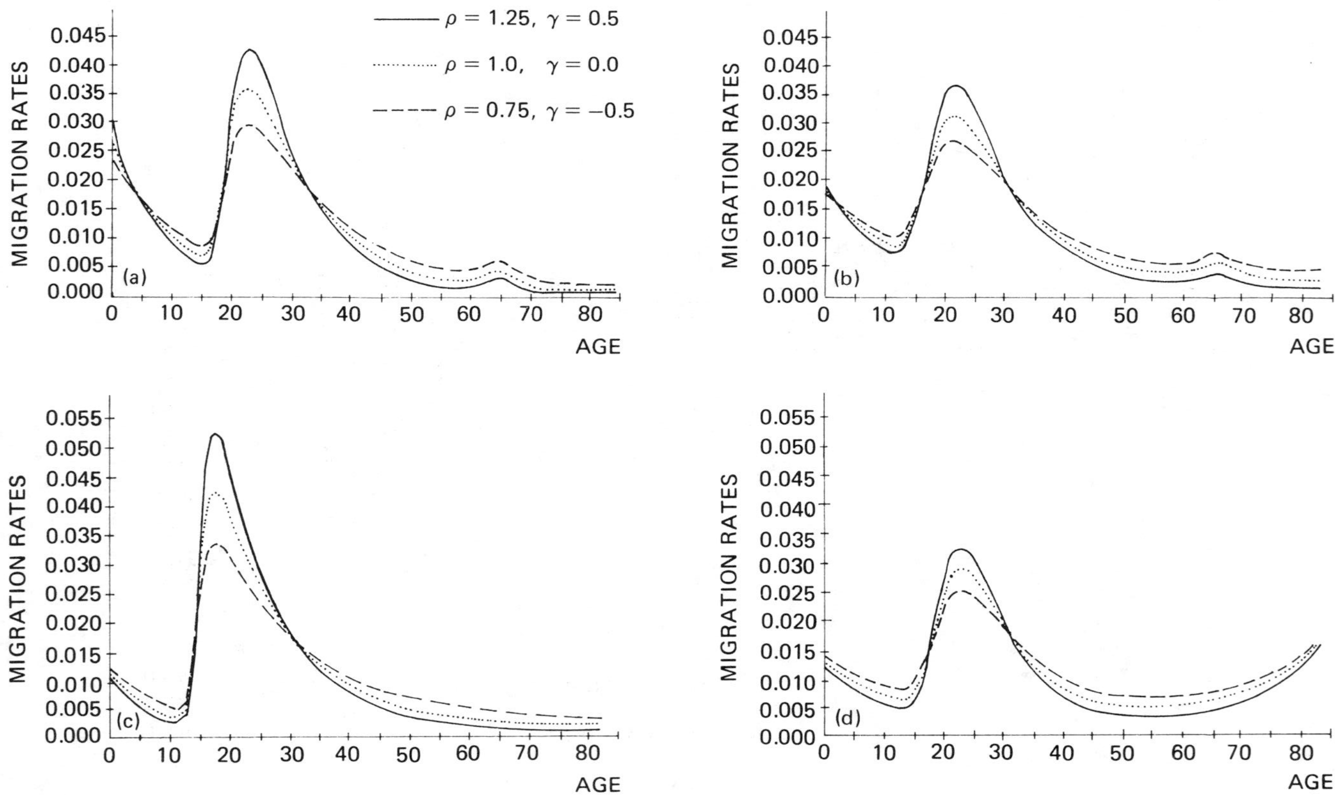

Fig. 8. Sensitivity to logit model schedule to variations in γ *and* ρ. *four national male standard schedules. (a) Sweden. (b) United Kingdom. (c) Japan. (d) The Netherlands.*

dominant profiles and the age patterns of migration schedules with a single open-ended age interval for the post-labor force population, for example, Japan's migration schedules. Finally, the existence of a monotonically rising tail in migration schedules such as those exhibited by the Dutch data indicates the need for a third profile: the nine-parameter *upward-sloping model migration schedule*. These three fundamental age profiles define our three families of model migration schedules.

Within each family of schedules, a number of key parameters or variables may be put forward in order to further classify different categories of migration profiles. The following aspects of shape and location along the age axis are especially important:

(1) Peaking: early peaking versus late peaking (μ_2)

(2) Dominance: child dominance versus labor dominance (δ_{12})

(3) Symmetry: labor symmetry versus labor asymmetry (σ_2)

(4) Regularity: parental regularity vs. parental irregularity (β_1)

These fundamental families and four key parameters give rise to a large variety of standard schedules. For example, even if the four key parameters are restricted to only dichotomous values, one already needs $2^4 = 16$ standard schedules. If, in addition, the sexes are to be differentiated, then 32 standard schedules are a minimum. A large number of standard schedules would make the logit approach a less desirable alternative. Hence, we shall examine the feasibility of adopting only a single standard for each sex and assume that the shape of the post-labor force part of the schedule may be determined exogenously.[6]

Table 5 presents the median parameter values of the 164 male and 172 female model schedules that have no retirement peak among the interregional schedules we have calculated for Sweden, the United Kingdom, and Japan. This data base is precisely the same one that was used earlier to develop the basic regression equations set out in Table 2.

2.4. *USING THE BASIC STANDARD SCHEDULE*

Given a standard schedule and a few observed rates, such as M(0-4) and M(20-24), for example, how can one find estimates for γ and ρ and, with those estimates, go on to obtain the entire synthetic schedule?

First, taking logits of the two observed migration rates gives Y(0-4) and Y(20-24), and associating these two logits with the pair of corresponding logits for the standard gives

$$Y(0\text{-}4) = \gamma + \rho\, Y_s(0\text{-}4) \;,$$

$$Y(20\text{-}24) = \gamma + \rho\, Y_s(20\text{-}24) \;.$$

Solving these two equations in two unknowns gives crude estimates for γ and ρ, and applying them to the standard schedule's full set of logits results in a set of logits for the synthetic schedule. From these one can obtain the migration rates, as shown in an earlier subsection. However, tests of such a

[6] *In tests of our logit migration system, therefore, we shall always set the post-labor force retirement peak or upward slope equal to observed model schedule values.*

TABLE 5. The Basic Standard Median Migration Schedule

A. Males		
$\delta_{12} = 0.33571$		$\mu_2 = 19.67385$
$\sigma_2 = 3.42123$	$a_1 = 0.01992$	$a_2 = 0.06471$
$\beta_{12} = 1.02442$	$\alpha_1 = 0.10390$	$\alpha_2 = 0.10618$
$\delta_{1c} = 6.79034$	$c = 0.00263$	$\lambda_2 = 0.37244$
B. Females		
$\delta_{12} = 0.32367$		$\mu_2 = 19.88280$
$\sigma_2 = 2.89784$	$a_1 = 0.02209$	$a_2 = 0.06935$
$\beta_{12} = 0.84944$	$\alpha_1 = 0.10883$	$\alpha_2 = 0.13434$
$\delta_{1c} = 5.95881$	$c = 0.00350$	$\lambda_2 = 0.37870$

procedure with the migration data for Sweden, the United Kingdom, Japan, and The Netherlands indicate that the method is very erratic in the quality of the fits that it produces and, therefore, more refined procedures are necessary. Such procedures (for the case of mortality) are described in the literature on the Brass logit system (for example, in Brass, 1975 and Carrier and Goh, 1972).

A reasonable first approximation to an improved estimation method is suggested by the regression approach described earlier. Imagine a regression of ρ on the M-ratio, M(0-4)/M(20-24). Starting with the basic standard median migration schedule and varying ρ within the range of observed values, one may obtain a corresponding set of M-ratios. Associating ρ and the M-ratio in this way, one may proceed further and use the relational equation to estimate $\hat{\gamma}$ from $\hat{\rho}$:

$$\hat{\gamma} = 2(\hat{\rho}-1) \ .$$

Using the basic median standard, for example, gives the following regression equation:

$$\hat{\rho}_F = 2.690 - 3.062\ M$$

for females, and

$$\hat{\rho}_M = 2.510 - 2.983\ M$$

for males.

A further simplification can be made by forcing the regression line to pass through the origin. Since the resulting regression coefficient has a negative sign and the intercept exhibits roughly the same absolute value, but with a positive sign, the regression equations take on the form

$$\hat{\rho}_F = 2.226(1-M)$$

for females, and

$$\hat{\rho}_M = 2.101(1-M)$$

for males.

Given a standard schedule and estimates for γ and ρ, one can proceed to compute the associated synthetic model migration schedule. Figure 9 illustrates representative examples of the quality of fit obtained using this procedure. Two synthetic schedules are illustrated with each observed model migration schedule: those calculated with the interpolated 85 single-year of age observations and the resulting least-squares estimates of γ and ρ, and those computed using the above regression equations of ρ on the M-ratio.

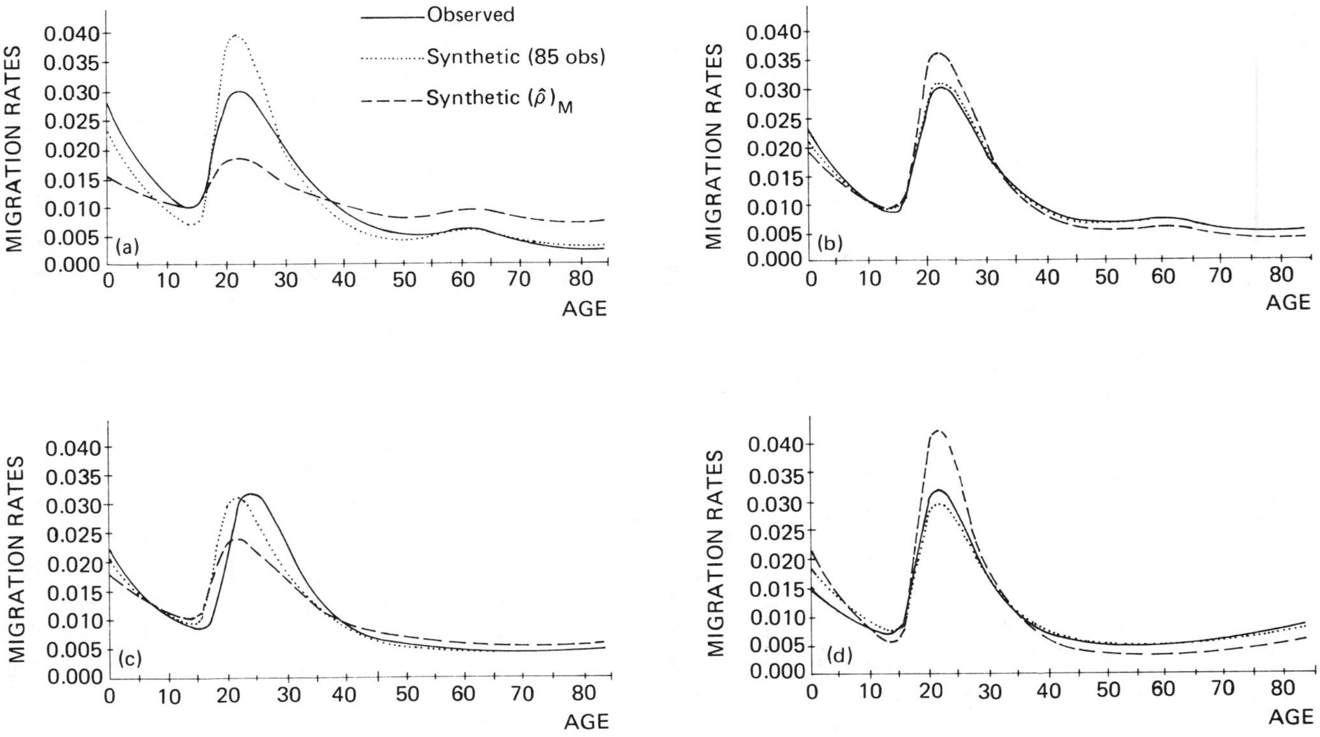

Fig. 9. The fits of relational synthetic model migration schedules to data for the female populations of (a) Stockholm, (b) London, (c) Tokyo, and (d) Amsterdam.

2.5. *APPLICATIONS*

The male and female median standard schedules set out in Table 5 are similar, and a simplified logit system could use their average parameter values to define a unisexual standard. A rough rounding of these averages would simplify matters even more. In applying the logit migration system to data on the Philippines, we shall adopt both of the above simplifications and use the simplified basic standard migration schedule presented in Table 6.

The simplified basic schedule in Table 6 together with estimates of $\hat{\rho}$ obtained with the pair of M-ratio regressions set out earlier produced the synthetic schedules for the Philippines illustrated in Fig. 10. As with the correlational perspective, the results are unsatisfactory and underscore the need to define a more appropriate standard for Third World countries.

3. CONCLUDING REMARKS

This paper began with the observation that empirical regularities characterize observed multistate schedules in ways that are no less important than the corresponding well-

TABLE 6. The Simplified Basic Standard Migration Schedule[a]

$\delta_{12} = 1/3$		$\mu_2 = 20$
$\sigma_2 = 4$	$a_1 = 0.02$	$a_2 = 0.06$
$\beta_{12} = 1$	$\alpha_1 = 0.10$	$\alpha_2 = 0.10$
$\delta_{1c} = 6$	$c = 0.003$	$\lambda_2 = 0.40$

[a]*The values of a_1, a_2, and c are initial values only and need to be scaled proportionately to ensure a unit GMR.*

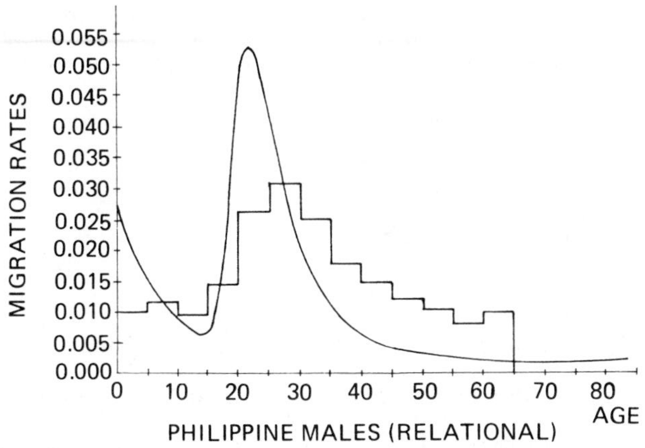

Fig. 10. A synthetic model migration schedule for Philippine males: the relational approach (del Mar Pernia, 1977).

established regularities in observed fertility or mortality schedules. Regularities in age profiles lead naturally to the development of hypothetical or synthetic model migration schedules that might be suitable for studies of populations with inadequate or defective data. Drawing on techniques used in the corresponding literature in fertility and mortality, we have outlined two alternative perspectives for inferring migration patterns in the absence of accurate migration data. Such model schedules may be used to assess the *reliability* of empirical migration data and indicate appropriate strategies for their *correction*, and they also may be used to help resolve problems caused by *missing data*.

The synthetic model migration schedules described in this study demonstrate the utility of examining the regularities in age profile exhibited by empirical schedules of interregional migration. Although, data limitations have restricted some of the findings to conjectures, a modest start has been made. It is hoped that the results reported here will induce others to devote more attention to this topic.

ACKNOWLEDGMENTS

The authors are grateful to the many national collaborating scholars who have participated in IIASA's Comparative Migration and Settlement Study. This paper could not have been written without the data bank produced by their collective efforts. Thanks also go to Richard Raquillet for his contributions to the early phases of this study and to Walter Kogler for his untiring efforts on our behalf in front of a console in IIASA's computer center.

REFERENCES

Brass, W., ed. (1971). On the scale of mortality. "Biological Aspects of Demography," pp. 69-110. London: Taylor and Francis, Ltd.

Brass, W. (1975). "Methods for Estimating Fertility and Mortality from Limited and Defective Data." Chapel Hill, North Carolina: Laboratories for Population Statistics, The University of North Carolina at Chapel Hill.

Brass, W., and Coale, Ansley (1968). Methods of analysis and estimation. "Demography of Tropical Africa" (William Brass, ed.), pp. 88-150. Princeton, New Jersey: Princeton University Press.

Carrier, N., and Hobcraft, J. (1971). "Demographic Estimation for Developing Societies." London: Population Investigation Committee, London School of Economics.

Carrier, N., and Goh, T. (1972). The validation of Brass's model life table system. *Population Studies 26(1)*, 29-51.

Castro, L. J., and Rogers, A. (1979). "Migration Age Patterns: Measurement and Analysis." WP-79-16. Laxenburg, Austria: International Institute for Applied Systems Analysis.

Coale, A. (1977). The development of new models of nuptiality and fertility. *Population, numéro spécial,* 131-154.

Coale, A., and Demeny, P. (1966). "Regional Model Life Tables and Stable Populations." Princeton, New Jersey: Princeton University Press.

Coale, A. J., and McNeil, D. R. (1972). The distribution by age of the frequency of first marriage in a female cohort. *Journal of the American Statistical Association 67,* 743-749.

Coale, A., and Trussell, J. (1974). Model fertility schedules: Variations in the age structure of childbearing in human populations. *Population Index 40(2),* 185-206.

del Mar Pernia, E. (1977). "Urbanization, Population Growth, and Economic Development in the Philippines." Westport, Connecticut: Greenwood Press.

Hill, K., and Trussell, J. (1977). Further developments in indirect mortality estimation. *Population Studies 31(2),* 313-334.

Krishnan, P., and Kayani, A. K. (1973). Model divorce tables. *Genus 32,* 109-127.

Rogers, A., Raquillet, R., and Castro, L. J. (1978). Model migration schedules and their applications. *Environment and Planning A 10,* 475-502.

United Nations (1955). "Age and Sex Patterns of Mortality: Model Life Tables for Underdeveloped Countries." New York.

Zaba, B. (1979). The four-parameter logit life table system. *Population studies 33(1)*, 79-100.

4

Multistate Life Table Methodology: A Probabilist Critique

Jan M. Hoem and Ulla Funck Jensen

1. INTRODUCTION

1.1. OUR PURPOSE

Multistate life tables are tabulations of values of functions defined for Markov chains with a continuous time parameter and a finite state space. In the simplest situation, there are only two states, called "alive" and "dead", of which the latter is of course absorbing, and the tabulation constitutes an ordinary life table. Almost equally easy to handle are hierarchical Markov chains, in which the states are ordered in a hierarchy and transitions can only lead upwards in the hierarchy (or to an absorbing state). In such a model, every nonabsorbing state is irretrievable, i.e., reentry into such a state is impossible. In (nonhierarchical) increment-decrement models, reentry is possible for at least one state, and the

MULTIDIMENSIONAL MATHEMATICAL DEMOGRAPHY

ISBN 0-12-435640-0

tabulation is a corresponding increment-decrement (life) table. The simplest example of such a Markov chain is the three state labor-force status model that underlies modern increment-decrement working life tables (Hoem and Fong, 1976; Hoem, 1977; Willekens, 1980; Smith, 1980; Schoen and Woodrow, 1980; Brouard, 1980, 1981), as well as other applications (Du Pasquier, 1912, 1913; Rogers, 1975; Schoen and Land, 1979).

Demographers have given the methodology of increment-decrement tables a lot of attention in later years. Compare Ledent (1978, 1980a,b), Oechsli (1979), Schoen (1979), Schoen and Land (1979), Rogers (1980), Ledent and Rees (1980), and their references, as well as many of the chapters in this volume. Most contributions have focused on the problem of computing tabular values accurately from data for given age intervals on the basis of as few explicit assumptions as possible about the underlying transition intensities. The data are sometimes taken to be gross flows, but mostly one assumes that occurrence/exposure rates have been observed. The several methods that have been proposed for the latter situation seem to have given sensible results in most cases. Frequently, there also seems to be little substantive importance in the numerical differences between results produced when two or more methods have been applied to the same data.[1] Occasionally,

[1]A few data sets have been analyzed by means of the linear integration hypothesis ("the linear method" of Section 3) as well as by the method of piecewise constant intensities ("the exponential method" of Section 4). For instance, Willekens (1980) has reanalyzed by the linear method the labor-force status data first analyzed by the exponential method by Hoem and Fong (1976), and Schoen and Land (1979) as well as Schoen (1979) have analyzed some marriage data for a Swedish cohort by both methods. For both data sets we fail to see the substantive significance of the differences in

however, some startling irregularity has been observed, such as a negative computed "probability"[2] or a computed mean of 9.13 in a distribution concentrated on the interval from 0 to 5

(footnote 1 continued) the results produced by the two methods. Schoen and Land (1979) have also applied a cubic (rather than linear) approximation to the ℓ-functions in an analysis of their marriage data, in our opinion without much change in the results. Furthermore, the same data have been analyzed once more by Schoen (1979), who combined piecewise quadratic intensities with a linear approximation to the $\{\ell^{i}_{x+t}\}$ *and with estimates of the* ${}_{n}a^{jk}_{x}$ *introduced below our (2.7), and by Land and Schoen (1982) by yet another method. Again the comparable results are very close to those of other methods. Similarly, Keyfitz and Frauenthal (1975, p. 893) report that changing over from a linear to a quadratic force of mortality made very little numerical difference in their analysis of an ordinary life table for Swedish males, 1965. They also compared other competing methods and got differences that similarly appear substantively insignificant. Ledent and Rees (1980) reach a corresponding conclusion in an extensive comparison of results from applications of a number of different methods to a set of Dutch migration data.*

[2]*In computations that at least have an illustrative value, Manninen (1979, p. 31, cited by Ledent, 1980a, p. 554), using the linear integration hypothesis, found a negative retention "probability" for age group 20-24 in a Finnish region of high outmigration. The corresponding computed retention probability for the neighboring age group of 25-29 years was positive but unreasonably small (Manninen, 1979, p. 31), and the computed matrix of transition "probabilities" for the latter age group had a negative determinant (equal to -0.008), which is impossible for a proper transition matrix. Compare Condition 2 in Singer and Spilerman (1976a, p. 11). Manninen (1979, Appendix 4) also computed some negative survivorship proportions (our Section 2.5). Ledent (1978, pp. 122-123) has reported negative computed outmigration rates and survivorship proportions for a four region system for the United States. Similarly, Liaw and Ledent (1980, Table 1) have demonstrated that the linear method applied to U.S. marriage data can lead to a negative computed retention "probability" for divorced females between ages 20 and 25, and a corresponding remarriage "probability" of over 1. See Ledent and Rees (1980, pp. 35-38) for a systematic discussion of these matters.*

(Schoen, 1979, p. 267), which demonstrates that the limits of applicability of these methods has been insufficiently charted.[3]

It is the purpose of this chapter to consider this literature in a wider perspective by exploiting the integrative power of mathematical statistics. We are worried about the distance that many demographic contributions evidently have to previous and current developments in other fields of statistical methodology, and we fear that the developing flora of competing special methods largely serving the same purposes may confuse potential users among practicing demographers or deter them from coming to grips with an essentially simple theory. Mathematical statistics suggests a single main approach to the issues investigated. The approach builds on the commonplace distinction between

(a) a probabilistic model,

(b) the numerical methods used to compute some model quantities from others (for instance the transition probabilities from the transition intensities), and

(c) problems and methods of statistical inference applied when the model is used to analyze real data.

We feel that this distinction is not kept sufficiently firmly in the foreground in the demographic literature. We also feel that some contributions are hard to understand because other useful distinctions are not made, or are made only tacitly. To spare others the effort we had to make to penetrate

[3] *The evident unease that follows from such disconcerting findings (Ledent, 1980a) may have helped motivate Ledent and Rees (1980) to start mapping these waters.*

this veil, we shall be more explicit in specifying some trivia than what may seem necessary to some readers.

We proceed as follows.

1.2. *MODEL CONSIDERATIONS*

To achieve a suitable level of precision, our presentation will be made within the framework of a time-continuous Markov chain model with a finite state space, which is the natural setting of increment-decrement theory. In this theory, the continuous time parameter, say x, represents biological age, duration since some initial event (duration of marriage, time since last previous birth, etc.), or some such fundamentally influential parameter. Let us call it *seniority*. The states in the finite state space I correspond to demographic statuses, and transitions between states correspond to demographic events. The notation, standard concepts, and some results of such models are reviewed in Section 2. Most of what we have to say there is well known in principle,[4] but we feel that our particular juxtaposition of results is useful in a discussion with mathematical demographers.

Within this framework, we feel that human behavior is reflected most easily in the specification of the state space and transition intensities, and that the fundamental assumptions of a model specification should be made in those terms, not by means of transition probabilities, survival or transfer

[4] *We believe that the multinomiality interpretation in (2.21) is new, that the convergence theorem below the proof of (2.11) is new in this formulation, and that the developments in Section 2.4 below (2.15) are new in their present generality.*

functions, or other derived quantities. Once the transition intensities are available, the transition probabilities can be computed as the solution to the Kolmogorov differential equations. From the intensities and probabilities, all other quantities can be computed subsequently.

In contrast, many of the methods found in the demographic literature are based on assumptions made on the behavior of transition probabilities or on the survival functions of the "stationary population," assumptions that we shall call *integration hypotheses* for reasons that will appear later. Beside the fact that usually it is difficult to see what such specifications say about human behavior, it turns out that they may have quite unreasonable consequences, as we show in Section 3. Because it figures so prominently in the demographic literature, we focus on the linear integration hypothesis, which states that over suitable intervals the transition probabilities are linear functions of model time (age). The transition "intensities" induced by this assumption may easily violate fundamental assumptions about intensity functions: The induced functions will not always be nonnegative; induced "intensity" functions that are not identically zero may sometimes represent impossible direct transitions; and quite realistic parameter values may lead not only to abnormities like negative probabilities, but also to other impossible transition matrices whose unsuitability is less easily detected. Similar problems are bound to appear with other integration hypotheses as well.[5]

[5] *Schoen (1979, pp. 262 and 264) seems to have discovered anomalies connected with the cubic integration hypothesis, where survival functions are assumed to be locally cubic polynomial functions of age. Compare also Liaw and Ledent (1980, p. 6).*

We suggest, therefore, that the integration hypotheses are regarded strictly as methods of numerical analysis (as they essentially are in most contributions) and should not be taken as part of the model specification. We also suggest that those who regard the integration hypotheses as an important part of this methodology and who (unlike us) want them to be used in the future as well, should delineate their applicability better than what has been done so far, following the way shown by Ledent and Rees (1980).

In this connection it should be noted that a linear integration hypothesis is inherent in one of the algorithms sometimes suggested for the numerical solution of the Kolmogorov differential equations. This may help explain why numerical results produced on the basis of the linear integration hypothesis are frequently close to those produced by some other methods.

As one can see already, the current theory of increment-decrement tables constitutes a complex pattern. Into this web, Ledent and his collaborators (Ledent, 1980a; Ledent and Rees, 1980) weaved another thread, in that they started to investigate the consequences of applying Markov chain based increment-decrement methods in a situation where the data have been generated from a more complex mechanism. As we understand it, Ledent and Rees (1980) feel that it may be inappropriate to use methods directly geared to the Markov chain assumptions for migration data because of the presence of such features as preferred patterns of moves between regions (e.g., returning to home base may be preferred to moving on to other regions; Ledent and Rees, 1980, Section 6.2); population heterogeneity in the propensity to migrate (Ledent and Rees, 1980, Section

6.3); overaggregation of regions that may ruin Markovian properties possibly holding for a more disaggregated spacial system (Ledent and Rees, 1980, p. 125); and perhaps duration-dependence of the propensity to move, e.g., cumulative inertia (McGuinness, 1968).

Their considerations lead them to propose the use of Markov chain based procedures in ways that deviate from what is sensible within the Markov chain framework. For example, they prefer methods based on gross flows (Section 5.1) to methods based on occurrence/exposure rates (Section 4), in spite of the fact that statistical theory would point to the latter in the Markovian situation. Similarly, they recommend the use of five-year age and time intervals for investigations of migration, although one would otherwise expect single-year intervals to be better. (Compare also Ledent, 1980a, Section 3.4.) We have sympathy for their sense of urgency and the feeling that planning agencies need computational recipes today rather than the day after tomorrow, as described to us by Ledent in private conversations, but we believe that real progress on this front needs a different strategy. When deviations from the Markov chain model are important, we would prefer to start with the specification of a model that better reflects the deviant features, in the manner, say, of Singer and Spilerman (1979), Cohen and Singer (1979), Ginsberg (1979), Heckman and Singer (1982), and Kitsul and Philipov (1982). Inference procedures would then be derived in terms of the more complex model, and prescriptions about methods of analysis when only Markov chain related data are available would be based on investigations of their robustness against the perceived deviations from the Markov chain model.

This does not mean that we fail to take the possibility of such deviations into account during our discussions of the virtues of the various approaches in the increment-decrement model methodology. One should keep in mind that the very specification of the Markov chain model in itself is often a very rough approximation to reality, made for convenience in the hope or conviction that it suffices for the application in hand. One case in point is our example of nineteenth century marital fertility in Section 4.1. In correspondence with the typical treatment given to illustrations in the increment-decrement model literature, we suppress a genuine underlying semi-Markov process model and get a Markovian model by disregarding all duration effects both for duration of marriage and for duration since last previous birth at any age. We also simplify the statistical algorithms by not accounting for parity. This is much the same as what happens when a one-sex marriage model accounts for duration and for order of marriage is replaced by the standard four or five-state one-sex Markovian model incorporating remarriage. Another example is the three-state working life table model, where all previous work experience (outside of current status) is disregarded at any age, in defiance of most known facts about labor-force participation. Apparently, for want of anything better, this suffices for the main purposes of such tables, as they have been described by Smith (1977).

In such situations, it cannot pay to focus on deviant details if this complicates empirical analysis. Quite on the contrary, one should exhibit bold flexibility and aim for manageable algorithms that will convey the macroscopic features of the situation in hand. This motivates some of our attitude concerning inference procedures, to which we turn next.

1.3. *INFERENCE CONSIDERATIONS*

We confine ourselves strictly to probability theory in Sections 2 and 3, and postpone all questions about statistical inference, including estimation, to Sections 4-6. In this connection, we note that much demographic analysis consists in the study of the behavior of relevant intensity functions. It may be suitable to partition the features of such a function into its *global, local,* and *sublocal behaviors*. Assuming that the complete seniority range can be partitioned into sensible seniority intervals of substantive interest, then this trichotomy corresponds to the distinction between (i) the intensity's macroscopic features, (ii) the way it changes over a short sequence of neighboring seniority intervals, including its local humps and dips, and so on, and (iii) the variation of the intensity within a basic seniority interval, microscopically, if you wish. To use adult male mortality as an example, perhaps single-year age intervals are appropriate, the global behavior is that of an (almost) uniformly increasing function, going to infinity as one approaches the upper limit of life. Locally, there may be features like a modern "accident hump" for young adult male mortality, or the "tuberculosis hump" of previous times. Sublocally, there may be various irregularities. If exact age is counted as reaching integer values at the end of calendar years rather than at birthdays (compare our Section 4.3), the mortality of males in the same age bracket may be dominated by seasonal variation, the winter and early spring months being harder on people's chances of survival than other times of the year, and by epidemics and other temporal features.

Sublocal variations are study objects in their own right (compare, e.g., Larsson, 1965, pp. 60-68), but let us suppose here that the investigator wants to focus on local and global intensity behavior, as seems to be the direction of interest in the increment-decrement model literature. Then sublocal variations only have nuisance value, and the investigator wants to eliminate their effect. One way of doing this is to work with transition intensities that are very regular over each seniority interval. A study of the ensuing inaccuracies may be based on ideas like those in Section 4.2, but they are not likely to be of great import. Beside the fact that the data may already have been organized into seniority intervals (by the collection procedure or the collecting agency) before they are submitted to the demographer for analysis, there may thus be good substantive grounds for such a grouping when the Markov chain model is reasonable. Since in addition demographers invariably think in terms of data grouped in this manner, it is convenient to frame much of the discussion of inference issues in this chapter in terms of such data.

Because such grouping goes against the grain of the attitudes of some mathematical statisticians, and because other possibilities deserve more attention from demographers, we note that the fundamental elements involved in statistical analysis by increment-decrement methods are the same as in any other statistical investigation: there is a *model* describing some segment of reality, an *observational plan* describing how the data relate to the model, and a set of *statistical algorithms* determining how inference is drawn from the data. In the present case, the *model specification* consists of

(i) a statement that we are dealing with probabilistically identical, independent sample paths of a Markov chain with certain general characteristics (time-continuity, existence of intensities, etc.);

(ii) a description of the state space I and of possible and impossible direct transitions, and

(iii) a set of assumptions about the intensity functions.

In some cases, prior knowledge (or the courage of the investigator) may be sufficient to specify one or more transition intensities as nice functions, known except for the value of some unknown parameters. The Gompertz-Makeham mortality formula $\mu(x) = \alpha + \beta c^x$ is a classical example, whose analysis by modern methods was described by Grenander (1956). For more recent cases in point, see Ginsberg (1978, 1979) and the review by Hobcraft and Rodriguez (1980, Chapter 4). Much of the current effort to develop parametric model schedules for demographic curves (of mortality, fertility, migration, and so on) can be seen as an endeavor to establish generally applicable formulas for transition intensities. Some recent contributions are Rogers and Castro (1982), Ewbank *et al.* (1981), Hoem *et al.* (1981), and Hartmann (1980, 1981).

When such model formulas are available, they should of course be exploited.[6] When they are not available, one may turn to completely nonparametric methods, in the manner of Nelson (1972), Aalen (1978), Aalen *et al.* (1980), Gill (1980), Ramlau-Hansen (1981), and others working in this blooming research direction. Under suitable conditions, these methods are as useful in demography as elsewhere.[6a] In demography, however, interest in macroscopic features rather than in local detail (not to mention sublocal variation) as well as sheer data size may make the computational effort involved in nonparametric procedures wasteful or prohibitive. In view of the shaky basis of the Markov chain specification and of the corresponding meaningfulness of the transition intensity studied, it may be sensible in some situations to spend available resources on other aspects of the investigation.[7] In addition, one should not be blind to the limitations of current nonparametric methods, in particular to the difficulties involved in inter-

[6]*Whenever suitable, their parameters should be estimated from data on the individual level, by methods such as maximum likelihood, in the manner described for the Gompertz-Makeham formula by Grenander (1956). In situations where there are good motives for working with aggregate data grouped by seniority intervals, however, we would instead resort to analytic graduation, i.e., to fitting the intensity curve to a sequence of occurrence/exposure rates or to some replacement for them (Hoem, 1976a).*

[6a]*One case in point is the analysis of mortality at the advanced ages, where the exposure is small and where mortality changes fast. For this case, modern statistical methods must be much more appropriate than the methods currently suggested by mathematical demographers.*

[7]*The same arguments may motivate the use of analytic graduation to fit a parametric intensity function rather than to base the estimation on individual level data.*

preting Nelson-Aalen plots.[7a] If all that is available beforehand and all that is needed from the empirical analysis is a general impression of the looks of the intensity function (modality, approximate location of maxima or minima, general level, and so on), then recourse may be had to approximations such as piecewise constant or piecewise polynomial intensities, provided natural seniority intervals are available over which the intensities can be taken as constant or polynomial. Our discussion in this chapter has this kind of situation in mind, although some of what we have to say has more general relevance.

In principle, the model is a simplified description of prior knowledge of the most important aspects of the real population process under investigation. New information about the process becomes available through data collected by some *observational plan*, which in a way acts as a filter between what is potentially observable and what is actually observed. The observational plan will describe such aspects as whether data are obtained for individual sample paths or only for aggregates; whether only segments of each life history are observed and by which principles the segments are chosen, including whether one is working with cohort or period data; whether observation is complete or fragmentary within each segment; whether the paths observed are selected and by what mechanism; and whether in principle all paths in the (possibly select) target population are included or whether "only" a sample has been surveyed. (In the latter case we shall sometimes find it convenient to

[7a]*Miller and Hickman (1980) report that estimators based on simple occurrence/exposure rates may actually be comparable, and often superior, to integrated intensity and product limit estimators as regards bias, standard deviation, skewness, kurtosis, and mean-square error.*

distinguish the *sampling plan* from the rest of the observational plan. See Section 6.) It may also describe the patterns of nonsampling errors and similar matters.

The observational plan influences the statistical analysis in many subtle ways, which need to be investigated for each separate case. Many more options are available than the simple Options 1 and 2 named by Rogers (1975) and discussed later by other mathematical demographers. Demography shares its problems in this area with many other disciplines that apply similar models and observational plans for follow-up studies: medical survival studies and epidemiology, the sociology of mobility, criminology, life insurance, biology, and reliability theory (life-testing), just to name some of them. There is a considerable and growing literature on the statistical theory involved, and one of us has already reviewed some of the aspects most directly relevant for applications in population studies (Hoem, 1976a). To illustrate the connection between this literature and increment-decrement life tables, we put the spotlight on a few items, most of which complement the latter review. In this manner we hope to demonstrate that increment-decrement model methodology involves much more than merely the computation of some multistate life tables, or the estimation of some transition probabilities from actual moves.

An assessment of the demographic literature needs to take into account the distinction between *complete* and *abridged tables*. Essentially, a complete table is the tabular representation of function values for a Markov chain model based on substantively meaningful, "short" seniority intervals that account for local intensity variations but cover up sublocal variations. In typical situations, and in particular for classical, ordinary life tables, single-year intervals are used.[8] An abridged table is one where longer intervals than this are used, typically five-year intervals instead of single-year intervals. In an abridged table, therefore, local intensity behavior is masked. Many of the proposals in the demographic literature should be understood as attempts to overcome this effect, even though this is often not said outright.

Long intervals may sometimes have been used deliberately to get rid of random fluctuations, which are more evident for short intervals. Perhaps long intervals are also seen as a way to reduce the overwhelming mass of statistics sometimes resulting from short intervals.[9] Of these, the latter item is of a pedagogical nature, and it may be the subject of a discussion in a different forum, but it need not concern us here. If there is enough random variation to preclude any use of short intervals, we would recommend other methods.[9a] A reasonable

[8]*Our definition of the terms "complete" and "abridged tables" tries to capture the general nature of a substantively useful distinction. It may deviate somewhat from general usage, where the differences between ordinary life tables with single-year and five-year age intervals (compare Shryock and Siegel, 1971, p. 429) seems to have rubbed off on other applications of the general theory. By our definition, a complete, ordinary life table should actually use several briefer intervals rather than one whole-year age interval for the first year of life, and single-year intervals for higher ages.*

[9]*In principle, longish intervals can be used to counteract reporting inaccuracy in the form of age or seniority heaping (digital preferences) as well, and they were used for that purpose by Cohen and Singer (1979, p. 78). Conventional choices of intervals will not have this effect.*

[9a]*The analysis of mortality at the advanced ages is one example. Compare footnote 6a.*

amount of random variation can be treated by graduation (as in Hoem and Fong, 1976) rather than by combining short seniority intervals into long ones. When warranted on substantive grounds, we would try to prevail upon data-producing agencies to supply the data for short rather than long intervals. Nevertheless, we must of course accept that there are situations where the data can be obtained for abridged tables alone. Our strategy for such cases is outlined in Section 4.4.

1.4. GENERAL CONSIDERATIONS

In our presentation, we have tried to strike a compromise between the notational conventions of demographers, actuaries, and mathematical statisticians, and our notation is very close to that of Land and Schoen (1982, Table 1). Our account proceeds by way of outline, indication, and example. This allows us to point out a few lacunas in existing theory and to fill a couple of them. Our main purpose, however, is to advocate the premise that demographic multistate life tables can be viewed as a particular field of application of ideas from mathematical statistics. Some particular issues arising in demographic applications may lead to extentions of statistical theory, but otherwise all its powerful tools are available to the demographer. Those required for increment-decrement models need not be developed over again.

2. THE MARKOV CHAIN MODEL

2.1. BASIC CONCEPTS

In our review of some theory of Markov chains, let x denote the continuous seniority parameter, say $0 \leq x \leq \zeta$, and let I be the finite state space. Consider a single sample path, and let $I_i(x) = 1$ if it is in state i at seniority x, with $I_i(x) = 0$ otherwise. The transition probabilities are

$$P_{ij}(x,y) = P\{I_j(y) = 1 | I_i(x) = 1\},$$

and we assume that the corresponding transition intensities

$$\mu_{ij}(x) = \lim_{y \downarrow x} P_{ij}(x,y)/(y-x)$$

exist for all x, i, and $j \neq i$, and that they are (say) piecewise continuous functions of x in the seniority interval $[0,\zeta\rangle$. We let

$$\mu_i(x) = \lim_{y \downarrow x}\{1 - P_{ii}(x,y)\}/(y-x) = \sum_{j \in I-i} \mu_{ij}(x),$$

and sometimes find it convenient to use $\mu_{ii}(x) = -\mu_i(x)$. Waiting times between transitions are assumed absolutely continuous.

We introduce the initial distribution

$$\ell_i(0) = P\{I_i(0) = 1\}, \quad \text{for } i \in I,$$

and define

$$\ell_i(x) = P\{I_i(x) = 1\} = \sum_{k \in I} \ell_k(0) P_{ki}(0,x).$$

The $\ell_i(0)$ are the radices of the corresponding (multistate) life table, and the functions $\{\ell_i(\cdot)\}$ are "the stationary population" corresponding to this Markov chain. For convenience, usually some multiple of the values of $\ell_i(\cdot)$, like $10^6\ell_i(\cdot)$, will be tabulated rather than values of $\ell_i(\cdot)$ itself.

The gross flows of the stationary population are the functions

$$\ell_{ij}(x,y) = \ell_i(x)P_{ij}(x,y).$$

Let $N_{jk}(x,y)$ be the number of direct transitions from state j to state k of a sample path between seniorities x and y, and let

$$d_{ijk}(x,y) = E\{I_i(x)N_{jk}(x,y)\} = \ell_i(x)\int_x^y P_{ij}(x,s)\mu_{jk}(s)ds.$$

(For an elementary proof of the integral formula, see Funck Jensen, 1981b.) Correspondingly, let

$$d_{jk}(x,y) = E\{N_{jk}(x,y)\} = \sum_{i\in I} d_{ijk}(x,y) = \int_x^y \ell_j(s)\mu_{jk}(s)ds.$$

It is convenient to have a second set of symbols for the same quantities when y = x + n for some fixed n, and we shall let

$$\ell^{ij}_{[x]+n} = \ell_{ij}(x,x+n),\quad {}_nd^{ij}_x = d_{ij}(x,x+n),\quad {}_np^{ij}_x = P_{ij}(x,x+n),$$

and so on, in correspondence with actuarial notation. We use the two sets of symbols interchangeably.

The transition probabilities satisfy the Kolmogorov forward differential equations:

$$\frac{\partial}{\partial y} P_{ij}(x,y) = -P_{ij}(x,y)\mu_j(y) + \sum_{k\in I-j} P_{ik}(x,y)\mu_{kj}(y). \tag{2.1}$$

Integrating these between $y = x$ and $y = x + n$, noting that $P_{ij}(x,x) = \delta_{ij}$, and multiplying the result by $\ell_x^i = \ell_i(x)$, we get one set of flow equations:

$$\ell^{ij}_{[x]+n} = \delta_{ij}\ell^i_x - \sum_{k\in I-j} {}_n d^{ijk}_x + \sum_{k\in I-j} {}_n d^{ikj}_x. \tag{2.2}$$

Adding over i, we get a second set:

$$\ell^j_{x+n} = \ell^j_x - \sum_{k\in I-j} {}_n d^{jk}_x + \sum_{k\in I-j} {}_n d^{kj}_x. \tag{2.3}$$

If we let $x = 0$ in (2.1), multiply through by $\ell_i(0)$, and then add over $i \in I$, we also get

$$\frac{d}{dy} \ell_j(y) = -\ell_j(y)\mu_j(y) + \sum_{k\in I-j} \ell_k(y)\mu_{kj}(y). \tag{2.4}$$

2.2. *EXPECTED SOJOURN TIMES*

The actual time which the sample path spends (its sojourn) in state j between seniorities x and x + n is the random variable $S = \int_0^n I_j(x+s)ds$. We let

$$e^{ij}_{x:\overline{n}|} = E\left\{\int_0^n I_j(x+s)ds \,|\, I_i(x) = 1\right\} = \int_0^n P_{ij}(x,x+s)ds$$

(where the integral formula follows by Fubini's theorem), and note that for $n > 1$, we may write

$$e^{ij}_{x:\overline{n}|} = e^{ij}_{x:\overline{1}|} + \sum_{k\in I} p^{ik}_x e^{kj}_{x+1:\overline{n-1}|}, \tag{2.5}$$

where we have followed the custom of deleting the left subscript when it equals 1, i.e., of letting ${}_1p_x^{ik} = p_x^{ik}$, ${}_1d_x^{ij} = d_x^{ij}$, and so on. This formula, which is useful for recursive computation of the values of the $e_{x:\overline{n}|}^{ij}$, can also be argued by direct reasoning concerning the contributions to $e_{x:\overline{n}|}^{ij}$ from the seniority intervals [x,x+1> and [x+1,x+n>. By a similar argument,

$$e_{x:\overline{n}|}^{ij} = \sum_{t=0}^{n-1} \sum_{k \in I} {}_tp_x^{ik} e_{x+t:\overline{1}|}^{kj} \tag{2.6}$$

for integer $n \geqq 2$. Another formula for $e_{x:\overline{n}|}^{ij}$ may be proved by partial integration, by noting that

$$\int_0^n P_{ij}(x,x+s)ds = \Big|_0^n s\, P_{ij}(x,x+s) - \int_0^n s \frac{\partial}{\partial s} P_{ij}(x,x+s)ds.$$

Substitution from (2.1) for $(\partial/\partial s)P_{ij}(x,x+s)$ gives

$$e_{x:\overline{n}|}^{ij} = n\, {}_np_x^{ij} + \int_0^n {}_tp_x^{ij} \mu_j(x+t)tdt - \sum_{k \in I-j} \int_0^n {}_tp_x^{ik} \mu_{kj}(x+t)tdt. \tag{2.7}$$

This result was noted by Ledent (1978, p. 38), who proved it in a manner which can be formalized as follows. If during the seniority interval [x,x+n> the sample path arrives in state j at seniorities $x + T_1'$, $x + T_2', \ldots$, and leaves state j at seniorities $x + T_1''$, $x + T_2'', \ldots$, simple accounting shows that the total sojourn time in j during [x,x+n> may also be written as $S = \Sigma_m T_m'' - \Sigma_m T_m' + nI_j(x+n)$. By formula (11) in Hoem and Aalen (1978), with $v = 1$ and $c_{k\ell}(s) \equiv s$, the expected value of this quantity, given that $I_i(x) = 1$, is (2.7).

Now let

$$ {}_nL_x^{ij} = E\left\{ I_i(x) \int_0^n I_j(x+s)\,ds \right\} = \ell_x^i e_{x:\overline{n|}}^{ij} , $$

and

$$ {}_nL_x^{j} = E\left\{ \int_0^n I_j(x+s)\,ds \right\} = \sum_{i\in I} {}_nL_x^{ij} = \int_0^n \ell_j(x+t)\,dt. $$

Schoen (1979) also introduces

$$ {}_na_x^{jk} = \int_0^n t\ell_{x+t}^j \mu_{jk}(x+t)\,dt \Big/ \int_0^n \ell_{x+t}^j \mu_{jk}(x+t)\,dt. $$

If we multiply (2.7) by ℓ_x^i and add over i,

$$ {}_nL_x^j = n\ell_{x+n}^j + \sum_{k\in I-j} {}_na_x^{jk}\,{}_nd_x^{jk} - \sum_{k\in I-j} {}_na_x^{kj}\,{}_nd_x^{kj} $$

results. Formulas of this type play a central part in a computational method suggested by Schoen (1979).

Typically, the state space I consists of two disjoint subsets, L and D, where D is absorbing as a whole and where it is possible to move from L to D. For the moment think of L as the collection of states corresponding to demographic statuses which the individual can have while alive, and D as the collection of states of death. This interpretation will be extended in Section 5.2. Let

$$ I_A(x) = \sum_{i\in A} I_i(x), \quad \text{for any subset } A \subseteq I, $$

so that $I_A(x) = 1$ if the sample path is in A at seniority x; $I_A(x) = 0$ otherwise. Then define

$$\ell_x = \ell(x) = P\{I_L(x) = 1\} = \sum_{i \in L} \ell_x^i,$$

and note that since $P_{ki}(x,y) = 0$ for any $k \in D$, $i \in L$, we get

$${}_nL_x^j = \sum_{i \in L} {}_nL_x^{ij}, \quad \text{for } j \in L.$$

If we define

$$e_{x:\overline{n}|}^j = E\left\{\int_0^n I_j(x+s)ds \,\middle|\, I_L(x) = 1\right\},$$

therefore, we get $e_{x:\overline{n}|}^j = {}_nL_x^j/\ell_x$. We shall prove that for integer $n \geq 1$ one may write

$$e_{x:\overline{n}|}^j = \sum_{t=0}^{n-1} L_{x+t}^j/\ell_x, \quad \text{for } j \in L. \tag{2.8}$$

Proof. We get

$$\ell_x e_{x:\overline{n}|}^j = {}_nL_x^j = \sum_{i \in I} \ell_x^i e_{x:\overline{n}|}^{ij} = \sum_{t=0}^{n-1} \sum_{k \in I} \sum_{i \in I} \ell_x^i \, {}_tp_x^{ik} e_{x+t:\overline{1}|}^{kj}$$

$$= \sum_{t=0}^{n-1} \sum_{k \in I} \ell_{x+t}^k e_{x+t:\overline{1}|}^{kj} = \sum_{t=0}^{n-1} L_{x+t}^j,$$

where we have used (2.6). □

For any $A \subseteq I$, let

$$\mu_{iA}(x) = \sum_{j \in A-i} \mu_{ij}(x).$$

Then $\mu_{iD}(x)$ is the force of "mortality" in state $i \in L$ at seniority x. Total "mortality" is nondifferential if this function of x is independent of $i \in L$, in which case we may denote it, say, by $\mu(x)$ as is customary, and then $\ell_x = \exp\{-\int_0^x \mu(s)ds\}$. Our use of the notation ℓ_x does *not* presuppose nondifferential mortality, however, and in the general case, an exponential formula for ℓ_x like the one just noted does not hold.

2.3. *FINDING TRANSITION PROBABILITIES FROM INTENSITIES*

Evidently, a complete knowledge of the $\{P_{ij}(x,y)\}$ and the $\{\ell_i(0)\}$ is enough to determine all functions in this theory Similarly, a complete specification of the $\{\mu_{ij}(x)\}$ along with the $\{\ell_i(0)\}$ are sufficient to define all others, for from the transition intensities, the transition probabilities can be found in principle by solution of the Kolmogorov differential equations (2.1). In some special cases, a compact analytic solution can be found, i.e., (2.1) provides a simple formula for the $\{P_{ij}(x,y)\}$ in terms of the $\{\mu_{ij}(x)\}$, involving nothing more difficult than a finite number of integral signs. This is the case for any hierarchical model (and in particular for the ordinary two-state life-table model), and also in the three-state labor-force status increment-decrement model with nondifferential mortality (see, e.g., Hoem and Fong, 1976, Chapter 6). If there is differential mortality in the latter model, however, a compact solution has not been found for general transition intensities, i.e., not even in so simple a case. A solution *has* been provided for the latter situation under particular assumptions about the intensities, such as if they are constant (see below) or linear (Diem, 1976, pp. 136-137), or, more generally, if there exist constants $a \geqq 0$ and b such that $\mu_{21}(x) = a\mu_{12}(x) > 0$ and $\mu_{23}(x) = \mu_{13}(x) + b\mu_{12}(x)$ for all relevant x, where state 3 is the absorbing state (Diem, 1976, pp. 128-129). Otherwise, one may resort to approximation formulas (e.g., Schoen and Land, 1979, Sec. 5.1), or to sums of infinite series, like $P_{ij}(x,y) = \sum_{m=0}^{\infty} P_{ij}^{(m)}(x,y)$, for $P_{ij}^{(m)}(x,y) = P\{N(x,y) = m,\ I_j(y) = 1 \mid I_i(x) = 1\}$, where $N(x,y)$ is the total number of transitions in a sample path between seniorities x and y. (Introduction of this random variable is essentially a trick that transforms a nonhierarchical Markov chain into a different, hierarchical one.)

If the transition intensities are constant over a seniority interval $(x,x+h)$, things simplify considerably. Assume that

$$\mu_{ij}(x+t) = c_{ij}, \quad \text{for all } i,j \in \mathcal{I},\ i \neq j,\ 0 < t < h, \tag{2.9}$$

let $c_{ii} = -\sum_{j \in \mathcal{I}-i} c_{ij}$, and let $\underline{\underline{C}}$ be the singular matrix (c_{ij}). Suppose that $\underline{\underline{C}}$ has the eigenvalues $\{\rho_i : i \in \mathcal{I}\}$ and that there exists a corresponding set of linearly independent eigenvectors $\{\underline{\underline{U}}_i : i \in \mathcal{I}\}$. Let $\underline{\underline{U}}$ be the matrix formed by these column vectors. If $\underline{\underline{D}}_t$ is a diagonal matrix with the values $\{\exp(\rho_i t) : i \in \mathcal{I}\}$ along its diagonal, then

$$\underline{\underline{P}}(t) = e^{\underline{\underline{C}}t} = \sum_{n=0}^{\infty} \frac{t^n}{n!} \underline{\underline{C}}^n = \underline{\underline{U}}\,\underline{\underline{D}}_t\,\underline{\underline{U}}^{-1}, \tag{2.10}$$

where $\underline{\underline{P}}(t) = \{P_{ij}(x+s,x+s+t)\}$ for $0 \leq s \leq s + t \leq h$. For general expositions of these matters, see Çinlar (1975, Appendix), Chiang (1980, Chapters 14-15), and Iosifescu (1980, Chapter 8). Funck Jensen (1981b) has given a particularly careful presentation geared to demographic applications and ready for computer programming.

In particular situations, compact explicit formulas can be derived for the eigenvalues $\{\rho_i\}$, and correspondingly for the P_{ij}. This is the case for the three-state increment-decrement labor-force status model; as reproduced by Schoen and Land (1979, Section 5.3). It has also been done for a marital status model with the states "unmarried", "married", "divorced", "widowed", and "dead", permitting remarriage and allowing for differential mortality (Halvorsen, 1970). In principle, such an explicit solution may be found as long as each communicating class consists of at most four states. Even if such a solution is unavailable, it is possible to use the exponential representation in the final member of (2.10). With this representation, further calculation of expected sojourn times, survival proportions (Section 2.5), and so on, is straightforward. As an alternative, one could work with (a finite number of terms of) the Taylor expansion in the middle member of (2.10), as seems to be done by some contributors. Liaw and Ledent (1980) suggest a sequence of approximations to $\exp(\underline{\underline{C}}t)$ based on a matrix continued fraction method (Shieh *et al.*, 1978).

It is possible to differentiate (2.10) with respect to a c_{ij} which is not zero by the nature of the model, and for later reference we note that

$$\frac{\partial}{\partial c_{\ell m}} p_{ij}(t) = \sum_{n=1}^{\infty} \frac{t^n}{n!} \sum_{k=1}^{n} c_{i\ell}^{(k-1)} \left(c_{mj}^{(n-k)} - c_{\ell j}^{(n-k)}\right), \qquad (2.11)$$

for $0 \leqq t \leqq h$, and $c_{\ell m} > 0$, $\ell \neq m$, where $c_{ij}^{(n)}$ is the (i,j)th element of $\underline{\underline{C}}^n$. Essentially the same formula appears as (20) in Coleman (1981). A similar formula can be derived for $e_{x:\overline{h}|}^{ij}$ by integration.

Proof of (2.11). It suffices to show that

$$\frac{\partial}{\partial c_{\ell m}} c_{ij}^{(n)} = \sum_{k=1}^{n} c_{i\ell}^{(k-1)} \left(c_{mj}^{(n-k)} - c_{\ell j}^{(n-k)} \right). \tag{2.12}$$

Fix ℓ and m, $\ell \neq m$, such that $c_{\ell m} > 0$, and denote the left-hand side of (2.12) by $a_{ij}^{(n)}$, with $a_{ij}^{(1)} = a_{ij}$. Since $c_{ij}^{(1)}$ for $i \neq j$, $c_{ii}^{(1)} = -\sum_{k \in I - i} c_{ik}$, we get $a_{ij} = \delta_{i\ell}(\delta_{jm} - \delta_{j\ell})$. For $n \geqq 2$,

$$a_{ij}^{(n)} = \frac{\partial}{\partial c_{\ell m}} \sum_{k \in I} c_{ik} c_{kj}^{(n-1)} = \sum_{k \in I} \left\{ a_{ik} c_{kj}^{(n-1)} + c_{ik} a_{kj}^{(n-1)} \right\},$$

so that

$$\underline{\underline{A}}^{(n)} = \underline{\underline{A}}\,\underline{\underline{C}}^{n-1} + \underline{\underline{C}}\,\underline{\underline{A}}^{(n-1)}$$

for $\underline{\underline{A}}^{(n)} = (a_{ij}^{(n)})$, $\underline{\underline{A}} = (a_{ij})$. Straightforward recursion gives

$$\underline{\underline{A}}^{(n)} = \sum_{k=1}^{n} \underline{\underline{C}}^{k-1} \underline{\underline{A}}\,\underline{\underline{C}}^{n-k},$$

from which (2.12) follows by simple computation. □

Now assume that the intensity functions $\{\mu_{ij}(\cdot)\}$ are specified to be piecewise constant over a fixed seniority interval (x,y), in the sense that this interval is partitioned into a finite number of subintervals J_k, and that $\mu_{ij}(s)$ is taken to equal some constant $b_{ij}^{(k)}$ for all $s \in J_k$ for each k, for all $i, j \in I$. If $\underline{\underline{B}}_k = (b_{ij}^{(k)})$, the elements $P_{ij}(s,t)$ of the matrix $\underline{\underline{P}}(s,t)$ may then be found for all $s \in J_k$, $t \in J_k$ from (2.10): $\underline{\underline{P}}(s,t) = \exp\{\underline{\underline{B}}_k(t-s)\}$ for $s \leqq t$. When s and t belong to different subintervals J_k, then $P_{ij}(s,t)$ may be found by chaining the intrainterval transition probabilities together by the Chapman-Kolmogorov equation. It may be convenient to regard such a procedure as a step in a sequence of successive approximations to "real" transition probabilities, based on underlying transition intensities $\{\mu_{ij}(\cdot)\}$ that are (say) continuous on $[x,y]$, as follows.

For each positive integer n, let a finite partition of (x,y) into subintervals $\{J_k^{(n)}\}$ be given and assume that $\max \delta(J_k^{(n)}) \to 0$ as $n \to \infty$, where $\delta(J_k^{(n)})$ is the length of subinterval $J_k^{(n)}$. Let $\{\mu_{ij}^{(n)}(s)\colon x < s < y;\ i,j \in \mathcal{I};\ i \neq j\}$ be a collection of transition intensities that are piecewise constant over $\{J_k^{(n)}\}$, and where $\mu_{ij}^{(n)}(s) = \mu_{ij}(s)$ for at least one $s = s_{ijkn} \in J_k^{(n)}$ for each (k,n); $i,j \in \mathcal{I}$; $i \neq j$. Let $S^{(n)} = \{S_s^{(n)}\colon x \leqq s \leqq y\}$ be a Markov chain over $\mathcal{I}$ corresponding to the intensities $\{\mu_{ij}^{(n)}(\cdot)\}$ and initial distribution $\{\ell_i(x)\colon i \in \mathcal{I}\}$ at seniority x, and let $S = \{S_s\colon x \leqq s \leqq y\}$ be the Markov chain one "really" wants to study, and which has the intensity functions $\{\mu_{ij}(\cdot)\}$. Then $S^{(n)}$ converges in distribution to S as $n \to \infty$.

If the transition probabilities of $S^{(n)}$ are $\{P_{ij}^{(n)}(s,t)\colon x \leqq s \leqq t \leqq y;\ i,\ j \in \mathcal{I}\}$, the essential part of the proof for this theorem is to show that $P_{ij}^{(n)}(s,t) \to P_{ij}(s,t)$ as $n \to \infty$. For details and a more general formulation, see Funck Jensen (1981b).

This essentially furnishes one method of numerical integration of the Kolmogorov forward differential equation (2.1). Let $\underline{\underline{\mu}}(s) = \{\mu_{ij}(s)\colon i,j \in \mathcal{I}\}$ be the matrix of intensity functions, and let $J_k^{(n)} = \langle y_k^{(n)}, y_{k+1}^{(n)}]$, and $z_k^{(n)} \in J_k^{(n)}$. If

$$x \leqq y_\alpha^{(n)} \leqq s < y_{\alpha+1}^{(n)} < \cdots < y_{\beta-1}^{(n)} < t \leqq y_\beta^{(n)} \leqq y,$$

then

$$\underline{\underline{P}}_n(s,t) = \exp\left[\underline{\underline{\mu}}\left(z_\alpha^{(n)}\right)\left(y_{\alpha+1}^{(n)} - s\right)\right]$$

$$\prod_{k=\alpha+1}^{\beta-2}\left\{\exp\left[\underline{\underline{\mu}}\left(z_k^{(n)}\right)\left(y_{k+1}^{(n)} - y_k^{(n)}\right)\right]\right\}\exp\left[\underline{\underline{\mu}}\left(z_{\beta-1}^{(n)}\right)\left(t - y_{\beta-1}^{(n)}\right)\right], \tag{2.13}$$

is an n-th approximation to $\underline{\underline{P}}(s,t)$. Another possibility is to use

$$\tilde{\underline{\underline{P}}}_n(s,t) = \left\{\underline{\underline{I}} + \underline{\underline{\mu}}\left(z_\alpha^{(n)}\right)\left(y_{\alpha+1}^{(n)} - s\right)\right\}$$

$$\prod_{k=\alpha+1}^{\beta-2}\left\{\underline{\underline{I}} + \underline{\underline{\mu}}\left(z_k^{(n)}\right)\left(y_{k+1}^{(n)} - y_k^{(n)}\right)\right\}\left\{\underline{\underline{I}} + \underline{\underline{\mu}}\left(z_{\beta-1}^{(n)}\right)\left(t - y_{\beta-1}^{(n)}\right)\right\}, \tag{2.14}$$

where $\underline{\underline{I}}$ is the identity matrix as usual. Compare Gantmacher [1959, XIV, §5-6, (49')]. This corresponds to taking $\tilde{\underline{\underline{P}}}_n(s,\cdot)$ to be piecewise linear over each subinterval $J_k^{(n)}$, as an alternative to letting the approximating intensities be piecewise constant, as in (2.13).

We mention these methods mainly for their theoretical interest and for later reference. For actual numerical computations, there are other methods as well, such as solving the integral equations that result from integrating the Kolmogorov backward differential equations (not given here).

2.4. MODEL TRANSITION RATES

If ${}_hL_x^{ij} > 0$, define the model transition rates

$$ {}_hm_x^{ijk} = \frac{{}_hd_x^{ijk}}{{}_hL_x^{ij}} = \frac{\int_0^h {}_tp_x^{ij}\,\mu_{jk}(x+t)\,dt}{\int_0^h {}_tp_x^{ij}\,dt}, \quad \text{for } j \neq k, $$

and let ${}_hm_x^{ijk} = 0$ if ${}_hL_x^{ij} = 0$. In general, ${}_hm_x^{ijk}$ depends on i. A corresponding i-independent quantity is

$$ {}_hm_x^{jk} = \frac{{}_hd_x^{jk}}{{}_hL_x^{j}} = \frac{\int_0^h \ell_j(x+t)\,\mu_{jk}(x+t)\,dt}{\int_0^h \ell_j(x+t)\,dt}, \quad \text{for } j \neq k, $$

which again is defined as 0 if the denominator (and thus also the numerator) equals 0. For convenience, let

$$ {}_hm_x^{j} = \sum_{k \in I - j} {}_hm_x^{jk}. $$

If ${}_hL_x^{ij} > 0$ and $\mu_{jk}(x+t) = c_{jk}$ for $0 < t < h$, then ${}_hm_x^{ijk} = {}_hm_x^{jk} = c_{jk}$, so in this case, corresponding model transition rates are equal to each other and to the (constant) intensity. If $\mu_{jk}(\cdot)$ is only piecewise continuous, both ${}_hm_x^{ijk}$ and ${}_hm_x^{jk}$ will converge to $\mu_{jk}(x)$ as $h \downarrow 0$ for all (i,j,k) where the rates have positive denominators for all $h > 0$. When they do converge in this manner, ${}_hm_x^{ijk}$ must be close to ${}_hm_x^{jk}$ for small $h > 0$. Sufficient conditions are easily derived as follows.

Let $a_{ij}(t) = {}_tp_x^{ij}$, note that $a_{ij}(0) = \delta_{ij}$, and use Kolmogorov's differential equation (2.1) to derive that

$$a'_{ij}(0) = (1-\delta_{ij})\mu_{ij}(x) - \delta_{ij}\mu_j(x)$$

and

$$a''_{ij}(0) = \mu'_{ij}(x) + \sum_{\alpha \in I-i-j} \mu_{i\alpha}(x)\mu_{\alpha j}(x) - \mu_{ij}(x)[\mu_i(x) + \mu_j(x)],$$

where the latter formula presupposes that the intensities are continuously differentiable. It follows that ${}_h m_x^{ijk} \to \mu_{jk}(x)$ as $h \downarrow 0$ provided either $a_{ij}(0) \neq 0$, or $a_{ij}(0) = 0$ but $a'_{ij}(0) \neq 0$, or $a_{ij}(0) = a'_{ij}(0) = 0$ but $a''_{ij}(0) \neq 0$, or if some corresponding higher order condition is satisfied.

If $i = j$, $a_{ij}(0) = 1$, and it follows that ${}_h m_x^{jjk} \to \mu_{jk}(x)$ as $h \downarrow 0$ without further conditions.

If $i \neq j$, $a_{ij}(0) = 0$. Then ${}_h m_x^{ijk} \to \mu_{jk}(x)$ as $h \downarrow 0$ provided $\mu_{ij}(x) > 0$, or else provided

$$\mu'_{ij}(x) + \sum_{\alpha \in I-i-j} \mu_{i\alpha}(x)\mu_{\alpha j}(x) > 0,$$

or else if some higher-order condition holds. Similarly, one sees that ${}_h m_x^{jk} \to \mu_{jk}(x)$ as $h \downarrow 0$ if either $\ell_j(x) > 0$, or else if

$$\sum_{\alpha \in I-j} \ell_\alpha(x)\mu_{\alpha j}(x) > 0,$$

or otherwise if some higher-order condition is fulfilled. Note that the conditions given have interesting interpretations in terms of needed direct transitions possible at age x.

Having studied what happens when $h \downarrow 0$, we now hold h fixed (and positive). Noting that $\frac{d}{dx}\,{}_nL_x^j = \ell_j(x+n) - \ell_j(x)$ and substituting ${}_nL_x^\alpha\,{}_nm_x^{\alpha\beta}$ for ${}_nd_x^{\alpha\beta}$ as well as h for n in (2.3), we get

$$\frac{d}{dx}\,{}_hL_x^j = -{}_bL_x^j\,{}_hm_x^j + \sum_{k\in I-j} {}_hL_x^k\,{}_hm_x^{kj}. \tag{2.15}$$

Note how similar (2.15) is to (2.4). The only difference is that the differential equations for $\ell_i(x)$ will have the $\{\mu_{ij}(x)\}$ in place of the $\{{}_hm_x^{ij}\}$. Since for fixed h the latter are *bona fide* intensity functions of (a continuous) x in their own right, this suggests solving the Kolmogorov forward differential equations with intensities $\{{}_hm_x^{ij}\}$ to get a different set of transition probabilities $\{{}_h\Pi_{ij}(x,y)\}$. (For the mathematics of these operations, see Iosufescu, 1980, pp. 262-264.) In the same manner as $\ell_j(y) = \sum_{k\in I} \ell_k(x)P_{kj}(x,y)$, we then get

$$ {}_hL_y^j = \sum_{k\in L} {}_hL_x^k\,{}_h\Pi_{kj}(x,y), \quad \text{for } j\in L,\ x \leqq y, \tag{2.16}$$

and in particular,

$$ {}_hL_y^j = \sum_{k\in L} {}_hL_0^k\,{}_h\Pi_{kj}(0,y), \quad \text{for } j\in L,\ y \geqq 0.$$

(It suffices to add over $k\in L$ here, for if $k\in D$ and $j\in L$, then ${}_h\Pi_{kj}(x,y) \equiv 0$ because ${}_hm_s^{kj} \equiv 0$.) This demonstrates that the $\{{}_hL_x^j\}$ may be constructed from a set of model transition rates $\{{}_hm_x^{ij}\}$ and an "initial distribution" $\{{}_hL_0^j\}$ in precisely the same manner as the $\{\ell_i(x)\}$ may be constructed from a set of intensities $\{\mu_{ij}(x)\}$ and an initial distribution $\{\ell_i(0)\}$. A computational method derived for one of these two cases may as well be used for the other. This may be convenient when the model transition rates have been specified and one is satisfied with computing the $\{{}_h\Pi_{ij}(x,y)\}$ and/or the $\{{}_hL_x^j\}$.

We get a connection to the $\{\ell_x^j\}$ by letting $n \to \infty$ in (2.3). This gives

$$\ell_x^j = \ell_\infty^j + \sum_{k \in I-j} {}_\infty d_x^{jk} - \sum_{k \in I-j} {}_\infty d_x^{kj},$$

where ℓ_∞^j is the probability that an individual will end his or her life in state j. (We assume that $\zeta = \infty$ for the rest of this section.) Since

$${}_\infty d_x^{jk} = \int_0^\infty \ell_j(x+s)\mu_{jk}(x+s)ds = \sum_{t \geq 0} {}_h d_{x+th}^{jk} = \sum_{t \geq 0} {}_h L_{x+th}^j \, {}_h m_{x+th}^{jk},$$

we get

$$\ell_x^j = \ell_\infty^j + \sum_{t \geq 0} {}_h L_{x+th}^j \, {}_h m_{x+th}^j - \sum_{t \geq 0} \sum_{k \in I-j} {}_h L_{x+th}^k \, {}_h m_{x+th}^{kj}. \tag{2.17}$$

For a transient state j, $\ell_\infty^j = 0$. Typically, L has only transient states, and $\sum_{i \in L} \ell_0^i = 1$. Leaving other cases aside, we get, in particular,

$$\ell_0^j = \sum_{t \geq 0} \left\{ {}_h L_{th}^j \, {}_h m_{th}^j - \sum_{k \in I-j} {}_h L_{th}^k \, {}_h m_{th}^{kj} \right\}, \quad \text{for } j \in L.$$

By (2.16), however,

$${}_h L_{th}^j = \sum_{k \in L} {}_h L_0^k \, {}_h \Pi_{kj}(0, th),$$

which, after some reorganization, gives

$$\ell_0^j = \sum_{k \in L} {}_h L_0^k \, b_{kj}, \quad j \in L, \tag{2.18}$$

for

$$b_{kj} = \sum_{t\geq 0} \left\{ {}_h\Pi_{kj}(0,th)\ {}_hm^j_{th} - \sum_{\alpha\in L-j} {}_h\Pi_{k\alpha}(0,th)\,{}_hm^{\alpha j}_{th} \right\}.$$

(Note that the summand equals $-(\partial/\partial y)_h\Pi_{kj}(0,th)$, where the derivative $\partial/\partial y$ is taken with respect to the second argument of the function.) If ℓ_0 and $\underline{L}_0$ denote vectors with elements $\{\ell^j_0\}$ and $\{_h\underline{L}^j_0\}$, respectively, and if $\underline{B} = (b_{kj})'$ is a nonsingular matrix of finite elements, (2.18) gives

$$\underline{L}_0 = \underline{B}^{-1}\underline{\ell}_0. \tag{2.19}$$

This permits the computation of a set $\{_hL^k_0\}$ that is consistent with the original $\{\ell^i_0\}$, and subsequently the computation of the $\{\ell^j_x\}$ by (2.17) with $\ell^j_\infty = 0$.

For practical applications one should note that values of the model transition rates $\{_hm^{ji}_x\}$ are needed for *all* values of x (where x is regarded as a continuous variable) in order to carry out the computations indicated, in the same manner as values of the transition intensities are needed for all x in Section 2.3.

It is an intriguing question which of these many functions determine which of the others. We have provided a partial answer above, following McCutcheon and Nesbitt (1973), who noted these kinds of relations for the ordinary (two-state) life table model. For that model, McCutcheon (1971) has also shown that the function q_x does not define the function ℓ_x uniquely, not even if q_x is known for *all* x, including all noninteger x. He also demonstrates that it is not enough to know the function m_x $(= {}_1m^{12}_x)$ for all $x \leq$ some x_0 smaller than the upper endpoint of the lifetime distribution if one wants to determine the function ℓ_x. It is necessary to have m_x specified for *all* x. For the magnitude of possible variations in ℓ_x for given "determining" functions, and for a partial extension to the case of multiple decrement, see McCutcheon (1975). For problems connected with the identification of *constant* intensities from a given matrix of transition probabilities, see Singer and Spilerman (1976a, Section 4).

It is a hopeless task, therefore, to try to recover the transition intensities and transition probabilities completely from no more than the values of the $\{{}_hm_x^{ij}: i,j \in I, i \neq j\}$ or the values of the $\{{}_hp_x^{ij}: i,j \in I, i \neq j\}$ for a few selected values of x, taken some h units apart. The most one can aim at in general in this direction, is to find some approximate values for the fundamental functions, which are the $\{P_{ij}(x,y)\}$, or alternatively (and more simply), the $\{\mu_{ij}(x)\}$.

2.5. *SURVIVAL PROPORTIONS*

It would be nice to have a substantive interpretation of the probability ${}_h\Pi_{ij}(x,y)$, but such an interpretation does not seem to be available at the moment, except in the case where L consists of a single state, say state 1. In that case, when $\ell_1(0) = 1$ and we use ordinary life table notation,

$$ {}_h\Pi_{11}(x,y) = \int_0^h \ell(y+t)dt \Big/ \int_0^h \ell(x+t)dt = {}_hL_y/{}_hL_x. \tag{2.20} $$

Proof. Call the right-hand side of (2.20) b(x,y). Since

$$ \frac{d}{dy}\int_0^h \ell(y+t)dt = -\int_0^h \ell(y+t)\mu(y+t)dt = -{}_hd_y = -{}_hm_y\ {}_hL_y, $$

we see that

$$(\partial/\partial y)b(x,y) = -{}_h m_y \; b(x,y),$$

which is the Kolmogorov forward differential equation for ${}_h\Pi_{11}(x,y)$ in this case. Because $b(x,x) = 1 = {}_h\Pi_{11}(x,x)$, ${}_h\Pi_{11}(x,y)$ and $b(x,y)$ coincide, as we claimed. □

The integral representation in (2.20) is a survival proportion of the form

$$ {}_h s_{ij}(x,y) = \frac{\int_0^h \ell_i(x+t)P_{ij}(x+t,y+t)\,dt}{\int_0^h \ell_i(x+t)\,dt}, \quad \text{for } i,j \in L,$$

written out for the special case in question, since $P_{11}(x+t,y+t) = \ell(y+t)/\ell(x+t)$ in that case. In deterministic terms, ${}_h s_{ij}(x,y)$ is the proportion of individuals in the stationary population, present in state i between ages x and x + h at any given moment, who move to state j and survive to be included in that state's population aged y to y + h at a moment y - x years later. (Compare, e.g., Ledent, 1980a, p. 545, above relation (56), and p. 546, relation (60).) In the simple case for which (2.20) holds, ${}_h s_{11}(x,y)$ is a transition probability in a Markov chain on I, precisely because of (2.20), and thus it satisfies the Chapman-Kolmogorov equation. This can also be seen directly in a trivial manner. Unfortunately, the $\{{}_h s_{ij}(x,y)\}$ are not *generally* transition probabilities of a Markov chain, as was pointed out by Pollard (1966, 1969). Since the $\{{}_h\Pi_{ij}(x,y)\}$ *are* a family of such transition probabilities, ${}_h s_{ij}(x,y)$ does not in general coincide with ${}_h\Pi_{ij}(x,y)$, the way it did in (2.20), as one might perhaps hope. A simple numerical illustration of the fact that the $\{{}_h s_{ij}(x,y)\}$ do not generally satisfy the Chapman-Kolmogorov equation has been given by Funck Jensen (1981a). Note in particular that if we define one-step survival proportions ${}_h s_x^{ij} = {}_h s_{ij}(x,x+h)$ in the usual manner, then one cannot always be sure that ${}_h s_{ij}(x,x+2h)$ equals $\Sigma_{k\in I}\, {}_h s_x^{ik}\, {}_h s_{x+h}^{kj}$. As a consequence, you cannot really always project the population aged x to x + h *in some state i* at time t several periods of length h into the future by projecting it step by step over periods each of length h by means of the survival proportions $\{{}_h s_x^{kj}\}$ in the usual manner, not even if you disregard the fact that the seniority distribution between seniorities x and x + h in any state i in a real population may deviate from the one implied by the mathematics of a stationary population. Such stepwise projection would be entirely permissible only if the $\{{}_h s_x^{ij}\}$ could be chained together over several periods of length h by matrix multiplication, and our comments show that this need not give the correct result. We do not want to overstress the practical consequences of this theoretical point, however, for two reasons. First, the numerical differences between the theoretically correct survival proportions and those produced by matrix multiplication over a limited number of periods were of little substantive significance in Funck Jensen's numerical example. They must be negligible as compared to the forecasting error caused by the fact that the survival proportions were kept constant over all one-step projection periods. Second, population projectors usually are not interested in following into the future the subpopulation at each age in each given state at some time t, but only in the projected *total* future size of the population in each state and each age interval, irrespective of their origin at time t. Luckily, although perhaps surprisingly, these totals *can* be computed *exactly* in the stationary population by chaining the one-step $\{{}_hs_x^{ij}\}$ together through matrix multiplication, for it is easy to prove both of the following relations:

$$ {}_hL_y^j = \sum_{k\in I} {}_hL_x^k \, {}_hs_{kj}(x,y), $$

$$ {}_hL_y^j = \sum_{k\in I} {}_hL_x^k \sum_{i\in I} {}_hs_{ki}(x,z)\,{}_hs_{ij}(z,y), $$

for $x \leq z \leq y$. Since the left-hand sides of these relations are the same, the right-hand sides must of course be equal. Incidentally, these relations show that the $\{{}_hL_x^k\}$ can be "projected" by means of the $\{{}_hs_{kj}(x,y)\}$ or the $\{\sum_{i\in I} {}_hs_{ki}(x,z)\,{}_hs_{ij}(z,y)\}$ in precisely the same manner as by means of the $\{{}_h\Pi_{kj}(x,y)\}$ of (2.16), even though the three sets of projection coefficients may differ from each other.

In spite of the difference between the s and the Π functions, the former do have a genuinely probabilistic interpretation, given by Funck Jensen (1981a) as follows:

Assume that a Poisson process with a constant parameter generates an otherwise closed population of independent individuals, all entering at seniority 0, and each with a probability of $\ell_i(0)$ of starting in state $i \in I$. After entry, each individual moves between the states in I in the manner of a sample path from a Markov chain with intensities $\{\mu_{ij}(\cdot)\}$. At a given moment t, some ${}_hN_x^i(t)$ individuals of this population are present in state i and have seniorities between x and x + h. Out of these, a number ${}_hN_{ij}(x,y,t)$ move to state j and survive to be included in that state's population at seniorities y to y + h at a moment y - x years later. Then, given the value of ${}_hN^i_x(t)$, the vector $\{{}_hN_{ij}(x,y,t);\ j \in \mathcal{I}\}$ is multinomially distributed, with

$$P\left\{{}_hN_{ij}(x,y,t) = m_j;\ j \in \mathcal{I} \,\middle|\, {}_hN^i_x(t) = m\right\} = \frac{m!}{\prod_{k\in\mathcal{I}} m_k!} \prod_{j\in\mathcal{I}} \left\{{}_hs_{ij}(x,y)\right\}^{m_j}. \tag{2.21}$$

In this context, ${}_hL^j_x$ has a second probabilistic interpretation, in addition to its original definition in Section 2.2 as an expected sojourn time. Assume that an individual is known to have entered the population (as an outcome of the Poisson process) during a given time interval from t_0 to $t_0 + h$. Then ${}_hL^j_x/h$ is the probability that this individual is in state j at time $t_0 + x + h$, at which time his age is between x and x + h. For if the actual time at his entry is T, then T is uniformly distributed between t_0 and $t_0 + h$ when it is known that $t_0 \leqq T \leqq t_0 + h$. Since the conditional probability of being in state j at time $t_0 + x + h$ is

$$\sum_{i\in\mathcal{I}} \ell_i(0)\ P_{ij}(0,\ t_0+h+x-t) = \ell_j(t_0+h+x-t),$$

given that T = t, the corresponding probability when we do not condition on T is

$$\int_{t_0}^{t_0+h} \ell_j(t_0+h+x-t)\ \frac{1}{h}\ dt,$$

which is seen to equal ${}_hL^j_x/h$ by a simple change of integration variable.

In the same manner as we derived lim ${}_hm^{jk}_x$ in Section 2.4, one may prove that

$$\lim_{h\downarrow 0}\ {}_hs_{ij}(x,y) = P_{ij}(x,y), \tag{2.22}$$

provided only $\ell_i(x) > 0$, or $\Sigma_{k\in I-i}\ell_k(x)\mu_{ki}(x) > 0$. For small h, therefore, it cannot matter much whether we use ${}_hs_{ij}(x,y)$ or, say, $P_{ij}(x+\frac{1}{2}h, y+\frac{1}{2}h)$ as projection coefficients. Note that (2.10) may be used to compute the survival proportions in the case of piecewise constant intensities.

3. INTEGRATION HYPOTHESES

3.1. *INTEGRATION HYPOTHESES AS MODELS*

It seems well recognized among demographers now that the assumption of piecewise constant transition intensities is a convenient basis for numerical computations, at least for complete tables, i.e., for tables based on "short", substantively meaningful intervals. For abridged tables (at least), many contributors dislike piecewise constancy, and a lot of effort has gone into developing alternative procedures.[10] It would be possible of course to formulate other assumptions about the behavior of the intensities in this situation, as we recommend (Section 4.4), but many demographers seem to prefer to formulate their assumptions in terms of functions at the probability level rather than at the "instantaneous" level of the intensities, usually in the form of hypotheses about the various ℓ-functions. In our account of this approach, we shall work in

[10] *The resulting methods have been used for complete tables as well, perhaps because corresponding computer programs have been readily available, or because piecewise constancy has not been entirely comme il faut in some circles. As noted in footnote 1, numerical differences between methods are small for short seniority intervals.*

terms of the transition probabilities $\{P_{ij}(x,y)\}$, partly because we guess that this may have been what some of the originators may really have intended, but mostly because it provides a convenient way of proving their main results.

Assume, therefore, that someone suggests, perhaps as a hypothesis, that

$$P_{ij}(x,x+t) = {}_hf_x^{ij}(t;\,\underline{\underline{\theta}}), \quad \text{for } 0 \leqq t < h,\ i,j \in I, \tag{3.1}$$

where each ${}_hf_x^{ij}(t;\,\underline{\underline{\theta}})$ is, say, a continuously differentiable function of t which is fully specified except for a vector $\underline{\underline{\theta}}$ of unknown parameters, to be estimated from the data. For consistency, ${}_hf_x^{ij}(0;\,\underline{\underline{\theta}}) = \delta_{ij}$. We shall call (3.1) an *integration hypothesis*, for it is used mainly to derive a corresponding formula for ${}_hL_x^{ij} = \int_0^h \ell_x^i \, {}_hf_x^{ij}(t;\,\underline{\underline{\theta}})dt$, which figures prominently in some procedures. Most demographic contributors seem to have overlooked the fact that integration hypotheses have consequences for other model functions, at least if they are taken seriously as part of the model. To study some such consequences, we suppress function arguments that are not needed for the moment, and write $\underline{\underline{P}}(t)$ for the matrix with elements $P_{ij}(t) = P_{ij}(x,x+t)$; $D\underline{\underline{P}}(t)$ for the matrix with elements $(d/dt)P_{ij}(t)$; $\underline{\underline{f}}(t) = \{{}_hf_x^{ij}(t;\,\underline{\underline{\theta}})\}$; and so on. If (3.1) is part of the model, the f^{ij} must satisfy the Kolmogorov forward differential equations for some matrix $\underline{\underline{M}}(t)$ of induced intensity functions $M_{ij}(t) = {}_hM_x^{ij}(t)$, i.e.,

$$D\underline{\underline{f}}(t) = \underline{\underline{f}}(t)\underline{\underline{M}}(t),$$

which means that

$$\underline{\underline{M}}(t) = \underline{\underline{f}}(t)^{-1}D\underline{\underline{f}}(t), \quad \text{for } 0 \leqq t < h. \tag{3.2}$$

Note that no iteration is needed to derive $\underline{\underline{M}}(\cdot)$ from $\underline{\underline{f}}(\cdot)$. These induced intensities $M_{ij}(t)$ need not coincide with the transition intensities $\mu_{ij}(x+t)$ of the "real" model, for (3.1) is only regarded as a local approximation; indeed we proceed to demonstrate that the $M_{ij}(t)$ may be meaningless as intensity functions, while the $\mu_{ij}(x+t)$ are patently not.

Various specifications of the f^{ij} have been suggested, usually in the form of polynomials in t, such as a quadratic (Land and Schoen, 1982), a cubic (Greville, 1943; Keyfitz, 1970; Schoen and Land, 1979; Schoen, 1979), or a quintic polynomial (Greville, 1967). For some very early references, see Seal (1981, p. 89). Most frequently, each $f^{ij}(t)$ is taken to be linear in t (*the linear integration hypothesis*). It is a generalization of the classical assumption of a uniform distribution of deaths[11] in the theory of the ordinary life table, where $t \cdot q_x$ is sometimes used to represent ${}_tq_x$ for $0 \leqq t \leqq 1$. It has been used recently by Rogers (1973), Keyfitz and Frauenthal (1975), Oechsli (1979), Schoen and Land (1979), Schoen (1979), Ledent (1980a), Willekens (1980), and surely by many others. The linear integration hypothesis can be written as

$$\underline{\underline{f}}(t) = \underline{\underline{I}} + \underline{\underline{A}}t \tag{3.3}$$

for a suitable matrix $\underline{\underline{A}} = (a_{ij})$. To be able to function in

[11] *See Hoem (1980) for a discussion of erroneous arguments connected with this assumption and the alternative Balducci assumption, where one lets* ${}_{1-t}q_{x+t} = (1-t)q_x$.

(3.3), $\underline{\underline{A}}$ must be an intensity matrix, i.e., it must have non-negative off-diagonal elements, nonpositive diagonal elements, and row sums of zero. By (3.2), (3.3) induces an intensity matrix

$$\underline{\underline{M}}(t) = (\underline{\underline{I}} + \underline{\underline{A}}t)^{-1}\underline{\underline{A}} \quad \text{for } 0 \leq t \leq h, \tag{3.4}$$

provided $\underline{\underline{I}} + \underline{\underline{A}}t$ remains nonsingular for all such t. Note that $\underline{\underline{M}}(0) = \underline{\underline{A}}$.

Various choices of $\underline{\underline{A}}$ are available. If $\underline{\underline{P}} = \underline{\underline{P}}(h)$ is known (or can be estimated directly), it may be convenient to let $\underline{\underline{A}} = (\underline{\underline{P}}-\underline{\underline{I}})/h$, which makes (3.3) a linear *interpolation* hypothesis. Another possibility is to start from $\underline{\underline{M}}(t_0)$ for some suitable $t_0 \in [0,h]$, solve (3.4) for $\underline{\underline{A}}$ to get

$$\underline{\underline{A}} = [\underline{\underline{I}} - t_0\underline{\underline{M}}(t_0)]^{-1}\underline{\underline{M}}(t_0),$$

and reinsert this into (3.4) to get

$$\underline{\underline{M}}(t) = [\underline{\underline{I}} + (t-t_0)\underline{\underline{M}}(t_0)]^{-1}\underline{\underline{M}}(t_0).$$

Three obvious choices of t_0 are $t_0 = 0$, $t_0 = \frac{1}{2}h$, and $t_0 = h$. Many "classical" results reappear if we let $t_0 = \frac{1}{2}h$ and $\overline{\underline{\underline{M}}} = \underline{\underline{M}}(\frac{1}{2}h)$, in which case

$$\underline{\underline{A}} = (\underline{\underline{I}}-\tfrac{1}{2}h\overline{\underline{\underline{M}}})^{-1}\overline{\underline{\underline{M}}}, \tag{3.5}$$

$$M(t) = [\underline{\underline{I}} + (t-\tfrac{1}{2}h)\overline{\underline{\underline{M}}}]^{-1}\overline{\underline{\underline{M}}}, \tag{3.6}$$

and

$$\underline{\underline{P}} = (\underline{\underline{I}}-\tfrac{1}{2}h\overline{\underline{\underline{M}}})^{-1}(\underline{\underline{I}}+\tfrac{1}{2}h\overline{\underline{\underline{M}}}). \tag{3.7}$$

We solve (3.7) for $\overline{\underline{\underline{M}}}$ to get, conversely,

$$\overline{\underline{\underline{M}}} = \frac{2}{h}\,(\underline{\underline{I}}+\underline{\underline{P}})^{-1}(\underline{\underline{P}}-\underline{\underline{I}}). \tag{3.8}$$

Compare, for instance, Ledent [1980a, Eqs. (85) and (93)], who uses the opposite sign for his intensity matrices. Liaw and Ledent [1980, relation (21)] show that (3.7) appears as an approximation to $\underline{\underline{P}} = \exp(\overline{\underline{\underline{M}}}h)$ in a sequence of approximations based on a matrix continued-fraction method. Note that (3.7) would also have resulted from introducing the linear interpolation hypothesis $\underline{\underline{A}} = (\underline{\underline{P}}-\underline{\underline{I}})/h$ into (3.4) with $t = \frac{1}{2}h$.

As is well recognized (compare Ledent, 1980a; Liaw and Ledent, 1980), there are several problems connected with the representation (3.3). For any intensity matrix $\underline{\underline{A}}$, let $||\underline{\underline{A}}|| = \max\{|a_{ii}|: i \in I\}$ be its largest diagonal element in absolute value. For $t > 1/||\underline{\underline{A}}||$, (3.3) makes $f^{ii}(t) < 0$ for some $i \in I$, so for such t, $\underline{\underline{I}} + \underline{\underline{A}}t$ is not a matrix of transition probabilities. Evidently, great care must be exercised if the linear hypothesis is taken in earnest: the interval length h should be small enough to keep $h||\underline{\underline{A}}||$ and $h||\overline{\underline{\underline{M}}}||$ under strict control. We prefer to regard the linear integration hypothesis not as a model element, but strictly as a means of furnishing a numerical approximation to $\underline{\underline{P}}(t)$ for small t, for example in an algorithm providing a numerical solution to the Kolmogorov equations, as in (2.14). If t grows too large, the approximation becomes progressively worse, and finally problems of implausibility manifest themselves, even in quite realistic situations.[12]

[12] *See footnote 2 for empirical examples. Negative retention "probabilities" may also appear for realistic parameter values in simpler models, such as the three-state working life table model. See footnote 13.*

The simplest and perhaps best understood example of these problems is the classical approximation formula for the nonsurvival probability of the ordinary life table, viz.,

$$ {}_hq_x = h\ {}_hm_x/(1+\tfrac{1}{2}h\ {}_hm_x). \tag{3.9} $$

This special case of (3.7) usually is regarded as acceptable for "small" ${}_hm_x$. As the latter quantity increases, the approximation becomes worse. When ${}_hm_x > 2/h$, the right-hand side of (3.9) exceeds 1, and the approximation is manifestly unacceptable. An alternative approximation would be to use

$$ {}_hq_x = 1 - \exp\{-h\ {}_hm_x\}, \tag{3.10} $$

to which Greville (1943) and Keyfitz and Frauenthal (1975) have suggested improvements. Formula (3.10) results from assuming the force of mortality μ_{x+t} to be constant for $0 < t < h$, in which case the constant value is ${}_hm_x$. For "large" values of $h\ {}_hm_x$, the characters of the two approximations are entirely different. If $h = 5$ (years), say, (3.9) gives a survival probability ${}_5p_x$ of 0 if ${}_5m_x = 0.4$ and a negative survival "probability" if ${}_5m_x > 0.4$. By contrast, the corresponding survival probability computed from (3.10) for ${}_5m_x = 0.4$ is ${}_5p_x = e^{-2} \approx 0.1353$. Note that this would be the *correct* value of the probability if μ_{x+t} were in fact equal to 0.4 for $0 < t < h$, while (3.9) would then be wide of the mark.

The linear integration model gives rise to additional problems, however, which present themselves no matter how strict the control of h is. As we shall show in Section 3.2, $M_{ij}(t)$ may become negative for $i \neq j$, $0 \leq t < h$, and one may have $M_{ij}(t) > 0$ even though a direct transition from i to j is impossible by the nature of the model. It may also happen that the representation in (3.3) breaks down in ways that are less easily detected than negative "probabilities": A fundamental requirement on $\underline{\underline{A}}$ is that it must at least be chosen in such a manner that for each t between 0 and h, $\underline{\underline{I}} + \underline{\underline{A}}t$ is embeddable in a Markov chain with (continuous) transition intensities. Singer and Spilerman (1976a, 1977) and Singer and Cohen (1980) give introductions to the embeddability problem for constant intensities. See Johansen (1973) for the general mathematical theory. Although it will not be demonstrated here,[13] it is easy to construct realistic examples where embeddability is violated.

These anomalies have been demonstrated for the linear integration hypothesis, but they are bound to appear for any integration hypothesis that does not ensure that (3.2) give meaningful intensity functions.[14] We cannot see that it pays to continue to pursue the research direction based on integration hypotheses. The problems inherent in that approach are not caused by the real-life phenomena studied or by the complexity of the theory of Markov chains, but are produced by the technicalities of the methodology.

3.2. A SIMPLE MARRIAGE MODEL

To conclude our criticism of the linear integration hypothesis, consider a hierarchical marriage model with the four states "unmarried" (state 1), "in first marriage" (state 2),

[13] *An example based on the working life table model is available from the authors. Compare also the negative determinant in Manninen's migration example, quoted in footnote 2.*

[14] *Compare footnote 5.*

"divorced, widowed, or remarried" (state 3), and "dead" (state 4). We let h = 1; let $\overline{M}_{14} = \overline{M}_{24} = \overline{M}_{34}$ to reflect an assumed nondifferential mortality; and let $\overline{M}_{13} = \overline{M}_{21} = \overline{M}_{32} = \overline{M}_{41} = \overline{M}_{42} = \overline{M}_{43} = 0$, because the corresponding direct moves are impossible. Then (3.6) implies that

$$M_{12}(t) = \frac{\overline{M}_{12}}{[1 - (t-\frac{1}{2})(\overline{M}_{12}+\overline{M}_{14})][1 - (t-\frac{1}{2})(\overline{M}_{23}+\overline{M}_{14})]}, \tag{3.12}$$

$$M_{13}(t) = \frac{\overline{M}_{12}\overline{M}_{23}(\frac{1}{2}-t)}{[1 - (t-\frac{1}{2})(\overline{M}_{12}+\overline{M}_{14})][1 - (t-\frac{1}{2})(\overline{M}_{23}+\overline{M}_{14})][1 - (t-\frac{1}{2})\overline{M}_{14}]}, \tag{3.13}$$

$$M_{i4}(t) = \frac{\overline{M}_{14}}{1 - (t-\frac{1}{2})\overline{M}_{14}}, \quad M_{4i}(t) \equiv 0, \quad \text{for } i = 1,2,3,$$

and

$$M_{23}(t) = \frac{\overline{M}_{23}}{[1 - (t-\frac{1}{2})(\overline{M}_{23}+\overline{M}_{14})][1 - (t-\frac{1}{2})\overline{M}_{14}]},$$

while $M_{21}(t) \equiv M_{32}(t) \equiv 0$. Assuming that none of these denominators become nonpositive for $0 \leqq t \leqq 1$, the outstanding feature of this representation is that

$$M_{13}(t) \gtreqless 0 \quad \text{as} \quad t \lesseqgtr \tfrac{1}{2}, \quad \text{for } t \in [0,1],$$

in glaring discrepancy with the fact that direct moves from state 1 to state 3 are impossible, and with the requirement that intensity functions be nonnegative. Thus, the linear integration hypothesis makes no sense at all as a model element in this example. One easily sees that this conclusion extends to any model where it is possible to move from some state to some other state, but not by a direct transition.

4. OCCURRENCE/EXPOSURE RATES

4.1. PIECEWISE CONSTANT INTENSITIES

In our account of issues of statistical inference, we first sketch some of the statistical theory of occurrence/exposure rates under the assumption of piecewise constant intensities, because they are so fundamental in the demographic literature. In the spirit of Section 2.3, we may regard this as a step on the way toward the "real" model, and in Section 4.3 we pursue some of the consequences of such a position. As we argued in Section 1.3, situations exist where an acceptable "real" model has piecewise constant intensities, in which case the present analysis has the character of an end product rather than of a step on the way toward a complete theory.[15]

Assume, then, that $\underline{\underline{\alpha}} = (\alpha_1, \alpha_2, \ldots, \alpha_K)'$ is a vector of parameters, each of which represents the value of a piecewise constant intensity over some seniority interval, for a time-continuous Markov chain model. The $\{\alpha_k\}$ may be the values of a single intensity function over a sequence of seniority intervals, or values of several intensity functions over one or more seniority intervals. At exact seniority x, $Y_k(x)$ individuals are exposed to the risk of a transition with intensity α_k. Very weak assumptions are needed concerning the processes $\{Y_k(\cdot)\}$: they may depend on each other and on the past in any way conceivable, as long as $Y(\cdot) = \{Y_1(\cdot), \ldots, Y_K(\cdot)\}'$ is defined to be continuous from the left and not influenced by the

[15] *A statistical theory for the case where some of the intensities are piecewise linear may be based on Diem (1976).*

future. (Influence from the future may arise, say, if only sample paths that end up in a particular part of the state space are included in the analysis. This may happen for instance if the inclusion of individual life history segments is conditional on survival up to some given age or some specified calendar date, or if maternity histories are grouped according to total number of births ever experienced at menopause.) In particular, we permit the *observed* exposure of one individual at a given seniority to depend on the life history of *other* individuals up to the same seniority.

Assume that a total of A_k transitions are observed corresponding to intensity α_k, and that the total number of seniority time units observed under this risk is $T_k = \int_0^\zeta Y_k(x)dx$. (Our total seniority interval is $[0,\zeta]$ for some positive $\zeta < \infty$.) Then the central rate or occurrence/exposure rate

$$\hat{\alpha}_k = A_k/T_k$$

is an estimator for α_k. Under certain conditions, which we need not explore here, it is even the maximum likelihood estimator of α_k, but we need not make use of the latter result.

Evidently, this formulation allows for the fact that $\hat{\alpha}_k$ may (and usually does) deviate from the estimand α_k, in the standard manner of mathematical statistics.

Assume that as the population size N increases without bounds, then $T_k/N \to$ some finite $\tau_k > 0$ in probability for each k. Then, asymptotically, the random variables $U_k = \sqrt{N}\,(\hat{\alpha}_k - \alpha_k)$ are independent and normally distributed, each with mean 0, and U_k with an asymptotic variance of $\sigma_k^2 = \alpha_k/\tau_k$, which can be estimated consistently by

$$\hat{\sigma}_k^2 = N\, \hat{\alpha}_k / T_k .$$

For the mathematics of these ideas, see Aalen and Hoem (1978, Sec. 4.6). Investigations by Schou and Væth (1980) suggest that the normality approximation is acceptable if $N\alpha_k$ exceeds about 10, and that the approximation is accurate more quickly for $\hat{\alpha}_k^{1/3}$ than for $\hat{\alpha}_k$ itself.

Through the well-known delta method, these fundamental asymptotic properties of the occurrence/exposure rates are inherited by their transformations, and in particular by the corresponding estimated transition probabilities and estimated mean sojourn times. Let $\gamma_j = g_j(\underline{\underline{\alpha}})$ (for $j = 1,2,\ldots,J$) be any set of derived model parameters, where each $g_j(\cdot)$ is a continuously differentiable function, and let

$$Dg_j(\underline{\underline{\alpha}}) = \left\{ \frac{\partial}{\partial \alpha_1} g_j(\underline{\underline{\alpha}}), \ldots, \frac{\partial}{\partial \alpha_K} g_j(\underline{\underline{\alpha}}) \right\}'.$$

Then $\sqrt{N}\,\{g_j(\hat{\underline{\underline{\alpha}}}) - g_j(\underline{\underline{\alpha}})\}$ is distributed asymptotically like $\sqrt{N}\,(\hat{\underline{\underline{\alpha}}}-\underline{\underline{\alpha}})'Dg_j(\underline{\underline{\alpha}})$. Moreover, the vector $\sqrt{N}\,(\hat{\underline{\underline{\gamma}}}-\underline{\underline{\gamma}})$ is multinormally distributed in the limit, with an asymptotic covariance matrix that is easily computed. Since $Dg_j(\hat{\underline{\underline{\alpha}}})$ is a consistent estimator of $Dg_j(\underline{\underline{\alpha}})$, it is also simple to estimate the covariance matrix. For the transition probabilities and mean sojourn times, the vectors of differentials can be found by means of our (2.11) and its integral.

To illustrate the usefulness of results of this nature, consider the comparison of the two sets of fertility rates in columns 5 and 9 of Table 1. These rates were computed from

TABLE 1. *Marital Fertility in Two Scandinavian Villages (Rautus and Rödön)*[a,b]

	Rautus				Rödön					
Age group at childbearing (1)	No. of women (2)	Years of exposure (3)	No. of births (4)	Fertility rate per 1000 (5)	No. of women (6)	Years of exposure (7)	No. of births (8)	Fertility rate per 1000 (9)	U_x (10)	V_x (11)
15-19	18	21.7	6	276	4	5.6	4	714	(1.1688)	(1.3984)
20-24	49	165.1	51	309	15	44.9	18	401	0.8852	0.9302
25-29	54	220.2	63	286	25	83.9	29	346	0.8089	0.8322
30-34	44	195.8	47	240	34	138.1	39	282	0.7407	0.7480
35-39	37	136.1	21	154	35	165.1	31	188	0.7023	0.6984
40-44	23	104.3	10	96	34	158.1	16	101	0.1348	0.1343
Marital TFR				6805				10160		

[a] Women married 1830-1831 in Rautus, and 1826-1832 in Rödön.

[b] Lithell (1981, a,b), and private communication.

data collected to investigate the connection between fertility and breastfeeding in nineteenth century Sweden and Finland (Lithell, 1981a,b). The investigator has obtained church records of 62 women who entered their first marriage during the years 1830 and 1831 in the rural parish of Rautus (in Karelen, then in Finland), and also of 41 women who married for the first time during 1826-1832 in the rural parish of Rödön (in Jämtland, Sweden). The records were followed until the women died, became widowed, or moved out of the parish, and the investigator has counted births and computed exact exposures, listed in Table 1. On account of background knowledge like the extreme poverty of the Rautus population, there is reason to expect to find a lower marital fertility there than in Rödön, an expectation that seems reflected in the data. With larger cohorts, the observed differences may prove significant, but for the population sizes in Table 1, they are just outside the range of significance. Disregarding the fact that no account has been taken of parity or duration effects in this particular subset of the data, we call the childbearing intensity for age group x in parish i $\phi_x^{(i)}$, with i = 1 for Rautus and i = 2 for Rödön. We expect *a priori* that $\phi_x^{(1)} \leqq \phi_x^{(2)}$ for all x, and want to test the hypothesis

$$H_0 : \phi_x^{(1)} = \phi_x^{(2)}, \quad \text{for all } x,$$

against the natural alternative that $\phi_x^{(1)} < \phi_x^{(2)}$ for at least some x. To this end, we form

$$U_x = \frac{\hat{\phi}_x^{(2)} - \hat{\phi}_x^{(1)}}{\left(\hat{\phi}_x^{(2)}/L_x^{(2)} + \hat{\phi}_x^{(1)}/L_x^{(1)}\right)^{\frac{1}{2}}} \tag{4.1}$$

and $U = \Sigma_x U_x/\sqrt{m}$, where the $\{\hat{\phi}_x^{(i)}\}$ are the empirical rates, $\hat{\phi}_x^{(i)} = B_x^{(i)}/L_x^{(i)}$ for a corresponding number of births $B_x^{(i)}$ and an observed exposure $L_x^{(i)}$. This m is the number of age groups involved. The denominator of U_x is a consistent estimator for the asymptotic standard deviation of the numerator (when both have been normalized by the same figure to account for population sizes). It could have been replaced by the square root of B_x/L_x, which (after normalization) would be a consistent estimator of the asymptotic standard deviation only under the hypothesis. Here, $B_x = B_x^{(1)} + B_x^{(2)}$ and $L_x = L_x^{(1)} + L_x^{(2)}$.

Then U can be used as an overall test statistic for H_0, and the $\{U_x\}$ can be used to locate any age groups x that can be safely said to have $\phi_x^{(2)} > \phi_x^{(1)}$. The test criterion utilizes the asymptotic normality (0.1) of U (and of each U_x) under the hypothesis. If u is the upper ε percentage point of the standard normal distribution, then H_0 is rejected when $U > u$.

We delete age group 15-19 from our test because it is so small in Rödön that the normality approximation is doubtful. For the 44 women in Rautus and the 37 women in Rödön who married at ages 20 and above, the value of U is 1.463, which only leads to the rejection of H_0 at levels of significance above 7.2%. More data are needed to really verify the substantive theory.

To exploit the Schou and Væth (1980) result that the normal approximation to the distribution of each $(\hat{\phi}_x^{(i)})^{1/3}$ may be better than that for $\hat{\phi}_x^{(i)}$, we may replace U_x by

$$V_x = \frac{\left(\hat{\phi}_x^{(2)}\right)^{1/3} - \left(\hat{\phi}_x^{(1)}\right)^{1/3}}{\left\{\frac{\left(\hat{\phi}_x^{(2)}\right)^{2/3}}{9B_x^{(2)}} + \frac{\left(\hat{\phi}_x^{(1)}\right)^{2/3}}{9B_x^{(1)}}\right\}^{1/2}} \tag{4.2}$$

and U by $V = \Sigma_x V_x/\sqrt{m}$. With the present data, V = 1.435, which is significant only at levels above 7.5%.

It is possible to study the asymptotic power of these tests and some competitors by investigating sequences of intensity parameters $\{\phi_x^{(i)}(N)\}$ converging in a balanced manner as the combined size N of the two populations increases beyond all bounds, such that $\phi_x^{(i)}(N) \to$ some ϕ_x, common for both populations, while $\sqrt{N}\{\phi_x^{(2)}(N) - \phi_x^{(1)}(N)\} \to$ some $\theta_x \geqq 0$. We hope to publish such an investigation elsewhere.

The applications of nonparametric methods to data of this nature might give further insight.

4.2. *GENERAL INTENSITIES*

Central rates $\{\hat{\alpha}_k\}$ are computed also when no credence is given to the assumption that intensities are piecewise constant. To see what $\hat{\alpha}_k$ then estimates, call the underlying, possibly nonconstant, intensity function $\alpha_k(\cdot)$, and assume that $\int_0^\zeta \alpha_k(x)dx < \infty$. Assume also that as $N \to \infty$, $Y_k(\cdot)$ increases as well, and in such a manner that $Y_k(x)/N$ converges in probability to some quantity $w_k(x)$ for each $x \in [0,\zeta]$, $w_k(\cdot)$ being an integrable function with $\int_0^\zeta w_k(x)dx > 0$. Then

$$\hat{\alpha}_k \to \frac{\int_0^\zeta w_k(x)\alpha_k(x)dx}{\int_0^\zeta w_k(x)dx}$$

in probability. In particular, if we are dealing with a central rate ${}_h\hat{\mu}_x^{ij}$ over the seniority interval from x to x + h for a transition intensity $\mu_{ij}(\cdot)$, then in probability,

$$
{}_h\hat{\mu}_x^{ij} \rightarrow \frac{\int_0^h w_i(x+t)\,\mu_{ij}(x+t)\,dt}{\int_0^h w_i(x+t)\,dt} \equiv {}_hm_x^{ij}(w_i), \tag{4.3}
$$

$w_i(y)$ being the probability limit of the mean number of individuals ever in state i at seniority y.

If $\mu_{ij}(\cdot)$ is constant over $\langle x,x+h\rangle$ after all, then ${}_hm_x^{ij}(w_i)$ equals this constant value, no matter what weight function $w_i(\cdot)$ is involved.

In a closed cohort, $w_i(\cdot) = \ell_i(\cdot)$, and ${}_hm_x^{ij}(\ell_i) = {}_hm_x^{ij}$ is the model transition rate defined in Section 2.4 above. Gardiner (1982) has studied the asymptotic statistical properties of central rates ${}_h\hat{\mu}_0^{0j}$ for a closed cohort subject simply to multiple decrement from an initial state 0 between seniorities 0 and h. If $\hat{\underline{\underline{\mu}}} = ({}_h\hat{\mu}_0^{01}, {}_h\hat{\mu}_0^{02}, \ldots, {}_h\hat{\mu}_0^{0J})'$ and $\underline{\underline{m}} = ({}_hm_0^{01}, {}_hm_0^{02}, \ldots, {}_hm_0^{0J})'$, he has proved that $\sqrt{N}(\hat{\underline{\underline{\mu}}}-\underline{\underline{m}})$ is asymptotically multinormal as $N \rightarrow \infty$, with mean $\underline{\underline{0}}$ and a covariance matrix $\underline{\underline{\Sigma}}$ for which we need not reproduce his formula. He proves that $\underline{\underline{\Sigma}}$ is a diagonal matrix if all intensities $\mu_{0j}(\cdot)$ are constant over $\langle 0,h\rangle$, in agreement with the asymptotic result stated for the $\{\hat{\alpha}_k\}$ in Section 4.1 above. The $\{{}_h\hat{\mu}_0^{0j}\}$ may be asymptotically independent even if the intensities are not constant, but they will not be so in general. Presumably, results of this nature can be extended to general transition rates $\{{}_h\hat{\mu}_x^{ij}\}$.

If the data are not for a closed cohort, indeed even if they only are for an *open* cohort, then ${}_h m_x^{ij}(w_i)$ will not coincide with ${}_h m_x^{ij}$ in general for nonconstant intensities. The discrepancy between the two depends of course on the "interaction" between the functions $w_i(\cdot)$ and $\mu_{ij}(\cdot)$ for the relevant seniorities. If $\mu_{ij}(\cdot)$ is continuous, then by the mean-value theorem,

$$ {}_h m_x^{ij}(w_i) = \mu_{ij}\left\{{}_h \xi_x^{ij}(w_i)\right\}, \tag{4.4}$$

for some seniority ${}_h \xi_x^{ij}(w_i)$ between x and x + h. This shows that ${}_h \hat{\mu}_x^{ij}$ estimates a value which $\mu_{ij}(\cdot)$ reaches over the seniority interval from x to x + h. If the intensity and the weight function behave reasonably well over the interval, then $\mu_{ij}\{{}_h \xi_x^{ij}(w_i)\}$ will be a sensible mean value to represent the intensity over the interval when we behave as if $\mu_{ij}(\cdot)$ were constant there. No matter whether they *are* well behaved or not, $\mu_{ij}\{{}_h \xi_x^{ij}(w_i)\}$ is an approximate value in a sequence on the way toward $\mu_{ij}(x)$ itself, in the spirit of the ideas at the end of Section 2.3. Any worries at this point will be unimportant if h is sufficiently small, for then any discrepancy $\sup\{|{}_h m_x^{ij}(w_i) - \mu_{ij}(x+t)|: 0 < t < h\}$ will be drowned by the estimation error caused by the finiteness of the study population.

Even though there is no guarantee that ${}_h \xi_x^{ij}(w_i)$ equals the midpoint x + ½h of the seniority interval, demographers will typically reason as if this is at least a good approximation, except in dramatically aberrant cases.[16] On occasion we shall do the same.

[16]*For mortality in the first year of life, a representative age much less than age ½ is usually selected, for instance.*

In line with what seems to be a convention among demographers, we shall use the symbol ${}_hM_x^{ij}$ for ${}_hm_x^{ij}(w_i)$ for a closed population if the central rate for a given seniority attained at transition has been computed for a calendar period. For an example, think of a fertility rate by age at childbearing for a given year. The central rate that estimates ${}_hM_x^{ij}$ will be denoted ${}_h\hat{M}_x^{ij}$. It is notable, and well recognized, that $w_i(\cdot)$ need not be equal to $\ell_i(\cdot)$ under this method of ascertainment.

The weight function $w_i(\cdot)$ should not be confused with, say, the density of the age distribution (in state i) in the closed population at the start of the observational period in question, as is sometimes done. If every member of the population has the same force of mortality $\mu(\cdot)$ and if everyone is exposed to the risk in question with a common intensity function, say $\lambda(\cdot)$, then we may drop the subscript i for our present purposes, and the density of the initial age distribution may be denoted $p(\cdot)$. If the observational period is taken to be of unit length, then for period rates,

$$w(y) = \ell(y) \int_{y-1}^{y} \frac{p(t)}{\ell(t)}\, dt, \quad \text{for } y \geq 1. \tag{4.5}$$

This holds both for events that occur at most once in a lifetime, such as a death [whence $\lambda(\cdot) = \mu(\cdot)$] or a first marriage (Hoem, 1971, p. 458), and for repeatable events like a childbirth (Hoem, 1971, p. 463). Similar formulas can be established for more complex models, like the three-state model of labor-force participation (Hoem, 1971, p. 467).

As is evident from (4.5), $w(y)$ equals $\ell(y)$ if

$$p(t) = \ell(t) \Big/ \int_0^\zeta \ell(s)ds, \quad \text{for } 0 \leqq x-1 < t < x+h \leqq \zeta. \tag{4.6}$$

The latter is an assumption of sectional stationarity. A corresponding assumption of sectional stability would be to let

$$p(t) = e^{-rt}\ell(t) \Big/ \int_0^\zeta e^{-rs}\ell(s)ds, \quad \text{for } 0 \leqq x-1 < t < x+h \leqq \zeta, \tag{4.7}$$

for some constant r which may depend on x and h. In general, $p(\cdot)$ and $w(\cdot)$ are different from each other, but under (4.6) or (4.7), $w(y) = p(y)$. Hoem (1971) has studied general conditions that make $w(\cdot)$ and $p(\cdot)$ coincide.

In the literature based on some integration hypothesis, it is regularly assumed that each ${}_hM_x^{ij}$ equals (or, presumably, is a good approximation to) the corresponding ${}_hm_x^{ij}$. The relations that set these functions pairwise equal to each other are called *orientation equations* (see Greville, 1943, 1967; Oechsli, 1975, 1979; Schoen, 1979; Schoen and Land, 1979). The assumption is not always made explicitly, but it is stated particularly lucidly by Willekens [1980, p. 572, after his Eq. (46)], and in the form of an assumption of sectional stationarity by Schoen and Land (1979, p. 766, Column 2).

Keyfitz (1970) made it clear that some assumption of this nature is needed for the methodology based on an integration hypothesis, linear of otherwise. Following up his own previous work, he suggested the adoption of the sectional stability assumption (4.7), an assumption also used by Keyfitz *et al.* (1972). Keyfitz and Frauenthal (1975, p. 893) proposed a linear approximation to $w(x+t)$ and found that experimenting with higher-order polynomial approximations to $w(x+t)$ (and $\mu(x+t)$)

made very little numerical difference to their results. Indeed, their linear approximation to w(x+t) did not seem to give results appreciably different from competing methods in their numerical experiments, in our opinion.

We do not want to overemphasize the theoretical or practical importance of the accuracy of these "assumptions" or approximations. In fact, we wonder whether they deserve all the attention they have got in some of the demographic literature, and whether the focus has been on the substantively important issues. Perhaps more thought should be given to the appropriate choice of seniority intervals rather than to overcoming the technical difficulties produced by the conventional manners of treating the data. The real need for particular care in the latter matters arises when $\mu_{ij}(x+t)$ changes much as t increases from 0 to h, if the weighting system $\{w_i(x+t): 0 < t < h\}$ is unfortunate at the same time. Even though this comment has certainly been made before, we are not aware that anyone has looked closely into the behavior of the approximations in such circumstances. The most instructive example of an accuracy test we know of uses very nice functions $\mu_{ij}(\cdot)$ and $w_i(\cdot)$, viz., Makeham mortality and a linear weight function (see Keyfitz and Frauenthal, 1975, p. 894).

The rest of our arguments have general interest beyond their value as reasons for our opinion on these issues and are collected in the next section.

4.3. PERIOD COHORT RATES

The theory above does not account for the real-time aspect of the transition intensities. To capture long-term trends, short-term period variations, and seasonal effects, each intensity $\mu_{ij}(\cdot)$ should be represented as a function $\mu_{ij}(x,\tau)$ of real-time τ as well as of achieved seniority x. This has a bearing on the accuracy of ${}_hM_x^{ij}$ as an approximation to ${}_hm_x^{ij}$, for the two quantities are influenced by real-time effects in different manners, in addition to the effects of the differences in the weight functions $w_i(\cdot)$ and $\ell_i(\cdot)$ involved in their definitions. If we are talking about fertility rates for single-year age groups for single-calendar-year periods, for instance, then of course the model cohort rate ${}_hm_x^{ij}$ involves the fertility for the relevant age group over two consecutive calendar years, while the model period rate ${}_hM_x^{ij}$ only depends on the fertility in the first year. Abrupt period changes in fertility may then make the two quantities disparate. They may also be differentially influenced by seasonal effects. Using one to approximate the other may not be the greatest of presumptions, but it is certainly a source of inaccuracy.

American-based and American-influenced mathematical demographers sometimes write as if the empirical period rates defined above (i.e., the ${}_h\hat{M}_x^{ij}$) are the only ones ever or regularly observed, and the cohort rates only appear as unobtainable theoretical constructs. It may be suitable at this stage to point out

(i) that empirical cohort rates of course can be computed when the investigator has access to individual life histories, as in the analysis of interview data, a situation that should not be forgotten in a general discussion of multistate life table methodology, and

(ii) that as a routine matter, even ordinary vital statistics is presented in a manner *different* from the one in which the empirical period rate ${}_h\hat{M}_x^{ij}$ appears, at least in Scandinavia, but surely elsewhere as well. While ${}_h\hat{M}_x^{ij}$ is computed for a period, by seniority (group) attained *at transition*, rates for a period can alternatively be obtained by seniority (group) attained *at the end of the period* instead. While the latter rates are for a calendar period, they refer to the data of a cohort, viz., the cohort that just reached the defining seniority group at the end of the period. Perhaps it is appropriate to call them (empirical) *period cohort rates*, to distinguish them from the "pure" empirical period rates and "pure" empirical cohort rates mentioned before.

If one insists on reckoning seniority in the same manner as biological age, then the theoretical counterparts of the empirical period cohort rates will satisfy (4.3) with a weight function $w_i(\cdot)$ generally different from $\ell_i(\cdot)$ and different from the one involved in ${}_hM_x^{ij}$. In the situation which lead to (4.5), the weight function for the model period cohort rate is

$$w(y;\ x,h) = \ell(y) \int_{\max(x,y-1)}^{\min(y,x+h)} \frac{p(u)}{\ell(u)}\, du, \quad \text{for } x \geqq 1. \qquad (4.8)$$

While the annual model period cohort birth rate for a single-year age group is influenced by fertility only in the year in question, the influence of the subpopulation age-and-state composition and of seasonal variations are different from that of ${}_hM_x^{ij}$. In all, we have a third concept entirely.

It is not at all certain, however, that exact biological age (or its seniority counterpart) is the most important influence on the development of the intensity functions for a cohort over a given period. It is quite conceivable in many situations that seasonal and period effects may be so strong that the behavior of people in the same rough age bracket may depend mostly on the time of the year. There may be preferential seasons to marry; new observable levels of education are reached at typical exam times; entries into and exits from the employed population, and possibly the labor force, have well-known seasonal variations; and so on. Such features may be caught by computing the seniority of all members of a cohort from a common calendar date, so that everyone in the cohort has the same exact seniority at any time. Time and seniority influences on the transition intensities will then coalesce. The period cohort rates will take the place of the pure cohort rates in the previous theory. The pure period rates will be without interest, except possibly as approximations to the period cohort rates (with a suitable age correction) when the latter cannot be obtained. An assessment of the adequacy of such an approximation may be based on formulas similar to (4.5) and (4.8). These are easily derived and are not given here.

This alternative definition of seniority has the potential advantage of being a better description of reality where our ideas are appropriate, and the sure advantage of simplifying possibly empirical analysis and certainly the groundwork for projections when period cohort rates are available.

Procedures essentially of this nature will have been used in innumerable investigations. They are particularly suitable for the analysis of gross flows (Section 5.1), and were used for this purpose by Hoem and Fong (1976, Fig. 14).

4.4. ABRIDGED TABLES

As we have made clear, we prefer complete tables to abridged tables when the choice is available. We see no intrinsic value in the latter.[17] Since on occasion the obtainable data are only sufficient for abridged tables, we briefly suggest our strategy for their construction, even though in our opinion it should be quite conventional.

In the spirit of Section 2.3, we see abridged tables computed as if intensities were constant over the relevant (long) seniority intervals as a first[18] approximation to the real thing. When this approximation is unacceptably inaccurate, we would use a nonconstant specification of the intensity function over each seniority interval and solve the Kolmogorov equations by a numerical method to get the transition probabilities and subsequently the other derived functions involved. The investigator should feel entitled to some daring in the specification of the intensity functions, at least if the specification retains a sensible amount of flexibility in the functional form. At least two different principles are available for making the intensity specification, neither of which is any radical innovation, and either of which may be appropriate according to the circumstances.

[17] *An assessment of the usefulness of an abridged working life table for the data in Hoem and Fong (1976) has been given by Hoem (1976b).*

[18] *Cohen and Singer (1979) and surely many others share this philosophy.*

One possibility is to represent the intensities as parametric functions over the entire seniority range and fit its parameters by some method such as analytic graduation. In demographic parlance, this would be to use a parametric model schedule, such as the Coale-Trussell (1974) fertility function, a Brass (1974) relational system, or the Rogers-Castro (1982) migration function. In accordance with (4.4), the curve-fitting needs representative seniorities ${}_h\xi_x^{ij}$ at which the occurrence/exposure rates are taken to estimate the values of the intensity functions. Unless we have strong reasons to do something else, we shall usually follow the convention of picking interval midpoints as approximations to the ${}_h\xi_x^{ij}$. The purpose of the exercise is to use function values of the fitted curve for intensities at all relevant seniorities, including seniorities other than the ${}_h\xi_x^{ij}$, in what may be described as a combination of graduation and interpolation.

Alternatively, one can specify a parametric function to represent the intensities locally over a few consecutive seniority intervals and fit its parameters to the observations over the relevant intervals alone, again by some method like analytic graduation. By application of ideas from moving average graduation, one might fit the parameters successively to partly overlapping sets of seniority intervals, perhaps utilizing the fitted curve only in the middle interval(s) of each set. Piecewise linear (Keyfitz and Frauenthal, 1975; Diem, 1976), piecewise quadratic (Schoen, 1979), or piecewise exponential function specifications are among those available.

Sectional stationarity or sectional stability assumptions, which play such a large part in methods suggested by mathematical demographers,[19] are not needed in the approach we advocate. Among such assumptions, made solely for mathematical convenience, without much substantive motivation and with badly charted limitations, we have only retained the use of seniority interval midpoints as approximations to the ${}_h\xi_x^{ij}$, an approximation that some demographic methods use while others do without. Like Ledent and Rees (1980, p. 25), we would sometimes apply (possibly piecewise) spline function representations for the intensities, in the manner described above. Unlike them, we would not subsequently iterate the parameter values to "agree with the data," for we do not see why the fitted curves need to agree with observed rates exactly, in the manner of a tradition going back to Keyfitz (1966). Beside the "assumptions" and approximations and model misspecifications involved, the empirical rates are subject to random variation[20] and perhaps also misreporting, so a bit of graduation may actually be preferable to an "exact" fit.

5. OTHER OBSERVATIONAL PLANS

5.1. *GROSS FLOWS*

For some analyses, and in particular to handle nonparametric assumptions about the transition intensities, data will be needed on the individual level. To carry out the kind of analysis mentioned in Section 4.1, "only" aggregate data are

[19] *Compare our discussion below (4.7) in Section 4.3.*

[20] *Note that throughout we use the standard statistical distinction between an empirical rate, say ${}_h\hat{\mu}_x^{ij}$, and its model counterpart, say ${}_h\mu_x^{ij}$, or ${}_hm_x^{ij}(w_i)$ as in (4.3).*

needed, but one needs to know the complete flows $\{(A_k, T_k);\ k = 1,2,\ldots,K\}$. In many cases, this information is not available, however. For instance the data may instead consist of counts of the numbers of individuals ${}_hN_x^{ij}$ who were in state i at some exact seniority x and in state j at a subsequent seniority x + h (gross flows), for any pair (i,j), $i \in I$, $j \in I$. Assume that the population is closed. Since for each $i \in I$, the set $\{{}_hN_x^{ij}: j \in I\}$ is multinomially distributed, given the number $N_x^i > 0$ of individuals in state i at seniority x, it is easy to estimate the transition probability ${}_hp_x^{ij}$ by

$$ {}_h\hat{p}_x^{ij} = {}_hN_x^{ij}/N_x^i \tag{5.1}$$

(provided one does not run into embeddability problems), and the (conditional) properties of such estimators are known from elementary statistics.

To estimate transition probabilities ${}_tp_x^{ij}$ for durations t different from integer multiples of h, a further specification of the underlying model and more sophisticated estimation methods are needed, however. Similar extras are required for the estimation of transition intensities and functions derived from them, such as the mean sojourn times. If all transition intensities are constant over the seniority interval from x to x + h and are collected in the intensity matrix $\underline{\underline{C}}$, one may try to invert the exponential relation $\underline{\underline{P}}(t) = \exp(\underline{\underline{C}}t)$ in our (2.10) and get, formally,

$$ \hat{\underline{\underline{C}}} = \frac{1}{h} \ln \hat{\underline{\underline{P}}}(t), \tag{5.2}$$

as was suggested for the general case by Zahl (1955). Introductions to problems arising in this connection have been given by Singer and Spilerman (1976a,b), Singer and Cohen (1980), and Singer (1981).

For purposes of illustration, it suffices to consider the special case of a homogeneous Markov chain with a state space of only two states, none of which is absorbing. As was demonstrated by Hoem and Fong (1976), such a model is fundamental in the study of the *three*-state increment-decrement model of labor-force participation with nondifferential mortality. The two-state model was used by Singer and Cohen (1980) and Singer (1981) as well.

The two-state model has only two transition intensities, say the intensity ν for going from state 1 to state 2, and the intensity ρ for transferring in the opposite direction. If $\gamma = \nu + \rho$, then the transition probabilities are

$$p_{12}(t) = \frac{\nu}{\gamma}\,(1-e^{-t\gamma}), \quad p_{21}(t) = \frac{\rho}{\gamma}\,(1-e^{-t\gamma}), \quad \text{for } 0 \leq t \leq h,$$

and $p_{11} = 1 - p_{12}$, $p_{22} = 1 - p_{21}$. Provided $p_{12}(h) + p_{21}(h) < 1$ (an embeddability condition), these relations for $t = h$ may be solved with respect to ν and ρ, and we get $\nu = bp_{12}$, $\rho = bp_{21}$, for

$$b = -\frac{1}{h}\,\frac{\ln(1-p_{12}-p_{21})}{p_{12} + p_{21}}, \tag{5.3}$$

where $p_{ij} = {}_hp_x^{ij} = p_{ij}(h)$. Corresponding estimators for the intensities are

$$\hat{\nu} = \hat{b}\hat{p}_{12}, \quad \hat{\rho} = \hat{b}\hat{p}_{21}, \quad \text{for } \hat{b} = -\frac{1}{h}\,\frac{\ln(1-\hat{p}_{12}-\hat{p}_{21})}{\hat{p}_{12} + \hat{p}_{21}}, \tag{5.4}$$

where $\hat{p}_{ij} = {}_h\hat{p}_x^{ij}$ from (5.1). These estimators are asymptotically binormally distributed with means ν and ρ, respectively, and with an asymptotic covariance matrix given by Hoem and Fong (1976, Correction Note of 9/8/78) and by Singer and Cohen (1980). (The corresponding results in Hoem and Fong, 1976, Section 6.6B are in error.) Variance estimates based on the formulas above, combined with other elements to account for subsequent graduation, etc., have been computed by Havning *et al.* (1979, Appendix 4) and reproduced by Linnemann (1981, Table 1).

Gross flows need not be specified as numbers of transitions between one exact *seniority* x and another (x+h), but are likely to be similar counts between some exact *time* t and a subsequent time t + h, for each of a number of seniority groups (x,y) at time t. Instead of the statistics $\{{}_hN_x^{ij}\}$ above (5.1), one will then have statistics $\{{}_hN_{ij}(x,y,t)\}$ as above (2.21). If the assumptions leading up to (2.21) hold, one may then compute

$$ {}_h\hat{s}_{ij}(x,y) = {}_hN_{ij}(x,y,t)/{}_hN_x^i(t), \tag{5.5} $$

which is an estimator with easily recognizable properties. If you want to make a projection with time interval length h, and if at time t the real population in question has a seniority-and-state distribution within each relevant seniority interval reasonably close to that of the corresponding stationary population, then the projection can be made in a straightforward manner. (Note our discussion in Section 2.5.) If any additional analysis is desired, one will most often find it convenient to estimate transition intensities first, for that is the simplest basis for a comparison between different populations and for the assessment of population trends, as well as for the computation of other multistate life table functions. In the present case, they must all be recovered from (5.5). As far as we know, no satisfactory general solution to this problem has been found to date, in spite of the efforts of Ledent (1982) and others, except possibly by way of numerical approximations whose accuracy still needs to be charted better.

If the stationarity assumption mentioned just above (5.5) does not hold, then (5.5) need not give a reasonable estimator for ${}_hs_{ij}(x,y)$. If the sectional stationarity assumption mentioned just *below* (5.5) breaks down, then the $\{{}_hs_{ij}(x,y)\}$ will not be appropriate projection coefficients, however accurately they are estimated.

These problems arise if you insist on treating seniority like exact biological age, for then gross flows data collected for a fixed calendar period with a grouping by initial seniority will lump individuals with somewhat different exact seniorities together in each group. For the reasons discussed in Section 4.3, these particular problems will disappear if exact seniority is counted, say, as starting at 0 on the same date for all members of each cohort involved. For gross flows, one would then be in the rather simpler situation leading up to (5.1).

5.2. *PURGED DATA*

Recall that in Section 2.2 we introduced a partition of the state pace I into an absorbing subset D and the rest, $L = I - D$. It happens that life histories that end up in D do not get analyzed (or not even collected) along with the rest of the data. This will typically be the case for data obtained through retrospective interviews, for then there is no information about those who died or otherwise left the population in question before the interview. Similarly, U.S. Census migration data will give changes of residence over the last previous five-year period, but only for individuals included in the census.

Conversely, it happens that only data for life histories ending in *D* is available, particularly if *D* contains states other than states of death. (Note that we have only assumed *D* to be absorbing as a whole. We have not assumed that each state of *D* is absorbing.) A typical case in demography is when data are collected only for ever-married women. Correspondingly, medical studies are sometimes based on data for individuals who have caught some chronic disease. In case-control studies, both types of data will be available but usually will be kept separate; the "cases" will all have got a disease (i.e., they will have ended in *D*), and the "controls" will not (i.e., they will have remained in *L*). A similar set-up, where life histories that end up in different parts of the state space are analyzed separately, occurs in demography when maternity histories are grouped according to the number of children ever born.[21]

Let us call a set of life histories *purged* if membership in a particular part of the state space at the end of observation is a condition for inclusion in the set. (The set is then purged of other types of life histories.) Such purging of the

[21]*That particular type of purging has the added disadvantage of being a grouping according to the outcome of a variable which is to be explained, a procedure discouraged in sociological methodology (see Blalock, 1964, pp. 107-110).*

data is prone to lead to selectivity biases that must be handled with great care. Note, for instance, the firm objection voiced by Hobcraft and Rodriguez (1980) against grouping birth histories by children ever born. Purging biases are studied in the theory of purged and partial Markov chains (Hoem, 1969), and has received the attention of Aalen *et al.* (1980), Borgan (1980), Sheps and Menken (1973, Chapters 7-9; they call an observational plan a sampling frame or a method of ascertainment), and others. More references are quoted by Hoem (1976a, p. 172). Similar problems occur for quite different types of models. In econometrics, the same phenomenon is called sample selection bias (Heckman, 1979).

If the condition for inclusion in the purged data set is that the life history ends up in an absorbing proper subset D of states in I, then behavior after inclusion in D is not affected by selection biases. As one might suspect, and as Hoem (1969) has demonstrated, one need not worry about such biases prior to entry either, nor for life histories remaining in $L = I - D$ throughout, if there is a nondifferential risk[22] of transferring into D. If we adopt the notation introduced at the end of Section 2.2, we may then write (for any x,y; $x \leqq y$)

$$P_{ij}(x,y) = \overline{P}_{ij}(x,y)\exp\left[-\int_x^y \mu(s)\,ds\right], \quad \text{for all } i,j \in L, \tag{5.6}$$

where $\overline{P}_{ij}(x,y)$ is the (partial) transition probability in a Markov chain with state space L and with transition intensities

[22] *Technically speaking, the intensity* $\mu_{iD}(\cdot)$ *must be the same for all* $i \in L$.

$\{\mu_{ij}(\cdot);\ i,j \in L\}$, i.e., what results if $\mu_{\ell d}(\cdot)$ is replaced by zero in $P_{ij}(x,y)$ for all $\ell \in L$, $d \in D$. Under the assumption of a nondifferential risk of moving into D, $\overline{P}_{ij}(x,y)$ has the additional interpretation as the probability of moving from state i at seniority x to state j at seniority y in the original Markov chain where transitions into D are possible, conditional on remaining in L at least until seniority y.

It is possible to get a multiplicative decomposition like (5.6) and a corresponding double interpretation of $\overline{P}_{ij}(x,y)$ *for a fixed x* if the transition intensities $\{\mu_{kD}(x+s)\colon k \in L,\ s \geq 0\}$ depend on the state occupied by the individual at seniority x, as long as otherwise they do not depend subsequently on the current state. For instance, mortality rates may depend on the place of residence at age x rather than on the place of occurrence. Ledent (1980a, p. 557), who may have been the first to realize this possibility, has suggested that a multiplicative decomposition may be used as a way out of some problems encountered in the use of retrospective migration data.

Except for special situations like the one just mentioned, there is no way around the existence of selectivity biases in purged data with differential risk of transferring into D. Cohen (1972) has essentially proved that $\overline{P}_{ij}(x,y)$ can have the given interpretation of a transition probability in the original chain, conditional on remaining in L at least until seniority y, *only* if there is a nondifferential D-risk.

5.3. *INTERACTION*

Another aspect of the great versatility of multistate life table methods is their ability to handle the interaction between separate population processes on the individual level, such as the interaction between marital status and childbearing, between labor-force participation and family building, between a medical condition and menopause (Aalen *et al.*, 1980), between childbearing and out-migration (Hoem, 1975), and between other processes that influence each other, possibly mutually. Schweder (1970) has studied possibilities of specifying independence and causality relationships in this connection. For illustration, we shall suggest how the multistate life model approach can be brought to bear on the interaction between education and childbearing, an interaction that has attracted much interest and whose implications for women's roles was discussed perceptively by Rindfuss *et al.* (1980).

To reduce technicalities and emphasize essentials, we shall simplify the model beyond realism. We focus on a single, closed birth cohort of women, disregard mortality both for the women and their children, and take no account of differential aspirations and other factors that might make the cohort probabilistically heterogeneous. At each age, the women are classified according to whether they have experienced childbearing or not. We shall reason as if children beyond the first one do not count in our arguments, and as if children always remain with their mothers. A nulliparous woman's intensity of a (first) birth will depend on her age as well as on her educational level.

We shall only count two educational levels. At each age we shall classify the women according to whether they have an education or not. While in reality educational levels are reached typically by taking degrees, most of which can be acquired only at certain times of the year, we shall reason as if a woman can reach the higher educational level here in principle at any time (beyond some minimal age), in the manner of a transition in a Markov chain with continuous time. At each age x, a woman without children has a "degree-taking intensity" $\lambda_0(x)$, and a woman with children has a corresponding transition intensity $\lambda_1(x)$. The first-birth intensities for the two educational levels are $\phi_0(x)$ and $\phi_1(x)$. We postulate a Markov chain model with these intensities and with states [22a] $\{0,1,2,3\}$, where a woman is

in state 0 as long as she has no children and no education,

in state 1 as long as she has no children but has an education,

in state 2 when she has experienced childbearing and has no education, and

in state 3 when she has both children and an education.

Popular wisdom will have it that children reduce a woman's chances to get an education, and that nulliparous women with an education have a lower fertility at each age than nulliparous women without an education. If this impression is correct, then $\lambda_0(x) > \lambda_1(x)$ for each age x, and $\phi_0(x) > \phi_1(x)$. For em-

[22a] *An interaction model of this type was used by Colding-Jørgensen and Simonsen (1940). A similar but nonhierarchical model appears in Coleman (1964a, p. 124), and it was used by Cohen and Singer (1979) in a recent exemplary empirical interaction study.*

pirical evidence, consult Rindfuss *et al.* (1980) and their references. They find that the reciprocal relationship between educational level at marriage and age at first birth is dominated by the (positive) effect from education to age at first birth with only a trivial effect in the other direction, in a linear regression analysis of data for ever-married women aged 35-44 at interview in the 1970 U.S. National Fertility Study. If this finding carries over to the life table analysis, we should expect that $\lambda_0(x) \equiv \lambda_1(x)$ and $\phi_0(x) > \phi_1(x)$, for all relevant x. Their data do not contain the complete educational histories that would be needed to check this, however. Only education (in completed years) at interview and education at marriage were obtained. As is well known, it can be very hard to disentangle cause-and-effect relationships between interacting processes if information on one of the processes (here, education) is limited to status at interview, in particular because temporal aspects of causality are upset. Compare, for instance, hesitation voiced by Trussell and Menken (1978) and a recent discussion by Leridon (1980). Because of its general interest, therefore, we show how these problems can be handled in our simplified model. We know of no other formal method that gives similar insight.

Assume, then, that a set of data contains the exact date at any first birth for each woman in our cohort, but that her educational level is known only at interview, which is when the cohort has reached some age z. The dates at which the higher educational level was reached is unknown for all educated women. Assume also that someone suggests that first-birth intensities be estimated in some conventional way, computed separately by educational level attained at age z. As is easily seen by the methods of purged Markov chains, this would amount to estimating *not* the intensities $\phi_0(\cdot)$ and $\phi_1(\cdot)$, but the possibly distorted intensities $\phi_0^*(\cdot)$ and $\phi_1^*(\cdot)$, defined as

$$\phi_0^*(x) = \phi_0(x) \frac{P_{22}(x,z)}{P_{00}(x,z) + P_{02}(x,z)} \tag{5.7}$$

and

$$\phi_1^*(x) = \frac{P_{00}(0,x)\phi_0(x)P_{23}(x,z) + P_{01}(0,x)\phi_1(x)}{P_{00}(0,x)[P_{01}(x,z) + P_{03}(x,z)] + P_{01}(0,x)} \tag{5.8}$$

If $\lambda_0 = \lambda_1$, the "distortion factor" in (5.7) equals 1, which means that the estimand is the undistorted ϕ_0 as desired. If $\lambda_0 > \lambda_1$, then $\phi_0^*(x) > \phi_0(x)$ for all x, so the (first-birth) fertility of uneducated women will be *overestimated* if children really reduce a woman's educational prospects. This is what we would expect on intuitive grounds, for women with children are likely to be overrepresented among those who have a low level of education at interview, if and only if studies are hindred by the presence of children. The mathematics of this argument is left to the reader.

To get some meat on these bones, consider a five-year unit seniority interval over which all intensities are taken to be constant for simplicity, and let x and z be the beginning and closing seniorities of the interval. In Table 2, Column 3 contains values of $\phi_0^*(x)$ for selected combinations of values for the intensity parameters ϕ_0, ϕ_1, λ_0, and λ_1. The values of ϕ_0 and ϕ_1 have been chosen as five times reasonably possible *annual* fertility rates for women without and with education, respectively. Thus, $\phi_0 = 1.0$ and $\phi_1 = 0.8$ correspond to annual rates of 200 and 160 per thousand. The values of λ_0 and λ_1 have been selected to give reasonable proportions of x-year-olds getting

TABLE 2. Values of ϕ_0^* and ϕ_1^* for $\phi_0 = 1$, $\phi_1 = 0.8$, $\lambda_0 = 0.4055\ldots$, and Selected Values of $\lambda_1 \leq \lambda_0$ for a Five-Year Unit Period with Constant Intensities

λ_1	$\eta_1 = 1 - \exp(-\lambda_1)$ (%)	ϕ_0^*	Overestimation of ϕ_0 (%)	ϕ_1^*	Overestimation of ϕ_1 (%)
(1)	(2)	(3)	(4)	(5)	(6)
0.1054...	10	1.2018	20.2	0.4719	-5.6
0.14	13.1	1.1773	17.7	0.4998	-0.0
0.2231...	20	1.1197	12.0	0.5605	12.1
0.4055...	33.3	1.0	0	0.6678	33.6

an education during the five-year seniority interval in the absence of other factors. For given λ_i, this proportion is $\eta_i = 1 - \exp(-\lambda_i)$, and conversely, $\lambda_i = -\ln(1-\eta_i)$; $i = 0,1$; where ln denotes the natural logarithm. In particular, $\eta_i = 1/3$ corresponds to $\lambda_i = 0.4055\ldots$. Columns 3 and 4 in Table 2 show that $\phi_0^*(x)$ may greatly overestimate ϕ_0. The values of parameters $\phi_0, \phi_1, \lambda_0$, and λ_1 used in Table 2, and similarly in Tables 3 and 4, have been selected from a wider range of trial values used by us to assess the generality of the features of these tables. The character of the computed results is similar to those of these tables throughout the range that we have investigated. The parameter values for Tables 2, 3, and 4 were *not* selected because they illustrated our points more clearly than other parameter values which we have tried.

To study the relation between $\phi_1^*(x)$ and $\phi_1(x)$ in the general situation, we note that $\phi_1^*(x) \gtreqless \phi_1(x)$ as

$$\phi_0(x)P_{23}(x,z) \gtreqless \phi_1(x)\{P_{01}(x,z) + P_{03}(x,z)\}. \tag{5.9}$$

TABLE 3. Values of ϕ_1^* for $\lambda_0 = \lambda_1 = 0.4055$ and Selected Combinations of Values of ϕ_0 and ϕ_1 with $\phi_1 \leq \phi_0$

ϕ_0	$\phi_1 = 0.5$		$\phi_1 = 0.8$	
	ϕ_1^*	Overestimation (%)	ϕ_1^*	Overestimation (%)
(1)	(2)	(3)	(4)	(5)
0.8	0.6084	21.7	0.8	0
0.9	0.6394	27.9	0.8387	4.8
1.0	0.6678	33.6	0.8749	9.4
1.2	0.7172	43.4	0.9394	17.4
2.0	0.8224	64.4	1.0992	37.4

If $\lambda_0 = \lambda_1$, then $P_{23}(x,z) = P_{01}(x,z) + P_{03}(x,z)$, in which case (5.9) implies that $\phi_1^*(x) > \phi_1(x)$. *Even if the presence of children has no effect on a woman's chances of improving her educational level, the estimation procedure is likely to*[23] *overestimate the fertility of women with an education,* therefore. In our numerical example, the overestimation of ϕ_1 can be serious (Table 3). Fortunately, the distortion will not be enough to reverse systematically the relation between the two levels of fertility, for $\phi_1^*(x) < \phi_0(x)$ for all x in the general case. Nevertheless, the "overfertility" of the uneducated will be underestimated.

If $\lambda_0 > \lambda_1$, then $P_{23}(x,z) < P_{01}(x,z) + P_{03}(x,z)$, and the size relation between the two sides of (5.9) depends on the relations between the four intensities in a nonsimple manner. Depending on the circumstances, $\phi_1(x)$ may be distorted downward, upward, or not at all. Compare Columns 5 and 6 in

Table 2. In the theoretical case where $\lambda_0(y)$ is larger than $\lambda_1(y)$ for most y between x and z, while $\phi_0(y) = \phi_1(y)$ for such y, then $\phi_1^*(x) < \phi_0(x)$. Since at the same time $\phi_0(x) < \phi_0^*(x)$, as we showed above, we realize that the estimation procedure would tend to "demonstrate" the conclusion that fertility decreases with an increasing educational level, a conclusion that would be erroneous under the premises, since we have assumed ϕ_0 and ϕ_1 to be equal in this segment of the discussion. Luckily, the assumptions leading to this problem may be untenable in practice for the two processes in question.

For the sake of argument, assume, however, that the role of the two processes were reversed in the observational plan. Suppose that one could get complete information on each woman's educational history, perhaps from school records or from a central register of examination records, but that the only information obtainable about her childbearing history were whether she had ever given birth before age z. Assume also (perhaps realistically) that $\lambda_0(y) = \lambda_1(y)$ but $\phi_0(y) > \phi_1(y)$ at all relevant ages y. One could then estimate intensities $\lambda_0^*(x)$ and $\lambda_1^*(x)$, similar to those in (5.7) and (5.8). Since $\lambda_0^*(x) > \lambda_1^*(x)$ in this situation, the likely conclusion[23] of the empirical investigation would be that children do in fact impair a woman's educational prospects, a conclusion that would be in error under the premises stated. See Table 4 for a numerical illustration.

[23] *We describe the outcome of an empirical study as only likely to go in the direction of the systematic errors, for random variation may of course throw it off target (even though it is the wrong target).*

TABLE 4. Values of λ_0^* *and* λ_1^* *for* $\lambda_0 = \lambda_1 = 0.4055$ *and Selected Combinations of Values of* ϕ_0 *and* ϕ_1 *with* $\phi_1 < \phi_0$

ϕ_0 (1)	ϕ_1 (2)	λ_0^* (3)	Overestimation of λ_0 (%) (4)	λ_1^* (5)	Overestimation of λ_1 (%) (6)
0.9	0.8	0.4400	8.5	0.3985	-1.7
1.0	0.5	0.6042	49.0	0.3705	-8.6
1.2	0.5	0.7034	73.5	0.3704	-8.6

5.4. THE MULTITUDE OF OBSERVATIONAL PLANS

A plethora of other ascertainment methods are used in demography and elsewhere to obtain data that can be analyzed by multistate life table models.

In the residence history study by Taeuber *et al.* (1968), observations were taken retrospectively on current residence, first and second prior residence, and birth place of individual in particular cohorts. The same restriction to the ascertainment of the most recent event(s) has been used for data on maternity histories in national contributions to the World Fertility Survey, and massive selection biases were demonstrate by Hobcraft and Rodriguez (1980) and by Page *et al.* (1980). Fo an overview, see Brass (1980, Section 6).

Braun and Hoem (1979) and Finnäs and Hoem (1980) have analyzed fertility data from the Danish fertility survey of 1975. It contained complete childbearing histories for women of all marital statuses, but data on cohabitation and marriage was mostly restricted to the latest cohabitation and the latest marriage, and no data on cohabitation was obtained from never-married women who did not report a current cohabitation at interview.

Sojourn intervals are sometimes obtained only when they overlap a set date or brief period of observation. Cohabitation intervals for the unmarried in the Danish data just mentioned is one case in point. The analysis of such sojourn times must account for an overrepresentation of long intervals. Among statisticians, this is known as the waiting time paradox (Feller, 1971, p. 11). Problems of this nature have been given considerable attention, also among demographers (see Henry, 1972; Sheps and Menken, 1973). Haldorsen (1974) handled them by means of multistate life table methodology in his analysis of lengths of periods spent in hospitals by patients registered in Norway as of 1 October 1970, with a prospective observational period up to the end of that year.

In an analysis of some experiments on mortality in laboratory mice, where the cause of death was ascertained only at death, Borgan *et al.* (1979) investigated the statistical theory of an observational plan with potential interest for studies of human cause-specific mortality.

Schoen and Woodrow (1980) had to impute some missing data to calculate their labor-force status life tables for the United States, 1972, on the basis of data from the Current Population Survey from January 1973. It contained information about labor-force status a year earlier, but only for persons who were *employed* in January 1973 (some 93 to 95% of the stock then in the labor force at every age).

It happens that while occurrences can be obtained with sufficient subspecification by relevant type of risk, the distribution of corresponding exposures over the same categories of risks are unobtainable, and only total exposure (the number of person-years lived under all risks taken together) is available for each seniority group. In the notation of Section 4.1, suppose that the $\{\alpha_i\}$ refer to different risks, but all for the same seniority interval. Suppose also that the $\{A_k\}$ are known, along with $T = \Sigma T_k$, but that the $\{T_k\}$ are otherwise unknown. Provided this is the case for a sequence of seniority intervals for cohort data, incidence rates of the form A_k/T may be analyzed by methods that are well known among demographers, and whose statistical properties have been investigated by Hoem (1978), Finnäs (1980), and Ramlau-Hansen (1980).

Sparre Andersen (1951) discussed the possibility of measuring the exposure by a sample when the corresponding occurrences are known for the total population.

Some of these and other observational plans used in socia[l] science projects have been cited by Singer and Spilerman (1976) and Tuma and Hannan (1978). Tuma (1979) reports computations tailored to the same pattern as in our Section 5.3. Every pla[n] has its own particular problems that must be studied on its ow[n] merits.

6. SAMPLING AND HETEROGENEITY

6.1. SAMPLE SURVEYS

Most of the empirical projects mentioned above have obtained their data from sample surveys, but some use data for complete populations or complete sections of populations. The labor-force status gross flows used by Hoem and Fong (1976) were of the latter type, for instance, for in principle they were counts for every person of working age who was a resident in Denmark and who had one out of a few purposively selected birthdays. Similarly, the data analyzed by Haldorsen (1974) was requested for all patients in hospitals in Norway as of the date of ascertainment. As long as we are dealing with populations that are probabilistically homogeneous (in theory), the problems that we have raised above pertain to both types of data sources and have the same solutions (if any), provided the sampling plan is noninformative and provided decisions about observation of life histories are independent across individuals.

We shall explain why this is so, and what the two latter prerequisites contain, in several steps. Let us first consider a simple example.

Assume that a birth cohort of stochastically independent women is followed until menopause or prior death, and let Z_i be the total number of children ever born to woman No. i. Define their completed parity distribution as $\pi(k) = P\{Z_i = k\}$. Assume that information is only obtained for a sample of n out of the total of N women, and that their completed parities are $Z_1', Z_2', \ldots, Z_n'$. The sample is selected without replacement by some standard plan, such as (possibly stratified) simple random sampling, in a manner that is independent of the $\{Z_i\}$. Then $Z_1', Z_2', \ldots, Z_n'$ may be regarded as independent and identically distributed with the distribution $\{\pi(k)\}$. Thus, the fact that we have got data from a sample and not for the total cohort influences the statistical analysis only via the sample size. There is no need to account for the possible complexities of the sampling procedure, in the manner of O'Brien and Suchindran (1980), nor can we agree that it is (most) sensible to let item selection be by simple random sampling with replacement, the way they seem to claim (for comparison of survival curves in their case).

We see this by computing the probability of selecting precisely women No. $i_1, i_2, \ldots, i_n$ and then observing that they have $k_1, k_2, \ldots, k_n$ children ever born, respectively. If we call the registration numbers of those actually selected $I_1, I_2, \ldots, I_n$, this is

$$P\left\{\bigcap_{j=1}^{n} (I_j = i_j \;\&\; Z_j' = k_j)\right\}$$

$$= P\left\{\bigcap_{j=1}^{n} (I_j = i_j)\right\} P\left\{\bigcap_{j=1}^{n} (Z_{i_j} = k_j) \;\middle|\; \bigcap_{j=1}^{n} (I_j = i_j)\right\}$$

because $Z_j' = Z_{I_j}$. Since $(I_1, \ldots, I_n)$ is stochastically independent of $(Z_1, \ldots, Z_n)$, and since the $\{Z_i\}$ are assumed mutually independent, the conditional probability above equals

$$P\left\{\bigcap_{j=1}^{n} (Z_{i_j} = k_j)\right\} = \prod_{j=1}^{n} \pi(k_j).$$

Adding over all possible values of $(i_1, \ldots, i_n)$ in the first relation above, therefore, we obtain

$$P\left\{\bigcap_{j=1}^{n} (Z_j' = k_j)\right\} = \prod_{j=1}^{n} \pi(k_j),$$

as desired.

In this argument, we assumed that the sampling was without replacement. Suppose now that it is *with* replacement instead.

Let $I_1,\ldots,I_M$ be the *different* registration numbers in the sample, after elimination of any doubles among the ones originally selected, say $J_1,J_2,\ldots,J_n$. The effective size M of the sample is a random variable whose value is determined by the $\{J_k\}$. If $Z_j' = Z_{I_j}$ as before, the same kind of argument gives the following relation:

$$P\left\{(M = m) \,\&\, \bigcap_{k=1}^{n} (J_k = j_k) \,\&\, \bigcap_{j=1}^{M} (Z_j' = k_j)\right\}$$

$$= P\left\{(M = m) \,\&\, \bigcap_{k=1}^{n} (J_k = j_k)\right\} \prod_{j=1}^{m} \pi(k_j).$$

Adding now over all possible values of $(j_1,\ldots,j_n)$ which give $M = m$, we get

$$P\left\{M = m \,\&\, \bigcap_{j=1}^{m} (Z_j' = k_j)\right\} = P\{M = m\} \prod_{j=1}^{m} \pi(k_j).$$

Thus

$$P\left\{\bigcap_{j=1}^{m} (Z_j' = k_j) \mid M = m\right\} = \prod_{j=1}^{m} \pi(k_j),$$

which means that the observed $\{Z_j'\}$ can be taken as i.i.d. with the completed parity distribution of the total cohort, conditional on the effective sample size M.

The above procedure eliminates rather than exploits the feature that the sampling was with replacement. As an alternative, one might try to work with $Z_k'' = Z_{J_k}$, for $k = 1,2,\ldots,n$, instead of removing all doubles. Unfortunately, this has the disadvantage that the $\{Z_k''\}$ are dependent, essentially because two Z_k'' may coincide. This is seen as follows:

Let σ^2 be the variance in the distribution $\{\pi(k)\}$, and assume that $\alpha_N = P\{J_a = J_b\} > 0$ for some selected a and b in $\{1,2,\ldots,n\}$, $a \neq b$. The probability α_N will depend on the population size N. If item selection is by simple random sampling with replacement, then $\alpha_N = 1/N$ for any distinct a and b. Otherwise, α_N may depend on a and b. Now,

$$P\{Z''_a = k, Z''_b = \ell\} = \sum_i \sum_{j \neq i} P\{J_a = i, J_b = j\} P\{Z_i = k, Z_j = \ell \mid J_a = i, J_b = j\}$$

$$+ \sum_i P\{J_a = J_b = i\} P\{Z_i = k, Z_i = \ell \mid J_a = J_b = i\}$$

$$= (1-\alpha_N)\pi(k)\pi(\ell) + \alpha_N \delta_{k\ell}\pi(k),$$

which means that $P\{Z''_a = k, Z''_b = \ell\}$ differs from $P\{Z''_a = k\}P\{Z''_b = \ell\}$ by the amount

$$\alpha_N \pi(k)\{\delta_{k\ell} - \pi(\ell)\}. \tag{6.1}$$

Except when $\pi(k) = 0$ or $\pi(\ell) = \delta_{k\ell}$, this discrepancy is non-zero. As $N \to \infty$, α_N is likely to converge to 0, as it will in common sampling plans, in which case this discrepancy disappears as well in the limit. But if $N \to \infty$, there is little practical difference between corresponding sampling schemes with and without replacement.

Multiplying (6.1) by $k\ell$ and adding over both k and ℓ, we get

$$\operatorname{cov}\left\{Z''_a, Z''_b\right\} = \sigma^2 \alpha_N, \tag{6.2}$$

in clear demonstration of the dependence (positive correlation) between the two random variables.

The reasoning in this section exploits some simple ideas from the superpopulation approach in the theory of survey sampling (see, e.g., Cassel *et al.*, 1977). In the following straightforward generalization of superpopulation ideas, some more mathematical finery is needed than above.

Assume that the target population consists of N probabilistically identical independent individuals, numbered from 1 to N. With reference to some stochastic process model, in our case a Markov chain model, individual No. i has a life history (sample path) Y_i that contains everything there is to know (with respect to the model) about this individual. A sampling plan is a specification of a random mechanism that selects a sample $\underline{\underline{S}} = (I_1,\ldots,I_{n(\underline{\underline{S}})})$ of distinct numbers from $\{1,2,\ldots,N\}$, and we define

$$p(\underline{\underline{s}}|\underline{\underline{y}}) = P\{\underline{\underline{S}} = \underline{\underline{s}}|\underline{\underline{Y}} = \underline{\underline{y}}\},$$

where $\underline{\underline{s}} = (i_1,\ldots,i_{n(\underline{\underline{s}})})$. We call the sampling plan *noninformative* if this function is independent of $\underline{\underline{y}}$. This means that $\underline{\underline{S}}$ and $\underline{\underline{Y}}$ are stochastically independent for a noninformative sampling plan. Assume for the moment that all of Y_i is obtained if individual No. i is sampled, and define $Y_j' = Y_{I_j}$. The data are the set $\underline{\underline{D}} = \{(I_j,Y_j'):j = 1,2,\ldots,n(\underline{\underline{S}})\}$. As our notation indicates, we permit the effective sample size to depend on $\underline{\underline{S}}$.

The probabilistic mechanism that governs $\underline{\underline{Y}}$ is determined by the assumption that $Y_1,Y_2,\ldots,Y_N$ are independent sample paths from the stochastic process in question, whose probability measure we now call $\xi(\cdot)$ in analogy with standard sampling theory notation. We assume that $\xi(\cdot)$ has a Radon-Nikodym derivative $\xi'(\cdot)$ with respect to some measure α. Then the likelihood of observing $\underset{=}{D} = \underset{=}{d}$ (for which $\underset{=}{S} = \underset{=}{s}$) is

$$\Lambda(\underset{=}{d}) = \int_A p(\underset{=}{s}\,|\,\underset{\sim}{y}^0) \prod_{j=1}^{N} \xi'(y_j^0)\,d\alpha^{*N}(\underset{\sim}{y}^0),$$

where the asterisk denotes a product measure. Here $A = \{\underset{\sim}{y}^0 : y_i^0 = y_i \text{ for all } i \in \underset{=}{s}\}$. If p is noninformative (and this is where we use that assumption), this becomes

$$\Lambda(\underset{=}{d}) = p(\underset{=}{s}) \prod_{i\in\underset{=}{s}} \xi'(y_i).$$

In the same manner as in the elementary example above, this means that we may treat the observed life histories $Y_1', \ldots, Y_{n(\underset{=}{s})}'$ as if they were $n(\underset{=}{s})$ independent observations coming from $\xi(\cdot)$.

Frequently, however, one does not obtain all the information potentially available about each sample path. The *individual level observational plan* acts as a filter, and "only" the possibly fragmentary information $Z_i = h_i(Y_1, \ldots, Y_N)$ is available for analysis.[24] Usually, Z_i depends mainly on Y_i. However, there may be *some* dependence on the other Y_j as well, perhaps because decisions concerning the extension or discontinuation of observation of an individual may be dynamic and may depend on the outcome observed for the whole population up to any moment. For instance, observation may be kept going until the time when the total exposure to risk (or the total num-

[24] *At this point, we find it useful to partition questions concerning the entire observational plan (Section 1.3) into those of the sampling plan and those of the individual level observational plan. The latter specifies what is observed from the individual sample path. The usefulness of this distinction is directly apparent and becomes even more evident at the end of this section (Section 6.1).*

ber of realizations of the risk event) reaches a predescribed level. For this reason, all Y_j appear as arguments in h_i. In addition the amount of information may vary between life histories, possibly because somewhat different seniority segments are observed.

Let us say that *the observation of life histories is independent across individuals* if and only if Z_i depends on Y_i alone, and not on any Y_j for $j \neq i$. In this case, we write $Z_i = h_i(Y_i)$.

Recall that if z is a possible value of Z_i, then in general, $h_i^{-1}(z) = \{\underline{y}: h_i(\underline{y}) = z\}$, and if B is a measurable event for Z_i, then $\xi h_i^{-1}(B) = \xi\{h_i^{-1}(B)\} = \xi\{\underline{\underline{Y}}: h_i(\underline{\underline{Y}}) \in B\}$, where ξ is now used for the *joint* distribution of $\underline{\underline{Y}} = (Y_1, \ldots, Y_N)$. Thus, Z_i has the distribution $\xi h_i^{-1}(\cdot)$.

Now the data are $\underline{\underline{D}} = \{(I_j, Z_j'): j = 1, 2, \ldots, n(\underline{\underline{S}})\}$, and the likelihood of getting $\underline{\underline{D}} = \underline{\underline{d}}$ for a noninformative sampling plan $p(\cdot)$ is

$$\Lambda(\underline{\underline{d}}) = p(\underline{\underline{s}}) \int_{A'} \prod_{j=1}^{N} \xi'(y_j^0)\, d\alpha^{*N}(\underline{y}^0),$$

where $A' = \{\underline{y}^0: h_i(\underline{y}^0) = z_i \text{ for all } i \in \underline{\underline{s}}\}$. If we assume that observation is independent across individuals at this point, then this expression reduces to

$$\Lambda(\underline{\underline{d}}) = p(\underline{\underline{s}}) \prod_{i \in \underline{\underline{s}}} (\xi h_i^{-1})'(z_i),$$

and we conclude that $Z_1', Z_2', \ldots, Z_{n(\underline{\underline{s}})}'$ may be regarded as independent observations of transformed variables, where Z_j' has the distribution it would have had if a total survey had been carried out instead of the sampling survey. Note that the essential part of this argument and result is the noninvolvement of the nonsampled $\{Y_i: i \notin \underline{s}\}$ in the likelihood $\Lambda(\underline{d})$. There is an evident extension to a situation where dependence of observation across individuals *in the sample* is permitted, as long as independence of observation is retained between individuals in the sample and individuals outside. This should cover most practical cases.

In this argument, we have disregarded sampling problems connected with entries and exits of individuals in open populations. Similarly, nonsampling errors have either been disregarded, or have implicitly been included in the sampling plan if they are noninformative, i.e., not connected to the individual life histories. Since nonsampling errors patently may be informative in this sense, their inclusion in the sampling plan may cause it to be informative, which may introduce an element of unrealism into the account above. Singer and Cohen (1980, Section 7.1) discuss misclassification errors in the labor-force status model. Williams and Mallows (1970) study more elaborate models of errors in the determination of transition probabilities due to differential nonresponse in two-wave, two-state panel surveys. An early reference is Coleman (1964b)

The above argument also assumes that the information on the $\{Z_i\}$ is collected equally accurately and equally completely[25] in a total enumeration and in a sample survey. Since organizational problems of the two situations may be quite different, it is possible that we are taking some liberties with reality at this point as well.

[25] *The assumption of equal accuracy refers to the data quality on the individual level. The assumption of equal completeness refers to coverage errors on the population level.*

Unfortunately, current theory does not account fully for the last two items above, as far as we know. On the other hand, our distinction between the sampling plan and the individual level observational plan enables us to handle with ease a couple of features that might otherwise be problematic.

First, note that the observational plan may result in a Z_i which is empty of information, and that this is permitted. For instance, no information was obtained on cohabitation for unmarried women who reported that they were not cohabitating on the date of the interview in the data analyzed by Finnäs and Hoem (1980).

Second, the observational plan may result in purged data, in the manner described in Section 5.2. Since you cannot of course sample from among the paths that have been purged away, at first glance the sampling plan may seem to be informative in this situation. This could be a serious defect, for it would cause problems for the analysis of data from retrospective interviews, since individuals who have died or have moved out of the population before the interview date, have been purged away. The theory is "saved," however, by defining the target population to be the set of purged life histories remaining in the total population, in which case the sampling plan can be noninformative.

Note how important it is for the analysis that the sampling plan has this property. This rules out any kind of oversampling of life histories with special outcomes, such as particularly frequent migrants or mothers with many children, *unless* this corresponds to the definition of the target population.

Also note that we take it for granted that the individual life histories fruitfully can be regarded as independent sample paths of some stochastic process. Since there are always finitely many individuals in any human population, there will then be some amount of random error in any usual statistical procedure. As we demonstrate in Section 6.2, some identifiable part of the random error may be due to the sampling procedure,[26] but another part is caused by the fundamental randomness of the individual sample paths. Occasionally,[27] one comes across the (explicit or implicit) opposite view that in demography, (interesting) stochastic variation can only arise from sampling variation, i.e., in survey data. Otherwise, demographers are said to encounter empirical intensity plots only for populations large enough to permit the investigator to disregard randomness, and any irregularities in the plotted curves are explained as (i) either local variations of substantive interest, or (ii) caused mainly by registration errors.

We accept that stochastic elements may be unimportant in intensity plots for large N, and act on that conviction when this is suitable. (Compare Hoem *et al.*, 1981.) Otherwise, we feel that the position mentioned disregards the usefulness of increment-decrement life table methods for small populations and for small segments of national populations, in which random variation can be prominent.[28] Typically, the random fluctuations in the curves of Hoem and Fong (1976), based on a *nonran-*

[26] *Compare (6.6) and footnote 29.*

[27] *We have not sought out offending literature references for documentation, but we have met with the opinions stated often enough on the grapevine, in discussions, and in referee reports, to name a few informal sources.*

[28] *An illustrative example of the role of random variation in fertility curves for small segments of national populations can be obtained from the authors on request. In our experience, such examples are abundant.*

dom population segment, are of the same size order as the corresponding fluctuations in the curves of Schoen and Woodrow (1980) and Brouard (1980, 1981), all of which were based on data from random samples. In this connection, it is the number of contributing individuals that is important, not whether the data come from a sample survey or not.

6.2. *POPULATION HETEROGENEITY*

Most of the theory of multistate life table models has been formulated for probabilistically homogeneous populations, and the account above is no exception. Formally, this disregards the important question of population heterogeneity, although this aspect can be accounted for to some extent by grouping the population on known background factors and applying the theory of homogeneous populations to each subpopulation. To avoid the biasing effects of purging and of conditioning on interacting simultaneous processes on the individual level, described in Sections 5.2 and 5.3, the values of the grouping variables should be constant by definition for the individual over the target period. With this limitation, the grouping variables may be extraneous to the model (parental background, own sex, and so on), or they may be features of the life history prior to the target period, or to the life segment currently investigated. In the terminology of Section 5.2, grouping according to behavior in L is permitted in an analysis of subsequent behavior in D, but grouping according to eventual entry or nonentry into D is ruled out in an investigation of behavior in L. The idea is to exploit the manner in which population heterogeneity manifests itself in individual behavior.

Some recent investigations using various grouping criteria have been made by Rodriguez and Hobcraft (1980), Hobcraft and Rodriguez (1980, section on demographic controls), and Finnäs and Hoem (1980).

As a complement or alternative to grouping, population heterogeneity may be (partially) accounted for by one kind of regression analysis or another, where the intensities or their logarithms are regressed with respect to a set of explanatory variables whose values are known on the individual level. Some references are Coleman (1964a, 1981), Spilerman (1972), Cox (1972), Singer and Spilerman (1974, Section 3.2), Kalbfleisch and Prentice (1979), and Wyman (1981).

Since the effect of population heterogeneity may be manifest even when grouping possibilities have been exhausted and information on concomitant variables is unavailable, many authors have introduced an unobservable parameter on the individual level, say θ_i for individual No. i, and have posited that the probabilistic properties of the individual depend on the value of θ_i. In line with ideas going back to the introduction of the concept of accident proneness (Greenwood and Yule, 1920), $\theta_1, \theta_2, \ldots, \theta_N$ are seen as independent realizations of a random variable, say Θ, with some probability distribution which we shall denote $\eta(\cdot)$, and which actuaries would call the *structure function* because it describes the structure of the population. This notion is used in many contexts (accident analysis, industrial quality control, actuarial credibility theory, and others), and it appears often in demography and in related fields. It is the basis of the mover-stayer model (Blumen *et al.*, 1955) and its extensions (Spilerman, 1972a; Singer and Spilerman, 1974, Section 3.1; 1979), it pervades the book on models of conception and birth by Sheps and Menken (1973), and it has been used for other purposes in demography by Ginsberg (1973), Hoem (1976b), Vaupel *et al.* (1979), Hobcraft and Rodriguez (1980, p. 34), Singer and Cohen (1980, Section 7.2), and Manton and Stallard (1981). In an exciting paper, Heckman and Singer (1982) have just pointed out a new avenue of research in this tradition. Sometimes, θ is modeled as taking only a finite number of values (Singer and Spilerman, 1974, pp. 31-35; Keyfitz and Littman, 1979; Kitsul and Philipov, 1982), as in the original mover-stayer model, but it is more often depicted as absolutely continuous. Given θ_i, the behavior of the i-th individual, represented now by a probability measure $\xi(\cdot|\theta_i)$, is a particular version of a model of the kind studied before. On the individual level, therefore, each life history has the same type of properties as those studied under the assumption of population homogeneity. On the population level, however, things can become quite different because high-risk individuals behave differently from low-risk individuals. In mortality analysis for instance, the changing population composition due to the progressive depletion of high-risk individuals can result in serious biases in standard methods of analysis, as has been described instructively by Vaupel *et al.* (1979). Fortunately, the survey sampling theorem of Section 6.1 continues to hold as stated. Under the conditions given, the sampled life histories can be regarded as representative of the target population, in the same sense as before. The reason is that the sample paths $Y_1, Y_2, \ldots, Y_N$ are i.i.d. with the mixed distribution

$$\xi(\cdot) = \int_{\Omega} \xi(\cdot|\theta)d\eta(\theta), \tag{6.3}$$

where Ω is the range of θ.

In the same manner as the superpopulation model in sample survey theory has a fixed-values counterpart, the individual $\theta_1,\theta_2,\ldots,\theta_N$ can be regarded alternatively as unknown fixed parameters rather than as unobservable realizations of a fictitious random variable. (This may have been the position taken implicitly by McFarland, 1970.) Then the representation (6.3) is unavailable and the survey sampling theorem of Section 6.1 is no longer valid. Instead, one gets a development similar to that of the classical theory of sampling from a finite population. It will still not be true that simple random sampling with replacement is the answer to our problems (neither that alone nor that at all), for the kind of reasons that lead up to (6.1) and (6.2). Some indication of what is involved will be given by reverting to our simple example of the total numbers of children ever born to women in a closed cohort, which appeared early in Section 6.1.

With a fixed parameter value θ_i for individual No. i, let Z_i have the distribution $\{\pi(k|\theta_i)\}$. For simplicity, assume that item selection is by simple random sampling without replacement, and define

$$\bar{\pi}(k) = \sum_{i=1}^{N} \pi(k|\theta_i)/N, \quad \lambda_i = EZ_i, \quad \bar{\lambda} = \sum \lambda_i/N = \sum_k k\bar{\pi}(k),$$

$$\sigma_i^2 = \text{var } Z_i^2, \quad \sigma^2 = \sum \sigma_i^2/N, \quad \text{and} \quad \tau^2 = \sum(\lambda_i - \bar{\lambda})^2/N.$$

If $Z_j' = Z_{I_j}$ as before, then $P\{Z_j' = k\} = \bar{\pi}(k)$. A parameter of central interest is the expected completed parity $\bar{\lambda}$ of the cohort, which is the expectation of Z_j', of the mean realized completed parity $\overline{Z} = \Sigma_{i=1}^{N} Z_i/N$, as well as of the sample mean $\overline{Z}' = \Sigma_{j=1}^{n} Z_j'/n$. The efficiency of the latter is a function of its variance, which is

$$\text{var } \overline{Z}' = \frac{\sigma^2}{n} + \frac{N-n}{N-1}\frac{\tau^2}{n} . \tag{6.4}$$

Relation (6.4) is proved most easily by noting that

$$\text{var } Z_j' = \tau^2 + \sigma^2, \quad \text{cov}(Z_a', Z_b') = -\frac{\tau^2}{N-1}, \quad \text{for } a \neq b, \tag{6.5}$$

developing the variance by the standard formula

$$\text{var } \overline{Z}' = \frac{1}{n^2}\left\{ \sum_{j=1}^{n} \text{var } Z_j' + \sum_i \sum_{j \neq i} \text{cov}(Z_i', Z_j') \right\},$$

and then collecting terms. Note how the second part of (6.5) shows that any two Z_j' are negatively correlated unless all λ_i are equal.

A firmly antisuperpopulationist survey statistician may perhaps prefer to regard the $\{Z_i: i = 1,2,\ldots,N\}$ as fixed and $\overline{Z}'$ as an estimator of $\overline{Z}$. According to this line of thought, the variance on which to focus is

$$\text{var}\{\overline{Z}' | Z_1,\ldots,Z_N\} = \frac{N-n}{N-1}\frac{1}{n}\frac{1}{N}\sum_{i=1}^{N}(Z_i - \overline{Z})^2 .$$

This attitude may have been the one adopted by Potter and Sagi (1962) in a study of the sampling fluctuations of a contraceptive failure rate.

It is instructive to pursue this notion and partition (6.4) into one part due to the sampling procedure and a second part due to the inherent variability of the individual Z_i, in the following standard manner:

$$\text{var } \overline{Z}' = E \text{ var}(\overline{Z}' | Z_1, \ldots, Z_N) + \text{var } E(\overline{Z}' | Z_1, \ldots, Z_N)$$

$$= \frac{N-n}{N-1} \frac{1}{N} \frac{1}{n} E \sum_{i=1}^{N} (Z_i - \overline{Z})^2 + \text{var } \overline{Z},$$

which gives the two parts as

$$\frac{N-n}{n} \left(\frac{\sigma^2}{N} + \frac{\tau^2}{N-1} \right) \text{ and } \frac{\sigma^2}{N}, \tag{6.6}$$

respectively.[29]

More complex sampling plans and more extensive life history information may be discussed by similar methods.

ACKNOWLEDGMENTS

We are grateful to Ulla-Britt Lithell for making the data of the example in Section 4.2 available to us in advance of her own publication of articles (Lithell, 1981a,b) on their analysis, and to Fjalar Finnäs for translating and explaining parts of Manninen's 1969 paper. Remarks by Robert Busby, Ralph

[29] *If all Z_i have the same distribution, or even if they only have the same mean, then $\tau^2 = 0$, and the two parts of var $\overline{Z}'$ are*

$$\sigma^2 (1-n/N)/n \quad \text{and} \quad \sigma^2/N,$$

respectively. As noted at the end of Section 6.1, therefore, this measure of the random error in $\overline{Z}'$ can be partitioned into one part due to the sampling procedure and another part caused by the fundamental randomness of the individual variables. The fact that the partitioning is trivial does not reduce its conceptual value.

Ginsberg, and Henrik Ramlau-Hansen on some technical points were useful. Long discussions with Kenneth C. Land, Jacques Ledent, and Robert Schoen were greatly helpful for our understanding of the demographic literature on increment-decrement tables. We hope that our critique has been purged of verbal misunderstandings, and that the remaining disagreements are real but soluble.

REFERENCES

Aalen, O. O. (1978). Nonparametric inference for a family of counting processes. *Annals of Statistics 6*, 701-726.

Aalen, O. O. and Hoem, J. M. (1978). Random time changes for multivariate counting processes. *Scandinavian Actuarial Journal 1978 (2)*, 81-101.

Aalen, O. O., Borgan, Ø., Keiding, N., and Thormann, J. (1980). Interaction between life history events. Nonparametric analysis for prospective and retrospective data in the presence of censoring. *Scandinavian Journal of Statistics 7 (4)*, 161-171.

Blalock, Hubert M. (1964). "Causal Inferences in Nonexperimental Research." Chapel Hill: University of North Carolina Press.

Blumen, J., Kogan, M., and McCarthy, P. J. (1955). "The Industrial Mobility of Labor as a Probability Process." Cornell Studies of Industrial and Labor Relations, No. 6. Ithaca, New York: Cornell University Press.

Borgan, Ø. (1980). Applications of non-homogeneous Markov chains to medical studies. Nonparametric analysis for prospective and retrospective data. University of Oslo, Institute of Mathematics, *Statistical Research Report* 1980:8.

Borgan, Ø., Liestøl, K., and Ebbesen, P. (1979). Observational plans for the analysis of disease development and cause specific mortality. Copenhagen University, Laboratory of Actuarial Mathematics, Working Paper No. 25.

Brass, W. (1974). Perspectives in population prediction: Illustrated by the statistics of England and Wales (with discussion). *Journal of the Royal Statistical Society, Series A 137(A)*, 532-583.

Brass, W. (1980). Birth history analysis. Methodology Session No. 3, World Fertility Survey Conference, London, July 1980.

Braun, H. I. and Hoem, J. M. (1979). Modelling cohabitational birth intervals in the current Danish population: A progress report. Copenhagen University, Laboratory of Actuarial Mathematics, Working Paper No. 24.

Brouard, N. (1980). Espérance de vie active, reprise d'activité féminine: un modèle. *Revue économique 31 (6)*, 1260-1287.

Brouard, N. (1981). Les tables de vie active déduites de la mobilité par âge. *Population 36 (6)*, 1085-1103.

Cassel, Claes-Magnus, Särndal, C.-E., and Wretman, J. H. (1977). "Foundations of Inference in Survey Sampling." New York: Wiley.

Chiang, Chin Long (1980). "An Introduction to Stochastic Processes and Their Applications." Huntington, New York: Krieger Publishing Co.

Çinlar, Erhan (1975). "Introduction to Stochastic Processes." Englewood Cliffs, New Jersey: Prentice Hall.

Coale, A. and Trussell, J. (1974). Model fertility schedules: Variations in the age structure of childbearing in human populations. *Population Index 40 (2)*, 185-206.

Cohen, J. E. (1972). When does a leaky compartment model appear to have no leaks? *Theoretical Population Biology 3*, 404-405.

Cohen, J. E. and Singer, B. (1979). Malaria in Nigeria: Constrained continuous-time Markov models for discrete-time longitudinal data on human mixed-species infections. *American Mathematical Society: Lectures on Mathematics in Life Sciences 12*, 69-133.

Colding-Jørgensen, H. and Simonsen, W. (1940). "Statistical Appendix." *In* "Graviditet og galdestensdannelse," (J. M. Wollesen), pp. 81-101. Copenhagen: Nyt Nordisk Forlag.

Coleman, James S. (1964a). "Introduction to Mathematical Sociology." New York: The Free Press.

Coleman, James S. (1964b). "Models of Change and Response Uncertainty." Englewood Cliffs: Prentice-Hall.

Coleman, J. S. (1981). Estimating individual-level transition probabilities for multi-state life tables. Paper presented at the College Park Conference.

Cox, D. R. (1972). Regression models and life tables (with discussion). *Journal of the Royal Statistical Society, Series B, 34*, 187-220.

Diem, Janet Hughes (1976). Estimation in a non-stationary Markov chain. Unpublished Ph.D. dissertation. Tulane University.

Du Pasquier, L. G. (1912, 1913). Mathematische Theorie der Invaliditätsversicherung. *Mitteilungen der Vereinigung schweizerischer Versicherungsmathematiker 7*, 1-7; *8*, 1-153.

Ewbank, D., Gomez de Leon, J., and Stoto, M. A. (1981). A reducible four parameter system of model life tables. Paper prepared for the Population Association of America, Annual Meeting, Washington, D.C.

Feller, William (1971). "An Introduction to Probability Theory and Its Applications." Volume 2. New York: Wiley.

Finnäs, F. (1980). A method to estimate demographic intensities via cumulative incidence rates. *Theoretical Population Biology 17 (3)*, 365-379.

Finnäs, F. and Hoem, J. M. (1980). Starting age and subsequent birth intervals in cohabitational unions in current Danish cohorts, 1975. *Demography 17 (3)*, 275-295.

Funck Jensen, U. (1981a). A stochastic projection model with implications for multistate demography and manpower analysis. Copenhagen University, Institute of Mathematical Statistics, Preprint 1981/10.

Funck Jensen, U. (1981b). Markov processes and branching processes in multistate demography (working title). Copenhagen University, Institute of Mathematical Statistics, M.Sc. Thesis, to appear.

Gantmacher, F. R. (1959). "Matrizenrechnung," Teil I und II. Berlin: Veb Deutscher Verlag der Wissenschaften.

Gardiner, J. C. (1982). The asymptotic distribution of mortality rates in competing risks analyses. *Scandinavian Journal of Statistics 9 (1)*, 31-36.

Gill, R. D. (1980). "Censoring and Stochastic Integrals." Amsterdam: Mathematical Centre Tracts 124.

Ginsberg, R. B. (1973). Stochastic models of residential and geographic mobility for heterogeneous populations. *Environment and Planning A 5*, 113-124.

Ginsberg, R. B. (1978). The relationship between timing of moves and choice of destination in stochastic models of migration. *Environment and Planning A 10*, 667-679.

Ginsberg, R. B. (1979). Timing and duration effects in residence histories and other longitudinal data. *Regional Science and Urban Economics 9*, 311-331; 369-392.

Greenwood, M. and Yule, G. U. (1920). An inquiry into the nature of frequency distributions representative of multiple happenings with particular reference to the occurrence of multiple attacks of disease or of repeated accidents. *Journal of the Royal Statistical Society 83*, 255-279.

Grenander, U. (1956). On the theory of mortality measurement. Part 1. *Skandinavisk Aktuarietidskrift 39*, 70-96.

Greville, T. N. E. (1943). Short methods of constructing abridged life tables. *Record of the American Institute of Actuaries 33 (1)*, 29-42.

Greville, T. N. E. (1967). Methodology of the National, Regional and State Life Tables for the United States, 1959-61. U.S. Department of Health, Education and Welfare: Public Health Service Publications No. 1252, 1 (4).

Greville, T. N. E. (1979). Estimation of the rate of mortality in the presence of in- and out-movement. Chicago, Illinois: Society of Actuaries, *ARCH 1979:1*, 41-56.

Haldorsen, T. (1974). Beregning av liggetider på grunnlag av data fra pasienttellingen i 1970. Oslo: Central Bureau of Statistics of Norway, Arbeidsnotat IO 74/10.

Halvorsen, T. (1970). En modell for analyse av inngåelse og oppløsning av ekteskap i en åpen befolkning. Oslo: Central Bureau of Statistics of Norway, Arbeidsnotat IO 70/4.

Hartmann, M. (1980). Infant and childhood mortality. University of Lund, Department of Statistics, Technical Report.

Hartmann, M. (1981). Laws of mortality on the logit scale. University of Lund, Department of Statistics, Technical Report.

Havning, M., Ramlau-Hansen, H., and Thomsen, B. L. (1979). Fornyet analyse af data fra danske beskæftigelsestællinger 1972-74. Copenhagen University, Institute of Mathematical Statistics. Examination Project Report.

Heckman, J. J. (1979). Sample selection bias as a specification error. *Econometrica 47 (1)*, 153-161.

Heckman, J. J. and Singer, B. (1982). Population heterogeneity in demographic models. In this volume.

Henry, Louis (1972). "On the Measurement of Human Fertility: Selected Writings." Amsterdam: Elsevier, for the Population Council.

Hobcraft, J. N. and Rodriguez, G. (1980). Methodological issues in life table analysis of birth histories. Prepared for the IUSSP-WFS-CPS Seminar on the Analysis of Maternity Histories, London, April 1980. To be published by Ordina Editions.

Hoem, J. M. (1969). Purged and partial Markov chains. *Skandinavisk Aktuarietidskrift 52*, 147-155.

Hoem, J. M. (1971). On the interpretation of certain vital rates as averages of underlying forces of transition. *Theoretical Population Biology 2 (4)*, 454-468.

Hoem, J. M. (1975). Fertility and outmigration. Reflections on research approaches in empirical investigations of the association between two demographic phenomena. *In* "Demographic, Economic and Social Interactions," (Åke E. Andersson and Ingvar Holmberg, eds.), pp. 55-83. Cambridge, Massachussetts: Ballinger.

Hoem, J. M. (1976a). The statistical theory of demographic rates: A review of current developments (with discussion). *Scandinavian Journal of Statistics 3,* 169-185.

Hoem, J. M. (1976b). A Markov chain model of working life tables. Report No. 3. The effects of age grouping. Copenhagen University, Laboratory of Actuarial Mathematics, Working Paper No. 7.

Hoem, J. M. (1977). A Markov chain model of working life tables. *Scandinavian Actuarial Journal,* pp. 1-20.

Hoem, J. M. (1978). Demographic incidence rates. *Theoretical Population Biology 14 (3),* 329-337.

Hoem, J. M. (1980). Exposed-to-risk considerations based on the Balducci assumption and other assumptions in the analysis of mortality. Chicago, Illinois: Society of Actuaries, *ARCH 1980:1*, xi, 47-51.

Hoem, J. M. and Aalen, O. O. (1978). Actuarial values of payment streams. *Scandinavian Actuarial Journal,* pp. 38-47.

Hoem, J. M. and Fong, M. S. (1976). A Markov chain model of working life tables. Report No. 1. A new method for the construction of tables of working life. Copenhagen University, Laboratory of Actuarial Mathematics, Working Paper No. 2, with supplementary tables separately issued, and with a Correction Note of 9 August 1978.

Hoem, J. M., Hansen, H. O., Madsen, D., Løvgreen Nielsen, J., Ohlsen, E. M., and Rennermalm, B. (1981). Experiments in modelling recent Danish fertility curves. *Demography 18 (2),* 231-244.

Iosifescu, Marius (1980). "Finite Markov Processes and Their Applications." New York: Wiley.

Johansen, S. (1973). The imbedding problem for finite Markov chains. *In* "Geometric Methods in System Theory" (Mayne and Brockett, eds.), pp. 227-236. Boston: Reidel.

Kalbfleisch, J. D. and Prentice, R. L. (1980). "The Statistical Analysis of Failure Time Data." New York: Wiley.

Keyfitz, N. (1966). A life table that agrees with the data. *Journal of the American Statistical Association 61,* 305-311.

Keyfitz, N. (1970). Finding probabilities from observed rates or How to make a life table. *The American Statistician 24 (1),* 28-33.

Keyfitz, N. and Frauenthal, J. (1975). An improved life table method. *Biometrics 31,* 889-899.

Keyfitz, N. and Littman, G. (1979). Mortality in a heterogeneous population. *Population Studies 33 (2),* 333-342.

Keyfitz, N., Preston, S. H., and Schoen, R. (1972). Inferring probabilities from rates: Extension to multiple decrement. *Skandinavisk Aktuarietidskrift 1972 (1)*, 1-13.

Kitsul, P. and Philipov, O. (1982). High- and low-intensity model of mobility. In this volume.

Land, K. C. and Schoen, R. (1982). Statistical methods for Markov-generated increment-decrement life tables with polynomial gross flow functions. In this volume.

Larsson, T. (1965). Mortality in Sweden. *Supplementum ad Acta Genetica et Statistica Medica, Vol. 15*, 143 pp.

Ledent, J. (1978). Some methodological and empirical considerations in the construction of increment-decrement life tables. Laxenburg, Austria: International Institute for Applied Systems Analysis, Research Memorandum RM-78-25.

Ledent, J. (1980a). Multistate life tables: Movement versus transition perspectives. *Environment and Planning A 12 (5)*, 533-562.

Ledent, J. (1980b). An improved methodology for constructing increment-decrement life tables from the transition perspectives. Laxenburg, Austria: International Institute for Applied Systems Analysis, Working Paper WP-80-104.

Ledent, J. (1982). Transition probability estimation in increment-decrement life tables: Old and new developments from the "transition" perspective. In this volume.

Ledent, J. and Rees, P. (1980). Choices in the construction of multiregional life tables. Laxenburg: International Institute for Applied Systems Analysis, WP-80-173.

Leridon, H. (1980). The analysis of maternity histories when data on intermediate or explicative variables are limited to the situation at the time of the survey. Presented to the IUSSP-WFS-CPS Seminar on the Analysis of Maternity Histories. To be published by Ordina Editions.

Liaw, K.-L. and Ledent, J. (1980). Discrete approximation of a continuous model of multistate demography. Laxenburg: International Institute for Applied Systems Analysis, PP-80-14.

Linnemann, P. U. K. (1981). A band matrix solution to the problem of the tails in moving average graduation. Copenhagen University, Laboratory of Actuarial Mathematics, Working Paper No. 34.

Lithell, U.-B. (1981a). Breast-feeding habits and their relation to infant mortality and marital fertility. *Journal of Family History 1981*, 182-194.

Lithell, U.-B. (1981b). Poverty and marital fertility; A low standard of living as a determinant of a low level of marital fertility and a high infant mortality. Uppsala University, History Department.

McCutcheon, J. J. (1971). Some remarks on the basic mortality functions. *Transactions of the Faculty of Actuaries 32 (5)*, 395-403.

McCutcheon, J. J. (1975). Some problems relating to the construction of life tables. *Transactions of the Faculty of Actuaries 33 (4)*, 350-368.

McCutcheon, J. J. and Nesbitt, C. J. (1973). Further remarks on the basic mortality functions. *Transactions of the Faculty of Actuaries 33 (1)*, 81-91.

McFarland, D. D. (1970). Intragenerational social mobility as a Markov process: Including a time-stationary Markovian model that explains observed declines in mobility rates over time. *American Sociological Review 35 (3)*, 463-476.

McGinnis, R. (1968). A stochastic model of social mobility. *American Sociological Review 33*, 712-722.

Manninen, R. (1979). Suomen väestön kehitysanalyysi neljän alueen järjestelmänä. (An analysis of the Finish population as a system of four regions.) Helsinki University, Geography Department.

Manton, K. G. and Stallard, E. (1981). Heterogeneity and its effect on mortality measurement. To appear in the Proceedings of the Seminar on Methodology and Data Collection in Mortality Studies sponsored by the International Union for the Scientific Study of Population, July 7-10, 1981, Dakar, Senegal.

Miller, R. B. and Hickman, J. C. (1980). A comparison of several life table estimation methods. University of Wisconsin-Madison, Department of Statistics, Technical Report No. 627.

Nelson, W. (1972). Theory and applications of hazard plotting for censored failure data. *Technometrics 14*, 945-966.

O'Brien, K. and Suchindran, C. M. (1980). A method for comparing life tables from complex survey data. Proceedings of the Social Statistics Section of the American Statistical Association.

Oechsli, F. W. (1975). A population model based on a life table that includes marriage and parity. *Theoretical Population Biology 7 (2)*, 229-245.

Oechsli, F. W. (1979). A general method for constructing increment-decrement life tables that agree with the data. *Theoretical Population Biology 16 (1)*, 13-24.

Page, H. J., Ferry, B., Shah, J. H., and Lesthaeghe, R. (1980). The most recent births: Analytical potential and some underlying problems. Prepared for the IUSSP-WFS-CPS Seminar on the Analysis of Maternity Histories, London, April 1980.

Pollard, J. H. (1966). On the use of the direct matrix product in analysing certain stochastic population models. *Biometrika 53 (3-4)*, 397-415.

Pollard, J. H. (1969). Continuous-time and discrete-time models of population growth. *Journal of the Royal Statistical Society, Series A, 132 (1)*, 80-88.

Potter, R. G., Jr., and Sagi, P. C. (1962). Some procedures for estimating the sampling fluctuations of a contraceptive failure rate. *In* "Research in Family Planning" (Clyde V. Kiser, ed.), pp. 389-407. Princeton University Press.

Ramlau-Hansen, H. (1980). The estimation of demographic intensities via cumulative incidence rates. Copenhagen University, Laboratory of Actuarial Mathematics, Working Paper No. 33.

Ramlau-Hansen, H. (1981). Udglatning med kernefunktioner i forbindelse med tælleprocesser. Copenhagen University, Laboratory of Actuarial Mathematics, Working Paper No. 41.

Rindfuss, R. R., Bumpass, L., and St. John, C. (1980). Education and fertility: Implications for the roles women occupy. *American Sociological Review 45*, 431-447.

Rodriguez, G. and Hobcraft, J. N. (1980). Illustrative analysis: Life table analysis of birth intervals in Columbia. World Fertility Survey, Scientific Report No. 16.

Rogers, Andrei (1973). The mathematics of multiregional demographic growth. *Environment and Planning A5*, 3-9.

Rogers, Andrei (1975). "Introduction to Multiregional Mathematical Demography." New York: Wiley.

Rogers, Andrei (ed.) (1980). Essays in multistate mathematical demography. *Environment and Planning A 12 (5)*, 485-622.

Rogers, A. and Castro, L. J. (1982). Model schedules in multistate demographic analysis: The case of migration. In this volume.

Rogers, A. and Ledent, J. (1976). Increment-decrement life tables: A comment. *Demography 13 (2)*, 287-290.

Schoen, R. (1979). Calculating increment-decrement life tables by estimating mean durations at transfer from observed rates. *Mathematical Biosciences 47*, 255-269.

Schoen, R. and Land, K. C. (1979). A general algorithm for estimating a Markov-generated increment-decrement life table with applications to marital-status patterns. *Journal of the American Statistical Association 74*, 761-776.

Schoen, R. and Woodrow, K. (1980). Labor force status life tables for the United States, 1972. *Demography 17 (3)*, 297-322.

Schou, G. and Væth, M. (1980). A small sample study of occurrence/exposure rates for rare events. *Scandinavian Actuarial Journal 1980 (4)*, 209-225.

Schweder, T. (1970). Composable Markov processes. *Journal of Applied Probability 7*, 400-410.

Seal, H. L. (1981). Graduation by piecewise cubic polynomials. A historical review. *Blätter, Deutsche Gesellschaft für Versicherungsmathematik 15 (1)*, 89-114.

Sheps, Mindel C. and Menken, J. A. (1973). "Mathematical Models of Conception and Birth." Chicago: University of Chicago Press.

Shieh, L. S., Yates, R., and Navarro, J. (1978). Representation of continuous-time state equations by discrete-time state equations. *Proceedings of the Institute of Electrical and Electronic Engineers 8 (6)*, 485-492.

Shryock, Henry S., Siegel, Jacob S. and Associates (1971). "The Methods and Materials of Demography." Washington, D.C.: U.S. Government Printing Office.

Singer, B. (1981). Estimation of nonstationary Markov chains from panel data. *In* "Sociological Methodology 1981," (S. Leinhardt, ed.). San Francisco: Jossey Bass.

Singer, B. and Cohen, J. E. (1980). Estimating malaria incidence and recovery rates from panel surveys. *Mathematical Biosciences 49*, 273-305.

Singer, B. and Spilerman, S. (1974). Social mobility models for heterogeneous populations. *In* "Sociological Methodology 1973-1974," (Herbert L. Costner, ed.), pp. 356-401. San Francisco: Jossey Bass.

Singer, B. and Spilerman, S. (1976a). The representation of social processes by Markov models. *American Journal of Sociology 82 (1)*, 1-54.

Singer, B. and Spilerman, S. (1976b). Some methodological issues in the analysis of longitudinal surveys. *Annals of Economic and Social Measurement 5 (4)*, 447-474.

Singer, B. and Spilerman, S. (1977). Fitting stochastic models to longitudinal survey data: Some examples in the social sciences. *Bulletin of the International Statistical Institute 47 (3)*, 283-300.

Singer, B. and Spilerman, S. (1979). Clustering on the main diagonal in mobility matrices. *In* "Sociological Methodology, 1979," (K. Schuessler, ed.), pp. 172-208. San Francisco: Jossey-Bass.

Smith, S. J. (1977). Liability cases: The use of working life tables in court. Presented to the Population Association of America, Annual Meeting, St. Louis, Mo.

Smith, S. J. (1980). Tables of working life for the United States, 1977: Substantive and methodological implications. Presented to the Population Association of America, Annual Meeting, Denver, Col.

Sparre Andersen, E. (1951). The influence on the observed death rate of measuring the exposure by a sample. *Transactions of the 13th International Congress of Actuaries, Vol. 1*, 593-606.

Spilerman, S. (1972a). Extensions of the mover-stayer model. *American Journal of Sociology 78 (3)*, 599-626.

Spilerman, S. (1972b). The analysis of mobility processes by the introduction of independent variables into a Markov chain. *American Sociological Review 37*, 277-294.

Taeuber, Karl E., Chiazze, L., Jr., and Haenszel, W. (1968). Migration in the United States. Washington, D.C.: U.S. Government Printing Office.

Tuma, N. B. (1979). When can interdependence in a dynamic system on qualitative variables be ignored? *In* "Sociological Methodology 1981," (Karl F. Schuessler, ed.), pp. 358-391. San Francisco: Jossey-Bass.

Tuma, N. B. and Hannan, M. T. (1978). Approaches to the censoring problem in analysis of event histories. *In* "Sociological Methodology 1979," (Karl F. Schuessler, ed.). San Francisco: Jossey-Bass.

Trussell, J. and Menken, J. (1978). Early childbearing and subsequent fertility. *Family Planning Perspectives 10 (4)*, 209-218.

Vaupel, J. W., Manton, K. G., and Stallard, E. (1979). The impact of heterogeneity in individual frailty on the dynamics of mortality. *Demography 16 (3)*, 439-454.

Willekens, F. J. (1980). Multistate analysis: Tables of working life. *Environment and Planning A12 (5)*, 563-588.

Williams, W. H. and Mallows, C. L. (1970). Systematic biases in panel surveys due to differential nonresponse. *Journal of the American Statistical Association 65*, 1338-1349.

Wyman, K. E. (1981). Application of Cox model and other life table techniques to the study of work-fertility relationship. Paper presented to the Annual Meeting of the Population Association of America, Washington, D.C.

Zahl, S. (1955). A Markov process model for follow-up studies. *Human Biology 27,* 90-120.

5

Statistical Methods for Markov-Generated Increment–Decrement Life Tables with Polynomial Gross Flow Functions

Kenneth C. Land and Robert Schoen

1. INTRODUCTION

Perhaps the most characteristic art form of multidimensional mathematical demography is the *increment-decrement life table* (IDLT). IDLTs superimpose a set of mutually exclusive life statuses (e.g., "currently married" and "not currently married" in a nuptiality table, or "currently in the labor force" and "not currently in the labor force" in a labor-force status table) on the natality (birth)--alive at age x--mortality (death) continuum of the classic single-decrement life table model of demography, thus combining the age dimension with a status dimension. Furthermore, IDLTs allow entrants (increments) to, as well as exits (decrements) from, various life statuses. If the increments are defined by advances of members of the life table population through successive statuses

ISBN 0-12-435640-0

with no reentry allowed, then the IDLT is *hierarchical*; if the increments are composed of both entrants and reentrants, then the IDLT is *nonhierarchical*.

During the past decade and a half, there has been considerable research interest in the analysis, estimation, and substantive application of IDLTs. This has led, for example, to a precise characterization of the Markov model underlying ordinary IDLTs (for statements, see Hoem, 1976, pp. 170-171; Schoen and Land, 1979, pp. 763-764; Ledent, 1980c, pp. 535-540). It has also produced some advances in methods for, and clarification of issues in, the estimation of IDLTs.

The clearest instance of such methodological advances--and the baseline case against which other model specifications and methods of estimation must be judged--pertains to the *classic Markov chain IDLT model* of Du Pasquier (1912, 1913), Fix and Neyman (1951), and Sverdrup (1965). This model specifies *piecewise-constant transition forces* or, equivalently, *piecewise-exponential survival (survivorship) functions* and will be referred to subsequently in this paper by either expression. In the context of estimators that use *occurrence/exposure rates* as input data, statistical methods of estimation, hypothesis testing, and graduation for this model have been developed, summarized, and applied to real data by Sverdrup (1965), Hoem (1970, 1972b, 1976), Krishnamoorthy (1979), and Hoem and Jensen (1981). For data in the form of *gross flow rates (survivorship proportions)*, statistical methods for estimating IDLTs for this model specification have also been developed and applied by Hoem and Fong (1976) and Hoem and Jensen (1981).[1]

Given the mathematical elegance of this classic model and given the existence of statistical methods for applying the models to the two main forms of data with which mathematical demographers must deal, it might appear that there is no need for the development of alternative model specifications and estimation methods. Unfortunately, the classic model embodies an assumption about the "local behavior" of forces of transition between states of the model--that they are piecewise-constant within the smallest time (age) intervals used in the estimation process--that is tenable for most demographic processes only if the estimation-age-intervals are of length one year or less. For instance, it is well recognized that the force of mortality increases continuously over most adult ages. Similarly, the assumption that forces of marriage, divorce, interregional migration, labor-force accession and separation, etc., are constant for any extended age interval can be regarded as only a first approximation. The consequence is that the classic model and its statistical methods are most appropriate for the construction of an *unabridged* IDLT (i.e., an IDLT in which single years of age define the estimation-age-

[1]*In mathematical sociology, Coleman (1964a,b, 1968, 1970, 1973, 1981) has developed an approach to panel analysis built around the constant-forces, continuous-time, discrete-state Markov chain model; see also Singer and Spilerman (1974, 1976a,b), Cohen and Singer (1979), and Singer and Cohen (1980). Thus, although the relationship seems not to have been greatly exploited, there are similarities between the piecewise methods developed by mathematical demographers to estimate this classic model from survivorship proportions and the methods of panel analysis in mathematical sociology.*

intervals). By contrast, this model and its methods may produce less accurate estimates of transition probabilities, survivorship functions, etc., in the context of *abridged* IDLTs in which estimation-age-intervals are (say) 5 years long.

But the fact is that much demographic data from which IDLTs are constructed are indexed by 5-yr, rather than 1-yr, age intervals. Furthermore, rather than estimate a large unabridged IDLT, demographers often want to produce a short abridged, but nonetheless, accurate, table. This motivation is similar to that behind the efforts of Reed and Merrell (1939), Greville (1943), Keyfitz and Frauenthal (1975), Schoen (1978), and others to develop methods for constructing accurate, abridged, single-decrement life tables. In the IDLT context, the result similarly has been the development of several alternatives to the classic model and methods (Rogers, 1973, 1975; Schoen and Nelson, 1974; Schoen, 1975, 1976, 1977a, 1979; Rogers and Ledent, 1976; Rees and Wilson, 1977; Schoen and Land, 1979; Schoen and Woodrow, 1980; Ledent, 1980a; Willekens, 1980).

While the latter models and methods have increased the applicability of IDLTs, they exhibit one or more of the following three *deficiencies*. *First,* those alternative methods that are expressible in explicit algebraic form are extremely limited in the types of "local behavior" allowed in the transition force functions. For instance, we shall show in Section 3.4 that the "linear survival function" assumption used in most of these methods requires, for mathematical consistency, the specification of strictly increasing transition force functions within estimation-age-intervals. But, for forces of transition other than mortality, this specification may be no more appropriate than the piecewise-constant forces specification.[2] *Second,* some of the alternative methods contradict the analytic relationships that exist, by definition, among the basic life table functions. In brief, the essence of a life table model is that instantaneous transition force functions appear as derivatives of natural logarithms of survivorship functions and that person-years functions appear as definite integrals of the survivorship functions. Although the practice of combining mathematically inconsistent specifications of life table functions has a long tradition in single-decrement mathematical demography (see, e.g., Keyfitz, 1977, p. 14), and although such a practice may be justifiable on empirical grounds of goodness of fit to observed rates, it is not consistent or aesthetically pleasing from a mathematical point of view. *Third,* none of the alternative methods for estimating IDLTs has been associated with a fully developed statistical theory of estimation and hypothesis testing. Indeed, the alternatives to the classic model and methods implicitly rest

[2]*Two other methods of estimation deserve brief mention here. First, although the cubic-person-years-function specification of the Schoen-Land (1979) general algorithm is capable of incorporating increasing, decreasing, or constant transition force functions (within age intervals), it requires a recursion solution that cannot be expressed in an explicit algebraic formula. Second, the estimator of Schoen (1979) similarly permits flexibility in the underlying force functions and provides explicit algebraic expressions for the survivorship and person-years functions. However, it does not lead to a unique specification of those forces. In the absence of explicit, unique algebraic expressions for estimators, it is difficult, if not impossible, to satisfy the third desirable property stated in the text, namely, to develop an associated statistical theory of estimation and hypothesis testing.*

on the assumptions that the IDLT model is validly specified and that completely accurate population-level data are available. It follows that the IDLT may best be estimated by fitting it piecewise to all of the available age-specific data. In other words, a model parameter is estimated for each observed rate. Therefore, there are no degrees of freedom left over for hypothesis testing. These characteristics of the methods often are reflected in the use of the expression "calculate an IDLT" rather than "estimate an IDLT" by their authors.

Again, this is a tradition with long roots in actuarial science and mathematical demography (cf., Keyfitz, 1977, p. 24). While it guarantees that an IDLT will reproduce the observed data exactly and remain faithful to whatever local irregularities appear in the data, it carries the cost of separating life table theory and methods from statistical theory and methods. Furthermore, it rests on the dubious assumptions that the rates used by demographers to estimate life tables are error-free and that the observed realization of the underlying transition forces is not subject to stochastic variability (cf., Chiang, 1961, p. 275). Finally, by facilitating a possibly spurious exact fit to the observed rates, it promotes an atheoretical *semiparametric* (Hoem, 1976, p. 171) view of the life table model that fails to exploit the model's full potential.[3] For future reference, and without meaning to be pejorative, we shall refer to this as the *demographic* approach

[3]By "semiparametric," Hoem (1976, p. 171) means an approach to the estimation of life tables in which the definitional relationships among the life table functions are acknowledged but no functional forms are explicitly specified and estimated.

to IDLT estimation as contrasted to the *statistical* approach in which statistical concepts are brought to bear on problems of estimation, hypothesis testing, and graduation.

To summarize: Existing methods of estimating IDLTs exhibit one or more of the following deficiencies: (1) they are *either* capable of incorporating transition forces that increase, remain constant, or decrease within estimation-age-intervals *or* are capable of being put in explicit algebraic form, but do not have both desirable features; (2) they are not faithful to the analytic relationships that exist among the transition force, survival, and person-years functions of the life table; or (3) they lack a fully developed statistical theory of estimation and hypothesis testing.

The purpose of this paper is to develop a general class of models and associated statistical methods for *abridged* IDLTs that is not subject to these flaws.[4] To begin with, we specify, in Section 2, a family of polynomial gross flow functions for Markov-generated IDLTs. The corresponding families of rational polynomial transition force functions are capable of local behavior that is increasing, decreasing, or constant within estimation-age intervals. Furthermore, as the estima-

[4] *It is useful to distinguish two forms of statistical estimation in life tables. The first, and by far the most common, is age-specific estimation of the transition probabilities (or gross flow functions), survival functions, transition force functions, and expected sojourn times. The second is analytic graduation of the force functions across age intervals. Because of space limitations, only the first type of estimation is addressed in the present paper. To complement this material on estimation, we also include some material on assessing sampling variability in the rates in Section 3.5, and we suggest, at the end of Section 3.4, how existing methods of hypothesis testing on the force functions may be adapted to the models developed herein.*

tion-age-intervals decrease in size, our class of models converges to the classic piecewise-constant forces model. Thus, if our models are used to estimate an *unabridged* IDLT, the numerical results will be very similar to those obtained with the classic model.

For purposes of estimation, we concentrate on the quadratic gross flow functions form of our class of models. By building on our earlier general algorithm for estimating Markov-generated IDLTs (Schoen and Land, 1979), we derive, in Section 3, age-specific estimators for this model when the data are occurrence/exposure rates. Section 4 reports our application of these age-specific methods to occurrence-exposure rate data on nuptiality from the 1930-1934 birth cohort of Swedish females. In addition, Section 4 compares the empirical performance of the quadratic model developed herein with the traditional exponential and linear survival function models applied to the same data in Schoen and Land (1979). Modifications of the methods necessary to estimate the quadratic model when the data are survivorship proportions are discussed in Section 5. Section 6 contains some concluding comments on what to do when model assumptions are violated and on alternative approaches to estimation.

This is our program. What remains to be done is to exhibit the details and show that the proposed methods perform well empirically. To help the reader follow our combined probabilistic/actuarial notation, the principal symbols used are described in Table 1.

TABLE 1. Summary of Principal Symbols Used

Symbol	Interpretation	Defined by equation(s)	Boundaries
${}_nA_x^{ab}$	For any function A: 1. Right superscript a represents the state of origin or the state in which the function resides 2. Right superscript b represents the state of destination 3. Right subscript x represents the age involved, or the age at the beginning of the interval 4. Left subscript n represents the width of the age interval	(2.2), (2.3), (3.1), etc.	--
${}_na_x^{ij}$	The mean duration into the interval $[x, x+n)$ at transfer from state i to state j	(3.15), (3.16)	≥ 0; $\leq n$
${}_nD_x^{jh}$	The number of transfers in the observed population from state j to state h between the ages of x and x+n	(3.3)	≥ 0
${}_nd_x^{jh}$	The number of transfers from state j to state h between the ages of x and x+n	(2.9)	≥ 0
${}_nd_{[x]}^{ijh}$	The number of transfers from state j to state h between the ages of x and x+n by members of the closed group of persons who were in state i at age x	(2.10)	≥ 0

Table 1 (Cont'd)

Symbol	Interpretation	Defined by equation(s)	Boundaries
${}_n g_x^{ij}$, ${}_n h_x^{ij}$	*Weighted occurrence/exposure rates used in the quadratic gross flows approach to IDLT construction*	(3.17)	≥ 0
${}_n K_x^{j}$	*The average number of persons in the observed population in state j between the ages of x and x+n*	(3.3)	≥ 0
${}_n K_{x+n}^{ij}(t)$	*The number of persons in the observed population in state j between the ages of x+n and x+2n at historical time t who were in state i exactly n years earlier*	(5.2)	≥ 0
${}_n L_x^{j}$	*The number of person-years lived (in one year) in state j between the ages of x and x+n*	(2.22)	≥ 0
${}_n L_{[x]}^{ij}$	*The number of person-years lived in state j between the ages of x and x+n by members of the closed group of persons who were in state i at age x*	(2.21)	≥ 0
${}_n L_{x+n}^{ij\#}$	*The number of persons in the life table population in state j between the ages of x+n and x+2n who were in state i exactly n years earlier*	(5.1)	≥ 0
ℓ_x^{i}	*The number of persons in state i at exact age x*	(2.6)	≥ 0
ℓ_x^{jh}	*The number of transfers from state j to state h at or above age x*	(2.12)	≥ 0

Table 1 (Cont'd)

Symbol	Interpretation	Defined by equation(s)	Boundaries
$\ell^{ij}_{[x]+n}$	The number of persons in the closed group of those in state i at exact age x who were in state j at exact age x+n	(2.7)	≥ 0
$\ell^{ijh}_{[x]+n}$	The number of transfers from state j to state h at or above exact age x+n by members of the closed group of persons who were in state i at age x	(2.11)	≥ 0
${}_nM^{jh}_x$	The observed occurrence/exposure rate for transfers from state j to state h between the ages of x and x+n	(3.3)	≥ 0
${}_nm^{jh}_x$	The life-table occurrence/exposure rate for transfers from state j to state h between the ages of x and x+n	(3.2)	≥ 0
${}_nm^{ijh}_{[x]}$	The life-table occurrence/exposure rate for transfers from state j to state h between the ages of x and x+n by those in state i at age x	(3.1)	≥ 0
${}_nR^{ij}_x(t)$	The observed survivorship ratio, or the number of persons in state j between the ages of x+n and x+2n at historical time t divided by the total number of persons alive at historical time t who were in state i n years earlier	(5.3)	$\geq 0; \leq 1$

Table 1 (Cont'd)

Symbol	*Interpretation*	*Defined by equation(s)*	*Boundaries*
${}_nS_x^{ij}(t)$	*The observed survivorship proportion for persons in a real population (or sample thereof) who are located in state j between ages x+n and x+2n at historical time t and who were located in state i between ages x and x+n at a point in time n years earlier*	*(5.2)*	$\geq 0; \leq 1$
${}_ns_x^{ij}$	*The life-table survivorship proportion for individuals, or the fraction of those present in state i between ages x and x+n at a given time who are in state j at a moment exactly n years later*	*(5.1)*	$\geq 0; \leq 1$
μ_x^{ij}	*The force of transition from state i to state j at exact age x*	*(2.3)*	≥ 0
${}_n\pi_x^{ij}$	*The probability that a person in state i at age x will be in state j at age x+n*	*(2.2), (2.8)*	$\geq 0; \leq 1$

2. MODEL SPECIFICATION

2.1. *MARKOV-GENERATED INCREMENT-DECREMENT LIFE TABLES*

In order to keep the derivations as simple as possible, we adopt, as a specification of the stochastic process corresponding to the IDLTs to be estimated herein, the Markov assumptions that have become conventional in multidimensional mathematical demography (cf., Hoem, 1976, p. 170; Schoen and

Land, 1979, pp. 763-764; Ledent, 1980c, pp. 535-540). It is well known that the Markov specification must be dealt with sensitively and/or modified in order to model some empirical processes. For example, probabilities of divorce and remarriage have been found to depend not only on age-time but also on duration-time in the relevant marital status (e.g., Jones, 1962; Land, 1971; Schoen, 1977b). This suggests, of course, that the proper stochastic process specification is semi-Markov (cf., Hoem, 1972a). By contrast, in the context of interregional migration studies, migration probabilities have been shown to be origin-dependent (Long and Hansen, 1975; Ledent, 1980a,b). Again, this may require modification of the Markov specifications. In either case, and in other empirical contexts, the Markov model provides a baseline from which empirical departures may be measured and model modifications made.

Following the Schoen-Land (1979, pp. 763-764) specification of the time-inhomogeneous, finite-space, continuous-time Markov process model corresponding to a k-table IDLT, we *assume* that the state-space Ω of the process has k + 1 states, where k is a positive integer greater than 1. One of these states, the (k+1)st, will be *assumed* to be an absorbing state. A k-table IDLT contains an implicit absorbing state of death that is identified with this (k+1)st state in the corresponding Markov model. At least two of the remaining k states of Ω will be *assumed* to intercommunicate in order to ensure increments to, as well as decrements from, some states of the model.

On the state space Ω, we *define* a stochastic process $\{S(x): x \geq 0\}$, where the continuous-time parameter x denotes the exact age attained. As noted above, in order to keep the derivations as simple as possible herein, we assume that S(·) is not conditioned by duration-time or origin. In fact, we *assume* that S(·) is a *time(age)-inhomogeneous Markov process.* Consequently, the *transition probabilities, assumed* absolutely continuous, are defined by

$$\Pi_{ij}(x,y) = \text{Prob}\{S(y) = j \mid S(x) = i\}, \tag{2.1}$$

for states i and j in Ω. When $y = x + t$ for some $t \geq 0$, we adopt actuarial notation[5] (cf., Jordan, 1975, pp. 29-30) and let

$${}_t\pi_x^{ij} = \Pi_{ij}(x,x+t). \tag{2.2}$$

In the latter notation, the right-hand subscript indicates the initial conditioning age, the left-hand subscript indicates the duration (length) of the age interval from age x, and the right-hand superscripts indicate the states between which transitions are made. We shall use the notations (2.1) and (2.2)

[5]*As noted by Schoen and Land (1979, p. 761), transition probabilities cannot be estimated by quotients of ordinary survival functions, because the former refer to closed groups who occupy given states at age x. This contrasts with the usual quotient estimates of survival (p) and death (q) probabilities in single- and multiple-decrement theory. For this reason, we use the π notation to distinguish these conditional probabilities from straightforward applications of p and q probabilities to an increment-decrement context (for a statement and derivation of algebraic inequalities relating the p's, q's, and π's, see Schoen and Land, 1979, p. 771). In addition, in the present paper, we write all state indices (i, j, etc.) as superscripts on the right-hand side of the transition probabilities and other similar functions. Although this departs somewhat from the "halo" notation of Schoen and Land (1979), it is consistent with actuarial notation and with the notation of Hoem and Jensen (1981).*

interchangeably, but we shall generally favor the actuarial system.

We similarly *assume* the existence and, in general, unconstrained continuity of all *forces of transition (transition intensities)*:

$$\mu_x^{ij} = \lim_{t \to 0} \frac{{}_t\pi_x^{ij}}{t}, \quad i \neq j, \tag{2.3a}$$

and

$$-\mu_x^{ii} = \lim_{t \to 0} \frac{1 - {}_t\pi_x^{ii}}{t} = \sum_{j \neq i}^{k+1} \mu_x^{ij}, \tag{2.3b}$$

where we again use actuarial notation. Finally, in order to rule out empirically unrealistic instantaneous states, we *postulate* a finite number of transitions almost surely in any bounded interval.

Two remarks are in order regarding this specification. First, it should be reiterated that the Markov assumption enters into the specification of the model through the assertion that the transition probabilities (2.1) and the transition forces in (2.3a) and (2.3b) depend *only* on the state occupied at age x and not on duration-time in that state or on states occupied at prior times (including age 0). Second, by combining an unconstrained age x and an unconstrained $t \to 0$ limit in (2.3a) and (2.3b), we follow the conventional practice in actuarial science (Jordan, 1975, p. 16) and mathematical demography (Keyfitz, 1977, p. 5; Ledent, 1980c, p. 537) of assuming that the transition force functions are continuous *throughout* the age range of the life table. For some functional specifications, however, such as the classic piecewise-constant specification, this *global continuity* condition must be replaced by the weaker condition of *piecewise-continuity on the right* (Hoem, 1976, pp. 170-173). Furthermore, since age-specific methods of life table estimation do not require the fitted force functions to be continuous in the global sense of (2.3a) and (2.3b) (cf., Batten, 1978, pp. 2-7), it follows that the weaker condition of piecewise-continuity on the right also is the proper specification for such methods (cf., Schoen and Land, 1979, p. 764). This is indicated by noting that the age x in (2.3a) and (2.3b) is constrained to fall in the half-open (on the right) interval [a,b) and by replacing the $t \to 0$ by $t \downarrow 0$.

2.2. *DERIVATION OF THE FLOW EQUATIONS*

Given the Markov chain specifications adopted above, it follows that the transition probabilities (2.1) satisfy the *Kolmogorov forward differential equations* (see, e.g., Cox and Miller, 1965, p. 181):

$$\frac{\partial}{\partial t}\, {}_t\pi_x^{ij} = {}_t\pi_x^{ij} \cdot \mu_{x+t}^{jj} + \sum_{h \neq j}^{k+1} {}_t\pi_x^{ih} \cdot \mu_{x+t}^{hj}, \qquad t > 0, \qquad (2.4)$$

for i, j = 1,...,k+1. One of the essential building blocks of the estimation algorithm that we developed in Schoen and Land (1979) and employ later in the present paper is a discrete-time (age) version of Eqs. (2.4) called the *flow equations*. To derive the flow equations from the Kolmogorov equations, we need some additional concepts and notation.[6]

[6]*The derivation given here flows more directly from the Markov chain model than that given in Schoen and Land (1979, pp. 765-766) and owes much to Hoem and Jensen (1981).*

First, we define the state distribution at the initial age (0) by

$$\ell_0^i = \text{Prob}\{S(0) = i\}, \quad i = 1,\ldots,k. \tag{2.5}$$

These ℓ_0^i are the *radices* of the corresponding IDLT. Similarly, we define

$$\ell_x^i = \text{Prob}\{S(x) = i\} = \sum_{j=1}^{k} \ell_0^j \cdot {}_x\pi_0^{ji} \tag{2.6}$$

for $x \geq 0$. The $\{\ell_x^i\}$ functions constitute the *stationary population* of the IDLT corresponding to this Markov chain. It is customary in life table analysis to tabulate some multiple of ℓ_x^i, like $10^5 \cdot \ell_x^i$, rather than ℓ_x^i itself. In this form, the $\{\ell_x^i\}$ usually are referred to as *survival (survivorship) functions*.

Next, the *gross flows* of the stationary population are the functions

$$\ell_{[x]+t}^{ij} = \ell_{[x]}^i \cdot {}_t\pi_x^{ij}, \tag{2.7}$$

for $i = 1,\ldots,k$ and $j = 1,\ldots,k+1$. In this notation, the square brackets around the right-hand subscripts indicate that the functions refer to the closed group of persons who were in state i at age x. To this age is added, outside the brackets, the time ($t \geq 0$) that has elapsed since age x, so that the total subscript denotes the attained age. Thus, $\ell_{[x]}^i = \ell_x^i$, because the number of persons in the closed group of those in state i at age x is the same as the number of persons in state i at age x. But $\ell_{[x]+t}^{ij}$ denotes the number of persons in state j at age x + t among those who started in state i at age x and is generally less than $\ell^{i}_{[x]}$. Note that (2.7) may be rearranged to give the IDLT definition of transition probabilities stated by Schoen and Land (1979, p. 764):

$$ {}_{t}\pi^{ij}_{x} = \ell^{ij}_{[x]+t}/\ell^{i}_{[x]} \tag{2.8} $$

for i = 1,...,k, j = 1,.i.,k+1.

Another useful class of IDLT functions can be derived by noting that the probability that an individual who starts in state i at age x, is in state j at age x + s, and makes a transition to state h at age x + s is defined by the products ${}_{s}\pi^{ij}_{x} \cdot \mu^{jh}_{x+s}$. To convert this to the probability of such a transition over the age interval x to x + n, we integrate:

$$ \int_0^n {}_{s}\pi^{ij}_{x} \cdot \mu^{jh}_{x+s}\, ds. $$

Then, the total number of decrements (moves, transfers) from state j to state h between the ages of x and x + n by members of the closed group of persons who were in state i at age x is obtained by multiplying this integral by ℓ^{i}_{x} and denoted

$$ {}_{n}d^{ijh}_{[x]} = \ell^{i}_{[x]} \int_0^n {}_{s}\pi^{ij}_{x} \quad \mu^{jh}_{x+s}\, ds, \tag{2.9} $$

for i, j = 1,...,k and h = 1,...,k+1. These are *origin-dependent decrement functions*. From the set of the ${}_{n}d^{ijh}_{x}$, we can obtain the corresponding *origin-independent decrement functions* for state j to state h transfers by summing (2.9) over all i:

$$ {}_{n}d^{jh}_{x} = \sum_{i=1}^{k} {}_{n}d^{ijh}_{x} = \int_0^n \ell^{j}_{x+s} \cdot \mu^{jh}_{x+s}\, ds, \tag{2.10} $$

$j = 1,\ldots,k, h = 1,\ldots,k+1$.

Note that there is no reason why the integrals in (2.9) and (2.10) must be stopped at a finite upper bound n. Also, we could replace the lower bound x on the integrals by x + t, $t \geq 0$. Doing this in (2.9), we obtain the following expression for the total number of transfers from state j to state h at or above exact age x + t by members of the closed group of persons who were in state i at age x:

$$ {}_{\infty}d^{ijh}_{[x]+t} = \ell^{ijh}_{[x]+t} = \ell^{i}_{[x]} \int_{t}^{\infty} {}_{s}\pi^{ij}_{x} \cdot \mu^{jh}_{x+s}\, ds, \qquad (2.11)$$

$i, j = 1,\ldots,k$, and $j = 1,\ldots,k+1$. To distinguish these functions from (2.9), we refer to them as *origin-dependent transfer functions*. Similarly, from (2.11), we obtain the *origin-independent transfer functions*:

$$ {}_{\infty}d^{jh}_{x} = \ell^{jh}_{x} = \sum_{i=1}^{k} {}_{\infty}d^{ijh}_{[x]} = \int_{0}^{\infty} \ell^{j}_{x+s} \cdot \mu^{jh}_{x+s}\, ds, \qquad (2.12)$$

$j = 1,\ldots,k, h = 1,\ldots,k+1$. These functions determine the number of transfers from state j to state h at or above age x.

Obviously, there is an intimate relationship between the decrement and transfer functions. In particular, the decrement functions can be defined as differences of the corresponding transfer functions:

$$ {}_{n}d^{ijh}_{x} = \ell^{ijh}_{[x]} - \ell^{ijh}_{[x]+n}, \qquad (2.13)$$

and

$$ {}_{n}d^{jh}_{x} = \ell^{jh}_{x} - \ell^{jh}_{x+n}, \qquad (2.14)$$

for $i, j = 1,\ldots,k$, and $h = 1,\ldots,k+1$.

With the foregoing concepts in hand, we return to the Kolmogorov equation (2.4). Integrating these between ages t = x and t = x+n, noting that

$$ {}_0\pi_x^{ij} = \delta_{ij} = \begin{cases} 1 & \text{if } i = j \\ 0 & \text{if } i \neq j \end{cases}, $$

multiplying the results by ℓ_x^i, and using (2.9), we get the *origin-dependent flow equations:*

$$ \ell_{[x]+n}^{ij} = \ell_{[x]}^{ij} - \sum_{h \neq j}^{k+1} {}_n d_{[x]}^{ijh} + \sum_{h \neq j}^{k} {}_n d_{[x]}^{ihj}, \qquad (2.15) $$

i = 1,...,k, j = 1,...,k+1. Similarly, by summing over i, we have the corresponding *origin-independent flow equations:*

$$ \ell_{x+n}^{j} = \ell_{x}^{j} - \sum_{h \neq j}^{k+1} {}_n d_x^{jh} + \sum_{h \neq j}^{k+1} {}_n d_x^{hj}, \qquad (2.16) $$

j = 1,...,k. Equations (2.16) are the flow equations derived by Schoen (1975) from discrete-time accounting notions. Both (2.15) and (2.16) were first derived from the Kolmogorov equations by Schoen and Land (1979). Subsequently, they have been used by Ledent (1980c), Willekens (1980), and others. Note that they apply generally to the class of Markov-generated IDLTs and are not specific to any particular parameterization of the life table functions. Furthermore, these equations exhibit the interrelationships among the transfer functions ($\ell_{[x]+n}^{ijh}$), the gross flow functions ($\ell_{[x]+n}^{ij}$), and the survival functions (ℓ_{x+n}^{j}) implied by the Kolmogorov equations.[7] Thus,

[7] *Failure to recognize the distinctiveness of these three classes of functions in an IDLT context (they become equivalent in single- and multiple-decrement theory) can be a source of endless confusion.*

their use in an estimation algorithm amounts to a numerical solution of the Kolmogorov equations.

2.3. *POLYNOMIAL GROSS FLOW FUNCTIONS*

The foregoing specification is by now fairly conventional in the IDLT literature. It asserts that the IDLT to be estimated is generated by a time(age)-inhomogeneous Markov process. Were we to go no further than this, we would be left in the semiparametric situation characterized by Hoem (1976, p. 171) as typical of demographic applications of life tables. To proceed to a fully parametric approach to IDLT estimation requires that we parameterize the forces of transition (2.3).

As noted in the introduction, the classic specification is that these forces are piecewise constant within estimation-age-intervals. But, for abridged IDLTs, this "local behavior" specification may produce less accurate estimates when the forces are changing rapidly within the estimation intervals. Therefore, we seek a family of force functions that is capable of exhibiting increasing, decreasing, or constant local behavior. From this perspective, we have examined the conventional Gompertz-Makeham, gamma, lognormal, Weibull and Rayleigh distributions of life table, and reliability theory (Mann *et al.*, 1974; Gross and Clark, 1975). Relative to the standards of estimation that we have adopted, a major drawback of these standard distributions and their associated transition forces in the IDLT context is that they do not lead to estimators that are expressible in explicit algebraic form.

A family of functions that meets this criterion is the following class of *piecewise-polynomial gross flow functions:*

$$\ell^{ij}_{[x]+t} = b^{ij}_0 + b^{ij}_1 t + b^{ij}_2 t^2 + \cdots + b^{ij}_r t^r, \tag{2.17}$$

$0 \le t < n$, $r \ge 1$, where b_0, b_1, ..., b_r are real numbers, $b_r \neq 0$, i and j are states between which transitions are made (i = .,...,k,j = 1,...,k+1), and t is the (variable) duration elapsed since the closed group was formed in state i at age x. Since the gross flow functions on the left-hand side are defined by (2.15) (the integrated form of the Kolmogorov equations), Eqs. (2.17) amount to postulating an r-th degree polynomial parameterization of those integral expressions. Furthermore, since integrals are likely to be "smoother" than the functions from which they were generated, polynomial expansions like (2.17) may be more appropriate when applied to the gross flow functions than to the transition forces.

To fix ideas, we focus on two special cases of Eqs. (2.17) in the remainder of this paper: (1) r = 1, and (2) r = 2. In the first case, we obtain the *piecewise-linear gross flow equations*:

$$\ell^{ij}_{[x]+t} = \ell^{ij}_{[x]} + b^{ij} t \tag{2.18}$$

and, in the second case, we have the *piecewise-quadratic gross flow functions*:

$$\ell^{ij}_{[x]+t} = \ell^{ij}_{[x]} + b^{ij} t + c^{ij} t^2 \tag{2.19}$$

i = 1,...,k,j = 1,...,k+1. Note that we have set the constant terms in these equations equal to their initial value at the age x at which the closed groups are formed. In accordance with the interpretation given to Eqs. (2.7), this implies

$\ell_{[x]}^{ij} = \ell_x^i$ for i = j and $\ell_{[x]}^{ij} = 0$ for $i \neq j$. Note also that the b^{ij} coefficients in (2.18) must be negative for i = j and positive for $i \neq j$, since, except in trivial cases, the gross flows must decrease with t in the former case and increase in the latter. By contrast, the coefficients in (2.19) may define functions that are strictly increasing, strictly decreasing, or both increasing and decreasing as t goes from 0 to n.

Several comments are in order regarding these parameterizations.

First, we shall derive, in Section 3.4, algebraic expressions of the transition forces corresponding to (2.18) and (2.19), and we shall argue that these forces, especially those corresponding to (2.19), provide more flexible "local behavior" specifications for abridged IDLTs than do the piecewise-constant forces of the classic model. At the same time, the former do not present problems of identification and estimation that are not also present with the latter. Furthermore, it is possible (see Sections 3.2 and 3.3) to derive estimators for the IDLT functions of the linear and quadratic models that are expressible in explicit algebraic form--another of the objectives stated in the introduction to this chapter. This is not true for $r \geq 3$ in (2.17), in which case the entire table must be iterated to produce each age-specific estimate. Therefore, and because it is not clear that polynomials of degree greater than 2 would achieve much more flexibility or accuracy (for, say, 5-yr age intervals), we use only the linear and quadratic models in the remainder of the paper.

Next, note that, because the survival functions (2.16) are defined by

$$\ell^j_{x+t} = \sum_i \ell^{ij}_{[x]+t} = \sum_i \left[\ell^{ij}_{[x]} + b^{ij}t + c^{ij}t^2\right]$$

$$= \ell^j_x + t \sum_i b^{ij} + t^2 \sum_i c^{ij}$$

$$= \ell^j_x + b^j t + c^j t^2, \tag{2.20}$$

$j = 1,\ldots,k$, the degrees of the polynomials postulated in (2.18) and (2.19) are preserved. Thus, the piecewise-linear gross flow functions (2.18) imply *piecewise-linear survival functions*, and the piecewise-quadratic gross flow functions (2.19) imply *piecewise-quadratic survival functions*. While it is convenient to refer to the former as the "linear survival function model," as do Schoen and Land (1979) and other authors, it should be remembered that this is a short-hand expression for the more fundamental parameterizations (2.18); similar cautions apply when the latter is called the "quadratic survival function model."

The linear (2.18) and quadratic (2.19) parameterizations of the gross flow functions also yield simple closed-form expressions for ${}_nL^{ij}_{[x]}$, the *number of person-years lived in state j between the ages of x and x + n by members of the closed group of persons who were in state i at age x*:

$$ {}_nL^{ij}_{[x]} = \ell^i_{[x]} \int_0^n {}_t\pi^{ij}_x \, dt = \int_0^n \ell^{ij}_{[x]+t} \, dt \tag{2.21}$$

$i = 1,\ldots,k, j = 1,\ldots,k+1$, and ${}_nL^j_x$, the *number of person-years lived (in one year) in state j between the ages of x and x + n:*

$$ {}_nL^j_x = \sum_i {}_nL^{ij}_{[x]} = \int_0^n \ell^j_{x+t} \, dt, \tag{2.22}$$

$j = 1,\ldots,k$. Specifically, for the linear model, we obtain the following *piecewise-quadratic person-years functions* by performing the integrations in (2.21) and (2.22):

$$_nL^{ij}_{[x]} = n \cdot \ell^{ij}_{[x]} + b^{ij} \cdot \frac{n^2}{2} = \frac{n}{2}\left[\ell^{ij}_{[x]} + \ell^{ij}_{[x]+n}\right], \qquad (2.23)$$

and

$$_nL^{j}_{n} = n \cdot \ell^{j}_{x} + b^{j} \cdot \frac{n^2}{2} = \frac{n}{2}\left[\ell^{j}_{x} + \ell^{j}_{x+n}\right], \qquad (2.24)$$

where the second equalities follow from recognizing that the trapezoidal rule of numerical integration theory is exact for a first-degree polynomial (Young and Gregory, 1972, p. 364).[8] Similarly, for the quadratic model (2.19), we obtain the *piecewise-cubic person-years functions*:

$$\begin{aligned} _nL^{ij}_{[x]} &= n \cdot \ell^{ij}_{[x]} + b^{ij} \cdot \frac{n^2}{2} + c^{ij} \cdot \frac{n^3}{3} \\ &= \frac{n}{6}\left[\ell^{ij}_{[x]} + 4\ell^{ij}_{[x]+\frac{n}{2}} + \ell^{ij}_{[x]+n}\right], \end{aligned} \qquad (2.25)$$

and

$$\begin{aligned} _nL^{j}_{x} &= n \cdot \ell^{j}_{x} + b^{j} \cdot \frac{n^2}{2} + c^{j} \cdot \frac{n^3}{3} \\ &= \frac{n}{6}\left[\ell^{j}_{x} + 4\ell^{j}_{x+\frac{n}{2}} + \ell^{j}_{x+n}\right], \end{aligned} \qquad (2.26)$$

where the second equalities follow from recognizing that Simpson's rule from numerical integration theory is exact

[8] *Because the linear model implies (2.23) and (2.24), Hoem and Jensen (1981) refer to it as an "integration hypothesis."*

for a second-degree polynomial (Young and Gregory, 1972, p. 366).[9]

3. AGE-SPECIFIC METHODS FOR OCCURRENCE/EXPOSURE RATES

3.1. *OCCURRENCE/EXPOSURE RATES AND THE SECTIONAL STATIONARITY ASSUMPTION*

Consider now the problem of estimating IDLT models of the forms specified in the preceding section from data in the form of age-specific occurrence/exposure rates. To understand the structure of this type of data, we begin by defining two classes of model parameters. First, corresponding to the definition of origin-dependent decrement functions (2.9), we have the (central) *origin-dependent model transfer rates*:

$$ {}_t m^{ijh}_{[x]} = \frac{{}_t d^{ijh}_{[x]}}{{}_t L^{ij}_x} = \frac{\ell^i_{[x]} \int_0^t {}_s\pi^{ij}_x \cdot \mu^{jh}_{x+s}\, ds}{\ell^i_{[x]} \int_0^t {}_s\pi^{ij}_x\, ds}, \quad \text{if } {}_t L^{ij}_x > 0, \qquad (3.1) $$

for $j \neq h$, with $i,j = 1,\ldots,k$, and $h = 1,\ldots,k+1$, and let ${}_t m^{ijh}_x = 0$ if

[9] *Note that the "cubic" person-years functions (2.25) and (2.26) corresponding to this quadratic model are quite distinct from the traditional "cubic" formulas, e.g.,*

$$ {}_n L^{ij}_x = \frac{13n}{24}\left[\ell^{ij}_x + \ell^{ij}_{x+n}\right] - \frac{n}{24}\left[\ell^{ij}_{x-n} + \ell^{ij}_{x+2n}\right] $$

used by Schoen and Land (1979, p. 766) and other authors. The latter formulas are obtained by passing a third-degree polynomial through four values l_{x-n}, l_x, l_{x+n}, l_{x+2n} and then integrating from x to x+n, whereas (2.25) and (2.26) are obtained by integrating, from x to x+n, quadratic functions that are defined locally only on the x to x+n interval.

${}_tL_x^{ij} = 0$. Similarly, the origin-independent decrement functions (2.10) yield the (central) *origin-independent model transfer rates*:

$$ {}_tm_x^{jh} = \frac{{}_td_x^{jh}}{{}_tL_x^j} = \frac{\int_0^t \ell_{x+s}^j \cdot \mu_{x+s}^{jh}\, ds}{\int_0^t \ell_{x+s}^j\, ds}, \quad \text{if } {}_tL_x^j > 0, \tag{3.2} $$

for $j \neq h$, $j = 1,\ldots,k$, $h = 1,\ldots,k+1$, and ${}_tm_x^{jh} = 0$ if ${}_tL_x^j = 0$.

With complete, continuous-time observations on all state transfers and all persons in a population exposed to the risk of transferring, it is possible to produce direct estimates of these transition rates. However, the aggregate, population-level data available to demographers usually fall far short of this ideal situation. The more typical circumstance is that vital statistics agencies provide data from which to compute occurrence/exposure rates for a sequence of age intervals $[x,x+t)$ that partition an age range $[x_0,x_\omega)$. By *occurrence/exposure rates*, we mean rates of the form

$$ {}_tM_x^{jh} = \frac{{}_tD_x^{jh}}{{}_tK_x^j}, \quad i = 1,\ldots,k, h = 1,\ldots,k+1, j \neq h, \tag{3.3} $$

where ${}_tD_x^{jh}$ denotes the number of transfers or moves from state j to state h of the state-space Ω occurring among members of the population who are age x to x + t during the period of observation, and ${}_tK_x^j$ denotes the average number of persons in the population living in state j during the observation period (and thus exposed to the risk of a state j to state h move). For calendar year rates, the numerator in (3.3) refers to persons making state j to state h moves during the year who were age x at last birthday at the time of transfer, not to moves by persons age x at the beginning of the year. Similarly, the denominator of (3.3) is taken to be the midyear population estimated to be in state j. Thus, the observed rates (3.3) are estimates of the model rates (3.2). To "orient" (fit) and IDLT model to the observed data, we express this by equating

$$ {}_tM_x^{jh} = {}_tm_x^{jh}, \quad j \neq h, \tag{3.4}$$

for j = 1,...,k, and h = 1,...,k+1.

In order to use the occurrence/exposure rates (3.3) to estimate the IDLT models specified in the preceding section, however, we make an assumption that is stronger than (3.4). To understand this assumption, note that the origin-dependent model rates (3.1) condition on the state occupied at age x. But, in the definition of the observed rates (3.3), we did not so condition, because vital statistics data usually are not available on population movements for persons who were in a given state at a given exact age prior to a state transfer. Consequently, we *assume*

$$ {}_tM_x^{jh} = {}_tm_{[x]}^{ijh}, \quad j \neq h, \tag{3.5}$$

i,j = 1,...,k,h = 1,...,k+1. This is equivalent to employing a k-table version of the sectionally stationary assumption of single-decrement life table theory, namely, that within each estimation-age-interval the observed population has a stationary age distribution, as is required by (3.4), and to assuming that, for relatively short-age intervals (e.g., 5-yr intervals), the observed rates (3.3) are reasonably good estimates of the origin-dependent model rates (3.1).[10] Furthermore, Ledent (1980c, p. 544) has shown that assumption (3.5) holds exactly when the transition forces are constant over estimation-age-intervals. This suggests that (3.5) also is approximately satisfied for transition forces that are slowly changing.[11] In any case, it must be emphasized that, for *any* IDLT model that postulates nonconstant forces of transition within estimation-age-intervals, some assumption like (3.5) is necessary, unless, of course, the observed rates (3.3) are indexed by state occupied at age x as well as by state occupied at the time of transfer.

[10] Keyfitz (1968) has shown that the sectional-stationarity part of this assumption can be replaced with a sectionally stable premise in single-decrement theory, and Preston et al. (1972) extended that work to include multiple decrements. Our methods of estimation are consistent in either case.

[11] Interestingly, the one empirical application to date of the major extant nonconstant transition forces IDLT model (the linear model) that appears to have led to negative estimated diagonal (retention) Markov transition probabilities ($_t\hat{\pi}^{ii}_{20}$), namely, Manninen (1979), used occurrence/exposure rates for interregional migration defined on 5-yr intervals. This suggests that the failure of the linear model in this case is not due solely to its inability to handle multiple moves as argued by Ledent (1980c, p. 559), but also to the inappropriateness of assumption (3.5) relative to the rapidly changing transition forces over the [20, 25) age interval.

3.2. *REVIEW OF ESTIMATION METHODS FOR EXPONENTIAL AND LINEAR MODELS*

Methods for estimating Markov-generated IDLT models piecewise from age-specific occurrence/exposure rates have been developed and refined for two extant model specifications that we have referred to in previous sections as the exponential and linear (survival function) models. Before going on to a derivation of comparable methods for the quadratic (survival function) model introduced in Section 2.3, it will be useful to summarize the main results for these models. This will help to establish notation and a consistent format for presentation of the estimation algorithms.

First, we need some matrix notation. We define a *matrix of transition forces* by collecting the functions defined in (2.3) into a matrix of k-rows and k-columns:[12]

$$\underset{\sim}{\mu}_{x+t} = \begin{bmatrix} -\mu_{x+t}^{11} & \mu_{x+t}^{12} & \cdots & \mu_{x+t}^{1k} \\ \mu_{x+t}^{21} & -\mu_{x+t}^{22} & \cdots & \mu_{x+t}^{2k} \\ \vdots & \vdots & & \vdots \\ \mu_{x+t}^{k1} & \mu_{x+t}^{k2} & \cdots & -\mu_{x+t}^{kk} \end{bmatrix} .$$

Similarly, by collecting the transition probabilities (2.2) into an array, we have the *transition probability matrix*:

[12] *Because the transition forces, transition probabilities, gross flows, etc., of the dead (k+1) state can be defined trivially or residually, it suffices to dimension all of the matrices defined here as k-by-k rather than (k+1)-by-(k+1).*

$$
{}_t\underset{\sim}{\Pi}_x = \begin{bmatrix} {}_t\pi_x^{11} & {}_t\pi_x^{12} & \cdots & {}_t\pi_x^{1k} \\ {}_t\pi_x^{21} & {}_t\pi_x^{22} & \cdots & {}_t\pi_x^{2k} \\ \vdots & \vdots & & \vdots \\ {}_t\pi_x^{k1} & {}_t\pi_x^{k2} & \cdots & {}_t\pi_x^{kk} \end{bmatrix},
$$

which, when multiplied by the appropriate scalar ($\ell^i_{[x]}$), becomes a *matrix of gross flows* (defined in (2.7)):

$$
\underset{\sim}{\ell}_{[x]+t} = \begin{bmatrix} \ell^{11}_{[x]+t} & \ell^{12}_{[x]+t} & \cdots & \ell^{1k}_{[x]+t} \\ \ell^{21}_{[x]+t} & \ell^{22}_{[x]+t} & \cdots & \ell^{2k}_{[x]+t} \\ \vdots & \vdots & & \vdots \\ \ell^{k1}_{[x]+t} & \ell^{k2}_{[x]+t} & & \ell^{kk}_{[x]+t} \end{bmatrix}.
$$

Summing across rows of this matrix and transposing, we have the corresponding (column) *vector of survival functions* defined in (2.6):

$$
\underset{\sim}{\ell}_{x+t} = \begin{bmatrix} \ell^{1}_{x+t} \\ \ell^{2}_{x+t} \\ \vdots \\ \ell^{k}_{x+t} \end{bmatrix}.
$$

Furthermore, by using the definitions (2.21), we similarly have a *matrix of origin-dependent person-years functions*:

$$
{}_t\underset{\sim}{L}[x] = \begin{bmatrix} {}_tL_x^{11} & {}_tL_x^{12} & \cdots & {}_tL_x^{1k} \\ {}_tL_x^{21} & {}_tL_x^{22} & & {}_tL_x^{2k} \\ \vdots & \vdots & & \vdots \\ {}_tL_x^{k1} & {}_tL_x^{k2} & \cdots & {}_tL_x^{kk} \end{bmatrix},
$$

and, after summing across rows and transposing, a (column) *vector of origin-independent person-years functions:*

$$
{}_t\underset{\sim}{L}_x = \begin{bmatrix} {}_tL_x^{1} \\ {}_tL_x^{2} \\ \vdots \\ {}_tL_x^{k} \end{bmatrix}.
$$

Finally, we collect the observed rates (3.3) into a *matrix of occurrence/exposure rates:*

$$
{}_t\underset{\sim}{M}_x = \begin{bmatrix} \sum_{j\neq 1} {}_tM_x^{1j} & -{}_tM_x^{12} & \cdots & -{}_tM_x^{1k} \\ -{}_tM_x^{21} & \sum_{j\neq 2} {}_tM_x^{2j} & \cdots & -{}_tM_x^{2k} \\ \vdots & \vdots & & \vdots \\ -{}_tM_x^{k1} & -{}_tM_k^{k2} & \cdots & \sum_{j\neq k} {}_tM_x^{kk} \end{bmatrix},
$$

and, correspoindingly, without exhibiting the elements, we define *the matrix of origin-independent model transition rates* ${}_t\underset{\sim}{m}_x$, by putting (3.2) into a k-by-k array.

With this notation in hand, the standard estimation algorithm for the classic exponential model can be derived and stated very concisely. In brief, for fixed age x, the Kolmogorov equations (2.4) for this model can be written as a system of ordinary differential equations:

$$\frac{d\ {}_t\boldsymbol{\Pi}_x}{dt} = {}_t\boldsymbol{\Pi}_x\ \boldsymbol{\mu}_{x+t}, \tag{3.6}$$

with the initial conditions ${}_0\boldsymbol{\Pi}_x = \mathbf{I}$, where $\mathbf{I}$ denotes the identity matrix of order k, and $\boldsymbol{\mu}_{x+t}$ reduces to a matrix of constant forces $\boldsymbol{\mu}_x$ for the estimation-age-interval $x \leq x+t < x+n$. Given this simplification, the system (3.6) has the unique exponential solution:

$${}_t\boldsymbol{\Pi}_x = \exp(t\boldsymbol{\mu}_x), \quad 0 \leq t < n, \tag{3.7}$$

where this matrix exponential function is defined by the series

$$e^{t\boldsymbol{\mu}_x} = \exp(t\boldsymbol{\mu}_x) = \sum_{r=1} \frac{t^r}{r!}\ \boldsymbol{\mu}_x^r$$

$$= \mathbf{I} + t\boldsymbol{\mu}_x + \frac{t^2}{2!}\boldsymbol{\mu}_x^2 + \frac{t^3}{3!}\boldsymbol{\mu}_x^3 + \frac{t^4}{4!}\boldsymbol{\mu}_x^4 + \cdots \tag{3.8}$$

(see, e.g., Cox and Miller, 1965, p. 182). Furthermore, by substitution of the assumption of constant forces of transition into (3.1) and (3.2), we find that

$${}_t m^{ijh}_{[x]} = {}_t m^{jh}_x = \mu^{jh}_x, \tag{3.9}$$

$i,j = 1,\ldots,k, h = 1,\ldots,k+1$.[13] Thus, if we take the observed

[13] *Note that these equalities hold exactly, illustrating that the sectional stationarity assumption (3.5) is not required as an independent assumption when constant forces are specified.*

occurrence/exposure rates (3.3) as estimates of the model transition rates (3.1), we also have directly estimated the transition forces. The simplicity and directness of this result has been noted by virtually every author who has ever written on the subject of this IDLT model (see the references cited in the introduction to this chapter). Finally, using $-{}_n\tilde{M}_x$ as an estimate of $\tilde{\mu}_x$, Krishnamoorthy (1979) notes that the person-years matrix can be expressed as

$$
\begin{aligned}
{}_n\tilde{L}[x] &= \tilde{\ell}[x]\left[\int_0^n \exp(-t\ {}_n\tilde{M}_x)\,dt\right] \\
&= \tilde{\ell}[x]\,[\tilde{I} - \exp(-n\ {}_n\tilde{M}_x)]\,{}_n\tilde{M}_x^{-1} \\
&= [\tilde{\ell}[x] - \tilde{\ell}[x+n]]\,{}_n\tilde{M}_x^{-1}\ , \qquad (3.10)
\end{aligned}
$$

and, therefore, the corresponding person-years vector is

$$
{}_n\tilde{L}_x = [\tilde{\ell}_x - \tilde{\ell}_{x+n}]\,{}_n\tilde{M}_x^{-1}. \qquad (3.11)
$$

In order to facilitate comparisons among alternatives, it will be useful to put these results into the Schoen and Land (1979) *general algorithm* (*GA*) format. Recall that the *GA* consists of (a) *orientation equations* for relating observed rates (3.3) to their parametric (life-table) counterparts, (b) *flow equations* for estimating values of gross flows and survivorship functions at successive ages, and (c) *person-years equations* for estimating the successive values of person-years lived in the life-table states by the life-table population.

Using this format, we have the following *algorithm for piecewise estimation of the classic exponential model*:

Orientation:

$$-{}_n\underset{\sim}{M}_x = -{}_n\hat{\underset{\sim}{m}}_x = -{}_n\hat{\underset{\sim}{m}}_{[x]} = \hat{\underset{\sim}{\mu}}_x, \tag{3.12a}$$

Flow:

$$\hat{\underset{\sim}{\ell}}_{[x]+n} = \hat{\underset{\sim}{\ell}}_{[x]}\ {}_n\hat{\underset{\sim}{\Pi}}_x = \hat{\underset{\sim}{\ell}}_{[x]}\, e^{-n\,{}_n\underset{\sim}{M}_x}, \quad 0 \leq t < n, \tag{3.12b}$$

$$\hat{\underset{\sim}{\ell}}_{x+n} = \hat{\underset{\sim}{\ell}}_x\ {}_n\hat{\underset{\sim}{\Pi}}_x = \hat{\underset{\sim}{\ell}}_x\, e^{-n\,{}_n\underset{\sim}{M}_x}, \quad 0 \leq t < n, \tag{3.12c}$$

Person-Years:

$${}_n\hat{\underset{\sim}{L}}_{[x]} = [\hat{\underset{\sim}{\ell}}_{[x]} - \hat{\underset{\sim}{\ell}}_{[x]+n}]\,{}_n\underset{\sim}{M}_x^{-1}, \tag{3.12d}$$

$${}_n\hat{\underset{\sim}{L}}_x = [\hat{\underset{\sim}{\ell}}_x - \hat{\underset{\sim}{\ell}}_{x+n}]\,{}_n\underset{\sim}{M}_x^{-1}, \tag{3.12e}$$

where the carets indicate estimated life-table functions. Given an initial state-distribution vector $\underset{\sim}{\ell}_0$, Eqs. (3.12) can be applied successively to estimate a piecewise-constant forces IDLT for all estimation-age-intervals, except possibly the first and the last. It often is the case that these age intervals must be treated uniquely because of rapidly changing forces (in the initial interval) or unboundedness (in the last interval); see Krishnamoorthy (1979) and Keyfitz (1977) for details. Finally, once Eqs. (3.12) have been used to estimate gross flows, survival, and person-years functions, other IDLT functions (e.g., sojourn times--expected durations in the life table states) can be estimated by the usual formulas (for expositions of these, see, e.g., Schoen and Land, 1979; Ledent, 1980c; Hoem and Jensen, 1981).

Corresponding to algorithm (3.12), we have the following *algorithm for piecewise estimation of the linear model:*

Orientation:

$$_n\underset{\sim}{M}_x = {}_n\underset{\sim}{\hat{m}}_x, \tag{3.13a}$$

Flow:

$$\underset{\sim}{\hat{\ell}}_{[x]+n} = \underset{\sim}{\hat{\ell}}_{[x]}\ {}_n\underset{\sim}{\hat{\Pi}}_x$$

$$= \underset{\sim}{\hat{\ell}}_{[x]}[(\underset{\sim}{I} - \frac{n}{2}\ {}_n\underset{\sim}{M}_x)(\underset{\sim}{I} + \frac{n}{2}\ {}_n\underset{\sim}{M}_x)^{-1}], \tag{3.13b}$$

$$\underset{\sim}{\hat{\ell}}_{x+n} = \underset{\sim}{\hat{\ell}}_x\ {}_n\underset{\sim}{\hat{\Pi}}_x$$

$$= \underset{\sim}{\hat{\ell}}_x[(\underset{\sim}{I} - \frac{n}{2}\ {}_n\underset{\sim}{M}_x)(\underset{\sim}{I} + \frac{n}{2}\ {}_n\underset{\sim}{M}_x)^{-1}], \tag{3.13c}$$

Person-Years:

$$_n\underset{\sim}{\hat{L}}_{[x]} = \frac{n}{2}\ [\underset{\sim}{\hat{\ell}}_{[x]} + \underset{\sim}{\hat{\ell}}_{[x]+n}], \tag{3.13d}$$

$$_n\underset{\sim}{\hat{L}}_x = \frac{n}{2}\ [\underset{\sim}{\hat{\ell}}_x + \underset{\sim}{\hat{\ell}}_{x+n}]. \tag{3.13e}$$

Most of the components of this algorithm have been stated and/o derived in prior sections of this paper. Equations (3.13a) is a matrix expression of assumption (3.5). Equations (3.13b) and (3.13c) are matrix expressions derived from the flow equations (2.15) and (2.16), respectively. The estimator of $_n\underset{\sim}{\Pi}_x$ they contain was initially derived by Rogers and Ledent (1976). The combined the flow equations (2.16) with the orientation equations (3.13a) to obtain

$$\underset{\sim}{\hat{\ell}}_{x+n} = \underset{\sim}{\hat{\ell}}_x - {}_n\underset{\sim}{\hat{L}}_x\ {}_n\underset{\sim}{M}_x, \tag{3.14}$$

substituted (3.13e), and solved for the estimator $_n\underset{\sim}{\hat{\Pi}}_x$ in (3.13c). Rogers and Ledent (1976) and Schoen (1977a) then extended this to (3.13b). The last two equations, (3.13d) and

(3.13e), similarly, are matrix expressions of equations (2.23) and (2.24), respectively.

Again, Eqs. (3.13) can be applied to estimate a piecewise-linear gross flows IDLT for all estimation-age-intervals, except the first and last. For the same reasons as cited above, these may need separate treatment; see Schoen and Land (1979, p. 774) and Keyfitz (1977). After the basic life table functions are estimated piecewise by Eqs. (3.13), other functions can be estimated by the methods cited above.

In brief, we now have two versions of the Schoen-Land *GA*: Eqs. (3.12) for the classic piecewise-constant forces/exponential survival functions IDLT model and Eqs. (3.13) for the piecewise-linear gross flows/linear survival function model. As we noted in the introduction to this paper, each of these models has its weaknesses. It is for this reason that we specified the wider class of piecewise-polynomial gross flows IDLT models in Section 2.3. We now turn to the development of a version of the *GA* for the quadratic member of this class.

3.3. *ESTIMATING THE QUADRATIC IDLT*

For both the classic exponential and the linear (survival function) IDLT models, the piecewise estimation algorithms derived in the preceding subsection amount to fitting one segment of the model transition force functions per observed occurrence/exposure rate, since these functions each have a single unknown parameter. In the quadratic (survival function) model specified in Section 2.3, however, each age-specific gross flows function (2.19) has two unknown parameters. Thus, for this model, it is impossible to fit uniquely one transition force function segment per occurrence/exposure rate. Nonetheless, the Schoen-Land *GA* can be adapted for estimation of the quadratic model along the following lines.

First, Chiang's (1960) single-decrement life table concept of the average number of years lived in an age interval [x,x+n) by those dying in the interval can be generalized to the IDLT case (Ledent, 1978; Schoen, 1979) by defining ${}_na_x^{ij}$ as the *mean duration,* into the interval, *at transfer* from state i to state j:

$$
{}_na_x^{ij} = \frac{\int_0^n t \cdot \ell_{x+t}^{i} \cdot \mu_{x+t}^{ij}\, dt}{\int_0^n \ell_{x+t}^{i} \cdot \mu_{x+t}^{ij}\, dt}
$$

$$
= \frac{\int_0^n t \cdot \ell_{x+t}^{i} \cdot \mu_{x+t}^{ij}\, dt}{{}_nd_x^{ij}}, \qquad (3.15)
$$

$i = 1,\ldots,k, j = 1,\ldots,k+1, i \neq j$. It should be emphasized that (3.15) defines ${}_na_x^{ij}$ as the mean duration at transfer, not the mean duration lived in state i (between the ages of x and x+n) by those transferring.[14]

Given numerical values of the ${}_na_x^{ij}$, the *GA* can be used to estimate quadratic IDLTs. Thus, we need to develop methods of estimating such values. This problem is complicated by the relatively complex transition force functions (to be derived in the next subsection) implied by the quadratic model. As a point of comparison, it should be noted that ${}_na_x^{ij}$ may be shown

[14] *Hoem and Jensen (1981) note that* ${}_na_x^{ij}$ *can also be derived from the notion of the expected duration (sojourn) in state j between ages x and x+n of an individual located in state i at age x, using an equation similar to (3.26).*

to be equal to $\frac{n}{2}$ if decrements were uniformly distributed over the interval. Moreover, given the structure of (3.15), for age intervals over which the force functions of this model are increasing, we should expect the ${}_na_x^{ij}$ to be greater than for age intervals over which the force functions are decreasing.

One possible approach to estimating numerical values of the ${}_na_x^{ij}$ is to try direct integration of (3.15). But this leads to an expression in terms of the coefficients of the force functions which themselves are unknown. An alternative approach is to express the ${}_na_x^{ij}$ as a weighted sum of the ℓ_x^i and ℓ_{x+n}^i:

$$ {}_na_x^{ij} = \frac{\ell_x^i \cdot {}_ng_x^{ij} + \ell_{x+n}^i \cdot {}_nh_x^{ij}}{{}_nd_x^{ij}}, \tag{3.16} $$

the existence of which is assured by properties of the real number system.

In brief, expression (3.16) reduces the problem of estimating the ${}_na_x^{ij}$ to the question of how the weights in (3.16) are to be calculated. Assuming that (a) ℓ_x^i is linear between the ages x and x+n, (b) for $0 \leq t < n$, μ_{x+t}^{ij} is quadratic, and (c) μ_{x+t}^{ij} can be fit through the values ${}_nM_{x-n}^{ij}$, ${}_nM_x^{ij}$, and ${}_nM_{x+n}^{ij}$, which are assumed equal to μ_t^{ij} at the midpoints $t = x - \frac{n}{2}$, $x + \frac{n}{2}$, $x + \frac{3n}{2}$, Schoen (1979, p. 258) derived the weight functions:

$$ {}_ng_x^{ij} = \frac{n^2}{240}\left({}_nM_{x-n}^{ij} + 38\,{}_nM_x^{ij} + {}_nM_{x+n}^{ij}\right), \tag{3.17a} $$

and

$$ {}_nh_x^{ij} = \frac{n^2}{240}\left(-6\,{}_nM_{x-n}^{ij} + 72\,{}_nM_x^{ij} + 14\,{}_nM_{x+n}^{ij}\right), \tag{3.17b} $$

$i = 1,\ldots,k, j = 1,\ldots,k+1, i \neq j$, and let

$$_n g_x^{ii} = -\sum_{j \neq i} {}_n g_x^{ij}$$

and

$$_n h_x^{ii} = -\sum_{j \neq i} {}_n h_x^{ij}.$$

In words, the first of these weight functions states that ℓ_x^i should be weighted about 38 times more heavily by $_n M_x^{ij}$ than by $_n M_{x-n}^{ij}$ and $_n M_{x+n}^{ij}$ and that each of the latter should be equally weighted. By contrast, in the second weight function, $_n M_{x+n}^{ij}$, which is "closer" to ℓ_{x+n}^i than is $_n M_{x-n}^{ij}$, is weighted relatively more heavily.

While these weights were derived under model specifications different from those in the present paper, the assumptions under which they were derived, nevertheless, are analytically justifiable as finite approximations for the present model. In particular, we have the following statement.

Proposition. Schoen's (1979) specifications of a linear ℓ_x^i function and a quadratic μ_{x+t}^{ij} function are equivalent to particular finite-difference approximations to Taylor series expansions of general nonlinear expressions for ℓ_x^i and μ_{x+t}^{ij}.

Proof. The linear Taylor series expansion of ℓ_{x+t}^i from the point ℓ_x^i for $0 \leq t < n$ is

$$\ell_{x+t}^i = \ell_x^i + t \cdot D\ell_x^i + R_2, \tag{3.18}$$

where D denotes the derivative operator and R_2 is the remainder term. This expansion assumes the existence of the first derivative of ℓ_x^i, but, since ℓ_{x+t}^i here is taken to be a general nonlinear function for which we have not specified a particular algebraic form, we cannot express $D\ell_x^i$ algebraically. On the other hand, if we have computed numerical values for ℓ_x and ℓ_{x+n}, we can approximate $D\ell_x^i$ by the finite first-difference quotient over the $[x,x+n)$ age interval:

$$\Delta\ell_x^i = \frac{\ell_{x+n}^i - \ell_x^i}{n} = \frac{-\left(\ell_x^i - \ell_{x+n}^i\right)}{n}. \tag{3.19}$$

Using (3.19) in (3.18) and dropping the remainder term, we then have

$$\ell_{x+t}^i = \ell_x^i - \frac{t}{n}\left(\ell_x^i - \ell_{x+n}^i\right), \tag{3.20}$$

which is Schoen's (1979) linear ℓ_x^i specification. Thus, Schoen's specification can be viewed as a finite-difference approximation to a Taylor polynomial for ℓ_{x+t}^i that passes through both ℓ_x^i and ℓ_{x+t}^i.

Similarly, assuming the existence of its first and second derivatives, the quadratic Taylor series expansion of a general nonlinear μ_{x+t}^{ij} from the point $\mu_{x-\frac{n}{2}}^{ij}$ for $0 \leq t < 2n$ is

$$\mu_{[x-\frac{n}{2}]+t}^{ij} = \mu_{x-\frac{n}{2}}^{ij} + t \cdot D\mu_{x-\frac{n}{2}}^{ij} + \frac{t^2}{2!} D^{(2)}\mu_{x-\frac{n}{2}}^{ij} + R_3. \tag{3.21}$$

Again, we cannot express the derivatives of μ_{x+t}^{ij} algebraically. But if we assume $\mu_{x-\frac{n}{2}}^{ij} = {}_nM_{x-n}^{ij}$, $\mu_{x+\frac{n}{2}}^{ij} = {}_nM_x^{ij}$, and $\mu_{x+\frac{3n}{2}}^{ij} = {}_nM_{x+n}^{ij}$, we have the following finite-difference approximations to the first and second derivatives of $\mu_{x-\frac{n}{2}}^{ij}$:

$$\Delta\mu^{ij}_{x-\frac{n}{2}} = \frac{1}{n}\left({}_nM^{ij}_x - {}_nM^{ij}_{x-n}\right), \tag{3.22}$$

and

$$\Delta^{(2)}\mu^{ij}_{x-\frac{n}{2}} = \frac{1}{n^2}\left({}_nM^{ij}_{x+n} - 2\,{}_nM^{ij}_x + {}_nM^{ij}_{x-n}\right). \tag{3.23}$$

Substituting these expressions into (3.21), using $\mu^{ij}_{x-\frac{n}{2}} = {}_nM^{ij}_{x-n}$, and dropping the remainder term, we obtain the following approximate Taylor polynomial:

$$\mu^{ij}_{[x-\frac{n}{2}]+t} = {}_nM^{ij}_{x-n} + \frac{t}{n}\left({}_nM^{ij}_x - {}_nM^{ij}_{x-n}\right)$$

$$+ \frac{t^2}{2!n^2}\left({}_nM^{ij}_{x+n} - 2\,{}_nM^{ij}_x + {}_nM^{ij}_{x-n}\right). \tag{3.24}$$

This equation is very close to the quadratic expression for $\mu^{ij}_{[x-\frac{n}{2}]+t}$ specified by Schoen (1979). The latter expression contains the following additional term:

$$C = \frac{-5}{8}\,{}_nM^{ij}_{x-n} + \frac{6}{8}\,{}_nM^{ij}_x - \frac{1}{8}\,{}_nM^{ij}_{x+n}. \tag{3.25}$$

Since this term is not multiplied by a power of t, it amounts to a correction of the initial value term ${}_nM^{ij}_{x-n}$ in (3.24). How is this correction factor to be interpreted? Since there is one and only one polynomial of degree r-1 that takes on the r ordinate values $y_1,\ldots,y_r$ at the r abscissa values $x_1,\ldots,x_r$ (Young and Gregory, 1972, p. 258), and since we have required that our quadratic (3.24) pass through ${}_nM^{ij}_{x-n}$, ${}_nM^{ij}_x$, and ${}_nM^{ij}_{x+n}$ at $x - \frac{n}{2}$, $x + \frac{n}{2}$, and $x + \frac{3n}{2}$, the correction (3.25) is the factor necessary to adjust (3.24) to ensure that this requirement is satisfied. This completes the proof.

In brief, while Schoen's (1979) assumptions taken in isolation are analytically inconsistent, the foregoing argument shows that they are analytically consistent finite approximations within the context of the present model. Furthermore, since the survival functions of this model exhibit quadratic "local behavior" while the force functions (to be derived in the next subsection) are capable of cubic- or more general polynomial-type "local behavior," it is appropriate to truncate expansions of the latter at the quadratic term if expansions of the former are truncated at the linear term. Why stop at those terms? While it is possible to take expansions (3.18) and (3.21) out to higher-order derivatives, this would require an iterative solution to the estimation algorithm (to be stated below) in order to obtain subsequent values of the survival function beyond ℓ^{i}_{x+n}. Since we have taken as one of our goals the production of estimators with explicit algebraic forms, we have opted to stop the expansions as indicated above.

To use the weight functions (3.17a) and (3.17b) in modifying the Schoen-Land *GA*, we first define the matrices

$$
{}_n\underset{\sim}{G}_x = \begin{bmatrix} {}_ng_x^{11} & -{}_ng_x^{12} & \cdots & -{}_ng_x^{1k} \\ -{}_ng_x^{21} & {}_ng_x^{22} & \cdots & -{}_ng_x^{2k} \\ \vdots & \vdots & & \\ -{}_ng_x^{k1} & -{}_ng_x^{k2} & \cdots & {}_ng_x^{kk} \end{bmatrix}
$$

and

$$
{}_n\underset{\sim}{H}_x = \begin{bmatrix} {}_nh_x^{11} & -{}_nh_x^{12} & \cdots & -{}_nh_x^{1k} \\ -{}_nh_x^{21} & {}_nh_x^{22} & \cdots & -{}_nh_x^{2k} \\ \vdots & \vdots & & \vdots \\ -{}_nh_x^{k1} & -{}_nh_x^{k2} & \cdots & {}_nh_x^{kk} \end{bmatrix}.
$$

Next, we note that a matrix form of the following version of the origin-independent person-years equations, which was derived by Ledent (1978, p. 45):

$$
{}_nL_x^i = n \cdot \ell_{x+n}^i + \sum_{j \neq i} {}_na_x^{ij} \cdot {}_nd_x^{ij} - \sum_{j \neq i} {}_na_x^{ji} \cdot {}_nd_x^{ji}, \tag{3.26}
$$

$i = 1,\ldots,k, j = 1,\ldots,k+1, i \neq j$, can be written as

$$
{}_n\underset{\sim}{L}_x = n\underset{\sim}{\ell}_{x+n} + \underset{\sim}{\ell}_x \, {}_n\underset{\sim}{G}_x + \underset{\sim}{\ell}_{x+n} \, {}_n\underset{\sim}{H}_x, \tag{3.27}
$$

by using Eqs. (3.16) and (3.17). Hence, following Schoen (1979, p. 259), (3.27) can be substituted into (3.14) to obtain

$$
\underset{\sim}{\ell}_{x+n} = \underset{\sim}{\ell}_x [\underset{\sim}{I} - {}_n\underset{\sim}{G}_x \, {}_n\underset{\sim}{M}_x][\underset{\sim}{I} + n \, {}_n\underset{\sim}{M}_x + {}_n\underset{\sim}{H}_x \, {}_n\underset{\sim}{M}_x]^{-1}, \tag{3.28}
$$

where I is identity matrix of order k. In this form, the product of the matrix expressions contained in brackets in (3.28) clearly is recognizable as the k-by-k transition probability matrix ${}_n\underset{\sim}{\Pi}_x$. Therefore, this equation also applies when the survival function vectors ℓ_x are replaced by the gross flow matrices $\underset{\sim}{\ell}_{[x]}$.

We summarize the foregoing results into the following *algorithm for piecewise estimation of the quadratic model:*

Orientation:

$$ {}_n\underset{\sim}{M}_x = {}_n\hat{\underset{\sim}{m}}_{[x]}, \tag{3.29a}$$

Flow:

$$\hat{\underset{\sim}{\ell}}_{[x]+n} = \hat{\underset{\sim}{\ell}}_{[x]}\ {}_n\hat{\underset{\sim}{\Pi}}_x,$$

$$= \hat{\underset{\sim}{\ell}}_{[x]}[\underset{\sim}{I} - {}_n\underset{\sim}{G}_x\ {}_n\underset{\sim}{M}_x][\underset{\sim}{I} + n\,{}_n\underset{\sim}{M}_x + {}_n\underset{\sim}{H}_x\ {}_n\underset{\sim}{M}_x]^{-1} \tag{3.29b}$$

$$\hat{\underset{\sim}{\ell}}_{x+n} = \hat{\underset{\sim}{\ell}}_x\ {}_n\hat{\underset{\sim}{\Pi}}_x$$

$$= \hat{\underset{\sim}{\ell}}_x[\underset{\sim}{I} - {}_n\underset{\sim}{G}_x\ {}_n\underset{\sim}{M}_x][\underset{\sim}{I} + n\,{}_n\underset{\sim}{M}_x + {}_n\underset{\sim}{H}_x\ {}_n\underset{\sim}{M}_x]^{-1}, \tag{3.29c}$$

Person-Years:

$$ {}_n\hat{\underset{\sim}{L}}_{[x]} = n\hat{\underset{\sim}{\ell}}_{[x]+n} + \hat{\underset{\sim}{\ell}}_{[x]}\ {}_n\underset{\sim}{G}_x + \hat{\underset{\sim}{\ell}}_{[x]+n}\ {}_n\underset{\sim}{H}_x, \tag{3.29d}$$

$$ {}_n\hat{\underset{\sim}{L}}_x = n\hat{\underset{\sim}{\ell}}_{x+n} + \hat{\underset{\sim}{\ell}}_x\ {}_n\underset{\sim}{G}_x + \hat{\underset{\sim}{\ell}}_{x+n}\ {}_n\underset{\sim}{H}_x. \tag{3.29e}$$

The orientation Eqs. (3.29a) are the same as those for the linear model (3.13a), whereas the flow equations (3.29b) and (3.29c) reduce to those for the linear model if

$$ {}_n\underset{\sim}{G}_x = {}_n\underset{\sim}{H}_x = \frac{n^2}{4}\ {}_n\underset{\sim}{M}_x.$$

Thus, just as the quadratic model (2.19) generalizes the linear model (2.18), so does this estimation algorithm (3.29) generalize (3.13). Furthermore, remarks made about adapting (3.13) for the first and last age intervals and estimating other life-table functions also apply here.

3.4. PROBLEMS OF EMBEDDABILITY, IDENTIFICATION, AND ESTIMATION OF TRANSITION FORCES IN THE LINEAR AND QUADRATIC MODELS

It is clear that algorithms (3.13) and (3.29) provide convenient computational devices for piecewise estimation of the linear and quadratic IDLTs. Nonetheless, the *GA* for the classic model (3.12) contains one element not found in either the linear or quadratic *GA*s: estimates of the transition forces. Under the assumption of piecewise-constant forces, these are equated to the observed rates. Their importance derives from the fact that they represent the most fundamental level at which an IDLT model can be formulated. Furthermore, for estimation of IDLT functions at ages other than integer multiples of the age intervals used in the algorithms (3.13) and (3.29), it is useful to obtain estimates of the underlying instantaneous model. We now address this and related issues for the linear and quadratic model.

To derive an estimator for the forces of transition in the quadratic model, note that, after application of algorithm (3.29), the $\ell^{ij}_{[x]+n}$ and $_nL^{ij}_{[x]}$ values of (2.19) and (2.25) have been estimated. Then (2.19) can be solved for b^{ij}:

$$b^{ij} = \frac{1}{n}\left(\ell^{ij}_{[x]+n} - \ell^{ij}_{[x]} - n^2 c^{ij}\right), \tag{3.30}$$

or, after rearranging and multiplying by $\frac{n^2}{2}$:

$$\frac{n}{2}\,\ell^{ij}_{[x]+n} = \frac{n}{2}\,\ell^{ij}_{[x]} + \frac{n^2}{2}\,b^{ij} + \frac{n^3}{2}\,c^{ij}. \tag{3.31}$$

Subtracting this from (2.25), we have

$$_nL^{ij}_{[x]} - \frac{n}{2}\,\ell^{ij}_{[x]+n} = \frac{n}{2}\,\ell^{ij}_{[x]} - \frac{n^3}{6}\,c^{ij}, \tag{3.32}$$

or, solving for c^{ij}:

$$c^{ij} = \frac{6}{n^3}\left[\frac{n}{2}\left(\ell^{ij}_{[x]} + \ell^{ij}_{[x]+n}\right) - {}_nL^{ij}_{[x]}\right]. \tag{3.33}$$

Next, replace $\frac{n}{2}$ in (3.31) by $\frac{n}{3}$ to obtain:

$$\frac{n}{3}\,\ell^{ij}_{[x]+n} = \frac{n}{3}\,\ell^{ij}_{[x]} + \frac{n^2}{3}\,b^{ij} + \frac{n^3}{3}\,c^{ij}. \tag{3.34}$$

Subtracting this from (2.25) and solving for b^{ij} yields:

$$b^{ij} = \frac{6}{n^2}\left[{}_nL^{ij}_{[x]} - \frac{n}{3}\left(2\ell^{ij}_{[x]} + \ell^{ij}_{[x]+n}\right)\right]. \tag{3.35}$$

Hence, by using these expressions in (2.19), we have

$$\ell^{ij}_{[x]+t} = \ell^{ij}_{[x]} + \frac{6t}{n^2}\left[{}_nL^{ij}_{[x]} - \frac{2n}{3}\,\ell^{ij}_{[x]} - \frac{n}{3}\,\ell^{ij}_{[x]+n}\right]$$

$$+ \frac{6t^2}{n^3}\left[\frac{n}{2}\left(\ell^{ij}_{[x]} + \ell^{ij}_{[x]+n}\right) - {}_nL^{ij}_{[x]}\right]. \tag{3.36}$$

Furthermore, the rate of change (derivative) of this gross flows expression then is

$$\frac{d}{dt}\,\ell^{ij}_{[x]+t} = \frac{6}{n^2}\left[{}_nL^{ij}_{[x]} - \frac{n}{3}\left(2\ell^{ij}_{[x]} + \ell^{ij}_{[x]+n}\right)\right]$$

$$+ \frac{12t}{n^3}\left[\frac{n}{2}\left(\ell^{ij}_{[x]} + \ell^{ij}_{[x]+n}\right) - {}_nL^{ij}_{[x]}\right] = b_{ij} + 2c_{ij}t, \tag{3.37}$$

where the coefficients in this last equation are defined by the corresponding terms in the first equality.

In matrix notation, we put the coefficients of (3.37) into matrices:

$$\underset{\sim}{B} = \begin{bmatrix} b_{11} & b_{12} & \cdots & b_{1k} \\ b_{21} & b_{22} & \cdots & b_{2k} \\ \vdots & \vdots & & \vdots \\ b_{k1} & b_{k2} & \cdots & b_{kk} \end{bmatrix} \quad \text{and} \quad \underset{\sim}{C} = \begin{bmatrix} c_{11} & c_{12} & \cdots & c_{1k} \\ c_{21} & c_{22} & \cdots & c_{2k} \\ \vdots & \vdots & & \vdots \\ c_{k1} & c_{k2} & \cdots & c_{kk} \end{bmatrix}$$

and then write the sets of Eqs. (3.36) and (3.37) as

$$\underset{\sim}{\ell}_{[x]+t} = \underset{\sim}{\ell}_{[x]} + \underset{\sim}{B}t + \underset{\sim}{C}t^2, \tag{3.38}$$

and

$$\frac{d}{dt}\underset{\sim}{\ell}_{[x]+t} = \underset{\sim}{B} + 2\underset{\sim}{C}t. \tag{3.39}$$

Next, we note that the transition probability matrix, ${}_{t}\underset{\sim}{\Pi}_{x}$, has the following expression in terms of the $\underset{\sim}{B}$ and $\underset{\sim}{C}$ matrices:

$${}_{t}\underset{\sim}{\Pi}_{x} = \underset{\sim}{\ell}^{-1}_{[x]}\underset{\sim}{\ell}_{[x]+t} = \underset{\sim}{I} + \underset{\sim}{\ell}^{-1}_{[x]}\underset{\sim}{B}t + \underset{\sim}{\ell}^{-1}_{[x]}\underset{\sim}{C}t^2. \tag{3.40}$$

Furthermore, the Kolmogorov equations (3.6) can be solved for the matrix of transition forces

$$\underset{\sim}{\mu}_{x+t} = {}_{t}\underset{\sim}{\Pi}_{x}^{-1}\frac{d}{dt}\,{}_{t}\underset{\sim}{\Pi}_{x} = \underset{\sim}{\ell}^{-1}_{[x]+t}\frac{d}{dt}\underset{\sim}{\ell}_{[x]+t}, \tag{3.41}$$

where the second equality follows from use of (3.40). Finally, by noting that estimates of the $\underset{\sim}{B}$ and $\underset{\sim}{C}$ coefficient matrices can be obtained from algorithm (3.29), we obtain the following matrix *estimator of the transition forces of the quadratic model:*

$$\hat{\underset{\sim}{\mu}}_{x+t} = \left[\hat{\underset{\sim}{\ell}}_{[x]} + \hat{\underset{\sim}{B}}t + \hat{\underset{\sim}{C}}t^2\right]^{-1}[\hat{\underset{\sim}{B}}+2\hat{\underset{\sim}{C}}t], \tag{3.42}$$

for $0 \leq t < n$. Several remarks will help to interpret this estimator.

First, observe that the derivation of the corresponding estimator for the linear model is a special case of the foregoing derivation. Specifically, since $c^{ij} = 0$ in the linear model, (3.30) becomes

$$b^{ij} = \frac{1}{n}\left(\ell^{ij}_{[x]+n} - \ell^{ij}_{[x]}\right), \tag{3.43}$$

so that (3.36) is

$$\ell^{ij}_{[x]+t} = \ell^{ij}_{[x]} + \frac{t}{n}\left(\ell^{ij}_{[x]+n} - \ell^{ij}_{[x]}\right), \tag{3.44}$$

and (3.37) correspondingly becomes

$$\frac{d}{dt}\ell^{ij}_{[x]+t} = \frac{1}{n}\left(\ell^{ij}_{[x]+n} - \ell^{ij}_{[x]}\right). \tag{3.45}$$

Using the right-hand side of this last equation to define the elements of the B matrix, we then obtain the following expressions corresponding to (3.38) and (3.39):

$$\underset{\sim}{\ell}_{[x]+t} = \underset{\sim}{\ell}_{[x]} + \underset{\sim}{B}t, \tag{3.46a}$$

and

$$\frac{d}{dt}\underset{\sim}{\ell}_{[x]+t} = \underset{\sim}{B}. \tag{3.46b}$$

Consequently, the matrix *estimator of the transition forces of the linear model is*

$$\hat{\underset{\sim}{\mu}}_{x+t} = \left[\hat{\underset{\sim}{\ell}}_{[x]} + \hat{\underset{\sim}{B}}t\right]^{-1}[\hat{\underset{\sim}{B}}], \tag{3.47}$$

for $0 \leq t < n$.

Second, because the transition forces (2.3) were defined in terms of limits on functions of the transition probabilities, it may be useful to reexpress these force estimators in terms of the probabilities. For the linear model, we have the following equivalent expression for (3.47):

$$\hat{\underset{\sim}{\mu}}_{x+t} = {}_t\hat{\underset{\sim}{\Pi}}_x^{-1} \frac{d}{dt} {}_t\hat{\underset{\sim}{\Pi}}_x$$

$$= \left[\hat{\underset{\sim}{\ell}}_{[x]}^{-1}\hat{\underset{\sim}{\ell}}_{[x]} + \hat{\underset{\sim}{\ell}}_{[x]}^{-1}\hat{\underset{\sim}{B}}t\right]^{-1}\left[\hat{\underset{\sim}{\ell}}_x^{-1}\hat{\underset{\sim}{B}}\right]$$

$$= \left[\underset{\sim}{I} - \frac{t}{n}(\underset{\sim}{I} - {}_n\hat{\underset{\sim}{\Pi}}_x)\right]^{-1}\left[-\frac{1}{n}(\underset{\sim}{I} - {}_n\hat{\underset{\sim}{\Pi}}_x)\right]$$

$$= -[n\underset{\sim}{I} - t(\underset{\sim}{I} - {}_n\hat{\underset{\sim}{\Pi}}_x)]^{-1}[\underset{\sim}{I} - {}_n\hat{\underset{\sim}{\Pi}}_x], \qquad (3.48)$$

where the second equality follows by premultiplying (3.46a) and (3.46b) by $\underset{\sim}{\ell}_{[x]}^{-1}$ to convert gross flows to transition probabilities, the third follows from substituting in the expressions for the components of $\underset{\sim}{B}$ from (3.45) and rearranging, and the fourth follows by simplifying. A corresponding derivation for the quadratic estimator (3.42) leads to

$$\hat{\underset{\sim}{\mu}}_{x+t} = \left[\underset{\sim}{I} + \hat{\underset{\sim}{\ell}}_{[x]}^{-1}\hat{\underset{\sim}{B}}t + \hat{\underset{\sim}{\ell}}_{[x]}^{-1}\hat{\underset{\sim}{C}}t^2\right]^{-1}\left[\hat{\underset{\sim}{\ell}}_{[x]}^{-1}\hat{\underset{\sim}{B}} + \hat{\underset{\sim}{\ell}}_{[x]}^{-1}\hat{\underset{\sim}{C}}t\right], \qquad (3.49)$$

which is not so readily interpretable.

In scalar terms, what do these expressions imply about the algebraic forms of the forces of transition in the linear and quadratic models? In the case of *linear gross flows*, (3.47) and (3.48), in general, *produce rational polynomial force functions of degree k-1 in the numerator and degree k in the denominator*, where k is the number of living states in the state space Ω.[15] This assertion follows by noting that the inverse of a k-by-k matrix that is linear in t (as in (3.47)) has a k-th degree polynomial in its determinant and a k-1 degree polynomial in its cofactor matrix, and then using Cramer's rule. Similar reasoning shows that the estimators for *quadratic gross flows*, (3.42) and (3.49), *produce rational polynomial force functions of degree 2k-1 in the numerator and degree 2k in the denominator.*

To illustrate these properties, consider the following explicit solution of the quadratic estimator (3.42) when k = 2:

$$\hat{\underset{\sim}{\mu}}_{x+t} = \frac{1}{\det}\begin{bmatrix} \hat{l}^{22}_{[x]} + \hat{b}_{22}t + \hat{c}_{22}t^2 & -\hat{b}_{12}t - \hat{c}_{12}t^2 \\ -\hat{b}_{21}t - \hat{c}_{21}t^2 & \hat{\ell}^{11}_{[x]} + \hat{b}_{11}t + \hat{c}_{11}t^2 \end{bmatrix}$$

$$\times \begin{bmatrix} \hat{b}_{11} + 2\hat{c}_{11}t & \hat{b}_{12} + 2\hat{c}_{12}t \\ \hat{b}_{21} + 2\hat{c}_{21}t & \hat{b}_{22} + 2\hat{c}_{22}t \end{bmatrix}, \tag{3.50}$$

where $\det = [\hat{\ell}^{11}_{[x]} + \hat{b}_{11}t + \hat{c}_{11}t^2][\hat{\ell}^{22}_{[x]} + \hat{b}_{22}t + \hat{c}_{22}t^2] - [\hat{b}_{21}t + \hat{c}_{21}t^2][\hat{b}_{12}t + \hat{c}_{12}t^2]$. Consistent with the foregoing assertion, this matrix equation yields rational polynomial expressions for the μ^{ij}_{x+t} of degree 3 in the numerator and degree

[15] *This characterization of the algebraic form of the forces of transition in the linear model corrects that given in Schoen and Land (1979, p. 767) in terms of the derivatives of the origin-dependent transfer functions. We are grateful to Hoem and Jensen (1981) for pointing out that the prior derivation erroneously assumed linearly distributed decrements. Linearity in the gross flows does not imply that individual decrement (d) functions are linear. Conversely, linearity in the decrements does not imply linear gross flows.*

4 in the denominator. Furthermore, given the composition of the b_{ij} and c_{ij} coefficients in (3.37), it is clear that the forces in (3.50) are not constrained to be strictly increasing or decreasing over the x to x+n age interval. Rather, they may increase, decrease, or remain essentially constant. By contrast, an examination of the estimator (3.48) shows that the forces of transition in the linear model must be strictly increasing over the interval x to x+n.

Although the foregoing estimators for the transition forces in the linear and quadratic models were derived under the Markov specifications adopted in Section 2, this is no guarantee that they will produce numerical estimates that are sensible transition forces (i.e., are nonnegative) when they are applied to a particular set of occurrence/exposure rates. The technical term for this question of whether the estimated transition matrix ${}_{n}\hat{\underset{\sim}{\Pi}}_{x}$ in algorithms (3.13) or (3.29) could have arisen via the evolution of an age-inhomogeneous continuous-time Markov process is *embeddability*. Singer and Spilerman (1976a,b) summarize the mathematical literature on the embedding problem and develop various testing and estimation strategies for the constant-forces model. They also show, by analysis of several numerical examples, that a transition matrix is not necessarily embeddable even in this simple, classic model. Similarly, Hoem and Jensen (1981) have shown, by numerical examples, that the transition matrices estimated under the linear algorithm (3.13) are not necessarily embeddable.

The linear model makes a strong assumption about the behavior of the gross flows functions within an estimation-age-interval--namely, that the gross flows between distinct states grow linearly with duration into the interval. Since that may, of course, be an erroneous characterization of the behavior of the flows implied by a given set of observed occurrence/exposure rates, the numerical examples of Hoem and Jensen (1981) are to be expected. Likewise, it is not surprising that at least one empirical study, that of Manninen (1979), has produced a set of rates that are not embeddable under the linear model.[11] Furthermore, even though the quadratic model developed herein makes a somewhat more flexible characterization of the gross flows (and, therefore, of the transition forces), it is surely the case that there are sets of numerical values of occurrence/exposure rates for which it is not embeddable.

In the face of this uncertainty with respect to embeddability, and in view of the absence of *sufficient* conditions for embeddability that lead to practical test procedures for empirically estimated transition matrices (Singer and Spilerman, 1976a, p. 10), we can only recommend that the age-specific transition matrices, ${}_n\hat{\underset{\sim}{\Pi}}_x$, estimated by application of algorithms (3.13) or (3.29) be tested for embeddability by application of one or more of the existing *necessary* conditions that have been found in the mathematical statistics literature (for a statement of these, see Singer and Spilerman, 1976a, p. 11). One of the most applicable of these is

$$\det {}_n\underset{\sim}{\Pi}_x > 0, \tag{3.51}$$

which is due to Kingman (1962). In the case of a 2-by-2 matrix, this reduces to

$$\operatorname{trace} {}_n\underset{\sim}{\Pi}_x > 1, \tag{3.52}$$

which is also sufficient in this case (Singer and Cohen, 1980, p. 279).[16]

Lest the reader be led, by the Hoem and Jensen (1981) numerical examples, to the conclusion that no sets of observed occurrence/exposure rates exist for which the transition matrices estimated under the linear model (3.13) are embeddable, it should be noted that the nuptiality table for Swedish females reported in Schoen and Land (1979, pp. 772-773) satisfies (3.52) for all estimation-age-intervals except the highest one for which marriages and divorces are nonzero (80-84). A similar statement can be made for the nuptiality table reported in Section 4, which is estimated by the quadratic model (3.29). Thus, just as there exist empirical circumstances under which these 2-living-state models are not embeddable, there are others under which they satisfy the criterion (3.52). Furthermore, while the general test condition (3.51) is only a necessary condition and thus cannot be used to prove that a k-living-state ($k > 2$) model is embeddable, it is reasonable to assume that the foregoing assertion also applies in this general case.

Assuming that a k-by-k transition matrix ${}_n\hat{\underset{\sim}{\Pi}}_x$ estimated by algorithms (3.13) or (3.29) satisfies the necessary condition for embeddability (3.51), there may be no other problems in identifying and/or estimating the corresponding forces of tran-

[16] *Actually, conditions (3.51) and (3.52) do not take sampling variability into account. Therefore, Singer and Cohen (1980, pp. 280-284) developed a statistical test based on (3.52) under the assumption of binomial sampling of individuals evolving independently and observed at two points in time. Such sampling considerations are especially important when relatively small samples are used in estimating the transition matrices, as opposed to the population-level data sets typically used in IDLT estimation.*

sition, as Eqs. (3.42) and (3.47) have unique solutions except under the extraordinary circumstances of exact linear dependence. Consequently, provided that these solutions yield transition force functions that are nonnegative throughout the x to x+n estimation-age-interval, there may be no further embeddability, identification, or estimation problems.

The exception to this statement, again illustrated by Hoem and Jensen (1981), is the case of a model that possesses (at least one instance of) states i and h between which *direct* transitions are impossible (i.e., the forces are identically zero), but in which it is possible to move from state i at age x to state h at age x+t (t > 0) *indirectly* through an intermediate state j. In a model of this type, Hoem and Jensen (1981) have shown that the estimator of the forces for the linear model (3.47) leads to an estimated force between states i and h that is nonzero except at the midpoint of the estimation-age-interval.

Again, this apparently pathological result is *not* unique to the linear model. Coleman (1964a, pp. 181-182) observed a similar problem in the classic constant-forces model long ago in the context of estimation from panel data, and the difficulty occurs in the quadratic model as well. From the point of view of estimation, this problem can be characterized as one of imposing *structural zeros* on the force function estimators. A satisfactory statistical solution to this problem has been achieved for the constant-forces model only recently by Cohen and Singer (1979). After obtaining a set of initial estimates of transition forces, Cohen and Singer (1979, pp. 124-126) develop an iterative procedure for minimizing, subject to nonnegativity and structural zeros constraints on the estimates of the forces, the statistic

$$G^2 = -2\Sigma[\text{observed flows}] \cdot \ln\left[\frac{\text{flows predicted by model}}{\text{observed flows}}\right],$$

where $\ln$ denotes natural logarithm, and the summation is over all cells in a flow matrix $\underset{\sim}{\ell}[x]$. Since G^2 has asymptotically, for large predicted flows, the distribution of a chi-square variate, this produces minimum chi-square estimates of the transition forces that satisfy the model constraints. It appears that the Cohen-Singer (1979) algorithm could be adapted for application to the linear and quadratic models developed in the present paper by using the transition matrices estimated from (3.13) or (3.29) to define the "observed flows" and using (3.42) or (3.47) to establish a set of initial estimates of the forces. To pursue this line of inquiry in detail, however, is beyond the scope of this chapter.

3.5. *APPROXIMATE SAMPLING VARIANCES AND STATISTICAL INFERENCE*

Up to this point, our discussion of statistical methods for IDLT models has focused primarily on the *estimation* of such models. It is appropriate, therefore, to end this section with a brief consideration of related topics in *hypothesis testing*. Ordinarily, in the demographic approach to IDLT calculation described in the introduction to this paper, it is assumed that the model is validly specified and that completely accurate population-level data are available. Consequently, conventional issues of statistical inference are irrelevant. However, in keeping with the more general statistical perspective taken herein, and in order to extend the applicability of the estimation methods developed above to data based on "less than complete" large populations, it is necessary that appropriate methods of inference be at least reachable, if not "ready to be taken off the shelf."

Recall that, in the classic piecewise-constant forces IDLT model, the observed occurrence/exposure rates (3.3) are taken as direct point estimates of the age-specific forces (3.12a). Under this specification, it is possible to derive an explicit estimator for the asymptotic variance of the rates (3.3). This theory is reviewed in Hoem and Jensen (1981).

By contrast, in the piecewise-rational-polynomial forces IDLT models studied herein, neither the transition forces nor the model transfer rates are constant within estimation-age-intervals. Furthermore, the asymptotic sampling theory for these models analogous to that for the classic constant-forces model has not been developed. Nonetheless, Aalen's (1975) investigations of the sampling distributions of nonparametric estimators for cumulative transition intensities are applicable here. For intensities that are continuously varying with age but not given a specific functional form, Aalen (1975, p. 66) suggests an estimator of the cumulative intensity defined by integrating from an initial age to age x (an indicator function of) the inverse of the (continuously varying) population exposed to risk of a specific transition with respect to the (continuously varying) cumulative function defined by the total number of occurrences of transitions of that type up to age x. Under the assumption that the population exposed to this risk over a unit age interval [x, x+n) does not vary much around its mean value there, Hoem (1976, p. 178) shows that first differences (defined on the unit age interval) of Aalen's estimator are approximately equal to the usual occurrence/exposure rate ${}_nM_x^{ij}$ for a state i to state j transition.

Using the same assumption, it may similarly be shown that first differences (defined again on the unit age interval) of Aalen's (1975, pp. 70-71) unbiased estimator of the sampling variance for his cumulative intensity estimator yield the following approximation to the asymptotic variances of ${}_nM_x^{ij}$:

$$\sigma^2\left({}_nM_x^{ij}\right) \cong {}_nD_x^{ij}/\left({}_nK_x^{i}\right)^2, \tag{3.54}$$

$i = 1,\ldots,k, j = 1,\ldots,k+1, i \neq j$. Although it may be possible to improve on these approximate estimators by using the specific properties of our parametric model, it is noteworthy that (3.54) reduces to Hoem's (1972b) estimator for the classic constant-forces IDLT model and to Chiang's (1968) nonparametric estimator in the single-decrement life table model. Finally, Aalen's (1975) investigations appear to support use of (3.54) to compute approximate asymptotic normal tests of significance on the ${}_nM_x^{ij}$. But the extent to which (3.54) can be used to generalize the conventional theory of inference for piecewise-constant forces summarized in Hoem and Jensen (1981) is an open research question.

4. MARITAL DISSOLUTION AND REMARRIAGE IN SWEDEN: APPLICATION AND COMPARISON OF METHODS

Consider now an application of the methods described in the preceding section to the two-table (three-state) marital-status system diagrammed in Fig. 1. Table 2 presents the results of applying the quadratic IDLT model to cohort data for females in Sweden born in the period 1930-1934. The data are the same as those employed in Schoen and Urton (1977) and use the period experience of the year 1973 to complete the cohort's life history.

The first tier of Table 2 presents an abridged life table for the birth cohort of 100,000 females. It shows estimates of the number of females surviving to subsequent ages ($\hat{\ell}^T$), the number of person-years lived by the cohort at and above each age ($\hat{T}^T$), and the number of person-years lived by the cohort at and above each age in the married ($\hat{T}^m$) and unmarried ($\hat{T}^u$) states. The observed occurrence/exposure rates, M^{Td}, M^{mu}, M^{md}, and M^{ud}, also are shown. The reader can verify that

$$\hat{\ell}^T_x = \hat{\ell}^m_x + \hat{\ell}^u_x, \qquad (4.1a)$$

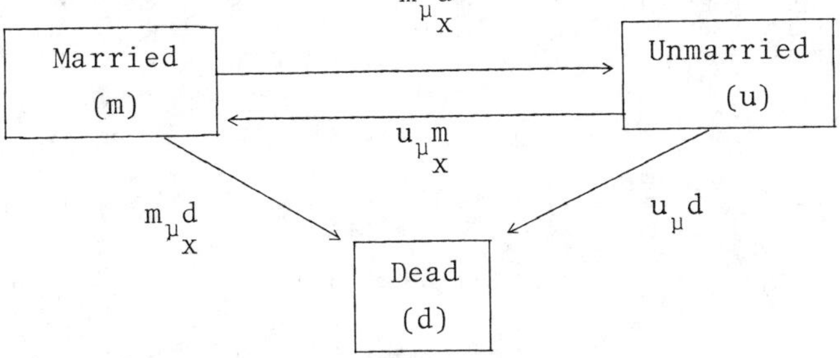

Fig. 1. Flow diagram for a marital status life table model.

TABLE 2. *Piecewise-Quadratic Survival Function Marital-Status Life Table, Females in Sweden, Cohort Born 1930-1934*[a]

A. *Aggregate life table for all ever-married persons*

Age (x)	Number of persons at age x ($\hat{\ell}^T$)	Number of person-years lived at and above the age shown ($\hat{T}^T$)	Number of person-years lived in m at and above the age shown ($\hat{T}^m$)	Number of person-years lived in u at and above the age shown ($\hat{T}^u$)	Occurrence/exposure rates (M^{Td})	(M^{mu})	(M^{md})	(M^{um})	(M^{ud})
0	100,000	7,424,987	3,558,270	3,866,718	0.040764	0.000000	0.000000	0.000000	0.040764
1	96,062	7,328,377	3,558,270	3,770,107	0.002944	0.000000	0.000000	0.000000	0.002944
5	94,939	6,946,938	3,558,270	3,388,668	0.001015	0.000000	0.000000	0.000000	0.001015
10	94,458	6,473,446	3,558,270	2,915,176	0.000776	0.000000	0.000000	0.000000	0.000776
15	94,092	6,002,071	3,558,270	2,443,802	0.000465	0.003191	0.000665	0.033278	0.000457
20	93,873	5,532,161	3,538,516	1,993,644	0.000572	0.010515	0.000429	0.183666	0.000680
25	93,606	5,063,452	3,335,805	1,727,647	0.000665	0.010894	0.000515	0.189127	0.001187
30	93,290	4,596,193	2,979,508	1,616,686	0.000778	0.009264	0.000618	0.091324	0.001724
35	92,930	4,130,586	2,579,972	1,550,614	0.001135	0.011609	0.000898	0.033658	0.002478
40	92,408	3,667,158	2,183,224	1,483,934	0.001560	0.013179	0.001284	0.019438	0.002888
45	91,687	3,206,760	1,803,772	1,402,988	0.002499	0.012014	0.002122	0.013481	0.004158
50	90,526	2,750,999	1,443,468	1,307,531	0.003815	0.012507	0.003359	0.007286	0.005491
55	88,787	2,302,420	1,103,665	1,198,755	0.005618	0.017602	0.005092	0.003105	0.007105
60	86,302	1,864,200	791,855	1,072,345	0.009004	0.025512	0.008225	0.001201	0.010504
65	82,481	1,441,343	519,120	922,223	0.015684	0.039434	0.014042	0.000494	0.017660
70	76,246	1,043,038	298,459	744,580	0.028180	0.059783	0.025723	0.000203	0.029869
75	66,197	684,815	141,382	543,434	0.051508	0.089778	0.048466	0.000094	0.052667
80	51,048	389,937	50,605	339,333	0.089098	0.126430	0.082431	0.000045	0.090402
85	32,369	179,879	11,727	168,152	0.181162	0.171942	0.153682	0.000000	[illegible]

B. Married (m)					C. Unmarried (u)				
Age (x)	Number of currently married persons at age x ($\hat{\ell}^m$)	Transition probabilities ($\hat{\pi}^{mm}$)	($\hat{\pi}^{mu}$)	($\hat{\pi}^{md}$)	Age (x)	Number of unmarried persons at age x ($\hat{\ell}^u$)	Transition probabilities ($\hat{\pi}^{uu}$)	($\hat{\pi}^{um}$)	($\hat{\pi}^{ud}$)
20	14,904	0.9637	0.0342	0.0022	0	100,000	0.9606	0.0000	0.0394
25	61,541	0.9623	0.0351	0.0026	1	96,062	0.9883	0.0000	0.0117
30	78,461	0.9600	0.0368	0.0032	5	94,939	0.9949	0.0000	0.0051
35	80,547	0.9435	0.0518	0.0047	10	94,458	0.9961	0.0000	0.0039
40	77,830	0.9332	0.0602	0.0066	15	94,092	0.8393	0.1584	0.0023
45	73,915	0.9336	0.0556	0.0108	20	78,969	0.3996	0.5974	0.0030
50	70,109	0.9246	0.0585	0.0170	25	32,065	0.3951	0.6001	0.0048
55	65,510	0.8929	0.0815	0.0256	30	14,829	0.6401	0.3524	0.0075
60	58,827	0.8442	0.1148	0.0410	35	12,382	0.8405	0.1478	0.0117
65	49,806	0.7635	0.1670	0.0695	40	14,579	0.8977	0.0884	0.0140
70	38,093	0.6477	0.2284	0.1239	45	17,772	0.9177	0.0621	0.0202
75	24,703	0.4923	0.2873	0.2204	50	20,417	0.9393	0.0338	0.0269
80	12,173	0.3332	0.3165	0.3502	55	23,277	0.9509	0.0142	0.0349
85	4,061	0.0000	0.0000	1.0000	60	27,475	0.9434	0.0053	0.0513
					65	32,676	0.9131	0.0020	0.0848
					70	38,152	0.8596	0.0007	0.1397
					75	41,494	0.7658	0.0003	0.2339
					80	38,876	0.6291	0.0001	0.3708
					85	28,308	0.0000	0.0000	1.0000

[a] *Data from Schoen and Urton (1977). Calculation procedures as described in text.*

and

$$\hat{T}_x^T = \hat{T}_x^m + \hat{T}_x^u, \tag{4.1b}$$

as must be the case in a valid IDLT.

The second and third tiers of the table exhibit information for the married and unmarried states. For each age, these panels show estimates of the numbers of females married ($\hat{\ell}^m$) and unmarried ($\hat{\ell}^u$) and the transition probabilities of being in a given state at the next age shown in the table ($\hat{\pi}^{mm}$, $\hat{\pi}^{mu}$, $\hat{\pi}^{md}$, $\hat{\pi}^{uu}$, $\hat{\pi}^{um}$, $\hat{\pi}^{ud}$).

Table 2 was computed using the piecewise-quadratic algorithm (3.29).[17] In previous research reports (Schoen and Land, 1979; Schoen, 1979), we have calculated abridged marital status life tables from the data of Table 2 using three alternative "traditional" specifications of our General Algorithm: (1) piecewise-exponential survival functions, (2) piecewise-linear survival functions, and (3) piecewise-cubic person-years functions.[9] These tables can be compared with Table 2 in order to assess the relative empirical performance of the piecewise-quadratic specification.

Such a comparison can be made either in terms of survival functions or transition probabilities. Among survival functions, those of the quadratic generally are closer to those produced by the cubic than are those produced by the exponential or linear specifications (cf., Schoen, 1979, p. 262). Since the cubic specification usually is regarded as producing more accurate (decrement-only) life tables than either the

[17] *For the 80-84 and the open-ended 85+ age interval, the modified weight functions and calculation formulas derived by Schoen (1978, 1979) were used.*

linear or the exponential specification, this bodes well for the quadratic. Similarly, the quadratic performs relatively well in comparisons of transition probabilities.[18] For instance, the exponential and, particularly, the linear specifications produce greater ${}_5\hat{\pi}_{30}^{um}$ values than the quadratic specification, which is capable of reflecting the downward trend in the age-specific rates of marriage from age 25 through age 39. At the higher ages, the major cause of marital-status changes is mortality, and death rates rise steeply at those ages. There the exponential specification, with its piecewise-constant forces assumption, is least appropriate, while work by Schoen (1978) suggests that the quadratic may be preferable to the linear.

Additional information can be distilled from Table 2 by using (3.42) or (3.49) to estimate the age-specific coefficients of the transition force functions. Since k = 2 in this model, these, in general, will be cubic-to-quartic rational polynomials by the reasoning summarized in Section 3.4. However, the numerators of the married-unmarried transition forces contain terms that cancel, thus reducing to quadratics. The resulting parameter estimates for the numerator and denominator polynomials are displayed in Table 3. As might be expected, the numerator constant terms for all forces tend to move monotonically over all age intervals from the lowest to the highest. On the other hand, the other estimated coefficients tend to oscillate, and the cubic and quartic terms are quite small.

[18] *Schoen (1979, pp. 262-264) shows that the cubic specification yields systematically biased estimates of transition probabilities.*

Table 3. Estimated values of the force function coefficients for the piecewise-quadratic gross flows IDLT for marital status of Swedish females, cohort born 1930-1934[a]

A. Denominator coefficients[b] for all transition forces

Age	t	t^2	t^3	t^4
15	0.012505	-0.008930	0.000000	0.000000
20	-0.163388	0.007618	-0.000003	-0.000000
25	-0.163896	0.010604	-0.000003	-0.000000
30	-0.072508	0.006344	0.000000	-0.000000
35	0.010622	0.002471	0.000001	-0.000000
40	0.030951	0.001062	0.000002	-0.000000
45	0.016182	0.000700	0.000002	-0.000000
50	0.009348	0.000121	0.000004	-0.000000
55	0.012853	-0.000464	0.000008	0.000000
60	0.008897	-0.001075	0.000021	0.000000
65	-0.005334	-0.001052	0.000046	0.000001
70	-0.039737	0.000233	0.000088	0.000000
75	-0.109606	0.006235	0.000029	-0.000003
80	-0.201550	0.016568	-0.000219	-0.000009

	B. Numerator coefficients for married (m) to unmarried (u) transition forces			C. Numerator coefficients for unmarried (u) to married (m) transition forces		
Age	Constant	t	t^2	Constant	t	t^2
15	0.000000	0.000000	0.000000	-0.012976	0.017863	0.000000
20	0.008961	-0.000852	0.000003	0.155137	-0.014261	0.000001
25	0.008970	-0.000779	-0.000024	0.170741	-0.020285	0.000031
30	0.007350	0.000007	-0.000047	0.102216	-0.012692	0.000053
35	0.010130	0.000091	-0.000027	0.042250	-0.005074	0.000031
40	0.013079	-0.000416	-0.000006	0.022514	-0.001936	0.000011
45	0.011798	-0.000273	-0.000005	0.016024	-0.001445	0.000009
50	0.010698	0.000397	-0.000007	0.009386	-0.001054	0.000010
55	0.014625	0.000671	-0.000004	0.004240	-0.000560	0.000008
60	0.020985	0.000792	0.000005	0.001661	-0.000239	0.000005
65	0.033640	-0.000100	0.000026	0.000663	-0.000102	0.000003
70	0.052399	-0.002690	0.000093	0.000259	-0.000044	0.000002
75	0.078089	-0.008249	0.000263	0.000107	-0.000020	0.000001
80	0.104500	-0.016477	0.000700	0.000047	-0.000010	0.000001

Table 3 (Cont'd.)

D. Numerator coefficients for married (m) to dead (d) transition forces				
Age	Constant	t	t^2	t^3
15	0.000000	0.000000	0.000000	0.000000
20	0.000420	-0.000065	0.000002	0.000000
25	0.000462	-0.000062	0.000001	0.000000
30	0.000492	-0.000003	-0.000003	0.000000
35	0.000714	0.000035	-0.000003	0.000000
40	0.000922	0.000109	-0.000005	0.000000
45	0.001562	0.000171	-0.000006	0.000000
50	0.002572	0.000242	-0.000007	0.000000
55	0.003741	0.000428	-0.000015	-0.000000
60	0.005748	0.000767	-0.000036	-0.000001
65	0.009428	0.001231	-0.000086	-0.000001
70	0.017621	0.001334	-0.000184	-0.000000
75	0.037266	-0.001967	-0.000181	0.000007
80	0.062571	-0.008233	-0.000028	0.000019

E. Numerator coefficients for unmarried (u) to dead (d) transition forces				
Age	Constant	t	t^2	t^3
15	0.000472	-0.000003	0.000000	0.000000
20	0.000562	-0.000057	0.000002	0.000000
25	0.000939	-0.000082	0.000001	0.000000
30	0.001342	-0.000000	-0.000003	0.000000
35	0.002180	0.000007	-0.000003	0.000000
40	0.002360	0.000119	-0.000005	0.000000
45	0.003502	0.000147	-0.000006	0.000000
50	0.004732	0.000172	-0.000007	0.000000
55	0.005701	0.000388	-0.000014	-0.000000
60	0.007641	0.000830	-0.000036	-0.000001
65	0.012879	0.001074	-0.000082	-0.000001
70	0.021775	0.000934	-0.000175	-0.000000
75	0.040633	-0.002234	-0.000171	0.000007
80	0.067153	-0.008416	-0.000016	0.000019

[a] *Source: See Table 2.*

[b] *The constant term is 1 at all ages.*

Note that, by applying the trace condition (3.52) to the diagonal probabilities of Table 2, it can be verified that th coefficient estimates of Table 3 define meaningful Markov tra sition forces for all bound age intervals except the last (80-84). In that age interval, the forces of mortality from the married and unmarried states become so strong that the functional form of the forces implied by the quadratic model i incapable of adequately reflecting the change. The simplest solution is to seek data for shorter age intervals in this las age group. Nonetheless, it is noteworthy that the coefficient for that age interval in Table 3 do not depart greatly from th trend in the prior ages.

In brief, it is clear that the quadratic model and its as sociated estimation methods developed herein produces an abridged IDLT from the data of Table 2 that is preferable to those produced by traditional models and methods. We do not claim absolute superiority of the quadratic over alternative models and methods, because the quadratic makes assumptions about the behavior of gross flows and transition forces that may not hold up in all empirical applications. But, because of its ability to incorporate forces that increase, remain constant, or decrease within estimation-age-intervals, the quadratic model certainly is a leading contender when the analyst's objective is the production of an accurate abridged IDLT.

5. APPLICATION OF THE METHODS TO SURVIVORSHIP PROPORTIONS

Heretofore we have assumed that occurrence/exposure rates (3.3) of movement between the states of an IDLT model are available. Such is not always the case, however, particularly for analyses of interregional migration and labor-force status. For those kinds of analyses, the available data more typically are in the form of population statistics that can be used to estimate the *model survivorship proportions:*

$$ {}_{n}s_{x}^{ij} = \frac{\int_0^n \ell_{x+t}^{i} \cdot {}_{n}\pi_{x+t}^{ij}\, dt}{\int_0^n \ell_{x+t}^{i}\, dt} = \frac{{}_{n}L_{x+n}^{ij\#}}{{}_{n}L_{x}^{i}}, \qquad (5.1) $$

$i,j = 1,\ldots,k$, where ${}_{n}\pi_{x+t}^{ij}$ denotes the probability of being in state i at age x+t and in state j at x+t+n, and ${}_{n}L_{x+n}^{ij\#}$ is the number of persons in state j between the ages of x+n and x+2n who were in state i exactly n years earlier. Deterministically, ${}_{n}s_{x}^{ij}$ denotes the proportion of individuals in the stationary population, present in state i between the ages of x and x+n at a given time, who are in state j at a moment exactly n years later (cf., Ledent, 1980c, p. 545; Hoem and Jensen, 1981).

It should be emphasized that ${}_{n}L_{x+n}^{ij\#}$ as defined here is not the same as the ${}_{n}L_{[x+n]}^{ij}$ defined in (2.21). In (5.1), ${}_{n}L_{x+n}^{ij\#}$ is specified in relation to the closed group of persons in state i *between* the ages x and x+n. On the other hand, ${}_{n}L_{[x+n]}^{ij}$ is specified in relation to $\ell_{[x+n]}^{i}$, the closed group of persons in state i *at exact age* x+n. Since there are persons in state i between the ages x and x+n who are not in state i at exact age x+n, the distinction is a significant one.[19] Another way of saying this is to note that (5.1) implicitly defines the survivorship proportions as origin-independent by use of ℓ^{i}_{x+t} rather than $\ell^{i}_{[x]+t}$ functions. Rather than repeat the entire development analogous to (3.1) - (3.5), we shall merely note that the data to be described next are also origin-independent and thus can be taken as estimates of (5.1). In order to use these data to estimate a nonconstant-forces IDLT, we again make the stronger assumption of sectional stationarity analogous to (3.5).

Corresponding to (5.1), we seek to estimate the *population survivorship proportions*:

$$ {}_{n}S^{ij}_{x}(t) = {}_{n}K^{ij}_{x+n}(t)/{}_{n}K^{i}_{x}(t-n), \tag{5.2}$$

for i,j = 1,...,k, where ${}_{n}K^{ij}_{x+n}(t)$ denotes the number of persons in a real population (or sample thereof) who are located in state j between ages x+n and x+2n at historical time t and who were located in state i exactly n years earlier, and ${}_{n}K^{i}_{x}(t-n)$ denotes the number of persons in state i between the ages of x and x+n at historical time t-n. If the exact ages at which an individual is located in states i and j are known, then (5.2) provides direct estimates of the transition probabilities (2.8). This is similar to the usual data situation of panel studies with microdata in sociology.[1]

In most cases, however, we do not observe the survivorship proportions (5.2) but rather the *survivorship ratios*:

[19] *Nevertheless, Rogers (1975, p. 79) provides a derivation of survivorship proportions in terms of person-year functions based on closed groups formed at exact ages.*

$$_nR_x^{ij}(t) = {_nK_{x+n}^{ij}(t)}/\sum_j {_nK_{x+n}^{ij}(t)}. \tag{5.3}$$

For a sequence of age intervals $[x,x+n)$ covering an age range $[0,\omega)$, this is the type of data available on interregional migration from the decennial census retrospective questions (Rogers, 1975) and on labor-force status from certain U.S. Current Population Surveys (Schoen and Woodrow, 1980). To transform the R^{ij} to the S^{ij}, it is necessary to "survive back" the population in the denominator of (5.3) to get the denominator of (5.2). Assuming that the relevant mortality experience follows that of the initial state, the desired survivorship proportions can be found from

$$_nS_x^{ij} = {_nS_x^{ij}(t)} = {_nR_x^{ij}(t)} \cdot \frac{_n\hat{L}_{x+n}^{i}}{_n\hat{L}_x^{i}}, \tag{5.4}$$

providing that an appropriate life table is available (cf., Ledent, 1980a).

There are several ways to estimate the transition probabilities from the survivorship proportions, and thus to "orient" the model to the data. If the matrix of population survivorship proportions is denoted by

$$_n\underset{\sim}{S}_x = \begin{bmatrix} _nS_x^{11} & _nS_x^{12} & \cdots & _nS_x^{1k} \\ _nS_x^{21} & _nS_x^{22} & \cdots & _nS_x^{2k} \\ \vdots & \vdots & & \vdots \\ _nS_x^{k1} & _nS_x^{k2} & \cdots & _nS_x^{kk} \end{bmatrix},$$

one estimator is

$$ {}_{n}\hat{\underset{\sim}{\Pi}}_{x} = \frac{1}{2}\left({}_{n}\underset{\sim}{S}_{x} + {}_{n}\underset{\sim}{S}_{x-n}\right), \tag{5.5} $$

That orientation equation was suggested by Rees and Wilson (1977) and used, for example, by Schoen and Woodrow (1980). Its rationale rests on the fact that the transition matrix ${}_{n}\hat{\underset{\sim}{\Pi}}_{x}$ pertains to state transitions between exact ages x and x+n, whereas ${}_{n}\underset{\sim}{S}_{x}$ pertains to state transitions occurring, on the average, between exact ages $x + \frac{n}{2}$ and $x + \frac{3n}{2}$ and the matrix ${}_{n}\underset{\sim}{S}_{x-n}$ to changes between exact ages $x - \frac{n}{2}$ and $x + \frac{n}{2}$. Hence, provided that the age distribution of the observed population is not greatly skewed, the average of those $\underset{\sim}{S}$ matrices (5.5) will provide a "good" estimator of ${}_{n}\hat{\underset{\sim}{\Pi}}_{x}$ (Ledent, 1980c, p. 556).

Given the estimated transition matrix ${}_{n}\hat{\underset{\sim}{\Pi}}_{x}$ in (5.5), the IDLT can be estimated from initial cohort (radix) values by means of the *General Algorithm*. For the linear gross flows case, the survivorship ($\underset{\sim}{\ell}$) matrices and vectors can be found from (3.13b) and (3.13c), the person-years ($\underset{\sim}{L}$) matrices and vectors from (3.13d) and (3.13e), and the occurrence/exposure ($\underset{\sim}{M}$) rate matrices from

$$ {}_{n}\hat{\underset{\sim}{M}}_{x} = {}_{n}\hat{\underset{\sim}{L}}_{[x]}^{-1}\left(\hat{\underset{\sim}{\ell}}_{[x]} - \hat{\underset{\sim}{\ell}}_{[x]+n}\right), \tag{5.6} $$

a generally applicable expression obtained by rearranging the matrix version of (3.14). For the quadratic gross flows case, the $\underset{\sim}{\ell}$ values can be found from (3.29b) and (3.29c) and the $\underset{\sim}{M}$ and $\underset{\sim}{L}$ values by iteration using (5.6) and (3.29d). [Initial values for $\underset{\sim}{L}$ can be obtained from (3.13d).] For the constant forces case, the $\underset{\sim}{\ell}$ values can be found from (3.12b) and (3.12c), the $\underset{\sim}{M}$ values by iteration using

$$ {}_n\hat{\underset{\sim}{\Pi}}_x = \underset{\sim}{I} - n\,{}_n\underset{\sim}{M}_x + \frac{n^2}{2!}\,{}_n\underset{\sim}{M}_x^2 - \frac{n^3}{3!}\,{}_n\underset{\sim}{M}_x^3 + \cdots \qquad (5.7) $$

which is obtained from (3.8) and the relationship $\underset{\sim}{\mu}_x = -{}_n\underset{\sim}{M}_x$, or, more generally, the $\underset{\sim}{M}$ values can be found by using the methods described in Singer and Spilerman (1976a) or Cohen and Singer (1979), and the $\underset{\sim}{L}$ values follow from (5.6). Finally, provided there are no embeddability problems, the transition forces can be estimated. For the piecewise-constant forces model, this can be done by using the $\underset{\sim}{M}$ values, and, for the linear and quadratic models, by the methods described in Section 3.4.

An alternative method for estimating the transition probability matrix is given by

$$ {}_n\hat{\underset{\sim}{\Pi}}[x + \tfrac{n}{2}] = {}_n\underset{\sim}{S}_x . \qquad (5.8) $$

That method is discussed in Hoem and Jensen (1981) and was used by Hoem and Fong (1976, Fig. 14). In essence, it follows directly from viewing ${}_n\underset{\sim}{S}_x$ as pertaining to state transitions that occur, on the average, between exact ages $x + \frac{n}{2}$ and $x + \frac{3n}{2}$. In employing (5.8), it is convenient to use age intervals going from $x + \frac{n}{2}$ to $x + \frac{3n}{2}$ rather than from x to x+n, in effect, to change the age-accounting convention. Given the $\hat{\underset{\sim}{\Pi}}$ values, the remaining IDLT functions can be found as described above.

Under (3.13), the linear gross flows version of the *GA*, (5.8) can be derived mathematically from the orientation equation

$$ {}_n\underset{\sim}{S}_x = {}_n\underset{\sim}{s}_x, \tag{5.9} $$

where ${}_n\underset{\sim}{s}_x$ is the matrix of model survivorship proportions of the same form as ${}_n\underset{\sim}{S}_x$. Paralleling Rogers (1975), (5.1) can be expressed in matrix form as

$$ {}_n\underset{\sim}{s}_x = ({}_n\underset{\sim}{L}_x^{\#})^{-1}\, {}_n\underset{\sim}{L}_{x+n}^{\#}, \tag{5.10} $$

where

$$ {}_nL_{x+n}^{\#} = \begin{bmatrix} {}_nL_{x+n}^{11\#} & {}_nL_{x+n}^{12\#} & \cdots & {}_nL_{x+n}^{1k\#} \\ {}_nL_{x+n}^{21\#} & {}_nL_{x+n}^{22\#} & \cdots & {}_nL_{x+n}^{2k\#} \\ \vdots & \vdots & & \vdots \\ {}_nL_{x+n}^{k1\#} & {}_nL_{x+n}^{k2\#} & \cdots & {}_nL_{x+n}^{kk\#} \end{bmatrix}, $$

and ${}_n\underset{\sim}{L}_x^{\#} = {}_n\underset{\sim}{L}_{x+0}^{\#}$. Now with linear gross flows, ${}_n\underset{\sim}{L}_x^{\#} = n\underset{\sim}{\ell}_{[x+\frac{n}{2}]}$ and ${}_n\underset{\sim}{L}_{x+n}^{\#} = n\underset{\sim}{\ell}_{[x+\frac{n}{2}]+n}$, hence

$$ {}_n\underset{\sim}{s}_x = \underset{\sim}{\ell}_{[x+\frac{n}{2}]}^{-1}\, \underset{\sim}{\ell}_{[x+\frac{n}{2}]+n} = {}_n\underset{\sim}{\Pi}_{[x+\frac{n}{2}]}, $$

which demonstrates the equivalence of (5.8) and (5.9). Hoem and Jensen (1981) have pointed out that, in general, the survivorship proportions are unlike Markov transition probabilities in that they do not satisfy the Chapman-Kolmogorov equation, i.e., that ${}_{2n}\underset{\sim}{S}_x$ is not necessarily equal to ${}_n\underset{\sim}{S}_x \; {}_n\underset{\sim}{S}_{x+n}$. From the above analysis, however, it can be seen that the Chapman-Kolmogorov equation does hold under the modified age-accounting convention in the case of linear gross flows and orientation equation (5.9).

In sum, a critical assumption in estimating an IDLT model from data in the form of survivorship proportions pertains to the nature of the orientation equation chosen to estimate the $\underset{\sim}{\Pi}$ from the $\underset{\sim}{S}$. Two simple and direct choices are shown in (5.5) and (5.8). At present, however, we do not have sufficient empirical experience from which to judge their performance relative to each other and to more complicated numerical procedures recently suggested by Ledent and Rees (1980). Thus, we regard the optimal choice of an orientation equation for the estimation of IDLT models from survivorship proportions as a question for future research.

6. CONCLUDING COMMENTS

Our objective in this chapter has been to advance the state-of-the-art in abridged increment-decrement life table methodology. Our goals have been threefold: (1) to specify a class of IDLT models for which the force of transition, gross flow, survival, and person-years functions are analytically consistent; (2) to ensure that this class of models is both capable of incorporating transition forces that increase, remain constant, or decrease within estimation-age intervals, and of producing age-specific estimators that can be put in explicit algebraic form; and (3) to develop ways in which this class of models can be related to a body of statistical theory of estimation and hypothesis testing. We feel that the polynomial gross flows models and methods developed in the preceding sections have fully achieved the first and second of these goals and have opened up some promising pathways for the third.

As with all demographic models, however, the applicability of our class of models rests on certain critical assumptions, the validity of which must be evaluated in any particular empirical application. One of these is the *sectional-stationarity/approximation assumption* (3.5). The validity of this assumption depends, in part, on the extent to which the relevant transition forces are nonconstant over an estimation-age interval. If the departure is substantial, the analyst may be well advised to either shorten the estimation-age interval to facilitate modeling the transition forces and reduce the effects of nonstationarity in the observed population, or obtain occurrence/exposure rates indexed by the state occupied at the beginning of the interval.

Two other assumptions derive from the *Markov property* specified above in Eqs. (2.1), (2.2), and (2.3). As noted there, this property *rules out duration-dependence,* such as is often found in nuptiality studies, *and origin-dependence,* such as is often found in interregional migration research. But Schoen and Land (1979, p. 774) have observed that it may be possible to handle duration effects relatively well by using real cohort data. The IDLT model then will reflect the experience of a real group of persons, and thus, at each age and within each life status, the duration composition of the model will be close to that of the actual population. This de facto standardization for duration will minimize the error involved in failing to recognize duration explicitly, as was the case in our empirical analysis in Section 4. Of course, an alternative approach is to seek occurrence/exposure rates that are indexed by duration-time as well as age-time and expand our Markov model to a semi-Markov scheme. This latter recommendation to "use more refined data" also has been explored by Ledent (1980b) in an effort to eliminate the distortions of origin-dependence in migration studies.

A final assumption underlying our models and methods is the implicit specification that the *populations* to which the models are applied *are homogeneous* in the sense that a common transition force regime applies to all its members. While the general subject of population heterogeneity in demographic models contains many issues that cannot be explored here, suffice it to say that methods for coping with population heterogeneity are as applicable to the models developed herein as to any other life table model.

It is appropriate to conclude this chapter with a comparison of the models and methods developed herein with extant alternatives. In particular, how do these models and methods compare to the "preferred method" of Hoem and Jensen (1981)? The latter consists of estimating the (constant or nonconstant) forces of transition directly from occurrence/exposure rates [e.g., as in (3.12) or in (3.24) and (3.25)] and using these together with a numerical integration of the Kolmogorov equations (2.4) to estimate the IDLT. To begin with, both alternatives rest upon the four assumptions just described-- the sectional stationarity/approximation assumption becomes unnecessary only if the transition forces are specified as constant, and, as we noted in the introduction, the piecewise-constant force specification generally yields accurate estimates of the transition probabilities and other life table functions only for unabridged IDLTs. Second, since, as we observed at the end of Section 2.2, our flow equations (2.15) and (2.16) may be regarded as finite-age-versions of the Kolmogorov equations, both alternatives rest on this bedrock of Markov chain models. But, third, whereas the linear and quadratic models developed herein lead to estimation algorithms (3.13) and (3.29) that are expressible in explicit algebraic form, the "preferred method" of Hoem and Jensen (1981) appears to produce estimators that cannot be so expressed if the assumption of constant forces is relaxed. Thus, our models are computationally simpler to estimate than those of the Hoem-Jensen (1981) "preferred method" if nonconstant forces are assumed, and are likely to be more sensitive to the nature of the underlying process if the constant forces assumption is retained. Nonetheless, because both alternatives converge numerically as the lengths of the estimation-age-intervals decrease, it is the similarities between them that should be emphasized.

ACKNOWLEDGMENT

The research reported here was supported, in part, by National Science Foundation Grants SES 77-13261 and SES 78-25472, and National Institute of Child Health and Human Development (DHHS) Grant 1 RO1 HD11756. Authors' names are ordered alphabetically to indicate the joint product of ongoin collaborative research in mathematical demography. This version of the paper has benefited greatly from conversations with Jan M. Hoem and Ulla Funck Jensen at the Conference.

REFERENCES

Aalen, Odd O. (1975). Statistical inference for a family of counting processes. Unpublished Ph.D. Dissertation. Berkeley: Department of Statistics, University of California.

Batten, Robert W. (1978). "Mortality Table Construction." Englewood Cliffs, New Jersey: Prentice-Hall.

Chiang, Chin-Long (1960). A stochastic study of the life table and its applications, II: Sample variance of the observed expectation of life and other biometric functions. *Human Biology 32,* 221-238.

Chiang, Chin-Long (1968). "Introduction to Stochastic Processes in Biostatistics." New York: Wiley.

Cohen, Joel E. and Singer, Burton (1979). Malaria in Nigeria: Constrained continuous-time Markov models for discrete-time longitudinal data on human mixed-species infections. *Lectures on Mathematics in the Life Sciences 12,* 69-133.

Coleman, James S. (1964a). "Introduction to Mathematical Sociology." New York: Free Press.

Coleman, James S. (1964b). "Models of Change and Response Uncertainty." Englewood Cliffs, New Jersey: Prentice-Hall.

Coleman, James S. (1968). The mathematical study of change. *In* "Methodology in Social Research" (H. M. Blalock, Jr., and A. B. Blalock, eds.), pp. 428-478. New York: McGraw-Hill.

Coleman, James S. (1970). Multivariate analysis for attribute data. *Sociological Methodology 1970,* 217-245.

Coleman, James S. (1973). "The Mathematics of Collective Action." Chicago: Aldine.

Coleman, James S. (1981). "Longitudinal Data Analysis." New York: Basic Books.

Cox, D. R. and Miller, H. D. (1965). "The Theory of Stochastic Processes." New York: Wiley.

Du Pasquier, L. G. (1912). Mathematische theorie der invaliditatsversicherung. *Mitt. Ver. Schweitzer. Versicherungsmath. 7,* 1-7.

Du Pasquier, L. G. (1913). Mathematische theorie der invaliditatsversicherung. *Mitt. Ver. Schweitzer. Versicherungsmath. 8,* 1-153.

Fix, E. and Neymann, J. (1951). A simple stochastic model of recovery, relapse, death and loss of patients. *Human Biology 23,* 205-241.

Greville, T. N. E. (1943). Short methods of constructing abridged life tables. *Record of the American Institute of Actuaries (Part I) 32,* 29-42.

Gross, A. J. and Clark, U. A. (1975). "Survival Distributions: Reliability Applications in the Biomedical Sciences." New York: Wiley.

Hoem, Jan M. (1970). Point estimation of forces of transition in demographic models. *Journal of the Royal Statistical Sociology, Series B 33,* 275-289.

Hoem, Jan M. (1972a). Inhomogeneous semi-Markov processes, select actuarial tables, and duration-dependence in demography. *In* "Population Dynamics" (T. N. E. Greville, ed.), pp. 251-296. New York: Academic Press.

Hoem, Jan M. (1972b). On the statistical theory of analytic graduation. *Proceedings of the Sixth Berkeley Symposium on Mathematical Statistics and Probability 1,* 569-600.

Hoem, Jan M. (1976). The statistical theory of demographic rates. *Scandinavian Journal of Statistics 3,* 169-185.

Hoem, J. M. and Fong, M. S. (1976). A Markov chain model of working life tables. Working Paper No. 2. Denmark: Laboratory of Actuarial Mathematics, University of Copenhagen.

Hoem, J. M. and Jensen, U. F. (1981). Multistate life table methodology: A probabilist critique. Paper presented at the Conference on Multidimensional Mathematical Demography, March 23-25, 1981, Center of Adult Education, University of Maryland, College Park, Maryland.

Jones, J. P. (1962). Remarriage tables based on experience under OASDI. U.S. Social Security Administration, Actuarial Study No. 55. Washington, D.C.: U.S. Government Printing Office.

Jordan, Chester W., Jr. (1975). "Life Contingencies," Second Edition. Chicago: Society of Actuaries.

Keyfitz, N. (1968). A life table that agrees with the data II. *Journal of The American Statistical Association 32,* 213-232.

Keyfitz, N. (1977). "Introduction to the Mathematics of Population," with revisions. Reading, Massachusetts: Addison-Wesley.

Keyfitz, N. and Frauenthal, J. (1975). An improved life table method. *Biometrics 21,* 889-899.

Kingman, J. F. C. (1962). The imbedding problem for finite Markov chains. *Z. Wahrscheinlichkeitstheorie und Verw. Gebiete 1,* 14-24.

Krishnamoorthy, S. (1979). Classical approach to increment-decrement life tables: Application to the study of the marital status of United States females, 1970. *Mathematical Biosciences 44,* 139-154.

Land, Kenneth C. (1971). Some exhaustible Poisson process models of divorce by marriage cohort. *Journal of Mathematical Sociology 7,* 213-232.

Ledent, Jacques (1978). Some methodological and empirical considerations in the construction of increment-decrement life tables. Research Memorandum RM-78-25, May, Laxenburg: International Institute for Applied Systems Analysis, Austria.

Ledent, Jacques (1980a). An improved methodology for constructing increment-decrement life tables from the transition perspectives. Working Paper WP-80-104, June, Laxenburg: International Institute for Applied Systems Analysis, Austria.

Ledent, Jacques (1980b). Constructing multiregional life tables using place-of-birth-specific migration data. Working Paper WP-80-96, May, Laxenburg: International Institute for Applied Systems Analysis, Austria.

Ledent, Jacques (1980c). Multistate life tables: Movement versus transition perspectives. *Environment and Planning A 12,* 533-562.

Ledent, J. and Rees, P. H. (1980). Choices in the construction of multiregional life tables. Working Paper WP-80-173, November, Laxenburg: International Institute of Applied Systems Analysis, Austria.

Long, L. H. and Hansen, K. A. (1975). Trends in return migration to the South. *Demography 12,* 601-614.

Manninen, R. (1979). Suomen Vaestön Kehitysanalyysi neljän alueen järjestelmäna (An Analysis of the Finnish Population as a System of Four Regions). Helsinki: Department of Geography, University of Helsinki, Finland.

Mann, N. R., Schafer, R. D., and Singpurwalla, N. D. (1974). "Methods for Statistical Analysis of Reliability and Life Data." New York: Wiley.

Preston, S. H., Keyfitz, N., and Schoen, R. (1972). "Causes of Death: Life Tables for National Populations." New York: Seminar Press.

Reed, L. J. and Merrell, M. (1939). A short method for constructing an abridged life table. *American Journal of Hygiene 30,* 33-62.

Rees, P. H. and Wilson, A. G. (1977). "Spatial Population Analysis." London: Edward Arnold.

Rogers, Andrei (1973). The multiregional life table. *The Journal of Mathematical Sociology 3,* 127-137.

Rogers, Andrei (1975). "Introduction to Multiregional Mathematical Demography." New York: Wiley.

Rogers, A. and Ledent, J. (1976). Increment-decrement life tables: A comment. *Demography 13,* 287-290.

Schoen, Robert (1975). California divorce rates by age at first marriage and duration of first marriage. *Journal of Marriage and the Family 37*, 548-555.

Schoen, Robert (1976). Reply to Rogers and Ledent. *Demography 13*, 291.

Schoen, Robert (1977a). Further reactions to Rogers and Ledent's comment. *Demography 14*, 591-592.

Schoen, Robert (1977b). On choosing an indexing variable in demographic analysis. *Social Science Research 6*, 246-256.

Schoen, Robert (1978). Calculating life tables by estimating Chiang's *a* from observed rates. *Demography 15*, 625-635.

Schoen, Robert (1979). Calculating increment-decrement life tables by estimating mean durations at transfer from observed rates. *Mathematical Biosciences 47*, 255-269.

Schoen, R. and Land, K. C. (1979). A general algorithm for estimating a Markov-generated increment-decrement life table with applications to marital status patterns. *Journal of the American Statistical Association 74*, 761-776.

Schoen, R. and Nelson, V. E. (1974). Marriage, divorce, and mortality: A life table analysis. *Demography 11*, 267-290.

Schoen, R. and Urton, W. (1977). Marriage, divorce, and mortality: The Swedish experience. *Proceedings of the General Conference of the International Union for the Scientific Study of Population 1*, 311-332.

Schoen, R. and Woodrow, K. (1980). Labor force status life tables for the United States, 1972. *Demography 17*, 297-322.

Singer, B. and Cohen, J. E. (1980). Estimating malaria incidence and recovery rates from panel surveys. *Mathematical Biosciences 49*, 273-305.

Singer, B. and Spilerman, S. (1974). Social mobility models for heterogeneous populations. *Sociological Methodology 74*, 356-401.

Singer, B. and Spilerman, S. (1976a). The representation of social processes by Markov models. *American Journal of Sociology 82*, 1-54.

Singer, B. and Spilerman, S. (1976b). Some methodological issues in the analysis of longitudinal surveys. *Annals of Economic and Social Measurement 5*, 447-474.

Sverdrup, E. (1965). Estimates and test procedures in connection with stochastic models for death, recoveries, and transfers between different states of health. *Skandinavisk Aktuarietidskrift 40*, 184-211.

Willekens, Frans (1980). Multistate analysis: Tables of working life. *Environment and Planning A 12*, 563-589.

Young, D. M. and Gregory, R. T. (1972). "A Survey of Numerical Mathematics." Volume I. Reading, Massachusetts: Addison-Wesley.

6

Transition Probability Estimation in Increment-Decrement Life Tables: Using Mobility Data from a Census or a Survey

Jacques Ledent

1. INTRODUCTION

Increment-decrement life tables, which are life tables that recognize entries as well as withdrawals from alternative states of existence, are used increasingly in various fields of demography, e.g., the analysis of marital status, labor force participation, and interregional migration.

In practice, the crux of their calculation lies in the estimation of a set of transition probabilities from which multistate life table functions that generalize the statistics contained in the columns of an ordinary life table can be calculated. For the purpose of this estimation, two general perspectives that stem from alternative conceptualizations of the "passage" between the different states can be distinguished (Ledent, 1980a).

ISBN 0-12-435640-0

One is the *movement* perspective that views "passage" as an instantaneous event, similar to a birth or a death. It calls for mobility data consisting of numbers of interstate moves (events) observed during a given period, which generally can be obtained from a population register. The other perspective is the *transition* perspective, one that conceives "passage" as the result of being present in a state distinct from the one occupied at an earlier date. It requires mobility data consisting of numbers of movers (or changes in individuals' state of presence) between two points in time, which are commonly supplied by a population census or survey.

Thus, for example, in the case of multiregional life tables (increment-decrement life tables applied to the analysis of interregional migration), the relevant perspective is the movement perspective if the mobility information comes from a population register, i.e., in the count of moves (migrations), whereas the transition perspective is the appropriate perspective if the mobility information comes from a population census, i.e., in the count of movers (migrants).

From a methodological viewpoint, the implementation of the movement perspective raises relatively few problems since satisfactory methods, generalizing those classically used for estimating the survival probabilities of an ordinary life table, have been recently developed (for a review of these methods, see Ledent and Rees, 1980, Section 3). By contrast, the implementation of the transition perspective, in its current state of development, is much less adequate because it often involves an approximation that is coarse or left unjustified.

Two alternative approaches to the implementation of the transition perspective, both of which have been initially developed by Rogers (1975), are currently available. The first approach, labeled approach A in this chapter, originates from an *ad hoc* adaptation of a particular estimation method of the movement perspective. The second approach, labeled approach B, is derived from the approach sometimes used by demographers to calculate an ordinary life table from census information in the form of survivorship proportions. Fundamentally, these two approaches use the same mobility information, which they convert into alternative input quantities, mobility rates and transition proportions, respectively, to be clarified later on.

Concerned with the case of mobility data in the count of movers, typically provided by a population census or survey, we seek to improve further the implementation of the transition perspective so as to confer on it a status equivalent to that accorded to the movement perspective. Approaches A and B are dealt with in Sections 1 and 2, respectively: an examination of their development and a presentation of the amendments that we propose are included. Finally, Section 3 sets out a comparison of the two approaches, a comparison that takes on a particular importance in the case of multiregional life tables.

2. APPROACH A: ESTIMATION FROM MOBILITY RATES

In its current state of development, approach A to the estimation of the transition probabilities of an increment-decrement life table from mobility data in the count of movers relies on an approximation, the validity of which is somewhat questionable. Thus below, after a description of the technique involved, an attempt is made to substitute a proper theoretical background for the currently weak rationale of this approach, which eventually leads to an improved estimation method.

CURRENT STATE OF DEVELOPMENT

Approach A was initially suggested by Rogers (1975, pp. 87-88) who, to calculate a two-region life table for West Virginia and the rest of the United States from data in the form of migrants, used his simplified version of the linear estimators pertaining to the movement perspective, the so-called "Option 1" estimators in the nomenclature of Rogers (1975) and Willekens and Rogers (1978).

The rationale for such a procedure readily follows from Rogers' assumption that no multiple moves can take place within each unit time interval (see, for example, Rogers, 1975, p. 59). Under such an assumption, there is equivalence of the numbers of moves and movers observed between alternative states during each unit age/time interval so that the Option 1 estimators can be applied to mobility data consistent with either the movement perspective or the transition perspective.

The "Option 1" Method

In view of some of the extensions that we propose later on, a rapid overview of the derivation of the Option 1 method (Rogers, 1975, pp. 82-84) is here in order.

First, Rogers depicts the evolution between ages x and x + n of the closed groups of people l_x^i present at age x in each state i, regardless of their past mobility history, by means of

$$\ell_x^{ii} = 1_x^i - \ell_x^{i\delta} - \sum_{\substack{k=1 \\ k \neq i}}^{r} \ell_x^{ik} , \quad i = 1,\ldots,r \tag{1}$$ [1]

where ℓ_x^{ik} is the number of the members of 1_x^i who survive to age x + n in state k and $\ell_x^{i\delta}$ the number of persons in the same closed group who die before reaching age x + n. Note that, because of Rogers' assumption of a single move per unit time interval, all the moves out of state i (including deaths) are necessarily made by members of 1_x^i. Under these conditions,

(a) $\ell_x^{i\delta}$ is equal to the number of deaths occurring in state i between ages x and x + n, and

(b) ℓ_x^{ij} (for $j \neq i$) is equal to the number of moves from state i to state j made by persons aged x to x + n, so that Eq. (1) represents the decrements and increments occurring to the cohort 1_x^i from both the movement and transition perspectives.

Second, Rogers defines the following age-specific exposure/occurrence rates (on an annual basis):

(a) mortality rates

$$m_x^{i\delta} = \ell_x^{i\delta}/L_x^{ii} , \quad i = 1,\ldots,r \tag{2}$$

(b) and mobility rates

$$m_x^{ij} = \ell_x^{ij}/L_x^{ii} , \quad i,j = 1,\ldots,r \quad (j \neq i) \tag{3}$$

where L_x^{ii}, the number of person-years lived in state i between ages x and x + n by the survivors of the closed group 1_x^i, is

[1] *r is the number of nonabsorbing states in the system.*

taken as

$$L_x^{ii} = (n/2)\left(l_x^i + \ell_x^{ii}\right), \quad i = 1,\ldots,r \tag{4}$$

Equations (1)-(4) thus define an increment-decrement life table, the calculation of which rests on the implementation of a linkage with the observed population. This linkage, as proposed by Rogers, is carried out by equating the life table rates defined in Eqs. (2) and (3) with their observed counterparts, i.e.,

$$m_x^{i\delta} = M_x^{\delta(i)}, \quad i = 1,\ldots,r \tag{5}$$

and

$$m_x^{ij} = M_x^{ij}, \quad i,j = 1,\ldots,r \quad (j \neq i) \tag{6}$$

where $M_x^{\delta(i)}$ is the observed mortality rate associated with age group x to x + n in state i, and M_x^{ij} the observed rate of transfer from state i to state j associated with age group x to x + n.

Appropriate combinations of Eqs. (1)-(6) then lead to formulas expressing various transition probabilities. Thus, the probability $p_x^{ii} = \ell_x^{ii}/l_x^i$ that a person aged x in state i will survive to age x + n in the same state is

$$p_x^{ii} = \frac{1 - \frac{n}{2}\left[M_x^{\delta(i)} + \sum_{\substack{k=1\\k\neq i}}^{r} M_x^{ik}\right]}{1 + \frac{n}{2}\left[M_x^{\delta(i)} + \sum_{\substack{k=1\\k\neq i}}^{r} M_x^{ik}\right]}, \quad i = 1,\ldots,r \tag{7}$$

and the probability $p_x^{ij} = \ell_x^{ij}/l_x^i$ that the same individual will survive in another state j is

$$p_x^{ij} = \frac{n\, M_x^{ij}}{1 + \frac{n}{2}\left[M_x^{\delta(i)} + \sum_{\substack{k=1 \\ k \neq i}}^{r} M_x^{ik}\right]}, \qquad i,j = 1,\ldots,r \,. \quad (j \neq i) \tag{8}$$

In addition, the probability $p_x^{i\delta} = \ell_x^{i\delta}/l_x^i$, that the individual will die before reaching x + n is

$$p_x^{i\delta} = \frac{n\, M_x^{\delta(i)}}{i + \frac{n}{2}\left[M_x^{\delta(i)} + \sum_{\substack{k=1 \\ k \neq i}}^{r} M_x^{ik}\right]}, \qquad i = 1,\ldots,r. \tag{9}$$

Since an individual who dies between ages x and x + n necessarily dies in the state in which he was present at age x (due to the assumption of a single move per unit time interval), the probability $p_x^{i\delta(j)}$ that an individual aged x in state i will die in a specific state j before reaching age x + n is equal to the right-hand side of (9) if j = i and to zero if j ≠ i.

From an applied viewpoint, the problem raised by formulas (7)-(9) is one of measuring the observed mobility rates. First, let us assume that the mobility data come from a population register (movement perspective). Then M_x^{ij} is readily derived as the ratio of the observed number of moves D_x^{ij} made from state i to state j over a given period (t, t+T) by persons aged x to x + n (at the time of the move) to the number of person-years $\hat{K}_x^i$ lived in state i during that period by people aged x to x + n. Generally, the latter number is taken as T times the arithmetic average of the beginning- and end-of-the-period populations aged x to x + n so that M_x^{ij} can be derived from

$$\bar{M}_x^{ij} = \frac{1}{T} \frac{D_x^{ij}}{\frac{1}{2}\left[K_x^i(t) + K_x^i(t+T)\right]} , \quad i,j = 1,\ldots,r. \quad (j \neq i) \qquad (10)^2$$

Alternatively, in the case the data come from a population census or survey (transition perspective), Rogers (1975, pp. 87-88) suggests that the number of movers O_x^{ij} from state i to state j over the observation period be simply substituted for the corresponding number of moves D_x^{ij}, which leads to the following observed rates

$$\hat{M}_x^{ij} = \frac{1}{T} \frac{O_x^{ij}}{\frac{1}{2}\left[K_x^i(t) + K_x^i(t+T)\right]} , \quad i,j = 1,\ldots,r. \quad (j \neq i) \qquad (11)^2$$

Note here the existence of a certain ambiguity regarding the measurement of the numerator of (11), i.e., the number of movers O_x^{ij}. Does age refer to the beginning of the period, the end of the period, or perhaps the midperiod?[3] The recent empirical work on various multiregional populations reviewed by Rees and Willekens (1981) indicates that, in most instances, this number of movers is measured with the age subscript referring to the end of the period when the length T of

[2]*To distinguish the rates pertaining to the alternative perspectives, we place, as done in formulas (10) and (11), a bar (case of the movement perspective) or a caret (case of the transition perspective) above the symbol M standing for the observed mobility rates.*

[3]*No such ambiguity exists regarding the measurement of the number of moves D_x^{ij} since those are made by people aged x to x + n at the time of the move.*

the observation period is less than the width n of each age group and to the beginning of the period when they are equal. Unfortunately, neither choice is correct because the transition perspective, unlike the movement approach, does not allow an equivalence of the age-time space in which the data are gathered, and that used in the model (Ledent and Rees, 1980, pp. 45-47).

A possible procedure, following Rees (1979), is to estimate the number of movers O_x^{ij} from adjacent age-group data, thus

$$O_x^{ij} = \left(1 - \frac{T}{2n}\right) K_{x-n.}^{ij} + \frac{T}{2n} K_{x.}^{ij} , \qquad i,j = 1,\ldots,r \quad (j \neq i) \tag{12}$$

where $K_{x.}^{ij}$ is the number of movers from state i to state j relating to people aged x to x + n at the beginning of the observation period.[4]

Of course, a more accurate estimate can be obtained by interpolating between the successive values of the number of movers O_x^{ij}, using a cubic spline function (see Shryock *et al.*, 1973, p. 689; McNeil *et al.*, 1977) rather than the linear function implied by Eq. (12). Specifically, if the number of movers $K_{x.}^{ij}$ is plotted at age $x + \frac{1}{2}n$ (and at age $-\frac{1}{2}n$ in the case of $K_{-n.}^{ij}$ corresponding to the infants born during the observation period), the number of movers O_x^{ij} can be taken as the value E_x^{ij} of the ordinate, at exact age x, of the cubic spline function fitted to the series of the $K_{x.}^{ij}$'s.

[4] *This formula must be modified for the first, the last but one, and the last age intervals (see Ledent and Rees, 1980, pp. 48-49).*

To summarize, in the case which preoccupies us here, namely, that of the transition perspective, the approach proposed by Rogers (1975) consists of using the estimators (7)-(9) in which the mobility rates are estimated, from adequately measured numbers of movers, according to formula (11).

The "Option 3" Estimators

Because of Rogers' assumption that only a single move can occur per unit time interval, the application of the Option 1 estimators to data consistent with either the movement perspective or the transition perspective is generally perceived as being little reliable.

Fortunately, in the case of the movement perspective, Rogers' restrictive assumption can be relaxed (Schoen, 1975). On doing so, it can be readily shown that the transition probability p_x^{ij} is the (j,i)th element of a matrix $\underset{\sim}{p}_x$ (Rogers and Ledent, 1976):

$$\underset{\sim}{p}_x = (\underset{\sim}{I}+\tfrac{1}{2}n\underset{\sim}{\overline{M}}_x)^{-1}(\underset{\sim}{I}-\tfrac{1}{2}n\underset{\sim}{\overline{M}}_x), \tag{12}$$

and that the probability $p_x^{i\delta(j)}$ is the (j,i)th element of a matrix $\underset{\sim}{p}_x^{\delta}$ (Ledent, 1978, p. 44):

$$\underset{\sim}{p}_x^{\delta} = n\underset{\sim}{M}_x^{\delta}(\underset{\sim}{I}+\tfrac{1}{2}n\underset{\sim}{\overline{M}}_x)^{-1}, \tag{13}$$

where $\underset{\sim}{M}_x^{\delta}$ is a diagonal matrix of the state-specific mortality rates $M_x^{\delta(i)}$, and $\underset{\sim}{\overline{M}}_x$ a matrix that adds to $\underset{\sim}{M}_x^{\delta}$ a matrix collecting the various mobility rates $\overline{M}_x^{ij}$. In the nomenclature of Willekens and Rogers (1978), these estimators, the full linear estimators of the movement approach, are referred to as the Option 3 estimators.

By contrast, in the case of the transition perspective, no real attempt has been made thus far to remove Rogers' restrictive assumption, which leaves us with no alternative other than use the Option 1 estimators. Naturally, the ruling out of multiple movers per unit time interval leads to values of the age-specific mortality probabilities $p_x^{i\delta} = 1 - \Sigma_{k=1}^{r} p_x^{ik}$ that are clearly underestimated. This has not gone unnoticed in the past, and this is why Willekens and Rogers (1978) recommended to substitute the Option 3 for the Option 1 estimators: as demonstrated by Ledent and Rees (1980, pp. 53-57), they generally yield more acceptable death probabilities $p_x^{i\delta}$ while producing very similar migration probabilities. However, such a recommendation, which was actually adopted in the calculation of multiregional life tables for several countries in which migration data are consistent with the transition perspective (see Rees and Willekens, 1981), does not remedy entirely the problem associated with Rogers' assumption.[5]

The conclusion here is that, at the present time, approach A to the estimation of the transition probabilities of an increment-decrement life table from mobility data in the form of movers, which are transformed into adequate transition rates, makes use of the linear estimators of the movement perspective: either the simplified Option 1 estimators or, preferably, the Option 3 estimators. The main drawback of this approach is, as indicated above, its reliance on a restrictive theoretical background caused by the ruling out of multiple moves within each unit time interval.

[5] *The substitution of the Option 3 for the Option 1 estimators recommended by Willekens and Rogers (1978) appears to follow from simple empirical considerations.*

Relaxing this assumption, we build upon the derivation of the Option 1 estimators reviewed earlier to derive a set of improved estimators.

IMPROVEMENTS SUGGESTED

In the context of the transition perspective, the removal of the no-multiple move assumption substantially modifies the nature of the elements appearing on the right-hand side of the accounting Eq. (1). First, the members $\ell_x^{i\delta}$ of the closed group of people l_x^i present at age x in state i who die before reaching age x + n can die in state i as well as in any other state of the system (which they may have entered after several successive interstate moves). Second, the number ℓ_x^{ij} of movers from state i to state j, which now differs from the total number of moves taking place from state i to state j, is equal to the balance of the moves made, in both directions, between states i and j, by those present in state i at age x.

As a result, approach A can be improved by bringing two straightforward modifications to the framework underlying the derivation of the Option 1 estimators: one concerns the treatment of mortality and one the treatment of mobility.

Derivation of New Estimators

The modification related to the treatment of mortality simply requires disaggregating the total number of deaths $\ell_x^{i\delta}$ according to the state of occurrence. Precisely, we decompose this number into r state-specific components $\ell_x^{i\delta(k)}$, thus

$$\ell_x^{i\delta} = \ell_x^{i\delta(.)} = \sum_{k=1}^{r} \ell_x^{i\delta(k)} , \quad i = 1,\ldots,r \tag{14}$$

where $\ell_x^{i\delta(k)}$ reflects the number of individuals in the group l_x^i who die in state k before reaching age x + n.

An immediate consequence of this modification is the necessary introduction of age-specific mortality rates that relate not only to the state of residence at age x but also to the state in which the deaths actually occur, i.e., we substitute the following for Eq. (2):

$$m_x^{i\delta(j)} = \ell_x^{i\delta(j)}/L_x^{ij}, \quad i,j = 1,\ldots,r \tag{15}$$

where L_x^{ij} is the number of person-years lived in state j between ages x and x + n by the survivors of the closed group l_x^i.

In accordance with the homogeneity assumption underpinning an increment-decrement life table, those life table mortality rates are naturally linked with the conventionally observed mortality rates pertaining to each state by simply setting

$$m_x^{i\delta(j)} = M_x^{\delta(j)}, \quad i,j = 1,\ldots,r. \tag{16}$$

Then, on assuming a linear calculation of the number of person-years L_x^{ij}, that is, formula (4) holds if j = i, and $L_x^{ij} = \frac{1}{2}n\ \ell_x^{ij}$ if $j \neq i$, and an unchanged analytical presentation of the transition mobility rates of the Option 1 method, it can be readily shown that the term $\ell_x^{i\delta}$, formerly equal to $M_x^{\delta(i)}L_x^{ii}$, now becomes equal to

$$\ell_x^{i\delta} = \left[M_x^{\delta(i)} + \tfrac{1}{2}n \sum_{\substack{k=1\\k\neq i}}^{r} M_x^{\delta(k)} M_x^{ik}\right] L_x^{ii}, \quad i = 1,\ldots,n. \tag{17}$$

It follows that, the formulas expressing the new estimators

sought can be derived from formulas (7)-(9) by simply substituting $M_x^{\delta(i)} + \frac{1}{2}n \Sigma_{\substack{k=1\\k\neq i}}^{r} M_x^{\delta(k)} M_x^{ik}$ for $M_x^{\delta(i)}$. After grouping terms containing similar elements and adding a caret on top of the mobility rates (since we are dealing with the transition perspective exclusively), we obtain

$$p_x^{ii} = \frac{1 - \frac{n}{2}\left[M_x^{\delta(i)} + \sum_{\substack{k=1\\k\neq i}}^{r}\left(1 + \frac{n}{2} M_x^{\delta(k)}\right)\hat{M}_x^{ik}\right]}{1 + \frac{n}{2}\left[M_x^{\delta(i)} + \sum_{\substack{k=1\\k\neq i}}^{r}\left(1 + \frac{n}{2} M_x^{\delta(k)}\right)\hat{M}_x^{ik}\right]}, \quad i = 1,\ldots,r \tag{18}$$

$$p_x^{ij} = \frac{n\,\hat{M}_x^{ij}}{1 + \frac{n}{2}\left[M_x^{\delta(i)} + \sum_{\substack{k=1\\k\neq i}}^{r}\left(1 + \frac{n}{2} M_x^{\delta(k)}\right)\hat{M}_x^{ik}\right]}, \quad i,j = 1,\ldots,r \quad (j \neq i) \tag{19}$$

$$p_x^{i\delta} = \frac{n\left[M_x^{\delta(i)} + \frac{n}{2}\sum_{\substack{k=1\\k\neq i}}^{r} M_x^{\delta(k)}\hat{M}_x^{ik}\right]}{1 + \frac{n}{2}\left[M_x^{\delta(i)} + \sum_{\substack{k=1\\k\neq i}}^{r}\left(1 + \frac{n}{2} M_x^{\delta(k)}\right)\hat{M}_x^{ik}\right]}, \quad i = 1,\ldots,r. \tag{20}$$

Note that, owing to the treatment of mortality taken above, the mortality probability $p_x^{i\delta}$ can be decomposed into n state-specific elements. The expression of the probability $p_x^{i\delta(k)}$ that a person alive at age x in state i will die within the next five years in state k follows readily from formula (20):

$$p_x^{i\delta(i)} = \frac{nM_x^{\delta(i)}}{1 + \frac{n}{2}\left[M_x^{\delta(i)} + \sum_{\substack{k=1\\k\neq i}}^{r}\left(1 + \frac{n}{2}M_x^{\delta(k)}\right)\hat{M}_x^{ik}\right]}, \qquad i = 1,\ldots,r \tag{21}$$

$$p_x^{i\delta(j)} = \frac{\frac{n^2}{2}M_x^{\delta(j)}\hat{M}_x^{ij}}{1 + \frac{n}{2}\left[M_x^{\delta(i)} + \sum_{\substack{k=1\\k\neq i}}^{r}\left(1 + \frac{n}{2}M_x^{\delta(k)}\right)\hat{M}_x^{ik}\right]}, \qquad i,j = 1,\ldots,r. \quad (j \neq i) \tag{22}$$

Measurement of the Mobility Rates

In deriving the new estimators just established, the analytical presentation of the mobility rates contained in the Option 1 estimation method was kept unchanged. However, the relaxation of the no-multiple move assumption entails a further modification, the second and last foretold modification of Option 1, that affects the interpretation and measurement of the mobility rates.

Because no restriction is now placed on the number of moves made by each individual in a unit time interval, the number of movers ℓ_x^{ij} is not assimilable to a number of events. Consequently, we cannot anymore view the age-specific mobility rates defined by Eq. (3) as occurrence/exposure rates. In fact, recalling that ℓ_x^{ij} reflects the balance of moves in two opposite directions, we are naturally led to reinterpret the mobility rates as quantities having the same nature as the *net* rates used in the analysis of migration. More exactly, since the mobility rate m_x^{ij} is now associated with people who are necessarily in state i at age x, we must now view the life table mobility rates of Eq. (3) as average annual values of net mover (migrant) rates.

Such a reinterpretation has two important consequences for the measurement of the observed rates to which the life table mobility rates are to be equated. First, in contrast to occurrence/exposure rates, net mover rates are strongly affected by the length of the observation period (Long and Boertlein, 1977; Rees, 1977), so that the choice of such a period in the implementation of the proposed revision of the Option 1 method is not an indifferent matter. Actually, returning to the accounting equation (1), we note that the number of movers ℓ_x^{ij} has an n-year dimension. Then we conclude that the measurement of the mobility rates in the observed population over a T-year period where T is different from the width n of each age group, is theoretically incorrect if no restriction exists about the number of moves allowed to each individual per unit time interval.

Second, because the life table mobility rates concern groups of people living in a specific state at the beginning of each unit time interval considered, the denominator of formula (11) used for the measurement of the mobility rate $\hat{M}_x^{ij}$ in the observed population should be modified. Specifically, it should be reduced to that part of the number of person-years $\hat{K}_x^i$ lived in state i by persons aged x to x + n *who were present in state i at the beginning of the observation period.* Such a quantity, in practice, can be approximated by T times the arithmetic average of the population of state i aged x to x + n at the beginning of the period and the part of this population that is still present in state i at the end of the period. Under these circumstances, an adequate measure of each observed mobility rate should be obtained from

$$\hat{M}_x^{ij} = \frac{1}{T}\,\frac{O_x^{ij}}{\frac{1}{2}\left[K_x^{i}(t) + K_{x.}^{ii}\right]}\,, \qquad i,j = 1,\ldots,r \quad (j \neq i) \tag{23}$$

where O_x^{ij} is obtained by interpolating through the various $K_{y.}^{ij}$ values $(y = -n,0,n,\ldots)$, either linearly, in which case

$$O_x^{ij} = \frac{1}{2}\left[K_{x-n.}^{ij} + K_{x.}^{ij}\right], \qquad i,j = 1,\ldots,r \quad (j \neq i) \tag{24}$$ [6]

or by means of a cubic spline function.

Finally, having determined earlier that our revision of the Option 1 method is theoretically not valid in case where the time and age intervals are different, let us ask ourselves: what can we do if $T \neq n$? A simple and apparently adequate possibility is to use an adequate interpolative method to transform the n-year quantities $K_{x.}^{ij}$ and $K_x^{i}(t)$ appearing in formula (23) into similar T-year quantities, thereby deriving mobility rates relating to T-year rather than n-year age groups.

In other words, regardless of the width n of each age interval in the observed data, the age-specific transition probabilities should be estimated for age-specific intervals whose width is necessarily equal to the length T of the observation period. In the case of n being different from T, a

[6] *This formula, valid under the same conditions as (12), follows from the latter where T is set equal to n.*

prior transformation of the original data using an adequate interpolation method is thus necessary.

3. APPROACH B: ESTIMATION FROM TRANSITION PROPORTIONS

The above approach to transition probability estimation from mobility data in the form of movers is an approach largely inspired from the classical estimation of survival probabilities in an ordinary life table: it is based on the assumption of equal life table and observed mobility rates.

The alternative approach that is the subject of this section, which we call approach B, relies on an estimation technique that parallels the technique sometimes used by demographers to calculate, from census information, an ordinary life table for countries in which proper mortality data are lacking. It makes use of the concept of transition or survivorship proportions and estimates the transition probability matrices $\underset{\sim}{p}_x$ on the assumption of equal life table and observed transition proportion matrices.

The current state of development of approach B is the result of successive efforts that are briefly reviewed below before new improvements are introduced.

GENESIS

The initial development of approach B is due to Rogers (1975, pp. 85-88) who devised as an alternative to his Option 1 method a method, which he called the Option 2 method, to deal more specifically with the case of migration data treated as reported changes of regions of residence from those at a prior fixed date.

The "Option 2" Method

The Option 2 method originates from the observation that, if the number of person-years lived in the multistate stationary population is a linear function of the ℓ-statistics, then the following relationship exists between the survivorship proportions $\underset{\sim}{s}_x$[7] and the transition probabilities $\underset{\sim}{p}_x$ (Rogers, 1975, p. 85):

$$\underset{\sim}{s}_x = (\underset{\sim}{I}+\underset{\sim}{p}_{x+n})\underset{\sim}{p}_x(\underset{\sim}{I}+\underset{\sim}{p}_x)^{-1} . \quad (25)$$

Equation (25) can be rearranged to yield either a formula for $\underset{\sim}{p}_x$ or one for $\underset{\sim}{p}_{x+n}$. On the one hand (the case originally considered by Rogers, 1975), postmultiplying both sides of Eq. (25) by $(\underset{\sim}{I}+\underset{\sim}{p}_x)$, bringing all the terms in $\underset{\sim}{p}_x$ to the left-hand side, and substituting the observed life table survivorship proportions $\underset{\sim}{S}_x$ for their life table counterparts, we obtain

$$\underset{\sim}{p}_x = [\underset{\sim}{I}+\underset{\sim}{p}_{x-n}-\underset{\sim}{S}_x]^{-1}\underset{\sim}{S}_x , \quad (26)$$

an equation that indicates that the series of transition probability matrices can be derived from the knowledge of the observed survivorship proportion matrices and a prior estimate of $\underset{\sim}{p}_{z-n}$ (the probability matrix relating to the last but one age group).

[7]*The (i,j)th element of* $\underset{\sim}{s}_x$ *represents the proportion of those present in state j between ages x and x + n who survive n years later to be present in state i.*

On the other hand (the case suggested by Ledent, 1978, p. 17), bringing $\underset{\sim}{p}_{x+n}$ rather than $\underset{\sim}{p}_x$ to the left-hand side leads to

$$\underset{\sim}{p}_{x+n} = \underset{\sim}{S}_x[\underset{\sim}{I}+\underset{\sim}{p}_x]\underset{\sim}{p}_x^{-1} - \underset{\sim}{I} , \tag{27}$$

an equation that indicates that the series of transition probability matrices can be derived from the knowledge of the observed survivorship proportion matrices and a prior estimate of $\underset{\sim}{p}_0$.[8]

The application of Eqs. (26) and (27) to actual situations raises the question of measuring or estimating the observed survivorship proportions. Two cases must be distinguished here depending on whether or not the mobility information available concerns age-specific numbers of movers over a fixed time period.

First, if no such information is available, estimates of the age-specific survivorship proportions can be obtained from data on lifetime movers measured at two different points in time, by application of the method developed by Rogers and von Rabenau (1971).[9] Second, if age-specific numbers of movers over a fixed time period are available, measures of the observed survivorship proportions can be obtained simply by dividing each number of movers by the relevant age-specific population

[8] *The latter can be easily derived from the knowledge of the survivorship proportion matrix relating to the infants born during the observation period.*

[9] *This method is a multistate generalization of the method used by demographers to estimate ordinary survivorship proportions from population data in two consecutive censuses.*

of the state of origin at the beginning of the period. However, in the case of incomplete information,[10] an accounting method (see Rees and Wilson, 1977) may be necessary to secure estimates of the necessary survivorship proportions.

Unfortunately, the application of the Option 2 method to practical situations commonly leads to unsatisfactory results,[11] not only when the observed survivorship proportions are not proper transition probability matrices (for example, in the case where they are estimated using the Rogers-von Rabenau procedure), but also when they are adequately measured; for an illustration of this statement, see Ledent and Rees (1980, p. 106).

We thus conclude that the faulty results following from the application of the Option 2 method are due to the method itself rather than to the measurement or estimation of the input data. Two main explanations can be offered for this. First, the Option 2 does nothing other than determine the simple Markov process that would yield survivorship proportions identical to those observed in the system at hand. Then, since the population homogeneity and Markovian assumptions that underpin a simple Markov process do not hold in actual population systems,[12] the "equivalent" Markov process is unlikely to

[10] *This case often occurs in the analysis of migration when (1) census tabulations do not include the numbers of people who are in the same area at the beginning and at the end of the observation period, and (2) detailed age-specific data on the beginning-of-the period population are not available.*

[11] *Note that the Option 2 method implicitly assumes an equality between the length T of the observation period (or the period between the two observations on lifetime movers) and the width n of each age group.*

[12] *This has been well documented in the case of interregional migration: see Goldstein (1964), Morrison (1971), and Long and Hansen (1975).*

reflect the actual mobility process that produced those observed survivorship proportions.

Second, the equivalent Markov process derived on the basis of Eq. (25) does not necessarily lead to transition probability estimates that lie between 0 and 1. As is well known, any operation on transition probability matrices other than an arithmetic averaging or a multiplication, does not necessarily lead to a proper transition probability matrix. Moreover, the inaccuracy problem here is amplified by the fact that the Option 2 method relies on a formula that links the statistics of two consecutive age groups: estimation errors related to a given age group are passed on to the next, so that the "noise" thus introduced is likely to increase as the estimation procedure is carried out.

Thus, the limited success of the Option 2 method is to be attributed not to the logic behind it, which is perfectly sound, but to the relation set out in Eq. (25) that links transition probabilities with survivorship proportions: this relation relies on rigid and unrealistic assumptions. This immediately suggests the development of a more satisfactory estimation method, one that adopts the logic of the Option 2 method but is based on an alternative relation linking transition probabilities with survivorship proportions.

The Averaging Method

One such estimation method has been proposed by Rees and Wilson (1977) who take $\tilde{p}_x$ as the arithmetic average of the observed survivorship proportion matrices associated with the two age groups located immediately below and above age x, i.e.,

$$\underset{\sim}{p}_x = \tfrac{1}{2}[\underset{\sim}{S}_{x-n} + \underset{\sim}{S}_x] \ . \qquad (28)^{13}$$

This relation, unlike the one in (26) or (27), always produces a proper transition probability matrix as long as the survivorship proportions are correctly estimated (i.e., are transition probability matrices themselves).

Note that the Rees-Wilson estimation method just described is not as crude an estimation method as may appear at first glance. Although it is not an exact estimation method following from well-defined assumptions, it is nevertheless a very reasonable approximate method that follows from obvious intuitive considerations for which no further elaboration is needed here.

Equation (28), like Eqs. (26) or (27), is applicable only in the case $T = n$. However, in the case $T \neq n$, it can be applied easily after the introduction of a proper adjustment. To see this, the best way is perhaps to start from the observation that the Rees-Wilson averaging method is a simple procedure that involves a linear interpolation between the observed survivorship proportions. More precisely, for each pair of nonabsorbing states i and j, the Rees-Wilson procedure involves the construction of a survivorship curve obtained by joining with straight lines consecutive values of the observed survivorship proportions S_x^{ij}, plotted on a graph of such proportions versus age at ages $-\tfrac{1}{2}n, \tfrac{1}{2}n, \ldots, x+\tfrac{1}{2}n, \ldots$, and then finding the transition probabilities p_x^{ij} related to ages $0, n, 2n, \ldots$ as

[13] *$\underset{\sim}{s}_{x-n}$ must be squared in the case of $x = 0$ so that it refers to n-year period (Ledent and Rees, 1980, p. 9): infants born during an n-year time interval are, on the average, alive $\tfrac{1}{2}n$ years during that period.*

the ordinates of this survivorship curve midway through each segment.

Then, the above observation readily suggests that, in the case of unequal time and age intervals ($T \neq n$), an increment-decrement life table can be calculated from T-year transition probabilities estimated as the ordinates at ages $0, T, 2T, \ldots,$ of a point-to-point curve constructed by plotting the T-year survivorship proportions observed for n-year age groups (again at ages $-\frac{1}{2}n, \frac{1}{2}n, \ldots$).

An Extension of the Averaging Method

An extension of the Rees-Wilson averaging method has been proposed by Ledent (1980a,b) who suggested that the point-to-point survivorship curves implicit to the Rees-Wilson method could be replaced by more realistic curves obtained by fitting appropriate functions to the observed survivorship proportions, e.g., cubic spline functions similar to those employed by McNeil *et al.* (1977).

Note that, in the case of age groups characterized by low mortality, the estimation of the transition probabilities $\underset{\sim}{p}_x$ as ordinates of such survivorship curves can be troublesome in that $\Sigma_{k=1}^{r} p_x^{ik} > 1$. Therefore, rather than estimate p_x^{ii} from a curve describing survivorship in state i, it is preferable to first estimate $p_x^{i\delta}$ from a nonsurvivorship curve fitted to the proportions $1 - \Sigma_{k=1}^{r} S_x^{ik}$ and then derive the retention probability p_x^{ii} as

$$1 - p_x^{i\delta} - \sum_{\substack{k=1 \\ k \neq i}}^{r} p_x^{ik}.$$

To what extent is the cubic spline interpolation an improvement of the Rees-Wilson linear interpolation? First, in the case of reliable input data, the survivorship curves obtained using a cubic spline function remain close to the corresponding point-to-point survivorship curves in all age brackets where the relevant mobility propensities vary monotonically with age. As one would expect, major differences occur only at the major turning points of the mobility propensity schedules (see Ledent and Rees, 1980, p. 97). Second, in the case of unreliable input data, i.e., observed survivorship proportions varying erratically with age, the survivorship curves based on the linear and cubic spline interpolations are likely to be further apart. Thus, we immediately see the advantage of the cubic spline model over the linear interpolation: it allows for the "smoothing" of the input data and the derivation of the transition probabilities in just one step instead of two as in Hoem (1977).

In practice, the derivation of the observed survivorship proportions necessary for the application of the above procedure (as well as of its predecessors) is a difficult task. First, the information commonly available does not allow for the measurement of the survivorship proportions required. Second, the use of accounts suggested earlier for completing the information available is not always an efficient means: it is not only resource-consuming but it also often does not generate acceptable results.

To circumvent this difficulty, Ledent (1980a,b) has proposed a further modification of the Rees-Wilson procedure, a modification that is tailored to the type of mobility data available, i.e., age-specific numbers of movers between the alternative nonabsorbing states. This modification starts with the observation that age-specific transition proportions $\bar{S}_x^{ij}$ conditional on survival (hereafter denoted as conditional transition proportions) can be immediately derived from the aforementioned data on the basis of the following relationship:

$$\bar{S}_x^{ij} = K_{x.}^{ij} \Big/ \sum_{k=1}^{r} K_{x.}^{ik} , \quad i,j = 1,\ldots,r . \tag{29}$$

Therefore, the various transition probability matrices $\underset{\sim}{p}_x$ can be obtained by first estimating from the set of conditional proportions $\underset{\sim}{\bar{S}}_x$ a set of conditional transition probabilities $\underset{\sim}{\bar{p}}_x$ and then transforming these into the required transition probabilities by introducing independent mortality information Analytically, the value of $\underset{\sim}{p}_x$ follows from

$$\underset{\sim}{p}_x = \underset{\sim}{\bar{p}}_x \underset{\sim}{\hat{p}}_x^{\sigma} , \tag{30}$$

where $\underset{\sim}{\bar{p}}_x$ is the corresponding conditional transition probabili ty matrix and $\underset{\sim}{\hat{p}}_x^{\sigma}$ is a diagonal survivorship matrix whose elements are similar to the survival probabilities of an ordinary life table.

How are the elements of (30) estimated? First, the condi tional transition probability matrices ${}^{i}\underset{\sim}{\bar{p}}_x^{j}$ can be derived from the observed values ${}^{i}\underset{\sim}{\bar{S}}_x^{j}$ of the conditional survivorship propor tions using the cubic spline interpolative procedure described above for all $j \neq i$; then conditional retention probabilities follow immediately from ${}^{i}\bar{p}_x^{i} = 1 - \Sigma_{j \neq i}\, {}^{i}\bar{p}_x^{j}$. Second, the estimation of the diagonal elements of $\hat{p}_x^{\sigma}$ is not that straightforward because Eq. (30) implicitly assumes that mortality rates are dependent on the place of residence at age x rather than on the place of occurrence. Ledent (1980b, pp. 24-26) has developed for this purpose an *ad hoc* method that makes use of the Markov process associated with the observed mobility process.

NEW DEVELOPMENTS

As it now stands, approach B to transition probability estimation from the transition perspective consists of the following two stages:

(a) the estimation of the conditional transition probability matrices $\bar{\underset{\sim}{p}}_x$ carried out in two successive steps: first, measurement of the conditional transition proportion matrices $\bar{\underset{\sim}{S}}_x$ and second, estimation of the conditional transition probability matrices $\bar{\underset{\sim}{p}}_x$ by interpolating through the $\bar{\underset{\sim}{S}}_x$ matrices using cubic spline functions;

(b) transformation of the $\bar{\underset{\sim}{p}}_x$ matrices into the requested $\underset{\sim}{p}_x$ matrices by an *ad hoc* procedure.

Of these two steps, the most problematic is certainly the second, which is unnecessarily complicated. As demonstrated below, this stage can be implemented in a simpler and more satisfactory way.

Let us recall that the conditional and unconditional transition probabilities are defined for all i,j = 1,...,r, by

$$\bar{p}_x^{ij} = \ell_x^{ij} \Big/ \sum_{k=1}^{r} \ell_x^{ik} \qquad (31a)$$

and

$$p_x^{ij} = \ell_x^{ij}/l_x^i \,, \tag{31b}$$

(where the quantities on the right-hand sides have the same meaning as in section 1), so that

$$p_x^{ij} = \bar{p}_x^{ij} \sum_{k=1}^{r} \ell_x^{ik} \Big/ l_x^i \,, \qquad i,j = 1,\ldots,r \,. \tag{32}$$

Since Eqs. (2), (15), and (16) can be combined to yield

$$\sum_{k=1}^{r} \ell_x^{ik} = l_x^i - \sum_{k=1}^{r} \ell_x^{i\delta}(k) = l_x^i - \sum_{k=1}^{r} M_x^{\delta(k)} L_x^{ik} \,, \qquad \forall i = 1,\ldots,r \tag{33}$$

Eq. (32) can be rewritten as

$$p_x^{ij} = \bar{p}_x^{ij} \left[1 - \frac{\sum_{k=1}^{r} M_x^{\delta(k)} L_x^{ik}}{l_x^i} \right] , \qquad i,j = 1,\ldots,r \,. \tag{34}$$

Let us now assume that the number of person-years lived between ages x and x + n is linearly calculated. Then, it is readily established that Eq. (34) leads to the following linear system of r^2 equations in r^2 unknowns p_x^{ij}:

$$p_x^{ij} = \bar{p}_x^{ij} \left[1 - nM_x^{\delta(i)} \frac{1 + p_x^{ii}}{2} - \frac{n}{2} \sum_{\substack{k=1 \\ k \neq i}}^{r} M_x^{\delta(k)} p_x^{ik} \right] , \qquad i,j = 1,\ldots,r \tag{35}$$

a system that, fortunately, can be solved easily. First, let us define

$$A_x^i = \sum_{k=1}^{r} M_x^{\delta(k)} p_x^{ik} , \qquad i = 1,\ldots,r \tag{36}$$

which allows us to rewrite (35) as

$$p_x^{ij} = \bar{p}_x^{ij}\left[1 - \frac{n}{2} M_x^{\delta(i)} - \frac{n}{2} A_x^i\right] , \qquad i,j = 1,\ldots,r . \tag{37}$$

Then, let us substitute (37) into (36) to obtain

$$A_x^i = \left[\sum_{k=1}^{r} M_x^{\delta(k)} \bar{p}_x^{ik}\right]\left[1 - \frac{n}{2} M_x^{\delta(i)} - \frac{n}{2} A_x^i\right] , \qquad i = 1,\ldots,r . \tag{38}$$

Next, on defining, by analogy with (36),

$$\bar{A}_x^i = \sum_{k=1}^{r} M_x^{\delta(k)} \bar{p}_x^{ik} , \qquad i = 1,\ldots,r \tag{39}$$

we can rewrite (38) as

$$A_x^i = \bar{A}_x^i\left[1 - \frac{n}{2} M_x^{\delta(i)} - \frac{n}{2} A_x^i\right] , \qquad i = 1,\ldots,r \tag{40}$$

so that

$$A_x^i = \bar{A}_x^i \, \frac{1 - \frac{n}{2} M_x^{\delta(i)}}{1 + \frac{n}{2} \bar{A}_x^i} , \qquad i = 1,\ldots,r . \tag{41}$$

Finally, on substituting (41) into (37), we obtain

$$p_x^{ij} = \bar{p}_x^{ij} \, \frac{1 - \frac{n}{2} M_x^{\delta(i)}}{1 + \frac{n}{2} \bar{A}_x^i} , \qquad i,j = 1,\ldots,r \tag{42}$$

and, after setting out $\bar{A}_x^i$,

$$p_x^{ij} = \bar{p}_x^{ij} \frac{1 - \frac{n}{2} M_x^{\delta(i)}}{1 + \frac{n}{2} \sum_{k=1}^{r} M_x^{\delta(k)} \bar{p}_x^{ik}}, \quad i,j = 1,\ldots,r . \tag{43}$$

In addition, the nonsurvival probability $p_x^{i\delta}$ can be derived from Eq. (42) on the basis of the following steps:

$$p_x^{i\delta} = 1 - \sum_{k=1}^{r} p_x^{ik}$$

$$= 1 - \left[\sum_{k=1}^{r} \bar{p}_x^{ik}\right] \frac{1 - \frac{n}{2} M_x^{\delta(i)}}{1 + \frac{n}{2} \bar{A}_x^{i}}$$

$$= 1 - \frac{1 - \frac{n}{2} M_x^{\delta(i)}}{1 + \frac{n}{2} \bar{A}_x^{i}}$$

$$= \frac{\frac{n}{2}\left[M_x^{\delta(i)} + \bar{A}_x^{i}\right]}{1 + \frac{n}{2} \bar{A}_x^{i}},$$

and finally

$$p_x^{i\delta} = \frac{\frac{n}{2}\left[M_x^{\delta(i)} + \sum_{k=1}^{r} M_x^{\delta(k)} \bar{p}_x^{ik}\right]}{1 + \frac{n}{2} \sum_{k=1}^{r} M_x^{\delta(k)} \bar{p}_x^{ik}}, \quad i = 1,\ldots,r . \tag{44}$$

Moreover, this probability can be decomposed into r state-specific elements, such that

$$p_x^{i\delta(i)} = \frac{M_x^{\delta(i)} \frac{n}{2}\left(1 + \bar{p}_x^{ii}\right)}{1 + \frac{n}{2} \sum_{k=1}^{r} M_x^{\delta(k)} \bar{p}_x^{ik}}, \quad i = 1,\ldots,r \tag{45}$$

and

$$p_x^{i\delta(j)} = \frac{\frac{n}{2} M_x^{\delta(j)} \bar{p}_x^{ij}}{1 + \frac{n}{2} \sum_{k=1}^{r} M_x^{\delta(k)} \bar{p}_x^{ik}} , \quad i,j = 1,\ldots,r . \quad (j \neq i) \tag{46}$$

4. A BRIEF COMPARISON OF THE TWO ALTERNATIVE APPROACHES

The principal conclusion that can be made regarding the alternative approaches to transition probability estimation from mobility data in the form of movers (transition perspective) is that they are not as disparate as a first impression might lead us to think. To clarify this point, this section contrasts the similarities and differences exhibited by the two approaches, as revised and improved in this paper.

First, the data input that they require is very similar. Both of them call for the availability of

(a) conventional age-specific mortality rates $M_x^{\delta(i)}$, and

(b) age-specific numbers of movers K_x^{ij} between the non-absorbing states.

In addition, approach A demands a knowledge of the age-specific population at the beginning of the observation period. The need for such additional information follows from the fact that whereas approach B includes, among the basic mobility quantities derived from the raw input data, a quantity relating to stayers, approach A does not.

Second, the two alternative approaches appear to operate in opposite directions. On the one hand, approach A focuses on the various state-specific groups of people at a given age x in the multistate stationary population and determines the state allocation of their survivors some n years later. On the other hand, approach B concentrates on the persons at age x + n in the same multistate stationary population and determines the state allocation of the persons at exact age x of whom they are the survivors. At the risk of simplifying a bit, approach A proceeds forward whereas approach B proceeds backward.

Note that the two polar views taken by the alternative approaches are equivalent in the case of a closed system but not in the case of an open system (i.e., for multiregional life tables as they have been implemented so far). This remark raises the question of the closure of the system, the importance of which has been recently stressed by Ledent and Rees (1980, pp. 72-86).

The theory behind increment-decrement life tables normally relates to a closed system. Thus, when one deals with interregional migration, another state (the Rest of the World) should be added to the system considered. In practice, however, the addition of such a state proves to be undesirable because the information needed concerns the spatial distribution of the population under study, with the effect of external migration removed. Interestingly enough, this is exactly the type of information provided by approach B, which uses mobility data not only conditional on survival but also *conditional on survival within the system.*

By contrast, approach A, as described in Section 1, neglects external migration altogether and does not provide information free of external effects. Within each age interval, the would-be external migrants remain in the system, (essentially in the region of residence at the beginning of the interval) with the result that the mobility (retention) probabilities are under (over) estimated. How can we modify approach A to exclude external effects? The logic behind the transition perspective suggests that the best way to achieve this is simply to remove external effects at the level of the population at risk in the definition of the age-specific mobility rates $\hat{M}_x^{ij}$: specifically, in Eq. (27), one should subtract from K_x^i the number of moves D_x^{iw} out of the system made during the observation period by the members of K_x^i. The difficulty here is that the value of D_x^{iw} is generally not available.

Finally, we conclude this section by contrasting the implementation of the two alternative approaches (in their updated versions). Both methods exhibit two similar stages:

1. *Measurement or estimation of several basic quantities from the raw data.* This first stage requires (a) use of an interpolative method to obtain some of the mobility statistics desired and (b) if $n \neq T$, the transformation of some of the data relating to n-year age groups into the corresponding numbers relating to T-year age groups. The interpolative method called for the derivation of the mobility statistics should be performed on the basis of cubic spline functions. But, in the special case $n = T$, it can be performed more rapidly (but also less accurately) on the basis of piecewise linear functions.

2. *Estimation of the transition probabilities.* This is a task that, once the basic quantities are known, simply requires the application of the formulas derived in Sections 1 and 2.

TABLE 1. A Tabular Comparison of the Two Alternative Approaches

	Approach A	Approach B
Input data	${}_nM_x^{\delta(i)}$, ${}_nK_x^{i}$ ${}_nK_x^{ij}$, ${}_nD_x^{iw}$	${}_nM_x^{\delta(i)}$, ${}_nK_x^{ij}$
Measurement or estimation of basic quantities	${}_T\hat{M}_x^{ij} = \frac{1}{T} \frac{{}_TE_x^{ij}}{\frac{1}{2}\left[{}_TK_x^{i} - {}_TD_x^{iw} + {}_TK_x^{ii}\right]}$ $(j \neq i)$	
	1 if $n = T$ ${}_TE_x^{ij} = \frac{1}{2}\left[{}_nK_{x-n}^{ij} + {}_nK_x^{ij}\right]$	1 if $n = T$ ${}_T\bar{p}_x^{ij} = \frac{1}{2}\left[{}_n\bar{S}_{x-n}^{ij} + {}_n\bar{S}_x^{ij}\right]$
	2 $\forall n$ (a) ${}_nK_x^{ij} \rightarrow {}_TE_x^{ij}$; ${}_nK_x^{i} \rightarrow {}_TK_x^{i}$; ${}_nD_x^{iw} \rightarrow {}_TD_x^{iw}$; ${}_nK_x^{ii} \rightarrow {}_TK_x^{ii}$; (b) ${}_nM_x^{\delta(i)} \rightarrow {}_TM_x^{\delta(i)}$ (if $n \neq T$)	2 $\forall n$ (a) ${}_n\bar{S}_x^{ij} \rightarrow {}_T\bar{p}_x^{ij}$; (b) ${}_nM_x^{\delta(i)} \rightarrow {}_TM_x^{\delta(i)}$ (if $n \neq T$)
Transition probabilities	${}_Tp_x^{ij} = \frac{T\,{}_T\hat{M}_x^{ij}}{1 + \frac{T}{2}\left[{}_TM_x^{\delta(i)} + \sum_{k=1}^{r} {}_TM_x^{\delta(k)}\hat{M}_x^{ik}\right]}$ $(j \neq i)$	${}_Tp_x^{ij} = {}_T\bar{p}_x^{ij} = \frac{1 - \frac{T}{2}\,{}_TM_x^{\delta(i)}}{1 + \frac{T}{2}\sum_{k=1}^{r} {}_TM_x^{\delta(k)}\,{}_T\bar{p}_x^{ik}}$
	${}_Tp_x^{ii} = \frac{1 - \frac{T}{2}\left[{}_TM_x^{\delta(i)} + \sum_{k=1}^{r} {}_TM_x^{\delta(k)}\hat{M}_x^{ik}\right]}{1 + \frac{T}{2}\left[{}_TM_x^{\delta(i)} + \sum_{k=1}^{r} {}_TM_x^{\delta(k)}\hat{M}_x^{ik}\right]}$	

1 Simplified case applicable if n = T. 2 General case

A perhaps more illuminating presentation of the contrast between the two approaches is provided in Table 1, where the various quantities introduced now have a left subscript representing the width of the age groups concerned. In particular, T appears more often than n, a reflection of the fact that, when mobility data refer to a T-year observation period, the transition probabilities to be estimated refer to T-year age groups (regardless of the width n of the age groups relating to the original mobility data).

5. CONCLUSION

This paper has been concerned with the estimation of transition probabilities in increment-decrement life tables in the case where the mobility data available come in the count of movers from a population census or survey. It has summarized, extended, and compared the two approaches proposed to date. The investigation points to the superiority of one approach over the other, namely, several reasons suggest that approach B is preferable:

(a) Approach B starts with a quantity ($\bar{\underset{\sim}{s}}_x$) that is close to the one to be estimated ($\underset{\sim}{p}_x$), whereas approach A first needs to ascertain the extent of total mobility out of each state.

(b) The transition proportion concept used in approach B has a more transparent interpretation than the mobility concept, assimable to a net migrant rate, used in approach A.

(c) In case of unequal time and age intervals, approach B

involves fewer transformations of data and thus fewer calculations than approach A.

These reasons, however, are not sufficient to reject approach A altogether. Nevertheless, if external migration is an important variable, approach B, which involves an estimation method unaffected by such a possibility, presents a decisive advantage over approach A: the nonexistence of additional information on external flows renders the necessary amendment of the latter approach virtually impossible.

REFERENCES

Goldstein, S. (1964). The extent of repeated migration: An analysis based on the Danish population register. *Journal of the American Statistical Association 59,* 1121-1132.

Hoem, J. (1977). A Markov chain model of working life tables. *Scandinavian Actuarial Journal,* 1-20.

Ledent, J. (1978). Some Methodological and Empirical Considerations in the Construction of Increment-Decrement Life Tables. RM-78-25. Laxenburg, Austria: International Institute for Applied Systems Analysis.

Ledent, J. (1980a). Multistate life tables: Movement versus transition perspectives. *Environment and Planning 12,* 533-562.

Ledent, J. (1980b). An Improved Methodology for Constructing Increment-Decrement Life Tables from the Transition Perspective. WP-80-104. Laxenburg, Austria: International Institute for Applied Systems Analysis.

Ledent, J. and Rees, P. H. (1980). Choices in the Construction of Multiregional Life Tables. WP-80-173. Laxenburg, Austria: International Institute for Applied Systems Analysis.

Long, L. H. and Hansen, K. A. (1975). Trends in return migration to the South. *Demography 12(4),* 601-614.

Long, L. H. and Boertlein, C. G. (1977). The geographical mobility of Americans - An international comparison. *Current Population Reports: Special Studies,* Series P-23, No. 64.

McNeil, D. R., Trussell, T. J., and Turner, J. C. (1977). Spline interpolation of demographic data. *Demography 14(2),* 245-252.

Morrison, P. A. (1971). Chronic movers and the future redistribution of population: A longitudinal analysis. *Demography 8,* 171-184.

Rees, P. H. (1977). The measurement of migration from census data and other sources. *Environment and Planning A9,* 247-272.

Rees, P. H. (1979). 1. Migration and Settlement in the United Kingdom. RR-79-3. Laxenburg, Austria: International Institute for Applied Systems Analysis.

Rees, P. H. and Willekens, F. (1981). Data Bases and Accounting Frameworks for IIASA's Comparative Migration and Settlement Study. CP-81-39. Laxenburg, Austria: International Institute for Applied Systems Analysis.

Rees, P. H. and Wilson, A. G. (1977). Spatial Population Analysis. London: Edward Arnold.

Rogers, A. (1975). Introduction to Multiregional Mathematical Demography. New York: Wiley.

Rogers, A. and Ledent, J. (1976). Increment-decrement life tables: A comment. *Demography 13(2)*, 287-290.

Rogers, A. and von Rabenau, B. (1971). Estimation from interregional migration streams from place of birth by place of residence data. *Demography 8*, 185-194.

Schoen, R. (1975). Constructing increment-decrement life tables. *Demography 12(2)*, 313-324.

Shyrock, H. S., Siegel, J. S., and associates (1973). The Methods and Materials of Demography, Vols. I and II. Second printing. Washington, D.C.: U.S. Government Printing Office.

Willekens, F. and Rogers, A. (1978). Spatial Population Analysis: Methods and Computer Programs. RR-78-18. Laxenburg, Austria: International Institute for Applied Systems Analysis.

7

Generalizing the Life Table Model to Incorporate Interactions between the Sexes

Robert Schoen

1. INTRODUCTION

Since its introduction over 300 years ago, the life table has been the central mathematical model of demography. It has proven to be a powerful and flexible tool, readily adaptable to extensions that allow it to incorporate more information on the vital processes that characterize human behavior. Many, if not most, generalizations of the life table model have served to extend it along one of the following three dimensions: (i) from stationary population models reflecting attrition alone to stable population models reflecting both attrition and renewal; (ii) from models with a single cause of decrement to models allowing any number of increments and decrements; and (iii) from one-sex models to models incorporating the interaction between the sexes.

MULTIDIMENSIONAL MATHEMATICAL
DEMOGRAPHY

ISBN 0-12-435640-0

The present paper focuses primarily on the third dimension and seeks to encompass two-sex models within a general algorithm for specifying and constructing life table models. Two-sex models reflect the interaction between the sexes with regard to either fertility or nuptiality, the two demographic behaviors that involve the joint action of both sexes. The difficulty in constructing two-sex models arises from the fact that while both stable and increment-decrement models can be constructed to reproduce all observed behavioral rates, two-sex models cannot simultaneously reflect observed male and female rates. In general, differences between the age compositions of the observed and model populations lead to inconsistent numbers of births or marriages when the observed male and female rates are applied to the model male and female populations. The resolution of the "two-sex problem" lies in the specification of an appropriate consistency condition that relates the observed and model male and female rates, and that question will be discussed in the section on Model V (TWOGRO).

The three-life table dimensions give rise to 10 different models. They are named in Table 1, which represents the first systematic attempt to identify all of the different types of two-sex models possible with the stationary/stable and decrement/increment-decrement dimensions. In the next section, each of these models will be discussed in turn, and related to the equations common to all life table models. As a numerical example, a two-sex fertility increment-decrement stable population (TWOFIDS) model will be presented, using data for the United States and California, 1970. As a large number of symbols are needed, a guide to the notation employed is given in Table 2.

TABLE 1. The Ten Life Table Models Implied by the Stationary/Stable, Decrement/Increment-Decrement, and One-Sex/Two-Sex Dimensions

Type of model		One-sex	Two-sex[a] fertility	Two-sex nuptiality
Decrement only	Stationary population	I. LT	--	VII. TWONUP
	Stable population	II. SP	V. TWOGRO	VIII. MSQUEEZ
Increment-decrement	Stationary population	III. IDLT	--	IX. TWOMSLT
	Stable population	IV. IDSP	VI. TWOFIDS	X. TWOMSSP

[a]*Two cells are empty because two-sex fertility models must permit population growth.*

2. LIFE TABLE MODELS

2.1. MODEL I: LT

The basic life table model (LT) dates back to the seventeenth century and the work of Graunt (1662) and Halley (1693). A birth cohort, a closed group of persons born in the same year, is followed from birth to the death of its last member, as it is subjected to a fixed age schedule of mortality rates. Alternatively, the basic life table can be seen as a stationary population, one that does not change with respect to either size or age composition, that arises from a history of unchanging mortality and a long series of identical birth cohorts.

There are many ways to specify and construct the basic life table model (Shryock and Siegel, 1973; Schoen, 1978a). Here the approach will be to use the algorithm of Schoen (1975) and Schoen and Land (1979), which identified three sets of

TABLE 2. Guide to the Notation Employed[a]

Summary of principal symbols		
Symbol	Meaning of root symbol	Defined by equation/in model
a	Mean duration at transfer	75/TWOFIDS example
B, b	Number of births	
${}_nB_x$, ${}_nb_x$		12/SP
$b(x,y)$		28/TWOGRO
$\underset{\sim}{b}(x,y)$		after 39/TWOFIDS
$\underset{\sim}{b}^*(x,y)$		39/TWOFIDS
$b(x,k;y,j)$		after 39/TWOFIDS
${}^ib(x,y)$		67/TWOMSSP
${}^{s;i}{}_nb_x$		68/TWOMSSP
C, c	Number of marriages	
$c(x,y)$		40/TWONUP
${}^sc(x,y)$		45/MSQUEEZ
$\underset{\sim}{C}, \underset{\sim}{c}$		A.1/TWONUP
D, d	Number of decrements	
${}_nd_x$		1/LT
${}_nD_x$		2/LT
${}_n\underset{\sim}{d}_x$		17/IDLT
${}^{ij}{}_nd^k_x$		after 19/IDLT
${}^s{}_nd_x$		29/TWOGRO
${}^s{}_n\underset{\sim}{d}_x$		34/TWOFIDS
${}^{s;i}{}_nd^j_x$		53/TWOMSLT
${}^{s;i}{}_nd^j(x,y)$		53/TWOMSLT
F, f	Fertility rate	
${}_nF_x$, ${}_n\hat{f}_x$		12/SP
${}_n\underset{\sim}{f}_x$, ${}_n\underset{\sim}{\hat{f}}_x$		23/IDSP
${}^i{}_n\hat{f}_x$		after 25/IDSP

Table 2 (Cont'd)

Symbol	Meaning of root symbol	Defined by equation/in model
${}^{s}_{n}F(x,y)$, ${}^{s}_{n}\hat{f}(x,y)$		28/TWOGRO
${}^{s}_{n}F_{\underset{\sim}{x}}$, ${}^{s}_{n}\hat{f}_{\underset{\sim}{x}}$		36/TWOFIDS
${}^{s}_{n}\hat{f}(x,k;y,j)$		after 39/TWOFIDS
ℓ	Number surviving to an exact age in the model	
ℓ_{x}		1/LT
$\ell_{\underset{\sim}{x}}$		17/IDLT
${}^{ij}\ell_{x+n}$		after 19/IDLT
${}^{i}\ell_{x}$		20/IDLT
${}^{s}\ell_{\underset{\sim}{x}}$		34/TWOFIDS
${}^{s;i}\ell_{x}$		53/TWOMSLT
${}^{s;i}\ell(x,y)$		55/TWOMSLT
L	Person-years lived or number of persons in the model population	
${}_{n}L_{x}$		2/LT
${}_{n}L_{\underset{\sim}{x}}$		18/IDLT
${}^{ij}_{n}L_{x}$		after 19/IDLT
${}_{n}L^{*}_{\underset{\sim}{x}}$		25/IDSP
${}^{i}_{n}L_{x}$		after 25/IDSP
${}^{s}_{n}L_{\underset{\sim}{x}}$		37/TWOFIDS
${}^{s}_{n}L^{*}_{\underset{\sim}{x}}$		38/TWOFIDS
${}^{s;k}_{n}L_{x}$		after 39/TWOFIDS
${}^{i}L(x,y)$		59/TWOMSLT
${}^{s;i}L(x,y)$		68/TWOMSSP
${}^{s}\underset{\sim}{L}$		A.1/TWONUP
M,m	Occurrence/exposure rate of transfer	

Table 2 (Cont'd)

Symbol	Meaning of root symbol	Defined by equation/in Model
${}_nM_x$, ${}_nm_x$		2/LT
${}_n\tilde{M}_x$, ${}_n\tilde{m}_x$		18/IDLT
${}^{i}_{n}m^{j}_{x}$		after 19/IDLT
${}^{s}_{n}M_x$, ${}^{s}_{n}m_x$		30/TWOGRO
${}^{s}_{n}\tilde{M}_x$, ${}^{s}_{n}\tilde{m}_x$		35/TWOFIDS
${}^{s;k}_{n}M^{j}_{x}$, ${}^{s;k}_{n}m^{j}_{x}$		57/TWOMSLT
${}^{s;k}_{n}M^{j}(x,y)$, ${}^{s;k}_{n}m^{j}(x,y)$		59/TWOMSLT
r	Intrinsic growth rate	11/SP
T_x	Person-years lived above age x in a model population	Table 2
${}^{s}W$, ${}^{s}w$	Marriage rate for sex s	42/TWONUP
μ	Force of transition	
μ_x		6/LT
${}^{i}\mu^{j}_{x}$		20/IDLT

[a]The paper has attempted to use a more or less consistent set of symbols based upon standard actuarial ("halo") notation, although the demands of some of the models go beyond standard usage, and a generally accepted system of notation, even for increment-decrement life tables, has yet to emerge. Some of the major conventions followed here are

(1) Capital letters are generally used for data functions, lower case letters for model functions (although L and T are model functions). (2) Right subscripts, frequently x or y, represent an exact or initial age. (3) Left subscripts, generally n, represent the width of an age interval. (4) Right superscripts designate the destination of a transfer (δ denotes a transfer to death; p, a marriage to a previously married person). (5) Left superscripts designate (a) a state of origin or residence (w for widowed, v for divorced, u for unmarried, and g for married); (b) the appropriate sex, when the superscript is s, m (male), or f (female); or (c) a compound of sex and/or states. (6) A caret (^) indicates a stable population function (e.g., $\hat{L}$) (7) A tilde (~) indicates a matrix (e.g., $\tilde{L}$).

equations governing life table models. The first set, the *flow equations*, specify the state structure of the model and the possible flows between states. The second set, the *orientation equations,* relate the "observed" (or input) occurrence/exposure rate of decrement to the analogous rates in the model. The third set, the *person-year equations,* relate the number of person-years lived in an age interval by the model population to the number of persons at each exact age.

To write out the three sets of equations for basic life table model LT, we have

A. Flow equation:

$$\ell_{x+n} = \ell_x - {}_nd_x \tag{1}$$

B. Orientation equation:

$${}_nD_x/{}_nP_x = {}_nM_x = {}_nm_x = {}_nd_x/{}_nL_x \tag{2}$$

C. Person-year equation:

$${}_nL_x = \int_0^n \ell_{x+t}dt \tag{3}$$

where ℓ_{x+n} represents the number of persons alive in the life table at exact age x+n; ${}_nd_x$, the number of decrements between ages x and x+n; ${}_nL_x$, the number of person-years lived between ages x and x+n (or the life table population aged x to x+n); ${}_nm_x$, the life table occurrence/exposure rate of decrement between ages x and x+n; ${}_nM_x$, the observed population occurrence/exposure rate of decrement between ages x and x+n; ${}_nD_x$, the observed number of decrements between ages x and x+n; and ${}_nP_x$, the observed population aged x to x+n.

To construct a life table from observed data using Eqs. (1) - (3), it is necessary to introduce a numerical integration procedure to evaluate the number of person-years lived in each interval in terms of values of the survivorship function ℓ_x. A number of numerical integration procedures have been used in life table construction. Probably the simplest is the linear assumption (in that ℓ_{x+t} is assumed to be a straight line for $0 \leq t \leq n$), which can be written as

$$ {}_nL_x = \tfrac{1}{2}n(\ell_x + \ell_{x+n}). \tag{4} $$

Using Eqs. (1), (2), and (4), we find the linear solution

$$ \ell_{x+n} = \ell_x \left[\frac{1 - \frac{1}{2}n \; {}_nM_x}{1 + \frac{1}{2}n \; {}_nM_x} \right], \tag{5} $$

which allows us to calculate, in turn, all of the survivorship values, and from them the remaining life table values. To begin, a round number, commonly 100,000, is taken as ℓ_0, the starting value or radix of the table. (In practice, different procedures are generally used for the youngest and oldest ages as indicated in the numerical example of the next section.) Different numerical integration procedures give rise to different numerical solutions, hence the three kinds of equations provide the structure from which the model can be constructed, rather than an explicit solution.

The emphasis is on constructing discrete models from discrete data, specifically data in the form of occurrence/exposure rates. Little will be said about other forms of input data, in part because they have been discussed elsewhere (Ledent, 1980; MacRae, 1977), and in part because fertility and marriage rates are frequently available. It is important to note, however, that the three sets of equations are based on an underlying Markov process model. The flow equations of a life table can be derived from the Kolmogorov forward differential equations of the Markov chain (Schoen and Land, 1979, p. 765). If we denote the instantaneous force of decrement (or transition intensity) at age x by μ_x, we have for a time inhomogeneous continuous-time Markov process model

$$\mu_x = \lim_{h \downarrow 0} \frac{{}_h m_x}{h} = -\frac{1}{\ell_x} \frac{d}{dx} \ell_x. \tag{6}$$

From Eq. (6), we find (Jordan, 1967, p. 14)

$$\ell_{x+n} = \ell_x \left(\exp - \int_0^n \mu_{x+t} dt \right). \tag{7}$$

The model transfer rates can be expressed in terms of the force of transition by

$${}_n m_x = \frac{\int_0^n \ell_{x+t} \mu_{x+t} dt}{\int_0^n \ell_{x+t} dt}. \tag{8}$$

If there are k_x persons in the observed population at exact age x, the observed population rate can be written as

$${}_n M_x = \frac{\int_0^n k_{x+t} \mu_{x+t} dt}{\int_0^n k_{x+t} dt}. \tag{9}$$

The orientation equations therefore assume that, within each age interval, the observed population has a stationary population age distribution. That assumption can be relaxed to permit the observed population to have a stable population age distribution within age intervals, but such a refinement will not be pursued here (Keyfitz, 1968a; Preston *et al.*, 1973).

2.2. *MODEL II: SP*

The development of stable population theory is closely associated with A. J. Lotka (Lotka, 1907a,b, 1939; Sharpe and Lotka, 1911), although the idea of a life table model with exponentially increasing birth cohorts and a fixed age distribution can be traced back to Euler (1760). To include population growth in our algorithm, we must add a fourth set of equations, the *renewal equations*. For the basic stable population (SP) model, we then have

A. Flow equation:

$$\ell_{x+n} = \ell_x - {}_nd_x \tag{10}$$

B. Orientation equations:

$${}_nM_x = {}_nm_x = {}_n\hat{m}_x = \frac{{}_n\hat{d}_x}{{}_n\hat{L}_x} = \frac{\exp[-r(x + \tfrac{1}{2}n)]\,{}_nd_x}{\exp[-r(x + \tfrac{1}{2}n)]\,{}_nL_x} \tag{11}$$

$${}_nB_x/{}_nP_x = {}_nF_x = {}_n\hat{f}_x = {}_nb_x/{}_n\hat{L}_x \tag{12}$$

C. Person-year equations:

$${}_nL_x = \int_0^n \ell_{x+t}\,dt \tag{13}$$

$$ {}_n\hat{L}_x = \int_0^n \exp[-r(x+t)]\ell_{x+t}dt = \exp[-r(x+\tfrac{1}{2}n)]\,{}_nL_x \tag{14} $$

D. Renewal equation:

$$ \ell_0 = \sum_x \exp[-r(x+\tfrac{1}{2}n)]\,{}_nL_x\,{}_n\hat{f}_x = \sum_x {}_nb_x, \tag{15} $$

where the caret (^) indicates a stable, as opposed to stationary, population function; r is Lotka's intrinsic rate of natural increase, or the growth rate of the stable population; ${}_n\hat{f}_x$ represents the fertility rate for persons aged x to x+n in the stable population; ${}_nb_x$, the number of births aged x to x+n in the stable population; ${}_nF_x$, the observed fertility rate for persons aged x to x+n; and ${}_nB_x$, the observed number of births to persons aged x to x+n.

Every cohort born into the stable population follows an identical life course, determined by the fixed age schedule of mortality. It is thus possible, as well as desirable for purposes of simplification, to use a flow equation for a birth cohort. The orientation equations, primarily for reasons of simplification, equate the observed rate with both the cohort rate and the period (stable population) rate, though the three rates need not be identical. Throughout the present paper, a stable population $\hat{L}$ or $\hat{d}$ function is assumed to be equal to the corresponding cohort function adjusted for population growth to the midpoint of the age interval. That approximation has proven to be quite accurate, particularly in the renewal equation (Keyfitz, 1968b, Chapter 11).

In continuous form, the renewal (or characteristic) equation is

$$\ell_0 = \int_0^\infty \exp(-rx)\ell_x \hat{f}_x dx. \tag{16}$$

By convention, the model applies to the year in which there are ℓ_0 births, that is, the year in which the number of births in the stable population equals the radix of the corresponding life table. While the number of births in the stable population will grow from year to year at exponential growth rate r, the relationships within the stable population, such as its crude birth and death rates and its age composition, will stay the same. In essence, that is what the renewal equation shows, as it requires that the intrinsic growth rate r be such that when the observed fertility rates are applied to the survivors of earlier birth cohorts, *adjusted for changes in cohort size*, ℓ_0 births will result.

2.3. MODEL III: IDLT

Increment-decrement life table (IDLT) models go back at least to Du Pasquier (1912, 1913), with subsequent methodological extensions by Fix and Neyman (1951), Chiang (1964), Sverdrup (1965), and Hoem (1970). It was not until recently, however, when computers became readily available, that the model attracted considerable attention (Rogers, 1973, 1975; Rogers and Ledent, 1976; Schoen, 1975; Schoen and Land, 1979; Schoen and Nelson, 1974). Like the basic life table, the IDLT model can follow the experience of an actual birth cohort. Its ability to allow increments (entrants), as well as decrements (exits) from different life statuses, gives it great flexibility, and IDLT models have been applied to analyses of migration, marriage and divorce, labor-force participation, and other areas.

The specification of a k+1 state IDLT, where there are k living states and the k+1st state "dead," is best done with the use of matrix notation. For simplicity, and with no loss of generality, we shall emphasize two-table (three-state) models. We can then write (Rogers and Ledent, 1976; Schoen, 1977a)

A. Flow equations:

$$\underset{\sim}{\ell}_{x+n} = \underset{\sim}{\ell}_{x} - {}_{n}\underset{\sim}{d}_{x} \tag{17}$$

B. Orientation equations:

$${}_{n}\underset{\sim}{M}_{x} = {}_{n}\underset{\sim}{m}_{x} = {}_{n}\underset{\sim}{d}_{x} \cdot {}_{n}\underset{\sim}{L}_{x}^{-1} \tag{18}$$

C. Person-year equations:

$${}_{n}\underset{\sim}{L}_{x} = \int_{0}^{n} \ell_{x+t}\,dt \tag{19}$$

where

$$\underset{\sim}{\ell}_{x} = \begin{bmatrix} {}^{11}\ell_{x} & {}^{21}\ell_{x} \\ {}^{12}\ell_{x} & {}^{22}\ell_{x} \end{bmatrix},$$

$${}_{n}\underset{\sim}{d}_{x} = \begin{bmatrix} {}^{11}_{n}d_{x}^{\delta} + {}^{11}_{n}d_{x}^{2} - {}^{12}_{n}d_{x}^{1} & {}^{21}_{n}d_{x}^{\delta} + {}^{21}_{n}d_{x}^{2} - {}^{22}_{n}d_{x}^{1} \\ {}^{12}_{n}d_{x}^{\delta} + {}^{12}_{n}d_{x}^{1} - {}^{11}_{n}d_{x}^{2} & {}^{22}_{n}d_{x}^{\delta} + {}^{22}_{n}d_{x}^{1} - {}^{21}_{n}d_{x}^{2} \end{bmatrix},$$

$${}_{n}\underset{\sim}{m}_{x} = \begin{bmatrix} {}^{1}_{n}m_{x}^{\delta} + {}^{1}_{n}m_{x}^{2} & -{}^{2}_{n}m_{x}^{1} \\ -{}^{1}_{n}m_{x}^{2} & {}^{2}_{n}m_{x}^{\delta} + {}^{2}_{n}m_{x}^{1} \end{bmatrix},$$

${}_n\underset{\sim}{M}_x$ is a matrix of the same form as ${}_n\underset{\sim}{m}_x$, with observed rather than IDLT rates; ${}_n\underset{\sim}{L}_x$, a matrix of the same form as $\underset{\sim}{\ell}_x$, with person-year (L) functions instead of survivorship (ℓ) functions; δ, as a right superscript represents a transfer to the dead state; ${}^{ij}\ell_{x+n}$ represents the number of persons in state j of the IDLT at exact age x+n who were in state i at exact age x; ${}^{ij}_{n}d^{k}_{x}$, the number of transfers from state j to state k between ages x and x+n among persons who were in state i at age x; ${}^{i}_{n}m^{j}_{x}$, the IDLT rate of transfer from state i to state j between ages x and x+n; and ${}^{ij}_{n}L_x$, the number of person-years lived in state j between ages x and x+n by persons who were in state i at age x.

For a discussion and comparison of IDLT models constructed from rates using different person-year equations, see Schoen (1979), and from census or retrospective data, see Ledent (1980) and Schoen and Woodrow (1980).

The Markov transition probability matrix is given by $\underset{\sim}{\ell}_{x+n}\underset{\sim}{\ell}_x^{-1}$, and the underlying time-inhomogeneous, finite-space, continuous-time Markov process model is described in Schoen and Land (1979). The instantaneous forces of transition from state i to state j are given by

$$ {}^{i}\mu^{j}_{x} = \lim_{h\downarrow 0} {}^{ij}\ell_{x+h}/h\,{}^{i}\ell_{x} , \tag{20}$$

where ${}^{i}\ell_x$ represents the number of persons in IDLT state i at exact age x, and procedures to estimate the matrix of forces are discussed in Land and Schoen (1982).

2.4. *MODEL IV: IDSP*

Work on increment-decrement stable population (IDSP) models was pioneered by Andrei Rogers (1975), who treated both the discrete and continuous cases in detail. In applying our algorithm, we have

A. Flow equations:

$$\underset{\sim}{\ell}_{x+n} = \underset{\sim}{\ell}_x - {}_n\underset{\sim}{d}_x \tag{21}$$

B. Orientation equations:

$${}_n\underset{\sim}{M}_x = {}_n\underset{\sim}{m}_x = {}_n\underset{\sim}{\hat{m}}_x \tag{22}$$

$${}_n\underset{\sim}{F}_x = {}_n\underset{\sim}{\hat{f}}_x \tag{23}$$

C. Person-year equations;

$${}_n\underset{\sim}{L}_x = \int_0^n \underset{\sim}{\ell}_{x+t}dt = \exp[r(x+\tfrac{1}{2}n)]\,{}_n\underset{\sim}{\hat{L}}_x \tag{24}$$

D. Renewal equations:

$$\underset{\sim}{\ell}_0 = \sum_x \exp[-r(x+\tfrac{1}{2}n)]\,{}_n\underset{\sim}{L}^*_x\,{}_n\underset{\sim}{\hat{f}}_x \tag{25}$$

where

$${}_n\underset{\sim}{\hat{f}}_x = \begin{bmatrix} {}^1_n\hat{f}_x & 0 \\ 0 & {}^2_n\hat{f}_x \end{bmatrix}, \qquad {}_n\underset{\sim}{L}^*_x = \begin{bmatrix} {}^1_nL_x & 0 \\ 0 & {}^2_nL_x \end{bmatrix},$$

${}_n\underset{\sim}{F}_x$ is a matrix of the same form as ${}_n\underset{\sim}{\hat{f}}_x$ with observed instead of IDSP age-state specific fertility rates; ${}^i_n\hat{f}_x$, the fertility rate for persons in state i between the ages of x and x+n; and ${}^i_nL_x$, the number of person-years lived in state i between the ages of x and x+n.

In the IDLT model, the radix (${}^{i}\ell_0$) values for the various states can be set arbitrarily, unless there is some logical reason for choosing a particular allocation, e.g., to reflect that all persons are unmarried at birth. In the IDSP model, however, the radix values can be determined by the rates. Equation (25) provides one equation for each living state, sufficient to determine the value of r and the proportional allocation of births. In the model presented above, births to persons in state i are allocated to state i. That allocation rule can be modified as the situation warrants, however, e.g., to put all births into the unmarried state in a marital status IDSP.

2.5. *MODEL V: TWOGRO*

The two-sex fertility stable population (TWOGRO) is the first of the six two-sex models to be considered. An awareness of the "two-sex problem" in the literature dates back at least to the papers of A. H. Pollard (1948) and D. G. Kendall (1949). Since then, a number of approaches to reconciling the inconsistent male and female age-specific fertility (or marriage) rates have been proposed, including those of Das Gupta (1978), Goodman (1967, 1968), Henry (1972), McFarland (1975), Mitra (1978), and J. H. Pollard (1975).

The approach to consistency followed here is taken from Schoen (1981). Let the number of births to males exact age x and females exact age y be $\beta(x,y)$. If we assume constant age-specific fertility preferences between males age x and females age y, the total change in $\beta(x,y)$--or the total differential of $\beta(x,y)$--can be written as (Granville *et al.*, 1941, p. 450)

$$d\beta(x,y) = \frac{\partial\beta(x,y)}{\partial\,^{m}\ell_x}\,\Delta^{m}\ell_x + \frac{\partial\beta(x,y)}{\partial\,^{f}\ell_y}\,\Delta^{f}\ell_y\,, \qquad (26)$$

where the left superscripts m and f represent the male and female populations, respectively. If we consider the case of equal changes, at the margin, in the number of males aged x and females aged y, Eq. (26) can be rewritten in the limit as

$$\frac{d\beta(x,y)}{d\lambda(x,y)} = \frac{\partial\beta(x,y)}{\partial\,^{m}\ell_x} + \frac{\partial\beta(x,y)}{\partial\,^{f}\ell_y}\,, \qquad (27)$$

where $d\lambda(x,y)$ represents either $d^{m}\ell_x$ or $d^{f}\ell_y$. (A similar analytic approach has been used to study the components of production functions in economics, e.g., Brems, 1968, p. 170.) Equation (27), in effect, expresses the total instantaneous rate of change in $\beta(x,y)$ as the sum of the *one-sex propensities* of males aged x and females aged y to have an (x,y) birth. Accordingly, as our consistency condition, we require that the observed and model populations have equal instantaneous rates of change in their number of (x,y) births, given equal changes at the margin in the number of males aged x and females aged y. In terms of continuous functions, that consistency condition *equates* measures that reflect the underlying fertility *preferences*, i.e., (i) the sum of the male and female propensities in the observed population, and (ii) the sum of those male and female propensities in the model. Using discrete functions, and again assuming that the observed and model populations have the same age composition within the age intervals considered, we have

$$^{m}F(x,y) + {}^{f}F(x,y) = {}^{m}\hat{f}(x,y) + {}^{f}\hat{f}(x,y) \qquad (28)$$

where

$$^m\hat{f}(x,y) = b(x,y)/^m\hat{L}_x, \quad ^f\hat{f}(x,y) = b(x,y)/^f\hat{L}_y,$$

$^iF(x,y)$ represents the corresponding observed age-sex-specific fertility rate; and b(x,y), the number of births in the model to males aged x to x+n and females aged y to y+n. [If the male age interval is x to x + u and the female age interval is y to y + v, a factor of (u/v) must be attached to the $^mF(x,y)$ and the $^m\hat{f}(x,y)$.]

Equation (28) specifies a "harmonic mean" consistency condition in that it is equivalent to equating the number of observed and model population (x,y) marriages divided by the harmonic mean of the respective male and female populations aged x to x+n and y to y+n. The harmonic mean had been suggested earlier (Das Gupta, 1972; Keyfitz, 1971), but had been rejected as unrealistic as it appears to be sensitive only to the number of males aged x and females aged y, and therefore incapable of capturing the competitive nature of the fertility "market". In spite of appearances, however, the harmonic mean consistency condition is capable of reflecting the change in the number of (x,y) births brought about by a change in the number of persons in any age-sex group.

For example, let us consider how an increase in the observed number of males aged z (z≠x) will affect the number of (x,y) births in the model. All other things remaining the same, including the number of (z,j) births (where j ranges over all female ages), the increase in males aged z means a decrease in the $^mF(z,j)$ rates. Thus, the sum of $^mF(z,j)$ and $^fF(z,j)$ will decline and accordingly $^m\hat{f}(z,j) + {^f\hat{f}}(z,j)$ will be smaller, since the two sums are equal. That implies a decline in the number of (z,j) births in the model for all j. With fewer (z,y) births, females aged y in the model are more available to have births by males aged x. Thus, the apparent decrease in competition from males aged z in the observed population is reflected by an increase in (x,y) births in the model, demonstrating the realistic nature of the seemingly "simple" harmonic mean consistency condition.

To apply our algorithm, we have

(A) Flow equations:

$$^{i}\ell_{x+n} = {}^{i}\ell_{x} - {}^{i}_{n}d_{x}, \quad i=m,f \tag{29}$$

(B) Orientation equations:

$$^{i}_{n}M_{x} = {}^{i}_{n}m_{x} = {}^{i}_{n}\hat{m}_{x}, \quad i=m,f \tag{30}$$

$$^{m}F(x,y) + {}^{f}F(x,y) = {}^{m}\hat{f}(x,y) + {}^{f}\hat{f}(x,y) \tag{31}$$

(C) Person-year equations:

$$^{i}_{n}L_{x} = \int_{0}^{n} {}^{i}\ell_{x+t}dt = \exp[r(x+\tfrac{1}{2}n)]\,{}^{i}_{n}\hat{L}_{x}, \quad i=m,f \tag{32}$$

(D) Renewal equation:

$$\begin{aligned} ^{m}\ell_{0} + {}^{f}\ell_{0} &= \sum_{x}\sum_{y} \exp[-r(x+\tfrac{1}{2}n)]\,{}^{m}_{n}L_{x} \cdot {}^{m}\hat{f}(x,y) \\ &= \sum_{x}\sum_{y} \exp[-r(x+\tfrac{1}{2}n)]\,{}^{f}_{n}L_{y} \cdot {}^{f}\hat{f}(x,y) \\ &= \sum_{x}\sum_{y} b(x,y). \end{aligned} \tag{33}$$

Since the sex ratio at birth is fairly constant at about 105 male births per 100 female births, $^{m}\ell_{0}$ can be set at

105,000, ${}^{f}\ell_0$ at 100,000, and all births allocated to the male and female populations in the ratio 105:100. (If it is desir to let the sex ratio at birth depend upon the ages of the parents, see Schoen, 1978b, p. 363.)

The TWOGRO model specified above, once established, is self-renewing in the sense that its age-sex composition will remain fixed over time. Its birth cohorts will increase in size exponentially, and it will maintain the same behavioral rates. One important property remains to be shown, however, for this and for all of the other two-sex models. That property is known as ergodicity, which states that any population will forget its initial composition and take on the age-sex composition specified above as, over a long period of time, it reflects the observed behavioral rates.

2.6. *MODEL VI: TWOFIDS*

The two-sex fertility increment-decrement stable population (TWOFIDS) is a model capable of capturing all of the thre basic elements of demography, as it can reflect the implicatio of male and female rates of birth, death, and migration. To apply our algorithm, retaining the two-table (three-state) model for convenience, we have

A. Flow equations:

$$ {}^{i}\ell_{\underset{\sim}{x}+n} = {}^{i}\ell_{\underset{\sim}{x}} - {}^{i}_{n}d_{\underset{\sim}{x}}, \quad i=m,f \tag{34}$$

B. Orientation equations:

$$ {}^{i}_{n}M_{\underset{\sim}{x}} = {}^{i}_{n}m_{\underset{\sim}{x}} = {}^{i}_{n}\hat{m}_{\underset{\sim}{x}}, \quad i=m,f \tag{35}$$

$$ {}^{m}\underset{\sim}{F}(x,y) + {}^{f}\underset{\sim}{F}(x,y) = {}^{m}\hat{\underset{\sim}{f}}(x,y) + {}^{f}\hat{\underset{\sim}{f}}(x,y) \tag{36} $$

C. Person-year equations:

$$ {}^{i}_{n}\underset{\sim}{L}_{x} = \int_{0}^{n} {}^{i}\underset{\sim}{\ell}_{x+t}\,dt = \exp[r(x+\tfrac{1}{2}n)]\,{}^{i}_{n}\hat{\underset{\sim}{L}}_{x}, \quad i=m,f \tag{37} $$

D. Renewal equations:

$$ \begin{aligned} \sum_{x}\sum_{y} \underset{\sim}{b}(x,y) &= \sum_{x}\sum_{y} \exp[-r(x+\tfrac{1}{2}n)]\,{}^{m}_{n}\underset{\sim}{L}^{*}_{x}\;{}^{m}\hat{\underset{\sim}{f}}(x,y) \\ &= \sum_{x}\sum_{y} \exp[-r(y+\tfrac{1}{2}n)]\,{}^{f}\hat{\underset{\sim}{f}}(x,y)\,{}^{f}_{n}\underset{\sim}{L}^{*}_{y} \end{aligned} \tag{38} $$

$$ {}^{m}\underset{\sim}{\ell}_{0} + {}^{f}\underset{\sim}{\ell}_{0} = \sum_{x}\sum_{y} \underset{\sim}{b}^{*}(x,y), \tag{39} $$

where

$$ {}^{i}\hat{\underset{\sim}{f}}(x,y) = \begin{bmatrix} {}^{i}\hat{f}(x,1;y,1) & {}^{i}\hat{f}(x,1;y,2) \\ {}^{i}\hat{f}(x,2;y,1) & {}^{i}\hat{f}(x,2;y,2) \end{bmatrix}, \quad i=m,f $$

$$ \underset{\sim}{b}(x,y) = \begin{bmatrix} b(x,1;y,1) & b(x,1;y,2) \\ b(x,2;y,1) & b(x,2;y,2) \end{bmatrix}, $$

$\underset{\sim}{b}^{*}(x,y)$ is the diagonal matrix that results when the elements of $\underset{\sim}{b}(x,y)$ are allocated to initial states in accordance with a specified allocation rule; ${}^{i}\underset{\sim}{F}(x,y), i = m$ or f, is a matrix of the same form as ${}^{i}\hat{\underset{\sim}{f}}(x,y)$ with observed instead of TWOFIDS fertility rates;

$$ {}^{m}\hat{f}(x,k;y,j) = b(x,k;y,j)/{}^{m;k}_{n}\hat{L}_{x} $$

and

$$ {}^{f}\hat{f}(x,k;y,j) = b(x,k;y,j)/{}^{f;j}_{n}\hat{L}_{y} $$

are, respectively, the TWOFIDS male and female age-state-of-father/age-state-of-mother specific fertility rates for males aged x to x+n in state k and females aged y to y+n in state j; b(x,k;y,j), the number of births in the model to males aged x to x+n in state k and females aged y to y+n in state j; and ${}^{i;k}_{n}L_x$, the number of persons of sex i in state k between the ages of x and x+n in the model population.

The next section of the paper discusses the calculation of the TWOFIDS model in more detail, and presents such a table based on the experience of the United States and California in 1970.

2.7. *MODEL VII: TWONUP*

The two-sex nuptiality-mortality life table (TWONUP) is probably the simplest of the two-sex models. While the number of marriages depends upon the whole age-sex composition of the model, the complications of growth are not present. In general, TWONUP is more appropriately viewed from a stationary population rather than a cohort perspective, however, as more than one male and one female cohort interact with one another (unless there is a constant age difference between brides and grooms).

In terms of our algorithm, we have

A. Flow equations:

$$ {}^{m}\ell_{x+n} = {}^{m}\ell_{x} - {}^{m}_{n}d^{\delta}_{x} - {}^{m}_{n}d^{p}_{x} - \sum_{j} c(x,j) \tag{40a} $$

$$ {}^{f}\ell_{x+n} = {}^{f}\ell_{x} - {}^{f}_{n}d^{\delta}_{x} - {}^{f}_{n}d^{p}_{x} - \sum_{i} c(i,x) \tag{40b} $$

B. Orientation equations:

$${}_n^iM_x^j = {}_n^im_x^j, \quad i=m,f;\ j=\delta,p \tag{41}$$

$${}^mW(x,y) + {}^fW(x,y) = {}^mw(x,y) + {}^fw(x,y) \tag{42}$$

$${}^mw(x,y) = c(x,y)/{}_n^mL_x, \quad {}^fw(x,y) = c(x,y)/{}_n^fL_y \tag{43}$$

C. Person-year equations:

$${}_n^iL_x = \int_0^n {}^i\ell_{x+t}\,dt, \quad i=m,f \tag{44}$$

where $c(x,y)$ represents the number of first marriages in the model between males aged x to x+n and females aged y to y+n; ${}^iw(x,y)$, i = m or f, is the male or female age-of-bride/age-of-groom specific first marriage rate in the model between males aged x to x+n and females aged y to y+n; ${}^iW(x,y)$, i = m or f, is the corresponding male or female observed population first marriage rate between males aged x to x+n and females aged y to y+n; and p, as a right superscript, indicates a decrement to marriage where the spouse is not marrying for the first time.

Since previously married persons are outside of the model, TWONUP captures the competitive nature of the "marriage market" only with respect to marriages where both bride and groom are marrying for the first time. For a further discussion of the TWONUP model and its application to Swedish data, see Schoen (1977b, 1981). A matrix algebra approach to calculating the number of first marriages by age-of-bride and age-of-groom is shown in the Appendix.

2.8. *MODEL XIII: MSQUEEZ*

The two-sex nuptiality-mortality stable population (MSQUEEZ) is a somewhat different sort of model because it is the only stable population model considered where the intrinsic growth rate r must be determined exogenously. The reason is that married persons cannot be included in the model since nuptiality involves unmarried persons, and a decrement-only model cannot follow persons from one marital status to another. Thus, the model can provide no information on the married population and the births attributable to them.

The fact that r must be obtained outside of the model does not mean the model cannot be useful. On the contrary, the ability to set r arbitrarily affords an opportunity to examine the effects of population growth on marriage. In short, it is a model to study the marriage squeeze, and hence its name.

To apply our algorithm,

A. Flow equations:

$$ {}^{m}\ell_{x+n} = {}^{m}\ell_{x} - {}^{m}_{n}d^{\delta}_{x} - {}^{m}_{n}d^{p}_{x} - \sum_{j} {}^{m}c(x,j) \tag{45a} $$

$$ {}^{f}\ell_{x+n} = {}^{f}\ell_{x} - {}^{f}_{n}d^{\delta}_{x} - {}^{f}_{n}d^{p}_{x} - \sum_{i} {}^{f}c(i,x) \tag{45b} $$

B. Orientation equations:

$$ {}^{i}_{n}M^{j}_{x} = {}^{i}_{n}m^{j}_{x} = {}^{i}_{n}\hat{m}^{j}_{x}, \quad i=m,f;\ j=\delta,p \tag{46} $$

$$ \begin{aligned} {}^{m}W(x,y) + {}^{f}W(x,y) &= {}^{m}\hat{w}(x,y) + {}^{f}\hat{w}(x,y) \\ &= {}^{m}w(x,y) + {}^{f}w(x,y) \end{aligned} \tag{47} $$

$$ {}^{m}\hat{w}(x,y) = \frac{\hat{c}(x,y)}{{}_{n}^{m}\hat{L}_{x}} = \frac{\exp[-r(x+\frac{1}{2}n)]\,{}^{m}c(x,y)}{\exp[-r(x+\frac{1}{2}n)]\,{}_{n}^{m}L_{x}} \qquad (48) $$

$$ {}^{f}\hat{w}(x,y) = \frac{\hat{c}(x,y)}{{}_{n}^{f}\hat{L}_{y}} = \frac{\exp[-r(y+\frac{1}{2}n)]\,{}^{f}c(x,y)}{\exp[-r(y+\frac{1}{2}n)]\,{}_{n}^{f}L_{y}} $$

C. Person-year equations:

$$ {}_{n}^{i}L_{x} = \int_{0}^{n} {}^{i}\ell_{x+t}\,dt = \exp[r(x+\tfrac{1}{2}n)]\,{}_{n}^{i}\hat{L}_{x}, \quad i=m,f \qquad (49) $$

where ${}^{i}c(x,y)$, i = m or f, represents the number of first marriages between males aged x to x+n and females aged y to y+n in a cohort of sex i.

Because of differences in cohort size in the stable population, ${}^{m}\hat{c}(x,y)$ equals ${}^{f}\hat{c}(x,y)$, but ${}^{m}c(x,y)$ is not generally equal to ${}^{f}c(x,y)$. A related consequence for two-sex nuptiality models, as opposed to two-sex fertility models, may be noted here. In two-sex *fertility* stable populations, the fertility rates determine r and the initial allocation of births to the states of the model. Given that allocation, however, the experience of each birth cohort is independent of r. In two-sex *nuptiality* stable populations, like MSQUEEZ, r does affect cohort experience because marriage typically involves members of different birth cohorts. It should also be noted that despite the strong assumption of constant rates underlying MSQUEEZ, the fact that the first marriage behavior of actual cohorts generally takes place over a very narrow span of ages suggests that the model is not nearly as unrealistic as it might appear to be at first.

Since the intrinsic growth rate r is known, MSQUEEZ can also be readily calculated using period, rather than cohort, flow equations. In that case we have

$$ {}^{m}\hat{\ell}_{x+n} = {}^{m}\hat{\ell}_{x} - {}^{m}_{n}\hat{d}^{\delta}_{x} - {}^{m}_{n}\hat{d}^{p}_{x} - \sum_{j} \hat{c}(x,j) - r\,{}^{m}_{n}\hat{L}_{x}, \tag{50a} $$

$$ {}^{f}\hat{\ell}_{x+n} = {}^{f}\hat{\ell}_{x} - {}^{f}_{n}\hat{d}^{\delta}_{x} - {}^{f}_{n}\hat{d}^{p}_{x} - \sum_{i} \hat{c}(i,x) - r\,{}^{f}_{n}\hat{L}_{x}. \tag{50b} $$

Because the population is growing at rate r, the number of persons at exact age x+n at time t would, with no decrements at all between ages x and x+n, be $\hat{\ell}_x e^{-rn}$. Thus an additional "decrement" of $r\hat{L}$ is needed in the period flow equation. The full derivation of the period flow equations is essentially the same as the Keyfitz (1968a) derivation of the basic calculation equation of an "iterative" life table.

2.9. *MODEL IX: TWOMSLT*

The two-sex marital status life table (TWOMSLT) reflects the competitive context of remarriages as well as first marriages, as it follows the married population and reflects the incidence of divorce and widowhood. Doing so presents problems that did not arise in TWOFIDS, however, because while two-sex fertility deals with an *event*, two-sex nuptiality involves a continuing *status*.

Divorce is essentially *not* a "two-sex" event, in that demographically the incidence of divorce can be related to a "one-sex population," the population of married persons. Each couple in that population, under our Markovian assumptions which distinguish only age, sex, and state, is identified by the ages of the husband and wife. The appropriate observed divorce rate for couples where the male is aged x to x+n and the female is aged y to y+n is thus found by dividing the number of divorces among such couples by the number of such couples in the population. It would not be correct to apply the observed divorce rates for all males aged x to x+n or all females aged y to y+n to the population of the model. That procedure does not ensure that the model reflects an equal number of divorces to males and females, a logical necessity.

In the case of widowhoods, it is necessary for the model to reflect one male widowhood for each married female death, and one female widowhood for each married male death. It does not seem necessary, however, to assume that the death rate for married persons depends upon the age of their spouse (Hoem, 1970, p. 12). Hence, the number of widowhoods among a model population of males aged x to x+n married to females aged y to y+n can be found by multiplying the number of (x,y) couples by the observed married death rate for females aged y to y+n. The female widowhoods can be found in a similar manner.

From the above considerations, it is evident that we need to determine the number of person-years lived in the married state (L values) for every existing (x,y) combination of male and female ages. To do so, cohort flow equations that reflect the experiences of (x,y) couples and provide survivorship (ℓ) values for them, will be needed. Previously, flow equations began with persons at exact age x and ended with persons at exact age x+n. Here, however, flow equations for (x,y) couples cannot begin with both the male exact age x and the female exact age y, as husband and wife generally do not share the same birthday.

A logical approach to finding flow equations for couples is to have male flow equations begin with males at exact age x married to females aged y to y+n, and female flow equations begin with females at exact age y married to males aged x to x+n. That approach will be followed, but it still leaves certain potential inconsistencies between period and cohort exposures to risk. The number of person-years lived during an n-year interval by the (x,y) couples, as seen from the male cohort perspective, is

$$A_{xy} = \int_0^n \int_0^n {}^g\ell_{x+t,y+s+t} \, ds\, dt,$$

and from the female cohort perspective is

$$B_{xy} = \int_0^n \int_0^n {}^g\ell_{x+s+t,y+t} \, ds\, dt,$$

with ${}^g\ell_{x+t,y+s}$ representing the number of married (state g) persons where the male is exact age x+t and the female is exact age y+s. However, the number of person-years lived in an n-year *period* by all couples where the husband is aged x to x+n and the wife is aged y to y+n is

$${}^g_nL(x,y) = \int_0^n \int_0^n {}^g\ell_{x+t,y+s} \, ds\, dt.$$

The value of ${}^g_nL(x,y)$ differs from A_{xy} because it includes the person-years lived by couples where the male attained exact age x during the n-year period and excludes the person-years lived by couples when the female's age was over y+n, and ${}^g_nL(x,y)$ differs from B_{xy} because it includes the person-years lived by couples where the female attained exact age x during the n-year period and excludes the person-years lived by couples when the male's age was over x+n. With single integrals and in the one-sex case, such inconsistencies do not arise because both period and cohort exposures span the same exact ages.

To reconcile the period and cohort exposures to risk in the married state, we need to express A and B in terms of L. Assuming linearity in the ℓ function,

$$A_{xy} = {}^{g}\ell_{x+\frac{1}{2}n,\,y+n},$$

$$B_{xy} = {}^{g}\ell_{x+n,\,y+\frac{1}{2}n}, \quad \text{and} \quad {}_{n}^{g}L(x,y) = {}^{g}\ell_{x+\frac{1}{2}n,\,y+\frac{1}{2}n},$$

which leads to

$$A_{xy} = \tfrac{1}{2}\,{}_{n}^{g}L(x,y) + \tfrac{1}{2}\,{}_{n}^{g}L(x,y+n),$$
$$B_{xy} = \tfrac{1}{2}\,{}_{n}^{g}L(x,y) + \tfrac{1}{2}\,{}_{n}^{g}L(x+n,y). \qquad (51)$$

If the data reflect an h-year period rather than the assumed n-year period, Eqs. (51) become

$$A_{xy} = \frac{2n - h}{2n}\,{}_{n}^{g}L(x,y) + \frac{h}{2n}\,{}_{n}^{g}L(x,y+n),$$
$$B_{xy} = \frac{2n - h}{2n}\,{}_{n}^{g}L(x,y) + \frac{h}{2n}\,{}_{n}^{g}L(x+n,y). \qquad (52)$$

The simplifying assumptions of Eqs. (52) will be used in the cohort flow equations for a two-table (three-state) TWOMSLT model recognizing the statuses unmarried (u) and married (g).

To apply our algorithm to TWOMSLT in the light of the previous discussion, we have

A. Flow equations:

$$ {}^{m;u}\ell_{x+n} = {}^{m;u}\ell_x - {}^{m;u}{}_n d_x^{\delta} - \sum_j {}^{m}c(x,j) $$

$$ + \sum_j {}^{m;g}{}_n d^{w}(x,j) + \sum_j {}^{m;g}{}_n d^{v}(x,j) \qquad (53) $$

$$ {}^{f;u}\ell_{x+n} = {}^{f;u}\ell_x - {}^{f;u}{}_n d_x^{\delta} - \sum_i {}^{f}c(i,x) $$

$$ + \sum_i {}^{f;g}{}_n d^{w}(i,x) + \sum_i {}^{f;g}{}_n d^{v}(i,x) \qquad (54) $$

$$ {}^{m;g}\ell(x+n,y+n) = {}^{m;g}\ell(x,y) + \left(\frac{2n-h}{2n}\right){}^{m}c(x,y) $$

$$ + \left(\frac{h}{2n}\right){}^{m}c(x,y+n) - \left(\frac{2n-h}{2n}\right){}^{m;g}{}_n d^{\delta}(x,y) $$

$$ - \left(\frac{h}{2n}\right){}^{m;g}{}_n d^{\delta}(x,y+n) - \left(\frac{2n-h}{2n}\right){}^{m;g}{}_n d^{w}(x,y) $$

$$ - \left(\frac{h}{2n}\right){}^{m;g}{}_n d^{w}(x,y+n) - \left(\frac{2n-h}{2n}\right){}^{m;g}{}_n d^{v}(x,y) $$

$$ - \left(\frac{h}{2n}\right){}^{m;g}{}_n d^{v}(x,y+n) \qquad (55a) $$

$$ {}^{m;g}\ell_{x+n} = {}^{m;g}\ell_x + \sum_j {}^{m}c(x,j) - \sum_j {}^{m;g}{}_n d^{\delta}(x,j) $$

$$ - \sum_j {}^{m;g}{}_n d^{w}(x,j) - \sum_j {}^{m;g}{}_n d^{v}(x,j) \qquad (55b) $$

$$
\begin{aligned}
{}^{f;g}\ell(x+n,y+n) = {}^{f;g}\ell(x,y) &+ \left(\frac{2n-h}{2n}\right){}^{f}c(x,y) + \left(\frac{h}{2n}\right){}^{f}c(x+n,y) \\
&- \left(\frac{2n-h}{2n}\right){}^{f;g}_{n}d^{\delta}(x,y) - \left(\frac{h}{2n}\right){}^{f;g}_{n}d^{\delta}(x+n,y) \\
&- \left(\frac{2n-h}{2n}\right){}^{f;g}_{n}d^{w}(x,y) - \left(\frac{h}{2n}\right){}^{f;g}_{n}d^{w}(x+n,y) \\
&- \left(\frac{2n-h}{2n}\right){}^{f;g}_{n}d^{v}(x,y) - \left(\frac{h}{2n}\right){}^{f;g}_{n}d^{v}(x+n,y)
\end{aligned}
\tag{56a}
$$

$$
\begin{aligned}
{}^{f;g}\ell_{x+n} = {}^{f;g}\ell_{x} &+ \sum_i {}^{f}c(i,x) - \sum_i {}^{f;g}_{n}d^{\delta}(i,x) \\
&- \sum_i {}^{f;g}_{n}d^{w}(i,x) - \sum_i {}^{f;g}_{n}d^{v}(i,x)
\end{aligned}
\tag{56b}
$$

B. Orientation equations:

$$ {}^{i;j}_{n}M^{\delta}_{x} = {}^{i;j}_{n}m^{\delta}_{x}, \quad i=m,f;\ j=u,g \tag{57} $$

$$ {}^{m}W(x,y) + {}^{f}W(x,y) = {}^{m}w(x,y) + {}^{f}w(x,y) \tag{58} $$

$$ {}^{m,g}_{n}M^{\delta}_{x} = \frac{{}^{f;g}_{n}d^{w}(x,y)}{{}^{g}_{n}L(x,y)} = {}^{f;g}_{n}m^{w}(x,y) $$

$$ {}^{f;g}_{n}M^{\delta}_{y} = \frac{{}^{m;g}_{n}d^{w}(x,y)}{{}^{g}_{n}L(x,y)} = {}^{m;g}_{n}m^{w}(x,y) \tag{59} $$

$$ {}^{i;g}_{n}M^{v}(x,y) = \frac{{}^{i;g}_{n}d^{v}(x,y)}{{}^{g}_{n}L(x,y)} = {}^{i;g}_{n}m^{v}(x,y), \quad i=m,f \tag{60} $$

C. Person-year equations:

$$ {}^{i;j}_{n}L_x = \int_0^n {}^{i;j}\ell_{x+t}\,dt, \quad i=m,f;\ j=u,g \tag{61} $$

$$ {}^{g}_{n}L(x,y) = \int_0^n {}^{g}\ell_{x+t,y+t}\,dt \tag{62} $$

where u,g, as left superscripts, refer to the unmarried and married states, respectively; m;j, f;j, j = u,g, as left superscripts, refer, respectively, to males and females in marital status j; δ,w,v, as right superscripts, refer to transitions due to death, widowhood, and divorce, respectively; h is the period over which the data are collected (typically 1 year), as distinct from n, the age interval over which the data are aggregated; ${}^{m;g}\ell(x,y)$, represents the number of married couples where the male is exact age x and the female is aged y to y+n; ${}^{f;g}\ell(x,y)$, the number of married couples where the female is exact age y and the male is aged x to x+n; ${}^{m;g}_{n}d^{k}(x,y)$, the number of transfers in the model from cause k among males aged x to x+n married to females aged y to y+n, and ${}^{f;g}d^{k}(x,y)$ is the corresponding expression for females; ${}^{i;g}_{n}M^{v}(x,y)$, i = m or f, is the observed population divorce rate for males aged x to x+n married to females aged y to y+n, and ${}^{i;g}_{n}m^{v}(x,y)$ is the corresponding rate in the model population; and ${}^{g}_{n}L(x,y)$ is the number of person-years lived in the married state by couples where the male is aged x to x+n and the female is aged y to y+n.

Equation (62) expresses ${}^{g}_{n}L(x,y)$ as a single integral, consistent with Eq. (61) and the linearity assumption previously introduced, so that the sum of the ${}^{g}_{n}L(x,y)$ over all female ages will be consistent with ${}^{m;g}_{n}L_x$ and the sum over all male ages will be consistent with ${}^{f;g}_{n}L_y$.

When TWOMSLT is extended to more than two marital statuses, for example, by introducing the statuses widowed and divorced, the complexities multiply. Two-sex nuptiality consistency conditions are required for each type of marriage, i.e., for each combination of previous marital statuses of the bride and groom. The model presented is already cumbersome because the need to partition the married population by the ages of both spouses means that it cannot be conveniently written in matrix form.

The TWOMSLT model specified above has also been simplified in the sense that it does not explicitly provide the number of persons of sex i in marital status j at age x+n by marital status at age x, and hence does not provide an explicit solution for the Markov transition probabilities. Those seeking a solution for the transition probabilities are advised to follow the procedures used in the earlier sections and discussed in Schoen and Land (1979).

2.10. MODEL X: TWOMSSP

While the two-sex marital status stable population (TWOMSSP) is the most complex of the ten life table models presented here, a one-age group version of the model was explored years ago by Kendall (1949). As in the case of TWOMSLT, we shall consider the two-stable (three-state) model, which recognizes the marital statuses of unmarried (u) and married (g).

The TWOMSSP model reflects the implications of an observed population's male and female rates of birth, death, marriage, and divorce. Because marital status is part of the model and the interaction between the sexes is explicitly recognized in the formation of married couples, "one-sex" fertility rates can be used. In other words, fertility rates need only be specific to each age-of-husband/age-of-wife pair, and age-specific for unmarried persons (of either sex). While it may be possible to do so, there does not seem to be any compelling reason (or obvious way) to relate out-of-wedlock births to reciprocal fertility preferences and the age-sex-marital status composition of the population.

To apply our algorithm along the lines followed in the TWOMSLT case, we have

A. Flow equations: Same as for TWOMSLT, Eqs. (53) - (56).

B. Orientation equations:

$$ {}^{i;j}_{\ n}M^{\delta}_{x} = {}^{i;j}_{\ n}m^{\delta}_{x} = {}^{i;j}_{\ n}\hat{m}^{\delta}_{x}, \quad i=m,f;\ j=u,g \tag{63} $$

$$ \begin{aligned} {}^{m}W(x,y) + {}^{f}W(x,y) &= {}^{m}\hat{w}(x,y) + {}^{f}\hat{w}(x,y) \\ &= \frac{\exp[-r(x+\frac{1}{2}n)]\,{}^{m}c(x,y)}{\exp[-r(x+\frac{1}{2}n)]\,{}^{m}_{n}L_{x}} + \frac{\exp[-r(y+\frac{1}{2}n)]\,{}^{f}c(x,y)}{\exp[-r(y+\frac{1}{2}n)]\,{}^{f}_{n}L_{y}} \\ &= {}^{m}w(x,y) + {}^{f}w(x,y) \end{aligned} \tag{64} $$

$$ {}^{m;g}_{\ n}M^{\delta}_{x} = {}^{f;g}_{\ n}{}_{m}w(x,y) = {}^{f;g}_{\ n}{}_{\hat{m}}w(x,y) $$

$$ {}^{f;g}_{\ n}M^{\delta}_{y} = {}^{m;g}_{\ n}{}_{m}w(x,y) = {}^{m;g}_{\ n}{}_{\hat{m}}w(x,y) \tag{65} $$

$$ {}^{i;g}_{\ n}{}_{M}v(x,y) = {}^{i;g}_{\ n}{}_{m}v(x,y) = {}^{i;g}_{\ n}{}_{\hat{m}}v(x,y), \quad i=m,f \tag{66} $$

$$ {}^{g}_{n}F(x,y) = {}^{g}_{n}\hat{f}(x,y) = {}^{g}b(x,y)/{}^{g}_{n}\hat{L}(x,y) \tag{67} $$

$$ {}^{i;u}_{n}F_{x} = {}^{i;u}_{n}\hat{f}_{x} = {}^{i;u}_{n}b_{x}/{}^{i;u}_{n}\hat{L}_{x}, \quad i=m \textit{ or } f \tag{68} $$

C. Person-year equations:

$$ {}^{i;j}_{n}L_{x} = \int_{0}^{n} {}^{i;j}\ell_{x+t}dt = \exp[r(x+\tfrac{1}{2}n)]\,{}^{i;j}_{n}\hat{L}_{x}, \quad i=m,f;\ j=u,g \tag{69} $$

$$ {}^{m;g}_{n}L(x,y) = \int_{0}^{n} {}^{m;g}\ell_{x+t,y+t}dt = \exp[r(x+\tfrac{1}{2}n)]\,{}^{g}_{n}\hat{L}(x,y) $$

$$ {}^{f;g}_{n}L(x,y) = \int_{0}^{n} {}^{f;g}\ell_{x+t,y+t}dt = \exp[r(y+\tfrac{1}{2}n)]\,{}^{g}_{n}\hat{L}(x,y) \tag{70} $$

D. Renewal equation:

$$ {}^{m}\ell_{0} + {}^{f}\ell_{0} = \sum_{x} {}^{i;u}_{n}b_{x} + \sum_{xy}\sum {}^{g}b(x,y) $$

$$ = \sum_{x} \exp[-r(x+\tfrac{1}{2}n)]\,{}^{i;u}_{n}L_{x}\,{}^{i;u}_{n}\hat{f}_{x} + \sum_{xy}\sum {}^{g}_{n}\hat{L}(x,y)\,{}^{g}_{n}\hat{f}(x,y) \tag{71} $$

where ${}^{g}_{n}\hat{L}(x,y)$ represents the number of person-years lived in the TWOMSSP stable population by married couples where the male was aged x to x+n and the female was aged y to y+n; and ${}^{i;g}_{n}L(x,y)$, i = m or f, represents the number of person-years lived in a cohort by married persons of sex i where the male was aged x to x+n and the female was aged y to y+n.

All births are allocated to the male and female unmarried states in proportion to the established sex ratio at birth.

3. A TWOFIDS MODEL FOR THE UNITED STATES/CALIFORNIA 1970

To go beyond the mathematical specifications of the previous section, describe the calculations involved in constructing one of the more complicated two-sex life table models, and consider some of the numerical results, a TWOFIDS model for the United States 1970 was prepared. Two regions, the state of California and the rest of the U.S., were recognized. (The Appendix provides a discussion of the data inputs.) The TWOFIDS model was selected as an example because it can be applied to a wide range of behaviors, rather than to marital status changes alone, and because no fully articulated TWOFIDS model has appeared in the literature. The calculations in TWOFIDS are complex enough to indicate the practical problems involved in model construction, although they avoid the difficulties of doubly-indexed survivorship (ℓ) functions.

A FORTRAN program was written to make the needed data adjustments, calculate the TWOFIDS tables, and perform several ancillary computations. Iterative procedures were substituted for the direct algebraic manipulation of matrices. The computations were performed in the following sequence:

(i) IDLTs were calculated for the four sex-region groups, U.S. males and females and California males and females;

(ii) the two-sex fertility consistency condition was applied to the four IDLTs to calculate the arrays of births, $\underset{\sim}{b}(x,y)$, with each $b(x,y)$ being found using Eq. (31) and both parents assumed living in the region of birth;

(iii) an improved value of the intrinsic growth rate (r^*) was found using the iterative equation

$$r^* = \frac{1}{27.5} \ln\left[\frac{\exp[27.5r \sum_{xy}\sum b(x,y)]}{{}^{m}\ell_0 + {}^{f}\ell_0}\right], \tag{72}$$

with r = 0 used for the first iteration;

(iv) maintaining the total number of births $({}^{m}\ell_0 + {}^{f}\ell_0)$ at 205,000 and the sex ratio at birth of 105 males per 100 females, the radix values were updated, beginning with the ℓ_0 value for U.S. males, which was taken as (105,000)·(U.S. births/total births); and

(v) using the new radix values, the cycle was repeated, beginning with step (i), until convergence on r to within 0.000000001 and on the U.S. male ℓ_0 to within 0.0001 was achieved.

The IDLTs themselves can be calculated in a number of ways, depending on the choice of numerical integration procedure to determine the person-year (L) values. The cubic method assumes that ${}^{ij}\ell$ is a third-degree polynomial and has generally been found to produce very accurate L values. It can be unstable in the presence of large transfer rates, however, and leads to biased values for the transition probabilities (Schoen, 1979, p. 264). The linear method (Schoen, 1975; Rogers and Ledent, 1976) and the exponential method (Krishnamoorthy, 1979) are available, but restrict the underlying transition forces to be, respectively, increasing or constant within each age interval. The method of calculating an IDLT by estimating the mean durations at transfer $({}^{i}_{n}a^{j}_{x})$ from the observed rates (Schoen, 1979; Land and Schoen, 1982) was chosen as it allows the pattern of the rates to determine the nature of the underlying transition forces within each age interval and provides an unbiased matrix solution for the Markov transition probabilities. The mean duration at transfer method can be implemented directly using the matrix equation

$$\underset{\sim}{\ell}_{x+n} = (\underset{\sim}{I} + n\,{}_n\underset{\sim}{M}_x + {}_n\underset{\sim}{M}_x\,{}_n\underset{\sim}{H}_x)^{-1}(\underset{\sim}{I} - {}_n\underset{\sim}{M}_x\,{}_n\underset{\sim}{G}_x)\underset{\sim}{\ell}_x, \tag{73}$$

where $\underset{\sim}{I}$ is the identity matrix of order equal to the number of living states, and ${}_n\underset{\sim}{G}_x$, ${}_n\underset{\sim}{H}_x$ are matrices of the form of ${}_n\underset{\sim}{M}_x$ [as defined in Eq. (18)] with

$${}^i_n g^j_x = \frac{n^2}{240}\left[{}^i_n M^j_{x+n} + 38\,{}^i_n M^j_x + {}^i_n M^j_{x-n}\right]$$

and

$${}^i_n h^j_x = \frac{n^2}{240}\left[14\,{}^i_n M^j_{x+n} + 72\,{}^i_n M^j_x - 6\,{}^i_n M^j_{x-n}\right].$$

In the present case, the IDLT was calculated iteratively using the relationships

$${}^i_n L_x = n\,{}^i\ell_{x+n} + \sum_{j \neq i} {}^{ij}_n a_x \cdot {}^{ij}_n d_x - \sum_{j \neq i} {}^{ji}_n a_x \cdot {}^{ji}_n d_x \tag{74}$$

and

$${}^i_n a^j_x = \frac{{}^i\ell_x \cdot {}^i_n f^j_x + {}^i\ell_{x+n} \cdot {}^i_n g^j_x}{{}^i_n d^j_x}, \tag{75}$$

with initial ℓ values calculated using the linear method [Schoen, 1975, Eq. (9)].

For the youngest and oldest ages, modified procedures were used. For age 0, the Keyfitz (1970) empirical regression equation

$${}^i a^\delta_0 = 0.07 + 1.7\,{}^i M^\delta_0 \tag{76}$$

was used for mortality, and ${}^{i}a_0^s = 0.5$ for the mean duration at migration. For age group 1 - 4, both mean durations at transfer were taken to be 1.5. The values of ${}^{i}\ell_{85}$ and ${}^{i}_{5}L_{80}$ were calculated using ${}^{i}g^{j}$ and ${}^{i}h^{j}$ values modified to reflect the open-ended nature of the 85 and over-age interval (Schoen, 1979, p. 260). For the 85 and over person-year values, the relationship

$$ {}_{\infty}\underset{\sim}{L}_{85} = {}_{\infty}\underset{\sim}{M}_{85}^{-1}\underset{\sim}{\ell}_{85}, \tag{77} $$

or rather its scalar counterparts (Schoen, 1975, p. 323), provided the person-year values.

The computations were carried out on a CDC CYBER 175. Approximately 2 seconds were required to compile the program and 5 seconds to execute it, at a cost of about \$2. The IDLT required 33 iterations for ${}^{i}\ell_{80}$ to converge to within 0.0001 on successive cycles, and the entire TWOFIDS model needed 29 iterations for convergence.

The TWOFIDS model for the U.S./California 1970 is shown in Table 3 for U.S. (excluding California) males, U.S. (excluding California) females, California males, and California females. Each of the four panels of Table 3 is divided into two tiers, one giving stable (period) population values and the other cohort values. The mean durations at outmigration (a^s) and death (a^δ) are shown because of their important role in the calculation procedures.

Table 4 presents some summary measures from the TWOFIDS model and compares them with male and female one-sex IDSP and IDLT models calculated using the same input data. The TWOFIDS intrinsic growth rate is 0.00797, which is between the male and

TABLE 3. *Two-Sex Fertility Multiregional Stable Population, U.S./California 1970*

Panel a. United States (excluding California) Males

Age	Survivors to exact age x	Outmigrations among persons aged x to x+n	Deaths among persons aged x to x+n	Births to persons aged x to x+n	Fertility rate for persons x to x+n	Population aged x to x+n	Populated aged x and over
	Stable Population (Period) Values						
(x)	$(\hat{\ell}_x)$	$({}_n\hat{d}^s_x)$	$({}_n\hat{d}^\delta_x)$	$({}_nb_x)$	$({}_n\hat{f}_x)$	$({}_n\hat{L}_x)$	$(\hat{T}_x)$
0	92299	205	2074	0		90091	4665727
1	89514	806	328	0		351779	4575637
5	86463	795	211	0		423418	4223858
10	82945	571	208	0		406382	3800440
15	79553	1012	613	9870	0.02542	388214	3394058
20	75627	2200	827	51005	0.13927	366244	3005844
25	70981	2049	700	56736	0.16439	345125	2639600
30	67173	1509	754	34155	0.10433	327371	2294475
35	63796	972	976	17130	0.05517	310472	1967104
40	60366	568	1420	7398	0.02528	292699	1656633
45	56651	473	2066	2582	0.00946	272938	1363934
50	52431	316	2952	812	0.00324	250203	1090996
55	47517	305	4148	515	0.00231	223220	840793
60	41638	206	5336	0		191431	617572
65	34821	250	6387	0		155049	426141
70	27188	160	6858	0		116314	271092
75	19411	93	6769	0		77979	154778
80	12028	45	5513	0		44486	76799
85	6161	15	6047	0		32313	32313

Table 3. Panel a (Cont'd)

Cohort Values									
Age (x)	Survivors to exact age x (ℓ_x)	Outmigrations among persons aged x to x+n $({}_nd_x^s)$	Deaths among persons aged x to x+n $({}_nd_x^\delta)$	Rate of outmigration among persons aged x to x+n $({}_nm_x^s)$	Mortality rate among persons aged x to x+n $({}_nm_x^\delta)$	Mean duration at outmigration for persons aged x to x+n $({}_na_x^s)$	Mean duration at death for persons aged x to x+n $({}_na_n^\delta)$	Population aged x to x+n $({}_nL_x)$	Population aged x and over (T_x)
0	92299	206	2082	0.00228	0.02302	0.5000	0.1091	90451	6131407
1	90230	826	336	0.00229	0.00093	1.5000	1.5000	360289	6040956
5	89978	844	224	0.00188	0.00050	2.3977	2.4179	449493	5680667
10	89824	631	230	0.00141	0.00051	2.7299	3.1493	448943	5231174
15	89653	1164	705	0.00261	0.00158	2.9458	2.6962	446303	4782232
20	88693	2632	989	0.00601	0.00226	2.5454	2.4904	438159	4335928
25	86627	2552	871	0.00594	0.00203	2.4239	2.5249	429675	3897769
30	85311	1955	976	0.00461	0.00230	2.3653	2.6206	424137	3468094
35	84317	1311	1316	0.00313	0.00314	2.3258	2.6883	418592	3043957
40	83026	798	1992	0.00194	0.00485	2.3917	2.6969	410670	2625366
45	81083	691	3016	0.00173	0.00757	2.3855	2.6887	398508	2214696
50	78093	481	4486	0.00126	0.01180	2.4580	2.6808	380162	1816187
55	73651	482	6558	0.00137	0.01858	2.3993	2.6403	352949	1436025
60	67161	340	8780	0.00108	0.02788	2.5556	2.6059	314988	1083076
65	58449	429	10937	0.00162	0.04120	2.3961	2.5591	265493	768088
70	47492	286	12220	0.00138	0.05896	2.3235	2.5268	207262	502595
75	35284	173	12552	0.00120	0.08680	2.2771	2.4604	144599	295333
80	22753	87	10639	0.00101	0.12393	2.2273	2.3745	85846	150735
85	12128	29	12144	0.00045	0.18715			64889	64889

Table 3. Panel b. United States (Excluding California) Females

Stable Population (Period) Values							
Age (x)	Survivors to exact age x $(\hat{\ell}_x)$	Outmigrations among persons aged x to x+n $({}_n\hat{d}^s_x)$	Deaths among persons aged x to x+n $({}_n\hat{d}^\delta_x)$	Births to persons aged x to x+n $({}_nb_x)$	Fertility rate for persons x to x+n $({}_n\hat{f}_x)$	Population aged x to x+n $({}_n\hat{L}_x)$	Population aged x and over $(\hat{T}_x)$
0	87904	179	1544	0		86172	4846418
1	85681	701	254	0		336866	4760247
5	82820	710	138	0		405732	4423380
10	79513	512	115	480	0.00123	389677	4017648
15	76346	884	231	27309	0.07313	373420	3627970
20	72973	1778	268	64883	0.18262	355294	3254550
25	69213	1722	296	51420	0.15227	337683	2899256
30	65936	1292	380	23833	0.07394	322305	2561573
35	63001	800	565	9700	0.03154	307570	2239269
40	60019	468	805	2433	0.00832	292379	1931699
45	56907	372	1168	145	0.00052	276218	1639320
50	53547	253	1604	0		258744	1363102
55	49903	293	2173	0		239566	1104358
60	45857	202	2874	0		218158	864792
65	41281	215	3943	0		193004	646634
70	35766	138	5284	0		162817	453630
75	29176	122	6810	0		126540	290813
80	21361	58	7521	0		85707	164273
85	13162	19	12915	0		78567	78567

Table 3. Panel b (Cont'd)

	Cohort Values								
Age (x)	Survivors to exact age x (ℓ_x)	Outmigrations among persons aged x to x+n ($_nd_x^S$)	Deaths among persons aged x to x+n ($_nd_x^\delta$)	Rate of outmigration among persons aged x to x+n ($_nm_x^S$)	Mortality rate among persons aged x to x+n ($_nm_x^\delta$)	Mean duration at outmigration for persons aged x to x+n ($_na_x^S$)	Mean duration at death for persons aged x to x+n ($_na_x^\delta$)	Population aged x to x+n ($_nL_x$)	Population aged x and over (T_x)
0	87904	179	1551	0.00207	0.01792	0.5000	0.1005	86515	6522591
1	86367	718	260	0.00208	0.00076	1.5000	1.5000	345016	6436076
5	86168	754	147	0.00175	0.00034	2.4023	2.3312	430718	6091060
10	86108	566	127	0.00131	0.00030	2.7145	2.8247	430488	5660341
15	86039	1016	265	0.00237	0.00062	2.8894	2.6191	429296	5229853
20	85580	2127	320	0.00500	0.00075	2.5554	2.5638	425059	4800557
25	84469	2144	368	0.00510	0.00088	2.4324	2.6196	420410	4375498
30	83741	1674	493	0.00401	0.00118	2.3595	2.6973	417573	3955089
35	83266	1078	761	0.00260	0.00184	2.3200	2.6878	414679	3537515
40	82548	657	1129	0.00160	0.00275	2.3796	2.6940	410221	3122836
45	81450	544	1706	0.00135	0.00423	2.3853	2.6696	403298	2712615
50	79755	384	2438	0.00098	0.00620	2.5233	2.6598	393139	2309317
55	77348	463	3436	0.00122	0.00907	2.4236	2.6483	378795	1916178
60	73967	332	4728	0.00092	0.01317	2.4974	2.6650	358965	1537383
65	69292	368	6751	0.00111	0.02043	2.3937	2.6583	330483	1178418
70	62475	245	9415	0.00085	0.03245	2.4309	2.6448	290125	847935
75	53034	226	12628	0.00096	0.05382	2.3070	2.5833	234648	557809
80	40407	113	14513	0.00068	0.08775	2.1898	2.4725	165389	323162
85	25909	38	25935	0.00024	0.16438			157773	157773

Table 3. Panel c. California Males

	Stable Population (Period) Values						
Age (x)	Survivors to exact age x ($\hat{\ell}_x$)	Outmigrations among persons aged x to x+n (${}_n\hat{d}^s_x$)	Deaths among persons aged x to x+n (${}_n\hat{d}^\delta_x$)	Births to persons aged x to x+n (${}_nb_x$)	Fertility rate for persons x to x+n (${}_n\hat{f}_x$)	Population aged x to x+n (${}_n\hat{L}_x$)	Population aged x and over ($\hat{T}_x$)
0	12701	218	255	0		12416	701941
1	12333	889	44	0		48238	689525
5	11822	861	27	0		57703	641287
10	11269	625	25	0		54966	583584
15	10752	790	81	1315	0.02491	52811	528618
20	10471	1300	122	6668	0.12493	53376	475806
25	10824	1693	104	7834	0.14551	53841	422430
30	10649	1495	106	4869	0.09361	52017	368590
35	10143	991	137	2476	0.05016	49360	316573
40	9595	604	194	1072	0.02306	46490	267213
45	8995	491	289	366	0.00844	43380	220723
50	8343	345	420	118	0.00297	39858	177344
55	7578	348	600	78	0.00218	35621	137486
60	6651	248	777	0		30629	101865
65	5589	239	961	0		25088	71236
70	4440	167	1044	0		19186	46148
75	3237	105	1078	0		13109	26962
80	2043	52	900	0		7636	13853
85	1074	22	1045	0		6217	6217

Table 3. Panel c (Cont'd)

Age (x)	Survivors to exact age x (ℓ_x)	Outmigrations among persons aged x to x+n $({}_nd_x^s)$	Deaths among persons aged x to x+n $({}_nd_x^\delta)$	Rate of outmigration among persons aged x to x+n $({}_nm_x^s)$	Mortality rate among persons aged x to x+n $({}_nm_x^\delta)$	Mean duration at outmigration for persons aged x to x+n $({}_na_x^s)$	Mean duration at death for persons aged x to x+n $({}_na_x^\delta)$	Population aged x to x+n $({}_nL_x)$	Population aged x and over (T_x)
	Cohort Values								
0	12701	219	256	0.01758	0.02055	0.5000	0.1049	12465	933913
1	12432	910	45	0.01842	0.00091	1.5000	1.5000	49405	921447
5	12303	914	29	0.01493	0.00047	2.3985	2.3875	61257	872042
10	12204	690	27	0.01137	0.00045	2.5661	3.2447	60723	810785
15	12117	908	93	0.01495	0.00154	2.7409	2.7450	60713	750063
20	12279	1555	146	0.02436	0.00228	2.6609	2.5116	63857	689349
25	13210	2107	130	0.03144	0.00193	2.4993	2.5015	67031	625493
30	13525	1936	138	0.02873	0.00205	2.3904	2.6097	67392	558462
35	13405	1336	184	0.02007	0.00277	2.3380	2.6765	66549	491070
40	13197	848	273	0.01299	0.00418	2.3922	2.7053	65227	424521
45	12874	717	422	0.01132	0.00666	2.3943	2.6984	63337	359293
50	12426	524	638	0.00865	0.01053	2.4802	2.6903	60560	295956
55	11745	551	949	0.00978	0.01684	2.4156	2.6443	56324	235396
60	10728	408	1278	0.00809	0.02537	2.4701	2.6198	50398	179072
65	9382	408	1646	0.00951	0.03832	2.4043	2.5653	42959	128675
70	7756	298	1861	0.00872	0.05442	2.3486	2.5444	34188	85716
75	5884	194	1998	0.00798	0.08220	2.2893	2.4698	24308	51528
80	3865	101	1736	0.00682	0.11780	2.2396	2.3707	14736	27220
85	2115	45	2100	0.00358	0.16817			12484	12484

Table 3. Panel d. California Females

	Stable Population (Period) Values						
Age (x)	Survivors to exact age x ($\hat{\ell}_x$)	Outmigrations among persons aged x to x+n ($_n\hat{d}^s_x$)	Deaths among persons aged x to x+n ($_n\hat{d}^\delta_x$)	Births to persons aged x to x+n ($_nb_x$)	Fertility rate for persons x to x+n ($_n\hat{f}_x$)	Population aged x to x+n ($_n\hat{L}_x$)	Population aged x and over ($\hat{T}_x$)
0	12096	192	189	0		11871	711478
1	11799	780	32	0		46173	699607
5	11320	775	15	0		55276	653434
10	10800	564	15	43	0.00081	52699	598157
15	10312	715	35	3601	0.07105	50689	545458
20	10040	1117	41	8644	0.17007	50828	494769
25	10254	1434	46	7278	0.14270	51000	443942
30	10092	1305	58	3515	0.07126	49327	392941
35	9628	832	81	1373	0.02927	46921	343614
40	9141	490	117	325	0.00731	44475	296693
45	8648	380	175	18	0.00042	41963	252218
50	8131	273	239	0		39254	210255
55	7560	327	326	0		36196	171001
60	6911	234	410	0		32804	134806
65	6207	177	548	0		29232	102002
70	5464	123	725	0		25138	72770
75	4555	122	989	0		19954	47632
80	3406	66	1137	0		13808	27677
85	2152	32	2096	0		13869	13869

Table 3. Panel d (Cont'd)

Cohort Values									
Age (x)	Survivors to exact age x (ℓ_x)	Outmigrations among persons aged x to x+n ($_nd_x^s$)	Deaths among persons aged x to x+n ($_nd_x^\delta$)	Rate of outmigration among persons aged x to x+n ($_nm_x^s$)	Mortality rate among persons aged x to x+n ($_nm_x^\delta$)	Mean duration at outmigration for persons aged x to x+n ($_na_x^s$)	Mean duration at death for persons aged x to x+n ($_na_x^\delta$)	Population aged x to x+n ($_nL_x$)	Population aged x and over (T_x)
0	12096	193	190	0.01618	0.01591	0.5000	0.0970	11918	966720
1	11893	798	33	0.01688	0.00069	1.5000	1.5000	47290	954802
5	11780	823	16	0.01402	0.00028	2.4026	2.3611	58680	907511
10	11695	623	17	0.01071	0.00029	2.5674	2.9399	58218	848831
15	11621	822	41	0.01411	0.00070	2.7160	2.6264	58274	790613
20	11774	1336	49	0.02198	0.00081	2.6500	2.5719	60808	732339
25	12515	1785	57	0.02811	0.00090	2.5080	2.6089	63495	671531
30	12817	1691	75	0.02646	0.00117	2.3856	2.6648	63907	608036
35	12724	1121	109	0.01772	0.00172	2.3258	2.6904	63261	544129
40	12572	688	164	0.01102	0.00263	2.3744	2.7086	62401	480868
45	12377	555	255	0.00905	0.00416	2.3952	2.6695	61269	418467
50	12111	415	363	0.00696	0.00608	2.5450	2.6642	59643	357198
55	11718	518	516	0.00905	0.00902	2.4352	2.6271	57231	297555
60	11147	386	675	0.00714	0.01250	2.3965	2.6483	53977	240324
65	10419	303	939	0.00605	0.01876	2.3818	2.6500	50054	186347
70	9545	219	1292	0.00490	0.02884	2.4788	2.6705	44793	136293
75	8279	226	1835	0.00612	0.04958	2.3408	2.6023	37002	91499
80	6444	128	2193	0.00480	0.08231	2.2429	2.4751	26645	54497
85	4235	64	4210	0.00228	0.15114			27852	27852

TABLE 4. Comparative Summary Measures from Life Table Models of Mortality and Migration, United States/California 1970

Measure	Life table model[a]		
		Male and female one-sex	
	TWOFIDS	IDSP	IDLT[b]
1. Intrinsic growth rate (r)	0.00797	0.00992 (male) 0.00584 (female)	0
2. Intrinsic birth rate (b)	0.01876	0.02083 (male) 0.01667 (female)	0.01486 (male) 0.01335 (female)
3. Intrinsic death rate (d)	0.01080	0.01090 (male) 0.01083 (female)	0.01486 (male) 0.01335 (female)
4. Radix (ℓ_0) values:			
a. California males	12701	12626	10500
b. California females	12096	12264	10000
c. Rest of U.S. males	92299	92374	94500
d. Rest of U.S. females	87904	87736	90000
5. Proportion of total population living in California	0.1294	0.1300 (male) 0.1292 (female)	0.1211 (male) 0.1179 (female)
6. Total fertility rates (TFRs)			
a. California males	2.38	2.51	--
b. California females	2.46	2.35	--
c. Rest of U.S. males	2.64	2.80	--
d. Rest of U.S. females	2.62	2.48	--
7. Life expectancy			
a. Male	67.29	67.29	67.28
b. Female	74.89	74.89	74.89
8. Number of outmigrations in the stable population by			
a. California males	11482	10811	13350
b. California females	9939	10672	11472
c. Rest of U.S. males	12554	11883	16129
d. Rest of U.S. females	10717	11391	13817
9. Stable population outmigration rate for			
a. California males	0.01636	0.01649	0.01560
b. California females	0.01397	0.01377	0.01300
c. Rest of U.S. males	0.00269	0.00271	0.00260
d. Rest of U.S. females	0.00221	0.00218	0.00209
10. Crude migration rate (total moves/total population)	0.00409	0.00450 (male) 0.00368 (female)	0.00416 (male) 0.00338 (female)

[a]Source: Life table models calculated as described in text.
[b]Radix values set arbitrarily to give California 10% of all births, roughly its proportion of the U.S. population in 1970.

female IDSP values. The TWOFIDS intrinsic death rate, however, is not bounded by the two IDSP values of d, indicating that there is no assurance that two-sex model values will be somewhere between the corresponding figures in the one-sex male and female models. [Using the approach described in the Appendix to Schoen (1977b), I have produced other examples demonstrating that the harmonic mean consistency condition used here does not always lead to intermediate values.]

The TWOFIDS model shows that 12.1% of all births occur in California, but that net migration results in 12.9% of the population residing in that state. The two IDSPs show similar proportions of the population living in California. However, they suggest that the sex ratio at birth there is only 102.9 males per every 100 females, an unrealistic value that reflects the inability of the one-sex models to reconcile male and female rates. The figures for the Total Fertility Rates (the average number of children a person would have under a given set of fertility rates) also reveal differences between the one-sex and two-sex models. The IDSP males have higher Total Fertility Rates than the TWOFIDS males, while the IDSP females have lower Total Fertility Rates than their TWOFIDS counterparts.

Methodologically, the TWOFIDS model has an advantage over the IDSP model because it avoids unrealistic or inconsistent values between male and female populations. Substantively, the numerical values produced by both models should be interpreted with care because they reflect the implications of a set of mortality, fertility, and state transfer rates under the very strong assumption that those rates do not change over time.

4. CONCLUSION

Given an appropriate consistency condition, such as that presented in Eqs. (27) and (28), two-sex life table models can be specified and constructed using the same algorithm that applies to one-sex models. That algorithm calls for four sets of equations:

(i) flow equations that specify the movements between states and from one age to the next;

(ii) orientation equations that relate the observed behavioral rates to the behavioral rates of the model;

(iii) person-year equations that lead to numerical solutions for the number of person-years lived in each relevant population subgroup; and

(iv) renewal equations that relate fertility rates to population growth and the state composition of succeeding birth cohorts.

The algorithm builds upon the underlying instantaneous Markov process, but focuses on the estimation of model functions in the discrete case.

This chapter has been concerned with bringing together three dimensions along which life table models have developed, the stationary/stable population dimension, the decrement/increment-decrement dimension, and the one-sex/two-sex population dimension. These three dimensions give rise to the ten different life table models shown in Table 1. Six of them are two-sex models, and aside from Models V and VII (TWOGRO and TWONUP), they have received very little, if any, attention in the literature. It is hoped that their identification and specification here will lead to greater interest in them and in their uses for demographic analysis. For example, Model VIII (MSQUEEZ) is clearly of value in analyses of the marriage squeeze, and I have already begun some work utilizing it to that end. To illustrate how such models can be constructed, birth, death, and migration rates for the U.S. and California, 1970, were used to construct the two-sex fertility increment-decrement stable population (TWOFIDS) model shown in Table 3.

Many additional dimensions along which life table models can be profitably extended remain. Compound models, for example, a TWOMSLT model recognizing male and female labor-force statuses, as well as marital statuses, can be accommodated within the framework presented here by increasing the number of states and considering one status change at a time. The two sexes represent only the simplest example of interacting populations. Models recognizing different ethnic groups are the next step. If the nature of the interactions can be spelled out, models incorporating different species are possible, linking up life table models with the literature on predator-prey and other ecological systems. All of the models discussed here have assumed homogeneous populations, but that assumption can be relaxed to allow a greater or lesser degree of population heterogeneity. In addition, the present Markovian model can be replaced by a semi-Markov one, and such characteristics as duration in a state considered.

The greatest restriction in life table models, however, is the use of an unchanging set of behavioral rates. While the social, economic, and biological underpinnings of demographic behavior pose great challenges to any attempt to bring the demographic rates themselves within the scope of the model, some advances are being made (Land, 1979). With further progress, and with the life table's protean capacity to expand and include new information, the life table model can become the basis for a comprehensive model of life.

APPENDIX

THE TWONUP FIRST MARRIAGE MATRIX

The calculation of the number of first marriages by age-of-bride and age-of-groom can be approached using matrix algebra. If there are p male ages at marriage and q female ages at marriage, the matrix equation for the simple harmonic mean consistency equation is

$$\underset{\sim}{C} \# [\underset{\sim}{1}_{pq} \underset{\sim}{F}^{-1} + \underset{\sim}{M}^{-1} \underset{\sim}{1}_{pq}] = \underset{\sim}{c} \# [\underset{\sim}{1}_{pq} {}^{f}\underset{\sim}{L}^{-1} + {}^{m}\underset{\sim}{L}^{-1} \underset{\sim}{1}_{pq}], \qquad (A.1)$$

where # indicates element-wise matrix multiplication (or the Schur or Hadamard product); $\underset{\sim}{C}[\underset{\sim}{c}]$ is the p × q matrix of observed [model] population marriages whose ij-th element is C(i,j) [c(i,j)]; $\underset{\sim}{1}_{pq}$ a p × q matrix all of whose elements are unity; $\underset{\sim}{F}$, the q × q diagonal matrix whose q-th diagonal entry is the female population aged q; $\underset{\sim}{M}$, the p × p diagonal matrix whose p-th diagonal entry is the male population aged p; ${}^{f}\underset{\sim}{L}$, the q × q diagonal matrix whose q-th diagonal entry is ${}^{f}L_{q}$; and ${}^{m}\underset{\sim}{L}$, the p × p diagonal matrix whose p-th diagonal entry is ${}^{m}L_{p}$.

INPUT DATA FOR THE TWOFIDS MODEL

Calculating a two-sex fertility increment-decrement stable population model for the U.S., 1970, that recognizes the regions California and the rest of the U.S. requires extensive data inputs on mortality, fertility, and migration. As a result, approximations were introduced at several points.

First, mortality rates for the U.S., by age and sex, were taken from the U.S. Life Tables for 1970 (U.S. National Center for Health Statistics, 1974), and, for California, from Schoen and Collins (1973). To simplify the data assembly, the experience of the U.S. as a whole was assumed to characterize the "rest of the U.S." region.

Second, births cross-tabulated by age-of-mother and age-of-father for the U.S. were obtained from the *Vital Statistics of the U.S. 1970* (U.S. National Center for Health Statistics, 1975, Table 1-53). Births to fathers of unknown age (8.8% of all births) were allocated in proportion to births where the father's age was known. Births by age of mother for California were taken from *Vital Statistics of California 1970* (California, 1973, Table 10), and the rest of the birth matrix was estimated on the basis of the U.S. data. To calculate fertility rates, male and female populations for the U.S. were taken from the *Historical Statistics of the U.S.* (U.S. Bureau of the Census, 1975, p. 15), and for California from California (1973, p. 9).

Finally, data on gross migration were taken from the 15% sample of the 1970 census and reflect differences in residence between April 1, 1965 and April 1, 1970 (U.S. Bureau of the Census, 1977a, Table 1). The data are thus subject to recall errors, do not indicate multiple moves between 1965 and 1970, and include persons who lived outside of the U.S. in 1965. Since only seven age groups were provided for California inmigrants and outmigrants and only the total figures were broken down by sex, the complete age-sex distribution was estimated using figures given for all movers between March 1975 and March 1976 (U.S. Bureau of the Census 1977b, Table 4). Annual rates were calculated using the appropriate population base and one-fifth the number of moves shown for the five-year period. While the magnitude of error in the migration rates cannot be stated with precision, it should be noted that the errors are in part offsetting, though the net result is likely to understate the actual amount of movement.

REFERENCES

Brems, Hans (1968). "Quantitative Economic Theory: A Synthetic Approach." New York: Wiley.

California Department of Public Health (1973). Vital Statistics of California, 1970. Sacramento.

Chiang, Chin-Long (1964). A stochastic model of competing risks of illness and competing risks of death. *In* "Stochastic Models in Medicine and Biology," (J. Gurland, ed.), pp. 323-354. Madison: University of Wisconsin Press.

Das Gupta, P. (1972). "On two-sex models leading to stable populations. *Theoretical Population Biology 3,* 358-375.

Das Gupta, P. (1978). An alternative formulation of the birth function in a two-sex model. *Population Studies 32,* 367-379.

Du Pasquier, L. G. (1912-1913). Mathematische theorie der invaliditätsversicherung. *Mitteilungen der Vereinigung der schweitzerische versicherungsmathematiker 7,* 1-7; *8,* 1-153.

Euler, L. (1760). Recherches générales sur la mortalité et la multiplication. *Mémoires de L'Académie Royale des Science et Belles Lettres 16,* 144-164.

Fix, E. and J. Neyman (1951). A simple stochastic model of recovery, relapse, death, and loss of patients. *Human Biology 23,* 205-241.

Goodman, L. A. (1967). On the age-sex composition of the population that would result from given fertility and mortality conditions. *Demography 4,* 423-441.

Goodman, L. A. (1968). Stochastic models for the population growth of the sexes. *Biometrika 55,* 469-487.

Granville, William A., P. F. Smith, and W. R. Longley (1941). "Elements of the Differential and Integral Calculus." Revised edition. Boston: Ginn.

Graunt, John (1662). "Natural and Political Observations Mentioned in a Following Index and Made upon the Bills of Mortality." London: Roycroft.

Halley, Edmund (1693). An estimate of the degrees of the mortality of mankind. *Philosophical Transactions of the Royal Society of London,* 17.

Henry, L. (1972). Nuptiality. *Theoretical Population Biology 3,* 135-152.

Hoem, J. M. (1970). A probabilistic approach to nuptiality. *Biométrie-Praximétrie 11,* 3-19.

Jordan, Chester W., Jr. (1967). "Life Contingencies." 2nd ed. Chicago: Society of Actuaries.

Kendal, D. G. (1949). Stochastic processes and population growth. *Journal of the Royal Statistical Society, Series B, 11,* 230-264.

Keyfitz, Nathan (1968a). A life table that agrees with the data, II. *Journal of the American Statistical Association 63,* 1253-1268.

Keyfitz, Nathan (1968b). "Introduction to the Mathematics of Population." Reading, Massachusetts: Addison-Wesley.

Keyfitz, Nathan (1970). Finding probabilities from observed rates, or how to make a life table. *American Statistician 24,* 28-33.

Keyfitz, Nathan (1971). "The Mathematics of Sex and Marriage," Vol. 4, pp. 89-108. Proceedings of the Sixth Berkeley Symposium on Mathematical Statistics and Probability. Berkeley: University of California Press.

Krishnamoorthy, S. (1979). Classical approach to increment-decrement life tables: An application to the study of the marital status of United States females, 1970. *Mathematical Biosciences 44,* 139-154.

Land, Kenneth C. (1979). "Modeling macro social change." *In* "Sociological Methodology 1980" (Karl F. Schuessler, ed.), pp. 219-278. San Francisco: Jossey-Bass.

Land, Kenneth C. and Robert Schoen (1982). Statistical methods for Markov-generated increment-decrement life tables with polynomial gross flow functions. *In* "Multidimensional Mathematical Demography" (Kenneth C. Land and Andrei Rogers, eds.). New York: Academic Press.

Ledent, Jacques (1980). Multistate life tables: Movement versus transition perspectives. *Environment and Planning A, 12,* 533-562.

Lotka, A. J. (1907a). Relation between birth rates and death rates. *Science, N.S. 26,* 21-22.

Lotka, A. J. (1907b). Studies on the mode of growth of material aggregates. *American Journal of Science 24,* 199-216.

Lotka, A. J. (1939). "Theorie Analytique des Associations Biologiques." Paris: Hermann.

MacRae, E. C. (1977). Estimation of time-varying Markov processes with aggregate data. *Econometrica 45,* 183-198.

McFarland, D. D. (1975). Models of marriage formation and fertility. *Social Forces 54,* 66-83.

Mitra, S. (1978). On the derivation of a two-sex stable population model. *Demography 15,* 541-548.

Pollard, A. H. (1948). The measurement of reproductivity. *Journal of the Institute of Actuaries 74,* 288-305.

Pollard, J. H. (1975). Modeling human populations for projection purposes--Some of the problems and challenges. *Australian Journal of Statistics 17*, 63-76.

Preston, Samuel H., N. Keyfitz, and R. Schoen (1973). Cause-of-death life tables: Application of a new technique to worldwide data. *Transactions of the Society of Actuaries 25*, 83-109.

Rogers, Andrei (1973). Estimating internal migration from incomplete data using model multiregional life tables. *Demography 10*, 277-287.

Rogers, Andrei (1975). "Introduction to Multiregional Mathematical Demography." New York: Wiley.

Rogers, Andrei and Jacques Ledent (1976). Increment-decrement life tables: A comment. *Demography 13*, 287-290.

Schoen, Robert (1975). Constructing increment-decrement life tables. *Demography 12*, 313-324.

Schoen, Robert (1977a). Further reactions to Rogers and Ledent's comment. *Demography 14*, 591-592.

Schoen, Robert (1977b). A two-sex nuptiality-mortality life table. *Demography 14*, 333-350.

Schoen, Robert (1978a). Calculating life tables by estimating Chiang's *a* from observed rates. *Demography 15*, 625-635.

Schoen, Robert (1978b). A standardized two-sex stable population. *Theoretical Population Biology 14*, 357-370.

Schoen, Robert (1979). Calculating increment-decrement life tables by estimating mean durations at transfer from observed rates. *Mathematical Biosciences 44*, 255-269.

Schoen, Robert (1981). The harmonic mean as the basis of a realistic two-sex marriage model. *Demography 18*, 201-216.

Schoen, Robert and Marion Collins (1973). "Mortality by Cause: Life Tables for California 1950-1970." Sacramento: California Department of Public Health.

Schoen, Robert and Kenneth C. Land (1979). A general algorithm for estimating a Markov-generated increment-decrement life table with applications to marital-status patterns. *Journal of the American Statistical Association 74*, 761-776.

Schoen, Robert and V. E. Nelson (1974). Marriage, divorce, and mortality: A life table analysis. *Demography 11*, 267-290.

Schoen, Robert and Karen Woodrow (1980). Labor force status life tables for the United States, 1972. *Demography 17*, 297-322.

Sharpe, F. R. and A. J. Lotka (1911). A problem in age-distribution. *Philosophical Magazine, Series 6, 21,* 435-438.

Shyrock, H. S., J. S. Siegel, and Associates (1973). "The Methods and Materials of Demography." Rev. ed. Washington, D.C.: U.S. Bureau of the Census (U.S. Government Printing Office).

Sverdrup, Erling (1965). Estimates and test procedures in connection with stochastic models for deaths, recoveries, and transfers between different states of health. *Skandinavisk Aktuarietidskrift 40,* 184-211.

U.S. Bureau of the Census (1975). "Historical Statistics of the United States, Colonial Times to 1970." Washington, D.C.: U.S. Government Printing Office.

U.S. Bureau of the Census (1977a). "Gross Migration by County: 1965 to 1970." Current Population Reports P-25, No. 701. Washington, D.C.: U.S. Government Printing Office.

U.S. Bureau of the Census (1977b). "Geographical Mobility: March 1975 to March 1976." Current Population Reports P-20, No. 305. Washington, D.C.: U.S. Government Printing Office.

U.S. National Center for Health Statistics (1974). "Vital Statistics of the United States 1970." Vol. 2, Section 5, Life Tables. Washington, D.C.: U.S. Government Printing Office.

U.S. National Center for Health Statistics (1975). "Vital Statistics of the United States 1970." Vol. 2, Fertility. Washington, D.C.: U.S. Government Printing Office.

8

Multiregional Population Projections by Place of Previous Residence

Dimiter Philipov and Andrei Rogers

1. INTRODUCTION

Much of mathematical demography is concerned with the measurement and projection of changes of state, or *status*, experienced by individuals during their lifetime, e.g., changes in marital status, in employment status, in educational status, and in residential location. The study of such transitions from state to state and the evolution of the associated status-specific populations is the focus of a growing body of methodological techniques and applications sometimes referred to as *multistate demography* (Rogers, 1980).

Recent work in multistate mathematical demography has identified a unifying matrix-based generalization of classical techniques, which illuminates the common features of many of the well-known methods for dealing with transfers between

ISBN 0-12-435640-0

multiple states of existence. For example, it is now understood that multiple decrement life tables, marital status life tables, tables of working life, tables of educational life, and multiregional life tables are all members of a general class of increment-decrement life tables known as *multistate life tables*. It also has become evident that projections of populations disaggregated by status can be carried out using a common methodology--*multistate projection*.

Although traditional single-state methods are more parsimonious in their data requirements and provide reasonably adequate results for many purposes, they cannot deal with interstate transitions differentiated by origins and destinations and must, therefore, account for changes in stocks by reference to *net* totals, e.g., net migration. In a recent paper, we have shown that such an approach may introduce biases and inconsistencies into a projection and that multistate models have a decisive advantage over single-state models as a consequence of their ability to produce disaggregated projections that follow the evolution of subcategories of a population over time and space (Rogers and Philipov, 1980; Philipov and Rogers, 1981). This feature of multistate projection methods is further developed in this chapter, in the particular context of *multiregional* demography.

2. STATIONARY AND STABLE POPULATION DISTRIBUTIONS

To make our argument less abstract, imagine a single-sex population (females) disaggregated into five-year age groups, and, for ease of exposition, consider its spatial distribution to extend over only two regions, North and South. For a numerical illustration, let us draw on 1965-1970 data for the United States previously examined in Rogers and Castro (1976) and, more recently, in Ledent (1981). These data are set out in the appendices of an earlier paper (Philipov and Rogers, 1981). The three census regions: Northeast, North Central, and West have been aggregated together to form a single region: the "rest of the United States" or, more simply, the North.

In 1968, the female population of the U.S. stood at 102.3 million, with 32.5 million in the South and 69.8 million in the North (Appendix A in Philipov and Rogers, 1981). Conventional single-region life table calculations give a Southern-born baby girl a life expectancy of 74.11 yr, just three months less than the corresponding life expectancy of a baby girl born in the North. The gross reproduction rates in the two regions are 1.18 and 1.16, respectively.

Consider next the results of a multiregional (two-state) analysis (Rogers, 1975). First, computing a biregional life table we find that about 27% of a Southern-born baby girl's life expectancy can be expected to be lived in the North. Projecting the biregional population 30 yr forward on the assumption of constant rates gives a 1998 national total of 138.6 million, with 33.0% residing in the South. Continuing this projection to stability yields an ultimate share for the South of 34.5%, an intrinsic national rate of growth of 4.361 per thousand, and a stationary biregional population that locates about 72.6% of the total Southern-born population in the South as resident *natives*. In contrast 84.8% of the Northern-born population lives in the North, leaving the remaining 15.2% to live in the South as *aliens* (i.e., individuals living in a place different from their place of birth).

Multiplying the stationary population in each age group by exp[-r(y+2.5)], where r is the national intrinsic rate of growth and y is the starting age of the age group, gives the relative age distribution of the place-of-birth-specific stable population resident in each region. Since r is relatively small in our U.S. illustration (r = 0.004361) the stable share of natives and aliens in each region differs only slightly from the stationary (life-table) share, with the above 72.6 and 84.8% natives totals shifting to 72.3 and 86.4%, respectively. Multiplying each of these by the stable shares of the national population in each region (i.e., 34.5 and 65.5%, respectively) gives the stable shares of the national population in each of the four place-of-residence-by-place-of-birth (PRPB) subcategories, as shown in the bottom line of Table 1.

Biregional life table populations normally are disaggregated by place of birth and denoted by ${}_{i0}L_j(y)$. However, such populations can be readily disaggregated by place of residence at age x instead, in which case they are then denoted by ${}_{ix}L_j(y)$. Multiplying the latter by exp[-r(y+2.5)] gives the relative age distribution of the stable population in each region, disaggregated by its previous region of residence at age x. An example of such place-of-residence-by-place-of-previous-residence (PRPPR) stable shares is presented in Table 2 for the U.S. data with x = 15 yr. Note that the percentage share of aliens, in each region, declines as age x increases.

TABLE 1. PRPB Distribution at Stability of National and Regional Female Population of the U.S. (r = 0.004361)

	Resident in South		Resident in North	
	Born in South (natives)	Born in North (aliens)	Born in North (natives)	Born in South (aliens)
Percentage of regional population	72.3	27.7	86.4	13.6
Percentage of national population[a]	34.5		65.5	
Percentage distribution of national population[a]	24.9	9.6	56.6	8.9

[a]In the aggregation, each of the two birth cohorts (South and North) was weighted by its associated stable equivalent births.

TABLE 2. PRPPR (at exact age 15) Distribution at Stability of National and Regional Female Population of the U.S. (r = 0.004361)

	Resident in South		Resident in North	
	Having lived in South at age 15 (natives)	Having lived in North at age 15 (aliens)	Having lived in North at age 15 (natives)	Having lived in South at age 15 (aliens)
Percentage of regional population	74.2	25.8	87.9	12.1
Percentage of national population[a]	34.6		65.4	
Percentage distribution of national population[a]	25.7	8.9	57.4	7.9

[a]In the aggregation, each of the two "cohorts" (in South and in North at exact age 15) was weighted by its associated stable equivalent survivors at exact age 15.

3. MULTIREGIONAL POPULATION PROJECTIONS BY PLACE OF BIRTH

Several recent studies of migration have emphasized the importance of analyzing the flow patterns of *return* migrants, pointing to the not-surprising empirical finding that the migration rates of people returning to their region of birth are significantly higher than the average (Ledent, 1981; Lee, 1974; Long and Hansen, 1975; Miller, 1977). In an earlier paper (Philipov and Rogers, 1981), we followed this advice by introducing higher transition probabilities for return migrants in the multiregional projection model. There we called the outputs of such models *native-dependent projections*. In this section, however, we shall treat only the simpler case of *native-independent projections*, i.e., projections carried out with models assuming that all of the individuals in a regional population experience identical age-specific probabilities of moving, dying, and bearing offspring. Native-dependent projections are considered in Section 5.

3.1. FERTILITY

In projecting a multiregional population forward over time, we shall at times refer to people by where they live and at other times by where they were born. This poses no difficulties when we are dealing with survivors of a current population; it simply becomes a matter of keeping track of individuals born in each region. It is the births of new individuals that needs to be examined, because babies may be born in the region of residence of their parents at the start or at the end of the unit interval of time, and they themselves may migrate during the same interval into yet another region.

In the conventional multiregional projection model, some of the babies born in a given region during a unit time interval (t, t+1) may be living in another region by the end of that interval. Consequently, at time t + 1 these babies can be distinguished both by their place of residence j and by their place of birth i. Moreover, they may also be classified by the region of residence, say k, of their parent at the *start* of the time interval, because each regional population of parents is a potential contributor of babies to each PRPB-specific category of babies. For example, in our two-region illustration based on U.S. data, we distinguish four categories of babies for each of the two residence-specific categories of parent. Figure 1 shows the four categories corresponding to parents initially resident in the South; there are of course four equivalent categories for babies born to parents initially resident in the North.

Let

$$b^{i}_{kj}(x) = \frac{{}_{i}B^{(t+1)}_{kj}(x)}{K^{(t)}_{k}(x)} \qquad (1)$$

denote the average number of babies born during the five-year time interval (t, t+1) in region i and alive in region j at time t + 1, per x to (x+4)-year-old individual living in region k at time t. Summing over all birth places i gives the conventional multiregional birth rate (Rogers, 1975; p. 121):

$$b_{kj}(x) = \frac{1}{2}\left[\frac{{}_{k0}L_{j}(0)}{\ell_{k}(0)}\,F_{k}(x) + \sum_{h=1}^{m} s_{kh}(x)\,\frac{{}_{h0}L_{j}(0)}{\ell_{h}(0)}\,F_{h}(x+5)\right], \qquad (2)$$

where $F_h(x)$ = annual birth rate of people aged x to x + 4 re-

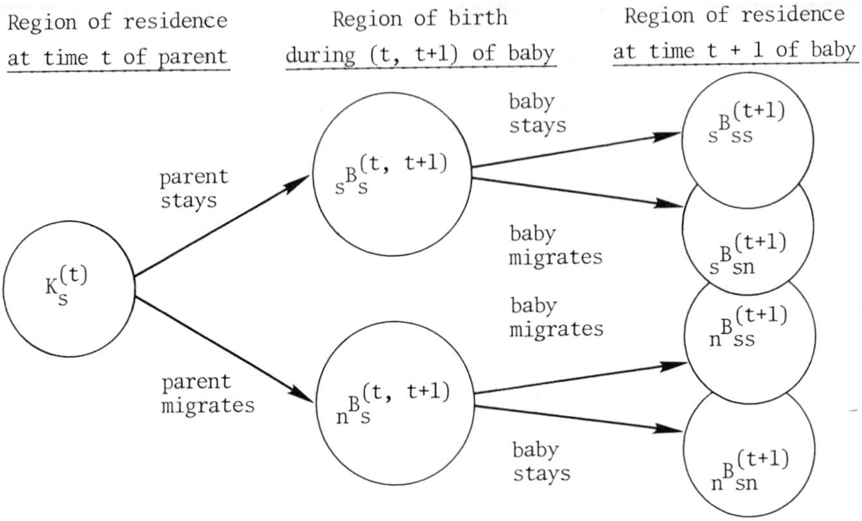

Fig. 1. The four categories of babies born to parents resident in the South at time t.

siding in region h; ${}_{h0}L_j(0)$ = total number of person-years lived between ages 0 to 5 in region j, per person born in region h (the stationary life table population); $s_{kh}(x)$ = proportion of people in region k and aged x to x + 4 that survive to be in region h and aged x + 5 to x + 9, five years later; $\ell_h(0)$ = radix of region h (set equal to unity in our calculations); and m = number of regions in the multiregional system.

Since, by definition,

$$b_{kj}(x) = \sum_{i=1}^{m} b_{kj}^{i}(x) \quad , \tag{3}$$

one can readily develop computational formulas for $b_{kj}^{i}(x)$ by taking the appropriate components from Eq. (2). For our two-region (South-North) example, this gives four equations of the form

$$b_{kj}^{k}(x) = \frac{1}{2}\,\frac{{}_{k0}L_j(0)}{\ell_k(0)}\,[F_k(x) + s_{kk}(x)F_k(x+5)] \ , \quad k,j = s,n \tag{4}$$

for parents in two regions who do not migrate between time t and the birth of the infant (i = k), but whose child may or may not migrate before t + 1 (j = k or j ≠ k); and four equations

$$b^{i}_{kj}(x) = \frac{1}{2}\,\frac{{}_{i0}L_j(0)}{\ell_i(0)}\,[s_{ki}(x)F_i(x+5)]\ , \quad k,i,j = s,n \quad (i \neq k) \tag{5}$$

corresponding to parents who do migrate between time t and the birth of the infant (i ≠ k), but whose child may or may not migrate before t + 1 (j = i or j = k). This implies that a child may migrate without its parents between the ages of 0 and 5.

3.2. SURVIVORSHIP

In order to complete the multiregional projection process, the generation of new births must be augmented with the survivorship of current residents disaggregated into natives and aliens. The Lexis diagram in Fig. 2 illustrates the different lifelines that can occur in our biregional example.

Equations (4) and (5) describe both the births and the survival of the babies until the end of the first unit time-interval. Whereas Fig. 1 shows how total births are allocated among categories of births, Fig. 2 illustrates their survival patterns.

Consider the babies born in the South during time interval (t, t+1). In the notation of Fig. 1, their number is equal to the sum of ${}_{s}B_{s}^{(t,\ t+1)}$ and ${}_{s}B_{n}^{(t,\ t+1)}$, i.e., the babies born to residents of the South at time t who stay and to residents of the North at time t who migrate before the

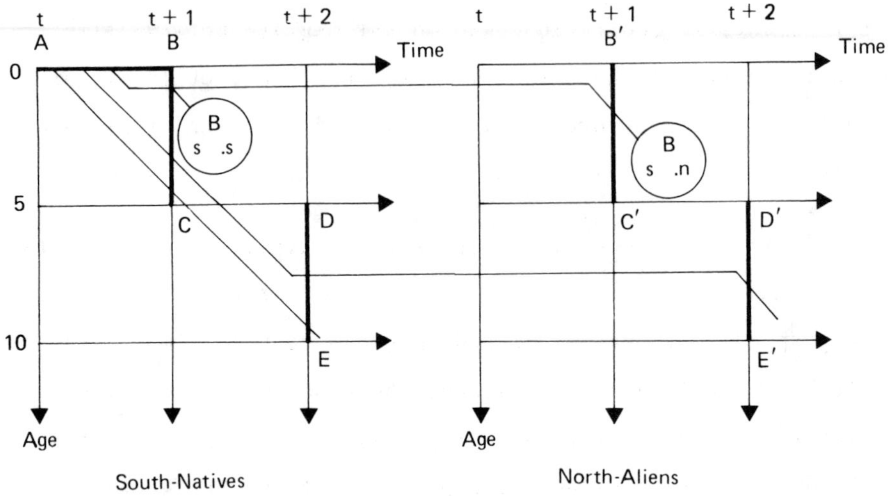

Fig. 2. Bistate Lexis diagram for Southern-born individuals.

birth of their baby. This total is represented by the segment AB in Fig. 2.

At time t + 1, the members of the cohort AB will survive to give BC [with a typical member ${}_sB^{(t+1)}_{.s}$) and B'C (with a typical member ${}_sB^{(t+1)}_{.n}$]. The place of residence of the parent at time t can be either the South or the North.

The cohort BC represents the 0 - 5-yr-old Southern natives at time t + 1, whereas B'C' represents the 0 - 5-yr-old Northern aliens. For the U.S. data and t + 1 = 1998, they are estimated to equal 3,565,044 and 104,007, respectively, by means of the birth coefficients b^s_{ss}, b^s_{sn}, b^s_{ns}, and b^s_{nn} set out in Eqs. (4) and (5).

The totals BC and B'C' may be survived forward to become DE and D'E', respectively, by keeping track of the events represented by the rhombuses BDEC, and B'D'E'C'. For example, D'E' is the sum of the survivors, in the same region, of B'C', and of arrivals from BC who at time t + 2 remained in the North.

The assumption characterizing the native-independent case allows one to assign the same region-specific survivorship proportions to both natives and aliens. This leads to the construction of the survivorship and projection matrices set out in Eqs. (A.3) and (A.5) of Appendix A.

3.3. *PROJECTION*

The age-specific birth rates, by location of birth, may be incorporated into the standard multiregional projection model (Rogers, 1975) transforming that model into a *multistate* projection model, where the states are places of birth. Such a transformation makes it possible to generate regional projection totals disaggregated by region of birth, i.e., place-of-residence-by-place-of-birth (PRPB) projections.

Appendix A describes the matrix model. Note that the Markovian assumption is still retained. All individuals in a region, recent inmigrants as well as old residents, aliens as well as natives, are assumed to experience identical probabilities of transition.

Table 3 presents the biregional age-disaggregated stable population by state that ultimately arises if the projection matrix defined by Eq. (A.5) and the U.S. data are applied to *any* initial population. This is because the stable distribution depends only on the elements of the growth matrix and not on the initial (base-year) population distribution.

The stable growth results in Table 3 are consistent with those presented earlier in Table 1. Note that the intrinsic rate of growth remains the same ($r = 0.004361$), as does the spatial distribution of the national population ($SHA_S = 34.5\%$

TABLE 3. PRPB Age and Regional Distributions at Stability of National Female Stable Equivalent Population of the U.S. (r = 0.004361).

	Resident in South		Resident in North	
Age	Born in South (natives)	Born in North (aliens)	Born in North (natives)	Born in South (aliens)
0-4	10.3	0.7	8.9	0.8
5-9	9.4	1.9	8.4	2.2
10-14	8.8	2.8	8.1	3.2
15-19	8.1	4.1	7.7	4.6
20-24	7.2	5.5	7.2	6.2
25-29	6.6	6.5	6.8	7.3
30-34	6.2	7.1	6.5	7.9
35-39	5.8	7.4	6.3	8.1
40-44	5.5	7.6	6.0	8.1
45-49	5.2	7.6	5.7	8.0
50-54	4.9	7.6	5.4	7.8
55-59	4.6	7.5	5.0	7.4
60-64	4.2	7.5	4.5	6.8
65-69	3.8	7.2	4.0	6.2
70-74	3.2	6.4	3.4	5.3
75-79	2.5	5.2	2.6	4.3
80-84	1.8	3.7	1.8	3.0
85+	1.8	3.8	1.7	2.9
Total	100.0	100.0	100.0	100.0
Mean age	33.7	49.0	35.1	46.5
Share	24.9	9.6	56.6	8.9

and $SHA_n = 65.5\%$). The multistate projection reveals, for example, that, at stability, the mean age of the alien population in the South will be 15.3 yr older than that of the native population and 2.5 yr older than the North's alien population. All of these stable growth quantities, however, could be obtained *without* the multistate growth matrix (if r is known) since a simple weighting of the stationary multiregional life table population gives identical results. The usefulness of the growth matrix, therefore, lies in generating projections and not stable population totals.

4. MULTIREGIONAL POPULATION PROJECTIONS BY PLACE OF PREVIOUS RESIDENCE

The PRPB model introduces heterogeneity to the population at exact age zero. The question naturally arises then whether this heterogeneity can be introduced at later ages. Such cases of heterogeneity may be more useful in situations where conditions in the region of childhood education, for example, could influence an individual's behavior more than those in the region of birth.

If the distinction between natives and aliens is introduced only after exact age x, then from birth until age x there is no need for disaggregation. For these ages the conventional multiregional projection model is valid, and only the regions of residence are recognized. Thus the biregional model with a single state (residents) is two-dimensional until age x and is four-dimensional after age x when two states, natives and aliens, are introduced. It therefore is sufficient to treat the residents as natives, keeping the alien states empty until age x. In such a case an inmigrant younger than age x will join the natives of the region of destination.

4.1. FERTILITY

The fertility discussion in the PRPB model is not relevant to the PRPPR model. This is because the birth coefficients are not changed in the latter model, since the age x at which heterogeneity is introduced is greater than zero. Therefore, births are calculated in the conventional manner, i.e., using Eq. (2). The increase in the dimensionality of the growth matrix, however, necessitates the proper positioning of the birth coefficients (see Appendix A).

4.2. SURVIVORSHIP

Survivorship in the PRPPR model can be illustrated by making use of the Lexis diagram once again. Figure 3 presents the case of Southern natives at time t at ages x - t to x (the population represented by the vertical line segment AB).

If heterogeneity is maintained at all ages above exact age x, then the Southern natives who outmigrate between ages x - 5 and x will join the state of North-Natives (line 2). Those who migrate between ages x and x + 5 will instead join the state of North-Aliens (line 3). It is evident that the survivorship of individuals in the age group immediately preceding exact age x is depicted in two different ways: by the events in triangle ABC on the one hand and by the events in the triangle BCD on the other. The events in the two triangles should not be added together, as was the case in the PRPB model (e.g., the rhombus ABCD in Fig. 2).

In the PRPB model the individuals represented by AB survive to become members of CD and C'D' five years later. In

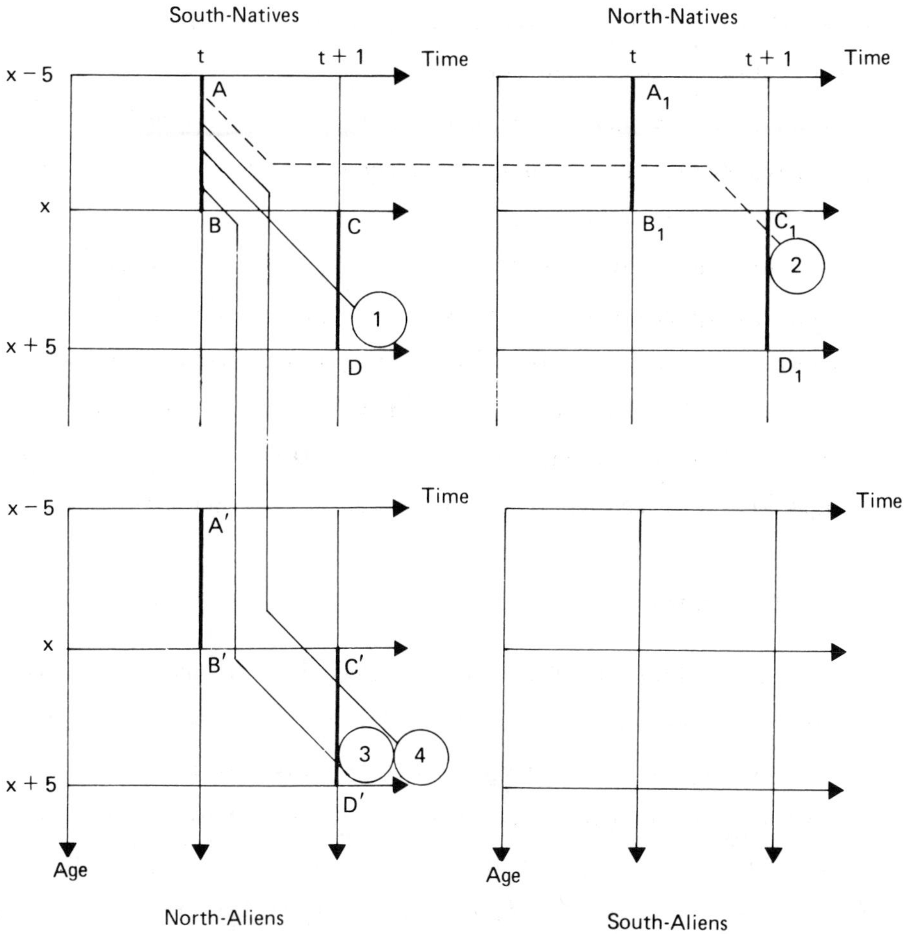

Fig. 3. Biregional bistate Lexis diagram.

the PRPPR case some of the members of C'D' must be reallocated to C_1D_1, dividing events into two parts, the events in the triangles ABC and BCD, respectively, by means of a separation factor α,

$$ABC = \alpha ABCD, \quad BCD = (1 - \alpha) ABCD, \qquad 0 \le \alpha \le 1$$

where the value of α is unknown (α = 0.5 gives the simplest approximation). Although the discussion thus far has referred to Southern natives at time t, it should be noted that a similar equation needs to be considered for Northern natives, involving an additional unknown parameter, β. The two parameters are independent of each other. Appendix B discusses their estimation in greater detail.

Until now the survivorship over one time interval of only one age group has been discussed. For the remaining age groups, things are simpler. The younger age groups are survived as in the conventional multiregional model by appropriately increasing the dimensionality of the matrix. The older age groups are survived as in the PRPB model (see Appendix A).

4.3. *PROJECTION*

The projection of the U.S. female population forward to stability using the growth matrix defined by Eqs. (A.7) and (A.8) produces regional totals that are disaggregated by region of previous residence at exact age x. The use of separation factors is necessary, and Appendix B describes the procedure that was used for the particular projection set out in Table 4, where $x = 15$.

The results in Table 4 are consistent with the aggregate totals presented earlier in Table 2, just as those in Table 3 were consistent with the totals in Table 1. Once again the same results could have been obtained, without the projection matrix, simply by scaling the life table population with $\exp[-r(y+2.5)]$. However, to obtain projections to years before stability, one must resort to the normal matrix projection model, using the rescaled life table population totals to estimate values for the two separation factors, α and β.

TABLE 4. PRPPR (at Exact Age 15) Age and Regional Distributions at Stability of National Female Stable Equivalent Population of the U.S. (r = 0.004361)[a]

	Resident in South		Resident in North	
Age	Having lived in South at age 15 (natives)	Having lived in North at age 15 (aliens)	Having lived in North at age 15 (natives)	Having lived in South at age 15 (aliens)
15-19	11.6	1.7	10.4	1.4
20-24	10.3	4.8	9.8	4.0
25-29	9.3	7.0	9.2	5.9
30-34	8.7	8.1	8.8	7.0
35-39	8.1	8.8	8.4	7.7
40-44	7.7	9.1	8.0	8.2
45-49	7.2	9.1	7.6	8.4
50-54	6.8	8.9	7.2	8.5
55-59	6.4	8.6	6.7	8.6
60-64	5.9	8.0	6.0	8.7
65-69	5.2	7.3	5.3	8.5
70-74	4.4	6.4	4.5	7.7
75-79	3.5	5.1	3.5	6.3
80-84	2.4	3.6	2.4	4.5
85+	2.5	3.5	2.3	4.6
Total	100.0	100.0	100.0	100.0
Mean age	44.0	51.6	44.4	54.2
Share	25.7	8.9	57.4	7.9

[a]*The two separation factors were estimated to be $\alpha = 0.32809$ and $\beta = 0.34329$ (Appendix B).*

5. NATIVE-DEPENDENT MULTIREGIONAL POPULATION PROJECTIONS

It is widely recognized that the migration rates of return migrants are significantly greater than the average rates of migration to the same destination (Ledent, 1981; Long and Hansen, 1975; Miller, 1977). An attractive feature of the multiregional, multistate population projection model is its ability to incorporate different probabilities for different subgroups in the population, for example, natives and aliens.

5.1. *FERTILITY*

The introduction of native-dependent migration behavior into the calculation of the fertility elements of the multistate growth matrix is straightforward and uses the native-dependent probabilities and survivorship proportions defined by a native-dependent life table (Ledent, 1981). In the case of PRPB projections, for example, the formulas for $b^i_{kj}(x)$ become

$$b^i_{kj} = \sum_{h=1}^{m} {}_h b^i_{kj}(x) , \tag{6}$$

where the rates now receive a subscript on the left-hand side to denote the place of birth of parent and hence the place-of-birth-specific probabilities used to calculate expected births.

The required computation procedure can be more readily understood if Eqs. (4) and (5) are first reexpressed in the alternative form (Willekens and Rogers, 1978, p. 59), where $p_{ij}(0)$ denotes the probability that a person at exact age 0 in region i will survive to be at exact age 5 in region j:

$$b^k_{kj}(x) = \frac{5}{4}\, p_{kj}(0)\,[F_k(x) + s_{kk}(x)F_k(x+5)],\ j \neq k \tag{7}$$

$$= \frac{5}{4}\,[1 + p_{kk}(0)]\,[F_k(x) + s_{kk}(x)F_k(x+5)],\ j = k \tag{8}$$

and

$$b^i_{kj}(x) = \frac{5}{4}\, p_{ij}(0)\,[s_{ki}(x)F_i(x+5)],\ j \neq i \tag{9}$$

$$= \frac{5}{4}\,[1 + p_{ii}(0)]\,[s_{ki}(x)F_i(x+5)],\ j = i \tag{10}$$

since

$$\frac{{}_{k0}L_j(0)}{\ell_k(0)} = \frac{5}{2}\, p_{kj}(0),\ k \neq j \tag{11}$$

and

$$\frac{{}_{k0}L_k(0)}{\ell_k(0)} = \frac{5}{2}\, [1 + p_{kk}(0)],\ k = j \tag{12}$$

when the linear integration formula is used to calculate person-years on a unit radix.

Equations (7) - (10) may be made native-dependent by replacing $p_{kj}(0)$ by ${}_hp_{kj}(0)$ and $s_{ki}(x)$ by ${}_hs_{ki}(x)$. The native-dependent probabilities and survivorship proportions may be obtained from a multistate life table. In our two-region U.S. numerical example, the birth rates with h equal to the baby's place of birth may be found as a residual:

$$ {}_hb^h_{kj}(x) = {}_hb_{kj}(x) - {}_hb^i_{kj}(x). \tag{13}$$

5.2. *SURVIVORSHIP*

The computation of a native-dependent life table is a straightforward exercise (Ledent, 1981). One simply calculates a separate table for each subgroup of individuals, applying to it the appropriate subgroup-specific probabilities. No conceptual innovations are required; indeed a standard multiregional life table program (Willekens and Rogers, 1978) may be used. A program of this type applied to the native-dependent data set out in Appendix C of Philipov and Rogers (1981) produced, for example, the native-dependent expectations of remaining lifetime at age 20 presented in Table 5. The table illustrates the striking effect that place of birth has on the locations where

TABLE 5. Expectations of Remaining Lifetime at Age 20, by Place of Birth and Place of Future Residence

		Residence at age 20	
		South	North
A. Southern-born population			
Place of future residence	South	46.41	32.43
	North	10.10	24.16
	Total	56.51	56.59
B. Northern-born population			
Place of future residence	South	13.06	5.08
	North	43.52	51.55
	Total	56.58	56.63

remaining lifetimes are expected to be lived. A Southern-born female living in the North at age 20 is likely to spend over half of her remaining expected lifetime of 56.59 yr back in her region of birth, about six times the corresponding duration of residence for a Northern-born female at the same age and location.

5.3. PROJECTION

Collecting the various native-dependent birth rates and survivorship proportions to form the matrices $\tilde{B}(x)$ and $\tilde{S}(x)$ defined in Eq. (A.9) of Appendix A and organizing them in the structure of the growth matrix defined in Eq. (A.5) yield a native-dependent multistate projection model that distinguishes among transition probabilities and regional populations according to place of birth. Such a model produces projections somewhat different to those of the native-independent counterpart discussed in Section 3. Table 6 compares selected outputs;

TABLE 6. Alternative PRPB Projections to 1998 and Stability: U.S. Females, 1968

Year	Population Residing in Region				Total
	South		North		
	Natives	Aliens	Natives	Aliens	
A. Native-dependent projections: r = 0.004360					
1968	28,885,548	3,586,779	63,662,232	6,142,451	102,277,016
%	(28.2)	(3.5)	(62.2)	(6.0)	(100.0)
1998	38.495,044	6,289,250	86,446,904	7,378,696	138,609,888
%	(27.8)	(4.5)	(62.4)	(5.3)	(100.0)
Stable %	(26.9)	(5.0)	(63.3)	(4.7)	(100.0)
B. Native-independent projections: r = 0.004361					
1968	28,885,548	3,586,779	63,662,232	6,142,451	102,277,016
%	(28.2)	(3.5)	(62.2)	(6.0)	(100.0)
1998	34,966,964	10,832,081	81,580,392	11,213,493	138,592,928
%	(25.2)	(7.8)	(58.9)	(8.1)	(100.0)
Stable %	(24.9)	(9.6)	(56.6)	(8.9)	(100.0)

[a]Totals may differ slightly due to independent rounding.

more detailed results from the native-dependent model are set out in Tables 7 and 8. The latter illustrates the results of a 30-yr projection.

Table 6 identifies two very important characteristics of native-dependent and native-independent projections. First, aggregate totals and growth rates are the same in the two kinds of projections if the Markovian assumption is retained for fertility and mortality rates. For example, in both projections, the U.S. total female population is expected to stand at 138.6 million in 1998 and ultimately to converge to an intrinsic rate of growth of 0.00436. Second, the percentage share of *natives* in each regional population is consistently underestimated in the native-independent projections because they do not

TABLE 7. Native-Dependent PRPB Age and Regional Distributions at Stability of National Female Stable Equivalent Population of the U.S. (r = 0.004360)

	Resident in South		Resident in North	
Age	Born in South (natives)	Born in North (aliens)	Born in North (natives)	Born in South (aliens)
0-4	8.8	1.7	8.2	1.8
5-9	8.3	2.9	7.8	3.0
10-14	7.9	3.8	7.6	3.9
15-19	7.4	5.3	7.3	5.5
20-24	6.9	6.6	7.0	7.3
25-29	6.6	6.9	6.8	8.0
30-34	6.3	6.9	6.6	8.2
35-39	6.1	6.8	6.4	8.1
40-44	5.9	6.7	6.2	8.0
45-49	5.6	6.6	5.9	7.7
50-54	5.4	6.6	5.6	7.3
55-59	5.1	6.8	5.3	6.8
60-64	4.7	7.1	4.8	6.1
65-69	4.3	7.0	4.3	5.3
70-74	3.7	6.2	3.6	4.5
75-79	2.9	5.0	2.8	3.6
80-84	2.0	3.5	1.9	2.5
85+	2.1	3.6	1.9	2.4
Total	100.0	100.0	100.0	100.0
Mean age	36.0	46.8	36.3	43.7
Share	26.9	5.0	63.3	4.7

take into account the higher migration probabilities of return migration. This suggests that disaggregations by place of birth may not lead to significant improvements in the accuracy with which national population *growth* is projected; however, they are important in analyzing projected *redistributions* of national populations.

TABLE 8. Native-Dependent PRPB Projection of Age and Regional Distributions in 1998 of National (1968) Female Population of the U.S.

	Resident in South		*Resident in North*	
Age	*Born in South (natives)*	*Born in North (aliens)*	*Born in North (natives)*	*Born in South (aliens)*
0-4	9.0	1.9	8.7	1.7
5-9	8.7	3.6	8.7	3.0
10-14	8.7	4.8	8.8	3.9
15-19	8.1	6.5	8.1	5.5
20-24	6.9	7.2	7.0	6.7
25-29	5.9	6.6	6.0	6.6
30-34	6.8	9.0	7.7	8.9
35-39	7.3	9.5	8.1	9.7
40-44	6.8	8.7	7.3	9.4
45-49	5.9	7.4	6.0	8.3
50-54	4.8	5.7	4.6	7.3
55-59	4.1	4.8	3.7	6.3
60-64	4.0	5.3	3.7	5.8
65-69	3.7	5.2	3.3	5.1
70-74	3.2	5.0	3.0	4.3
75-79	2.7	4.2	2.5	3.6
80-84	1.7	2.4	1.5	2.0
85+	1.7	2.3	1.4	1.9
Total	100.0	100.0	100.0	100.0
Mean age	34.4	42.6	33.7	43.3
Share	27.8	4.5	62.4	5.3
Annual growth rate	0.0072	0.0123	0.0083	0.0053

Note that in the native-dependent projection the South's share of the national population consistently hovers at the level of 32%, whereas in the native-independent projection it increases slightly over time to an ultimate share of just over 34%. A comparison of the mean ages of natives and aliens suggests that the native-dependent projection generates a slightly *older* native population and a *younger* alien population in each region.

6. CONCLUSION

Multistate population projections disaggregate conventional population projections into a number of state-specific subcategories, such as region of residence, region of birth, and region of previous residence. To the extent that interstate transition probabilities vary with such statuses, disaggregated native-dependent projections should produce more accurate results. This appears to be particularly the case in projections of the allocation of an aggregate population across several status categories. Because in our numerical example it was necessary to assume native-independent fertility and mortality rates, the aggregate growth rate of the population, not surprisingly, was unaffected by the disaggregation. However, it is likely that this would no longer be the case, for example, were disaggregated rural and urban data on fertility used in a projection for a typical developing country.

The fundamental concepts discussed in this paper have been illustrated with a four-state projection model in which two of the states referred to were regions of residence and the other two, regions of birth or regions of previous residence. This disaggregation produced projections of regional populations disaggregated into *natives* and *aliens*. The extension of this projection methodology to a larger number of states is relatively straightforward. For example, we may further disaggregate natives into *stayers*,[1] who have never left the region of birth, and *returners* who have left the region of birth and come back again. Similarly, aliens may be disaggregated into *recent aliens*, aliens who have arrived during the most recent time interval and *established aliens*, who arrived previously.

Finally, both the PRPB and the PRPPR models are exact age models inasmuch as x refers to an exact age and not to an age group. This creates complications that require a decomposition of the normal fertility coefficients in the PRPB model and of the normal survivorship proportions (using separation factors) in the PRPPR model. Considerable simplification may be achieved by adopting an age group model that keeps track of the place of previous residence at age x to x + 4. In such a case, the PRPPR (age group) model becomes a special case of the PRPB model in that an analogous disaggregation between natives and aliens is maintained for ages beyond the specified age groups.[2] Prior to this age group, there is no disaggregation.

[1] *Stayers can only be approximated by assuming that individuals present in a region both at the beginning and end of a unit interval of time did not leave the region during that time period.*

[2] *It should be noted that results for the PRPPR (age group) model cannot be obtained simply by deleting the first several age groups of the PRPB model, because the process of accumulating the alien population starts at a different age.*

APPENDIX A: NATIVE-INDEPENDENT MULTISTATE PROJECTION: BIREGIONAL MODEL

Expressing each set of four age-specific birth rates defined in Eqs. (4) and (5) in the form of a matrix, with the place-of-birth dependence (the subscript on the left-hand side) suppressed by assumption, gives

$$ {}_{s}\underset{\sim}{B}^{s}(x) = {}_{n}\underset{\sim}{B}^{s}(x) = {}_{\cdot}\underset{\sim}{B}^{s}(x) = \begin{bmatrix} b^{s}_{ss}(x) & b^{s}_{ns}(x) \\ b^{s}_{sn}(x) & b^{s}_{nn}(x) \end{bmatrix}, \qquad \text{(A.1)} $$

$$ {}_{s}\underset{\sim}{B}^{n}(x) = {}_{n}\underset{\sim}{B}^{n}(x) = {}_{\cdot}\underset{\sim}{B}^{n}(x) = \begin{bmatrix} b^{n}_{ss}(x) & b^{n}_{ns}(x) \\ b^{n}_{sn}(x) & b^{n}_{nn}(x) \end{bmatrix}, \qquad \text{(A.2)} $$

and setting out the corresponding survivorship proportions[3] as the matrix

$$ {}_{s}\underset{\sim}{S}(x) = {}_{n}\underset{\sim}{S}(x) = {}_{\cdot}\underset{\sim}{S}(x) = \begin{bmatrix} s_{ss}(x) & s_{ns}(x) \\ s_{sn}(x) & s_{nn}(x) \end{bmatrix}, \qquad \text{(A.3)} $$

with the place-of-birth dependence suppressed once again, gives the usual population growth process defined as the matrix multiplication:

$$ \{\underset{\sim}{K}^{(t+1)}\} = \underset{\sim}{G}\{\underset{\sim}{K}^{(t)}\}, \qquad \text{(A.4)} $$

where

[3] *Survivorship proportions are defined in the normal way (Rogers, 1975, p. 79) as*

$$ \underset{\sim}{S}(x) = \underset{\sim}{L}(x+5)\underset{\sim}{L}^{-1}(x). $$

$$\underset{\sim}{G} = \begin{bmatrix} \underset{\sim}{B}(0) & \underset{\sim}{B}(5) & \cdots \\ \underset{\sim}{S}(0) & \underset{\sim}{0} & \cdots \\ \underset{\sim}{0} & \underset{\sim}{S}(5) & \\ \cdot & & \cdot \\ \cdot & & \cdot \\ \cdot & & \cdot \end{bmatrix}, \tag{A.5}$$

$$\underset{\sim}{B}(x) = \begin{bmatrix} \cdot\underset{\sim}{B}^s(x) & \cdot\underset{\sim}{B}^s(x) \\ \cdot\underset{\sim}{B}^n(x) & \cdot\underset{\sim}{B}^n(x) \end{bmatrix}, \quad \underset{\sim}{S}(x) = \begin{bmatrix} \cdot\underset{\sim}{S}(x) & \underset{\sim}{0} \\ \underset{\sim}{0} & \cdot\underset{\sim}{S}(x) \end{bmatrix}, \tag{A.6}$$

and

$$\{\underset{\sim}{K}^{(t)}\} = \begin{bmatrix} \{\underset{\sim}{K}^{(t)}(0)\} \\ \{\underset{\sim}{K}^{(t)}(5)\} \\ \cdot \\ \cdot \\ \cdot \\ \cdot \end{bmatrix}, \quad \{\underset{\sim}{K}^{(t)}(x)\} = \begin{bmatrix} {}_sK_s^{(t)}(x) \\ {}_sK_n^{(t)}(x) \\ {}_nK_s^{(t)}(x) \\ {}_nK_n^{(t)}(x) \end{bmatrix}$$

The extension to the PRPPR model is straightforward. The needed increase of the dimensionality of the matrices gives

$$\underset{\sim}{B}(x) = \begin{bmatrix} b_{ss}(x) & b_{ns}(x) & b_{ss}(x) & b_{ns}(x) \\ 0 & 0 & 0 & 0 \\ 0 & 0 & 0 & 0 \\ b_{sn}(x) & b_{nn}(x) & b_{sn}(x) & b_{nn}(x) \end{bmatrix},$$

$$\underset{\sim}{S}(x) = \begin{bmatrix} s_{ss}(x) & 0 & 0 & s_{ns}(x) \\ 0 & 0 & 0 & 0 \\ 0 & 0 & 0 & 0 \\ s_{sn}(x) & 0 & 0 & s_{nn}(x) \end{bmatrix}. \tag{A.7}$$

The matrix $\underset{\sim}{B}(x)$ is included in the $\underset{\sim}{G}$ matrix defined by Eq. (A.5). This is also the case for the matrix $\underset{\sim}{S}(x)$ for ages before the disaggregation is introduced. Thus if the latter age is 15 in the PRPPR (exact age) model or the age group 10-15 in the PRPPR (age group) model, then $\underset{\sim}{S}(0)$ and $\underset{\sim}{S}(5)$ in $\underset{\sim}{G}$ from (A.5) are as given in (A.7). For the subsequent ages, $\underset{\sim}{S}(x)$ is given by

$$\underset{\sim}{S}(x) = \begin{bmatrix} s_{ss} & s_{ns} & 0 & \beta s_{ns} \\ (1-\alpha)s_{sn} & s_{nn} & 0 & 0 \\ 0 & 0 & s_{ss} & (1-\beta)s_{ns} \\ \alpha s_{sn} & 0 & s_{sn} & s_{nn} \end{bmatrix}, \tag{A.8}$$

where α and β are both greater than zero and less than unity in the projection of age group $(x-5, x)$ with the PRPPR (exact age x) model. In all other cases, $\alpha = \beta = 0$ and $\underset{\sim}{S}(x)$ then is reduced to the $\underset{\sim}{S}(x)$ in (A.6).

The extension to the native-dependent case is straightforward. The subscript on the left-hand side is then no longer suppressed and Eq. (A.6) becomes

$$\underset{\sim}{B}(x) = \begin{bmatrix} {}_s\underset{\sim}{B}^s(x) & {}_n\underset{\sim}{B}^s(x) \\ {}_s\underset{\sim}{B}^n(x) & {}_n\underset{\sim}{B}^n(x) \end{bmatrix}, \quad \underset{\sim}{S}(x) = \begin{bmatrix} {}_s\underset{\sim}{S}(x) & \underset{\sim}{0} \\ \underset{\sim}{0} & {}_n\underset{\sim}{S}(x) \end{bmatrix}. \tag{A.9}$$

APPENDIX B: SEPARATION FACTORS

When the parameters α and β, introduced in Section 4, are unknown they must be approximated. To develop a procedure for this, we first recall the problem of estimating infant mortality, described in Keyfitz (1968, p. 11), who discusses the use of separation factors

$$f_x^z = {}_\delta D_x^z / ({}_\alpha D_x^z + {}_\delta D_x^z) ,$$

where ${}_\alpha D_x^z$ denotes deaths of individuals who passed their xth birthday in the given calendar year (z, z+1), and ${}_\delta D_x^z$ denotes the deaths of those who passed their birthday during the preceding calendar year. The infant mortality problem is put forward: if for x = 0 the above two figures are not available, a value for the separation factor f_0^z can be adopted to divide the sum in its denominator (assumed to be available) into its two component parts.

Applying the separation factor approach to the case of migration instead of deaths, defined in the notation of Fig. 3,

$$\alpha_x^t = ABC/(ABC+BCD)$$

and proceed analogously.

It is likely that α_x^t is more strongly dependent on the age structure than is f_x^z. Consequently, the approximation $\alpha_x^t = 0.5$ is in general not a satisfactory approximation. A better estimate can be derived from the multistate life table. One can make use of the number of years lived in each status by a person of age x. For example, a person at exact age x = 10 in the South will live 4.99568 yr during the next 5 yr, 0.10718 out of which will be lived in the North. At exact age

$x = 15$, the latter quantity is 0.2195. Hence, we obtain the approximation

$$\alpha_{15} = 0.10718/(0.10718+0.2195) = 0.32809 \ .$$

An analogous approximation for β gave the value 0.34329.

REFERENCES

Keyfitz, N. (1968). "Introduction to the Mathematics of Population." Reading, Massachusetts: Addison-Wesley.

Ledent, J. (1981). Constructing multiregional life tables using place-of-birth-specific migration data. *In* "Advances in Multiregional Demography" (A. Rogers, ed.), RR-81-6. Laxenburg, Austria: International Institute for Applied Systems Analysis.

Lee, A. S. (1974). Return migration in the United States. *International Migration Review 8,* 283-300.

Long, L. H., and Hansen, K. A. (1975). Trends in Return Migration to the South. *Demography 12,* 601-614.

Miller, A. R. (1977). Interstate Migrants in the United States: Some social-economic differences by type of move. *Demography 14,* 1-17.

Philipov, D., and Rogers, A. (1981). Multistate population projections. *In* "Advances in Multiregional Demography" (A. Rogers, ed.), RR-81-6. Laxenburg, Austria: International Institute for Applied Systems Analysis.

Rogers, A. (1975). "Introduction to Multiregional Mathematical Demography." New York: Wiley.

Rogers, A., ed. (1980). "Essays in Multistate Demography." RR-80-10. Laxenburg, Austria: International Institute for Applied Systems Analysis, reprinted from a special issue of *Environment and Planning A* XII (May 1980), 5.

Rogers, A., and Castro, L. J. (1976). "Model Multiregional Life Tables and Stable Populations." RR-76-9. Laxenburg, Austria: International Institute for Applied Systems Analysis.

Rogers, A., and Philipov, D. C. (1980). Multiregional methods for subnational population projections. *Sistemi Urbani 2(3)*, 151-170.

Willekens, F., and Rogers, A. (1978). "Spatial Population Analysis: Methods and Computer Programs." RR-78-18. Laxenburg, Austria: International Institute for Applied Systems Analysis.

9

Multiregional Age-Structured Populations with Changing Rates: Weak and Stochastic Ergodic Theorems

Joel E. Cohen

1. INTRODUCTION

A biological population, human or nonhuman, may experience multiple states in two ways.

First, it may visit different states in the course of time, the whole population experiencing the same (possibly age-specific) vital rates at any one time. For example, a troop of baboons moves from one area to another of its range, with associated changes in food supply and risks of predation (Altmann and Altmann, 1970). A human population experiences fluctuating crop yields from one year to the next, with associated effects on childbearing and survival. These are *serial* changes of state of a *homogeneous* population.

Second, the population may be subdivided into *inhomogeneous* subpopulations that experience different states in *parallel*.

ISBN 0-12-435640-0

Individuals may migrate from one state to another in the course of time. The states may correspond to geographical regions, work status, marital status, health status, or other classifications (Rogers, 1980). Individuals within a given state at a given time are assumed to be homogeneous with respect to their vital rates.

The purposes of this chapter are to describe some population models in which serial and parallel inhomogeneity are combined, and to state some ergodic theorems for these models. In demography, ergodic theorems describe long-run behavior that is independent of initial conditions. Weak ergodic theorems assume that the rates that govern a population's evolution themselves follow some deterministic trajectory. Le Bras (1977) gave the first weak ergodic theorem for multiregional age-structured populations. We shall give four weak ergodic theorems that are more general than that of Le Bras. Stochastic ergodic theorems assume that the rates that govern a population's evolution are selected from a set of possible rates by some stochastic process. We shall state a stochastic ergodic theorem that assumes that the rates of birth, death, and migration or other transition are selected by a Markov chain.

2. THE FORMALISM OF MULTIREGIONAL POPULATION MODELS

Following Rogers (1966), we now describe a formalism commonly used for projecting multiregional age-structured pulations. Though we speak of regions and of migration, ap-iate terminology for other states could be substituted.

Let r be the number of regions and k be the number of age classes. A census by age and region Y(t) is an (rk)-vector partitioned into r k-vectors $Y_j(t, \ )$, j = 1,...,r, in which the i-th element $Y_j(t,i)$, i = 1,...,k, is the number of individuals at time t in region j in age class i. X is a set of (rk) × (rk) nonnegative matrices. A typical matrix $\underset{\sim}{x}$ in X is partitioned into r^2 k×k submatrices $\underset{\sim}{x}_{gh}$, g, h = 1, ...,r, one such submatrix for each ordered pair (g,h) of regions.

Censuses are assumed to evolve according to the recursion

$$Y(t+1) = \underset{\sim}{x}(t+1)Y(t), \quad t = 0,1,2,..., \tag{2.1}$$

where $\underset{\sim}{x}(t+1)$ is a matrix chosen from X. If $\underset{\sim}{x}(t+1) = \underset{\sim}{x}$, then the element $\underset{\sim}{x}_{gh}(1,j)$ of the submatrix $\underset{\sim}{x}_{gh}$ is the average number of individuals born from t to t+1, per individual in region h and age class j at time t, who are alive in region g at t+1; g, h = 1,...,r; j = 1,...,k. Also $x_{gh}(j+1,j)$ is the proportion of individuals in age class j and region h at time t who are alive in age class j+1 and region g at time t+1; j = 1,...,k-1. The remaining elements of $\underset{\sim}{x}_{gh}$ are zero.

In the case of two regions, r = 2, and two age classes, k = 2, $\underset{\sim}{x}$ and Y(t) have the form

$$x = \left(\begin{array}{cc|cc} \underset{\sim}{x}_{11}(1,1) & \underset{\sim}{x}_{11}(1,2) & \underset{\sim}{x}_{12}(1,1) & \underset{\sim}{x}_{12}(1,2) \\ \underset{\sim}{x}_{11}(2,1) & 0 & \underset{\sim}{x}_{12}(2,1) & 0 \\ \hline \underset{\sim}{x}_{21}(1,1) & \underset{\sim}{x}_{21}(1,2) & \underset{\sim}{x}_{22}(1,1) & \underset{\sim}{x}_{22}(1,2) \\ \underset{\sim}{x}_{21}(2,1) & 0 & \underset{\sim}{x}_{22}(2,1) & 0 \end{array}\right)$$

$$Y(t) = \left(\begin{array}{c} Y_1(t,1) \\ Y_1(t,2) \\ \hline Y_2(t,1) \\ Y_2(t,2) \end{array}\right).$$

There is a 2 × 2 submatrix of $\tilde{x}$ for each region and the elements within each submatrix refer to age classes. An alternate arrangement of elements by age class is described, e.g., by Willekens and Rogers (1978), following Feeney (1970).

3. WEAK ERGODIC THEOREMS FOR MULTIREGIONAL POPULATION MODELS

We now introduce some concepts needed to state ergodic theorems for multiregional (or multistate) populations.

For any nonnegative vectors u and v of the same length, with elements u_i and v_i, respectively, define the Hilbert projective pseudometric d(u,v) by

$$d(u,v) = \log[\max_{v_i > 0}(u_i/v_i)/\min_{v_j > 0}(u_j/v_j)],$$

if u and v have positive elements in corresponding positions; and by

$$d(u,v) = \infty \text{ if } (u_i = 0 \text{ and } v_i > 0) \text{ or } (u_i > 0 \text{ and } v_i = 0)$$

for some i. Here d measures how nearly the elements of u are proportional to the corresponding elements of v; $d(u,v) = 0$ if and only if $u = cv$ for some scalar $c > 0$. Thus if $Y_1(t)$ and $Y_2(t)$, $t = 0,1,2,\ldots$ are two sequences of positive age censuses, then as $t \to \infty$, $d(Y_1(t), Y_2(t)) \to 0$ if and only if the corresponding distributions of the population by age and region eventually differ by a vanishingly small amount.

We now define four kinds of sets of nonnegative matrices and discuss the relations among them: a contracting set, an exponentially contracting set, a primitive set, and an ergodic set.

A contracting set S (as defined in Cohen, 1979, p. 354) is a set of $n \times n$ matrices ($1 \leq n \leq \infty$) such that if u and v are any two positive n-vectors, then for any $\varepsilon > 0$ there is an integer N (possibly depending on u and v) such that for all $q \geq N$ and for any sequence $x_1, \ldots, x_q, \ldots$ of matrices chosen from S, if $H(1,q) = x_q \ldots x_1$, then $d(H(1,q)u, H(1,q)v) < \varepsilon$.

A contracting set S is an exponentially contracting set (Cohen, 1979, p. 354) if, for any positive n-vectors u and v, there exist positive constants $K < 1$ and D (with D possibly depending on u and v) such that for any products $H(1,t)$ of t arbitrary matrices from S, $d(H(1,t)u, H(1,t)v) \leq DK^t$.

A primitive set S with parameters (n,q), where n and q are positive integers, is a set of $n \times n$ nonnegative matrices such that any product of q factors that are matrices in S is positive (i.e., every element of the product is positive). An ergodic set S (Hajnal, 1976) with parameters (n,q,R) where $R > 0$ is a primitive set with parameters (n,q) such that for any matrix $m \in S$, $\min^+(m)/\max(m) > R > 0$. Here $\min^+(m)$ and $\max(m)$ are the smallest and largest of the positive elements of m.

Every matrix m in an ergodic set must be primitive, that is, have some power that is positive. But not every collection of primitive matrices is an ergodic set. For example, if

$$m_1 = \begin{pmatrix} + & 0 & + \\ + & 0 & 0 \\ 0 & + & 0 \end{pmatrix}, \quad m_2 = \begin{pmatrix} 0 & + & + \\ + & 0 & 0 \\ 0 & + & 0 \end{pmatrix},$$

where the + sign indicates some positive number, both $\tilde{m}_1$ and $\tilde{m}_2$ are primitive matrices in Leslie form. But

$$\tilde{m}_1^2\tilde{m}_2 = \begin{matrix} + & + & + \\ 0 & + & + \\ 0 & + & + \end{matrix}$$

is reducible, so that no matrix of the form $(\tilde{m}_1^2\tilde{m}_2)^n$, $n \geq 0$, is positive or even irreducible. Hence $\{\tilde{m}_1, \tilde{m}_2\}$ is not an ergodic set.

An ergodic set is an exponentially contracting set (Hajnal, 1976). But ergodic sets have a uniform property not necessarily enjoyed by exponentially contracting sets in general. If S is an ergodic set with parameters (n,q,R), then there exist constants $D > 0$ and $K \in (0,1)$ such that for all initial n-vectors u, v, if $u \geq 0$, $v \geq 0$, $u \neq 0$, $v \neq 0$, then $d(H(1,t)u, H(1,t)v) \leq DK^t$, as soon as $t \geq q$. The point here is that D does not depend on the initial u and v. This fact is stated by Golubitsky *et al.* (1975, p. 89) for products of matrices $\tilde{x}$ satisfying $\tilde{A} \leq \tilde{x} \leq \tilde{B}$, where $\tilde{A}$ and $\tilde{B}$ are fixed primitive matrices. Their argument carries over immediately to ergodic sets. In particular, even if $d(u,v) = \infty$, $\tilde{H}^* = H(1,q) > 0$ implies $d(\tilde{H}^*u, \tilde{H}^*v) \leq \sup_{H^*} \max_{g,h,i,j} H^*_{gh}H^*_{ij}/(H^*_{ih}H^*_{gj}) \leq (n/R)^{2q} < \infty$, where the supremum is taken over every possible product $\tilde{H}^*$ of q arbitrary matrices from S.

Exponentially contracting sets need not display such uniformity. For example, the set S containing only the matrix

$$\tilde{x} = \begin{pmatrix} 1 & 0 \\ 1 & \frac{1}{2} \end{pmatrix}$$

is an exponentially contracting, but not ergodic, set. Let $u^T = (0,1)$, $v^T = (1,1)$. Then $\underset{\sim}{x}^t u = (0,2^{-t})^T$ while $\underset{\sim}{x}^t v > 0$ for all t, so $d(\underset{\sim}{x}^t u, \underset{\sim}{x}^t v) = \infty$ for all t. If $u(\varepsilon) = (\varepsilon,1)^T$, then $\underset{\sim}{x}^t u(\varepsilon) = (\varepsilon, \delta+2^{-t})$, where δ can be made arbitrarily small by taking ε small. Consequently, for any fixed t, $d(\underset{\sim}{x}^t u(\varepsilon), \underset{\sim}{x}^t v)$ can be made arbitrarily large by making ε small enough.

An obvious way to assure that D in the upper bound DK^t is independent of the initial vectors u, v is to take initial vectors only from the set $Y(\delta) = \{y > 0;\ \min_i y_i / \max_j y_j \geq \delta\}$. In this case, D depends on δ, not on u, $v \in Y(\delta)$.

Of the four kinds of sets just defined, only ergodic sets and exponentially contracting sets will appear in the following theorems. We still need two more concepts, that of an incidence matrix and that of a state connection matrix.

The incidence matrix $k(\underset{\sim}{A})$ of any matrix $\underset{\sim}{A} = (a_{ij})$ is the matrix whose elements $k_{ij}(\underset{\sim}{A})$ satisfy $k_{ij}(\underset{\sim}{A}) = 1$ if $a_{ij} \neq 0$ and $k_{ij}(\underset{\sim}{A}) = 0$ if $a_{ij} = 0$. Hajnal (1976) observed that if S is a set of square nonnegative matrices $\underset{\sim}{s}$, all of which have a common incidence matrix $\underset{\sim}{k}$ which is primitive, and if $\min^+(\underset{\sim}{s})/\max(\underset{\sim}{s}) > R > 0$ for all $\underset{\sim}{s}$ in S, then S is an ergodic set.

The state connection matrix is a generalization of the incidence matrix.

If $\underset{\sim}{x}$ is a $kr \times kr$ multistate projection matrix, as described earlier, define the state connection matrix $c(\underset{\sim}{x})$ to be the $r \times r$ matrix with $c_{gh}(\underset{\sim}{x}) = 0$ if every element of the $k \times k$ submatrix $\underset{\sim}{x}_{gh}$ of $\underset{\sim}{x}$ is zero, and $c_{gh}(\underset{\sim}{x}) = 1$ if there is at least one positive element in $\underset{\sim}{x}_{gh}$.

We can now state a weak ergodic theorem.

Theorem 3.1. Let X be a set of multiregional projection matrices for r states with k age classes. Suppose that

(i) for every $\underset{\sim}{x} \in X$, $\min^{+}(\underset{\sim}{x})/\max(\underset{\sim}{x}) > R > 0$;

(ii) all matrices $\underset{\sim}{x}$ in X have the same incidence matrix κ;

(iii) each diagonal $k \times k$ submatrix κ_{gg} of κ is primitive, $g = 1,\ldots,r$ and $c(\kappa)$ is irreducible.

Then X is an ergodic set with parameters (kr,q,R), where $q = (r-1)(2k^2-4k+5)$.

Theorem 3.1 goes beyond the weak ergodic theorem of Le Bras (1977). Our assumption (i) is a bound only on the ratios of the positive elements within one matrix. Over the set X matrix elements may be arbitrarily large or small. Le Bras, like Golubitsky *et al.* (1975), assumes fixed upper and lower bounds on the elements of the multistate projection matrices.

Proof of Theorem 3.1. Correcting an assertion of Le Bras (1971), Feeney (1971) proved that if every diagonal submatrix $\underset{\sim}{x}_{gg}$, $g = 1,\ldots,r$, of a multistate projection matrix is primitive and if $c(\underset{\sim}{x})$ is irreducible, then $\underset{\sim}{x}$ is primitive. Therefore, by (iii), the common incidence matrix of every matrix in X is primitive, hence X is an ergodic and exponentially contracting set (Hajnal, 1976).

To derive q, we note that if $\underset{\sim}{A}$ is $n \times n$ and primitive, then $\underset{\sim}{A}^p > 0$ for $p \leq n^2 - 2n+2$ (Berman and Plemmons, 1979, p. 48). Take $p = k^2 - 2k + 2$. If $H(1,p)$ is a product of p arbitrary matrices chosen from X, then the diagonal $k \times k$ submatrices of $H(1,p)$ are positive. Therefore the g,h submatrix of $H(1,p+1)$ has a strictly positive column if $c_{gh}(\kappa) = 1$, so $H(1,p+1+p) = H(1,2p+1)$ has a positive g,h submatrix if

$c_{gh}(\kappa) = 1$. Now since $c_{gg}(\kappa) = 1$, $g = 1,\ldots,r$, $[c(\kappa)]^{r-1} > 0$ (Berman and Plemmons, 1979, p. 27). Since the product of any two positive (sub)matrices of the same size is positive, and since positive elements of $c(\kappa)$ correspond to positive submatrices of $H(1,2p+1)$, we see that every element of $H(1,(r-1)(2p+1))$ is positive. Thus $g = (r-1)(2k^2 - 4k+5)$, as asserted. This proves Theorem 3.1.

Since κ is primitive, by the result of Feeney (1971), we could have immediately written $q = (kr)^2 - 2kr + 2$. However, it is easy to show that if $r > 1$ and $k > 1$, then $(kr)^2 - 2kr + 2 > (r-1)(2k^2 - 4k + 5)$, so the value of q stated in the theorem is preferable. For $r = 4$, $k = 10$, $(kr)^2 - 2kr + 2 = 1522$, whereas $(r-1)(2k^2 - 4k + 5) = 495$.

We now weaken conditions (ii) and (iii) of Theorem 3.1.

Theorem 3.2. Let X be a set of multistate projection matrices for r states with k age classes. Suppose, in addition to (i) of Theorem 3.1, that (ii) for each $g = 1,\ldots,r$, $\{\underset{\sim}{x}_{gg};\ \underset{\sim}{x} \in X\}$ is a primitive set with parameters (k,q_g); (iii) $\{c(\underset{\sim}{x});\ \underset{\sim}{x} \in X\}$ is a primitive set with parameters (r,q_0). Then X is an ergodic set with parameters (kr,q,R) where $q = q_0(1 + 2\max_{g=1,\ldots,r} q_g)$.

Le Bras (1977) assumes that there is a primitive $r \times r$ state connection matrix, call it $\underset{\sim}{a}$, such that if $\underset{\sim}{x}$ is any multistate projection matrix, $\underset{\sim}{a} \leq c(\underset{\sim}{x})$. In Theorem 3.2, we require only that the set of all state connection matrices be an ergodic set. To see that this requirement is weaker, suppose the state connection matrix of a three-regional population at any given time were either $\underset{\sim}{c}_1$ or $\underset{\sim}{c}_2$, where

$$\underset{\sim}{c_1} = \begin{pmatrix} 1 & 1 & 0 \\ 0 & 1 & 1 \\ 1 & 0 & 1 \end{pmatrix}, \quad \underset{\sim}{c_2} = \begin{pmatrix} 1 & 0 & 1 \\ 1 & 1 & 0 \\ 0 & 1 & 1 \end{pmatrix},$$

and that the state connection matrix could change from time to time. The largest matrix that is elementwise less than $\underset{\sim}{c_1}$ and $\underset{\sim}{c_2}$ is $\underset{\sim}{I}$, the 3×3 identity matrix, which is not primitive. Thus the population just described is not covered by the results of Le Bras (1977). But it is readily checked that $\underset{\sim}{c_1^2} > 0$, $\underset{\sim}{c_2^2} > 0$, $\underset{\sim}{c_2}\underset{\sim}{c_1} > 0$, and $\underset{\sim}{c_1}\underset{\sim}{c_2} > 0$, so $\{\underset{\sim}{c_1}, \underset{\sim}{c_2}\}$ is an ergodic set and the population described may be covered by Theorem 3.2.

Proof of Theorem 3.2. Let $Q = \max_{g=1,\ldots,r} q_g$. Then $H(1,Q)$ has strictly positive diagonal $k \times k$ submatrices. Then suppose some matrix $\underset{\sim}{x}^{(a)} \in X$ has $c_{gh}(\underset{\sim}{x}^{(a)}) = 1$. Then in the g,h submatrix of $H(1,Q)\underset{\sim}{x}^{(a)}$ there is at least one positive column. Hence $H(1,Q)\underset{\sim}{x}^{(a)}H'(1,Q)$, where $H'(1,Q)$ is any product of Q matrices from X, chosen independently of the Q factors in $H(1,Q)$, has a positive $k \times k$ submatrix in the g,h position. Thus wherever $c_{gh}(\underset{\sim}{x}^{(a)}) = 1$, there is a positive submatrix in the g,h position of $H(1,Q)\underset{\sim}{x}^{(a)}H'(1,Q) \equiv H_a(1,2Q+1)$, where the subscript a shows that $\underset{\sim}{x}^{(a)}$ is the $(Q+1)$th factor in this product of $2Q + 1$ otherwise arbitrary matrices from X. Now let $\underset{\sim}{x}^{(a)}, \ldots, \underset{\sim}{x}^{(q_0)}$ be any q_0 elements of X and form $H_a(1,2Q+1), \ldots, H_{q_0}(1,2Q+1)$ where the factors other than the $(Q+1)$th are arbitrary. By (iii), $c(\underset{\sim}{x}^{(a)})\ldots c(\underset{\sim}{x}^{(q_0)}) > 0$. Hence $H_a(1,2Q+1)\ldots H_{q_0}(1,2Q+1) > 0$. Since $\underset{\sim}{x}^{(a)}, \ldots, \underset{\sim}{x}^{(q_0)}$ are arbitrary, we have shown that an arbitrary product of $q_0(2Q+1)$ matrices from X is positive. This proves Theorem 3.2.

Condition (ii) of Theorem 3.2 permits an element of a diagonal submatrix of the multistate projection matrices to be

0 at some times and positive at others. For application to real matrices used for multiregional projection, it is desirable to weaken (ii) further.

If the k age classes include post-reproductive ages, then $\underset{\sim}{x}_{gg}$ need not be primitive. Suppose that the last age class with positive effective fertility is the same in every region; call this age class β. Assume positive survival proportions up to age β. Formally, suppose $\underset{\sim}{x}_{gh}(1,\beta) > 0$; $\underset{\sim}{x}_{gh}(1,j) = 0$, $j > \beta$; $\underset{\sim}{x}_{gh}(j+1,j) > 0$, $0 < j < \beta$. Then Ledent (1972) proved that a cogredient permutation of rows and columns can put $\underset{\sim}{x}$ in the form

$$\underset{\sim}{x}' = \begin{pmatrix} M & 0 \\ A & B \end{pmatrix}, \tag{3.1}$$

where $\underset{\sim}{M}$ is $(r\beta) \times (r\beta)$ and $\underset{\sim}{B}$ is $r(k-\beta) \times r(k-\beta)$. The r^2 $\beta \times \beta$ submatrices $\underset{\sim}{M}_{gh}$ of $\underset{\sim}{M}$ are the northwest $\beta \times \beta$ submatrices of $\underset{\sim}{x}_{gh}$. The $(k-\beta) \times \beta$ submatrices $\underset{\sim}{A}_{gh}$ of $\underset{\sim}{A}$ are the southwest $(k-\beta) \times \beta$ submatrices of $\underset{\sim}{x}_{gh}$ and are zero everywhere except possibly for $\underset{\sim}{A}_{gh}(1,\beta) \geq 0$. The $(k-\beta) \times (k-\beta)$ submatrices $\underset{\sim}{B}_{gh}$ of $\underset{\sim}{B}$ are the southeast $(k-\beta) \times (k-\beta)$ submatrices of $\underset{\sim}{x}_{gh}$ and are zero except possibly for $\underset{\sim}{B}_{gh}(j+1,j) \geq 0$, $j = 1,\ldots,k-\beta-1$. The northeast $r\beta \times r(k-\beta)$ submatrix of $\underset{\sim}{x}'$ is zero. Ledent (1972) observed that if $\underset{\sim}{x}$ is a multiregional projection matrix for a real human population, then $\underset{\sim}{M}$ as described may be assumed to have primitive diagonal submatrices $\underset{\sim}{M}_{gg}$ and $c_{ij}(\underset{\sim}{M}) = 1$, $i,j = 1,2,\ldots,r$, so that $\underset{\sim}{M}$ is primitive by Feeney's (1971) result.

Theorem 3.3 generalizes Ledent's (1972) observation to inhomogeneous matrix products.

Theorem 3.3. Let X be a set of multistate projection matrices for r states with k age classes. Each $\underset{\sim}{x} \in X$ can be partitioned into r^2 $k \times k$ submatrices $\underset{\sim}{x}_{gh}$.

(i) Suppose there is an integer β, $1 \leq \beta < k$, such that, for g, h = 1,...,r, each $k \times k$ submatrix $\underset{\sim}{x}_{gh}$ can be partitioned in the form

$$\underset{\sim}{x}_{gh} = \begin{pmatrix} \underset{\sim}{M}_{gh} & \underset{\sim}{0} \\ \underset{\sim}{A}_{gh} & \underset{\sim}{B}_{gh} \end{pmatrix} \tag{3.2}$$

where $\underset{\sim}{M}_{gh}$ is $\beta \times \beta$, $\underset{\sim}{B}_{gh}$ is $\gamma \times \gamma$ with $\beta + \gamma = k$, and the zero matrix $\underset{\sim}{0}$ is $\beta \times \gamma$. Moreover, suppose there exists $R > 0$ such that, for all $\underset{\sim}{x} \in X$ and all g, h = 1,...,r, $\min^+(\underset{\sim}{M}_{gh})/\max(\underset{\sim}{M}_{gh}) > R$.

(ii) Suppose that, for each g, $\{\underset{\sim}{M}_{gg};\ \underset{\sim}{x} \in X\}$ is a primitive set with parameters (β, q_g).

(iii) Let $c^{(\underset{\sim}{M})}_{g,h}(\underset{\sim}{x}) = 1$ if $\underset{\sim}{M}_{gh}$ has at least one positive element and $c^{(\underset{\sim}{M})}_{g,h}(\underset{\sim}{x}) = 0$ if $\underset{\sim}{M}_{gh} = \underset{\sim}{0}_{\beta\times\beta}$, g, h = 1,...,r. Then suppose that $\{c^{(\underset{\sim}{M})}(\underset{\sim}{x});\ \underset{\sim}{x} \in X\}$ is a primitive set with parameters $(r, q_0, 1)$.

(iv) For all g, h = 1,...,r, let $\underset{\sim}{A}_{gh}(1,\beta) > 0$; i.e., the northeast element of every $\underset{\sim}{A}_{gh}$ is positive. The other elements of $\underset{\sim}{A}_{gh}$ may be 0 or positive.

(v) For all g, h = 1,...,r, let $\underset{\sim}{B}_{gh}$ be strictly lower triangular with positive subdiagonal, i.e.,

$\underset{\sim}{B}_{gh}(i,j) = 0$, $i = 1,\ldots,\gamma$; $j = i,\ldots,\gamma$;

$\underset{\sim}{B}_{gh}(i+1,i) > 0$, $i = 1,\ldots,\gamma-1$.

Then X is an exponentially contracting set.

We cannot conclude X is an ergodic set because the northeast $\beta \times \gamma$ corner of every $k \times k$ submatrix will always be 0.

We have not assumed any quantitative restrictions on the elements of $\tilde{A}_{gh}$ and $\tilde{B}_{gh}$. When each submatrix $\tilde{x}_{gh}$ is interpreted as a Leslie matrix, (iv) assumes a positive proportion surviving from age class β to $\beta + 1$, and (v) assumes positive proportions surviving from age class $\beta + 1$ to age class k. These conditions are met by human populations.

Proof of Theorem 3.3. By a cogredient permutation of rows and columns, each $\tilde{x} \in X$ takes the form $\tilde{x}'$ in (3.1) described by Ledent (1972). Then assumptions (ii) and (iii) impose on the set of all matrices that occupy the position of $\tilde{M}$ in (3.1) exactly the same conditions that assumptions (ii) and (iii) of Theorem 3.2 impose on all $\tilde{x} \in X$. Consequently, by Theorem 3.2 $\{\tilde{M}; \tilde{x} \in X\}$ is an ergodic set. If $H'(1,q)$ is the cogrediently permuted form of the product of q arbitrary $\tilde{x}$ X, then the northwest $r\beta \times r\beta$ submatrix of $H'(1,q)$ is positive for $q \geq Q = \max[\gamma, q_0(1+2\max_{g=1,\ldots,r} q_g)]$, again by Theorem 3.2. Also since the product of any γ strictly lower triangular $\gamma \times \gamma$ matrices is $\tilde{0}$, columns $r\beta + 1$, $r\beta + 2, \ldots, rk$ are 0 in $H'(1,q)$ for $q \geq Q$. It remains only to describe what happens to the southwest $r\gamma \times r\beta$ submatrix of $H'(1,q)$, $q \geq Q$, in the position corresponding to $\tilde{A}$ in (3.1). Assumptions (iv) and (v) imply that, as q increases from Q + 1 to Q + γ, the minimum number of positive elements in the βth column of each $\gamma \times \beta$ submatrix of the $r\gamma \times r\beta$ southwest corner of $H'(1,q)$ increases from 1 to γ. Thus as q increases from Q + 1 to Q + γ, each of columns $h\beta$, h = 1,...,r has at least $r, 2r, \ldots, \gamma r$ positive elements. Thus for $q \geq Q + \gamma$, $H'(1,q)$ has at least r positive columns in positions $h\beta$, h = 1,...,r; has 0 everywhere in columns $r\beta + 1, \ldots, rk$; and is strictly positive in the intersection of rows and columns $1, \ldots, r\beta$.

The proof of Theorem 6 of Cohen (1979, p. 362) therefore applies to H(1,q) and $q \geq Q+\gamma$ and shows that X is an exponentially contracting set. This proves Theorem 3.3.

When the states of a multistate projection matrix correspond to geographical regions, to being employed or unemployed, or to being married or unmarried, it is reasonable to suppose that, in the course of time, there is a positive migration from each state to every other state, in age classes prior to the last age of reproduction, as in Theorem 3.3 (iii). But when the states are {without high school diploma; with high school diploma} or {never married; ever married}, some states cannot be reentered, once they are left. Even so, there are conditions on multistate projection matrices sufficient to guarantee that a set of these will be exponentially contracting. For simplicity, we describe here only the special case of r = 2 states.

Theorem 3.4. Let X be a set of $2k \times 2k$ two-state projection matrices with k age classes. Partition each $\underset{\sim}{x} \in X$ into four $k \times k$ submatrices:

$$\underset{\sim}{x} = \begin{pmatrix} \underset{\sim}{x}_{11} & \underset{\sim}{x}_{12} \\ \underset{\sim}{x}_{21} & \underset{\sim}{x}_{22} \end{pmatrix},$$

(i) Let $\{\underset{\sim}{x}_{11};\ \underset{\sim}{x} \in X\}$ be an ergodic set with parameters (k,q_1,R_1). (ii) Let $\underset{\sim}{x}_{12} = \underset{\sim}{0}_{k\times k}$, for all $\underset{\sim}{x} \in X$; there are no transitions from state 2 to state 1.

(iii) Assume there is at least one positive element in each row of $\underset{\sim}{x}_{21}$ for all $\underset{\sim}{x} \in X$. (This means there are positive flows from state 1 to every age class of state 2.) (iv) Suppose there exist constants K_1, K_2, and K_3 such that $0 \leq kK_1 \leq 1$,

$0 < K_2 \leq K_3 < \infty$, and, for all $\underset{\sim}{x} \in X$, (a) $0 \leq \max(\underset{\sim}{x}_{22})\min^+(\underset{\sim}{x}_{11}) \leq K_1$; (b) $K_2 \leq \min^+(\underset{\sim}{x}_{21})/\max(\underset{\sim}{x}_{11})$; (c) $\max(\underset{\sim}{x}_{21})/\min^+(\underset{\sim}{x}_{11}) \leq K_3$. Then K is an exponentially contracting set.

Proof of Theorem 3.4. Theorem 3.4 is just a restatement, in the context of multistate projection matrices, of Theorem 5 of Cohen (1979, p. 359).

In applying Theorem 3.4 to real sets of multistate projection matrices, condition (i) can usually be assured by truncating after the largest age class with positive fertility. Condition (iii) assumes positive transitions from state 1 to every age class of state 2. For states defined in terms of education, employment, or marriage, very young children usually do not change states. If, for example, a 5-yr age class and time unit are used, some newborn individuals will change educational, employment, or marriage status after 20 yr, so all products of four matrices from X will have at least one positive element in each row of $\underset{\sim}{x}_{21}$ corresponding to young ages. Thus X can be replaced by all products of four matrices from X. If adults past a certain age do not change states, these age classes can be truncated, as is commonly done for post-reproductive age classes. Condition (iv,a) requires that the largest survival and effective fertility coefficients in state 2 all be small compared to the smallest coefficients in state 1. Thus the dynamics of state 1 dominate the projection under the conditions assumed in Theorem 3.4.

Le Bras (1977, p. 274) mentions qualitatively the case we consider in Theorem 3.4, but he offers no analysis of it.

None of Theorems 3.1 - 3.4 requires the set X of multistate projection matrices to be finite, or even countably infinite.

4. STOCHASTIC ERGODIC THEOREMS

So far, we have assumed that the sequence $\underset{\sim}{x}(t)$ of multistate projection matrices was chosen by some deterministic mechanism. Now we assume that the sequence $\underset{\sim}{x}(t)$ represents the sample path of a Markov chain. We have chosen a Markov chain as the process governing $\underset{\sim}{x}(t)$ because a Markov chain can represent sequential dependence of $\underset{\sim}{x}(t+1)$ on $\underset{\sim}{x}(t)$, yet is simple enough to be analyzed in detail. Whether the dependence of $\underset{\sim}{x}(t)$ on the past is really Markovian remains to be determined.

We shall proceed naively, without specifying which sets and functions are assumed to be measurable. Readers who recognize the need for such qualifications can supply them from the results already obtained for a single-regional, age-structured population (Cohen, 1977a,b).

We recall some definitions from the theory of finite Markov chains. Following Kemeny and Snell (1960), a Markov chain is ergodic if it is possible to go, directly or indirectly, from any state to any other state. A cyclic or periodic chain is an ergodic chain in which each state can only be entered at certain periodic intervals. A regular chain is an ergodic cha that is not cyclic.

Theorem 4.1. Let X be an exponentially contracting set containing s (s finite) multistate projection matrices $\underset{\sim}{x}^{(1)},\ldots,\underset{\sim}{x}^{(s)}$, each of which is $(kr) \times (kr)$. Let $P[\underset{\sim}{x}(t+1) = \underset{\sim}{x}^{(j)} | \underset{\sim}{x}(t) = \underset{\sim}{x}^{(i)}] = p_{ij}$, $i,j = 1,\ldots,s$, where $\underset{\sim}{P} = (p_{ij})$ is the (primitive) transition probability matrix of a regular Markov chain. Let $Y = \{y;\ y$ is a kr-vector, $y \geq 0$ and $||y|| = 1\}$, where $||y|| = \sum_i |y_i|$. For any kr-vector $Y(0) > 0$, define $Y(t)$ by (2.1) and define $y(t) = Y(t)/||Y(t)|| \in Y$. Then:

(i) The bivariate process $(\tilde{x}(t), y(t))$ is a Markov chain (with uncountably many states) on the state space $X \times Y$. If T is the transition probability function of the bivariate chain $(\tilde{x}(t), y(t))$, that is, $T(\tilde{x}^{(i)}, y, \tilde{x}^{(j)}, B)$ is the probability of a transition from $(\tilde{x}^{(i)}, y)$ into $(\tilde{x}^{(j)}, B)$, then T may be expressed explicitly in terms of $\tilde{P}$ and of matrix multiplication as $T(\tilde{x}^{(i)}, y, \tilde{x}^{(j)}, B) = p_{ij} I_B(\tilde{x}^{(j)} y / ||\tilde{x}^{(j)} y||)$, and for $B \subset Y$, $I_B(y) = 1$ if $y \in B$, $I_B(y) = 0$ if $y \notin B$.

(ii) There is a limiting probability distribution $F(A,B)$ defined on subsets A of X and subsets B of Y such that $\lim_{t\to\infty} P[\tilde{x}(t) \in A, \tilde{y}(t) \in B] = F(A,B)$, independent of initial conditions. F may be calculated numerically by solving the renewal equation

$$F(\tilde{x}^{(j)}, B) = \sum_{i=1}^{s} \int_{y\in Y} F(\tilde{x}^{(i)}, dy)\, T(\tilde{x}^{(i)}, y, \tilde{x}^{(j)}, B) .$$

(iii) Let $Y_\delta = \{y;\ y$ is a kr-vector, $y \geq 0$, and $\min_i y_i / \max_j y_j \geq \delta\}$. If X is an ergodic set, let $\delta = 0$. If X is not an ergodic set (but still is exponentially contracting, as assumed at the outset), fix $0 < \delta < 1$. Then there exist positive constants a (depending on δ and X) and b (depending only on X) such that, for any initial census $Y(0)$ in Y_δ, any initial projection matrix $\tilde{x}^{(i)}$ in X, and any subset B of Y,

$$|P[\tilde{x}(t) = \tilde{x}^{(j)}, y(t) \in B \,|\, \tilde{x}(1) = \tilde{x}^{(i)}, y(0) = Y(0)/||Y(0)||]$$
$$- F(\tilde{x}^{(j)}, B)| < ae^{-bt} .$$

(iv) For a scalar or vector-valued function g with domain $X \times Y$,

$$\lim_{t\to\infty} t^{-1} \sum_{\theta=1}^{t} g(\underset{\sim}{x}(\theta), y(\theta)) = \sum_{i=1}^{s} \int_Y g(\underset{\sim}{x}^{(i)}, y) F(\underset{\sim}{x}^{(i)}, dy)$$

whenever the right side of the equation exists. This means that long-run averages (left side) equal ensemble averages (right side).

(v) There is a constant $\lambda > 0$ such that, for any initial census $Y(0)$ and for almost all sample paths of the $\underset{\sim}{x}(t)$ chain,

$$\log \lambda = \lim_{t\to\infty} t^{-1} \log \|Y(t)\| = \lim_{t\to\infty} t^{-1} E[\log \|Y(t)\|].$$

This $\log \lambda$ is the asymptotic almost-sure growth rate of Furstenberg and Kesten (1960). A formula for calculating $\log \lambda$ is

$$\log \lambda = \sum_{i=1}^{s} \sum_{j=1}^{s} \int_Y \log(\|\underset{\sim}{x}^{(j)} y\|) p_{ij} F(\underset{\sim}{x}^{(i)}, dy).$$

If $c_{(i)}$ is the smallest of the column sums of $\underset{\sim}{x}^{(i)}$ and $c^{(i)}$ is the largest of the column sums of $\underset{\sim}{x}^{(i)}$, then

$$-\infty < \sum_{i=1}^{s} \pi_i \log c_{(i)} \leq \log \lambda \leq \sum_{i=1}^{s} \pi_i \log c^{(i)} < \infty,$$

where

$$\pi_i = \lim_{t\to\infty} P[\underset{\sim}{x}(t) = \underset{\sim}{x}^{(i)}].$$

(vi) There is a constant $\mu \geq \lambda > 0$ such that

$$\log \mu = \lim_{t\to\infty} t^{-1} \log E\|Y(t)\|,$$

where

$$E\|Y(t)\|$$

is just the average (over all sample paths) total population size of the census at time t. Thus μ is the asymptotic growth rate of the average population size, while λ is the average of the growth rates along each sample path. μ is the dominant eigenvalue of the (skr) $\times$ (skr) matrix $P^T \otimes X = \underset{\sim}{M}$, defined as consisting of s^2 submatrices $\underset{\sim}{M}_{ij} = p_{ji}\underset{\sim}{x}^{(i)}$, each of order kr $\times$ kr.

When X contains only a single matrix $\underset{\sim}{x}$, λ and μ are both the dominant eigenvalue of $\underset{\sim}{x}$.

(vii) If X is an ergodic set, then all regions grow asymptotically at the same rate, i.e., for i,j = 1,2,...,kr,

$$\log \mu = \lim_{t\to\infty} t^{-1} \log E(\underset{\sim}{x}_{ij}(t)), \quad \log \lambda = \lim_{t\to\infty} t^{-1} E(\log \underset{\sim}{x}_{ij}(t)).$$

(viii) The asymptotic variance in the logarithm of the increase per unit time in population size is

$$\sigma^2 = \lim_{t\to\infty} (E[\log(\|Y(t+1)\|/\|Y(t)\|)]^2$$

$$-\{E[\log(\|Y(t+1)\|/\|Y(t)\|)]\}^2),$$

where

$$\lim_{t\to\infty} E[\log(\|Y(t+1)\|/\|Y(t)\|)]^2$$

$$= \sum_{i=1}^{s} \sum_{j=1}^{s} \int_Y [\log\|x^{(j)}y\|]^2 p_{ij} F(x^{(i)}, dy)$$

and

$$\lim_{t\to\infty} E[\log(\|Y(t+1)\|/\|Y(t)\|)] = \log \lambda.$$

(Note that σ^2 is *not* the variance of $\lim_{t\to\infty} t^{-1}\log\|Y(t)\|$. For all sample paths, except those belonging to a set of probability 0, $\lim_{t\to\infty} t^{-1}\log\|Y(t)\|$ is the constant $\log \lambda$ and the variance of $\lim_{t\to\infty} t^{-1}\log\|Y(t)\|$ is 0.)

(ix) Let v be a real kr-vector. (If every element of v is 1, $v^TY(t)$ is the total population size at time t. If v^T contains the labor-force participation rates, assumed constant, by age and state, $v^TY(t)$ is the labor force at time t.) Lange and Hargrove (1980) give explicit recursive formulas for computing the right side of

$$\mathrm{var}(v^TY(t)) = (v^T \otimes v^T)[E(Y(t) \otimes Y(t)) - E(Y(t)) \otimes E(Y(t))],$$

where $\otimes$ is the ordinary tensor or Kronecker product. Thus the mean and variance of any homogeneous linear function of the census Y(t) can be calculated at any time t.

The proof of this theorem is so close to the proofs in Cohen (1977a,b) and Lange and Hargrove (1980) that we do not repeat the details. The only significant change is that we have replaced the requirement that X be an ergodic set by the conditions that X be an exponentially contracting set and, in part (iii), $Y(0) \in Y_\delta$.

5. RELATIVE RATES OF CONVERGENCE

Suppose the multiregional projection matrix $\underset{\sim}{x}$ (defined in Section 2) is constant in time and an initial census Y(0) by age and region is not a multiple of the dominant right eigenvector of $\underset{\sim}{x}$. In a numerical example based on Canadian data from 1966 to 1971, using eight regions and 14 age classes, Liaw (1980) found that the age structures within each region moved rapidly toward their stable limits, but that the proportions of the total population found within each region approached their stable limits much more slowly. Liaw interpreted these differences in rates of convergence in terms of the eigenvalues of the multiregional projection matrix.

Keyfitz (1980, p. 620) offered a more intuitive account of the differences in rates of convergence:

> "If a matrix can be rearranged in blocks [corresponding to regions in this example] within which the connectivity is strong but between which the connections are relatively weak, then when it is taken to successively high[er] powers the numbers within blocks will settle down quickly to constant ratios, and only some time after they have done so will the ratios of numbers in different blocks stabilize. The matrix is like a building with a good mixing of air within each room but little circulation between rooms; we can expect that after any disturbance the within-room variation will settle down to the stable form more quickly than the between-room variation."

In inhomogeneous products of multiregional projection matrices, there is no stable limit of age structure within regions *or* of proportions of total population between regions, although there is a stationary probability distribution of these quantities in some stochastic models.

The inhomogeneous analog of the phenomenon described by Liaw (1980) would be this: Let H(1,p) be a product of p matrices chosen from a set X of permissible multiregional projection matrices. Then for two different initial censuses Y(0) and Y'(0) by age and region such that Y(0) is not proportional to Y'(0), the Hilbert distance between a region's age census in H(1,p)Y(0) and the same region's age census in H(1,p)Y'(0) decreases more quickly as p increases than the Hilbert distance decreases between the vector of proportions of total population by region at time p, starting from Y(0), and the vector of proportions of total population by region at time p, starting from Y'(0).

I am not aware of numerical examples of inhomogeneous products of multiregional projection matrices that could test this expectation. Even if it is true, it does not follow from any obvious analysis of eigenvalues, for one reason. If A is a square nonnegative matrix with positive dominant eigenvalue, let R(A) be the ratio of the magnitude of the eigenvalue of A with second largest magnitude to the dominant eigenvalue; thus $R(A) \leq 1$. If one were to use eigenvalues to study the convergence of inhomogeneous products of positive matrices, one would like to have, for any two positive square matrices A and B of the same size, that $R(AB) \leq R(A)R(B)$. Unfortunately, this inequality is not always true. Such a submultiplicative inequality is true, however, for other real-valued functions of matrices that measure how near a matrix is to being of rank 1 (Hajnal, 1976). It seems likely that these "coefficients of ergodicity" could be used to develop a theory of relative rates of convergence of regional age structures and proportions among regions. Until such a theory is developed, the informal account of Keyfitz (1980), quoted above, seems a reasonable guide to what to expect, provided that "higher powers" is replaced by "longer inhomogeneous products."

6. EXTENSIONS AND APPLICATIONS

In this section I review briefly some possible extensions of this multiregional stochastic theorem that have already been worked out in the single-regional case, and then indicate what it would take to put the stochastic model to work with real data.

The Markov chain that governs the succession of multiregional projection matrices could be extended from a finite-state chain to a countably infinite (Cohen, 1976) or uncountably infinite (Cohen, 1977a) chain. The restriction to a time-homogeneous chain could be dropped (Cohen, 1977a,b) at the price of losing an invariant long-run distribution of vital rates and census structure. If the chain is homogeneous, ergodic, and periodic, the distributions of vital rates and census structure converge in Cesaro sums (Lange, 1979). The assumption of a single sex could be replaced by various linear two-sex models (Pollard, 1973, pp. 82-95). Immigration into the multiregional population could be considered (Lange and Hargrove, 1980). The interaction of demographic with exogenous environmental variables could be considered (Land, 1980) to integrate this demographic model into a larger social and economic framework. Although the explicit formulas for calculating long-run growth rates depend on a Markovian assumption, the existence of the long-run growth rates can be proved if a stationary stochastic process, not necessarily Markovian, is assumed to choose successive projection matrices (Lange and Holmes, 1981).

I have already described (Cohen, 1976, pp. 335-336; 1977a, pp. 24-25) how this stochastic model suggests a scheme for the analysis of historical data and for the construction of probabilistically interpretable projections. To estimate the Markov chain, one requires a sequence of observed projection matrices; ten would be a minimum. To reduce the dimensionality of the fertility, mortality, and migration schedules, one would fit curves, based on closed-form or relational models, that are specified by a small number of parameters. One would then fit some Markov process to the time series of estimated parameters. It would be important to test first that a Markovian model is an appropriate description of the time series of parameters, and second that the predictions of fertility, mortality, and migration rates resulting from such a model are better, or at least not worse, than those obtained by current simpler methods Such a comparison of new and old models should use various criteria of performance, because different models might be superior for different purposes. To prepare projections, one requires as a starting point a current census by age and region.

Although only a first-order Markovian model has been studied here as the stochastic process underlying successive projection matrices, it might turn out empirically that a more complex model is required by the data, e.g., a second-order Markov process, or that a simpler model without sequential dependence suffices. Whatever model is used in practice for projections of a given population, it would make sense continually to update both the estimates of the model's parameters and the form of the model according to the sequence of vital rates that actually occurs. The stochastic model used in projection should adapt to successive observations of demographic events.

ACKNOWLEDGMENTS

Jacques Ledent generously guided me to most of the works on multiregional demography cited here. W. Brian Arthur arranged an opportunity to work in and enjoy the hospitality of the Systems and Decision Sciences Area of the International Institute for Applied Systems Analysis, Laxenburg, Austria, where most of this chapter was written. Emmett B. Keeler detected and showed how to fill a gap in one argument in an earlier draft. The work was also partly supported by the U.S. National Science Foundation grant DEB 80-11026.

REFERENCES

Altmann, S. A., and Altmann, J. (1970). "Baboon Ecology: African Field Research." Basel: S. Karger.

Berman, A., and Plemmons, R. J. (1979). "Nonnegative Matrices in the Mathematical Sciences." New York: Academic Press.

Cohen, J. E. (1976). Ergodicity of age structure in populations with Markovian vital rates, I: Countable states. *Journal of the American Statistical Association 71,* 335-339.

Cohen, J. E. (1977a). Ergodicity of age structure in populations with Markovian vital rates, II: General states. *Advances in Applied Probability 9,* 18-37.

Cohen, J. E. (1977b). Ergodicity of age structure in populations with Markovian vital rates, III: Finite-state moments and growth rates; illustration. *Advances in Applied Probability 9,* 462-475.

Cohen, J. E. (1979). Contractive inhomogeneous products of non-negative matrices. *Mathematical Proceedings of the Cambridge Philosophical Society 86,* 351-364.

Feeney, G. M. (1970). Stable age by region distributions. *Demography 6,* 341-348.

Feeney, G. M. (1971). Comment on a proposition of H. Le Bras. *Theoretical Population Biology 2,* 122-123.

Furstenberg, H., and Kesten, H. (1960). Products of random matrices. *Annals of Mathematical Statistics 31,* 457-469.

Golubitsky, M., Keeler, E. B., and Rothschild, M. (1975). Convergence of the age-structure: applications of the projective metric. *Theoretical Population Biology 7,* 84-93.

Hajnal, J. (1976). On products of non-negative matrices. *Mathematical Proceedings of the Cambridge Philosophical Society 79,* 521-530.

Kemeny, J. G., and Snell, J. L. (1960). "Finite Markov Chains." New York: Springer (1976 reprint).

Keyfitz, N. (1980). Multistate demography and its data: A comment. *Environment and Planning A12,* 615-622.

Land, K. C. (1980). Modelling macro social change. "Sociological Methodology" (Karl F. Schuessler, ed.). San Francisco: Jossey-Bass.

Lange, K. (1979). On Cohen's stochastic generalization of the strong ergodic theorem of demography. *Journal of Applied Probability 16,* 496-504.

Lange, K., and Hargrove, J. (1980). Mean and variance of population size assuming Markovian vital rates. *Mathematical Biosciences 52,* 289-301.

Lange, K., and Holmes, W. (1981). Stochastic stable population growth. *Journal of Applied Probability 18,* 325-334.

Le Bras, H. (1971). Équilibre et croissance de populations soumises à des migrations. *Theoretical Population Biology 2,* 100-121.

Le Bras, H. (1977). Une formulation générale de la dynamique des populations. Population, special number: "La mesure des phénomènes demographiques," 261-290.

Ledent, J. P. (1971). On the life table and stable growth of a multiregional population experiencing internal migration. M.S. thesis, Department of Civil Engineering, Northwestern University, Evanston, Illinois.

Liaw, K. L. (1980). Multistate dynamics: The convergence of an age-by-region population system. *Environment and Planning A12,* 589-613.

Pollard, J. H. (1973). "Mathematical Models for the Growth of Human Populations." London: Cambridge University Press.

Rogers, A. (1966). The multiregional growth operator and the stable interregional age structure. *Demography 3,* 537-544.

Rogers, A. (ed.) (1980). Essays in multistate mathematical demography. (Special issue). *Environment and Planning A12(5),* 485-622.

Willekens, F., and Rogers, A. (1978). "Spatial Population Analysis: Methods and Computer Programs." Laxenburg, Autria: International Institute for Applied Systems Analysis RR-78-18.

10

High- and Low-Intensity Model of Mobility

P. Kitsul and Dimiter Philipov

1. INTRODUCTION

The analysis of a population's mobility is often restricted by the unavailability of data. This drawback is frequently overcome by using cross-sectional data to approximate longitudinal patterns, but problems still arise because such data may refer to different periods of time. For example, a model might require transition data over a five-year time period, whereas the available information might only be available from registration statistics for one-year transitions. With these one-year, origin-destination flow table data, an estimation of a five-year time period may be made by assuming that the mobility process is linear--the one-year-flows may be simply multiplied by five and the results entered into the model.

ISBN 0-12-435640-0

Thus the problem of data in the above example is eased by making an assumption. The accuracy of this assumption may be evaluated by a comparison of five-year data that might exist from other sources--census, interviews, etc.--with the results of the analysis based on one-year data. (Problems of data compatibility are, of course, considered first.)

Scientists are well aware that the above assumption is crude and have therefore suggested alternatives. An especially popular hypothesis is that the mobility process is Markovian. Rogers (1965) and Rees (1977) employed Markov chains in analyzing interregional migration; Bartholomew (1973) and Staroverov (1979) used it for a large number of social mobility models; and Blumen *et al.* (1955) incorporated it in the study of the industrial mobility of labor.

Similarly, the Markovian process may be applied to problems arising from incomplete or cross-sectional data. In such a case, let $\underset{\sim}{P}_\tau(t)$ be the matrix of transition probabilities over the time period $(t,t+\tau)$. Then for $\tau = 1$ yr and $\tau = 5$ yr, the Markovian assumption gives

$$\underset{\sim}{P}_5(t) = [\underset{\sim}{P}_1(t)]^5 \ . \tag{1}$$

Such a Markovian model has been found satisfactory in some cases of mobility, as reported by Bartholomew (1973) and Staroverov (1979). Unfortunately, it is not always adequate. Rees (1977) has applied the approach to two sets of data for Great Britain: data from a questionnaire referring to the migration of heads of households and census data of interregional migration. In the first case, the results obtained were satisfactory but in the second analysis, which included ten regions of Great Britain, the calculated rates differed significantly from the observed rates. After a detailed examination of the problem the author concludes that "... a more complex (than the Markovian) process is involved when an interregional framework is employed" (Rees, 1977, p. 262).

In both linear and Markovian models, the population is considered homogeneous with respect to mobility. Heterogeneity was introduced by Blumen *et al.* (1955) into what is now known as the mover-stayer model, which has since been elaborated on by Goodman (1961), Spilerman (1972), Bartholomew (1973), and Boudon (1975).

The mover-stayer model is based on the assumption that a certain part of the population has a zero probability of moving (*stayers*), and the remaining part has a positive probability of moving (*movers*). The formal description is

$$\underset{\sim}{P}_{\tau}(t) = \underset{\sim}{\alpha}\ \underset{\sim}{\pi}_{\tau}(t) + (\underset{\sim}{I}-\underset{\sim}{\alpha}) , \tag{2}$$

where $\underset{\sim}{\pi}_{\tau}(t)$ is the transition matrix of the movers, $\underset{\sim}{I}$ is the identity matrix, and $\underset{\sim}{\alpha}$ is a diagonal matrix of the proportions of the movers in each state at time t.

When the Markovian assumption is applied to the matrix $\underset{\sim}{\pi}_{\tau}(t)$, we have

$$\underset{\sim}{P}_{5}(t) = \underset{\sim}{\alpha}[\underset{\sim}{\pi}_{1}(t)]^{5} + (\underset{\sim}{I}-\underset{\sim}{\alpha}) .$$

It should be noted that the mover-stayer model is Markovian only if $\underset{\sim}{\alpha} = \underset{\sim}{I}$, when it reduces to (1).

Spilerman (1972) considered the extension of the mover-stayer model by developing the suggestion proposed by Blumen *et al.* (1955) to consider a range of intensities of moving.

He postulated that individuals move in accordance to a Poisson process and that the transition matrix would be the same for each transition. In the particular case where the number of transitions for each individual would be described by the same Poisson distribution, the model would be Markovian. A solution was also proposed for the more general case where several types of individuals with different rates of mobility exist. The implementation of this approach, however, demands statistical information that is unavailable in our case.

Boudon (1975), on the other hand, suggests that two homogeneous populations should be considered, both with nonzero probabilities of moving and focuses his work basically on intergenerational occupation tables. The solution of the resulting model is based on the maximum likelihood principle, which causes substantial computational difficulties when dealing with a large number of equations and unknowns.

In this chapter we shall assume, like Boudon, that the population consists of two groups with different intensities of mobility, and a different method of solution will be used.

It is clear from this brief survey that one of the major problems in the construction of mobility models is caused by the incompatibility of different transition time periods. It is obvious also that the problem is not relevant to inaccuracy or incompleteness of data. Rather, the nature of the process of mobility should be studied and more fully understood.

2. THE HIGH- AND LOW-INTENSITY MODEL OF MOBILITY

The inclusion of the time-period effect in a mobility model depends on certain assumptions: linearity, the Markovian property, heterogeneity, etc. The model considered here is based on the following assumptions:

(a) The population subject to mobility consists of two homogeneous groups with no interactions.

(b) The mobility of each group can be described by a Markovian process with different transition probability matrices, $\underset{\sim}{\pi}_\tau(t)$ and $\underset{\sim}{\rho}_\tau(t)$, say.

(c) The Markovian processes defined by $\underset{\sim}{\pi}$ and $\underset{\sim}{\rho}$ are strictly stationary.

The first two assumptions allow us to represent informally the mobility process as a mixture of Markovian processes

$$\underset{\sim}{P}_\tau(t) = \underset{\sim}{\alpha}(t)\underset{\sim}{\pi}_\tau(t) + [\underset{\sim}{I} - \underset{\sim}{\alpha}(t)]\underset{\sim}{\rho}_\tau(t) \ , \tag{3}$$

where $P_\tau(t)$ and $\underset{\sim}{\alpha}(t)$ are defined analogously to the mover-stayer model (2). Here $\underset{\sim}{\alpha}(t)$ depends on time.

The model will be derived formally by making use of the following notation:

H = a set of individuals who are high-intensity movers;

L = a set of individuals who are low-intensity movers.

The sum of H + L gives the total population.

$\{\text{indiv} \in H\}$: Denotes the event that an individual belongs to the group of high-intensity movers.

$\{\text{indiv} \in L\}$: Denotes the event that an individual belongs to the group of low-intensity movers.

$i,j = 1,\ldots,n$: Denote the states.

$\{\text{indiv}_t \in i\}$: Denotes an event that an individual is in state i at time t.

$\alpha = P(\text{indiv} \in H)$: Denotes the probability of $\{\text{indiv} \in H\}$.

$\alpha(t,i) = P(\text{indiv} \in H/\text{indiv}_t \in i)$: Denotes the above probability conditional to the event $\{\text{indiv}_t \in i\}$ and expresses the time dependency of the proportion of high-intensity movers in state i.

According to assumption (c), the elements of the matrices $\underset{\sim}{\pi}$ and $\underset{\sim}{\rho}$ can now be written as $\pi_{ij}(\tau-t)$ and $\rho_{ij}(\tau-t)$ for $\tau > t$. The first element, for example, denotes the probability that an individual from H who is in state i at time t will be in state j at time τ. In the above notation,

$$\pi_{ij}(\tau-t) = P(\text{indiv}_\tau \in j/\text{indiv}_t \in i,\ \text{indiv} \in H), \tag{4}$$

and, analogously,

$$\rho_{ij}(\tau-t) = P(\text{indiv}_\tau \in j/\text{indiv}_t \in i,\ \text{indiv} \in L). \tag{5}$$

These two expressions are used to obtain the transition probability matrix $\underset{\sim}{P}_\tau(t)$ for the total population, whose typical element is $P_{ij}(\tau,t)$:

$$P_{ij}(\tau,t) = P(\text{indiv}_\tau \in j/\text{indiv}_t \in i),$$

$$P_{ij}(\tau,t) = P(\text{indiv} \in H/\text{indiv}_t \in i)\cdot\pi_{ij}(\tau-t)$$

$$+ P(\text{indiv} \in L/\text{indiv}_t \in i)\cdot\rho_{ij}(\tau-t). \tag{6}$$

Equation (6) was obtained by using (4) and (5) and by considering the definition of conditional probabilities

$$P(A/B) = P(AB)/P(B)$$

as well as the law of total probabilities.

Further, by applying Bayes' formula and the law of total probabilities once again, we have

$$\alpha(t,i) = P(\text{indiv} \in H/\text{indiv}_t \in i)$$

$$= \frac{P(\text{indiv} \in H)P(\text{indiv}_t \in i/\text{indiv} \in H)}{P(\text{indiv}_t \in i)}$$

$$= \frac{\alpha \cdot P(\text{indiv}_t \in i/\text{indiv} \in H)}{P(\text{indiv}_t \in i/\text{indiv} \in H) \in P(\text{indiv} \in H) + P(\text{indiv}_t \in i/\text{indiv} \in L) \cdot P(\text{indiv} \in L)}$$

$$= \frac{\alpha}{\alpha + (1-\alpha)\dfrac{P_i^L(t)}{P_i^H(t)}}$$

where $P_i^H(t)$ is the probability that an individual from set H is in state i at time t,

$$P_i^H(t) = P(\text{indiv}_t \in i/\text{indiv} \in H),$$

and $P_i^L(t)$ is analogously defined for the individuals from state L. Note that these two probabilities represent the distribution of the movers among the states at time t in the corresponding groups H and L. The above is immediately followed by

$$P(\text{indiv} \in L/\text{indiv}_t \in i) = 1 - \alpha(t,i) = \frac{1-\alpha}{(1-\alpha) + \alpha\dfrac{P_i^H(t)}{P_i^L(t)}}$$

Taking into account that

$$P_i^H(t) = \sum_{k=1}^{n} \pi_{ki}(t)\ P_k^H(0)$$

and

$$P_i^L(t) = \sum_{k=1}^{n} \rho_{ki}(t)\ P_k^L(0)\ ,$$

the following expression for the transition probabilities $P_{ij}(\tau,t)$ is obtained from (6):

$$P_{ij}(\tau,t) = \frac{\alpha}{\alpha + (1-\alpha)\dfrac{\sum_k \rho_{ki}(t) P_k^L(0)}{\sum_k \pi_{ki}(t) P_k^H(0)}}\ \pi_{ij}(\tau-t)$$
$$+ \frac{1-\alpha}{(1-\alpha) + \alpha\dfrac{\sum_k \pi_{ki}(t) P_k^H(0)}{\sum_k \pi_{ki}(t) P_K^L(0)}}\ \rho_{ij}(\tau-t)\ . \qquad (7)$$

Equation (7) defines the high- and low-intensity model of mobility. Note that the groups H and L have been considered differently according to the probability of moving, but the essence of the difference has not yet been discussed.

The formally derived model (7) differs from its informal version (3) in that the $\underset{\sim}{\alpha}(t)$ are now explicitly given.

3. SOLUTION OF THE MODEL

The formal model (7) is too sophisticated for our purposes, and finding a solution is difficult if only conventional demographic data are available. One must be aware of the difficulties in the estimation of the matrices $\underset{\sim}{\pi}$ and $\underset{\sim}{\rho}$, of the proportion α, and of the initial distributions $P_i^H(0)$ and $P_i^L(0)$, $i = 1,\ldots,n$. Certain assumptions have again to be introduced.

The first assumption should introduce some "natural" hypothesis concerning the general features of the mobility process. For example, the concept of "attractiveness" of states (or regions) is often used because it is intuitively clear. A plausible hypothesis is that the attractiveness of any state does not change over a certain period of time.

For the purposes of modeling, attractiveness of states must be quantitatively expressed. Different measures of attractiveness have been suggested, but they all incorporate the effect of exogenous factors (social, economic, etc.) on mobility. The discussion in this chapter, however, depends on a measure that is dependent only on mobility characteristics. For this, origin-destination mobility rates are used, but they depend on the width of the time period over which the observations are taken. Therefore, intensities (also referred to as a measure, or force, of mobility) are preferred.

In the case of a continuous stationary Markovian model, the transition matrix is represented as

$$\underset{\sim}{P}(\tau) = e^{\underset{\sim}{\mu}\tau} , \tag{8}$$

where $\underset{\sim}{\mu}$ is the matrix of intensities. Its nondiagonal elements may be treated as quantitative measures of attractiveness since intensities do not depend on time. The usage of the intensity of migrating to the construction of multiregional life tables is discussed, for instance, by Keyfitz (1980) and Ledent and Rees (1980).

In this chapter we hold to the hypothesis that the attractiveness of each state remains constant over a certain period of time (say, 5-7 yr) regardless of how this attractiveness is quantitatively expressed. We presume that instantaneous mobility rates are a measure of attractiveness. The following two assumptions are then added to those on p. 519.

(d) The proportion of high-intensity movers $\alpha(t,i)$ are approximately equal for different states i and are constant over a certain interval of time. Then $\alpha(t,i) \doteq \alpha$. Therefore from (7) we have, in matrix form,

$$\underset{\sim}{P}_{\tau}(t) = \alpha\underset{\sim}{\pi}(\tau-t) + (1-\alpha)\underset{\sim}{\rho}(\tau-t). \tag{9}$$

(e) The matrices of intensities $\underset{\sim}{\mu}_{\pi}$ and $\underset{\sim}{\mu}_{\rho}$ that correspond to $\underset{\sim}{\pi}$ and $\underset{\sim}{\rho}$ are proportional:

$$\underset{\sim}{\mu}_{\rho} = k\underset{\sim}{\mu}_{\pi} ,$$

where $k > 0$ is a scalar. Therefore, Eq. (9) can be represented as

$$\underset{\sim}{P}_{\tau}(t) = \alpha \exp[(\tau-t)\underset{\sim}{\mu}_{\pi}] + (1-\alpha)\exp[k(\tau-t)\underset{\sim}{\mu}_{\pi}]. \tag{10}$$

These two assumptions have a transparent demographic interpretation. From the first assumption, it follows that the initial distribution of high-intensity movers is uniform over the states. The second assumption indicates that the attractiveness of any state is independent of the type of movers.

In order to check the assumptions, one needs detailed data, which are usually not available. Nevertheless, it is possible to verify these assumptions at least indirectly.

Recalling the definition of a function of matrices (Gantmacher, 1959, Chapter V), from assumption (e) we find that all the matrices--$\underset{\sim}{\mu}_\rho$, $\underset{\sim}{\mu}_\pi$, $\exp(\underset{\sim}{\mu}_\rho)$, and $\exp(\underset{\sim}{\mu}_\pi)$--are diagonalized by the same transformation, say $\underset{\sim}{T}$. Then the same is true for the matrix $\underset{\sim}{P}_\tau(t)$ whose elements are given in (7), and since $\underset{\sim}{\pi}$ and ρ are Markovian, Eq. (8) applies. Assumption (d) allows the matrix $\underset{\sim}{P}_\tau(t)$ to be diagonalized by the same transformation $\underset{\sim}{T}$ for different values of τ.

The assumptions (d) and (e) can be verified by checking how the matrix $\underset{\sim}{P}_\tau(t)$ is diagonalized for different values of τ. If the diagonalization transformation does not depend on τ, then it can be stated that the assumptions are correct. Obviously a certain degree of approximation has to be admitted.

4. VERIFICATION OF THE MODEL

Two sets of British migration data have been used to test the above assumptions. They will be used also to illustrate the estimation of the unknown parameters. The data from the first set refer to the five-year period from 1966 to 1971 and are taken from Rees (1978). The second set refer to the single year 1970 and are taken from Rees (1979).

Both sets of data are adjusted, where necessary, to refer to 15 age groups of five-year intervals (0-4, 5-9, ..., 70-74, 75+) and to three regional systems: East Anglia, South East, and the rest of Britain.

Let $p_{ij}(\tau,x)$ be the probability that an individual at exact age x in region i will be in region j in τ years. Let $\Sigma_{j=1}^{n} p_{ij}(\tau,x) = 1$, where n = number of regions. The last equation states that the effect of mortality is not accounted for in the estimation of $p_{ij}(\tau,x)$. This assumption is made for convenience, since the matrix of the $p_{ij}(\tau,x)$ is stochastic, hence its properties are easier to describe and understand.

Note that the probabilities $p_{ij}(\tau,x)$ as described here, are linked with the estimated probabilities $\hat{p}_{ij}(1,x)$ from

$$\hat{\underset{\sim}{P}}(x) = [\underset{\sim}{I} + \tfrac{1}{2}\underset{\sim}{M}_1(x)^{-1}[\underset{\sim}{I} - \tfrac{1}{2}\underset{\sim}{M}_1(x)], \tag{11}$$

where $\hat{\underset{\sim}{P}}(x) = [\hat{p}_{ij}(1,x)]$, with the following equality:

$$p_{ij}(1,x) = \frac{\hat{p}_{ij}(1,x)}{1 - \hat{p}_{i\delta}(1,x)}$$

where $\hat{p}_{i\delta}(\tau,x)$ is the probability of dying in region i between ages x and x + τ.[1]

Having in mind that

$$\sum_{j=1}^{n} \hat{p}_{ij}(1,x) + p_{i\delta}(1,x) = 1,$$

obviously

$$\sum_{j=1}^{n} p_{ij}(1,x) = 1.$$

[1] *The matrix formula (11) was introduced by Rogers and Ledent (1976).*

According to (9), the formal description of the age-disaggregated high- and low-intensity model is

$$\underset{\sim}{P}_\tau(x) = \alpha(x)\pi_\tau(x) + [1 - \alpha(x)]\underset{\sim}{\rho}_\tau(x).$$

Using the empirical data, it is necessary to check whether the matrices $\underset{\sim}{P}_1(x)$ and $\underset{\sim}{P}_5(x)$ are diagonalized by the same transformation.

Let the eigenvalues of $\underset{\sim}{P}_1$ be different and n in number.[2] Then the transformation $\underset{\sim}{T}_1$, which diagonalized $\underset{\sim}{P}_1$, is defined by the different n right eigenvectors. Analogously, let $\underset{\sim}{P}_5$ be diagonalized by $\underset{\sim}{T}_5$. By $\underset{\sim}{T}^{-1}$ we denote the inverse of the matrix $\underset{\sim}{T}$. Hence $\underset{\sim}{T}_1^{-1}$ and $\underset{\sim}{T}_5^{-1}$ are constructed by the left eigenvectors of $\underset{\sim}{P}_1$ and $\underset{\sim}{P}_5$, respectively. For more details about diagonalization, see for instance, Bellman (1960), Chiang (1968), and Gantmacher (1959).

Let $\underset{\sim}{T}_1^{-1}\ \underset{\sim}{P}_1\ \underset{\sim}{T}_1 = \text{diag}(\underset{\sim}{P}_1) = \underset{\sim}{\Lambda}_1$, where $\underset{\sim}{\Lambda}_1$ is a diagonal matrix of the eigenvalues of $\underset{\sim}{P}_1$, and correspondingly, let $\text{diag}(\underset{\sim}{P}_5) = \underset{\sim}{\Lambda}_5$. We shall assume further that the transformations $\underset{\sim}{T}_1$ and $\underset{\sim}{T}_5$ are empirically close enough if

$$\hat{\underset{\sim}{P}}_1 = \underset{\sim}{T}_5\ \underset{\sim}{\Lambda}_1\ \underset{\sim}{T}_5^{-1} \doteq \underset{\sim}{P}_1 \tag{12}$$

and

$$\hat{\underset{\sim}{P}}_5 = \underset{\sim}{T}_1\ \underset{\sim}{\Lambda}_5\ \underset{\sim}{T}_1^{-1} \doteq \underset{\sim}{P}_5 \tag{13}$$

are true. The approximations in (12) and (13) provide a measure of the validity of the model proposed here.[3] The authors

[2] *For simplification, the notation of age-groups will be omitted.*

[3] *Some theoretical aspects of this approximation are considered in Appendix A of Kitsul and Philipov (1981).*

consider such a measure to be only an empirical one, i.e., the numerical expressions for $\hat{P}$ and P have to be compared. Such a comparison was made by Kitsul and Philipov (1981). For different age groups, detailed numerical tests of these approximations were presented and for convenience the estimated results (for the age group 15-19 only) are given in the Appendix.

Considering that $T_1 \doteqdot T_5$ in the sense of (12) and (13), the system of equations

$$P_1(x) = \alpha \exp[\mu(x)] + (1-\alpha)\exp[k\mu(x)]$$

$$P_5(x) = \alpha \exp[5\mu(x)] + (1-\alpha)\exp[5k\mu(x)],$$

which is derived from (10), can be transformed into

$$\Lambda_1 = \alpha e^{v} + (1-\alpha)e^{kv},$$
$$\Lambda_5 = \alpha e^{5v} + (1-\alpha)e^{5kv}, \tag{14}$$

where $v = \text{diag}\ \mu = T_1 \mu T_1^{-1}$. Further,

$$\lambda_i(P_1) = \alpha \exp(\nu_i) + (1-\alpha)\exp(k\nu_i), \quad i = 1,\ldots,n$$

$$\lambda_i(P_5) = \alpha \exp(5\nu_i) + (1-\alpha)\exp(5k\nu_i), \quad i = 1,\ldots,n$$

where $\lambda_i(P)$ is the i-th eigenvalue of P, and ν_i is the eigenvalue of v. If the matrices P_1 and P_5 are given, then the above system can be solved with respect to α, k, and ν_i $(i = 1,\ldots,n)$. As an example, consider the two matrices P_1 and P_5 for the age group 15-19 of the three regions of Great Britain considered here. Let the effect of mortality be eliminated, so that the two matrices are stochastic, that is, with row elements summing up to unity. Their numerical expressions then are

$$\underset{\sim}{P}_1 = \begin{bmatrix} 0.96614 & 0.01829 & 0.01556 \\ 0.00220 & 0.98320 & 0.01460 \\ 0.00114 & 0.00997 & 0.98889 \end{bmatrix},$$

and

$$\underset{\sim}{P}_5 = \begin{bmatrix} 0.90131 & 0.05361 & 0.04508 \\ 0.00706 & 0.95184 & 0.04109 \\ 0.00308 & 0.03056 & 0.96635 \end{bmatrix}.$$

The eigenvalues are

$$\lambda_1(\underset{\sim}{P}_1) = 1, \; \lambda_2(\underset{\sim}{P}_1) = 0.96405, \; \lambda_3(\underset{\sim}{P}_1) = 0.97419 \; ,$$

$$\lambda_1(\underset{\sim}{P}_5) = 1, \; \lambda_2(\underset{\sim}{P}_5) = 0.89477, \; \lambda_3(\underset{\sim}{P}_5) = 0.92473 \; .$$

The eigenvalues of each matrix are different, hence the eigenvectors are also different, and they define the diagonalization transformations.

The system (14) now will be

$$\begin{bmatrix} 1.0 & 0 & 0 \\ 0 & 0.96405 & 0 \\ 0 & 0 & 0.97419 \end{bmatrix} = \alpha \exp \begin{bmatrix} 0 & 0 & 0 \\ 0 & \nu_2 & 0 \\ 0 & 0 & \nu_3 \end{bmatrix} + (1-\alpha) \exp k \begin{bmatrix} 0 & 0 & 0 \\ 0 & \nu_2 & 0 \\ 0 & 0 & \nu_3 \end{bmatrix}$$

$$\begin{bmatrix} 1.0 & 0 & 0 \\ 0 & 0.89477 & 0 \\ 0 & 0 & 0.92473 \end{bmatrix} = \alpha \exp 5 \begin{bmatrix} 0 & 0 & 0 \\ 0 & \nu_2 & 0 \\ 0 & 0 & \nu_3 \end{bmatrix} + (1-\alpha) \exp 5k \begin{bmatrix} 0 & 0 & 0 \\ 0 & \nu_2 & 0 \\ 0 & 0 & \nu_3 \end{bmatrix} \qquad (15)$$

For the system (15), a unique value for k was found: 0.01. For this k, $\alpha = 0.0233$, $\nu_2 = -1.6848$, and $\nu_3 = -1.0051$.

The values for α and k allow us to state that a subgroup, which is 2.3% of the total population of Great Britain, aged 15-19, has a mobility intensity 100 times as large as that of the remaining population. Note that this large difference in intensities does not imply the same differences in the probabilities to migrate! Recalling that the matrices $\underset{\sim}{\pi}_1(x)$ and $\underset{\sim}{\rho}_1(x)$ are Markovian,

$$\underset{\sim}{\pi}_1(x) = e^{\underset{\sim}{\mu}} , \tag{16a}$$

and

$$\underset{\sim}{\rho}_1(x) = e^{k\underset{\sim}{\mu}} . \tag{16b}$$

It is possible then, to estimate these matrices and find the numerical expressions for $\underset{\sim}{P}_5(x)$ and $\underset{\sim}{P}_1(x)$.

First note that if $\underset{\sim}{P}_1(x)$ is diagonalized with the tranformation $\underset{\sim}{T}_1(x)$, then $\underset{\sim}{\pi}_1(x)$ and $\underset{\sim}{\rho}_1(x)$ are diagonalized with the same transformation. Thus (16a) yields

$$\mathrm{diag}(\underset{\sim}{\pi}_1) = \underset{\sim}{T}_1^{-1}\ \underset{\sim}{\pi}_1\ \underset{\sim}{T}_1 = \underset{\sim}{T}_1^{-1}\ e^{\underset{\sim}{\mu}}\ \underset{\sim}{T} = e^{\underset{\sim}{V}} ,$$

and similarly from (16b),

$$\mathrm{diag}(\underset{\sim}{\rho}_1) = \underset{\sim}{T}_1^{-1}\ \underset{\sim}{\rho}_1\ \underset{\sim}{T}_1 = e^{k\underset{\sim}{v}} .$$

Then

$$\mathrm{diag}(\underset{\sim}{\pi}_1) = \begin{bmatrix} 1 & 0 & 0 \\ 0 & e^{\nu 2} & 0 \\ 0 & 0 & e^{\nu 3} \end{bmatrix} ,$$

and

$$\operatorname{diag}(\underset{\sim}{\rho}_1) = \begin{bmatrix} 1 & 0 & 0 \\ 0 & e^{k\nu_2} & 0 \\ 0 & 0 & e^{k\nu_3} \end{bmatrix} .$$

From the last two expressions, $\underset{\sim}{\pi}_1$ and $\underset{\sim}{\rho}_1$ can be found by applying the reverse transformations

$$\underset{\sim}{\pi}_1 = \underset{\sim}{T}_1 \operatorname{diag}(\underset{\sim}{\pi}_1)\underset{\sim}{T}_1^{-1} .$$

and

$$\underset{\sim}{\rho}_1 = \underset{\sim}{T}_1 \operatorname{diag}(\underset{\sim}{\rho}_1)\underset{\sim}{T}_1^{-1} .$$

The estimated values for $\underset{\sim}{\pi}_1$ and $\underset{\sim}{\rho}_1$ are

$$\underset{\sim}{\pi}_1 = \begin{bmatrix} 0.23138 & 0.38506 & 0.38366 \\ 0.04575 & 0.58615 & 0.36809 \\ 0.02863 & 0.25083 & 0.72054 \end{bmatrix} ,$$

and

$$\underset{\sim}{\rho}_1 = \begin{bmatrix} 0.98373 & 0.00952 & 0.00675 \\ 0.00116 & 0.99271 & 0.00614 \\ 0.00048 & 0.00421 & 0.99531 \end{bmatrix} .$$

While $\underset{\sim}{\rho}_1$ is structured similarly to $\underset{\sim}{P}_1$, this is not the case with $\underset{\sim}{\pi}_1$. The elements on the main diagonal of $\underset{\sim}{\pi}_1$ reflect the probabilities for the high-intensity movers to remain in the region of origin over a period of one year. These numbers are by far lower than usual. Note that these kinds of probabilities depend substantially on the size of the regional populations, thus explaining the comparatively high out-migration probabilities of the smaller region of East Anglia.

For $(\underset{\sim}{\pi}_1)^5$ and $(\underset{\sim}{\rho}_1)^5$, the following expressions may be derived:

$$(\underset{\sim}{\pi}_1)^5 = \underset{\sim}{T}_1 \operatorname{diag}[(\underset{\sim}{\pi}_1)^5]\underset{\sim}{T}_1^{-1} ,$$

and

$$(\underset{\sim}{\rho}_1)^5 = \underset{\sim}{T}_1 \operatorname{diag}[(\underset{\sim}{\rho}_1)^5]\underset{\sim}{T}_1^{-1} ,$$

where

$$\operatorname{diag}[(\underset{\sim}{\pi}_1)^5] = \begin{bmatrix} 1 & 0 & 0 \\ 0 & e^{5\nu_2} & 0 \\ 0 & 0 & e^{5\nu_3} \end{bmatrix} ,$$

and

$$\operatorname{diag}[(\underset{\sim}{\rho}_1)^5] = \begin{bmatrix} 1 & 0 & 0 \\ 0 & e^{5k\nu_2} & 0 \\ 0 & 0 & e^{5k\nu_3} \end{bmatrix} .$$

The final numerical estimation for $\underset{\sim}{P}_5(x)$ using

$$\underset{\sim}{P}_5(x) = \alpha[\underset{\sim}{\pi}_1(x)]^5 + (1-\alpha)[\underset{\sim}{\rho}_1(x)]^5 , \quad x = 15$$

is

$$\begin{bmatrix} 0.90092 & 0.05367 & 0.04541 \\ 0.00645 & 0.95098 & 0.04257 \\ 0.00332 & 0.02909 & 0.96760 \end{bmatrix} = 0.0233 \begin{bmatrix} 0.04468 & 0.38844 & 0.56692 \\ 0.04450 & 0.38908 & 0.56640 \\ 0.04397 & 0.38425 & 0.57179 \end{bmatrix}$$

$$+ 0.9767 \begin{bmatrix} 0.92142 & 0.04566 & 0.03292 \\ 0.00554 & 0.96443 & 0.03003 \\ 0.00234 & 0.02058 & 0.97707 \end{bmatrix},$$

while

$$\underset{\sim}{P}_1(x) = \alpha \underset{\sim}{\pi}_1(x) + (1-\alpha) \underset{\sim}{\rho}_1(x), \quad x = 15$$

is

$$\begin{bmatrix} 0.96614 & 0.01830 & 0.01556 \\ 0.00220 & 0.98320 & 0.01460 \\ 0.00114 & 0.00997 & 0.98889 \end{bmatrix} = 0.0233 \begin{bmatrix} 0.23138 & 0.38506 & 0.38360 \\ 0.04575 & 0.58615 & 0.36809 \\ 0.02863 & 0.25083 & 0.72054 \end{bmatrix}$$

$$+ 0.9767 \begin{bmatrix} 0.98373 & 0.00952 & 0.00675 \\ 0.00116 & 0.99271 & 0.00614 \\ 0.00048 & 0.00421 & 0.99531 \end{bmatrix}$$

Note that the estimated matrix $\underset{\sim}{P}_5(15)$ is very close to the observed one, while $\underset{\sim}{P}_1(15)$ is exactly the same. It may therefore be concluded that the assumptions are valid since the errors that they introduce are negligible. The same result was proved to hold for all other age groups (Kitsul and Philipov, 1981).

The matrix $[\underset{\sim}{\pi}_1(15)]^5$ deserves special attention in the last numerical equality because its columns have approximately equal numbers. This is a consequence of $\underset{\sim}{\pi}_1$ referring to the group having approximately a 100 times larger mobility intensity than the other group. Since $[\underset{\sim}{\pi}_1]^\tau = \exp(\underset{\sim}{\mu}\tau)$, and $[\underset{\sim}{\rho}_1]^\tau = \exp(k\underset{\sim}{\mu}\tau)$, both processes tend to the same asymptote, but the first approaches it more rapidly.

Therefore, $[\underset{\sim}{\pi}_1]^5$ is very close to the asymptotic distribution denoted by $[\underset{\sim}{\pi}_1]$, say. But $[\underset{\sim}{\pi}_1]^\infty$ defines the stable state of the high-intensity movers, hence, even if this part of the population is not stable in the initial period of time, it will reach spatial stability over a period of 5-10 yr.

5. IMPLEMENTATION OF THE MODEL

The previous two sections set out the mathematical and numerical descriptions of the high- and low-intensity model of mobility. The numerical results verify the assumptions made, thus also verifying the model itself. They were derived, however, on the basis of two sets of data--from one-year and five-year observations--both disaggregated by age.

In order to make use of the model, we must assume that only one set of data is available, and then implement it to obtain approximations for the other set. Since one-year data are usually available from vital statistics in most countries, they will be assumed to be given, but parameters α and k must be specified exogenously. This is in fact the basic point in the implementation of the model.

The estimations from the previous section were repeated for all age groups. It was found that k changed insignificantly while α changed according to a migration schedule. From this starting point, it seems reasonable to search for values for α and k that might refer even to the aggregated-by-age population, say, α_{TOT} and k_{TOT}. Then two approaches are possible: either keep these values constant for all ages or disaggregate them [i.e., k_{TOT} may be kept constant, and α_{TOT} may be used to generate a set $\alpha(x)$ for all x, such that $\alpha(x)$ form a curve similar to that of the observed migration rates and such that the arithmetic mean of $\alpha(x)$ be equal to α_{TOT}].

In either case, values for α_{TOT} and k_{TOT} are sufficient. How these are derived will be discussed later in this section, but now we assume they are somehow available. If so, k_{TOT} and α_{TOT}, or $\alpha(x)$, can be entered in the system used to derive the matrix $\underset{\sim}{v} = \text{diag}\ \underset{\sim}{\mu}$. After that, using equation

$$\underset{\sim}{\Lambda}_5 = \alpha e^{5\underset{\sim}{v}} + (1-\alpha)e^{5k\underset{\sim}{v}}\ , \tag{17}$$

the diagonalized matrix $\underset{\sim}{\Lambda}_5 = \text{diag}(\underset{\sim}{P}_5)$ becomes available. In order to find $\underset{\sim}{P}_5$, it is necessary to have its diagonalizing transformation. But the discussion here suggests that $\underset{\sim}{T}_5 = \underset{\sim}{T}_1$. Hence

$$\underset{\sim}{P}_5 = \underset{\sim}{T}_1\ \underset{\sim}{\Lambda}_5\ \underset{\sim}{T}_1^{-1}\ .$$

What remains unclear is how values for α and k, even for the aggregated-by-age population, could become available. One way to find them is to look at sociological studies; α can be inferred from statements concerning the part of the population that moves most frequently, and k can be inferred from how much larger this frequency is, keeping in mind that k indicate intensity and not probability differences.

Here another, much more preferable way of deriving α and will be discussed. In many countries data are available on interregional migration flows aggregated by age (the migration flow matrix) stemming from censuses or inquiries that are usually held every five or ten years. Since the midperiod multiregional population data are usually available, one can estimate an age-aggregated matrix of the origin-destination migration rates. Let this matrix be denoted by $\underset{\sim}{M}_5(\mathrm{TOT})$. For the three regions of Great Britain, it was estimated as follows:

$$\underset{\sim}{M}_5(\mathrm{TOT}) = \begin{bmatrix} 0.92659 & 0.03618 & 0.03724 \\ 0.00694 & 0.95628 & 0.03678 \\ 0.00267 & 0.01750 & 0.97982 \end{bmatrix} .$$

The same matrix, for a one-year time period is as follows:

$$\underset{\sim}{M}_1(\mathrm{T)T}) = \begin{bmatrix} 0.97494 & 0.01290 & 0.01217 \\ 0.00214 & 0.98606 & 0.01180 \\ 0.00075 & 0.00581 & 0.99344 \end{bmatrix}$$

Note that these matrices have the same structure as those from p. 519. Their eigenvalues are

$$\lambda_1(\underset{\sim}{M}_5) = 1, \quad \lambda_2(\underset{\sim}{M}_5) = 0.91973, \quad \lambda_3(\underset{\sim}{M}_5) = 0.94296 ,$$

$$\lambda_1(\underset{\sim}{M}_1) = 1, \quad \lambda_2(\underset{\sim}{M}_1) = 0.97286, \quad \lambda_3(\underset{\sim}{M}_1) = 0.98159 .$$

Repeating further the procedures from Section 3, one receives the following values for the unknown parameters:

$$\alpha_{TOT} = 0.02198, \quad k_{TOT} = 0.01049 ,$$

$$\nu_2(TOT) = -1.1735, \quad \nu_2(TOT) = -0.7092 .$$

These values will be used to derive the age-specific migration-rate matrices $\underset{\sim}{M}_5(x)$. This can be done in two different ways. First, for each x the value for the parameter α_{TOT} is kept constant. Consider further only the case when $x = 15$. Values for $\nu_2(15)$ and $\nu_3(15)$ may be estimated from $\underset{\sim}{\Lambda}_1 = \alpha \exp[\underset{\sim}{v}(15)] + (1-\alpha)\exp[k\underset{\sim}{v}(15)]$. Recall that $\nu_1(x) = 0$ since $\lambda_1[\underset{\sim}{M}_1(x)] = 1$, and that $\underset{\sim}{M}_1(x)$ is available. Then, values for $\lambda_2[\underset{\sim}{M}_5(15)]$ and $\lambda_3[\underset{\sim}{M}_5(15)]$ are found correspondingly equal to 0.89003 and 0.92254. Thus the diagonalized matrix $\underset{\sim}{\Lambda}_5(15) = \text{diag}[\underset{\sim}{M}_5(15)]$ becomes available, bearing in mind that $\lambda_1[\underset{\sim}{M}_5(15)] = 1$. Then the transformation $\underset{\sim}{T}_1(15)$, which diagonalizes $\underset{\sim}{M}_1(15)$, may be used to obtain

$$\underset{\sim}{M}_5(15) = \underset{\sim}{T}_1(15)\underset{\sim}{\Lambda}_5(15)\underset{\sim}{T}_1^{-1}(15) = \begin{bmatrix} 0.89647 & 0.05640 & 0.04714 \\ 0.00679 & 0.94911 & 0.04411 \\ 0.00343 & 0.03015 & 0.96642 \end{bmatrix} .$$

The second way of deriving the matrices $\underset{\sim}{M}_5(x)$ for all x is to use α_{TOT} and the observed migration schedules to yield values for $\alpha(x)$ for each x. This method of estimation was used but the results obtained were not better than those given by the previous method. The elements of the matrix $\underset{\sim}{M}_5(15)$ received by either method then are rearranged as suggested by Rogers and Ledent (1976) and used to estimate $\underset{\sim}{P}_5(15)$ from

$$\underset{\sim}{P}_5(15) = [\underset{\sim}{I} + \tfrac{1}{2}\underset{\sim}{M}_5(15)]^{-1}[\underset{\sim}{I} - \tfrac{1}{2}\underset{\sim}{M}_5(15)] .$$

Numerical results can be found in Kitsul and Philipov (1981).

6. A POSSIBLE EXTENSION

One of the basic assumptions in the construction of model (7) is that the matrices $\underset{\sim}{\pi}_\tau(t)$ and $\underset{\sim}{\rho}_\tau(t)$ are Markovian. This assumption assures that one of the basic properties of social mobility models will hold--ergodicity. Indeed, as τ tends to infinity in Eq. (10), it becomes obvious that the matrix $\underset{\sim}{P}_\tau(t)$ stabilizes. The ergodicity of Markov chains is used for this.

Another class of stochastic matrices, which is also relevant to the discussion in this paper, has the ergodic property. It is introduced by the following theorem.

Theorem. Let a stochastic matrix of transition probabilities $\underset{\sim}{P}_t$ have the following properties:

(1) It can be diagonalized by a time-independent transformation T.

(2) Its eigenvalues tend to zero with time tending to infinity, but the largest eigenvalue always remains equal to 1.

Then the distribution vector

$$\{X_t\} = \underset{\sim}{P}_t\{X_o\} \tag{18}$$

has a limit

$$\{X_\infty\} = \lim_{t\to\infty}\{X_t\} ,$$

which is independent of the initial distribution $\{X_o\}$.

Proof. Let

$$\underset{\sim}{P}_\infty = \lim_{t\to\infty} \underset{\sim}{P}_t .$$

Then

$$\underset{\sim}{P}_t \underset{\sim}{P}_\infty = \underset{\sim}{T} \operatorname{diag}\{\lambda_t^i\}\underset{\sim}{T}^{-1}\underset{\sim}{T} \operatorname{diag}\{\lambda_\infty^i\}\underset{\sim}{T}^{-1}$$

$$= \underset{\sim}{T} \operatorname{diag}\{\lambda_\infty^i\}\underset{\sim}{T}^{-1} = \underset{\sim}{P}_\infty$$

or

$$\underset{\sim}{P}_t \underset{\sim}{P}_\infty = \underset{\sim}{P}_\infty ,$$

hence

$$\underset{\sim}{P}_t \underset{\sim}{P}_\infty\{X_0\} = \underset{\sim}{P}_\infty\{X_0\} . \tag{19}$$

Consider further the distribution vector (18). Going to the limit when $t \to \infty$ holds,

$$\{X_\infty\} = \underset{\sim}{P}_\infty\{X_0\} . \tag{20}$$

From (19) and (20), we have

$$\underset{\sim}{P}_t\{X_\infty\} = \{X_\infty\} .$$

Thus it is proved that $\{X_\infty\}$ is an eigenvector of $\underset{\sim}{P}_t$ corresponding to the eigenvalue equal to unity. Obviously, $\{X_\infty\}$ depends on the structure of the matrix $\underset{\sim}{P}_t$ but not on the initial distribution $\{X_0\}$.

The high- and low-intensity model can be derived on the basis of matrices $\underset{\sim}{\pi}$ and $\underset{\sim}{\rho}$ that belong to the class defined above. Then the process represented by the resulting matrix $\underset{\sim}{P}$ will be ergodic. This result can be considered as a complement to the weak ergodic theorem used in demography. The latter assures that a stable age distribution, which is independent of the initial one, will be achieved for a wide variety of fertility and mortality rates in the Markovian case. In the single-region case, the result is based on the work of Lopez (1961), and it has been extended to the multiregional case by Kim (1980). The results allow for the application of multiregional stable population theory, developed by Rogers (1975), over a wider class of mobility models than the Markovian.

APPENDIX

This Appendix contains data verifying the assumption that the transition matrices $\underset{\sim}{P}_1(x)$ and $\underset{\sim}{P}_5(x)$ can be diagonalized by the same transformation matrix $\underset{\sim}{T}(x)$ for each age group. The following matrices for the age group 15-19 are compared:

$\underset{\sim}{P}_5$ (five-year observed migration probabilities)

$\hat{\underset{\sim}{P}}_5 = \underset{\sim}{T}_1 \underset{\sim}{\Lambda}_5 \underset{\sim}{T}_1^{-1}$ (five-year estimated migration probabilities)

$\underset{\sim}{P}_1$ (one-year observed migration probabilities)

$\hat{\underset{\sim}{P}}_1 = \underset{\sim}{T}_5 \underset{\sim}{\Lambda}_1 \underset{\sim}{T}_5^{-1}$ (one-year estimated migration probabilities)

Migration probabilities calculated using the Markovian approximation

$$\tilde{\underset{\sim}{P}}_5 = (P_1)^5$$

$$\tilde{\underset{\sim}{P}}_1 = (P_5)^{1/5}$$

are also given (fifth degree and fifth root).

Age group: 15-19

Five-year obs.			Five-year est.		
0.89593	0.05704	0.04704	0.89551	0.05717	0.04733
0.00755	0.94978	0.04267	0.00688	0.94890	0.04421
0.00318	0.03178	0.96504	0.00344	0.03023	0.96634

Fifth degree

0.83971	0.08572	0.07457
0.01030	0.91949	0.07021
0.00548	0.04795	0.94657

One-year obs.			One-year est.		
0.96553	0.01869	0.01578	0.96567	0.01866	0.01566
0.00225	0.98296	0.01479	0.00246	0.98326	0.01427
0.00115	0.01010	0.98874	0.00107	0.01062	0.98831

Fifth root

0.97812	0.01208	0.00981
0.00146	0.98941	0.00913
0.00071	0.00625	0.99305

REFERENCES

Bartholomew, D. (1973). Stochastic Models for Social Processes. Chichester: Wiley.

Bellman, R. (1960). Introduction to Matrix Analysis. New York, Toronto, London: McGraw-Hill.

Blumen, I., Kogan, F., and McCarthy, P. (1955). The Industrial Mobility of Labor as a Probability Process. Cornell Studies of Industry and Labor Relations, 4. Ithaca, New York.

Boudon, R. (1975). A model for the analysis of mobility tables. *In* Quantitative Sociology (H. Blalock, A. Aganbegian, F. Borodkin, Boudon, R. and V. Capecchi, eds.). New York, San Francisco, London: Academic Press.

Chiang, C. (1968). Introduction to Stochastic Processes in Biostatistics. New York: Wiley.

Gantmacher, F. R. (1959). The Theory of Matrices. New York: Chelsea Publishing Company.

Goodman, L. (1961). Statistical methods for the mover-stayer model. *Journal of the American Statistical Association 56,* 841-868.

Keyfitz, N. (1980). Multidimensionality in Population Analysis, RR-80-13. Laxenburg, Austria: International Institute for Applied Systems Analysis. Reprinted from *Sociological Methodology*.

Kim, J. (1980). Multiregional Zero Growth Populations with Changing Rates, WP-80-46. Laxenburg, Austria: International Institute for Applied Systems Analysis.

Kitsul, P. and Philipov, D. (1981). The one-year/five-year migration problem. Pages 1-34 in Advances in Multiregional Demography (A. Rogers, ed.), RR-81-6. Laxenburg, Austria: International Institute for Applied Systems Analysis.

Ledent, J. and Rees, P. (1980). Choices in the Construction of Multiregional Life Tables, WP-80-173. Laxenburg, Austria: International Institute for Applied Systems Analysis.

Lopez, A. (1961). Problems in Stable Population Theory. Princeton Office of Population Research, Princeton University.

Rees, P. H. (1977). The measurement of migration, from census data and other sources. *Environment and Planning A9*, 247-272.

Rees, P. H. (1978). Problems of multiregional analysis: data collection and demographic accounting. Working Paper 221. Leeds: School of Geography, University of Leeds.

Rees, P. H. (1979). Migration and settlement in the United Kingdom, unpublished paper. Leeds: School of Geography, University of Leeds.

Rogers, A. (1965). A Markovian policy of interregional migration. Papers, *Regional Science Association 17,* 205-224.

Rogers, A. (1975). Introduction to Multiregional Mathematical Demography. New York: Wiley.

Rogers, A. and Ledent, J. (1976). Increment-decrement life tables: A comment. *Demography 13(2),* 287-290.

Spilerman, S. (1972). Extensions of the mover-stayer model. *American Journal of Sociology 78(3).*

Staroverov, O. (1979). Population Mobility Models. Nauka, Moscow (in Russian).

11

Increment–Decrement Life Tables and Semi-Markovian Processes from a Sample Path Perspective

Charles J. Mode

Underlying both increment-decrement life table methodology and semi-Markovian processes is the notion of a set of states among which an individual moves over a period of time. The set of states visited by an individual and the sojourn times in these states constitute his sample path. Because sample paths are a primary concern when designing and implementing computer microsimulation models with a view toward coming to grips with the problem of deciphering patterns in data against a background of intrinsic variation or perhaps filling gaps in existing data, when designing macrosimulation models that capture broad trends in populations or when merely thinking about a set of models that may have generated a set of data, stochastic processes based on probability distributions defined directly on sample paths are of basic interest. In the case of microsimulation, distributions defined directly on sample paths suggest algorithms

ISBN 0-12-435640-0

needed to simulate these paths with a computer. For the case of macrosimulation, the sample path approach frequently suggests intuitive arguments for deriving integral and other types of equations satisfied by the summary measures of the process. In large measure, macrosimulation consists of solving these equations numerically. Discussed in this chapter is a class of stochastic processes based on probability distributions defined directly on the sample paths.

The substantive material begins in Section 2 with a discussion of assigning probabilities directly on sample paths through a conditioning scheme. Also discussed in this section is the way this scheme differs from the one used in assigning probabilities for Markov processes in continuous time. Singled out for discussion in section 3 are two types of semi-Markovian processes defined in terms of one-step transition matrices. Several parametric forms of these one-step transition matrices, along with covariates to accommodate population heterogeneity, are discussed in Section 4. In Section 5, connections among one-step transition matrices, multiple decrement life tables, and increment-decrement life table analyses are suggested. Section 6 contains a discussion of the Kolmogorov differential equations and their connection with renewal-type integral equations, a basic analytic tool for semi-Markovian processes. Displayed in Section 7 are the basic renewal type integral equations for the semi-Markovian processes defined in Section 4. Finally, the paper ends with Section 8, containing a discussion of efficient numerical algorithms for repeatedly solving systems of renewal type integral equations, an operation that becomes necessary when studying the implications of a model for social policy.

1. INTRODUCTION

A type of data analysis, referred to as increment-decrement life tables, has received considerable attention in recent years. Used in this type of analysis are data on sporadic episodes of contraceptive use, switching among methods of contraception, partial marriage histories involving one or more partners, and partial migration or perhaps job histories. Among the first to study such data under the title increment-decrement life tables were Schoen and Nelson (1974), Schoen (1975), and Rogers and Ledent (1976). An independent approach to analyzing incomplete longitudinal data, using semi-Markov processes, was reported in Littman and Mode (1977). Used in this analysis were data from the Taichung Medical IUD experiment. Although these data were incomplete in the sense that women were followed only for periods ranging from six to nine years, the observations on sample paths within periods were regarded as complete. In a substantively different but in a conceptually and methodologically similar vein, Wachter *et al.* (1978) have reported on extensive microsimulation experiments, pertaining to a host of questions in European historical demography, in which artificial data on sample paths for entire life spans were analyzed. Among the questions dealt with were the number of ancestors a modern English man had at the time of the Norman conquest and age pyramid variances.

The type of conceptual structure dealt with under increment-decrement life table analysis may be viewed as an extension of both single- and multiple-decrement life tables. In a single-decrement table, an investigator estimates a survival function $S(t)$, the fraction alive at time $t > 0$, who were born at $t = 0$. Either period or incomplete cohort data may be used to estimate $S(t)$ at selected values of t. A natural extension of the survival function, when there is movement among states (tables), is the current state probability $P_{ij}(t)$. Given that a process begins in state i at $t = 0$, $P_{ij}(t)$ is the conditional probability it is in state j at time $t > 0$. Current state probabilities involve multiple transitions among states. One-step transitions out of one state into others involve multiple-decrement life tables.

Various types of techniques based on incomplete data have been used to estimate current state probabilities. However, if it were possible to obtain a complete set of data on the phenomena considered in increment-decrement life tables, a rather simple picture emerges. An investigator considers a finite set of states ℓ, called the state space. In studies of nuptuality, for example, a possible choice for the states of ℓ could be never married, married, separated, and divorced. Now think of a set of individuals who evolve among the states of ℓ over a period of time. Each individual will generate a sample path. At some initial epoch, a particular individual enters state i_0; after a random sojourn time in i_0, he moves to state i_1; and so he continues. A record of the states visited by an individual, along with the sojourn times in each state, is his sample path. A complete data set consists of the sample paths of the individuals in a sample.

In this chapter, connections among ideas underlying increment-decrement life tables and semi-Markovian processes will be discussed from the perspective of defining the basic probabilities underlying a stochastic process on sample paths. Some discussion of this perspective can also be found in Singer and Spilerman (1976).

To be sure, in many cases, complete sample paths of individuals are not observed. Nevertheless, if problems are approached by thinking about basic probabilities on sample paths, a rich framework for formulating and testing hypotheses about data emerges. Moreover, under certain simplifying assumptions, this approach yields systems of renewal-type integral equations that are useful for implementing a class of macrosimulation models on a computer. If increment-decrement life tables are interpreted in a certain way, they also belong to this class of models.

2. DEFINING BASIC PROBABILITIES ON SAMPLE PATHS

As a first step in developing ideas, it will be helpful to set down some notation for sample paths. Let i_ν, $\nu \geq 0$, be states of ℓ in a particular sample path; and, let y_ν be the time taken to go from $i_{\nu-1}$ to i_ν, $\nu \geq 1$. Note y_ν is the sojourn time in $i_{\nu-1}$. The pair $\langle i_\nu, y_\nu \rangle$, describing the ν-th step among states of ℓ, $\nu \geq 1$, will be denoted by ω_ν. Age is an important variable in demography. Consequently, if an individual is of age x when entering an initial state i_0, then we shall write $\omega_0 = \langle i_0, x \rangle$. Sample paths consist of sequences of the form $\omega = \langle \omega_0, \omega_1 \ldots \rangle$. The first n terms in such sequences will be denoted by $\omega^{(n)}$, $n \geq 0$.

At this juncture, it should be pointed out that the approach of defining basic probabilities directly on sample paths differs fundamentally from approaches depending on Markov processes in continuous time. In an approach suggested by Hoem (1972), for example, a pair of random functions $\langle Z(t), U(t) \rangle$ defined for $t \geq 0$ was considered. The function $Z(t)$ indicated the state occupied at time t; $U(t)$ represented the duration of stay in the current state at time t. The basic probabilities underlying the process were

$$P_{ij}(s,t,u,v) = P[Z(t) = j, U(t) \leq v | Z(s) = i, U(s) = u], \quad (2.1)$$

with the following interpretation. Suppose at time $s \geq 0$ an individual is in state i and has been there for u time units. Given this event, $P_{ij}(s,t,u,v)$ is the conditional probability of being in state j at time $t > s$ and his duration of stay in j at t is less than or equal to v time units. By assuming that a Markov property holds not only with respect to states but also in continuous time, it is possible to use the functions in (2.1) to define the joint distributions of the vectors $\langle Z(t_i), U(t_i) \rangle$, $1 \leq i \leq n$, for any $n \geq 1$ and $0 \leq t_1 < t_2 < \ldots < t_n$. Such an approach can lead to theoretically interesting results but tends to obscure what is actually being assumed, explicitly or implicitly, about sample paths, the basic objects when one thinks about data analysis. By assigning the basic probabilities of the process through the abstract probabilities in (2.1), it is also unclear how one would develop computer algorithms for generating realizations of sample paths. Rather than associating risk functions with the abstract probabilities in

(2.1), it also seems preferable to define these functions in terms the distributions defined directly on sample paths.

Defining probabilities directly on sample paths is easy in principle. Suppose the first n-1 steps of a sample path have been observed, $n \geq 1$. Given $\omega^{(n-1)}$, let $P_n(\omega^{(n-1)}; i_n, t)$ be the conditional probability that the next state visited is i_n and the sojourn time in state i_{n-1} was less than or equal to t. For each $n \geq 1$, it is assumed that

$$\sum_{i_n} P_n(\omega^{(n-1)}; i_n, \infty) = 1, \tag{2.2}$$

where $P_n(\omega^{(n-1)}; i_n, \infty) = \lim P_n(\omega^{(n-1)}; i_n, t)$ as $t \to \infty$, and $i_n \in I$.

It will also be useful to interpret these conditional probabilities in terms of pairs of random variables $\langle X_n, Y_n \rangle$, describing the process at the n-th step. The random variable X_n indicates the state entered at the n-th step; Y_n is the sojourn time in state X_{n-1}, $n \geq 1$. The function $P_n(\omega^{n-1)}; i_n, t)$ is the conditional distribution of the pair $\langle X_n, Y_n \rangle$, given the history $\omega^{(n-1)}$ of the process in the first n-1 steps. In symbols,

$$P[X_n = i_n, Y_n \leq t \mid \omega^{(n-1)}] = P_n(\omega^{(n-1)}; i_n, t). \tag{2.3}$$

Relation (2.3) may be used to determine the joint distribution of the pairs $\langle X_{n_\nu}, Y_{n_\nu} \rangle$, $1 \leq \nu \leq k$, for any $k \geq 1$ and integers $1 \leq n_1 < n_2 < \ldots < n_k$. Readers interested in the technical details may consult Tulcea's theorem (see Loève, 1960, p. 137). It is also interesting to observe that once particular forms of the probabilities on the right in (2.3) are given, then, by

Tulcea's theorem, an algorithm for generating realizations of the sample paths in microsimulation experiments is made explicit.

Because the class of stochastic processes under discussion evolve in continuous time, it is of interest to consider a random function $Z(t)$, indicating the state in ℓ an individual occupies at time $t > 0$. Suppose state i_0 is entered at $t = 0$ by an individual of age x. If $t < Y_1$, the time of the first step, then the individual is still in state i_0 at t and $Z(t) = i_0$. The time the second step occurs is $Y_1 + Y_2$. Thus, if $Y_1 \leq t < Y_1 + Y_2$, then $Z(t) = i_1$. By continuing this line of reasoning, it can be seen that after the first step, $Z(t) = j$ if, and only if,

$$X_n = j \quad \text{and} \quad Y_1 + \ldots + Y_n \leq t < Y_1 + \ldots + Y_{n+1}, \tag{2.4}$$

for some $n \geq 1$. The age of our individual at time t is $x + t$.

To make the present general discussion useful from the point of view of thinking about and analyzing data, special cases of the conditional probabilities on the right in (2.3) need to be considered. The general discussion in this section will prove to be informative, however, because it helps clarify assumptions being made about sample paths in special cases.

As the terminology suggests, the above discussion refers to a particular individual in a population. In a homogeneous population, individuals may be viewed as evolving according to the same stochastic process; in a heterogeneous population, individuals or perhaps groups of individuals are viewed as evolving according to different stochastic processes.

3. SEMI-MARKOVIAN PROCESSES

Two special cases of the conditional probabilities on the right in (2.3) will be singled out for discussion in this section. For every pair of states i and j in $\mathcal{I}$, let $A_{ij}(t)$ be nonnegative functions, nondecreasing in t, such that the limits,

$$A_{ij}(\infty) = \lim_{t\uparrow\infty} A_{ij}(t), \tag{3.1}$$

have the property

$$\sum_j A_{ij}(\infty) = 1, \quad j \in \mathcal{I}, \tag{3.2}$$

for every $i \in \mathcal{I}$. Except for the case $A_{ii}(t) = 1$ and $A_{ij}(t) = 0$, $j \neq i$, for $t \geq 0$, i.e., i is an absorbing state, the functions $A_{ij}(t)$ may be defined in terms of nonnegative densities $a_{ij}(t)$ so that

$$A_{ij}(t) = \int_0^t a_{ij}(s)ds. \tag{3.3}$$

Some explicit forms of these functions will be given in the next section. Usually, $a_{ii}(t) = 0$ for all $t \geq 0$ when i is a nonabsorbing state.

A widely studied case arises if it is assumed that for every $n \geq 1$ and sample path $\omega^{(n-1)} = \langle\langle i_0,x\rangle,\langle i_1,y_1\rangle,\ldots,\langle i,y_{n-1}\rangle\rangle$

$$P_n(\omega^{(n-1)};\ j,t) = P[X_n=j, Y_n \leq t \mid X_{n-1}-i] = A_{ij}(t), \tag{3.4}$$

for all $i,j \in \mathcal{I}$. According to assumption (3.4), the conditional probability of going to state j in t or less time units does not depend on the step $n \geq 1$ or the age at which an individual enters state i. Furthermore, the sequence of random variables $\langle X_n \rangle$ is a Markov chain with stationary transition probabilities $\pi_{ij} = A_{ij}(\infty)$. The sequence $\langle Y_n \rangle$ of sojourn times in states are independent random variables. Assumption (3.4) is the basic one underlying the Markov renewal theory considered by Cinlar (1969, 1975). The random function $Z(t)$, $t \geq 0$, indicating the state occupied at time t, is called a semi-Markov process.

Because age is an important variable in demography, it is of interest to extend (3.4) to the case the one-step transition function on the right in (3.4) depends on the age of an individual when entering state i. In the age-dependent case, for each pair of states i and j in I, let the nonnegative function $A_{ij}(x,t)$ be defined for $x \geq 0$ and $t \geq 0$, where x is age at entrance into state i. For each x, the limits $A_{ij}(x,\infty)$ satisfy (3.2). When i is not an absorbing state, it will be supposed that there are nonnegative densities $a_{ij}(x,t)$ such that $A_{ij}(x,t)$ may be expressed in form (3.3).

An interesting case arises when, for each sample path of the form $\omega^{(n-1)}$ considered in (3.4), it is assumed that

$$P_n(\omega^{(n-1)};\ j,t) = P[X_n = j, Y_n \leq t \mid \omega^{(n-1)}]$$

$$= A_{ij}(x+y_1+\ldots+y_{n-1}, t) \qquad (3.5)$$

for all $n \geq 1$. Assumption (3.5) is semi-Markovian in the sense that the sequence $\langle X_n \rangle$ of states visited enjoys the Markov property. But, the sequence $\langle Y_n \rangle$ of sojourn times in states are neither independently distributed nor do they enjoy the Markov property.

Further insights into the nature of assumption (3.5) may be gained if the random variables

$$T_\nu = x + Y_1 + \ldots + Y_\nu, \quad 1 \leq \nu \leq n, \tag{3.6}$$

are considered. Note T_ν is the age an individual enters state i_ν at the ν-th step. According to (3.5), the joint density of the pairs of random variables $\langle X_\nu, Y_\nu \rangle$, $1 \leq i \leq n$, is

$$a_{i_0 i_1}(x, y_1) a_{i_1 i_2}(x+y_1, y_2) \ldots a_{i_{n-1} i_n}(x+y_1+\ldots+y_{n-1}, y_n). \tag{3.7}$$

Therefore, by well-known mathematical procedures, it follows from (3.7) that the joint density of the pairs $\langle X_\nu T_\nu \rangle$, $1 \leq \nu \leq n$, is

$$a_{i_0 i_1}(x, t_1 - x) a_{i_1 i_2}(t_1, t_2 - t_1) \ldots a_{i_{n-1} i_n}(t_{n-1}, t_n - t_{n-1}). \tag{3.8}$$

Observe that the Jacobian of the transformation in (3.6) is one.

From (3.8), it follows that the conditional density of the pair $\langle X_n, T_n \rangle$, given that $\langle X_\nu, T_\nu \rangle = \langle i_\nu, t_\nu \rangle$, $1 \leq \nu \leq n-1$, is $a_{i_{n-1} i_n}(t_{n-1}, t_n - t_{n-1})$. Consequently, the sequence of pairs $\langle X_\nu, T_\nu \rangle$, $\nu \geq 1$, enjoys the Markov property, a property that is useful in deriving both likelihood functions and integral equations. Under assumption (3.5), $Z(t)$, $t \geq 0$, will be called an age-dependent semi-Markov processes.

The two cases just described merely scratch the surface of the many cases embedded in the formulation considered in Section 2. Fragmentary data will usually force an investigator to confine his attention to a few special cases of the functions on the right in (2.3). It is easy to imagine situations, however, in which the probabilistic laws governing the movement of individuals among states depend not only on the number of states visited but also on their ages when entering a state. Furthermore, when viewed from some time origin, these laws may change in time. No attempt will be made here to even outline these more complex cases. Conditioning schemes of the type outlined in Section 2 should, however, be useful in coming to grips with these more complex cases. It should also be mentioned that schemes in which the variable x in $A_{ij}(x,t)$ is vector-valued could be considered.

4. PARAMETRIC FORMS OF ONE-STEP TRANSITION MATRICES, COMPETING RISKS, AND LIKELIHOOD FUNCTIONS

Considered in this section is the problem of designing parametric forms of the functions in the one-step transition matrix $\underline{A}(x,t) = (A_{ij}(x,t))$. Attention will be focused on the age-dependent case, since (3.4) is a special case of condition (3.5). For each $i \in \mathcal{I}$, the functions $A_{ij}(x,t)$, $j \in \mathcal{I}$, may be viewed as a model of competing risks. There exists a considerable literature on competing risks; for example, see David and Moeschberger (1978). In his treatment of the mathematical theory of competing risks, Birnbaum (1979) included some historical material.

The simplest model of competing risks is based on the following notions. Suppose an individual of age x enters state i. Given this event, let $\pi_{ij}(x)$ be the conditional probability of eventually moving to state j. To take the timing of the move into account for every j such that $\pi_{ij}(x) \neq 0$, let

$G_{ij}(x,t)$ be the conditional probability that the move to j occurs during a time interval of length $t > 0$. Then

$$A_{ij}(x,t) = \pi_{ij}(x)G_{ij}(x,t). \tag{4.1}$$

The functions $G_{ij}(x,t)$ are assumed to be proper in the sense that $G_{ij}(x,t) \to 1$ as $t \to \infty$ for every $x \geq 0$. Hence, as $t \to \infty$, $A_{ij}(x,t) \to \pi_{ij}(x) = A_{ij}(x,\infty)$, which satisfies a condition of form (3.2) for every $x \geq 0$. From (4.1), it follows that the conditional distribution of the sojourn time Y_ν in state i, given that $X_{\nu-1} = i$ and $T_{\nu-1} = x$, is

$$P[Y_\nu \leq t | X_{\nu-1}=i, T_{\nu-1}=x] = A_i(x,t) = \sum_j \pi_{ij}(x)G_{ij}(x,t), \quad j \in I, \tag{4.2}$$

for every $\nu \geq 1$.

Various choices of parametric forms are possible. Hennessey (1980), for example, in his study of work histories of the disabled based on data collected by the Social Security Administration, chose the density of the function in (4.1) to be

$$a_{ij}(x,t) = \pi_{ij}(x)g(\alpha_{ij}(x), \beta_{ij}(x);\ t), \tag{4.3}$$

where $g(\alpha,\beta;\ t)$ is the gamma density $g(\alpha,\beta;\ t) = (\beta^\alpha/\Gamma(\alpha))t^{\alpha-1} \exp[-\alpha t]$, $\alpha,\beta,t > 0$. If only the class of unimodel densities on $(0,\infty)$ were being considered, a lognormal density on the right in (4.3) might serve equally well. In Hennessey's study, the parameters in (4.3) were estimated by the method of maximum likelihood based on likelihood functions on the sample paths of individuals. If, in such studies, the sample paths of individuals were observed for short periods of time, serious truncation biases could arise in estimating the probabilities $\pi_{ij}(x)$ in (4.3).

An alternative approach to constructing one-step transition matrices is based on the classical theory of competing risks as suggested by Berman (1963). According to this theory, if an individual of age x enters state i, there are independent latent sojourn times T_{ij} with distribution functions $F_{ij}(x,t)$, $j \neq i$. Associated with these distribution functions are negative latent risk functions $\eta_{ij}(x,t)$ such that

$$F_{ij}(x,t) = 1 - \exp\left[-\int_0^t \eta_{ij}(x,s)ds\right]. \tag{4.4}$$

It is assumed that for every $x \geq 0$, the integral on the right in (4.4) diverges as $t \to \infty$.

The individual is still in state i at age $x + t$ if, and only if, $T_{ij} > t$ for all $i \neq j \in I$. Because latent sojourn times are independent, it follows that the conditional probability that he is still in state i at age $x + t$ is

$$1 - A_i(x,t) = \prod_j (1-F_{ij}(x,t)), \quad i \neq j \in I. \tag{4.5}$$

Given that the individual is still in state i at age $x + s$, $\eta_{ij}(x,s)ds$ is approximately the conditional probability of a transition to state j during a small time interval ds. Integration on s yields the formula

$$A_{ij}(x,t) = \int_0^t (1-A_i(x,s))\eta_{ij}(x,s)ds \tag{4.6}$$

for a one-step transition function with the density

$$a_{ij}(x,t) = (1-A_i(x,t))\eta_{ij}(x,t). \tag{4.7}$$

Formula (4.6) reduces to a simple closed form when there are positive functions $\beta_{ij}(x)$, such that $\eta_{ij}(x,t) = \beta_{ij}(x)$ for all $t \geq 0$. Let $\beta_i(x) = \Sigma_j \beta_{ij}(x)$, $i \neq j$. Then, formula (4.6) becomes

$$A_{ij}(x,t) = \pi_{ij}(x)(1-\exp[-\beta_i(x)t]), \quad t \geq 0, \tag{4.8}$$

where $\pi_{ij}(x) = \beta_{ij}(x)/\beta_i(x)$.

A simple and straightforward way of introducing age dependence is to assume that there are latent risk functions $\theta_{ij}(x)$ governing an individual's transitions among states as a function of his age x. The latent risk function $\eta_{ij}(x,t)$ is then determined by translating the function $\theta_{ij}(x)$. Thus,

$$\eta_{ij}(x,t) = \theta_{ij}(x+t). \tag{4.9}$$

With the latent risk functions specified as in (4.9), formulas (4.4), (4.5), and (4.6) could, in principle, be used to calculate all transition functions in the matrix $\underline{A}(x,t) = (A_{ij}(x,t))$ on some lattice of $\langle x,t \rangle$-points. Singer and Spilerman (1976) have used a notion similar to (4.9) in their discussion of a non-time-stationary Markov model [see their Eq. (4.14)].

When there is heterogeneity in the population, a vector $\underline{z} = \langle z_0, z_1, \ldots, z_n \rangle$ of covariates may be associated with each individual. Usually, $z_0 = 1$. Included in these covariates could be such variables as race, education, and age. In (4.8), for example, the parameters β_{ij} could be thought of as functions of the vector $\underline{z}$. Among the functional forms considered by Coleman (1981), as well as by many other investigators, was the exponential decomposition

$$\beta_{ij}(\underline{z}) = \exp\left[\sum_{\nu=0}^{m} \gamma_{ij\nu} z_\nu\right], \tag{4.10}$$

where the γ's are parameters to be estimated. As we shall see in Section 6, the one-step transition function in (4.8) has a close connection with the time-homogeneous Markov process considered by Coleman.

For those situations in which age is not one of the variables in the vector $\underline{z}$ and (4.9) seems a reasonable assumption regarding its effect, the latent risk function $\eta_{ij}(x,\underline{z};\ t)$, depending on a vector $\underline{z}$ of covariates, could assume the form

$$\eta_{ij}(x,\underline{z};\ t) = \beta_{ij}(\underline{z})\theta_{ij}(x+t), \tag{4.11}$$

where $\beta_{ij}(\underline{z})$ is the exponential decomposition in (4.10). Multiplicative models of the type in (4.11) were discussed in an influential paper by Cox (1972). At least two forms of the θ's could be considered.

A widely used risk function is that of the Weibull type: $\theta(\alpha,\beta;\ t) = \alpha\beta t^{\alpha-1}$, $\alpha,\beta > 0$. This function is decreasing in t if $\alpha < 1$; if $\alpha > 1$, it is increasing in t. Thus, for $\theta_{ij}(t) = \theta(\alpha_{ij},\beta_{ij};\ t)$, either $\alpha_{ij} < 1$ or $\alpha_{ij} > 1$, depending on whether the risk of moving from state i to state j decreases or increases with age. If the state j is death and ages past thirty are considered, then it may be reasonable to use a Gompertzian risk function of the form $\theta(\alpha,\beta;\ t) = \alpha \exp[\beta t]$, $\alpha,\beta > 0$, because there is good empirical evidence that risk of death increases exponentially with age. Evidently, the parameters in these risk functions could be viewed as functions of covariates. This view as yet, however, does not seem to be in wide use.

Many computing laboratories have canned programs for finding the maxima of a function of several variables. The existence of such programs makes the method of maximum likelihood a feasible alternative for estimating parameters in models of the type just described. A sharp conception of the structure of the underlying stochastic process will be necessary to write down an appropriate likelihood function associated with each individual in the sample. Likelihood functions will vary, depending on the state space of the process and the sampling framework. Briefly, for an age-dependent semi-Markov process, suppose the sample path of the ν-th individual has the form $\langle X_j, T_j \rangle = \langle i_j, t_j \rangle$, $1 \leq j \leq n_\nu$. Because these pairs are Markovian, the likelihood function for the ν-th individual will be a product like that in (3.8), with the density depending on a vector $\underline{z}_\nu$ of covariates. Hennessey (1980) has provided examples as to how these products need to be modified for the case when an individual is still in a state when last observed as well as for other cases. Under the assumption of independence, the likelihood function of the sample is the product of the likelihoods for individuals.

5. ONE-STEP TRANSITION MATRICES AND MULTIPLE DECREMENT LIFE TABLES

In many applications, an investigator will not have much information on sample paths of individuals. Just as in the construction of period life tables, he may have to base his calculations on data across age groups during a given period. The principal purpose of this section is to discuss briefly how estimates based on incomplete period information may be connected with the one-step transition matrices discussed in previous sections. Since age at entrance into a state may not be known, only matrices of the form $\underline{A}(t) = (A_{ij}(t))$ for the non-age-dependent case will be considered.

For each nonabsorbing state i, the values of the functions $A_{ij}(t)$, $i \neq j \in I$, at the points $t = t_\nu$, $\nu = 0,1,2,\ldots$, where $0 = t_0 < t_1 < t_2 < \ldots$, could be viewed as a multiple-decrement life table. Let $q_{ij}(t_\nu)$ be the conditional probability of moving to state $j \neq i$ during an age interval $(t_{\nu-1}, t_\nu]$, given that an individual was in state i at age $t_{\nu-1}$. Then

$$q_{ij}(t_\nu) = \frac{A_{ij}(t_\nu) - A_{ij}(t_{\nu-1})}{1 - A_i(t_{\nu-1})} . \tag{5.1}$$

The probabilities in (5.1) are the focus of attention in life table procedures. Estimates $q_{ij}(t_\nu)$ of these probabilities are transformed into estimates of the function in $\underline{A}(t)$, using the following relationships.

Let

$$q_i(t_\nu) = \sum_j q_{ij}(t_\nu), \quad i \neq j \in I, \tag{5.2}$$

and $p_i(t_\nu) = 1 - q_i(t_\nu)$. Define $P_i(t_\nu)$, but putting $P_i(0) = 1$ and $P_i(t_\nu) = p_i(t_1)p_i(t_2) \ldots p_i(t_\nu)$ for $\nu \geq 1$. Then,

$$A_{ij}(t_n) = \sum_{\nu=1}^{n} P_i(t_{\nu-1}) q_{ij}(t_\nu), \tag{5.3}$$

for $n \geq 1$ with $A_{ij}(0) = 0$. An estimate $\hat{A}_{ij}(t)$ of $A_{ij}(t)$ is obtained by substituting $\hat{q}_{ij}(t_\nu)$ for $q_{ij}(t_\nu)$ throughout.

Schoen (1979) described a procedure for estimating life table rates ${}_n^iM_x^j$ (see his Eq. 6) by estimating mean durations in state i when transferring to j during an age interval (x,x+n]. Although Schoen used these estimated rates in connection with a rate matrix that seemed to be associated with a discretized version of the Kolmogorov differential equations, they apparently could have been used to get estimates of the q-probabilities in (5.1) by utilizing actuarial methods for converting rates into probabilities. Consult, for example, formula (10.12) on p. 297 of Elandt-Johnson and Johnson (1980). Specifically, such a procedure would yield an estimate of $q_{ij}(t_\nu)$ with $t_{\nu-1} = x$ and $t_\nu = x + n$ for some $\nu \geq 1$. To avoid inconsistencies, before doing extensive calculations, an investigator should make sure that all estimates of the q-probabilities lie in the interval (0,1) as they should.

The estimation procedure just outlined suffers from a number of limitations. Only two of these limitations will be mentioned. Because period estimates can differ markedly from estimates based on longitudinal sample paths, as is widely recognized, caution should be exercised in making longitudinal interferences for cohorts based on period estimates. A second limitation concerns the width of the age intervals under study in period data. If these intervals are quite wide, say five years, then multiple steps rather than single steps among states may, to some extent, contaminate the data. An investigator will have to exercise some judgment regarding the seriousness of the biases introduced by multiple steps on rates that are interpreted in terms of single steps.

6. THE KOLMOGOROV DIFFERENTIAL EQUATIONS

Several authors have mentioned connections between the Kolmogorov differential equations and increment-decrement life tables. Schoen and Land (1979), for example, make explicit mention of the forward Kolmogorov differential equations in connection with their equation (4.3). Krishnamoorthy (1979) and Keyfitz (1980) also mention differential equations of the Kolmogorov type. Differential equations of this type involve current state probabilities $P_{ij}(t)$, mentioned in the introduction, for a time-homogeneous Markov process on a finite state space I.

Unlike those processes discussed in previous sections, whose finite-dimensional distributions were determined by conditional distributions on sample paths, finite-dimensional distributions for a time-homogeneous Markov process, $Z(t)$, $t \geq 0$, are determined by the current state probabilities $P_{ij}(t), i,j \in I$, $t \geq 0$. Thus, for any $n \geq 1$, states $i_0, i_1, \ldots, i_n$, and times such that $0 \leq t_0 < t_. \ldots < t_n$, the conditional probability that $Z(t_\nu) = i_\nu$, $1 \leq \nu \leq n$, given that $Z(t_0) = i_0$, is assumed to be

$$P[Z(t_\nu) = i_\nu, 1 \leq \nu \leq n \mid Z(t_0) = i_0] = \prod_{\nu=1}^{n} P_{i_{\nu-1} i_\nu}(t_\nu - t_{\nu-1}). \tag{6.1}$$

Singer and Cohen (1980) have presented a strategy for deciding whether longitudinal data could have been generated by a time-homogeneous Markov process or a mixture of such processes. Works of this type are of basic importance, because they address the question of whether such processes are plausible models for interpreting and understanding a set of data.

The matrix $\underline{P}'(0) = (P'_{ij}(0)) = (q_{ij}) = \underline{Q}$ of derivatives at $t = 0$ plays an important role in the theory of time-homogeneous Markov processes. For $j \neq i$, $q_{ij} \geq 0$, $q_{ii} \leq 0$, and

$$-q_{ii} = q_i = \sum_j q_{ij}, \quad j \neq i. \tag{6.2}$$

Probabilists have investigated the implications of assumption (6.1) on the distributions of sojourn times in states. As Doob (1953, Chapter VI) and other probabilists have shown, assumption (6.1) implies that sojourn times in states are distributed independently according to exponential distributions with parameters depending only on the states. The parameter for state i is the q_i defined in Eq. (6.2). Furthermore, the conditional probability of moving from state i to state $j \neq i$ is $\pi_{ij} = q_{ij}/q_i$, $q_i \neq 0$. Consequently, a time-homogeneous Markov process is probabilistically equivalent to a semi-Markov process whose one-step transition matrix $\underline{A}(t) = (A_{ij}(t))$ in (3.4) is determined by

$$A_{ij}(t) = \pi_{ij}(1-\exp[-q_i t]), \tag{6.3}$$

where $t \geq 0$, $\pi_{ii} = 0$, and $i,j \in I$. It is interesting to note that (6.3) is equivalent to (4.8) when the parameters $\beta_{ij}(x)$ do not depend on x.

In increment-decrement life table analysis, estimates of rates are frequently interpreted as estimates of the elements in the rate matrix $\underline{Q}$ (see Krishnamoorthy, 1979; Schoen, 1979). Given the matrix $\underline{Q}$, the Kolmogorov differential equations provide a means for expressing the matrix $\underline{P}(t) = (P_{ij}(t))$ of current state probabilities in terms of $\underline{Q}$. Accounts of these differential equations may be found in well-known books (e.g., Feller, 1968). In the present notation, the Kolmogorov differential equations are

$$P'_{ij}(t) = -q_i P_{ij}(t) + \sum_{\nu \neq i} q_i \pi_{i\nu} P_{\nu j}(t) \tag{6.4}$$

and

$$P'_{ij}(t) = -P_{ij}(t) q_j + \sum_{\nu \neq j} P_{i\nu}(t) q_\nu \pi_{\nu j}, \tag{6.5}$$

for $t > 0$, where $P_{ij}(0) = \delta_{ij}$, the Kronecker delta. Equation (6.4) is easy to work with from a sample path perspective; it is known as the backward equation. The forward equation (6.5) is the one frequently used in increment-decrement life-table analysis. Equations (6.4) and (6.5) have the exponential matrix $\underline{P}(t) = \exp[\underline{Q}t] = (P_{ij}(t))$, $t \geq 0$, as their common solution.

Backward equations (6.4) are more informative from the sample path perspective if they are converted into integral equations. By multiplying by the integrating factor $\exp[q_i t]$, Eq. (6.4) may be transformed into the system of integral equations:

$$P_{ij}(t) = \delta_{ij} \exp(-q_i t) + \sum_{\nu \neq i} \int_0^t q_i \exp(-q_i s) \pi_{i\nu} P_{\nu j}(t-s) ds, \tag{6.6}$$

for $t \geq 0$. Equation (6.6) exhibits $P_{ij}(t)$ as the sum of the probabilities of two complementary events, given that state i is entered at $t = 0$. One event occurs if at time $t > 0$ an individual is still in state i. If $i = j$, the probability of this event is $\exp[-q_i t]$; if $i \neq j$, this event has probability zero. Hence, the term $\delta_{ij}\exp[-q_i t]$ on the right in (6.6).

A second event occurs when an individual leaves the initial state i at least once during $(0,t]$, $t > 0$. Recall that $q_i \exp[-q_i t]$ is the probability density function (pdf) of an exponential distribution with parameter q_i. Therefore, viewed from the perspective of being in state i at time $t = 0$, $q_i \exp[-q_i s]ds$ is approximately the probability of leaving state i during a small time interval ds. Given that the process leaves i, $\pi_{i\nu}$ is the conditional probability of moving eventually to state $\nu \neq i$. Having entered state ν at time s, $P_{\nu j}(t-s)$ is the conditional probability of being in state j at time t. Integrating on s and summing over $\nu \neq i$ yields the second term on the right in (6.6). Adding the probabilities of the two complementary events yields Eq. (6.6), which is valid for all i and j.

Equations of type (6.6) are known as renewal-type integral equations. Discussions like that in the two preceding paragraphs are referred to as renewal arguments. Renewal-type integral equations have been used extensively in multitype branching processes (Mode, 1971); related equations have also arisen in multidimensional mathematical demography (Rogers, 1975; Rogers and Willekens, 1978).

7. INTEGRAL EQUATIONS FOR AGE-DEPENDENT SEMI-MARKOV PROCESSES

Renewal-type arguments of the type used in the discussion of Eq. (6.6) can easily be extended to derive integral equations for current state probabilities of an age-dependent semi-Markov process, see Section 3. Suppose the finite state space I is partitioned into a set I_1 of absorbing states and a set I_2 of communicating transient states. In the model of work histories of the disabled considered by Hennessey (1980), for example, I consisted of four states. The states E_1 (recovered) and E_2 (diseased) were absorbing; while the states E_3 (not working, receiving benefits) and E_4 (working, receiving benefits) were communicating transient states.

Let $(A_{ij}(x,t))$ be the one-step transition matrix of an age-dependent semi-Markov process. Current state probabilities for an age-dependent semi-Markov process are defined as follows. Suppose that at epoch $t = 0$, an individual of age x enters state i. Given this event, let $P_{ij}(x,t)$ be the conditional probability that he is in state j at epoch $t > 0$. At epoch $t > 0$, our individual is age $x + t$.

Two cases need to be considered in deriving integral equations for $P_{ij}(x,t)$, $i,j \in I$. Consider first the case where i and j are transient states in I_2. If an individual of age x enters state i at epoch $t = 0$, then $1 - A_i(x,t)$ is the conditional probability that he is still in state i at epoch $t > 0$. The other possibility is that he moves to another transient state on the first step sometime during the time interval $(0,t]$, $t > 0$. Because the sequence of pairs $\langle X_\nu, T_\nu \rangle$, $\nu \geq 1$, representing the states visited and the ages at entrance into these states, enjoys the Markov property, a renewal argument yields the integral equation

$$P_{ij}(x,t) = \delta_{ij}(1-A_i(x,t)) + \sum_{\nu} \int_0^t a_{i\nu}(x,s)P_{\nu j}(x+s,t-s)ds, \quad (7.1)$$

where $i \neq \nu \in I_2$.

Considered next is the case $i \in I_2$, a transient state, and $j \in I_1$, an absorbing state. The conditional probability that our individual moves to absorbing state j on the first step sometime during the time interval (0,t] is $A_{ij}(x,t)$. The other possibility is that he moves to some transient state on the first step sometime during (0,t], $t > 0$. Another renewal argument yields the integral equation

$$P_{ij}(x,t) = A_{ij}(x,t) + \sum_{\nu} \int_0^t a_{i\nu}(x,s)P_{\nu j}(x+s,t-s)ds, \qquad (7.2)$$

where $i \neq \nu \in I_2$.

Equations (7.1) and (7.2) will be useful only if efficient numerical algorithms for solving them can be found and implemented on a computer. Efficient algorithms would be particularly important if the a-densities in (7.1) and (7.2) depended on a vector $\underline{z}$ of covariates, making it necessary to solve these equations repeatedly for different values of $\underline{z}$ relevant to policy considerations.

8. NUMERICAL ALGORITHMS FOR SOLVING RENEWAL-TYPE EQUATIONS

When Eq. (7.1) and (7.2) are viewed on continuous time, solving them appears quite formidable. As we shall see, however, their discrete time analogues can be managed numerically. Throughout this section, both the variables x and t will vary over some discrete time points 0,1,2,..., representing a scale of interest. Because individuals do not leave transient states instantaneously, $a_{ij}(x,0) = 0$ for all x and j whenever $i \in I_2$.

The simplest case occurs when Eqs. (7.1) and (7.2) do not depend on x. The discrete time analogue of Eq. (7.1) is then

$$P_{ij}(t) = \delta_{ij}(1-A_i(t)) + \sum_{\nu} \sum_{s=1}^{t} a_{i\nu}(s)P_{\nu j}(t-s), \tag{8.1}$$

where $i \neq \nu \in I_2$ and $i,j \in I_2$. Equation (8.1) is a discrete time generalization of Eq. (6.6), which was derived from the backward Kolmogorov differential equations, in that sojourn times in states do not necessarily have exponential distributions. It could thus serve as a substitute for differential equations of the Kolmogorov type in increment-decrement life table analysis. Indeed, Eq. (8.1) seems preferable when an investigator suspects that sojourn times in states are not exponentially distributed. When, as described in Section 5, an investigator has derived estimates of the functions $(A_{ij}(t))$ on a course time (age) scale from period data, it would be advisable to interpolate them down to a finer time scale before using them in Eq. (8.1). A monotone-increasing interpolation scheme for the elements of the matrix $(A_{ij}(t))$ would ensure nonnegative estimates of the a-densities in (8.1) determined by $a_{ij}(t) = A_{ij}(t) - A_{ij}(t-1)$, $t \geq 1$.

Because $P_{ij}(0) = \delta_{ij}$, $i,j \in I_2$, and only the probabilities $P_{ij}(s)$, $s = 0,1,2,\ldots,t-1$ occur on the right in Eq. (8.1), it may be solved recursively. That is, given $P_{ij}(0) = \delta_{ij}$, all $P_{ij}(1)$ may be computed. Then, given $P_{ij}(0)$ and $P_{ij}(1)$, $i,j \in I_2$, all $P_{ij}(s)$ may be computed, and so on.

For the case $i \in I_2$, a transient state, and $j \in I_1$, an absorbing state, $P_{ij}(0) = 0$ and $P_{ij}(1) = A_{ij}(1)$. Therefore, for $t \geq 2$ the discrete time analogue of Eq. (7.2) is

$$P_{ij}(t) = A_{ij}(t) + \sum_{\nu} \sum_{s=1}^{t-1} a_{i\nu}(s) P_{\nu j}(t-s), \tag{8.2}$$

where $i \neq \nu \in I_2$. Clearly, Eq. (8.2) may be solved recursively for $t \geq 2$.

At this juncture, two points regarding Eq. (8.1) and (8.2) should be mentioned. First, estimates of the functions $a_{ij}(t)$ for all values of t are not required to use Eqs. (8.1) and (8.2). For example, if estimates of the $a_{ij}(s)$ are available only for those s, such that $1 \leq s \leq r$ when r is a finite integer, then the current state probabilities $P_{ij}(t)$ may be estimated for $1 \leq s \leq r$ for each pair $i \in I_2$ and $j \in I$. A second point is that all these calculations involve only nonnegative numbers. Calculations involving only nonnegative numbers are known to have greater numerical stability than those involving mixtures of negative and positive numbers. Such mixtures frequently arise, for example, in calculating inverses of matrices.

Equations (7.1) and (7.2) cannot be solved recursively for the case when they depend on x. They may, however, be solved by first calculating the renewal density $m_{ij}(x,t)$, $i,j \in I_2$. By generalizing an argument outlined in the appendix of Mode and Pickens (1979), it can be shown that the renewal density $m_{ij}(x,t)$, defined for $x,t \geq 0$ and $i,j \in I_2$, satisfies the equation

$$m_{ij}(x,t) = a_{ij}^{(0)}(x,t) + \sum_{\nu} \sum_{s=0}^{t} m_{i\nu}(x,s) a_{\nu j}(x+s,t-s), \tag{8.3}$$

where $t \geq 0$ and $\nu \in I_2$. For all x and $i,j \in I_2$, $a_{ij}^{(0)}(x,0) = \delta_{ij}$ and $a_{ij}^{(0)}(x,t) = 0$ if $t \neq 0$. Because $a_{ij}(x,0) = 0$ for all x and

$i,j \in \mathcal{I}_2$, it follows that (8.3) is a recursive system that may be solved recursively in t for each x.

After calculating the renewal density $m_{ij}(x,t)$ according to Eq. (8.3), the discrete time version of (7.1) may be solved by calculating

$$P_{ij}(x,t) = \sum_{\nu} \sum_{s=0}^{t} m_{i\nu}(x,s)\delta_{\nu j}(1-A_{\nu}(x+s,t-s))$$

$$= \sum_{s=0}^{t} m_{ij}(x,s)(1-A_j(x+s,t-s)), \qquad (8.4)$$

where $\nu \in \mathcal{I}_2$ and $t \geq 0$. Similarly, the discrete time version of Eq. (7.2) may be solved by calculating

$$P_{ij}(x,t) = \sum_{\nu} \sum_{s=0}^{t} m_{i\nu}(x,s)A_{\nu j}(x+s,t-s). \qquad (8.5)$$

In (8.5), $t \geq 0$ and $\nu \in \mathcal{I}_2$.

The algorithm just outlined was used extensively in Mode and Soyka (1980), where age-dependent semi-Markov processes of the type just described were linked in a kind of time series in analyzing longitudinal data collected in the Taichung Medical IUD experiment. In this study, estimates of the functions in the one-step transition matrices were derived from sample path data, using a modification of a life table procedure discussed in Section 5.

ACKNOWLEDGMENT

The author expresses his warm thanks to Professor Burton Singer of Columbia and Rockefeller University for several lengthy telephone conversations, for reading the manuscript, and for suggesting key references. Although the author is grateful to him for his help, he is absolved of all responsibility for the technical contents of the paper.

Research supported in part by National Institute of Child Health and Human Development Grant R01 HD 09571.

REFERENCES

Berman, S. M. (1963). Notes on extreme values, competing risks, and semi-Markov processes. *Annuals of Mathematical Statistics 34,* 1104-06.

Birnbaum, Z. W. (1979). On the mathematics of competing risks. DHEW Publication No. (PHS) 79-1351.

Cinlar, Erhan (1969). Markov renewal theory. *Advances in Applied Probability 1,* 123-187.

Cinlar, Erhan (1975). "Introduction to Stochastic Processes." Englewood Cliffs, New Jersey: Prentice-Hall.

Coleman, J. S. (1981). Estimating individual-level transition probabilities for multistate life tables. Paper presented at Conference on Multidimensional Mathematical Demography.

Cox, D. R. (1972). Regression models and life tables. *Journal of the Royal Statistical Sociology Series B 33,* 187-202.

David, H. A., and Moeschberger, M. L. (1978). "The Theory of Competing Risks." Griffin's Statistical Monographs, No. 39, New York: Macmillan.

Doob, J. L. (1953). "Stochastic Processes." New York and London: Wiley.

Elandt-Johnson, R. C., and Johnson, N. L. (1980). "Survival Models and Data Analysis." New York: Wiley.

Feller, William (1968). "An Introduction to Probability Theory and Its Applications," Vol. 1. Third ed. New York and London: Wiley.

Hennessey, John C. (1980). An age-dependent, absorbing semi-Markov model of work histories of the disabled. *Mathematical Biosciences 51,* 283-304.

Hoem, J. M. (1972). Inhomogeneous semi-Markov processes, select actuarial tables, and duration-dependence in demography. *In* "Population Dynamics" (T. N. E. Greville, ed.), pp. 251-296. New York: Academic Press.

Keyfitz, Nathan (1980). "Multidimensionality in Population Analysis." International Institute for Applied Systems Analysis. Laxenburg, Austria. RR-80-33. (Reprinted from Sociological Methodology 1980.)

Krishnamoorthy, S. (1979). Classical approach to increment-decrement life tables--An application to the study of the marital status of United States females, 1970. *Mathematical Biosciences 44,* 139-154.

Littman, Gary S., and Mode, C. J. (1977). A non-Markovian model of the Taichung Medical IUD experiment. *Mathematical Biosciences 34*, 279-302.

Loève, M. (1960). "Probability Theory." New York: D. Van Nostrand.

Mode, Charles J. (1971). "Multiple Branching Processes--Theory and Applications." New York: Elsevier.

Mode, C. J., and Pickens, G. (1979). An analysis of postpartum contraceptive strategies--Policies for preventive medicine. *Mathematical Biosciences 47*, 91-113.

Mode, Charles J., and Soyka, Michael G. (1980). Linking semi-Markov Processes in time series--An approach to longitudinal data analysis. *Mathematical Biosciences 51*, 141-164.

Rogers, Andrei (1975). "Introduction to Multiregional Mathematical Demography." New York, London, Sydney, Toronto: Wiley-Interscience.

Rogers, Andrei, and Ledent, Jacques (1976). Increment-decrement life tables--A comment. *Demography 11*, 267-290.

Roger, Andrei, and Willekens, Frans (1978). "Migration and Settlement: Measurement and Analysis." International Institute for Applied System Analysis A-2361, Laxenburg, Austria.

Schoen, Robert (1975). Constructing increment-decrement life tables. *Demography 12*, 313-324.

Schoen, Robert (1979). Calculating increment-decrement life tables by estimating mean durations at transfer from observed rates. *Mathematical Biosciences 47*, 255-269.

Schoen, Robert, and Land, Kenneth C. (1979). A general Algorithm for estimating a Markov-generated increment-decrement life table with applications to marital-status patterns. *Journal of the American Statistical Association 74*, 761-776.

Schoen, Robert, and Nelson, Verne E. (1974). Marriage, divorce, and mortality--A life table analysis. *Demography 11*, 267-290.

Singer, Burton, and Cohen, Joel E. (198). Estimating malaria incidence and recovery rates from panel surveys. *Mathematical Biosciences 49*, 273-305.

Singer, Burton, and Spilerman, S. (1976). Some methodological issues in the analysis of longitudinal surveys. *The Annals of Economic and Social Measurement 5*, 447-474.

Wachter, Kenneth W., Hammel, Eugene A., and Laslett, Peter (1978). "Statistical Studies in Historical Demography." New York: Academic Press.

12

Population Heterogeneity in Demographic Models

James J. Heckman and Burton Singer

1. INTRODUCTION

Most specifications of the single decrement life table together with the more recently developed multistate increment-decrement life tables share two basic features. They describe the dynamics of populations where individuals are assumed to be homogeneous with respect to unobserved characteristics, and the underlying stochastic process is in most instances a time-inhomogeneous Markov process or, more generally, an age-dependent semi-Markov process (Hoem, 1972; Hoem and Fong, 1976; Mode and Soyka, 1980; Ledent, 1980; Keyfitz, 1980; Schoen and Land, 1979). In a recent review of the methods of multidimensional population analysis, it is stated that

> The main limit to their application is the Markov assumption that the history of the process affects each transi-

ISBN 0-12-435640-0

tion only through the state distribution immediately before that transition (Keyfitz, 1980, p. 216).

An important stimulus for a reconsideration of the basic assumptions underlying models of population dynamics has been the recent availability of large longitudinal data files on human populations. Using repeated observations on the same individuals over long periods of time, such diverse processes as interindustry occupational mobility (Blumen *et al.*, 1955), contraceptive usage-pregnancy sequences (Littman and Mode, 1977), job switching in work careers (Tuma, 1976), and malarial infection histories (Cohen and Singer, 1979), to name only a few, have been found to exhibit violations of first-order Markov dependence. Among the many proposals that have been put forth to account for deviations of observed data from Markovian models, the most common parsimonious alternatives seem to be

1. Mixtures of Markov and semi-Markov processes (Spilerman, 1972; Coleman, 1964a,b; Sheps and Menken, 1973; Hoem, 1975; Kitsul and Philipov, 1981; Manton and Stallard, 1980).

2. Markov and semi-Markov processes in random environments and/or with deterministic time trends (Cohen, 1979; Charlesworth, 1980).

3. Treating the observed process as one (or several) coordinates of a higher-dimensional Markovian process (Tuma, 1980).

4. Treating the observed process as a functional of an underlying latent stochastic process (Wiggins, 1973; Coleman, 1964a,b; and portions of Heckman, 1978).

5. Markov processes subject to measurement error (Baum *et al.*, 1970).

6. Homogeneous population models incorporating very restrictive forms of dependence across time where the parametrizations are guided by a social or biological theory (Heckman and Borjas, 1980).

The purpose of this chapter is to describe some strategies for and raise some questions concerning population heterogeneity as it pertains to alternatives 1, 2, 5, and 6. Because of the complexity of the issues involved and the large number of currently unresolved problems, we shall concentrate on mixtures of waiting time distributions. These distributions only characterize single episodes (spells) in what may be a multiple-episode process. An analogous discussion for multiple episodes in semi-Markov processes lies in the future.

In Section 2 we describe some problems in medical epidemiology, demography, and economics where the duration time until the occurrence of an event is the primary dependent variable of interest. In each of the examples, an unobserved variable plays a central role in a proposed theory about the structure of a conditional duration distribution given the unobservable and possibly some observed covariates. However, there is often very little *a priori* theory about the form of the unconditional distribution for the unobservable. This situation, which arises across a multiplicity of fields, has resulted in *ad hoc* parametric families of mixing distributions being incorporated in duration models to facilitate estimation of parameters in conditional duration distributions given observed and unobserved covariates. It is not widely appreciated that parameter estimates in such structural models can be extremely sensitive to assumed choices for the distribution of unobservables. This sensitivity is exhibited in Section 3 in the context of durations of spells of unemployment.

Our example suggests the need for estimation methods for structural parameters that are insensitive to the distribution of unobservables. Furthermore, if the actual distribution of unobservables is of interest, then it would be desirable to have simple criteria for assessing some qualitative characteristics, e.g., number of modes and their amplitude, directly from the estimated duration distribution. The assessment of such qualitative characteristics is the subject of Section 4.

In Section 5 we exhibit a nonparametric maximum likelihood estimator (NPMLE) for the distribution of an unobservable which simultaneously estimates parameters in a wide class of conditional duration distributions given observed covariates and the unobservable. A limited Monte Carlo study, described in Section 6, indicates that our implementation of the NPMLE using the EM algorithm has the desired insensitivity to the distribution of unobservables while doing a good job of estimating structural parameters in a conditional duration distribution given the unobservable and some observed covariates.

It is interesting that the NPMLE is a consistent estimator of both the distribution of unobservables and the coefficient vector associated with the covariates. However, in the Monte Carlo evidence the vector of coefficients is estimated well while the distribution function of the unobservables is not. Although we currently lack a full understanding of the reasons for this difficulty, some insight might be provided by considering the analogous problem for another class of estimators. In particular, nonparametric estimation of mixing distributions, in the context of duration models, can be viewed as a process of numerical inversion of integral transforms, typically a very ill-conditioned problem. Successful inversion requires the use of smoothing operators, accompanied by a rationale for their use, which resides in some substantive theory or in empirical evidence external to the given data set. In most social science problems where unobservables are incorporated in duration models, the necessary external evidence is not currently available. This presents a major challenge for future research, not only in the modeling of duration data but for the analysis of longitudinal data generally.

2. DURATION MODELS AND UNOBSERVABLES

Let T be a positive random variable representing an individual's waiting time until the occurrence of an event, e.g., death, detection of a complication due to a chronic disease, first live birth to a woman following initiation of cohabitation, etc. The distribution of T will be denoted by $G(t) = \text{Prob}(T \leq t)$ and, as in most of the applications discussed below, we shall assume that G(t) has an associated density g(t) and hazard rate h(t) related via

$$G(t) = 1 - \exp\left(-\int_0^t h(u)\,du\right),$$

with

$$h(t) = g(t)/[1 - G(t)] .$$

The level of model complexity that often must be dealt with in attempts to account for estimated duration distributions G is the introduction of an observed vector of variables $\underline{Z}$, and an unobserved variable θ in a representation of the form

$$G(t\ \underline{Z}) = \int_{\theta} F(t|\underline{Z},\theta)d\mu(\theta) ,$$

where $F(t|\underline{Z},\theta)$ is interpreted as the conditional duration distribution given values of $(\underline{Z},\theta)$, and $\mu(\theta)$ is an *a priori* unknown probability distribution of the unobservable θ. We are assuming throughout that $\underline{Z}$ and θ are independent. Then the unconditional duration distribution is given by

$$G(t) = \int_{Z} G(t|\underline{Z})d\nu(\underline{Z}) ,$$

where ν is the distribution of the observables.

The following examples illustrate the diversity of substantive contexts in which unobservables play a central role.

1. Manton and Stallard (1980), hereafter referred to as MS, formulate a quite general discrete-state continuous-time stochastic model for mortality due to chronic diseases that formally incorporates dependencies between multiple disease processes. Unfortunately, age of onset of various chronic diseases is either not known reliably or simply unavailable in primary data bases on mortality. Thus, susceptibility to the diseases themselves must be incorporated as an unobserved variable in duration models for mortality. Two formulations for heterogeneity in susceptibility are considered by MS:

(i) In a study of stomach cancer it is assumed that there are only two types of individuals: those who could not contract the disease and those who could. The latter group progressed toward death via a stochastic model of the intraindividual evolution of stomach cancer. The unobservable is

$$\theta_j = \begin{cases} 1, & \text{if individual } j \text{ is susceptible to stomach cancer} \\ 0, & \text{otherwise} \end{cases}$$

Some possible rationales for this proposal would be that special genetic factors are necessary for initiation of the disease or that a single exposure to a specific toxic substance is necessary and sufficient. In this situation some theory is guiding the specification of heterogeneity.

(ii) When modeling duration until onset of a chronic disease, it is assumed that the hazard function for individual j is of the form $h^{(j)}(t) = \theta_j \bar{h}(t)$. The variable θ is unobservable and is interpreted as the ratio of biological to chronological age. $\bar{h}(t)$ is the hazard function for what is referred to as a standard individual, see MS (1980) for details on the notion of "standard individual." To facilitate estimation of parameters in $\bar{h}(t)$, θ is assumed to be gamma distributed in the population. This specification was employed by MS in a study of lung cancer mortality.

2. In a study of birth intervals in the current Danish population, Braun and Hoem (1979) propose a hazard function for the duration of the first interval for parity 0 women following the initiation of cohabitation of the form

$$h(t,x|\theta) = \rho d\lambda(x,\theta)(d\lambda(x,\theta)t)^{p-1} \exp[-d\lambda(x,\theta)t] .$$

Here t measures duration of the interval from initiation of cohabitation, and x is the woman's age; ρ, d, and p are parameters to be estimated. The dependence of fertility on age is incorporated in a fecundity function

$$(x,\theta) = \begin{cases} 0, & \text{if } x \leq 14 \\ 1, & \text{if } 14 < x \leq 25 \\ \left[1 - \left(\frac{x-25}{20}\right)^{\theta}\right]^2, & \text{if } 25 < x \leq 45,\ \theta > 0 \\ 0, & \text{if } x > 45 \end{cases}$$

The shape parameter θ may be interpreted as an unobservable indicator of fecundity, which is distributed in the Danish population according to some unknown distribution $\mu(\theta)$. See Sheps and Menken (1973) for further discussion of fecundity in heterogeneous populations.

3. In contemporary theories of labor-force dynamics, the duration of spells of nonemployment is governed by an individual's reservation wage, defined to be the minimal wage offer that the person will accept in order to terminate a spell. It is further hypothesized that the reservation wage decreases during spells of nonemployment, thereby giving rise to a hazard rate for the duration of such spells that increases with time. Some other covariates influencing the duration of spells of nonemployment are marital status, years of education, age at initiation of the spell, and the local unemployment rate. One parametrization of these ideas is a hazard rate of the form

$$h(t|\underline{Z},\theta) = t^{\beta} \exp\left(\sum_{i=1}^{K} \alpha_i Z_i + c\theta\right),$$

where $\underline{Z} = (Z_1,\ldots,Z_k)$ are observed covariates, t^{β} with $\beta > 0$ captures the notion of a declining reservation wage during the spell, and θ is an unobservable proxy for perceived ability and other attitudinal variables that influence an individual's decision to accept a wage offer and terminate a spell of nonemployment. c is a scale parameter. The distribution of θ is *a priori* unknown. For further details on economic theories that lead to this and other parametrizations of durations of spells of nonemployment, see Lippman and McCall (1976) and Flinn and Heckman (1981).

4. J. Hoem (1975) presents analytical strategies for studying the relationships between fertility and outmigration, both of which are under the influence of common unobservable background variables. He gives a lucid discussion of biases and misinterpretations of the relationship between fertility and outmigration, which can result from neglect of heterogeneity. The outmigration-fertility process is modeled as a mixture of continuous-time Markov chains. The hazard rates describing duration in each state are assumed to depend on an unobservable variable θ that is interpreted as "upward mobility ambition" and is a surrogate for attitudinal variables governing fertility and migration decisions. No theory is available to guide the specification of the distribution of θ.

These examples illustrate a key feature of the modeling of longitudinal data in medicine and the social sciences. There is sometimes a theoretical basis, however crude, for selecting parametric families of conditional distributions $F(t|\underline{Z},\theta)$ for modeling duration data. On the other hand, there is virtually no theory that guides the choice of mixing distribution $\mu(\theta)$. Current practice across a multiplicity of fields is usually to select gamma, log normal, beta, or some other simple parametric family of distributions to describe the distribution of unobservables. Justification for the choice is usually on the basis of ability of the family to reproduce a considerable variety of shapes, analytical simplicity, and considerations of computational cost. Unfortunately, this practice can lead to very misleading conclusions about the key "structural" parameters in a model, as we shall now demonstrate.

3. SENSITIVITY OF PARAMETER ESTIMATES

We illustrate the sensitivity of parameter estimates in $F(t|\underline{Z},\theta)$ to *ad hoc* choices for the distribution $\mu(\theta)$ by reexamining data on durations of spells of unemployment assembled by Kiefer and Neumann (1979). The hazard rate for $F(t|\underline{Z},\theta)$ is assumed to be of the form

$$h(t|\underline{Z},\theta) = t^{\beta} \exp\left[\alpha_0 + \sum_{i=1}^{6} \alpha_i Z_i + \alpha_7 Z_1 Z_2 + c\theta\right],$$

a slight extension of the parametrization in example 3, Section 2. The vector $\underline{Z}$ is described in Table 1. Three parametric families of mixing distributions $\mu(\theta)$ were utilized to describe the distribution of the unobservable, θ: normal, log normal, and gamma distributions. The entries in the first three columns of Table 1 are the coefficients $\alpha_0,\ldots,\alpha_7$, β, and c--with standard errors in parentheses--estimated via maximum likelihood, using each of the indicated mixing distributions. The point estimates in the fourth column will be discussed in Section 5. Notice that qualitatively different interpretations about the influence of observed covariates on the dura-

TABLE 1. Kiefer-Neumann Data[a]

	Normal heterogeneity	Log normal heterogeneity	Gamma heterogeneity	Nonparametric maxim likelihood estimation
Intercept	-3.92	-13.2	5.90	--
	(2.8)	(4.7)	(3.4)	
ln duration	-0.066	-0.708	-0.576	0.494
	(0.15)	(0.17)	(0.17)	
Age	0.0036	-0.106	-0.202	-0.0396
	(0.048)	(0.03)	(0.06)	
Education	0.0679	-0.322	-0.981	-0.156
	(0.233)	(0.145)	(0.301)	
Tenure on	-0.0512	0.00419	-0.034	-0.041
previous job	(0.0149)	(0.023)	(0.016)	
Unemployment	-0.0172	0.0061	-0.003	-0.0174
benefits	(0.0036)	(0.0051)	(0.004)	
Married	0.833	0.159	-0.607	0.124
(0.1)	(0.362)	(0.30)	(0.496)	
Unemployment	-26.12	25.8	-17.9	-24.61
rate	(9.5)	(10.3)	(11.2)	
Ed. x age	-0.00272	0.00621	0.0152	0.0011
	(0.0044)	(0.034)	(0.0053)	
Heterogeneity	5.16	5.7	4.62	--
(C)	(0.567)	(0.42)	(0.790)	

[a]*For definitions of variables, see Kiefer and Neumann (1979). Sample size is 456; reduced form estimates. (Standard errors in parentheses.)*

tion of spells of unemployment arise simply as a result of the *ad hoc* choice of the distribution of the unobservable θ. Furthermore, the negative sign for ℓn (duration) suggests that the data are not consistent with the declining reservation wage hypothesis generated by many theories of search unemployment (see Lippman and McCall, 1976). The opposite conclusion arises from the techniques described in Section 5.

In response to the sensitivity exhibited in Table 1, it is natural to seek a procedure that estimates μ in a nonparametric fashion, together with parameters such as $\alpha_0,\ldots,\alpha_7$, β, and c in the above model. A prior question to the utilization of such a technique is to ask whether any qualitative properties of μ can be inferred simply from examination of the raw duration data, while invoking minimal assumptions about $F(t|\underline{Z},\theta)$. Furthermore, it would be useful to have simple nonparametric test criteria to assess whether given duration data are compatible with any member of a wide class of heterogeneous population models. This is the subject of the next section.

4. QUALITATIVE PROPERTIES OF MIXTURES

Qualitative restrictions on the structure of mixing distributions that are consistent with observed duration distributions G can frequently be inferred under rather mild regularity conditions on the assumed conditional distribution $F(t|\theta)$.[1] We illustrate the use of such conditions in two contexts: (i) assessment of oscillation properties of mixing densities and (ii) testing whether observed duration data could have been generated from a mixture of first passage time distributions for continuous-state processes crossing a threshold.

[1] *For the present discussion we suppress the dependence of the conditional duration distributions on observed covariates.*

4.1. *ASSESSING MODALITY OF MIXING DENSITIES*

We consider some classes of mixtures of duration distributions for which modality characteristics of the density $g(t)$ of observed durations imply modality properties of the density $m(\theta)$ of the mixing distribution $d\mu(\theta) = m(\theta)d\theta$. To this end let

$$G_1 = \{G\colon G(t) = \int_0^t g(u)du \text{ and } g(t) = \int_\Theta f(t|\theta)m(\theta)d\theta \text{ for some probability density } m(\theta) \text{ and } f(t|\theta) = k(t|\theta)v(t), \text{ where } k(t|\theta) \text{ is sign regular of order 2 } (SR_2)\}.$$

Sign regularity means that if $t_1 < t_2$ and $\theta_1 < \theta_2$, then

$$\varepsilon_2 \det\begin{pmatrix} k(t_1|\theta_1) & k(t_1|\theta_2) \\ k(t_2|\theta_1) & k(t_2|\theta_2) \end{pmatrix} \geq 0 ,$$

where ε_2 is either +1 or -1. If $\varepsilon_2 = +1$, then $k(t|\theta)$ is called *totally positive* of order 2, abbreviated TP_2. As an indication of the generality of models for which $k(t|\theta) = f(t|\theta)/v(t)$ is in SR_2, observe that this includes all members of the exponential family. In particular, if $d\nu(t)$ is a measure on $[0,+\infty)$ with density $v(t)$ and such that $\int_0^\infty e^{t\theta}v(t)dt < \infty$ for $\theta \in \Theta$, let

$$\beta(\theta) = \left[\int_0^\infty \exp(t\theta)v(t)dt\right]^{-1}$$

and $f(t|\theta) = \beta(\theta)v(t)\exp(t\theta)$. Then the density

$$g(t) = \int_\Theta \beta(\theta)\exp(t\theta)v(t)m(\theta)d\theta$$

governs observable durations, $f(t|\theta)$ is a member of the exponential family, and $k(t|\theta) = \beta(\theta)\exp(t\theta)$ is TP_2 (see, e.g., Karlin, 1968).

The essential point in isolating the class of duration densities in G_1 is that oscillation properties of g/v imply minimal oscillation properties of $m(\theta)$. For example, if g/v is unimodal with a mode at some finite $t_0 > 0$, then m cannot be monotonic; it must have at least one mode in the interior of the parameter space Θ. More generally, if a is an arbitrary positive level and $[g(t)/v(t)] - a$ changes sign k times as t increases from 0 to $+\infty$, then $m(\theta) - a$ must change sign at least k times as θ traverses the parameter set Θ from left to right (Karlin, 1968, p. 21).

The importance of this variation-diminishing character of the transformation $\int_\Theta k(t|\theta)m(\theta)d\theta$ for modeling purposes is that if we assess the modality of g, using, for example, the procedure of Larkin (1979), then since v is a member of an *a priori* given restricted parametric family of functions, we know the oscillation properties of g/v. These, in turn, imply restrictions on $m(\theta)$ in fitting mixing densities. In terms of fitting finite mixtures, a bimodal g/v suggests fitting a measure with support at, say, 5 points to the data but subject to the constraint that $p_1 < p_2$, $p_2 > p_3$, $p_3 < p_4$, $p_4 > p_5$, where

$$d\mu(\theta) = \begin{cases} p_i, & \text{if } \theta = \theta_i \\ 0, & \text{otherwise} \end{cases}, \quad \theta_1 < \theta_2 < \cdots < \theta_5$$

Subsequent specification of a mixing density $m(\theta)$ to describe the same data could proceed by fitting spline polynomials with knots at $\theta_1,\ldots,\theta_5$ to the estimated mixing distribution.

4.2. *FIRST PASSAGE DISTRIBUTIONS: AN EXAMPLE*

In economic theories of job search (see, e.g., McCall, 1970; Mortensen, 1970), an individual's reservation wage is an important unobservable. We consider a simple, but proto-typical, example of the relationship of reservation wages to models for the duration of spells of nonemployment. To this end, let θ represent an individual's reservation wage, and let $X(t)$ be a diffusion process on $[0,+\infty]$ governing the dynamics of market wages that the individual confronts. For the present discussion we assume that θ does not depend on time.[2] Then for $X(0) = x < \theta$, the duration of a spell of nonemployment is defined to be

$$T_{x,\theta} = \inf(t\colon X(t) = \theta \mid X(0) = x) \ . \tag{4.1}$$

For diffusions having reflecting barrier at $x = 0$ with local variance $\sigma^2(x)$ and local nonnegative drift $b(x)$ having bounded, continuous first derivatives, i.e., the infinitesimal generator is of the form

[2] *This discussion is for duration times consistent with the constant reservation wage hypothesis. For the declining reservation wage theory, we must consider $\theta(t)$ decreasing for t increasing and*

$$T_{x,\theta} = \inf(t\colon X(t) = \theta(t) \mid X(0) = x < \theta(0)).$$

This entails a more complicated discussion, which we defer to a separate work.

$$\sigma^2(x)d^2/dx^2 + b(x)d/dx, \quad x > 0 \ , \tag{4.2}$$

the distribution of $T_{x,\theta}$ has a density $q(t;x,\theta)$ with respect to Lebesque measure. In particular,

$$P(T_{x,\theta} > t) = \int_t^\infty q(s;x,\theta)ds$$

and, in addition, $q(t+s;x,\theta)$ is sign regular of all orders in t and s with sign sequence $\varepsilon_m = (-1)^{m(m-1)/2}$. This means that for $0 < s_1 < \ldots < s_m$ and $0 < t_1 < \ldots < t_m$

$$\varepsilon_m \det \begin{pmatrix} q(s_1+t_1;\cdot) & \ldots & q(s_1+t_m;\cdot) \\ \vdots & & \vdots \\ q(s_m+t_1;\cdot) & \ldots & q(s_m+t_m;\cdot) \end{pmatrix} \geq 0$$

for $m = 1,2,\ldots$ (see Karlin, 1964, p. 59).

This general property of first passage time distributions for diffusions with smooth coefficients provides a necessary condition on duration densities for them to be generated by random variables of the form (4.1).

In order to introduce population heterogeneity into this formulation, let $m(\theta)$ be a probability density such that $m(\theta+\phi)$ is TP_2 (or SR_2 with $\varepsilon_2 = -1$) in the variables θ and ϕ. Then let T_x be the duration of a spell of nonemployment for an individual in a heterogeneous population where the reservation wage has probability density $m(\theta)$. For the present discussion, but with no loss of generality in the principle indicated below, assume that $x = 0$. Then

$$P(T_0 > t) = \int_0^\infty \left(\int_t q(s;0,\theta)ds \right) m(\theta)d\theta \ . \tag{4.4}$$

Since $q(t;0,\theta)$ is totally positive of all orders in t and θ (Karlin, 1964, p. 59), the density $g(t) = \int_0^\infty q(t;0,\theta)m(\theta)d\theta$ has the property that $g(t+s)$ is TP_2 (or SR_2 with $\varepsilon_2 = -1$) according as $m(\theta+\phi)$ is TP_2 (or SR_2 with $\varepsilon_2 = -1$). Thus rejection of the null hypothesis that the density of observed durations satisfied $g(t+s) \in TP_2$ or SR_2 with $\varepsilon_2 = -1$ implies that the data are not consistent with a job search theory where $X(t)$ is any member of a very wide class of diffusion processes and where the unobserved reservation wage is distributed in the population according to a density with $m(\theta+\phi)$ being TP_2 or SR_2 with $\varepsilon_2 = -1$.

From the perspective of proposing classes of mixing distributions to be fit to duration data in conjunction with parametric families of conditional distributions $F(t|\underline{Z},\theta)$, determining that data are consistent with (4.4) for several values of Z greatly restricts the parametric families that might be utilized in the procedures described in Section 5.

The above discussion immediately raises the question of how easy it might be to generate densities $m(\theta)$ such that $m(\theta+\phi)$ is TP_2 or SR_2. To this end observe that any density of the form

$$m(\theta) = \int_{-\infty}^{+\infty} \exp(\theta z)w(z)dz$$

has the property that $m(\theta+\phi)$ is TP_2. In particular, if $w(z)$ is a probability density on $(-\infty,0]$, then $m(\theta)$ is just a mixture of exponentials. (For detailed proofs of these facts, see Karlin, 1968, p. 70.)

5. ESTIMATION IN MIXTURE MODELS

As demonstrated in Section 3, alternative choices of functional forms for $\mu(\theta)$ can lead to parameter estimates in $F(t|\underline{Z},\theta)$ with dramatically different interpretations. Thus we require nonparametric estimators of μ to be utilized in conjunction with estimators of parameters in $F(t[\underline{Z},\theta)$ in order to obtain estimated values in which we can have some confidence. Elsewhere (Heckman and Singer, 1981), we have verified consistency of the nonparametric maximum likelihood estimator (NPMLE) of $\mu(\theta)$ in the model (6.1). Furthermore, under mild regularity conditions, Laird (1978) has shown the NPMLE of μ to be a distribution with only a finite number of points of increase. With this motivation, our strategy is to represent the density $g(t\ \underline{Z})$ in the form

$$g(t|\underline{Z}) = \sum_{i=1}^{I} f(t|\underline{Z},\theta_i)p_i , \tag{5.1}$$

where $p_i = d\mu(\theta_i)$. We estimate parameters in f, together with θ_i and p_i, by maximum likelihood.

An immediate problem with (5.1) is that I is usually *a priori* unknown. An exception to this is the two point mixture, I = 2, mentioned in example 1, Section 2 and treated in greater detail in Tolley *et al.* (1978). Thus, in order to avoid imposing false constraints on μ, we estimate p_i and θ_i starting initially with a large value of I and then estimate successively simpler models while assessing the deterioration in fit of the overall model to the original duration data. A difficulty with this approach is that if I is selected to exceed its true value, the likelihood function is maximized on a ridge in the parameter space. In this case, standard gradient procedures are computationally unstable. For this reason, we advocate implementation of the EM algorithm which, as shown by Dempster *et al.* (1977) and in much greater detail by Wu (1981), guarantees convergence to local maxima, some point on a ridge when it is present, of the likelihood function. Some experimentation with starting values in the EM algorithm iteration cycle seems to be necessary to ensure confidence in the designation of a global maximum.

To illustrate how the algorithm is applied in the present setting, consider the estimation of parameters in a duration model with

$$F(t|\underline{Z},\theta) = 1 - \exp(-t^{\alpha_1}\exp[(\underset{\sim}{\alpha}_2,\underline{Z}) + \theta]) , \tag{5.2}$$

where α_1 and $\underset{\sim}{\alpha}_2 = (\alpha_2^{(1)},\ldots,\alpha_2^{(k)})$ are structural coefficients to be estimated and

$$(\underset{\sim}{\alpha}_2,\underline{Z}) = \sum_{j=1}^{k} \alpha_2^{(j)} Z_i .$$

Define

$$\lambda_{i\ell} = \exp[(\underset{\sim}{\alpha}_2,Z_\ell) + \theta_i], \quad i = 1,2,\ldots,I ,$$

where $\ell = 1,2,\ldots,L$ indexes individuals in the sample. Let $\underset{\sim}{\lambda}_\ell$ be an I-dimensional vector of the $\lambda_{i\ell}$. It will be convenient to reexpress the duration density $g(t|\underline{Z})$ in terms of $\underset{\sim}{\lambda}_\ell$ as

$$g(t_\ell|\underset{\sim}{\lambda}_\ell) = \sum_{i=1}^{I} p_i \left(\alpha_1 t_\ell^{\alpha_1 - 1}\right)\lambda_{i\ell} \exp\left(-t_\ell^{\alpha_1}\lambda_{i\ell}\right) .$$

The duration density for person ℓ conditional on membership in component population i is

$$f(t_\ell \mid \lambda_{i\ell}) = \alpha_1 t_\ell^{\alpha_1 - 1} \lambda_{i\ell} \exp\left(-t_\ell^{\alpha_1} \lambda_{i\ell}\right).$$

We wish to maximize the log likelihood

$$\tilde{\mathcal{L}} = \sum_{\ell=1}^{L} \ln g(t_\ell \mid \lambda_\ell)$$

with respect to p_i, θ_i, and $\underset{\sim}{\alpha} = (\alpha_1, \underset{\sim}{\alpha}_2)$.

The following iteration cycle produces a local maximum for the log likelihood. At the m-th stage of iteration, denote the current estimates as $\lambda_i^{(m)}$, $p_i^{(m)}$, and $\underset{\sim}{\alpha}^{(m)}$. Then define

$$p_i^{(m+1)} = \frac{1}{L} \sum_{\ell=1}^{L} p_i^{(m)} \frac{f\left(t_\ell \mid \lambda_{i\ell}^{(m)}\right)}{\sum_{i=1}^{I} p_i^{(m)} f\left(t_\ell \mid \lambda_{i\ell}^{(m)}\right)} .$$

The expression

$$\phi_{i\ell}^{(m+1)} = p_i^{(m)} \frac{f\left(t_\ell \mid \lambda_{i\ell}^{(m)}\right)}{\sum_{i=1}^{I} p_i^{(m)} f\left(t_\ell \mid \lambda_{i\ell}^{(m)}\right)}$$

can be interpreted as the posterior probability that observation ℓ is generated by a member of the i-th component population of the mixture given values of the parameter estimates at iteration stage m. Then $p_i^{(m+1)}$ is simply an unweighted mean of these posterior probabilities.

Given $p_i^{(m+1)}$, we form the function

$$\tilde{\mathcal{L}}^{(m+1)} = \sum_{\ell=1}^{L} \sum_{i=1}^{I} [\ell n\ f(t_\ell | \lambda_{i\ell})] \phi_{i\ell}^{(m+1)}$$

and maximize it with respect to θ_i, $i = 1,\ldots,I$ and $\underset{\sim}{\alpha}$

Given initial values for $\underset{\sim}{\alpha}$, θ_i, and p_i, $i = 1,\ldots,I$, one first computes $\{p_i^{(0)}\}$, then maximizes $\tilde{\mathcal{L}}^{(1)}$ with respect to $\underset{\sim}{\alpha}$ and $\{\theta_i\}$, then forms $\{p_i^{(1)}\}$, then maximizes $\tilde{\mathcal{L}}^{(2)}$, and so forth. This procedure produces a local optimum for $\mathcal{L}$. The estimated values of p_i are constrained to lie in the unit interval. To guard against failure to locate a global optimum, it is wise to run the EM iteration cycles from a variety of starting values. For detailed illustrations of the importance of varying the starting values, see Heckman and Singer (1982).

6. PERFORMANCE OF THE EM ALGORITHM AND REVISED ESTIMATES FOR THE KIEFER-NEUMANN DATA

In Heckman and Singer (1982), we verified the regularity conditions of Kiefer and Wolfowitz (1956) to prove that the supremum of a likelihood function is a consistent estimator of the parameters $\underset{\sim}{\alpha}$ and the mixing distribution μ for duration models of the form

$$P(T \leq t | \underline{Z}) = \int_\Theta \{1 - \exp(-t^{\alpha_1} \exp(\underset{\sim}{\alpha}_2, \underline{Z}) + \theta)\} d\mu(\theta) \quad , \qquad (6.1)$$

where Θ is a finite interval. This fact, together with the characterization of the nonparametric maximum likelihood estimator (NPMLE) in the present problem as a finite mixture (as discussed in Section 5) suggests that for increasing sample sizes one might expect the number of points of increase of the estimated mixing distributions to increase and become dense in θ when $d\mu(\theta) = m(\theta)d\theta$. Furthermore, good estimates of $\underset{\sim}{\alpha}$ should simultaneously be produced.

In order to investigate this conjecture, we performed a small Monte Carlo study of the EM algorithm on duration models where $\mu(\theta)$ either had a truncated gamma or truncated normal density[3] or was a distribution with a small number of points of increase, i.e., less than five. Our results from this study are as follows. In all runs that incorporate covariates, the structural parameters are precisely estimated. If $d\mu(\theta) = m(\theta)d\theta$ and there are no covariates, then $m(\theta)$ is poorly estimated even in samples of size 5000. When covariates are included, then the mixing distribution always tends to be poorly estimated. The interesting aspect of our Monte Carlo study is that the structural parameters $\underset{\sim}{\alpha}$ are accurately estimated while at the same time the EM algorithm is not correctly estimating μ. The original duration distribution is always closely approximated by the corresponding distribution in the estimated mixture model. Furthermore, the estimated mixing distribution produces good forecasts of duration distributions from fresh data.

We further clarify the nature of our results by exhibiting a small portion of a larger Monte Carlo study that is described in detail in Heckman and Singer (1982). To this end let

[3] *Truncated distributions are utilized herein to satisfy the requirements of Laird, 1978 that θ lie in a bounded interval. However, we have subsequently found that such a restriction is unnecessary (Heckman and Singer, 1982).*

$$F(t|Z,\theta) = 1 - \exp[-t^{\alpha_1} \exp(\alpha_0+\alpha_2 Z+\theta)] \ . \qquad (6.2)$$

We assume that $\phi = e^{\theta}$ is truncated gamma distributed.[4]

Following the procedure outlined in Section 5, the EM algorithm is used to estimate the P_i, θ_i, $i = 1,\ldots,I$ and the structural parameters $\underset{\sim}{\alpha}$

Our artificial samples are generated by the following procedure. To generate each observation, we begin by drawing a uniform random variable in the interval (0,1). From the cdf of θ, we solve for the implied θ. Values of scalar Z are taken from a standard normal random number generator. We then draw another uniform random number in the interval (0,1). Given θ, Z, and specified values of $\underset{\sim}{\alpha}$, (6.2) is solved for the implied t. No censoring or truncation is imposed. The results reported below are for samples of size one thousand ($L = 1000$). Analogous results for other sample sizes are reported in Heckman and Singer (1982). Since the estimation procedure does not restrict the mean of θ, α_0 is set to zero (the mean of θ is implicit in our estimates). In each run ten mass points for θ were selected to commence the iterations.

We first present estimates of a model in which $\alpha_0 = 0$, $\alpha_1 = 2$, $\alpha_2 = 0.5$. The results are displayed in Table 2.

The agreement between fitted and true values of $\underset{\sim}{\alpha}$ is very high. Next we consider estimates of θ_i and P_i. These are

[4]*For the computation we use a truncated distribution for* e^{θ} *of the form*

$$d\mu(\theta) = \frac{\exp(\Delta\theta)\exp(-e^{\theta})d\theta}{\Gamma(\Delta)\,Prob(-\theta^* \leq \theta \leq \theta^*)}$$

with $\theta^* = 10^{72}$. *This is virtually indistinguishable from the untruncated distribution.*

TABLE 2.

True model	$\alpha_1 = 2$	$\alpha_2 = 0.5$
Estimated model	$\hat{\alpha}_1 = 1.947$ (0.12)	$\hat{\alpha}_2 = 0.484$ (0.053)
	$L = 1000$	

Estimated mixing measure

Starting values for θ_i are $\theta = (1,\ldots,10)$, $P_i = 0.1$, $i = 1,\ldots,10$.

Estimated θ_i	Estimated P_i	Estimated CDF	True CDF	Observed CDF
0.0483	0.0063	0.0063	0.0011	0.002
0.2734	0.0918	0.0981	0.0312	0.042
1.2376	0.6057	0.7038	0.3509	0.370
4.0582	0.2961	1.000	0.9152	0.917

Estimated cumulative distribution of durations versus actual [$\hat{G}(t)$ vs. $G(t)$]

Value of t	Estimated t cdf	Observed cdf
0.25	0.1321	0.1380
0.50	0.3775	0.3720
0.75	0.5878	0.5890
1.00	0.7339	0.7290
1.25	0.8285	0.8270
1.50	0.8876	0.8970
1.75	0.9242	0.9280
2.00	0.9471	0.9430
3.00	0.9833	0.9850
4.00	0.9933	0.9920

reported below the subheading "Estimated mixing measure." For the starting values recorded in the first line, the EM algorithm converged to the estimates shown in the first two columns. A remarkable finding in all of our runs is a clustering phenomenon. Even though we start with ten distinct values of θ_i, the algorithm eventually produces fewer than ten distinct values in the sense that there are several values of θ_i that are indistinguishable given the inherent numerical accuracy of the computational procedure. A comparison between the estimated cdf, the true cdf, and the sample cdf (based on the realized θ) is given in the final three columns. The agreement is rather poor.

Next we consider the agreement between the calculated cdf for duration times and the sample cdf. The calculated cdf is computed conditional on Z values. For each observation, we compute the probability that durations are less than the values of t reported in the table. In this calculation we used estimated values of θ_i, P_i, and $\underset{\sim}{\alpha}$. Summing up all observations produces the numbers reported in the first column under the subheading "Estimated cumulative distribution of durations versus actual [$\hat{G}(t)$ vs. $G(t)$]. The sample histogram is recorded in the second column. The agreement between the estimated and empirical histogram is remarkably good. These findings have been duplicated for numerous other values of $\underset{\sim}{\alpha}$. The structural parameters are always estimated rather precisely, the cdf of θ is estimated rather imprecisely, and the estimated model fits the duration data rather well.

With the Monte Carlo evidence indicating that the EM algorithm reliably estimates structural parameters $\underset{\sim}{\alpha}$, regardless of what mixing distribution governs the unobservable θ, we estimated the parameters in the unemployment model in Section 3 from the data of Kiefer and Neumann (1979). This produced the point estimates in column 4 of Table 1. The most striking feature of these estimates is the positive coefficient on ℓn(duration). In the language of search theory, the Kiefer-

Neumann data now indicate that a declining reservation wage describes an unemployed worker's strategy. This finding is in accord with the predictions of several models of search unemployment (see Lippman and McCall, 1976). The coefficient estimates of the other variables display a distinct pattern of signs and magnitudes that are not captured by any single parametric duration model presented in Table 1.

7. DISCUSSION AND CONCLUSIONS

We indicated, by example, some of the diverse contexts in medicine and the social sciences in which unobserved variables play a key role in duration models. Then a reanalysis of data on duration of spells of unemployment indicated the extreme sensitivity of structural parameters in conditional duration distributions $F(t|\underline{Z},\theta)$ to assumed parametric families of mixing distributions $\mu(\theta)$. This sensitivity suggested the desirability of estimating structural parameters in $F(t|\underline{Z},\theta)$ reliably while simultaneously estimating $\mu(\theta)$ in a nonparametric fashion.

Some qualitative properties, e.g., number of modes, of the distribution of an unobserved variable can be inferred from the oscillation properties of the density of observed durations, provided some substantive theory supports a conditional duration distribution having sign regular density $f(t|\theta)$. For direct estimation of structural parameters and the mixing distribution, a nonparametric maximum likelihood estimator (NPMLE) was implemented using the EM algorithm. This procedure, studied in a prototypical class of models via a Monte Carlo experiment, indicated that structural parameters tend to be reliably estimated while the underlying mixing distribution is not recovered, even when the sample size is increased from a few hundred to five thousand. Thus the NPMLE is a very robust estimator of structural parameters in duration models with general distributions of unobservables.

A detailed explanation for the inability of the EM algorithm to recover mixing densities with any accuracy lies in the future. Since estimation via inversion formulas encounters the same difficulties, it is useful to consider the issues in that context. First, it is well known that numerical inversion of Fredholm integral operators (see, e.g., Anderssen and Bloomfield, 1973) is an unstable process. The simplest version of this problem in the setting of duration models arises if we consider the specification

$$P(T > t) = \int_0^\infty e^{-\theta t} d\mu(\theta) \quad , \qquad (7.1)$$

where μ is an *a priori* unknown probability distribution. Then using an empirical survivor function to estimate (7.1), e.g., the Kaplan-Meier estimator, estimation of $\mu(\theta)$ amounts to doing numerical inversion of a Laplace transform. It is well known (see Bellman *et al.*, 1966 for a lucid discussion) that numerical inversion of a Laplace transform is typically a very ill-conditioned problem.

Smoothing procedures must be incorporated with inversion formulas if interpretable mixing distributions are to be recovered. A sensitive aspect of the use of smoothing operators to invert integral transforms is that some substantive theory about the nature of μ is *required* in order to justify any one of a wide variety of smoothing procedures used to estimate a mixing distribution. As we have indicated throughout this chapter, *a priori* theory about the structure of $\mu(\theta)$ is the missing element in many of the problems where unobserved heterogeneity is being incorporated in duration models. It is our view that effective estimation of mixing distributions in the whole range of problems discussed in this chapter will require an infusion of theoretical and/or empirical information from sources *external* to a given data set. The external information must be the basis of a rationale for smoothing operators used in the inversion process. For a very instructive example of the delicate interplay between data, theory, and smoothing operations to facilitate numerical inversion of Laplace transforms, see Lax and Zwanziger (1973). An analogous discussion for a variety of contexts in demography, medical epidemiology, economics, and sociology lies in the future.

As a final point, it is important to observe that the mathematical property of consistency of the NPMLE, used with the models in this paper, is a poor guide to the quality of estimates of mixing distributions, even in samples of size 5000. A full understanding of estimation and testing of models with unobservables requires a deep integration of numerical analysis, statistics, and subject matter theory that has yet to be carried out. This is a major challenge for the future.

ACKNOWLEDGMENTS

This research was supported by NSF Grant SOC 77-27136. We are indebted to George Yates for numerous valuable comments and excellent computational assistance. We greatly benefited from conversations on an earlier draft with Henry Braun, Mel Lax, and Nancy Tuma.

REFERENCES

Anderssen, R. S. and Bloomfield, P. (1974). Numerical differentiation procedures for nonexact data. *Numerische Mathematik 22,* 157-182.

Baum, L., Petrie, T., Soules, G., and Weiss, N. (1970). A maximization technique occurring in the statistical analysis of probabilistic functions of Markov chains. *Annals of Mathematical Statistics 41,* 164-171.

Bellman, R., Kalaba, R. E., and Lockett, J. A. (1966). "Numerical Inversion of the Laplace Transform." New York: American Elsevier.

Blumen, I., Kogan, M., and McCarthy, P. J. (1955). "The Industrial Mobility of Labor as a Probability Process," Cornell Studies of Industrial and Labor Relations," No. 6, Ithaca, New York: Cornell University Press.

Braun, H. and Hoem, J. (1979). Modelling cohabitational birth intervals in the current Danish population: A progress report. Working Paper 24, Laboratory of Actuarial Mathematics, University of Copenhagen.

Charlesworth, Brian (1980). "Evolution in Age-Structured Populations." Cambridge: Cambridge University Press.

Cohen, Joel (1979). Ergodic theorems in demography. *Bulletin of the American Mathematical Society 1, 2,* 275-295.

Cohen, Joel and Singer, Burton (1979). Malaria in Nigeria: Constrained continuous-time Markov Models for discrete-time longitudinal data on human mixed-species infections. *In* "Lectures on Mathematics in the Life Sciences," Vol. 12 (S. Levin, ed.), pp. 69-133. Providence: American Mathematical Society.

Coleman, James (1964a). "Introduction to Mathematical Sociology." New York: The Free Press.

Coleman, James S. (1964b). "Models of Change and Response Uncertainty." Englewood Cliffs, New Jersey: Prentice-Hall.

Dempster, A. P., Laird, N., and Rubin, D. (1977). Maximum likelihood from incomplete data via the EM algorithm. *Journal of the Royal Statistical Society B,* 1-38.

Flinn, C. and Heckman, J. J. (1981). New methods for the analysis of labor force dynamics. Working Paper, NORC-Economics Research Center, University of Chicago.

Heckman, J. (1978). Simple statistical models for discrete panel data developed and applied to test the hypothesis of true state dependence against the hypothesis of spurious state dependence. *Annals de l'INSEE BO-31, 227-270.*

Heckman, J. and Borjas, G. (1980). Does unemployment cause future unemployment? Definitions, questions and answers from a continuous-time model of heterogeneity and state dependence. *Economica 47,* 247-283.

Heckman, J. and Singer, B. (1982). A method for minimizing the impact of distributional assumptions in econometric models for duration data. Forthcoming in *Econometrica.*

Hoem, Jan (1972). Inhomogeneous semi-Markov processes, select actuarial tables, and duration dependence in demography. *In* "Population Dynamics," (T. N. E. Greville, ed.), pp. 251-296. New York: Academic Press.

Hoem, Jan (1975). Fertility and out-migration. Reflections on research approaches in empirical investigations of the association between two demographic phenomena. *In* Demographic, Economic and Social Interactions," (Å. E. Anderson and I. Holmberg, eds.), pp. 55-83. Cambridge, Massachusetts: Ballinger.

Hoem, Jan and Fong, M. S. (1976). A Markov chain model of working life tables. Report No. 1, A new method for the construction of tables of working life. Working Paper 2, Laboratory of Actuarial Mathematics. University of Copenhagen.

Karlin, Samuel (1964). Total positivity, absorption probabilities and applications. *Transactions of the American Mathematical Society 111,* 33-107.

Karlin, Samuel (1968). "Total Positivity." Stanford University Press.

Keyfitz, Nathan (1980). Multidimensionality in population analysis. *In* "Sociological Methodology, 1980" (K. Schuessler, ed.), pp. 191-218. San Francisco: Jossey-Bass.

Kiefer, J. and Wolfowitz, J. (1956). Consistency of the maximum likelihood estimator in the presence of infinitely many incidental parameters. *Annals of Mathematical Statistics 27,* 887-906.

Kiefer, N. and Neumann, G. (1979). An empirical job search model with a test of the constant reservation wage hypothesis. *Journal of Political Economy,* 69-82.

Kitsul, Pavel and Philipov, Dimiter (1981). "The one-year/five-year migration problem. *In* "Advances in Multiregional Demography" (A. Rogers, ed.), pp. 1-34. Laxenburg: Int. Inst. for Applied System Analysis.

Laird, Nan (1978). Nonparametric maximum likelihood estimation of a mixing distribution. *Journal of the American Statistical Association 73, 364,* 805-811.

Larkin, R. (1979). An algorithm for assessing bimodality versus unimodality in a univariate distribution. Unpublished memorandum, Rockefeller University.

Lax, M. and Zwanziger, M. (1973). Exact photo count statistics: Lasers near threshold. *Physical Review A 7, 2,* 750-771.

Ledent, Jacques (1980). Multistate life tables: Movement versus transition perspective. *Environment and Planning A 12,* 533-562.

Lippman, S. and McCall, J. (1976). The economics of job search: A survey. *Economic Inquiry 14,* 113-126.

Littman, G. S. and Mode, C. J. (1977). A non-Markovian stochastic model for the Taichung medical IUD experiment. *Mathematical Biosciences 34,* 279-302.

Manton, K. G. and Stallard, E. (1980). A stochastic compartment model representation of chronic disease dependence: Techniques for evaluating parameters of partially unobserved age inhomogeneous stochastic processes. *Theoretical Population Biology 18, 1,* 57-75.

McCall, John J. (1970). Economics of information and job search. *Quarterly Journal in Economics 84,* 113-126.

Mode, C. J. and Soyka, M. G. (1980). Linking semi-Markov processes in time series - An approach to longitudinal data analysis. *Mathematical Biosciences 51,* 141-164.

Mortensen, Dale T. (1970). Job search, the duration of unemployment, and the Phillips curve. *American Economics Review 60,* 847-862.

Schoen, R. and Land, K. C. (1979). A general algorithm for estimating a Markov-generated increment-decrement life table with applications to marital-status patterns. *Journal of the American Statistical Association 74,* 761-776.

Sheps, Mindel C. and Menken, Jane (1973). "Mathematical Models of Conception and Birth." Chicago: University of Chicago Press.

Spilerman, S. (1972). Extensions of the mover-stayer model. *American Journal of Sociology 78, 8,* 599-626.

Tolley, H. D., Burdich, D., Manton, K. G., and Stallard, E. (1978). A compartment model approach to the estimation of tumor incidence and growth: Investigation of a model of cancer latency. *Biometrics 34,* 377-389.

Tuma, Nancy (1976). Rewards, resources, and the rate of mobility: A nonstationary multivariate stochastic model. *American Sociological Review 41,* 338-360.

Tuma, Nancy (1980). When can interdependence in a dynamic system of qualitative variables be ignored? *In* "Sociological Methodology, 1980" (K. Schuessler, ed.), p. 358-391. San Francisco: Jossey-Bass.

Wiggins, Lee (1973). "Panel Analysis - Latent Probability Models for Attitude and Behavior Processes." San Francisco: Jossey-Bass.

Wu, C. F. (1981). On the convergence of the EM algorithm. Technical Report No. 642, Department of Statistics, University of Wisconsin.

Index

M

N

O

P

Q

R

S

Participants

Robert C. Busby, *Drexel University*
Luis J. Castro, *International Institute for Applied Systems Analysis*
Joel E. Cohen, *The Rockefeller University*
James S. Coleman, *University of Chicago*
Thomas J. Espenshade, *The Urban Institute*
V. Jeffrey Evans, *National Institutes of Health*
Ralph B. Ginsberg, *University of Pennsylvania*
Jan M. Hoem, *University of Stockholm*
George C. Hough, Jr., *University of Texas, Austin*
Ulla Funck Jensen, *University of Copenhagen*
Pavel Kitsul, *International Institute for Applied Systems Analysis*
Kenneth C. Land, *University of Texas, Austin*
Jacques Ledent, *Université du Québec*
Marilyn M. McMillen, *U.S. Social Security Administration*
Jane A. Menken, *Princeton University*
Charles J. Mode, *Drexel University*
David Myers, *Social Science Research Council*
Dimiter Philipov, *International Institute for Applied Systems Analysis*
Samuel H. Preston, *University of Pennsylvania*
Andrei Rogers, *International Institute for Applied Systems Analysis*
Robert Schoen, *University of Illinois, Urbana*
Burton Singer, *Columbia University*
Nancy Brandon Tuma, *Stanford University*
Frans F. Willekens, *Netherlands Interuniversity Demographic Institute*
James J. Zuiches, *National Science Foundation*

STUDIES IN POPULATION

Under the Editorship of: H. H. Winsborough

Department of Sociology
University of Wisconsin
Madison, Wisconsin

Samuel H. Preston, Nathan Keyfitz, and Robert Schoen. **Causes of Death:** ***Life Tables for National Populations.***

Otis Dudley Duncan, David L. Featherman, and Beverly Duncan. **Socioeconomic Background and Achievement.**

James A. Sweet. **Women in the Labor Force.**

Tertius Chandler and Gerald Fox. **3000 Years of Urban Growth.**

William H. Sewell and Robert M. Hauser. **Education, Occupation, and Earnings:** *Achievement in the Early Career.*

Otis Dudley Duncan. **Introduction to Structural Equation Models.**

William H. Sewell, Robert M. Hauser, and David L. Featherman (Eds.). **Schooling and Achievement in American Society.**

Henry Shryock, Jacob S. Siegel, and Associates. **The Methods and Materials of Demography.** ***Condensed Edition by Edward Stockwell.***

Samuel H. Preston. **Mortality Patterns in National Populations:** ***With Special Reference to Recorded Causes of Death.***

Robert M. Hauser and David L. Featherman. **The Process of Stratification:** ***Trends and Analyses.***

Ronald R. Rindfuss and James A. Sweet. **Postwar Fertility Trends and Differentials in the United States.**

David L. Featherman and Robert M. Hauser. **Opportunity and Change.**

Karl E. Taeuber, Larry L. Bumpass, and James A. Sweet (Eds.). **Social Demography.**

Thomas J. Espenshade and William J. Serow (Eds.). **The Economic Consequences of Slowing Population Growth.**

Frank D. Bean and W. Parker Frisbie (Eds.). **The Demography of Racial and Ethnic Groups.**

Joseph A. McFalls, Jr. **Psychopathology and Subfecundity.**

Franklin D. Wilson. **Residential Consumption, Economic Opportunity, and Race.**

Maris A. Vinovskis (Ed.). **Studies in American Historical Demography.**

Clifford C. Clogg. **Measuring Underemployment: Demographic Indicators for the United States.**

Doreen S. Goyer. **International Population Census Bibliography:** ***Revision and Update,*** **1945-1977.**

David L. Brown and John M. Wardwell (Eds.). **New Directions in Urban–Rural Migration:** ***The Population Turnaround in Rural America.***

A. J. Jaffe, Ruth M. Cullen, and Thomas D. Boswell. **The Changing Demography of Spanish Americans.**

Robert Alan Johnson. **Religious Assortative Marriage in the United States.**

Hilary J. Page and Ron Lesthaeghe. **Child-Spacing in Tropical Africa.**

Dennis P. Hogan. **Transitions and Social Change:** ***The Early Lives of American Men.***

F. Thomas Juster and Kenneth C. Land (Eds.). **Social Accounting Systems:** ***Essays on the State of the Art.***

M. Sivamurthy. **Growth and Structure of Human Population in the Presence of Migration.**

Robert M. Hauser, David Mechanic, Archibald O. Haller, and Taissa O. Hauser (Eds.). **Social Structure and Behavior:** ***Essays in Honor of William Hamilton Sewell.***

Valerie Kincade Oppenheimer. **Work and the Family:** ***A Study in Social Demography.***

Kenneth C. Land and Andrei Rogers (Eds.). ***Multidimensional Mathematical Demography.***